WORLD WORDS

Recommended Pronunciations

W. CABELL GREET

Associate Professor of English in Barnard College, Columbia University

CBS Speech Consultant

19 CBS 44

Published for the COLUMBIA BROADCASTING SYSTEM

by COLUMBIA UNIVERSITY PRESS · NEW YORK

First Printing May, 1944
Second Printing June, 1944
Third Printing September, 1944
Fourth Printing January, 1945

FOREIGN AGENT: OXFORD UNIVERSITY PRESS, Humphrey Milford, Amen House, London, E.C., 4, England, AND B. I. Building, Nicol Road, Bombay, India

MANUFACTURED IN THE UNITED STATES OF AMERICA

To the Memory of

GEORGE PHILIP KRAPP

LATE PROFESSOR OF ENGLISH, COLUMBIA UNIVERSITY IN THE CITY OF NEW YORK

and

ARTHUR LLOYD JAMES

LATE PROFESSOR OF PHONETICS, UNIVERSITY OF LONDON

"Speak the speech, I pray you, as I pronounced it to you, trippingly on the tongue . . ." HAMLET, III. 2

PREFACE

SINCE the publication of *War Words* a year ago, the relentless battle fronts have brought more strange names into communiqués and press dispatches. Names long alien have now become hallowed in the English language as the places where American soldiers fought and died—*Tarawa, Arawe, Salerno, Garigliano, Carroceto.* The list is daily lengthening.

In this book of *World Words*, about twelve thousand names and words are pronounced. They include the battlefields and air force objectives of the past two years, the likely places of attack during the coming months, names that will figure in the peace and appear on the air routes, names of important persons, and words that are difficult for broadcasters. Pronunciations for two thirds or three quarters of these cannot be found in any other volume of easy access.

Whatever the defects of this book, it shows the need of pronunciations as well as of accurate spellings in all reference works, and particularly in gazetteers and map indexes. The construction of pronunciations is a fascinating business; it combines the interest of making crossword puzzles with the excitement of betting on an election. Nevertheless, every branch of lexicography is better pursued at leisure. This book has been prepared in great haste. To be readily understood and, in radio parlance, to be on the nose, were its prime requirements. It is desirable that the United States Board on Geographical Names and the Permanent Committee on Geographical Names for British Official Use be granted the necessary funds to give reasonable pronunciations for all names that are spelled on maps. Or in the absence of government support, perhaps the National Geographic Society and the boards of the Encyclopedia Britannica Atlas and similar organizations will undertake to complete their indexes by supplying pronunciations. In this radio-minded world, pronunciations are quite as important as spelling.

To anyone who works with pronunciation and the other parts of rhetoric, the nicest fable for critics is in Holofernes' speech, beginning "He draweth out the thread of his verbosity finer than the staple of his argument" (*Love's Labor's Lost*, Act V, scene 1); Holofernes in lambasting Don Adriano's rhetoric shows himself just as fantastic, and pedantic to boot. For effective radio (or so we believe at CBS), pronunciation is not an opportunity to be elegant but an everyday problem of what to do with difficult names and debatable words. This book is an effort to find reasonable solutions, fanciful as some of the respellings may at first seem.

The pleasures of working with learned experts are great and long remembered. A hundred or more busy professors, consular agents, and foreign correspondents have directly contributed to these judgments on pronunciation. Professor L. Carrington Goodrich and Professor Cyrus H. Peake of Columbia University and Dr. Lin Lin of the Chinese Ministry of Information showed the patience of the East before hundreds of queries. Dr. J. van Beusekom of the Netherlands Information Bureau and Mr. Chris O'Sullivan and Mr. Alwyn Lee of the Australian News and Information Bureau gave in their pronunciations a sense of nearness to the life of the South Pacific. Professor Einar Haugen of the University of Wisconsin, Dr. F. G. Nelson of the University of Minnesota, and Mr. Oka Fen of the Royal Norwegian Information Service provided authority for many Scandinavian pronunciations and evidence of a great variety of usage. Mr. A. E. Gilliat of the Burma Civil Service, Mr. T. A. Raman, head of the Indian Information Service, Washington, Mr. Paul A. Eakin of the Presbyterian Mission, Bangkok, and Mr. and Mrs. J. J. Van Hine of the Christian and Missionary Alliance, Tonkin, had much more to say of east Asia than could be set down in phonetics. Mr. Jonas Budrys, Consul General of Lithuania, Mr. Ernst Jaakson of the Estonian Consulate General, Mr. Harry W. Lielnors, Mr. Otto G. Lindberg, and Dr. Thomas A. Sebeok of Indiana University, interpreted the names of the Baltic languages and Hungarian. Dr. Fred Householder was ever the admirable consultant on Greek. Professor Clarence A. Manning and Professor Arthur P. Coleman of the Department of East European Languages, Columbia University, Mr. Vladimir Alexieff, and members of the American Association of Teachers of Slavonic and East European Languages made an indispensable contribution to the difficult problems of comparative Slavonic pronunciations. Dr. J. A. W. Bennett of Queens College, Oxford, and the British Library of Information, Dr. Charles E. Funk of the Funk & Wagnalls Company, and Mr. Edward Artin and Dr. John P. Bethel of G. & C. Merriam Co. contributed good cheer when the burdens were heavy. Mr. Ambrose Lansing and Mr. C. K. Wilkinson of the Metropolitan Museum of Art were delightful instructors in the ways of Arabic and Persian. Professor Oswaldo Serpa of Rio de Janeiro sent a phonograph recording of his own pronunciation of important Brazilian names. Prof. Leon Feraru, Long Island University, chanted the Rumanian list like a medieval epic. Mr. Solomon V. Arnaldo, director of the Philippine Bureau of Information checked the pronunciation of Philippine names; Mr. Raif Erisken of the Turkish Consulate General passed on the Turkish. Professor Harry Morgan Ayres, Professor Adriaan J. Barnouw, Professor Carl F. Bayerschmidt, Professor Dino Bigongiari, Dr. William Bridgwater, Professor Elliott V. K. Dobbie, Professor Robert Herndon Fife, Mr. Philip Hayden, Professor Frederick W. Heuser, Professor Frédéric Hoffherr, Mr. Roger Howson, Mr. André Mesnard, Professor Tomás Navarro, and Professor Henry H. L. Schulze—to these and to other colleagues and masters at Columbia University the debt is deeper than probably they realize. Professor Ayres, Mr. Alexieff, Professor Bigongiari, Professor Dobbie, Professor Haugen, Dr. Householder, Mr. Mesnard, and Dr. Sebeok—bless them—read the proofs.

When such men are the consultants for a little dictionary, it is obvious that any merits of the work are their due. Blame for faults is the due of the editor, but he will pass it on to Mr. Roy Langham and Mr. James Seward of the Columbia Broadcasting System, for they have abetted the work since its small beginnings two years ago as a mimeographed bulletin.

So many languages are represented on these pages, it will do no harm to add Old English of the time when the Danes were invading England. To all who labor at meritorious works that cannot be perfected even in a life time, the words of King Alfred, brilliant leader and noble scholar, bring comfort, as he wrote in his preface to the Anglo-Saxon Translation of Boethius' *Consolation of Philosophy:* "King Alfred was the translator of this book, and he turned it from Latin into English, as it now is done. Sometimes he translated word for word, sometimes meaning for meaning, just as he could tell it most clearly and distinctly, despite the various and manifold worldly ills which troubled him either in mind or in body. Our troubles are difficult to count that in his days came upon the kingdom he had undertaken. Nevertheless he studied this book and translated it from Latin to English speech and published it again for the nation, just as it is now done. He asks and, in God's name, he entreats each man who is pleased to read the book that he pray for him and not blame him if he understands it more correctly than Alfred could; for each man must, according to the measure of his understanding and according to his leisure, speak what he speaks, and do what he does."

Ælfred Kuning wæs wealhstod thisse bec, and hie of boc-lædene on englisc wende, swa hio nu is gedon. Hwilum he sette word be worde, hwilum andgit of andgite, swa swa he hit tha sweotolost and andgitfullicast gereccan mihte for tham mistlicum and manigfealdum weoruldbisgum the hine oft ægther on mode ge on lichoman bisgodan. Tha bisgu us sint swithe earfoth-rime the on his dagum on tha ricu becoman the he underfangen hæfde, and theah tha thas boc hæfde geleornode and of lædene to engliscum spelle gewende, and geworhte hi eft to leothe, swa swa heo nu gedon is; and bit and for Godes naman he halsath ælcne thara the thas boc rædan lyste, thæt he for hine gebidde, and him ne wite gif he hit rihtlicor ongite thonne he mihte; forthamthe ælc mon sceal be his andgites mæthe and be his æmettan sprecan thæt he sprecth, and don thæt thæt he deth.

At the end of a section in his Anglo-Saxon Reader, George Philip Krapp put this passage. It serves as a requiescat for him, for Lloyd James, and for all good workers.

W. Cabell Greet

Columbia University
February, 1944

INTRODUCTION

ENGLISH PRONUNCIATION

Correct English

This pronouncing dictionary is designed to assist speakers of the Columbia Broadcasting System. They have the problems of correct usage that every American has, with this difference—that as radio speakers they meet their problems in public while millions are listening in. Naturally no group has greater desire to be right.

The recurring question "Which is correct?" is best met by the doctrine of "levels of usage." Ask not only which is *correct*, but *correct for what purpose.* To the styles appropriate for the pulpit, the Supreme Court, after-dinner speaking, conversation, familiar speech, and so on, we must add the styles appropriate to radio. Radio is peculiar: though the subject matter may be serious and formal, the radio audience hears it in the familiar surroundings of home. The platform and pulpit styles become incongruous; the listeners wish the broadcaster to be natural and friendly, but well spoken and easily understood. And so he pays attention to pronunciation, for agreeable pronunciation is one part of an agreeable oral style. It is probably not the most important part, but it is the most easily questioned and often the most difficult to maintain before a wide audience in a nation where there are regional types of speech.

Included here with the names that the War has made prominent are certain common English words whose alternative pronunciations cause domestic conflict of a different order. The debates as to which pronunciation is "correct" can be settled only by future generations, for in 1944 these words actually have two or more pronunciations and each of them is held by millions of Americans to be "correct." It is not the province of CBS to regulate the English language, but it is desirable to avoid the awkwardness that conflicting pronunciations on one program may cause. A choice therefore has been made in the light, we hope, of common sense, guided by the fact that CBS is a national American network. Without seeking to impair any citizen's right to be his own professor of English, we look for what is national, contemporary, and reputable.

The English Pronunciation of Foreign Names

Just as the names of the older countries and the principal regions of Europe have English variants—as Germany, Italy, and Spain for Deutschland, Italia, and España—many European cities, provinces, and rivers have, during the centuries, acquired English pronunciations and even English spellings, which are commonly preferred in English contexts. But of course for the most formal occasions and for musical programs, and also in the case of foreign speakers, the nuance of foreign pronunciations may be desirable. Broadcasters, particularly announcers, should know both.

Although the English forms are stable, there is here, as in all other aspects of language, the possibility of change. Nowadays the "French" pronunciations of *Marseille* and *Lyon* are probably better American usage than the Anglicized *Marseilles* and *Lyons*. We now pronounce *Prague* in the French style, ignoring the time-honored English variant, as well as the Czech and the German. One sign of the falling off of classical studies is a general ignorance of the English pronunciation of Greek place names. The press reports usually give English spellings which don't quite make sense if they are pronounced as modern Greek, as, for example, *Piraeus* and *Athens*. If the classical traditions grow even weaker, such forms may be displaced. *Piraeus*, especially, gives trouble now.

When faced with the necessity of choosing between English and foreign pronunciations, broadcasters should of course use the pronunciations commonly employed in the comfortable English of educated people acquainted with the place and the subject. Names that are not Anglicized in English dictionaries probably have no English pronunciation, and they should be pronounced in foreign style. We cannot be so conservative (or so radical?) as the English family who, according to Ned Calmer, spoke of happy holidays in Brittany and pronounced *Saint Michel* as if it were English *Saint Mitchell*.

Why Don't We Anglicize All Foreign Names?

The language of a strong and confident people usually has the power to take over and "domesticate" foreign names. Why cannot we say *Saint Mitchell* or *Michael* for French *Saint Michel?* In the past English borrowed and domesticated thousands of foreign names. It was as easy for English to absorb them as for French to Gallicize names today. But the present generations of English speakers are remarkably curious about the native pronunciations of foreign places. In the case of names that are not already Anglicized they are inclined to prefer the foreign pronunciations, especially on formal and semiformal occasions. English and especially American reference books and maps give native pronunciations and spellings much more often than do similar French works. Our public speakers and editors are rebuked by audiences if they freely Anglicize foreign names. For one reason or another there is a new and somewhat foreign standard of correctness or appropriateness of pronunciation.

Perhaps today we are more aware of foreign cultures, but familiarity alone has never preserved foreign names in English or in any European language. There is a higher degree of literacy and education among speakers of English than ever before. Yet educated Frenchmen do not hesitate to pronounce all foreign names as French. Professor H. M. Ayres suggests that when the schools gave up the "English" pronunciation of Latin and adopted the so-called "Roman" pronunciation, English speakers lost their model and the necessary precedents for Anglicizing foreign names. Our spelling of English words is eccentric and there are many exceptions to the rules. Perhaps because we don't know what to do with foreign names we ask the "correct" or foreign pronunciation. Uncertainty as to whether *Cracow* should be pronounced krā′-kō, krăk′-ou (*ou* as in *house*), or krăk′-ō, has not yet driven us to *Kraków*, krä′-ko͝of, but it may! Or, with the Great War to preserve democracy, did a belief in the linguistic rights of small nations grow along with world combines and rapid communication? In other centuries some travelers and "foreign correspondents" liked to use foreign pronunciations. Nowadays radio offers an opportunity to parade such pronunciations before a public that, it may be said, cannot easily object. Radio provides an ideal vehicle for popularizing new pronunciations, but the audience can object if it wishes. Radio may have implemented, but it did not inaugurate, the present movement to foreignisms.

Whatever the causes, there is established today a learned standard of handling newly arrived foreign names. We may well call it a new kind of Anglicizing: the rule, or the aspiration, is to adopt the foreign pronunciation insofar as it can be rendered by customary English sounds in the phrasing and rhythm of an English sentence. It is not good taste to introduce sounds that are foreign to English. Often, as with strange Chinese names, we succeed only in giving what seems to us a "foreign" flavor that means nothing whatever to a Chinese. Nevertheless the tendency is commendable as the opposite of a smug, indifferent attitude. It may well lead to a growth of understanding and sympathy. So far as radio is concerned, the tendency has to be taken as a fact, with such disturbing inconsistencies as the occasional preservation of native stress in *Tárawá* and an Englishing of *Truk*, "truck."

I have learned to respect the new rule for Anglicizing because of a bad guess I made as to what the public would do with foreign names as they became familiar. For centuries Russian *kh* as in *Kharkov* has been Anglicized as *k*. In *War Words* I therefore transcribed Russian *kh* as *k*. To my surprise when *Kharkov* became a daily headline, there was a strong drift to "Harkof." Russian *kh* is neither English *k* nor English *h*, but when Anglicized one would expect *k* as in the past on the analogy of the spelling, *h* on the analogy of the sound. We are evidently an ear-minded generation. Because *Kharkov* is an old name in English, I am still inclined to prefer *k*, but I have found great difficulty in defending any recommended pronunciation of a foreign name that is not as close as may be convenient to the native. Our bright people are more interested in the present international world than in the traditions of English.

But a word of caution must be added. Absurd foreignisms will be labeled pretentious and asinine, fine as the line is between what seems absurd and what seems "correct." The pronunciations must conform to the customs of idiomatic English. The "Parisian" *r*, for instance, is not welcomed. As Fowler cogently put it: "To say a French word in the middle of an English sentence exactly as it would be said by a Frenchman in a French sentence is a feat demanding an acrobatic mouth; the muscles have to be suddenly adjusted to a performance of a different nature, and after it as suddenly recalled to the normal state; it is a feat that should not be attempted; the greater its success as a *tour de force*, the greater its failure as a step in the conversational progress; for your collocutor, aware that he could not have done it himself, has his attention distracted, whether he admires or is humiliated."[1] To this Lloyd James added: "A technique that obtrudes, in speech as in most other forms of human activity, is offensive; it should be the aim of those who have to handle the spoken word to evoke neither admiration nor humiliation."[2]

FOREIGN LANGUAGES

The principal element in our idea of a foreign pronunciation is that the vowels a, e, i, o, u, are pronounced ah, eh, ee, oh, o͞o. In the following notes on foreign languages this is taken for granted and comment is made on the vowels when they do not follow this expectation. Only the unusual consonants are treated, and they are equated with the nearest English sounds. In most foreign languages *r* is a trill or rolled sound made with the tip of the tongue; occurence of uvular or "Parisian" *r* is mentioned. These notes are intended to inform the user of the book of the premises underlying the pronunciations given in the list and to enable him in some languages to construct pronunciations of names that, unfortunately, will have been omitted. The notes are not designed for consultants who know the languages. They are so simplified that they may irritate the learned.

Sometimes, as in the case of German *ch* and the "Parisian" *r*, an effort is made to describe the sounds, completely foreign to English, because they serve as touchstones in phonetics. As they are famous because we cannot pronounce them and the similar sounds, the descrip-

[1] H. W. Fowler, *A Dictionary of Modern English Usage*, p. 194.
[2] A. Lloyd James, *Broadcast English VI* (BBC, 1937), p. 16.

tions are awkward and probably fruitless. "Go and hear them" is the best advice for any one who is interested in foreign languages. Foreign broadcasts and recordings, such as the Linguaphone Persian records, can tell more of sounds than volumes of printed words.

On a world scale the problem of whether a foreign vowel is close or open, tense or slack, is nigh insoluble. When you first use the lists of the British Permanent Committee on Geographical Names, you may complain that vowel values are not indicated in the International Phonetic Alphabet or by English ā and ĕ, ō and ô, ē and ĭ, and so on. When you try to solve the problem yourself, you may decide that the PCGN chose the wise course in setting down merely *e* and *o* and *i*. Professor Bigongiari remarked, when I grumbled at the uncertainty of vowel-quality in lesser-known Italian names, "Why should Americans complain if the Italians are satisfied?" And he might have added—"particularly when Americans tolerate several varieties of English and seldom speak foreign languages well." I tried to use colorless symbols, but after hearing in one evening six instances of *Stalin* pronounced stä-leen′ (on other networks of course) I felt obliged to bring back ĭ for the unstressed *i* in Slavic names such as *Stalin* and *Mihailovich*. The pronunciations -lēn and -vēch cannot be recommended as acceptable English. The object of this book is to assist American speakers about to go before a microphone—speakers moreover who are used to the symbols in old-fashioned reference books. An effort has been made, however, to improve the English pronunciation of foreign *e* and *o* by avoiding wherever possible the symbols ā and ō. See the discussion of Italian and the note on page 34.

ALBANIAN

Albanian names have two forms, the indefinite and the definite; e.g., *Tiranë* and *Tirana*. The indefinite forms seem better suited to the habits of English speech. Unfortunately our atlases are inconsistent. If Albanian names crowd the news, our best chance of avoiding confusion is to follow the PCGN and adopt as standard the indefinite forms of the Geg dialect.

Pronunciation

In words of more than one syllable the accent is usually on the next to the last syllable.

Albanian	*Explanation*
c	*ts* as in *rats*.
ç	*ch* as in *church*.
dh	*th* as in *this*. (Cf. *th*)
ë	ə (schwa) or *uh*.

gj	*gy*, like the *g* of *legume* or of "gyarden" (for *garden*).
j	*y* as in *yet*.
l	the "bright *l*" of *lit*.
ll	the "dark *l*" of *wall*.
nj	*ny* as in Spanish *cañón*. (French *gn*). Cf. English *canyon*.
q	*ky*, like the k-sound of *cue* or of "kyard" (for *card*).
th	"*th*" as in *thin*. (Cf. *dh*.)
x	*dz* as in *adze*.
xh	*j* as in *joy*.
y	ü as in French *lune* and German *über*.
zh	*zh*, the medial consonant of *leisure* and *pleasure*.

ARABIC

The pronunciation of names on the African front was determined after consultation with Mr. Ambrose Lansing of the Metropolitan Museum of Art and Mr. Amin A. Dahab, Vice-Consul of Egypt, New York City. It necessarily represents a compromise between various dialects of Arabic, Italian, French, and the resources of American English. The diphthong *ei* is subject to various renderings; the best general rule is to pronounce it ā (as in *Beirut*).

BULGARIAN. See *Slavic Languages*

BURMAN

The principal advisor on Burmese names was Mr. A. E. Gilliat of the British Embassy, Washington, for many years Financial Commissioner at Rangoon. All or almost all the pronunciations recommended will pass current among English speakers in Burma. It seemed wise at this time and for the purposes of this list to attempt nothing more, but here is an interesting field for investigation.

The Burman stress is often on the last syllable. As in other eastern languages "short *a*" lies between schwa [ə] (the *a* of *about*) and the ä of *father* and the ă of *rat*. Any one of these symbols seems to be misleading. In transcribing Burman names, I have employed the symbol that seemed to recreate the most vivid pronunciation that I heard—not to correct other pronunciations but to present at least one acceptable pronunciation. See also the note on the names of India.

th is pronounced as in English *thin* or *this*, contrary to the Indian usage, q.v.
gy is pronounced practically *j* as in *jill*.
ky is pronounced *ch* as in *chill*.
See also the note on Indian names.

CHINESE

The phonetics of Chinese are so different from English phonetics that we should gratefully accept the English pronunciation of all names that have acquired an English pronunciation. Fantastic as some of these pronunciations are, they are no stranger to the Chinese than some of our unlearned attempts to give a "Chinese" pronunciation of their familiar names. The modern ideal that in English the "correct" pronunciation of a place name is that current in the place itself is never more severely tested than in the case of China; here it is sometimes absurd.

English-speaking traders and travelers have given English pronunciations to seaports and river ports, to provinces and many large cities, and radio speakers may wisely adopt them, just as we use English pronunciations or names of Paris, Rome, Florence, and Munich. The old capital Peiping is an exception, for we pronounce it in Chinese fashion bā-pĭng (bay-ping), probably because as a new name of political importance it was described in the news a few years ago. These English pronunciations are, or were, current in Chinese railroad and steamship offices, and we may expect to hear them from our correspondents in the East. However, the wide choice of pronunciation that a Chinese name affords—even in China, because of the variety of dialects—makes a forecast uncertain.

As the most reasonable course under the circumstances the following list gives English pronunciations wherever they are acceptable. The Chinese names that have not acquired English pronunciations are transcribed in the conventional Mandarin style of Western dictionaries. English speakers should try to pronounce Chinese names with level stress, giving to each syllable a full share of force and time. The list has been prepared in consultation with Professor L. Carrington Goodrich, head of the Department of Chinese and Japanese, Columbia University.

Unfortunately our periodicals and popular books omit the diacritical marks necessary for the interpretation of the Roman spelling of Chinese. The reader therefore cannot distinguish sounds almost as different as *p* and *b*, *t* and *d*, and so on. The value of a scholarly work like Herrmann's *Atlas of China* (Harvard University Press, 1936) is that the accents are marked and the place names located on maps. The index of the Atlas can serve fairly well as a pronouncing dictionary of Chinese place names, if the following rules are observed.

Rules for the Pronunciation of Non-Anglicized Chinese Names

When Chinese is spelled in our alphabet, with appropriate accents, the symbols have approximately these values:

VOWELS

Chinese	*Explanation*
a	ä as in *father*.
ao	ou as in *out*.
e	ĕ as in *let*.
ê	ŭ as in *cut*.
eh	ĕ (as in *let*) in some syllables; ŭ (as in *cut*) in others.
ho, ko *or* he, ke	hŭ, kŭ (with the vowel of *cut*).
i	ē as in *machine*.
ih	û as in *urn*.
o	ô as in *more*; but see *ho, ko*.
ou, ow	ō as in *go*.
u	o͞o as in *mood*.
ü	like Ger. *ü* or Fr. *u*.
ŭ	ə (schwa) or ŭ as in *cut*.

CONSONANTS

Aspirated		*Unaspirated*	
ch'	*ch* as in *chin*.	ch	*j* as in *jin*.
k'	*k* as in *koko*.	k	*g* as in *go*.
p'	*p* as in *pay*.	p	*b* as in *bay*.
t'	*t* as in *too*.	t	*d* as in *do*.
ts', tz'	*ts* as in *rats*.	ts, tz	*dz* as in *adz*.

j is a uvular sound like the "Parisian *r*" and the *j* of Spanish. English *r* is a poor rendering but almost inevitable with English speakers.

hs is properly pronounced as though spelled *hsh*, but for convenience it is equated to *sh*.

sh and the other consonants are pronounced much as in English.

STRESS

The syllables may be pronounced with level stress. Without special training we cannot attempt the Chinese tones.

NOTE

The CBS Program Department has a limited number of copies of "A Practical Romanized List of Words and Syllable Sounds for Aid in the Pronunciation of Chinese" by Harry S. Aldrich, U.S.A. It will be useful to anyone who has access to publications in which the accents are marked, and it will be sent to any station that requests it.

CROAT. See *Slavic Languages*

CZECH. See *Slavic Languages*

DANISH. See *Scandinavian Languages*

DUTCH AND FLEMISH

The accent is usually on the first syllable.

aa is pronounced ä as in *father*.

ch is pronounced as in Scottish *loch* and German *ach*.

e and *u* unstressed are pronounced ə (uh).

eeuw is similar to āo͝o.

ei and *ij* are transcribed ī (ai) rather than ĕĭ, which seemed beyond our resources, or ā (ay), which proved misleading.

g, voiced or voiceless, is similar to the *ch* of Scottish *loch* and German *ach*. It is here transcribed *k*(*h*). It may be Anglicized to *g* (voiced) or *k* (voiceless).

j is pronounced *y* as in *yes*.

n when final in word or syllable is often lost.

oe is pronounced o͞o as in *boom*. With lack of stress it tends to become the o͝o of *book*.

oo has the sound of English ō as in *go*.

ou and *au* are pronounced like the *ou* of *house* and *out*.

sch is *sk*(*h*) or, when final, *s*. Du. *Schelde*, sk(h)ĕl′-də; *Bosch*, bôs′.

u when followed by a consonant in the same syllable is pronounced between the û or *urn* and the ŭ of *but*.

u when not followed by a consonant in the same syllable, and *uu* are pronounced ü (like Fr. *u* and Ger. *ü*).

The dipthong in *huis* is here transcribed ûĭ [œi], a sound reminiscent of *oi* (as in *oil*) pronounced by some New Yorkers. Dutch *ui* is often Anglicized to *oi*, but Professor Elliott V. K. Dobbie and Dutch friends insisted that we should try a diphthong combining the vowel of *urn* and the vowel of *hit*.

w (labio-dental stop) is here given the sound of English *w*, though in many dictionaries rendered *v*.

y is a common variant of *ij* (see above).

ESTONIAN

Estonian is always stressed on the first syllable.

Vowel and consonant quantity is important in Estonian. A long vowel is indicated by doubling the symbol, *aa*, *ii*, etc. Estonian, like Finnish, q.v., has a number of diphthongs without English parallel.

õ is pronounced very like û in *urn*.

ä is pronounced ă as in *hat*.

FINNISH

The Finnish accent is on the first syllable. Compound words also have secondary accents. In this list the secondary accent is marked only when it does not agree with the usual English pattern of ′x ′x, stressed, unstressed, stressed, unstressed.

Vowel and consonant quantity is important in Finnish. A long vowel and a long consonant are both indicated by doubling the symbol, *aa*, *ee*, *ii*, *pp*, *tt*, etc. Finnish has a large number of diphthongs without English parallel, such as *uo* and *ie*. In these diphthongs, the two vowels have approximately equal importance, and it seemed better to transcribe them, when stressed, o͞o′-ô′ and ē′-ĕ′ than wô′ and yĕ′.

ä or *ae* is pronounced *ă* as in *hat*.

j has the value of *y* as in *yet*.

The influence of Sweden is very strong in Finland and many places have Swedish as well as Finnish names, especially where Swedish is the language spoken by the majority. In a few instances the Swedish names are better known than the Finnish.

FRENCH

It is the practice of American dictionaries to indicate the accent of a French word; but we should remember that from the point of view of English speakers, a French word has a level stress—i.e., each vowel (except schwa) receives practically the same time and energy. The last syllable in a phrase is uttered with a little more force and on a higher tone, while the final syllable in a sentence is on a lower tone. However, in the emphatic pronunciation of a single word, the first syllable may be stressed. When a Frenchman is asked the pronunciation of a single name or word, he will often give this emphatic form. But neither this nor an English heavy stress on the last syllable is so generally appropriate as a level stressing. (See Webster's [1934], Sec. 272, p. lv for an excellent account of the French "accent".)

An accent mark placed above a vowel in French spelling indicates quality, not stress.

VOWELS

See also *Nasalized Vowels.*

French	*Explanation*
â, a + s	ä as in *father*. Fr. *Châlons*, shä-lôN′.
a	a sound lying between the ä of *father* and the ă of *fat*. Fr. *Laval*, lä-väl′ or lă-văl′.
ai	ĕ as in *bed*. Fr. *Calais*, kä-lĕ′ or kă-lĕ′.
aï, aill-, -ail (final)	ī (practically) as in *ice* or ä + y as in *yes*. Fr. *Versailles*, vĕr-sī′ or vĕr-sä′(y).

au	ō as in *go*. Fr. *de Gaulle*, də gōl′; *Giraud*, zhē-rō′.
e (stressed), é, ê, è	ĕ as in *bed*. Fr. *Angers*, äN-zhĕ′; *Pétain*, pĕ-tăN′; *Angoulême*, äN-gōō-lĕm′; *Sète*, sĕt′.
e (unstressed)	ə (schwa) like the *e* of *moment*, mō′-mənt. Silent when final (Fr. *Curie*, kü-rē′) and when, within a word, it is not needed for an easy pronunciation of the adjacent consonants. Fr. *Abbeville*, äb-vēl′.
eau	ō as in *go*. Fr. *Clemenceau*, klĕ-mäN-sō′. See *au*.
eill-, eil (final), ey	ĕĭ or ĕy. Fr. *Marseille*, mär-sĕĭ′ or măr-sĕ′(y).
eu	û as in *urn*. Fr. *Honfleur*, ôN-flûr′.
ey	See *eill-*.
i before a consonant	ē as in *machine*. Fr. *Lille*, lēl′.
before a vowel	y as in *yet*. Fr. *St. Pierre*, săN pyĕr′.
ill-, il (final)	ē + y (as in *yes*). Fr. *Billancourt*, bē-yäN-kōōr′. Exception: Fr. *ville*, vēl′.
ô, o (final), o + s	ō as in *go*. Fr. *Bône*, bōn′; *St. Malo*, săN mä-lō′; *rose*, rōz′; *Rosny*, rō-nē′.
otherwise	ô as in *more* or ŭ as in *but*. Fr. *Somme*, sôm′ or sŭm′.
œ, œu	û as in *urn*. Fr. *Sacre Cœur*, sä-krĕ′ kûr′. See *eu*.
oi	wä as in *waft*. Fr. *Oise*, wäz′.
ou	ōō as in *pool*, (Fr. *Cherbourg*, shĕr-bōōr′); but before a vowel pronounced *w*. Fr. *oui*, wē′.
u	ü (ē pronounced with the lips rounded as for ōō). May be Anglicized as the front ōō of Eng. *toot*. Fr. *Debussy*, də-bü-sē′.
ue	A variant of *eu*. Fr. *Arcueil*, är-kûĭ′ or är-kû′(y).
ui	wē
y (final)	A variant of *i*, pronounced ē. Fr. *Puy*, pwē′.

NASALIZED VOWELS

The French nasalized vowels are somewhat like a nasal American pronunciation of l*ong*, s*ang*, and *urn* (with *r* silent as in the South). Nasalized *e*, *a*, *o* are pronounced like l*ong;* Nasalized *i*, *ai*, *ei*, *y* like s*ang*. Nasalized *ie* like *yang*, yăng; nasalized *oi* and *ui* like *wang*, wăng; nasalized *u*, *eu* like *urn*. The symbol N indicates that the preceding vowel is nasalized.

A single *m* and *n* not followed by a vowel, and *ng* nasalize the preceding vowel. French *vingt*, văN′; *Paimpol*, păN-pôl′; *Reims*, răNs′;

Amiens, ä-myăN′; *un*, ûN′; *Meung*, mûN′; *Rouen*, *rwäN*′; *Caen*, käN′; *Clermont-Ferrand*, klĕr-môN′ fĕ-räN′. (The nasal äN is between a nasalized ä of *father* and a nasalized ô of *orb*. The nasal ôN is between a nasalized ô of *orb* and a nasalized ō of *go*.)

CONSONANTS

The consonants *c*, *f*, *l*, and *r* are pronounced when final in monosyllables. Fr. *Cher*, shĕr′. Otherwise consonants, singly or in groups, when final are usually silent. (But *l* and *r* provide exceptions.) In some family names and some place names, final *-s* is pronounced. Fr. *Noguès*, nô-gĕs′; *Aix*, ĕks′.

c before e, i, y	*s* as in *see*. Fr. *Cette*, sĕt′.
otherwise	*k* as in *koko*. Fr. *Mâcon*, mä-kôN′.
ç	*s* as in *see*. Fr. *Monluçon*, môN-lü-sôN′.
ch	*sh* as in *shall*. Fr. *Chartres*, shär′tr.
g before e, i, y	*zh*, the medial consonant of *pleasure* and *leisure*. Fr. *Angers*, äN-zhĕ′.
otherwise (except *gn*, *ng*)	*g* as in *go*. Fr. *Gounod*, go͞o-nō′.
gn	*ny* as in Sp. *cañón*, almost Eng. *canyon*. Fr. *Avignon*, ä-vē-nyôN′.
gu before e, i, y	*g* as in *get*. Fr. *guerre*, gĕr′.
h	silent. Fr. *Henri*, äN-rē′.
j	*zh*, the medial consonant of *pleasure* and *leisure*. Fr. *Jean*, zhäN′.
l	*l* as in *lip*, except in *-ill-* and *-il* (which see). Often pronounced when final. Fr. *Toul*, to͞ol′. Pronounced in Fr. *ville*, vēl′.
m, n, ng	nasalize a preceding vowel in the same syllable. See *Nasalized Vowels*. Doubled, *mm*, *nn* are pronounced as in English. Fr. *Rennes*, rĕn′.
q, qu	*k* as in *key*. Fr. *Quimper*, kăN-pĕr′; *cinq*, săNk′.
s initial and final, and *ss*	*s* as in *see*. Fr. *Sousse*, so͞os′.
between vowels	*z* as in *zebra*. Fr. *Toulouse*, to͞o-lo͞oz′; *maison*, mĕ-zôN′.
th	*t* as in *Tom*. Fr. *Thierry*, tyĕ-rē′.
w	*v* as in *very*. Fr. *Weygand*, vĕ-gäN′.

NOTE ON "R"

For American radio it is usually desirable to use an American *r*. The "Parisian" *r* has no parallels in American English. If the *h* in *hole* is made further back so that the breath causes audible friction, or still further back so that the breath causes the uvula to vibrate, the sounds are voiceless correspondents to two types of Parisian *r* (customarily voiced). In many parts of France, *r* is a tip-of-tongue trill.

GERMAN

Names are accented upon the first syllable or, after the prefixes *be-*, *ent-* (*emp-*), *er-*, *ge-*, *ver-*, upon the second syllable.

VOWELS

Vowels are pronounced long when stressed before *h* and before one consonant, short before two or more consonants and when unstressed. However before *ch* and *ss*, a vowel may be long or short (thus leading to a recent disagreement on the pronunciation of *Bochum*—bō′-k(h)o͝om or bôk(h)′-o͝om).

German	*Explanation*
a, aa	ä as in *father*.
ä, ae	ĕ as in *bed* or ă as in *care*.
ai	ī as in *aisle* and *ride*. See *ei*.
au	ou as in *out*.
äu	oi as in *oil*. See *eu*.
e stressed	ā as in *late*, when long; ĕ as in *let*, when short.
unstressed	ə (schwa) or sometimes silent.
ei	ī as in *ride* and *aisle*. See *ai*.
eu	oi as in *oil*. See *äu*.
i	ē as in *meet*, when long; ĭ as in *sit*, when short.
ie	ē as in *eve*, *meet*.
ö, oe	û as in *urn* (or ā as in *may* pronounced with lips rounded).
ü, ue	ē as in *eve* pronounced with lips rounded. May be Anglicized as the front o͞o of Eng. *toot*.
y	a variant of *i*, pronounced ē when long; ĭ when short.

CONSONANTS

Except for indicating the length of preceding vowels there is no distinction between doubled or single consonants.

b	when initial or followed by vowel, like Eng. *b*; otherwise tends to *p*.
c before e, i (y), ä, ë	*ts* as in *rats*.
before a, o, u, or cons.	*k* as in *koko*.
ch after a, o, u (but not *äu*, *eu*)	*k(h)* as in Scot. *loch*; like Eng. *ck* as in *lock*, except that the sound continues. The back

	of the tongue approaches the velum but does not cut off the breath.
otherwise	like Eng. *k* in *kit* or Virginian *kyard* (for *card*) but a continuant reminiscent of Eng. *h* in *hue* or *sh* in *shall.* The diminutive *-chen* always has this front *ch.* The pronounciation of *ch* varies in Germany according to dialect areas. It is Anglicized to *k.*
ck	*kk*
d	when initial or followed by vowel, like English *d*; otherwise tends to *t.*
dt	*t* as in *set.*
g initial	*g* as in *go* and *get.*
between vowels	as above in Austria and southern Germany; in the north pronounced like Ger. *ch,* which see, but voiced.
final	*k* in Austria and southern Germany; in the north like Ger. *ch,* which see.
h initial	*h* as in *hat.*
after a vowel	silent but in stressed syllables indicates a long vowel.
j	*y* as in *yes.*
ng	*ng* as in *singer,* not as in *finger.*
qu	*kv*
r	uvular *r* (like the "Parisian" *r* of French) or a trilled or rolled *r* made with the tip of the tongue.
s before a vowel and initial	*z* as in *zone.*
otherwise (and *ss*)	*s* as in *so.*
sp, st initial in stressed syllable (or root)	*shp* and *sht*; otherwise *sp* and *st. Strasse* shträs′-ə, but *Fürsten,* für′-stən.
sch	*sh* as in *shall.*
t	as in English, except before *i* it is pronounced *ts.*
th	*t* as in *tat.*
tz	*ts* as in *rats.*
v	*f* as in *father.*
w	*v* as in *very.* Final *-ow* is ō as in *go.*
y	variant of *i.*
z	*ts* as in *rats.*

GREEK

There is no simple rule for the accenting of Greek names.

VOWELS

Greek (Romanized)	*Explanation*
a	ä as in *father*.
ai	ĕ as in *bet*.
e (epsilon)	ĕ as in *bet*.
e (eta), i, y	ē as in *beet*.
o	ô as in *on* (rounded).
ou	o͞o as in *boot*.
ei, oi, yi, ui	ē as in *beet*.
av (au), ev (eu) before b, g, d, z, l, m, n, r	äv, ĕv (*v* as in *every*).
before th, k, x, p, s, t, f, h (kh), ps	äf, ĕf (*f* as in *off*).

CONSONANTS

b (v)	*v* as in *very*.
kh (ch) before vowels	*h* as in *he*.
otherwise	*k(h)* as in Scot. *loch* and Ger. *ach*.
d (dh)	*th* as in *then*. (Cf. *th*.)
g (gh) before ē and ĕ	*y* as in *yes*.
before ä, ô, o͞o, and all consonants	properly "gh" (voiced velar fricative), but here transcribed *g* as in *go*.
gi (ghi) before vowels	*y* as in *yes*.
gg (ng), gk (nk)	*ngg* as in *stronger*.
gch (nch, nkh)	*ngh* as in *bring' her'*
h	When initial, *h* is sometimes silent.
mb, mp	*mb* or *b*
nd, nt	*nd* or *d*

Final *n* after *o*, and final *on* after a vowel are frequently not pronounced.

ph	*f* as in *ferry*.
ps	*ps* as in *leaps*.
r (rh)	*r* trilled with tip of tongue.
s before b, d, g, m, n, r	*z* as in *maze*.
otherwise	*s* as in *so* and *yes*.

In the names of islands of the Aegean, final *s* is frequently not pronounced.

th	"th" as in *thin*. (Cf. *d*.)

HUNGARIAN

In Hungarian or Magyar the accent is normally on the first syllable. In compound words, the first syllable of each component after the first receives secondary stress. Note that an acute accent placed above a vowel in the spelling indicates a long vowel, not a stress.

Hungarian	*Explanation*
a	ŏ as in *odd* (with some rounding).
á	ä as in *father*.
c, cz	*ts* as in *rats*.
cs	*ch* as in *church*.
gy	*d(y)* or by assimilation to following voiceless consonants, *t(y)*. Compare *duty* and *tune* pronounced dyōō′-tĭ and tyōōn′.
h	*h* as in *hat*, but silent after *g* and *t*.
j	*y* as in *yes*. Sometimes this sound occurs after a vowel. It seems odd to an English speaker but it is similar to the vowel ĭ as in *it*.
ö, ő	û as in *urn*, ö being short and ő long.
s	*sh* as in *shall*.
sz	*s* as in *sit*.
y	"liquifies" a preceding *g*, *l*, *n*, *t*. Compare the *ny* of English *canyon* with the *n* of *can*, and the *li* of *million* with the *l* of *mill*. See *gy* above. Otherwise *y* is ĭ or ē.
zs	*zh*, the medial consonant of *leisure*.

In Hungarian as in English there is much assimilation of consonants, as some of the names show. A voiceless consonant (p, t, k, s, f, *etc.*) will cause a preceding voiced consonant (b, d, g, z, v, *etc.*) to become voiceless. Likewise a voiced consonant voices a preceding voiceless consonant.

NAMES OF INDIA

The names of India are continually more and less Anglicized. It is often difficult to tell which is the most suitable of the various pronunciations a name has. For example, the "short *a*" is pronounced in the neighborhood of ŭ (the vowel of *but*) or schwa (the *a* of *about* and *sofa*). When it is Anglicized, it is pronounced like the *a* of *bat*. Thus every name with short *a* has at least two pronunciations of that vowel, ŭ and ă, and sometimes a third, ä. It is usually safer to take a recognized English pronunciation than to attempt to construct a native one from the accepted spelling, for the spelling is often an English corruption, misleading except for an English pronunciation.

The syllables of Indian names are accented almost evenly. The placing of an accent mark, therefore, is often an effort to prevent false stressing, and sometimes it is unfortunate. But one cannot omit the marks, as in the case of Chinese, because many of the names have been spelled and pronounced as if they were English, or half-English. Many Indians in the civil services have accepted the Anglicized forms.

In India *th* is an aspirated *t*. It is not *th* as in *thin* or as in *this*. Compare the usage of Burman.

ITALIAN

Words of more than one syllable are frequently accented on the next to the last; there are, however, many exceptions. A mistaken accent is made more painful by the American habit of overstressing foreign words. It is always better to stress lightly.

As an authority on the accenting of place names, we have, on Professor Dino Bigongiari's advice, followed the *Indice Generale della Carta d'Italia del T. C. I.* (Touring Club Italiano).

VOWELS

Italian has two or three qualities of *e* and of *o*. The American English sounds which most closely approach all of them are ĕ as in *bed* and ô as in *bawd*, though these vowels are more "open" than Italian "close *e*" and "close *o*". American ā (as in *ate*) and ō (as in *go*) are diphthongal—āĭ and ōo͝o, and quite out of place in Italian words. A skilled speaker of Italian will of course make subtle distinctions in vowels. An American, not very familiar with the language, had better stick to ä, ĕ, ē, ô, o͞o. There is no other error so bad as *Enna* pronounced ā'-nä, for this pronunciation is not Italian and not English.

In vowel compounds, *a*, *e*, and *o* keep their own values; *i* and *u*, unstressed, become glide sounds, *y* and *w*. It. *Gaeta*, gä-ĕ'-tä; *Leone*, lĕ-ô'-nĕ; *Scuola*, skwô'-lä; *Pistoia*, pē-stô'-yä; but note *Pavia*, pä-vē'-ä.

CONSONANTS

Italian consonants are not difficult to pronounce, but the spelling may mislead Americans. An Italian makes doubled consonants long.

Italian		*Explanation*
c, cc	before a, o, u, or cons.	*k* as in *kit*. It. *Capri*, kä'-prē; *Croce*, krô'-chĕ.
	before e, i	*ch* as in *church*. It. *Cenci*, chĕn'-chē. Followed by *a*, *o*, and *u*, the *i* is practically silent. It. *Ciano*, chä'-nô; *Boccaccio*, bôk-kät'-chô.
ch, cch		*k* as in *kit*. The *k*- sound is indicated by *c* before *o*, *a*, and *u*, and by *ch* before *i* and *e*. It. *bianco*, byän'-kô; *bianchi*, byän'-kē (*or*

		byä′-nkô, byä′-nkē); *vecchio*, vĕk′-kyô. Note also the pronunciation of *i* as a glide in *Chianti*, kyän′-tē (*or* kyä′-ntē); *Chiesa*, kyĕ′-zä; *Chioggia*, kyôd′-jä; *Chiusa*, kyo͞o′-sä.
g, gg	before a, o, u, or cons.	*g* as in *go*. It. *Gaeta*, gä-ĕ′-tä; *Grancia*, grän′-chä. See also *gh*, *gli*.
	before e, i	*j* as in *judge*. It. *Genova*, jĕ′-nô-vä. Followed by *a*, *o*, and *u*, the *i* is practically silent. It. *Giovanni*, jô-vän′-nē; *Perugia*, pĕ-ro͞o′-jä; *Foggia*, fôd′-jä.
gh		*g* as in *go*. This sound is indicated by *g* before *o*, *a*, and *u*, and by *gh* before *i* and *e*. It. *Ghigo*, gē′-gô. Note also the pronunciation of *i* as a glide in *Ghiaia*, gyä′-yä.
gli		*ly* as in Eng. *hellion*. It. *Ventimiglia*, vĕn-tē-mē′-lyä; *Gigli*, jē′-lyē.
gn		*ny* as in Sp. *cañón* (French *gn*), almost Eng. *canyon*. It. *Foligno*, fô-lē′-nyô.
gu		*gw* as in *Gwendolyn*. It. *Guardia*, gwär′-dyä; *Guido*, gwē′-dô. (In French and Spanish, to the contrary, *gu* before *e* and *i* is pronounced simply *g* as in *get*, the *u* being silent.)
i		ē, when alone and with consonants; *y* in the neighborhood of vowels. It. *Pistoia*, pē-stô′-yä; *Siena*, syĕ′-nä; *Fiume*, fyo͞o′-mĕ.
j		a variant spelling of *i*.
qu		*kw* as in *question*. It. *Quirinale*, kwē-rē-nä′-lĕ. (In French and Spanish, to the contrary, *qu* before *e* and *i* is pronounced simply *k* as in *kit*, the *u* being silent.)
s		*s* as in *sit*, except it becomes *z* before voiced consonants and, from Naples to the south, between vowels. It. *Sbarco*, zbär′-kô; *Cosenza*, kô-zĕn′-tsä.
sc	before a, o, u, or cons.	*sk* as in *sky*. It. *Scuola*, skwô′-lä.
	before e, i	*sh* as in *shall*. It. *Bisceglie*, bē-shĕ′-lyĕ. Followed by *a*, *o*, *u*, the *i* is practically silent. It. *Sciacca*, shäk′-kä.
sch		*sk* as in *sky*. The *sk*- sound is indicated by *sc* before *a*, *o*, and *u*, and by *sch* before *i* and *e*. It. *Scalea*, skä-lĕ′-ä; *scherzo*, skĕr′-tsô. Note

	also the pronunciation of *i* as a glide in *Ischia*, ē′-skyä.
z, zz	*ts* as in *rats*. It. *Spezia*, spĕ′-tsyä; *Arezzo*, ä-rĕt′-sô.
	dz, occasionally, as in *beds*. It. *mezzo*, mĕd′-zô; *Gozzano*, gôd-zä′-nô.

JAPANESE

In the "Roman" spelling of Japanese, the vowels have values similar to those of Spanish and Italian. They may be approximately rendered in English as follows: *a* as in *father*, *e* as in *men*, *i* as in *machine*, *o* as in *more*, *u* like the vowel of *pool*. Final *e* is pronounced schwa.

There is no strong accent, and the best rule for speakers of English is to pronounce the names with level stress, giving to each syllable a full share of time and force. This may prove difficult if not impossible in an English sentence, but for the sake of attaining something like uniformity CBS speakers should not emphasize the stresses they add. Names of four syllables like *Yokohama* will fall into the pattern of ′ x ′ x, stressed, unstressed, stressed, unstressed.

There is dialectal variety, but *j* may be pronounced as in *jam*, *g* as in *go*, *ch* as in *cheap*.

The combinations *ae*, *ai*, *oi*, *ui* are not true diphthongs but two separate vowels with the second weaker than the first. However, it is not unreasonable for us to pronounce both *ae* and *ai* as "long ī."

KOREAN

The names should be pronounced with level stress, each syllable receiving its full share of force and time.

LATVIAN

Lettish or Latvian is always stressed on the first syllable.

A long vowel is indicated by the macron, ā, ē, ī, *etc.*

Diphthongs such as *ie* are transcribed, when stressed, ē′-ĕ′ rather than yĕ, for the elements are of approximately equal importance. Compare the Finnish diphthongs.

Latvian	*Explanation*
c before e, i	*ts* as in *rats*.
otherwise	*k* as in *koko*.
j	*y* as in *yet*.
ņ	*ny* as in Sp. *cañón* (Fr. *gn*), almost Eng. *canyon*.

v	final	*f* as in *off*.
	otherwise	*v* as in *very*.
ž		*zh*, the medial consonant in *pleasure* and *leisure*.

LITHUANIAN

Lithuanian has both stress and pitch accents which can not be reduced to English rules.

In the pronunciation of the Lithuanian informants *ai* was nearer to ĕĭ than to ī, the transcription here used for convenience.

Lithuanian may employ *i* to indicate the palatal quality of a preceding consonant. It is here transcribed *y*, although one may not be conscious of its effect in listening to the speech of Lithuanians. *Šiauliai* sounds like a Virginian's shou′-lī *or* -lĕĭ, quite as much as shyou′-lyī *or* -lyĕĭ. Similarly one may hear palatal quality where the spelling does not indicate it (as before high and mid front vowels). For example *Panëvežis*, q.v.

Lithuanian *e* indicates an open vowel, ĕ or ă, while *ė* indicates a close vowel like the first part of English ā [ay]. Both are here transcribed ĕ, except that stressed *ė*, like *ei*, is transcribed ā [ay].

j is pronounced *y*.

š and ž are pronounced, respectively, *sh* as in *shall* and *zh* like the medial consonant of *leisure* and *pleasure*.

y is a vowel pronounced ē as in English *beet*.

MALAYAN

The Indonesian or Malayan languages are spoken in Madagascar, the Malay Peninsula, the East Indies, Formosa, and the Philippines. The place names that appear in the news are spelled and usually pronounced according to the usage of European nations that controlled these territories—France, England, Holland, Portugal, China, and Spain. The Indonesian languages and the Oceanic together form the Austronesian family. See *Languages of the Pacific*.

NORWEGIAN. See *Scandinavian Languages*

LANGUAGES OF THE PACIFIC

It is important to remember that the accent usually falls on the next to the last syllable in names of the East Indies and the myriad islands of Oceania. This is the most comfortable accent for Americans, but in an effort to be correct, we frequently are overcorrect and stress the last syllable of names that are properly accented on the penult, as in Bandung, Balik-Papan, Balabac, Denpasar. The vowels have the "continental" values of Spanish or Italian. The consonants we may pronounce as in English, with *g* as in *get* and *ng* as in *singer* (seldom as in *finger*). See *Tahiti.*

PERSIAN or IRANIAN

"Persian orthography is by no means fixed and consistent, and especially is there uncertainty about the identity and length of many vowels." *PÇGN.*

In Persian the sound of "long *a*" may suggest English ô, or, in poetry, ôu, rather than English ä, but the transcription ä is here employed as more suitable for American radio speakers.

The pronunciations were prepared in consultation with Mr. C. K. Wilkinson of the Metropolitan Museum of Art, New York.

PHILIPPINES. *See note appended to the section on Spanish*

POLISH. See *Slavic Languages*

PORTUGUESE

Words ending in vowels, except ã, or in *m* or *s*, are accented on the next to the last syllable. Words ending in consonants, except *m* or *s*, or in ã, are accented on the last syllable. Words that do not conform to these rules carry in Portuguese orthography a written accent (circumflex ê or acute é). See the last paragraph.

Unstressed vowels tend, like unstressed vowels in English, to become "centralized." That is to say, they tend towards schwa (ə or *uh*) or short *i* (ĭ).

VOWELS

Portuguese		*Explanation*
a	stressed	ä (ah) as in *father*. Before *l* it becomes ô as in Eng. *all.* Port. *Natal,* nä-tôl′.
	unstressed, expecially if final	tends to become ə (*uh*) as in *tellable* and *sofa.* In Brazil, often remains ä.
ã		See *Nasalized Vowels and Diphthongs.*
e	stressed	ĕ as in *edify.*
	unstressed, especially if final	ə (uh) in Portugal, ĭ in the islands and in Brazil. Practically silent or ĭ when initial in words like *espirito* (ĭ)spē′-rē-tŏŏ [(i)spee′-ree-tu].
ei		ā as in *aid.* However it may be reduced to ĕ in unstressed syllables. Port. *Figueiredo,* fē-gĕ-rĕ′-dŏŏ.

o	stressed	ô as in *more.*
	unstressed, especially if final	o͝o as in *pull.*
oi		ŏĭ as in *oil,* but sometimes the *o* is "weak" and *oi* is pronounced wē. Port. *Coimbra,* kwēm′-brə.
ou		ō as in *go.*

NASALIZED VOWELS AND DIPHTHONGS

Vowels marked with a til, for example ã, õ, and vowels before *m* + cons., *n* + cons., or final *m* are strongly nasalized.

ã	ûN. Like a Virginian's nasal pronunciation of *long.* In Brazil, almost ĕ as in nasal *men.*
ãe, ãi	ã (as above) + ĭ. Not far from a Virginian's nasal pronunciation of *mind;* and (for Brazil) Eng. *aim* (or āng).
ão	ã (as above) + ŭ. Similar to Virginian nasal pronunciations of the diphthong in *house.*
-em (final)	ã (as above) + ĭ. Similar to nasal American *mind;* and (for Brazil) Eng. *aim* (or āng).
õe	o + ĭ. Similar to a nasal pronunciation of Eng. *poem,* pō′-ĭm (or -ĭng). (Port. *põem* is another story.)

CONSONANTS

c	before e, i	*s* as in *so.*
	otherwise	*k* as in *koko.*
ç		*s* as in *so.*
ch		*sh* as in *shall.*
g	before e, i	*zh,* the medial consonant of *pleasure* and *leisure.*
	otherwise	*g* as in *go.*
h		silent
j (only before a, o, u)		*zh,* the medial consonant of *pleasure* and *leisure.*
lh		*ly* as in *million.* Cf. It. *gli.*
m		For *-em* see *Nasalized Vowels* above.
nh		*ny* as in Sp. *cañón.* Almost Eng. *canyon.*
qu	before e, i	*k* (the *u* is silent)
	otherwise	*kw*
s	initial, following a consonant, and when doubled (ss)	*s* as in *so.*

between vowels	*z* as in *zebra.*
before c, f, p, q, t, and when final	*sh* as in *shall,* but in Brazil usually *s* as in *so.*
before b, d, g (as in *go*), or any voiced cons.	*zh,* the medial consonant of *leisure* and *pleasure,* but in Brazil usually *z* as in *zebra.*

Note: The pronunciation of final *s* and *z* will be affected by the initial sound of the next word in the same phrase.

x	*sh* or *s* or *ks;* there is no dependable rule.
z initial and between vowels	*z* as in *zebra.*
before c, f, p, q, t, s	*sh* as in *shall,* but in Brazil usually *s.*
before b, d, g (as in *go*) or any voiced cons.	*zh,* the medial consonant of *leisure* and *pleasure,* but in Brazil usually *z.*

NOTE

No distinction is here made between close and open vowels. In Portuguese orthography a circumflex accent indicates a stressed close vowel. An acute accent indicates a stressed open vowel. A grave accent is placed only on an unaccented vowel to indicate that it receives special attention. For a much more detailed account of the pronunciation of Portuguese, see Joseph Dunn, *Grammar of the Portuguese Language* (New York, Hispanic Society of America; London, D. Nutt, 1930); Edwin B. Williams, *Introductory Portuguese Grammar* (New York, 1942).

RUMANIAN

There is no simple rule of accent in Rumanian.

With the following exceptions, Rumanian spelling has usual English values.

Rumanian	*Explanation*
ă stressed	û as in *urn.*
unstressed	ə (uh) as in *about.*
â	û as in *urn.*
c before e, i	*ch* as in *church.* Compare Italian.
otherwise	*k* as in *kit.*
ch	*k* as in *kit.* Compare Italian.
e	sometimes, esp. when initial, pronounced yĕ as in *yes.*
e unstressed before a vowel	*y* as in *you.* After *c* (see above) and *g* (see the following), it is practically silent.
g before e, i	*j* as in *judge.* Compare Italian.
otherwise	*g* as in *go.*

gh	*g* as in *go*. Compare Italian.
h	*h* before vowels, otherwise *k*(*h*) as in Scottish *loch*.
i unstressed before a vowel	*y* as in *yes*. After *c* and *g* (see above), it is practically silent. Compare Italian.
final	ĭ or *y* pronounced so short that it practically disappears. Rumanian *Ploeşti*, plô-yĕsht′.
î	variant of â (see above).
j	*zh*, the medial consonant in *pleasure* and *leisure*.
o unstressed before *a*	*w* as in *wash*.
ou	ō as in *both*.
ş	*sh* as in *shall*.
ţ	*ts* as in *rats*.
u unstressed before a vowel	*w* as in *wash*. Compare Italian.
final	o͝o (very short).

NOTE

In Rumanian the definite article is a suffix *-l*, *-ul*, *-le* (masculine) and *-a* (feminine). It may or may not be added to the names of rivers and mountains when they are referred to in the news. Compare the definite and indefinite forms of Albanian names.

RUSSIAN. *See Slavic Languages*

SCANDINAVIAN LANGUAGES

Usually the first syllable bears the principal accent of the word.

VOWELS

In stressed syllables a vowel is long if it is final or followed by one consonant; otherwise, and in unstressed syllables, a vowel is short.

Spelling		*Norwegian*	*Swedish*	*Danish*
a	long	ä	ä or ô	ä or ă
	short	ä or ŭ	ä or ŭ	ä or ŭ
aa, å		ô or ō	ō or ô	ô
æ, ä (long and short)		ĕ or ă	ĕ or ă	ĕ or ă
Sometimes *e* is written for *æ*.				
e	long	ā or ĭ	ā or ĭ	ā or ĭ
	short	ĕ (or ă)	ĕ	ĕ or ĭ
	unstressed	ə	ə	ə

i	long	ē	ē	ē
	short	ē	ē	ē or ĭ
o	long	ō or o͞o	o͞o	ō
	short	o͝o or o͞o	o͞o	ō

Sometimes *o* is pronounced ô, as if it were *aa* or *å*.

ö, ø, œ (long and short)		û	û	û
u	long	o͞o or ü	ü	o͞o
	short	o͞o or ü	o͝o	o͞o
y		ü	ü	ü

CONSONANTS

In Norwegian and Swedish all doubled consonants are pronounced long.

Spelling		*Norwegian*	*Swedish*	*Danish*
b		As in English.	As in English.	*b* or *p*
c	Before *e, i, y, æ, ä*, in all *c* is pronounced *s*; otherwise in all pronounced *k*.			
d		Silent after *l* and *n* and often when final in word or syllable.	As in English.	Initially *d* or *t*. After vowels, *th* as in *this*. Silent as in Norwegian.
f		As in English.	As in English.	As in English, but silent in the word *af*.
g	pronounced as in *go*	before *a, o, u, e æ, ø, å*, and cons.	before *a, o, u, å*, and cons.	before all vowels and consonants. May suggest *k* as in *koko*.

In all, *g* pronounced *ng* before *n* (but occasionally ĭ in Danish and Norwegian).

g	pronounced *y* as in *yet*	before *i, y, j*. Silent in *og, -ig, fugl, søndag*, etc.	before *e, i, y, ä, ö, j* and after *l, r*. Silent in *-ig, -igt, morgon, dag*, etc.	pronounced voiced *k*(*h*) or velar *y* after vowels and *l, r*. Sometimes silent. *k*(*h*) before *t*. *gg* is pronounced *kk*.
h		Silent before *j, v*.	Silent before *j*.	Silent before *j, v*.
j	In all, pronounced *y* as in *yet*.			

k as in *koko*	before *a*, *e*, *o*, *u*, *æ*, *ø*, *å* and consonants including *n*. before *i*, *y*, *j*, suggests *ky* or *ch* or *h*. Before these vowels *sk* is pronounced *sh*.	before *a*, *o*, *u*, *å*, and consonants, including *n*. before *e*, *i*, *y*, *ä*, *ö*, *j*, pronounced like the *ch* of *church*. Before these vowels *sk* is pronounced *sh*.	As in English but pronounced before *n*.
r	trilled	trilled	uvular or "Parisian" *r*.
rs	sh	sh	unvoiced uvular *r* + *s*.
s	In all three, pronounced *s* as in *so* except in *rs*, *sj*, which see. Never pronounced *z*.		
sj	sh	sh	sh
skj	sh	sh	sk(y)-
v	Oc. silent when final.	As in English.	Oc. silent when final.
w	In all, pronounced *v*.		
x	In all, pronounced *ks*.		
z	In all, pronounced *s* as in *so*.		

NOTE ON "EI, EJ" AND "AU, AV"

The diphthong *ei*, *ej* is here transcribed ā (ay) though it varies in dialects from ī (ai) to ā (ay). The diphthong *au*, *av* is pronounced ǎu or, as in Oslo, ǎv. The nearest English sound is the *ou* [*au*] of *house*, and it is so transcribed.

NOTE

This outline is based on materials provided by Prof. Einar Haugen. While it is too complicated to follow easily, it will explain contradictory transcriptions of Scandinavian place names. Convenient grammars in English are Einar Haugen, *Beginning Norwegian* (New York, 1937); W. G. Johnson, *Beginning Swedish* (Rock Island, 1939); and Ingeborg Stemann, *A New Danish Reader* (Copenhagen, 1939).

SERBIAN. See *Slavic Languages*.

SLAVIC LANGUAGES

There is no simple rule for the accenting of Russian and Bulgarian. Polish is accented on the syllable next to the last. Czech (Bohemian) and

Slovak are accented on the first syllable. Serb-Croat values of intonation and quantity are foreign to English. However, in English contexts an accent is given, usually to the first or the second syllable. Occasionally in this list two accents are marked to prevent mispronunciation or to reconcile contradictory authorities, each of which in its way is right.

In Czech and Slovak spelling an acute accent placed above a vowel is a sign of length, not stress. An apostrophe indicates a liquid sound. The accent of Polish ó indicates quality not stress.

In the following table are explained symbols of the official roman spelling of Czechoslovakia, Poland, and Yugoslavia (which also has an official Cyrillic spelling). Added in parenthesis are comments on difficult points in the customary American transliteration of the official Cyrillic spelling of Russia and Bulgaria.

Czechosl.	*Polish*	*Serb-Croat*	*Explanation*
	ą		ôN as in Fr. *bon*.
c	c	c	*ts* as in *rats*. In Polish before *i* or *j* + vowel it tends to ć.
	ć	ć	*ch* as in *cheese* (or *tsy*).
č	cz	č	*ch* as in *choke*.
ch *or* h	ch (Also Russian and Bulgarian *kh*.)	h	*h* (as in *hat*) before a vowel; otherwise *k*(*h*), as in Scot. *loch*. Rus. and Bulg. *kh* is Anglicized as *k*.
	dz		*dz* as in *buds;* when final, *ts* as in *rats;* before *i* it is pronounced *j* as in *judge*.
dž	dż	dž	*j* as in *judge*.
d'	dź	đ, dj, gj	nearly *j* as in *jill* (or *dy*).

(Russian *e* is sometimes pronounced yô as in English *yawl*. For example, *Orel*, ŏr-yôl′.)

	ę		ăN as in Fr. *fin*.
ě			yĕ as in *yet*.
h		h	(See *ch* above.)
j	j i + vowel	j	*y* (consonant) as in *yes;* but when after a vowel and followed by a consonant, or final, it forms a diphthong: *ej* = ā (ay).
	ł		(Pronounce *ł* and *l*, like English *l*. See note on page 28 below.)

(For Russian and Bulgarian *kh*, see *ch* above.)

l			when a vowel, pronounced as in English *cradle*.

ň	ń	nj	*ny* as in Sp. *cañón* (Fr. *gn*), almost English *canyon*.
ou			ō as in *go*.
	ó		o͝o as in pull (or o͞o as in *food*).
r	r	r	when a vowel, pronounced like Am. Eng. *err*, ûr. When a cons., pronounced as a trilled *r*.
ř			*rzh* (*r* + *zh* as below)
	rz		*zh*, the medial consonant of *leisure* and *pleasure*. When final in word or syllable it tends toward *sh* as in *show*.
	ś		*sh* as in *sheen* (or *sy*).
	s + i + vowel		
š	sz	š	*sh* as in *show*.
t'			nearly *ch* as in *chill* (or *ty*).
ů			o͞o as in *food*.
	w (Russian *v*)		*v* as in *very;* when final *f* as in *off*.
y, ý	y		ĭ as in *it* or ē as in *beet* or wē.
(Also Russian and Bulgarian *y*.)			
	z		*z* as in *zebra* except after *r*. See *rz*.
ž	ż	ž	*zh*, the medial consonant of *leisure* and *pleasure*. When final in word or syllable it may become *sh* as in *shall*.
	ź		*zh*, as described above (or *zy*).

Otherwise the letters have approximately the usual English values except that the voiced consonants (b, d, dz, dž, g, v, w, z, ž) tend to become the corresponding voiceless consonants (p, t, c, č, k, f, s, š) if followed by a voiceless consonant or if final. This tendency is not marked in Serb-Croat.

NOTE ON POLISH "Ł"

In English usage Polish *ł* and *l* should both be pronounced *l*, not *w* and *l* respectively. Polish speakers make a distinction between *l* and *ł*, something like the difference between the usual English *l's* in *lip* and *old*. The question is whether this distinction is important enough for English speakers to use *w* for *ł*, as is the recommendation in many dictionaries. Our consultants inform us that in the pronunciation of Polish cultivated by Polish radio announcers, singers, and clergymen, *l* and *ł*, though different, will be heard by English listeners as *l*. Polish friends say that *w* for *ł* sounds as odd to them as to other Americans. So *Łuck* should be simply lo͞otsk (lutsk), which isn't too simple after all. And the learned can try to give this *ł* the quality of the *l* in *old*.

NOTE ON ENGLISH, FRENCH, AND GERMAN SPELLINGS

Because of the peculiarities of the Roman alphabets of Czechoslovak, Polish, and Serb-Croat, and in the absence of official Roman spellings of Russian and Bulgarian, the sounds of these languages may be spelled according to English, French, or German conventions. Accordingly we find *Drazha*, *Draja*, and *Drascha* for *Draža; Chetnik*, *Tchetnik*, and *Tschetnik* for *Četnik; Kiev* or *Kieff*, *Kiev* or *Kief*, and *Kijew; Lapats* and *Lapatz* for *Lapac;* and so on. *Moscow*, *Moscou*, and *Moskau* for *Moskva* (Rus. transliterated) show older variations of sound as well as of spelling.

For English speakers the English spellings are comparatively simple, though we need a better indication than *e* for the sound yô in *Orel*. The French spellings sometimes mislead us, as for instance in *Chaliapin*, a Russian name that we should spell *Shalyapin*. Even the official British PCGN continues to use *j* with its French value in spelling *Jitomir*, which is familiar to American readers as *Zhitomir*. In our press dispatches the spelling of place names usually follows, within typographical limitations, the examples of the National Geographic Society, Webster's Dictionary, and other standard American reference works. Personal names, however, are often spelled as if they were French, because the French cultural tradition is strong in Europe and these names have not been respelled by the editors of our reference works.

NOTES ON RUSSIAN

Because of the gender of words understood but not expressed, the names of small villages may end in *a* (or *aya*), and the names of large villages in *o;* the names of cities may lack a suffix. As a community grows, it may pass through all three stages: *Gavrilova*, *Gavrilovo*, and *Gavrilov*. This and another picturesque habit—that of changing the names to honor new heroes—cause maps and sometimes dispatches to disagree. The forms preferred here are those of the recent map of the National Geographic Society.

The Russian *a*, stressed and unstressed, is here transcribed ä, though its quality may approach ŭ, the vowel of *but*, especially as pronounced by an Englishman. Whether the spelling *o* is to be rendered in phonetics ŏ, ô, ō, or ŭ is a problem that has confused makers of dictionaries. This editor has tried to follow a consistent practice, stressed *o* being usually rendered as ô, unstressed *o* as ŏ. Many phoneticians would prefer the use of ŭ for the sounds of *a* and unstressed *o*, but for the purpose of this list it seemed wise not to depart too far from present dictionary transcription and from customary spelling. Most Russian unstressed vowels in rapid speech will sound to a foreign ear like schwa.

Between a consonant and a following vowel, *y* is written to indicate a soft sign in the Russian Cyrillic spelling. If a vowel does not follow, *y* is written for the soft sign only with *l*, *m*, and *n*. A soft vowel is indicated by prefixing *y*, as in *Orel*, ŏr-yôl′. Russian *e* is "softer" to American ears than ĕ; hence the frequent spellings of *ie* and *ye* as in *Dniepr* for *Dnepr; Izvyestia* for *Izvestia;* and *Soviet*. In this list, however, *y* is not used to show this quality of *e*.

SPANISH

Words ending in a vowel, or in *n* or *s*, stress the next to the last syllable. Words ending in a consonant, except *n* or *s*, stress the last syllable. Words not following these rules bear an accent mark. The *Pequeño Larousse Ilustrado*, in the second or encyclopedic half, shows the exceptional accents of almost all Spanish names that will appear in the news, e.g. *Ávila, Cárdenas, Nájera.*

Spanish		*Explanation*
b		See note on page 31.
c	before e, i	*s* (Am. Sp.) as in *so*, or "th" (Castilian) as in *thin*.
	otherwise	*k* as in *koko*. Sp. *cocer*, kô-sĕr′ *or* -thĕr′; *acción*, äk-syôn′. The *k*-sound before *e* and *i* is indicated by *qu*, which see.
d	initial	very like English *d*.
	medial	*th* as in *gather*. Sp. *dedo*, dĕ′-*th*ô.
	final and in *-ado*	*th* as in *gather*, or it may disappear, as is amiably illustrated in the last phrases of the song *La Paloma*.
g	before e, i	*h* as in *heat* (or a voiceless uvular sound similar to the voiced Parisian *r*.) Sp. *gente*, hĕn′-tĕ. For the *h*-sound before a, o, u, see *j*.
	otherwise	*g* as in *go*. Sp. *gato grande*, gä′-tô grän′-dĕ. See *gu*.
gu	before e, i	*g* as in *go*. Sp. *guerra*, gĕ′-rä. The *u* is silent.
	before a, o	*gw* or, esp. when intervocalic, *w*. Sp. agua, ä′-wä, *Guadalajara* (g)wä′-*th*ä-lä-hä′-rä.
h		silent. Sp. *Chihuahua*, chē-wä′-wä.
j		*h* as in *hot* (or a voiceless uvular sound similar to the voiced Parisian *r*). Sp. *Jorge*, hôr′-hĕ.
ll		*y* (Am. Sp.) as in *yet*, or *ly* (Castilian) like *li* in Eng. *million* and like It. *gli*. In Argentina and Uruguay often *j* as in *just* or *zh*, the medial consonant of *leisure* and *pleasure*.
ñ		*ny* as in Eng. *canyon*, *ni* as in Eng. *onion*. Fr. and It. *gn*.

qu	before e, i	*k* as in *kit*. Sp. *que*, kĕʹ. This convention of silent *u* French shares, but not Italian. The *k*-sound before *a* and *o* is indicated by *c*, which see.
s		*s* as in *so*.
v		See note below.
x	between vowels	*ks*. Sp. *éxito*, ĕkʹ-sē-tô.
	before consonants	*s*. Sp. *extranjero*, ĕs-trän-hĕʹ-rô.
	for *j*	*h*, formerly *sh*. *México* or *Méjico*, mĕʹ-hē-kô. *Oaxaca*, wä-häʹ-kä. *Quixote* or *Quijote*, kē-hôʹ-tĕ, *formerly* kē-shôʹ-tĕ. *Jerez*, hĕ-rĕthʹ, formerly *Xeres*, shĕʹ-rĕs. But *Xochimilco*, sô-chē-mēlʹ-kô *or* shô- *or* hô-.
y (consonant)		*y* as in *yes*. In Argentina and Uruguay often *j* as in *judge* or *zh*, the medial consonant of *leisure* and *pleasure*. Sp. *yo*, yô; Arg., Urug. jô *or* zhô.

VOWELS AND DIPHTHONGS

Weak vowels *i* (*y*) and *u* combine with strong vowels *a*, *e*, *o* and with one another to form diphthongs. In these the strong vowel takes the stress or, in the case of *iu* and *ui*, the second vowel. Sp. *Teruel*, tĕ-rwĕlʹ; *baile*, bīʹ-lĕ; *hay*, īʹ; *Ruiz*, rwēsʹ *or* rwēthʹ. Exceptions are indicated by an accent. Sp. *Pía*, pēʹ-ä.

Strong vowels remain distinct from one another. Spanish *creer*, crĕ-ĕrʹ; *faena*, fä-ĕʹ-nä; *Saavedra*, säʹ-ä-vĕʹ-*th*rä.

NOTE ON "B" AND "V"

b is usually a spirant sound like English *v* but made with both lips instead of the lower lip and the upper teeth. It is like *b* (*bb*) in our southern dialect pronunciation of *river*, often spelled "ribber." In Spanish, *b* and *v* are alternatives in spelling. They are usually Anglicized, however, as English *b* and English *v* respectively, according to the Spanish form most familiar in English; e.g., *Havana* rather than *Habana*.

CASTILIAN AS A STANDARD

American Spanish is related to Castilian Spanish much as American English is related to the "Received Standard" of England. In the new world, the dialects of Spanish provinces, particularly in southern Spain, and the Midland dialects of England formed the basis of the Spanish of Latin American capitals and the American English of the great cities of the United States. Thus what had been provincial speech in the homelands became metropolitan speech in America. Meanwhile in Spain the dialect of Castile and in England the dialect of London literary and political circles gained still more prestige at the expense of provincial dialects. At home the provincial accents more or less lost the battle, in the former colonies they won it. However, Castilian Spanish still has a prestige in the Spanish-speaking world that may seem curious to the proud or satisfied speakers of American English. If you ask the correct pronunciation of the Spanish name of a prominent leader, it will often be given in the Castilian form without regard to the speech of his constituents. Thus recently the female secretaries of both President Quezon and Senator Chavez gave me a detailed description of the Castilian quality of *z* in these names, although it is rare in the Rio Grande Valley and in the Philippines. But this phenomenon is not exactly parallel to an American's acquiring a broad *a*, for a remarkable number of non-Castilian speakers of Spanish regard Castilian as the standard. If you ask for a pronunciation, they wish to give you the best. Nevertheless this courtesy complicates the making of dictionaries where what is current in educated speech of the region is "standard" and "correct." For American radio the Spanish American *s* for *c* and *z* is certainly preferable for programs concerned with Spanish America. In pronouncing the names of famous cities and persons in Spain the circumstances of the broadcast should determine the accent.

SPANISH IN THE PHILIPPINES

The popular languages of the Philippines are Indonesian or Austronesian. Tagalog is especially important. English and Spanish are predominantly the languages of the schools, the government, and the churches. Place names and family names are Hispanicized Indonesian or Spanish. Spanish has controlled the spelling of the local languages, which, in turn, have probably influenced the pronunciation of Spanish in the Philippines.

a in unaccented syllables tends to become schwa (the *a* of *about* and of *sofa*).

c before *e* and *i*, and *z* are pronounced *s* rather than "th" as in *thin.*

d has less tendency to become *th.*

SWEDISH. See *Scandinavian Languages*

THAI or SIAMESE

Like Chinese, Thai is a tonal language with at least five, and in some dialects, seven tones. As the tone changes, the meaning of a syllable is changed. There is no accent in the English sense, but to our ear the tone itself, especially the high-pitched tone, may give the impression of an accent. Accent marks have here been used to assist pronunciation or at least to prevent greater mispronunciation.

One characteristic that Thai shares with English is a number of seemingly useless letters in its spelling. Some of the pronunciations here set forth may arouse disbelief, but our consultant, the Rev. Paul A. Eakin of Bangkok, said them so, and he was born there. Moreover I have found no one to say him nay. Mr. Eakin writes, "Each tone is indicated in the written language by combinations of different class consonants with long and short vowels and by use of about three tonal marks placed over the syllable. There are definite rules for tones, and there are practically no exceptions. Difficulties arise mainly in connection with the 'silent' letters, which are retained in words originating in the Pali or Sanskrit to indicate the origin of the word. The alphabet is an adaptation of the Cambodian script existing in the middle of the thirteenth century. It contains some 44 consonants and as many vowel sounds. Since there are but 21 consonant sounds, this means that in many cases one sound is represented by several letters. The Thai Government is attempting to reduce the number of these consonants and so simplify the alphabet." See also Thomas A. Sebeok, "The Languages of Southeastern Asia," *The Far Eastern Quarterly*, August, 1943. There is no distinction between White Thai and Black Thai.

l, *r*, *y*, when final in a syllable, have the sound of *n*.

ch, *chj*, *d*, *dt*, *s*, *st*, when final in a syllable, have the sound of *t*.

b, *bp*, when final in a syllable, have the sound of *p*.

TURKISH

Turkish has no accent in the English sense of the word. The stresses here marked will serve to prevent mis-stressing, if they are not overemphasized, but they may be ignored in favor of a level pronunciation—so far as that is possible in an English sentence. The Turkish informants did not recommend a slight accent upon final syllables.

The circumflex is a sign of length and in the case of â it may indicate the sound *yah*.

Turkish	*Explanation*
c	*j* as in *just*.
ç	*ch* as in *church*.
g	*g* as in *go*.
ğ after a, ı, o, u ("hard" vowels)	silent
after e, i, ö, ü ("soft" vowels)	forms a diphthong: eğ = ā [ay]; öğ = ûĭ; üğ = üĭ; iğ is practically ē.
i (with dot)	ē as in *beet* or ĭ as in *sit*.
ı (without dot)	ĭ as in *bit*. (The Turkish sound, called "hoarse," "guttural," and "retracted," has no equi-

valent in English. It lies between ĭ and û. It may be transcribed schwa.)

j — *zh*, the medial consonant of *leisure* and *pleasure*.

ş — *sh* as in *shall*.

y — *y* introducing a diphthong, as in *you*, and *y* (or ĭ) completing a diphthong, as in *joy*, *oil*, *day*, *aid*.

A NOTE ON THE TRANSCRIPTION OF "E" AND "O"

English ĕ (eh) is usually preferable to English ā (ay) to indicate the pronunciation of French *é* and the close *e* of many other non-Germanic languages. The diphthongal character of English ā (ay), and its inevitable stress and length, is more painful than a failure to distinguish close and open *e*'s, at least in the pronunciation of occasional foreign names in an English context. The use of ĕ (eh) rather than ā (ay) is a departure from the practice of *War Words* (1st edition)—made at some cost. It was necessary when one heard on the same program the French learned in America and the French learned, by Americans, in France.

The use of ĕ (eh) rather than ā (ay) may also help to change the notion that every Italian *e* should be pronounced ā. The pronunciation of *Enna* as ā′-nä (ay′-nah), was the most unfortunate episode of the Sicilian verbal campaign. Insistence upon ĕ (eh) as the value of Italian *e* will extend to *Grosseto* and *Velletri*, where the vowel certainly is close, but in a stressed open syllable the symbol ĕ, interpreted by American speakers with our usual linguistic habits, may be sounded not too far from a close *e*. In any case this must be our reliance if we are to avoid a greater error.

Likewise ĕ (eh) has been preferred to ā (ay) in the transcription of Slavic languages. In the case of Russian, ā (ay) for stressed *e* and ĕ (eh) for unstressed *e*, worked well enough, but when it was necessary to devise a system for names in all the Slavic languages, it seemed better to use one symbol for stressed and unstressed *e*. If one symbol is used, ĕ (eh) is better than ā (ay).

The sound of ō as in *go* in American English is diphthongal ōŏŏ, in British English triphthongal or more. The associations of ô as it may occur in *orb*, *more*, *often*, *all* are nearer than ō to the sounds spelled *o* in many foreign languages.

At any time, of course, one could have adopted or devised special symbols for these foreign sounds. They would, however, have no special meaning for the users of this handbook. To the contrary, elaboration of symbols, a comfort to phoneticians, usually confuses and discourages everybody who has not a technical interest in phonetic problems. One man's meat is another man's person, as they say in New York.

USEFUL REFERENCE WORKS

The following reference books are all but indispensable for a study of pronunciation:

British Broadcasting Corporation, *Broadcast English* (London, 1932-1939). Seven pamphlets prepared for the BBC by A. Lloyd James.

Canadian Broadcasting Corporation, *Handbook for Announcers* (Ottawa, 1942). For Canadian place names.

Columbia Encyclopedia, The (New York, 1935).

Fowler, H. W., *A Dictionary of Modern English Usage* (Oxford, 1926).

Funk, Charles E., *What's the Name, Please?* (New York, 1936).

Funk and Wagnalls' New Standard Dictionary (New York, 1925).

Holt, Alfred H., *American Place Names* (New York, 1938).

Jones, Daniel, *An English Pronouncing Dictionary* (4th ed., New York, 1937).

Kenyon, J. S., *American Pronunciation* (8th ed., Ann Arbor, Mich., 1940).

Kenyon, J. S., and Knott, T. A., *A Pronouncing Dictionary of American English* (Springfield, Mass., 1944). This excellent dictionary, employing the alphabet of the International Phonetic Association, was received too late to be cited except in a few postscripts.

Krapp, G. P., *The English Language in America* (New York, 1925).

Mawson, C. O. Sylvester, *International Book of Names* (New York, 1933).

Permanent Committee on Geographical Names for British Official Use, *Lists* (Royal Geographical Society, London).

Thorndike-Century Senior Dictionary (New York, 1941).

U. S. Board on Geographical Names, *Reports* (Washington, D. C.)

Webster's New International Dictionary (2d. ed., Springfield, Mass., 1934), as interpreted by its prefatory "Guide to Pronunciation" (pp. xxii-lxxviii). Section 277 (pp. lix *ff*) lists for about 1100 debatable words the pronunciations given in seven authoritative dictionaries.

Webster's Biographical Dictionary (Springfield, Mass., 1943).

Consult also the files of the journal *American Speech*.

INDEX TO ABBREVIATIONS

Afghan.	Afghanistan
Afr.	Africa
Ala.	Alabama
Alb.	Albania
	Albanian
Alg.	Algeria
Am.	American
Arg.	Argentina
Austral.	Australia
Baluch.	Baluchistan
Belg.	Belgium
Braz.	Brazilian
Brit.	British
Bulg.	Bulgaria
	Bulgarian
Calab.	Calabria
Calif.	California
Ch.	China
co.	county
Col.	Colombia
collab.	collaborator with the Axis powers
Conn.	Connecticut
cons.	consonant
Cz.	Czechoslovakia
Del.	Delaware
Den.	Denmark
	Danish
dist.	district
Dodec.	Dodecanese Isls.
Du.	Dutch
Du. W. I.	Dutch West Indies
E. Afr.	East Africa
Eng.	England
	English
Est.	Estonia
	Estonian
Europ.	European
Fil.	Filipino
Fin.	Finland
	Finnish
Flem.	Flemish
for.	foreign
Fr.	France
	French
Fr. Eq. Afr.	French Equatorial Africa
Fr. Som.	French Somaliland
Ger.	Germany
	German
Gr.	Greece
	Greek
Hung.	Hungary
	Hungarian
Icel.	Iceland
Indo.	Indonesian
Indo-Ch.	Indo-China
Ind. Oc.	Indian Ocean
isl.	island
It.	Italy
	Italian
Jap.	Japan
	Japanese
Liecht.	Liechtenstein
Lith.	Lithuania
	Lithuanian
Madag.	Madagascar
Manchu.	Manchuria
Mass.	Massachusetts
Mex.	Mexico
Mich.	Michigan
Mo.	Missouri
Mon.	Monaco
Mor.	Morocco
mt.	mountain
N. C.	North Carolina
NEI	Netherlands East Indies
Neth.	Netherlands
N. J.	New Jersey
N. Mex.	New Mexico
Nor.	Norway
	Norwegian
N. Y.	New York
N. Z.	New Zealand
Oc.	Oceania
oc.	occasionally
Pa.	Pennsylvania
PCGN	Permanent Committee on Geographical Names for British Official Use
pen.	peninsula

Per.	Persian
P. I.	Philippine Islands
pl.	plural
Pol.	Poland
	Polish
Port.	Portugal
	Portuguese
Pres.	President
protec.	protectorate
prov.	province
repub.	republic
Rh.	Rhodes
riv.	river
Rum.	Rumania
	Rumanian
Rus.	Russia
	Russian
S. A.	South America
S. Afr.	South Africa
Sard.	Sardinia
S. C.	South Carolina
S.-C.	Serb-Croat
Scot.	Scotland
	Scottish
Sp.	Spain
	Spanish
Sp. Mor.	Spanish Morocco
str.	strait
Sw.	Sweden
	Swedish
Switz.	Switzerland
Tenn.	Tennessee
Tex.	Texas
Tun.	Tunisia
Turk.	Turkey
	Turkish
U. of S. A.	Union of South Africa
Urug.	Uruguay
U. S.	United States
Ven.	Venezuela
Vt.	Vermont
Wash.	Washington
W. Asia	West Asia
W. I.	West Indies
Wis.	Wisconsin
Yugosl.	Yugoslavia

KEYS TO PRONUNCIATION

In the first column is the word to be pronounced. In the second column the pronunciation is given by a simplified Websterian alphabet, and in the third column by a phonetic respelling without special accents.

The symbols of the second column, except ə, should present no difficulty to those who are familiar with American dictionaries. The symbol ə, which is named *schwa*, is used for unstressed vowels, however spelled, which in speech are sounded "uh"—for example, *a*bout, tak*e*n, penc*i*l, lem*o*n, circ*u*s.

The spelling of the third column should be self-evident. With only two or three exceptions the letters have customary *English* values. "*Th*" (italic) is the initial sound of *then:* "th" (roman) is the initial sound of *thin.*

There is often no exact equivalent in English for the sounds of foreign languages. Therefore the symbols in the third group (Foreign Sounds) are only desperate reachings for a sign that will suggest to an American a sound not too far removed from the foreignism. See also the discussions in the Introduction.

The accent mark is placed after the syllable to be stressed. Where it is difficult to decide which syllable more often bears the principal stress of a word, both syllables have been accented. No orthographic distinction is made between primary and secondary accents. In American speech the distinction is idiomatic and will usually take care of itself. For Chinese and Japanese, no accent is indicated unless the word has been Anglicized. In foreign words the stress accent should not be emphasized.

ENGLISH VOWELS

Key Word	*Key 1*	*Key 2*
*a*t, b*a*ton	ăt′, bă-tŏn′	at′, ba-ton′
*a*te	āt′	ayt′
f*a*ther	fä′-*th*ər	fah′-*th*uhr
c*a*re	kăr′	kehr′
*e*vent	ĭ-vĕnt′	i-vent′
*e*ve	ēv′	eev′
th*e*re	*th*ĕr′	*th*ehr′
*c*it*y*	sĭt′-ĭ	sit′-i
f*ea*r	fĭr′	fihr′
*i*ce	īs′	ais′
*o*dd	ŏd′	od′
g*o*	gō′	goh′

Key Word	*Key 1*	*Key 2*
*aw*e	ô′	o′ *or* aw′
p*u*ll	po͝ol′	pul′
p*oo*l	po͞ol′	pool′
b*u*t	bŭt′	buht′
*u*rn	ûrn′ *or* ərn′	uhrn′
*u*se	ūs′	yoos′
*oi*l	oil′	oil′
*ou*t	out′	aut′
*a*bove, sof*a*, furth*e*r, tak*e*n, char*i*ty, c*o*nvey, *u*ntil	ə (*schwa*)	uh

ENGLISH CONSONANTS

*ch*at	chăt′	chat′
*g*et	gĕt′	get′
*j*et	jĕt′	jet′
si*ng*er	sĭng′-ər	sing′-uhr
fi*ng*er	fĭng′-gər	fing′-guhr
plea*s*ure	plĕzh′-ər	plezh′-uhr
*th*in	thĭn′	thin′
*th*is	*th*ĭs′	*th*is′
*y*et	yĕt′	yet′

The other consonant symbols have the usual English value.

FOREIGN SOUNDS

	Key 1	*Key 2*	*Often Anglicized*
Fr. s*u*d	süd′	süd′	o͞o *or* ū as in *rude*
Fr. p*eu*r	pûr′	pœr′	û as in *purr*
Fr. b*on*	bôN′	boN′	ôn as in *wrong*
Fr. f*in*	făN′	faN′	ăn as in *sang*
Du. h*ui*s	hûĭs′	hœis′	oi as in *hoist*
Scot. lo*ch*	lôk(h)′	lok(h)′	k (*or* ck) as in *lock*
Sp. ca*ñ*ón	kä-nyôn′	kah-nyon′	ny as in *canyon*
It. *gl*i	lyē′	lyee′	ly (*or* li) as in *million*

See the Introduction for descriptions of foreign sounds.

RECOMMENDED PRONUNCIATIONS

a	ə	uh
The indefinite article *a* should be pronounced schwa [ə], not ā, in order to give the effect of speech and not of awkward, even childish reading aloud. There is of course a place for an emphatic ā-pronunciation of even an indefinite article, but this headline style is seldom safe from abuse, and it is an awkward way of securing emphasis. Stressing the article breaks up the characteristic pattern of spoken English, and radio speakers do this at the risk of losing their audience.		
aa, å		
The spelling *aa* in Danish represents the sound ô. The same spelling was formerly common in Norway, but has now largely given way to the Swedish spelling å, which is pronounced more like ō. (There are many Swedish place names in Finland.) In Dutch and German *aa* is pronounced *ah* (as in *father*).		
Aabenraa (Den.)	ô′-bən-rô′	o′-buhn-ro′
Aabo (Fin.) See *Åbo.*		
Aachen (Ger.)	äk(h)′-ən	ahk(h)′-uhn
French *Aix la Chapelle*, ĕks lä shä-pĕl′ [eks lah shah-pel′].		
Aagtekerke (Neth.)	äk(h)′-tə-kĕr′-kə	ahk(h)′-tuh-kehr′-kuh
Aahus (Sw.) See *Åhus.*		
Aal (Nor.)	ôl′	ol′
Aaland (Fin.) See *Åland.*		
Aalborg (Den.)	ôl′-bôr	ol′-bor
Aalesund (Nor.)	ô′-lə-so͝on	o′-luh-sun
Aalsmeer (Neth.)	äls-mār′	ahls-mayr′
Aalst (Belg.)	älst′	ahlst′
French *Alost*, ä-lôst′ [ah-lost′].		
Aalten (Neth.)	äl′-tən	ahl′-tuhn
Aamli (Nor.)	ôm′-lē	om′-lee
Aamot (Nor.)	ô′-mo͝ot	o′-mut
Aandalsnes (Nor.)	ôn′-däls-nĕs	on′-dahls-nes
aan Zee	än zā′	ahn zay′
An element, meaning *by the sea*, in Dutch place names.		
Aardal (Nor.)	ôr′-däl	or′-dahl
Aarhus (Den.)	ôr′-ho͞os	or′-hoos
Aasgaardsstrand (Nor.)	ôs′-gôrs-strän	os′-gors-strahn
Aavasaksa (Fin.)	ä′-vä-säk-sä	ah′-vah-sahk-sah

Abadan (Iran)	*Per.* ä-bä-dän′	ah-bah-dahn′
	Eng. ăb-ă-dăn′	ab-a-dan′
Abagaituev (Rus.)	ä-bä-gī-to͞o′-yĕf	ah-bah-gai-too′-yef
Abaiang (Oc.)	ä-bī′-äng	ah-bai′-ahng
Abakan (Rus.)	ä-bä-kän′	ah-bah-kahn′
Abau (New Guinea)	ä′-bou	ah′-bau
Abava (Latvia, riv.)	ä′-bä-vä	ah′-bah-vah
Abbeville	*Eng.* ăb′-ĭ-vĭl	ab′-i-vil
	Fr. äb-vēl′	ahb-veel′
Abd el Krim (Mor. leader)	äb dĕl krēm′	ahb del kreem′
Abdul Hussein Aziz (Afghan leader)	äb-do͝ol′ ho͝os-sān′ ä-zēz′	ahb-dul′ hus-sayn′ ah-zeez′
Abemama (Oc.)	ä-bĕ-mä′-mä	ah-beh-mah′-mah
Abernethy, Thomas G. (U.S. representative)	ăb′-ər-nĕth′-ĭ	ab′-uhr-neth′-i
Aberystwith (Wales)	Eng. ăb′-ə-rĭst′-wĭth	ab′-uh-rist′-with
	Welsh ä-bər-ŭst′-wĭth	ah-buhr-uhst′-with
Abganerovo (Rus.)	äb-gä-nĕ′-rŏ-vŏ	ahb-gah-neh′-ro-vo
Also called *Abganerova.*		
Abkoude (Neth.)	äp-kou′-də	ahp-kau′-duh
Åbo (Fin.)	*Sw.* ō′-bo͞o	oh′-boo
Finnish *Turku,* q.v.		
Abrud (Rum.)	ä-bro͝od′	ah-brud′
Hungarian *Abrudbánya,* ŏb′-ro͝od-bä′-nyŏ [ob′-rud-bah′-nyo].		
absorb, -ing	ăb-sŏrb′, -ĭng	ab-sorb′, -ing
The *s* should not be pronounced *z.*		
Abu Hashaifa (Egypt)	ä′-bo͞o hä-shī′-fä	ah′-boo hah-shai′-fah
Abukir (Egypt)	ä-bo͝o-kēr′	ah-bu-keer′
Accra (Gold Coast)	ə-krä′	uh-krah′
Achaia and Elis (Gr.)	*Eng.* ə-kā′-yə *and* ē′-lĭs	uh-kay′-yuh *and* ee′-lis
Also called in English *Achaea,* ə-kē′-ə [uh-kee′-uh]. Greek *Achaia kai Elis,* ä-hī′-ä kĕ ē′-lēs [ah-hai′-ah keh ee′-lees].		
Achaia kai Elis (Gr.)	ä-hī′-ä kĕ ē′-lēs	ah-hai′-ah keh ee′-lees
Also called in English *Achaea,* ə-kē′-ə [uh-kee′-uh].		
Acheloos (Gr., riv.)	ä-hĕ-lô′-ôs	ah-heh-lo′-os
Achinsk (Rus.)	ä′-chĭnsk	ah′-chinsk
Achuev (Rus.)	ä-cho͞o′-yĕf	ah-choo′-yef
Acireale (Sicily)	ä′-chē-rĕ-ä′-lĕ	ah′-chee-reh-ah′-leh
Acquapendente (It.)	äk-kwä-pĕn-dĕn′-tĕ	ahk-kwah-pen-den′-teh
Acre (Brazil)	ä′-krĭ	ah′-kri
Acroceraunia (Alb., pen.)	*Eng.* ăk′-rô-sĭ-rô′-nĭ-ə	ak′-ro-si-ro′-ni-uh
Albanian *Karaburun,* q.v. See also Cape *Glossa.*		
Acroma (Libya)	ä-krô′-mä	ah-kro′-mah

Ada (Yugosl.)	ä′-dä	ah′-dah
Adak (Alaska, isl.)	ā′-dăk	ay′-dak
Adalia (Turk.)	ə-däl′-ĭ-ə	uh-dahl′-i-uh

Also called *Antalya*, q.v.

Adanà (It., riv.)	ä-dä-nä′	ah-dah-nah′
Adana (Turk.)	ä′-dä-nä	ah′-dah-nah
Adapazarı (Turk.)	ä-dä-pä-zä′-rĭ	ah-dah-pah-zah′-ri
Addis Ababa (Ethiopia)	äd′-dĭs ä′-bə-bä	ahd′-dis ah′-buh-bah
Adem, el (Libya)	ă′-dĕm, ĕl	a′-dem, el
Adernò (Sicily)	ä-dĕr-nô′	ah-dehr-no′
Adige (It., riv.)	ä′-dē-jĕ	ah′-dee-jeh
Adler (Rus.)	äd′-lər	ahd′-luhr
Adour (Fr., riv.)	ä-do͞or′	ah-door′
Adowa (Ethiopia) See *Aduwa*.		
Adrano (Sicily)	ä-drä′-nô	ah-drah′-no
Adrianople (Turk.)	*Eng.* ā′-drĭ-ə-nō′-pəl	ay′-dri-uh-noh′-puhl

Turkish *Edirne*, q.v.

Aduwa (Ethiopia)	ä′-do͝o-wä	ah′-du-wah
advertisement	ăd′-vər-tīz′-mənt *or* ăd-vûr′-tĭs-mənt	ad′-vuhr-taiz′-muhnt ad-vuhr′-tis-muhnt

The first is the pronunciation of most educated Americans and is therefore preferable for network usage. It is placed first by the *Thorndike-Century Senior Dictionary* (1941), and by Kenyon and Knott (1944).

Adžibegovac, Stari (Yugosl.)	ä′-jĭ-bĕ′-gô-väts	ah′-ji-beh′-go-vahts
Æbeltoft (Den.)	ĕ′-bəl-tôft	eh′-buhl-toft
Aegadian Isles (It.)	*Eng.* ĭ-gā′-dĭ-ən	i-gay′-di-uhn

Italian *Egadi*, q.v.

Aegean Sea	ĭ-jē′-ən	i-jee′-uhn
Aegina (Gr.)	*Eng.* ĭ-jī′-nə	i-jai′-nuh

Greek *Aigina*, ā′-yē-nä [ay′-yee-nah].

aerial	ăr′-ĭ-əl	ehr′-i-uhl

The old learned pronunciation ā-ē′-rĭ-əl has been displaced as the word has become popular. The first syllable of ăr′-ĭ-əl, the common pronunciation today, is to be pronounced like the word *air*. It should not be pronounced ār.

Æroe *or* Ærö (Den., isl.)	ĕr′-û	ehr′-œ
aeroplane	ăr′-ə-plān′	ehr′-uh-playn′

The spelling *aeroplane* and its pronunciations have been displaced generally by the dissyllable *airplane*, ăr′-plān [ehr′-playn]. Sometimes the old-fashioned spelling *aeroplane* is given the pronunciation of *airplane*.

Aetolia and Acarnania (Gr.)	*Eng.* ē-tō′-lĭ-ə *and* ăk′-ər-nā′-nĭ-ə	ee-toh′-li-uh *and* ak′-uhr-nay′-ni-uh

Greek *Aitolia kai Akarnania*, ĕ-tô-lē′-ä kĕ ä-kär-nä-nē′-ä [eh-to-lee′-ah keh ah-kahr-nah-nee′-ah].

Aetos (Gr.)	ä-ĕ-tôs′	ah-eh-tos′
Afghanistan (W. Asia)	ăf-găn′-ĭ-stăn *or* ăf-gän′-ĭ-stän′	af-gan′-i-stan af-gahn′-i-stahn′
Afyon Karahisar (Turk.)	äf-ūn′ kä-rä-hĭ-sär′	ahf-yoon′ kah-rah-hi-sahr′
Also called *Karahisar*, q.v.		
Aga (Rus.)	ä-gä′	ah-gah′
Agadir (Mor.)	ä-gä-dēr′	ah-gah-deer′
Agaña (Guam)	ä-gä′-nyä	ah-gah′-nyah
Agareb (Tun.)	ä′-gä-rĕb	ah′-gah-reb
Agattu (Alaska)	ăg-ă-tōō′	ag-a-too′
Agde (Fr.)	ägd′	ahgd′
Agdenes (Nor.)	äg′-də-nĕs	ahg′-duh-nes
Agedabia (Libya)	ä-jĕ-dä′-byä	ah-jeh-dah′-byah
Agelat, el (Libya)	ä-gĕ-lăt′, ĕl	ah-geh-lat′, el
Agen (Fr.)	ä-zhäN′	ah-zhahN′
Agheila, el (Libya)	ä-gā′-lä, ĕl	ah-gay′-lah, el
Agiguan (Oc.)	ä-gē-gōō-än′	ah-gee-goo-ahn′
Aginsk (Rus.)	ä-gēnsk′	ah-geensk′
Aginskoe (Rus.)	ä-gēn′-skŏ-yĕ	ah-geen′-sko-yeh
Agioi Saranta (Alb.)	See *Saranta* and *Saranda*.	
agios, agioi (Gr.)	ī′-yôs, ī′-yē	ai′-yos, ai′-yee
An element, meaning *saint(s)*, in Greek place names. Look up the other part of the name. *Agios* is an alternative spelling of *hagios*, q.v. Similarly *Agia*.		
Agira (Sicily)	ä-jē′-rä	ah-jee′-rah
Agosta (Sicily)	ä-gôs′-tä	ah-gos′-tah
Also called *Augusta*, q. v.		
Agoulinitsa (Gr.)	ä-gōō-lē-nē′-tsä	ah-goo-lee-nee′-tsah
Agra (India)	ăg′-rə *or* ä′-grə	ag′-ruh *or* ah′-gruh
Agria (Crete, pen.)	ä′-grē-ä	ah′-gree-ah
Agrigento (Sicily)	ä-grē-jĕn′-tô	ah-gree-jen′-to
Also called *Girgenti*, jēr-jĕn′-tē [jeer-jen′-tee].		
Agrihan (Oc.)	ä-grē-hän′	ah-gree-hahn′
Agrinion (Gr.)	ä-grē′-nē-ô(n)	ah-gree′-nee-o(n)
Also called *Vrakhori*, vrä-hô′-rē [vrah-ho′-ree].		
Agropoli (It.)	ä-grô′-pô-lē	ah-gro′-po-lee
Águila (Mex.)	ä′-gē-lä	ah′-gee-lah
Aguinaldo, Emilio (Fil. leader)	ä-gē-näl′-dô, ĕ-mē′-lyô	ah-gee-nahl′-do, eh-mee′-lyo
Agyia (Gr.)	ī-yä′	ai-yah′
Ahe (Oc.)	ä′-hĕ	ah′-heh
Ahmedabad (India)	ăm′-ə-də-băd′	am′-uh-duh-bad′
Ahmed Kavam (Iran)	ä′-mĕd kä-väm′	ah′-med kah-vahm′

Ahmednagar (India)	ăm′-əd-nŭg′-ər	am′-uhd-nuhg′-uhr
Åhus (Sw.)	ō′-hüs	oh′-hüs
Ahvenanmaa (Fin., isls.)	ä′-vĕ-nän-mä′	ah′-veh-nahn-mah′
Also called *Åland*, q.v.		
Ahwaz (Iran)	ä-wäz′	ah-wahz′
Aigila (Gr., isl.)	ā′-yē-lä	ay′-yee-lah
Also called *Antikythera*, q.v., and *Tserigoto*, tsĕ-rē-gô′-tô [tseh-ree-go′-to], and *Lious*, lē-o͞os′ [lee-oos′].		
Aigina (Gr.) See *Aegina*.		
Aigion (Gr.)	ā′-yôn	ay′-yon
English *Aegion*, ē′-jĭ-ŏn [ee′-ji-on].		
Aigoudista (Gr.)	ĕ-go͞o′-*th*ē-stä	eh-goo′-*th*ee-stah
Aiguesmortes (Fr.)	ĕg-môrt′	eg-mort′
Aigun (Manchu.)	ī-go͝on	ai-gun
Also called *Aihun*, ī-ho͝on [ai-hun].		
Aikaterine (Gr.) See *Katerine*.		
Ailinginae (Oc.)	ä-ē′-lĭng-ē-nä′-ĕ	ah-ee′-ling-ee-nah′-eh
Ailinglapalap (Oc.)	ä-ē′-lĭng-lä′-pä-läp	ah-ee′-ling-lah′-pah-lahp
Ai-ling Soong (Mme H. H. Kung)	ī-lĭng so͝ong	ai-ling sung
Ailuk (Oc.)	ī′-lo͞ok	ai′-look
Ainaži (Latvia)	ī′-nä-zhē	ai′-nah-zhee
Russian *Gainasch*, q.v.		
Ain Beida (Alg.)	ān bā′-dä	ayn bay′-dah
Ain Draham (Tun.)	ān drä′-häm	ayn drah′-hahm
Ain Mestour (Tun.)	ān mĕs-to͞or′	ayn mes-toor′
Ainos (Turk.) See *Enez*.		
Ain Rhelal (Tun.)	ān rə-lăl′	ayn ruh-lal′
Aio (Oc.)	ī-ô′	ai-o′
Aisne (Fr., riv.)	*Eng.* ān′	ayn′
	Fr. ĕn′	en′
Aïstrates (Gr., isl.) See *Evstratios, Agios*.		
Aitape (New Guinea)	ī-tä-pĕ′	ai-tah-peh′
Aitara (Oc.)	ī-tä′-rä	ai-tah′-rah
Aitolia (Gr.) See *Aetolia and Acarnania*.		
Aitos (Bulg.)	ī′-tŏs	ai′-tos
Aitutake (Oc.)	ī-to͞o-tä′-kĕ	ai-too-tah′-keh
Aiud (Rum.)	ä′-yo͝od	ah′-yud
Aix (Fr.)	*Eng.* āks′	ayks′
	Fr. ĕks′	eks′
Aix la Chapelle (Ger.)	*Eng.* āks′ lä shä-pĕl′	ayks′ lah shah-pel′
	Fr. ĕks lä shä-pĕl′	eks lah shah-pel′
German *Aachen*, äk(h)′-ən [ahk(h)′-uhn].		

Aizpute (Latvia)	īz'-po͝o-tĕ	aiz'-pu-teh
Russian *Gasenpot*, q.v. German *Hasenpoth*, q.v.		
Ajaccio (Corsica)	ä-yät'-chô	ah-yaht'-cho
Ajmer (India)	ăj-mēr'	aj-meer'
Ajoe *or* Ayu (NEI)	ä'-yo͞o	ah'-yoo
Ajud (Rum.)	ä-zho͝od'	ah-zhud'
Ak. The abbreviation of Greek *akroterion*, q.v.		
Akarit, el (Tun.)	ä-kä-rēt', ĕl	ah-kah-reet', el
Akarnania (Gr.) See *Aetolia and Acarnania.*		
Akçehisar (Alb.) See *Krujë.*		
Akershus (Nor.)	ä'-kərs-ho͞os	ah'-kuhrs-hoos
Akhtopol (Bulg.)	äk(h)'-tŏ-pŏl(y)	ahk(h)'-to-pol(y)
Akhtyrka (Rus.)	äk-tĭr'-kä	ahk-tihr'-kah
Akhtyrskaya (Rus.)	äk-tĭr'-skä-yä	ahk-tihr'-skah-yah
Akita (Jap.)	ä-kē-tä	ah-kee-tah
Akkerman (Rum.) See *Cetatea Albă.*		
Ak Mechet (Rus.)	äk mĕ-chĕt'	ahk meh-chet'
Akmolinsk (Rus.)	äk-mŏ-lēnsk'	ahk-mo-leensk'
Akouda (Tun.)	ä-ko͞o'-dä	ah-koo'-dah
Akritas (Gr., cape)	ä-krē'-täs	ah-kree'-tahs
Also called *Gallo*, gä'-lô [gah'-lo].		
Akrokeraunia (Alb.) See *Acroceraunia.*		
akroterion	ä-krô-tē'-rē-ô(n)	ah-kro-tee'-ree-o(n)
An element, meaning *cape* or *point*, in Greek place names. Look up the other part of the name.		
Aksha (Rus.)	äk'-shä	ahk'-shah
Ak Sheikh (Rus.)	äk' shāk'	ahk' shayk'
Aksu (Ch., Sinkiang)	äk-so͞o	ahk-soo
Akte (Crete, point)	ä-ktē'	ah-ktee'
Aktyubinsk (Rus.)	äk-tū'-bĭnsk	ahk-tyoo'-binsk
Akutan (Alaska, isl.)	ä-ko͞o-tăn'	ah-koo-tan'
Akyab (Burma)	ăk-yăb' *or* äk-yäb'	ak-yab' *or* ahk-yahb'
Alagir (Rus.)	ä-lä-gēr'	ah-lah-geer'
Alagoas (Brazil)	ä-lə-gô'-əs	ah-luh-go'-uhs
Alamagan (Oc.)	ä-lä-mä-gän'	ah-lah-mah-gahn'
Alamein, el (Egypt)	ä-lä-mān', ĕl	ah-lah-mayn', el
Åland (Fin., isls.)	ō'-län	oh'-lahn
The Swedish name for islands which the Finns call *Ahvenanmaa*, q.v.		
Alanya (Turk.)	ä-län-yä'	ah-lahn-yah'
Also called *Alaiye.*		
Alas, Antonio de las (Fil. leader)	ä'-läs, än-tô'-nyô dĕ läs	ah'-lahs, ahn-to'-nyo deh lahs

Alaska	ə-lăs′-kə	uh-las′-kuh
Alatyr (Rus.)	ä-lä-tĭr′	ah-lah-tihr′
Álava (Sp., prov.)	ä′-lä-vä	ah′-lah-vah
Albacete (Sp.)	äl-bä-thĕ′-tĕ *or* -sĕ′-	ahl-bah-theh′-teh *or* -seh′-
Albacore	ăl′-bə-kôr′	al′-buh-kor′

British naval carrier-plane.

Alba Julia (Rum.)	äl′-bä yŏŏ′-lyä	ahl′-bah yu′-lyah

Inevitably English ăl′-bə jōōl′-yə [al′-buh jool′-yuh]. Hungarian *Gyulafehérvár*, dyŏŏ′-lŏ-fĕ′-hār-vär [dyu′-lo-feh′-hayr-vahr].

Albania	*Eng.* ăl-bān′-yə	al-bayn′-yuh

The pronunciation ôl-bān′-yə [awl-bayn′-yuh] is not recommended. The Albanians call their country *Shqipni*, q.v., or a variant thereof.

Albano (It.)	äl-bä′-nô	ahl-bah′-no

In Sicily *Albano* is stressed on the first syllable.

Albay (P.I.)	äl-bī′	ahl-bai′
Alberto, João (Braz. leader)	äl-bĕr′-tŏŏ, zhô-ouN′	ahl-behr′-tu, zho-auN′
Albuquerque (N.Mex.)	ăl′-bə-kûr′-kĭ	al′-buh-kuhr′-ki
Alburquerque (Sp.)	äl-bōōr-kĕr′-kĕ	ahl-boor-kehr′-keh
Alcalá (Sp.)	äl-kä-lä′	ahl-kah-lah′
Alcamo (Sicily)	äl′-kä-mô	ahl′-kah-mo
Alcántara (Sp.)	äl-kän′-tä-rä	ahl-kahn′-tah-rah
Alcázar (Sp.)	*Sp.* äl-kä′-thär *or* -sär	ahl-kah′-thahr *or* -sahr
	Eng. ăl-kăz′-ər	al-kaz′-uhr
Aleksandriya (Rus.)	ä-lĕk-sän-drē′-yä	ah-lek-sahn-dree′-yah
Aleksandrovac (Yugosl.)	ä′-lĕk-sän′-drô-väts	ah′-lek-sahn′-dro-vahts
Aleksandrovsk (Rus.)	ä-lĕk-sän′-drŏfsk	ah-lek-sahn′-drofsk
Aleksandrów (Pol.)	ä-lĕk-sän′-drŏŏf	ah-lek-sahn′-druf
Aleksikovo (Rus.)	ä-lĕk′-sĭ-kŏ-vŏ	ah-lek′-si-ko-vo
Aleksin (Rus.)	ä-lyŭk′-sĭn	ah-lyuhk′-sin
Aleksinac (Yugosl.)	ä′-lĕk′-sĭ-näts	ah′-lek′-si-nahts
Alemtejo (Port., prov.)	ä-lĕN-tĕ′-zhŏŏ	ah-leN-teh′-zhu
Aléria (Corsica)	*Eng.* ə-lē′-rĭ-ə	uh-lee′-ri-uh
	It. ä-lĕ′-ryä	ah-leh′-ryah
Alès (Fr.)	ä-lĕs′	ah-les′
Alessio (Alb.)	*It.* ä-lĕs′-syô	ah-les′-syo

Albanian *Lesh*, q.v.

Ålesund (Nor.) See *Aalesund*.

Aleut	ăl′-ĭ-ōōt *or* ăl′-yōōt	al′-i-oot *or* al′-yoot

Aleutian Isls. (Alaska)	ə-lū′-shən	uh-lyoo′-shuhn
Alexandretta (Turk.)	*Eng.* ăl′-ĕg-zăn-drĕt′-ə	al′-eg-zan-dret′-uh

French Alexandrette, ä-lĕk-säN-drĕt′ [ah-lek-sahN-dret′]. Turkish *Iskenderun*, q.v.

Alexandroupolis (Gr.)	ä-lĕk-sän-dro͞o′-pô-lē(s)	ah-lek-sahn-droo′-po-lee(s)

Formerly *Dede Agach*, dĕ-dĕ′ ä-gäch′ [deh-deh′ ah-gahch′].

Alexishafen (Oc.)	ä-lĕk′-sĭs-hä′-fən	ah-lek′-sis-hah′-fuhn
Alfedena (It.)	äl-fĕ-dĕ′-nä	ahl-feh-deh′-nah
Alfen (Neth.)	äl′-fən	ahl′-fuhn
Algarve (Port., prov.)	äl-gär′-vĕ	ahl-gahr′-veh
Algeciras (Sp.)	*Eng.* ăl′-jə-sĭr′-əs	al′-juh-sihr′-uhs
	Sp. äl-hĕ-thē′-räs	ahl-heh-thee′-rahs
	or äl-hĕ-sē′-rä	ahl-heh-see′-rah
Alghero (Sard.)	äl-gĕ′-rô	ahl-geh′-ro
Algiers	ăl-jĭrz′	al-jihrz′

French *Alger*, äl-zhĕ′ [ahl-zheh′]. Arabic *Al Jezair*, äl jə-zīr′ [ahl juh-zair′].

Al Hammam (Egypt)	äl häm-măm′	ahl hahm-mam′
Alia (Sicily)	ä-lē′-ä	ah-lee′-ah
Alia, el (Tun.)	ä′-lĭ-ä, ĕl	ah′-li-ah, el
Aliakmon (Gr., riv.)	ä-lē-äk′-môn	ah-lee-ahk′-mon
Alibunar (Yugosl.)	ä′-lē-bo͞o-när′	ah′-lee-boo-nahr′
Alicante (Sp.)	ä-lē-kän′-tĕ	ah-lee-kahn′-teh
Alice (It., Calab.)	ä-lē′-chĕ	ah-lee′-cheh

Elsewhere in Italy *Alice* is customarily stressed on the first syllable.

Alice Springs (Austral.)	ă′-lĭs	a′-lis
Alicudi (It., isl.)	ä-lē-ko͞o′-dē	ah-lee-koo′-dee
Alife (It.)	ä-lē′-fĕ	ah-lee′-feh
Aligarh (India)	ăl-ē-gûr′	al-ee-guhr′
Alika (Gr.)	ä′-lē-kä	ah′-lee-kah
Alikyanou (Crete)	ä-lē-kyä-no͞o′	ah-lee-kyah-noo′
Alim (Oc.)	ä′-lĭm	ah′-lim
Alince (Yugosl.)	ä′-lĭn-tsĕ	ah′-lin-tseh
Ali Soheily (Per. leader)	ä-lē′ sô-hā′-lē	ah-lee′ so-hay′-lee
Alkmaar (Neth.)	älk′-mär	ahlk′-mahr
Allanmyo (Burma)	ă′-lən-myō′	a′-luhn-myoh′
Allekakat (Alaska)	ăl′-ə-kăk′-ət	al′-uh-kak′-uht
Allenkul (Est.)	*Rus.* äl′-lĕn-kūl(y)	ahl′-len-kyool(y)

Estonian *Türi*, q.v. German *Allenkühl*, äl′-ən-kül [ahl′-uhn-kül].

Allenstein (Ger.)	äl′-ən-shtīn	ahl′-uhn-shtain

Allxhinë (Alb.) See *Llixhë*.

Alma Ata (Rus.)	äl′-mä ä′-tä	ahl′-mah ah′-tah

Almeloo (Neth.)	äl′-mə-lō	ahl′-muh-loh
Almería (Sp.)	äl-mĕ-rē′-ä	ahl-meh-ree′-ah
Almyron (Crete, gulf)	äl-mē-rô(n)′	ahl-mee-ro(n)′
	or är-mē-rô(n)′	ahr-mee-ro(n)′
Also called *Amphimallikos*, äm-fē-mä-lē-kôs′ [ahm-fee-mah-lee-kos′].		
Almyros (Crete) See *Georgioupolis.*		
Alonesos (Gr., isl.)	ä-lô′-nē-sôs	ah-lo′-nee-sos
Also called *Khiliodromia*, hē-lē-ô-*th*rô′-mē-ä [hee-lee-o-*th*ro′-mee-ah] or *Liadromia*, lē-ä-*th*rô′-mē-ä [lee-ah-*th*ro′-mee-ah].		
Alor Star (Malaya)	ä′-lôr stär′	ah′-lor stahr′
Alost (Belg.) See *Aalst.*		
Alpujarras (Sp.)	äl-po͞o-hä′-räs	ahl-poo-hah′-rahs
Als (Den., isl.)	äls′	ahls′
German *Alsen*, äl′-zən [ahl′-zuhn].		
Alta (Nor.)	äl′-tä	ahl′-tah
Altanski (Rus.)	äl-tän′-skĭ	ahl-tahn′-ski
Altona (Ger.)	äl′-tô-nä	ahl′-to-nah
Alu (Oc.)	ä′-lo͞o	ah′-loo
Alupka (Rus.)	ä-lo͝op′-kä	ah-lup′-kah
Alūksne (Latvia)	ä′-lo͞oks-nĕ	ah′-looks-neh
Russian and German *Marienburg*, q.v.		
Alunan, Rafael (Fil. leader)	ä-lo͞o′-nän, rä-fä-ĕl′	ah-loo′-nahn, rah-fah-el′
Alushta (Rus.)	ä-lo͞osh′-tä	ah-loosh′-tah
Alytus (Lith.)	ä-lē′-to͞os	ah-lee′-toos
Russian *Olita*, q.v.		
Amadeus (Austral., lake)	ə-măd′-ĭ-əs	uh-mad′-i-uhs
Amalfi (It.)	ä-mäl′-fē	ah-mahl′-fee
Amalias (Gr.)	ä-mäl-yäs′	ah-mahl-yahs′
Amalienborg (Den.)	ä-mä′-lĭ-ən-bôr	ah-mah′-li-uhn-bor
A Manhã (Braz. newspaper)	ä mə-nyäN′	ah muh-nyahN′
Amantea (It.)	ä-män-tĕ′-ä	ah-mahn-teh′-ah
Amarillo (Tex.)	ăm′-ə-rĭl′-ə	am′-uh-ril′-uh
Amazonas (Brazil)	ä-mə-zô′-nəs	ah-muh-zo′-nuhs
Ambala (India)	əm-bä′-lä	uhm-bah′-lah
Ambedkar, Bhimrao Ramji (Indian leader)	äm-bĕd′-kär, bēm′-rou räm′-jē	ahm-bed′-kahr, beem′-rau rahm′-jee
Ambitle (Oc.)	äm-bēt-lĕ′	ahm-beet-leh′
Ambleteuse (Fr.)	ämbl-tûz′	ahmbl-tœz′
Amboina (NEI)	*Eng.* ăm-boi′-nə	am-boi′-nuh
Ambon (NEI)	äm-bôn′(y)	ahm-bon′(y)
English *Amboina*, q.v.		
Ambunti (New Guinea)	äm-bo͞on′-tē	ahm-boon′-tee

Amchitka (Alaska, isl.)	ăm-chĭt′-kə	am-chit′-kuh
Ameland (Neth., isl.)	ä′-mə-länt	ah′-muh-lahnt
amen	ä′-mĕn′	ah′-men′
	or ā′-mĕn′	ay′-men′

The first is expected in song and usually in liturgical use. The latter is the old-fashioned English pronunciation, and it persists in some Protestant groups and often in everyday speech.

Ameri (Per. leader)	ä-mə-rē′	ah-muh-ree′
America	ə-mĕr′-ə-kə	uh-mehr′-uh-kuh

A British pronunciation with a "single-tap *r*" (similar to *d*) was once cultivated by American singers and announcers; it was as obvious as a sore thumb, if not indecent. The equally painful "Uh-muhrr′-ruh-kuh" is avoided by announcers.

Amerongen (Neth.)	ä′-mə-rông′-ən	ah′-muh-rong′-uhn
Amersfoort (Neth.)	ä′-mərs-fōrt	ah′-muhrs-fohrt
Amezaga, Juan José (Uruguayan leader)	ä-mĕ-sä′-gä (*or* -thä′-), whän′ hô-sĕ′	ah-meh-sah′-gah (*or* -thah′-), whahn′ ho-seh′
Amgun (Rus., riv.)	äm-gōōn′	ahm-goon′
Amiens (Fr.)	*Fr.* ä-myăN′	ah-myaN′
	Eng. ăm′-ĭ-ĕnz	am′-i-enz

The French pronunciation is probably the more common even in English contexts.

Åmli (Nor.) See *Aamli.*

Ammokhostos (Cyprus)	ä-mô′-hô-stôs	ah-mo′-ho-stos
Amorgos (Gr., isl.)	*Eng.* ə-môr′-gəs	uh-mor′-guhs
	Gr. ä-môr-gô(s)′	ah-mor-go(s)′
Amory (Brit.)	ā′-mə-rĭ	ay′-muh-ri
Amoy (Ch., Fukien)	ä-moi	ah-moi
Ampelakia (Gr.)	äm-bĕ-lä′-kyä	ahm-beh-lah′-kyah
Amphilokhia (Gr.)	äm-fē-lô-hē′-ä	ahm-fee-lo-hee′-ah

Also called *Karvasaras,* kär-vä-sä-räs′ [kahr-vah-sah-rahs′].

Amphimallikos (Crete, gulf) See *Almyron.*

Amphissa (Gr.)	äm′-fē-sä	ahm′-fee-sah

Also called *Salona,* sä′-lô-nä [sah′-lo-nah].

Amritsar (India)	əm-rĭt′-sər	uhm-rit′-suhr
Amselfeld (Yugosl.)	*Ger.* äm′-səl-fĕlt	ahm′-suhl-felt

Serb-Croat *Kosovo Polje,* q.v.

Amsterdam (Neth.)	*Eng.* ăm′-stər-dăm	am′-stuhr-dam
	Du. äm′-stər-däm′	ahm′-stuhr-dahm′
Amstetten (Austria)	äm′-stĕt-ən	ahm′-stet-uhn
Amur (Ch. and Rus., riv.)	ä-mōōr′	ah-moor′

Cf. *Heilungkiang.*

Anam (Indo-Ch.) See *Annam.*

Anambas (NEI)	ä-näm′-bäs	ah-nahm′-bahs
Ananda Mahidol (King of Siam)	ə-nän′ mä-hē-dōn′	uh-nahn′ mah-hee-dohn′
Ananev (Rus.)	ä-nän′-yĕf	ah-nahn′-yef
Anapa (Rus.)	ä-nä′-pä	ah-nah′-pah
Anaphe (Gr., isl.)	ä-nä′-fē	ah-nah′-fee
Anastasievskaya (Rus.)	ä-näs-täs′-yĕf-skä-yä	ah-nahs-tahs′-yef-skah-yah
Anatahan (Oc.)	ä-nä-tä-hän′	ah-nah-tah-hahn′
An-chi (Ch., Chekiang)	än-jē	ahn-jee
An-ch'ing (Ch., Anhwei) Also called *An-k'ing*, q. v.	än-chĭng	ahn-ching
Ancona (It.)	än-kô′-nä	ahn-ko′-nah
Åndalsnes (Nor.) See *Aandalsnes.*		
Andaman (India, isls.)	ăn′-də-măn	an′-duh-man
Andamsk (Rus.)	än-dämsk′	ahn-dahmsk′
Anderlecht (Belg.)	än′-dər-lĕk(h)t	ahn′-duhr-lek(h)t
Andersen, H. Carl (U.S. representative)	ăn′-dər-sən	an′-duhr-suhn
Andimiskh (Iran)	än-dĭm′-ĭsk(h)	ahn-dim′-isk(h)
Andoey *or* Andöy (Nor., isl.)	än′-ûĭ	ahn′-œi
Andorra (Sp.)	än-dô′-rä	ahn-do′-rah
Andravida (Gr.)	än-drä-vē′-*th*ä	ahn-drah-vee′-*th*ah
Andreanof (Alaska, isls.)	än-drĕ-ä′-nŏf	ahn-dreh-ah′-nof
Andreas, Agios (Cyprus, cape)	än-drĕ′-äs, ī′-yôs	ahn-dreh′-ahs, ai′-yos
Andreev (Pol.) See *Jędrzejów.*		
Andreevka (Rus.)	än-drĕ′-yĕf-kä	ahn-dreh′-yef-kah
Andresen, August H. (U.S. representative)	än-drē′-sən	ahn-dree′-suhn
Andria (It.)	än′-dryä	ahn′-dryah
Andrijevica (Yugosl.)	än′-drē′-yĕ-vĭ-tsä	ahn′-dree′-yeh-vi-tsah
Andros (Gr., isl.)	*Eng.* ăn′-drŏs *Gr.* än′-drô(s)	an′-dros ahn′-dro(s)
Andrychów (Pol.)	än-drĭ′-hŏŏf	ahn-dri′-huf
Aneta (Du. News Agency)	ä-nā′-tä	ah-nay′-tah
An-fu (Ch., Kiangsi)	än-fōō	ahn-foo
Angara (Rus., riv.)	än-gä-rä′	ahn-gah-rah′
Angarita, Isaías Medina (Ven. leader) See *Medina Angarita, Isaías.*		
Angaur (Oc.)	äng-our′	ahng-aur′
Angers (Fr.)	*Eng.* ăn′-jĭrz′ *Fr.* äN-zhĕ′	an′-jihrz′ ahN-zheh′

Angitola (It.)	än-jē′-tô-lä	ahn-jee′-to-lah
Angkor Thom (Indo-Ch.)	ăng′-kōr tôm′	ang′-kohr tawm′
Angkor Wat (Indo-Ch.)	ăng′-kōr wät′	ang′-kohr waht′
Angoulême (Fr.)	äN-gōō-lĕm′	ahN-goo-lem′
Angvik (Nor.)	äng′-vēk	ahng′-veek
Anholt (Den., isl.)	än′-hôlt	ahn′-holt
An-hsi (Ch.) See *Ansi*.		
An-hsiang (Ch., Hunan)	än-shyäng	ahn-shyahng
An-hwei (Ch., prov.)	än-whā	ahn-whay
An-i (Ch., Chekiang, Kiangsi, Shansi)	än-ē	ahn-ee
Aniche (Fr.)	ä-nēsh′	ah-neesh′
Anina (Rum.)	ä-nē′-nä	ah-nee′-nah
Anir (Oc.)	ä-nēr′	ah-neer′
Also called *Feni*, q.v.		
Anjou (Fr.)	*Eng.* ăn′-jōō	an′-joo
	Fr. äN-zhōō′	ahN-zhoo′
Ankara (Turk.)	äng′-kä-rä	ahng′-kah-rah

Another form of the word, with different accent, *Angora*, ăng-gō′-rə [ang-goh′-ruh], is a familiar attributive.

An-k'ing (Ch., Anhwei)	än-kĭng	ahn-king
Anklam (Ger.)	än′-kläm	ahn′-klahm
Annam (Indo-Ch.)	ə-năm′	uh-nam′
Annamese (Indo-Ch.)	ăn′-ə-mēz′ *or* -mēs′	an′-uh-meez′ *or* -mees′
An-ning (Ch., Yünnan)	än-nĭng	ahn-ning
Annovka (Rus.)	än′-nŏf-kä	ahn′-nof-kah
Anogia (Crete)	ä-noi′-yä	ah-noi′-yah
A Noite (Braz. newspaper)	ä noi′-tĭ	ah noi′-ti
Anosova (Rus.)	ä-nô′-sŏ-vä	ah-no′-so-vah
An-shu (Korea)	än-shū	ahn-shyoo
An-si *or* An-hsi (Ch., Kansu)	än-sē *or* än-shē	ahn-see *or* ahn-shee
Anska (Yugosl.)	än′-skä	ahn′-skah
Antalaha (Madag.)	än′-tə-lä′-hə	ahn′-tuh-lah′-huh
Antalya (Turk.)	än-täl-yä′	ahn-tahl-yah′
Also called *Adalia*, q.v.		
Anterion (Gr., cape)	än-dē′-rē(-ôn)	ahn-dee′-ree(-on)
anti-	ăn′-tĭ-	an′-ti-

In compounds, such as *anti-aircraft*, the *i* of *anti-* should be short, not long. The long *i* (as in *tie*) is overemphatic and characteristic of reading aloud rather than of speaking. It should be avoided on the radio.

Antibes (Fr.)	äN-tēb′	ahN-teeb′
Antikythera (Gr., isl.)	än-dē-kē′-thē-rä	ahn-dee-kee′-thee-rah
Also called *Aigila*, q.v.		

Antimakhia (Dodec., Cos)	än-dē-mä′-hē-ä	ahn-dee-mah′-hee-ah
Antiskari (Crete)	än-dē-skä′-rē	ahn-dee-skah′-ree
Antivari (Yugosl.)	*It.* än-tē′-vä-rē	ahn-tee′-vah-ree
Serb-Croat *Bar*, q.v.		
Antrodoco (It.)	än-trô-dô′-kô	ahn-tro-do′-ko
Antsirabe (Madag.)	än′-tsĭ-rä′-bĕ	ahn′-tsi-rah′-beh
Antsirane (Madag.)	än′-tsĭ-rä′-nĕ	ahn′-tsi-rah′-neh
An-tung (Manchu.)	*Eng.* ăn-to͝ong	an-tung
	Ch. än-do͝ong	ahn-dung
Antwerp (Belg.)	*Eng.* ănt′-wərp	ant′-wuhrp
Flemish *Antwerpen*, änt′-vĕr-pən [ahnt′-vehr-puhn]. French *Anvers*, äN-vĕr′ [ahN-vehr′].		
An-yi (Ch.) See *An-i*.		
An-yüan (Ch., Kiangsi)	än-yüän	ahn-yü-ahn
Anzio (It.)	än′-tsyô	ahn′-tsyo
Aola (Oc.)	ä-ô′-lä	ah-o′-lah
Aomori (Jap.)	ä-ô-mô-rē	ah-o-mo-ree
Aoos (Balkan riv.)	*Gr.* ä-ô′-ôs	ah-o′-os
Albanian *Vijosë*, q.v.		
Aosta (It.)	ä-ô′-stä	ah-o′-stah
Aouana, el (Tun.)	ä-wă′-nä, ĕl	ah-wa′-nah, el
Aouaria, el (Tun.)	ä-wä-rē′-yä, ĕl	ah-wah-ree′-yah, el
Apanasenko, J. R. (Rus. general)	ä-pä-nä′-sĕn-kŏ	ah-pah-nah′-sen-ko
Aparri (P.I.)	ä-pä′-rē	ah-pah′-ree
Apatin (Yugosl.)	ä′-pä-tĭn	ah′-pah-tin
Apeldoorn (Neth.)	äp′-əl-dōrn	ahp′-uhl-dohrn
Apennines (It., mts.)	ăp′-ə-nīnz	ap′-uh-nainz
Italian *Appennino*, äp-pĕn-nē′-nô [ahp-pen-nee′-no].		
Apia (Oc.)	ä-pē′-ä	ah-pee′-ah
Apollonia (Alb.)	*Eng.* ăp′-ə-lōn′-yə	ap′-uh-lohn′-yuh
Albanian *Pojan*, q.v.		
Appelscha (Neth.)	äp′-əl-sk(h)ä	ahp′-uhl-sk(h)ah
Appian Way (It., road)	ăp′-ĭ-ən	ap′-i-uhn
Appingedam (Neth.)	äp′-ĭng-ə-däm′	ahp′-ing-uh-dahm′
apricot	ā′-prĭ-kŏt *or* ăp′-rĭ-kŏt	ay′-pri-kot *or* ap′-ri-kot
Seven out of eight authoritative dictionaries list first the pronunciation with ā-. See *economic(s)* and the note thereon.		
Aprilia (It.)	ä-prē′-lyä	ah-pree′-lyah
Apsos (Alb., riv.)	*Gr.* äp′-sôs	ahp′-sos
Albanian *Berat*, q.v., and *Seman*, q.v.		
Apulia (It.)	*Eng.* ə-pū′-lyə	uh-pyoo′-lyuh
Italian *Puglia*, po͞o′-lyä [poo′-lyah].		

Aquila (It.)	ä′-kwē-lä	ah′-kwee-lah
Aquino, Benigno (Fil. leader)	ä-kē′-nô, bĕ-nēg′-nô	ah-kee′-no, beh-neeg′-no
Aquino (It.)	ä-kwē′-nô	ah-kwee′-no
Arabatskaya Strelka (Rus.)	ä-rä-bät′-skä-yä strĕl′-kä	ah-rah-baht′-skah-yah strel′-kah
Aracajú (Brazil)	ä-rə-kä-zho͞o′	ah-ruh-kah-zhoo′
Arad (Rum.)	*Rum.* ä-räd′	ah-rahd′
	Hung. ŏ′-rŏd	o′-rod
Arafura Sea (Austral.)	ä-rə-fo͞o′-rə	ah-ruh-foo′-ruh
Aragón (Sp.)	ä-rä-gôn′	ah-rah-gon′
Aragona (Sicily)	ä-rä-gô′-nä	ah-rah-go′-nah
Arakan (Burma)	ă′-rə-kăn′	a′-ruh-kan′
Araks *or* Aras (W. Asia, riv.)	ä-räks′ *or* ä-räs′	ah-rahks′ *or* ah-rahs′
English *Araxes*, q.v.		
Arambeï (Gr., mt.)	ä-rä-bā′	ah-rah-bay′
Aranci (Sard.)	ä-rän′-chē	ah-rahn′-chee
Aranđelovac (Yugosl.)	ä′-rän′-dyĕ-lô-väts	ah′-rahn′-dyeh-lo-vahts
Aranha, Oswaldo (Braz. leader)	ä-rä′-nyə, ŏz-väl′-do͝o	ah-rah′-nyuh, oz-vahl′-du
Aranha may approach ə-rĕ′-nyə [uh-reh′-nyuh].		
Aranjuez (Sp.)	ä-rän-hwĕth′ *or* -hwĕs′	ah-rahn-hweth′ *or* -hwes′
Aranya Prades (Thai)	ä-rŭn′-yə prä-tāt′	ah-ruhn′-yuh prah-tayt′
Aras (W. Asia) See *Araks.*		
Arawe (Oc.)	ä-rä′-wĕ	ah-rah′-weh
Araxes (W. Asia, riv.)	ä-răk′-sĭs	ah-rak′-sis
Also called *Aras* and *Araks.*		
Araxos (Gr.)	ä′-rä-ksôs	ah′-rah-ksos
Arbatax (Sard.)	är-bä′-täks	ahr-bah′-tahks
Arbe (Yugosl.)	*It.* är′-bĕ	ahr′-beh
Serb-Croat *Rab*, q.v.		
Arca, Rt (Yugosl.)	är′-tsä, ərt′	ahr′-tsah, uhrt′
Arcachon (Fr.)	är-kä-shôN′	ahr-kah-shoN′
arch-	ärch-	ahrch-
Exceptions, *archangel*, ärk′-ān′-jəl [ahrk′-ayn′-juhl], and derivatives. See also *archetype* and *archi-*.		
Archangel (Rus.)	*Eng.* ärk-ān′-jəl	ahrk-ayn′-juhl
Russian *Arkhangelsk*, är-hän′-gĕlsk [ahr-hahn′-gelsk].		
archetype	är′-kĭ-tīp	ahr′-ki-taip

archi-	är′-kĭ-	ahr′-ki-
As in *archipelago, architect, architectonic.*		
archipelago	är′-kĭ-pĕl′-ə-gō	ahr′-ki-pel′-uh-goh
This word trips many good men.		
Arcot (India)	är′-kŏt	ahr′-kot
arctic, antarctic	ärk′-tĭk, ănt-ärk′-tĭk	ahrk′-tik, ant-ahrk′-tik
Both *c's* must be pronounced.		
Arda (Balkan riv.)	är′-dä	ahr′-dah
Årdal (Nor.) See *Aardal.*		
Ardatov (Rus.)	är-dä′-tŏf	ahr-dah′-tof
Ardea (It.)	är′-dĕ-ä	ahr′-deh-ah
Ardres (Fr.)	är′dr	ahr′dr
Arendal (Nor.)	ä′-rən-däl	ah′-ruhn-dahl
Arends, Leslie C. (U.S. representative)	ăr′-əndz	ehr′-uhndz
Arensburg (Est.)	*Ger.* ä′-rĕns-bo͝ork(h)	ah′-rens-burk(h)
Estonian *Kuresaari,* q.v.		
Arents Eilanden (NEI)	ä′-rĕnts ā′-län-dən	ah′-rents ay′-lahn-duhn
Areopolis (Gr.)	ä-rĕ-ô′-pô-lē(s)	ah-reh-o′-po-lee(s)
Arezzo (It.)	ä-rĕt′-sô	ah-ret′-so
Argao (P.I.)	är-gou′	ahr-gau′
Argenta (It.)	är-jĕn′-tä	ahr-jen′-tah
Argentan (Fr.)	är-zhäN-täN′	ahr-zhahN-tahN′
Argenteuil (Fr.)	är-zhäN-tû′ĭ	ahr-zhahN-tœ′i
Argenton sur Creuse (Fr.)	är-zhäN-tôN′ sür krûz′	ahr-zhahN-toN′ sür krœz′
Arges (Rum., riv.)	är′-jĕsh	ahr′-jesh
Argine (It.)	är′-jē-nĕ	ahr′-jee-neh
Argolis (Gr.)	*Eng.* är′-gō-lĭs	ahr′-goh-lis
	Gr. är-gô-lēs′	ahr-go-lees′
Argos (Gr.)	är′-gô(s)	ahr′-go(s)
Argostolion (Gr.)	är-gôs-tô′-lē(-ôn)	ahr-gos-to′-lee(-on)
Argun (Rus., riv.)	är-go͞on′	ahr-goon′
Argyle (Austral.)	är′-gīl′	ahr′-gail′
Argyrokastron (Alb.)	*Gr.* är-yē-rô′-käs-trô(n)	ahr-yee-ro′-kahs-tro(n)
Albanian *Gjinokastër,* q.v.		
Ariana (Tun.)	ä-rĭ-ă′-nä	ah-ri-a′-nah
Ariano (It.)	ä-ryä′-nô	ah-ryah′-no
Arielli (It.)	ä-ryĕl′-lē	ah-ryel′-lee
Arilje (Yugosl.)	ä′-rĭ-lyĕ	ah′-ri-lyeh

Arima, el (Tun.)	ä-rē′-mä, ĕl	ah-ree′-mah, el
Aris (Oc.)	ä′-rēs	ah′-rees
Arish, el (Egypt)	ä-rēsh′, ĕl	ah-reesh′, el
Arkhanes (Crete)	är-hä′-nĕs	ahr-hah′-nes
Arkhara (Rus.)	är-hä′-rä	ahr-hah′-rah
Arles (Fr.)	*Eng.* ärlz′	ahrlz′
	Fr. ärl′	ahrl′
Arlon (Belg.)	är-lôN′	ahr-loN′
armada	*Eng.* är-mä′-də	ahr-mah′-duh
	or är-mā′-də	ahr-may′-duh
	Sp. är-mä′-*th*ä	ahr-mah′-*th*ah
Armavir (Rus.)	är-mä-vēr′	ahr-mah-veer′
Armeni (Crete)	är-mĕ′-nē	ahr-meh′-nee
Armentières (Fr.)	*Eng.* är′-mən-tĭrz′	ahr′-muhn-tihrz′
	Fr. är-mäN-tyĕr′	ahr-mahN-tyehr′
Armorica (Fr.)	är-môr′-ĭ-kə	ahr-mor′-i-kuh
French *Armorique*, är-mô-rēk′ [ahr-mo-reek′].		
Armyansk (Rus.)	är-myänsk′	ahr-myahnsk′
Arnavon (Oc.)	är-nä′-vôn	ahr-nah′-von
Arnhem (Austral.)	ärn′-əm	ahrn′-uhm
Earlier, ärn′-hĕm [ahrn′-hem].		
Arnhem (Neth.)	ärn′-hĕm	ahrn′-hem
Arno (It., riv.)	är′-nô	ahr′-no
Arno (Oc.)	är′-nô	ahr′-no
Aroe *or* Aru (NEI)	ä′-ro͞o	ah′-roo
Arorae (Oc.)	ä-rô′-rä-ĕ *or* -rī	ah-ro′-rah-eh *or* -rai
Aroussa, el (Tun.)	ä-ro͞o′-sä, ĕl	ah-roo′-sah, el
Arras (Fr.)	*Eng.* ăr′-əs	ehr′-uhs
	Fr. ä-räs′	ah-rahs′
Arta (Alb., lake)	*Eng.* är′-tä	ahr′-tah
Albanian *Knetë e Nartës.*		
Arta (Gr. riv.)	är′-tä	ahr′-tah
Artemov (Rus.)	är-tyô′-mŏf	ahr-tyo′-mof
Artemovsk (Rus.)	är-tyô′-mŏfsk	ahr-tyo′-mofsk
Artigas (Uruguay)	är-tē′-gäs	ahr-tee′-gahs
Aru (NEI) See *Aroe.*		
Aruba (Sp.)	ä-ro͞o′-bä	ah-roo′-bah
Arundel	*U.S.* ə-rŭn′-dəl	uh-ruhn′-duhl
	Eng. ăr′-ən-dəl	ehr′-uhn-duhl
Also ə-rŭn′-əl [uh-ruhn′-uhl] and ärn′-dəl [ahrn′-duhl].		
Arzamas (Rus.)	är-zä-mäs′	ahr-zah-mahs′
Arzen (Alb., riv.) See *Erzen.*		
Arzeu (Alg.)	är-zĕ-o͞o′	ahr-zeh-oo′
Arzgir (Rus.)	ärz′-gēr′	ahrz′-geer′

Aschersleben (Ger.)	äsh′-ərs-lā′-bən	ahsh′-uhrs-lay′-buhn
Ascoli (It.)	ä′-skô-lē	ah′-sko-lee
Asénsio Cabanillas, Carlos (Sp. leader)	ä-sĕn′-syô kä-bä-nē′-lyäs (*or* -yäs), kär′-lôs	ah-sen′-syo kah-bah-nee′-lyahs (*or* -yahs), kahr′-los
Aseri (Est.)	ä′-sĕ-rĭ	ah′-seh-ri
Åsgårdsstrand (Nor.) See *Aasgaardsstrand.*		
Ashishina (Tun.)	ä-shē-shē′-nä	ah-shee-shee′-nah
Ashkhabad (Rus.)	äsh-kä-bäd′	ahsh-kah-bahd′
Asinara (Sard., isl.)	ä-sē-nä′-rä	ah-see-nah′-rah
Asine (Gr.) See *Korone.*		
Asinello (It., isl.) Serb-Croat *Sveti Petar.*	ä-sē-nĕl′-lô	ah-see-nel′-lo
Asker (Nor.)	äs′-kər	ahs′-kuhr
Assam (India)	ăs-săm′	as-sam′
Assen (Neth.)	äs′-ən	ahs′-uhn
Assisi (It.)	äs-sē′-zē	ahs-see′-zee
Assling (Yugosl.) Serb-Croat *Jesenica,* q.v.	*Ger.* äs′-lĭng	ahs′-ling
Astakos (Gr.)	ä-stä-kôs′	ah-stah-kos′
Asterabad *or* Astrabad (Iran) See *Gurgan.*		
Astrakhan (Rus.)	*Eng.* ăs′-trə-kăn′	as′-truh-kan′
	Rus. ä′-strä-hän(y)	ah′-strah-hahn(y)
Astrid	*Eng.* ăs′-trĭd	as′-trid
(Nor. princess)	*Nor.* äs′-trē	ahs′-tree
Astritsi (Crete)	ä-strē′-tsē	ah-stree′-tsee
Astrolabe (New Guinea, bay)	ăs′-trō-lāb	as′-troh-layb
Astropalea (Dodec.) See *Astypalea* and *Stampalia.*		
Asturias (Sp., prov.)	*Eng.* ăs-tū′-rĭ-əs	as-tyoo′-ri-uhs
	Sp. äs-to͞or′-yäs	ahs-toor′-yahs
Astypalea (Dodec.)	ä-stē-pä-lĕ′-ä	ah-stee-pah-leh′-ah

Also called *Astropalea,* ä-strô-pä-lyä′ [ah-stro-pah-lyah′]. Italian *Stampalia,* q.v.

Asunción (Sp; Oc.)	ä-so͞on-syôn′ *or* -thyôn′	ah-soon-syon′ *or* -thyon′
Asyut (Egypt, prov.)	ä-syo͞ot′	ah-syoot′
Atafu (Oc.)	ä-tä-fo͞o′	ah-tah-foo′
Atalante (Gr.)	*Gr.* ä-tä-län′-dē	ah-tah-lahn′-dee
	Eng. ăt-ə-lăn′-tĭ	at-uh-lan′-ti
Ataliklikun (Oc.)	ä-tä-lĭk′-lē-ko͞on	ah-tah-lik′-lee-koon
Atavyri (Dodec., Rh., mt.)	ä-tä-vē′-rē	ah-tah-vee′-ree

Italian *Attairo,* ät-tī′-rô [aht-tai′-ro].

Atet (Burma)	ə-tĕt′	uh-tet′

An element in place names meaning *lower.*

Ath (Belg.)	ät′	aht′
Athenai (Gr.) See *Athens.*		
Athens (Gr.)	*Eng.* ăth′-ĭnz	ath′-inz
Greek *Athenai,* ä-thē′-nĕ [ah-thee′-neh]—often *Athena,* ä-thē′-nä [ah-thee′-nah].		
Athos (Gr., pen., mt.)	*Eng.* ăth′-ŏs	ath′-os
	or ā′-thŏs	ay′-thos
	Gr. ä′-thôs	ah′-thos
Also called *Agion Oros,* ī′-yôn ô′-rôs [ai′-yon o′-ros].		
Atina (It.)	ä-tē′-nä	ah-tee′-nah
Atka (Alaska, isl.)	ăt′-kə	at′-kuh
Atkarsk (Rus.)	ät-kärsk′	aht-kahrsk′
Atna (Nor.)	ät′-nä	aht′-nah
atoll	ăt′-ŏl *or* ə-tŏl′	at′-ol *or* uh-tol′
Attairo (Dodec., Rh., mt.) See *Atavyri.*		
Attu (Alaska, isl.)	ăt′-to͞o′	at′-too′
Aua (Oc.)	ou′-ä	au′-ah
Aur (Oc.)	our′	aur′
Auby (Fr.)	ō-bē′	oh-bee′
Auch (Fr.)	ōsh′	ohsh′
Auchel (Fr.)	ō-shĕl′	oh-shel′
Auchincloss, James C. (U.S. representative)	ô′-kĭn-klŏs	aw′-kin-klos
Auchinleck (Scot.)	ô′-kĭn-lĕk	o′-kin-lek
The old pronunciation ă-flĕk′ is associated with James Boswell.		
Auckland (N.Z.)	ôk′-lənd	awk′-luhnd
Aude (Fr., riv.)	ōd′	ohd′
Audruicq (Fr.)	ō-drwēk′	oh-drweek′
Auegia (Libya)	ä-wā′-jä	ah-way′-jah
Also called *Marsa* (q.v.) *el Auegia.*		
Aubsburg (Ger.)	*Eng.* ôgz′-bûrg	ogz′-buhrg
	Ger. ouk(h)s′-bo͝ork(h)	auk(h)s′-burk(h)
Augusta (Sicily)	*Eng.* ə-gŭs′-tə	uh-guhs′-tuh
	It. ou-go͞o′-stä	au-goo′-stah
Augustów (Pol.)	ou-go͝o′-sto͝of	au-gu′-stuf
Russian *Avgustov,* äv-go͞o′-stŏf [ahv-goo′-stof].		
Augustowski, Kanał (Pol.)	ou-go͝o-stôf′-skĭ, kä′-näl	au-gu-stof′-ski, kah′-nahl
Russian *Avgustovski Kanal,* äv-go͞o-stôf′-skĭ kä-näl′ [ahv-goo-stof′-ski kah-nahl′].		
Auki (Oc.)	ou′-kē	au′-kee
Auletta (It.)	ou-lĕt′-tä	au-let′-tah
Ault (Fr.)	ō′	oh′
Aunus (Fin., isthmus)	ou′-no͝os	au′-nus
Russian *Olonets,* q.v.		

Aur (Oc.)	our′	aur′
Aurangabad (India)	ô-rŭng′-gə-băd′	o-ruhng′-guh-bad′
	or ou-rŭng-gä-bäd′	au-ruhng-gah-bahd′
Auray (Fr.)	ō-rĕ′	oh-reh′
Aurignac (Fr.)	ō-rē-nyäk′	oh-ree-nyahk′
Aurillac (Fr.)	ō-rē-yäk′	oh-ree-yahk′
Aurland (Nor.)	our′-län	aur′-lahn
Aurskog (Nor.)	our′-skōg	aur′-skohg
	or oush′-kōg	aush′-kohg

Formerly spelled *Oerskog* or *Örskog* and pronounced ûr′-skōg [œr′-skohg] or ûsh′-kōg [œsh′-kohg].

Aurunci (It., mt.)	ou-ro͞on′-chē	au-roon′-chee
Ausonia (It.)	ou-sô′-nyä	au-so′-nyah
auspices	ôs′-pĭ-sĭz	os′-pi-siz

The plural ôs′-pĭ-sēz [os′-pi-seez] is incorrect. The singular is *auspice*; the plural therefore should be formed, not on the analogy of *basis*, *bases* (bā′-sĭs, -sēz), but of *base*, *bases* (bās, bā′-sĭz).

Aust Agder (Nor.)	oust′ äg′-dər	aust′ ahg′-duhr
Austerlitz (Cz.)	*Eng.* ôs′-tər-lĭts	os′-tuhr-lits
	Ger. ous′-tər-lĭts	aus′-tuhr-lits

Czech *Slavkov*, släv′-kôf [slahv′-kof].

Austraat (Nor.)	ou′-strôt	au′-strot
Auteuil (Fr.)	ō-tû′ĭ	oh-tœ′i
Autun (Fr.)	ō-tûN′	oh-tœN′
Auxerre (Fr.)	ō-sĕr′	oh-sehr′
Avala (Yugosl.)	ä′-vä-lä	ah′-vah-lah
Avdeevka (Rus.)	äv-dĕ′-yĕf-kä	ahv-deh′-yef-kah
Aveiro (Port.)	ä-vā′-ro͝o	ah-vay′-ru
Aversa (It.)	ä-vĕr′-sä	ah-vehr′-sah
Avesnes (Fr.)	ä-vĕn′	ah-ven′
Avezzano (It.)	ä-vĕt-sä′-nô	ah-vet-sah′-no
Avgustov (Pol.) See *Augustów*.		
Avignon (Fr.)	ä-vē-nyôN′	ah-vee-nyoN′
Ávila (Sp.)	ä′-vē-lä	ah′-vee-lah
Ávila Camacho	ä′-vē-lä kä-mä′-chô	ah′-vee-lah kah-mah′-cho

The President of Mexico should always be called by both names: *Ávila Camacho*, ä′-vē-lä kä-mä′-chô [ah′-vee-lah kah-mah′-cho], not simply *Camacho*, kä-mä′-chô [kah-mah′-cho].

Avlon (Alb.) See *Vlonë*.		
Avola (Sicily)	ä′-vô-lä	ah′-vo-lah
Aweleng (Oc.)	ä-wĕ-lĕng′	ah-weh-leng′
Axios (Balkan riv.)	*Gr.* ä-ksē-ôs′	ah-ksee-os′

Also called *Vardar*, q.v.

Axos (Crete)	ä-ksôs′	ah-ksos′
Ayan (Rus.)	ä-yän′	ah-yahn′
Aydın (Turk.)	ī-dēn′	ai-deen′
Ayr (Austral.)	ăr′	ehr′
Ayu (NEI) See *Ajoe*.		
Ayudhya (Thai)	*Eng.* ä-yōō′-thē-ä	ah-yoo′-thee-ah
	Thai ä-yōō′-tē-ä	ah-yoo′-tee-ah
Also spelled *Ayuthya* and *Ayuthia*.		
Ayuthya (Thai) See *Ayudhya*.		
Azad, Abdul Kalam (Indian leader)	ä-zäd′, äb′-do͝ol kə-läm′	ah-zahd′, ahb′-dul kuh-lahm′
Azali (Crete)	ä-zä′-lē	ah-zah′-lee
Azanja (Yugosl.)	ä′-zä′-nyä	ah′-zah′-nyah
Azbukovica (Yugosl.)	äz′-bōō-kô-vĭ-tsä	ahz′-boo-ko-vi-tsah
Azeis (Libya)	ä-zās′	ah-zays′
Azerbaijan (Iran, Rus.)	ä-zər-bī-jän′	ah-zuhr-bai-jahn′
Azib, el (Tun.)	ä′-zĭb, ĕl	ah′-zib, el
Azizia, el (Libya)	ă-zĭ-zē′-ä, ĕl	a-zi-zee′-ah, el
Azores (Port., isls.)	*Eng.* ə-zōrz′	uh-zohrz′
Portuguese *Açores*, ä-sô′-rĭsh [ah-so′-rish], and ə-sô′-rĕzh [uh-so′-rezh].		
Azov *or* Azof (Rus.)	ä-zôf′	ah-zof′

b, *bh*, and *v* are interchangeable in Greek; *b* and *v* in Spanish and other languages. It may be necessary to look up all these spellings.

Baafjellmoen (Nor.)	bô-fyĕl-mo͝o′-ən	bo-fyel-mu′-uhn
Baambrugge (Neth.)	bäm-brûk(h)′-ə	bahm-brœk(h)′-uh
Baba (Yugosl., mts.)	bä′-bä	bah′-bah
Babadag (Rum.)	bä-bä-däg′	bah-bah-dahg′
Babaevo (Rus.)	bä-bä′-yĕ-vŏ	bah-bah′-yeh-vo
Babase (Oc.)	bä′-bä-sĕ	bah′-bah-seh
Babelthuap (Oc.)	bä-bĕl-tōō′-äp	bah-bel-too′-ahp
Also called *Babeldoab*, bä-bĕl-dô-äb′ [bah-bel-do-ahb′].		
Babička Gora (Yugosl.)	bä′-bĭch-kä gô′-rä	bah′-bich-kah go′-rah
Babo (Oc.)	bä′-bô	bah′-bo
Babol (Iran)	bä-bôl′	bah-bawl′
Also called *Babul*, bä-bo͝ol′ [bah-bul′] and *Barfrush*, q.v.		
Babol Sar (Iran)	bä-bôl′ sär′	bah-bawl′ sahr′
Also called *Babul Sar*.		
Babul (Iran) See *Babol*.		
Babul Sar (Iran)	bä-bo͝ol′ sär′	bah-bul′ sahr′
Babuna (Yugosl., riv. and mts.)	bä′-bōō-nä	bah′-boo-nah
Babušnica (Yugosl.)	bä′-bōōsh′-nĭ-tsä	bah′-boosh′-ni-tsah

Babuyán (P.I.)	bä-bo͞o-yän′	bah-boo-yahn′
Bacău (Rum.)	bä-kû′-o͝o	bah-kuh′-u
Bache (Art collection)	bāch′	baych′
Bacher Gebirge (Yugosl.)	*Ger.* bä′-k(h)ər gə-bēr′-gə	bah′-k(h)uhr guh-beer′-guh
Serb-Croat *Pohorje*, q.v.		
Bačina (Yugosl.)	bä′-chĭ-nä	bah′-chi-nah
Bačka (Yugosl.)	bäch′-kä	bahch′-kah
Bačko Gradište (Yugosl.)	bäch′-kô grä′-dĭ-shtĕ	bahch′-ko grah′-di-shteh
Baclieu (Indo-Ch.)	bäk-lyû′	bahk-lyœ′
Bacolod (P.I.)	bä-kô′-lôd	bah-ko′-lod
Bacuit (P.I.)	bä-kwēt′	bah-kweet′
Badajos (Sp., prov.)	bä-dä′-hôs	bah-dah′-hos
Badgastein (Austria)	bät′-gä′-stīn	baht′-gah′-stain
Bad Ischl (Austria)	bät′ ĭsh′l	baht′ ish′l
Badnjevac (Yugosl.)	bäd′-nyĕ-väts	bahd′-nyeh-vahts
Badoglio, Pietro (It general)	bä-dô′-lyô, pyĕ′-trô	bah-do′-lyo, pyeh′-tro
Badovinci (Yugosl.)	bä′-dô′-vĭn-tsĭ	bah′-do′-vin-tsi
Baga (Oc.)	bä′-gä	bah′-gah
Bagabag (New Guinea)	bä-gä-bäg′	bah-gah-bahg′
Baganga (P.I.)	bä-gäng′-gä	bah-gahng′-gah
Bagehot (Eng. name)	băj′-ət *or* băg′-ət	baj′-uht *or* bag′-uht
The first is preferred for Walter Bagehot, the economist.		
Bagheria (Sicily)	bä-gĕ-rē′-ä	bah-geh-ree′-ah
Bagnara (It.)	bä-nyä′-rä	bah-nyah′-rah
Bagnara Calabra (It.)	bä-nyä′-rä kä′-lä-brä	bah-nyah′-rah kah′-lah-brah
Bagrdan (Yugosl.)	bä′-gər′-dän	bah′-guhr′-dahn
Baguio (P.I.)	*Eng.* băg′-ē-ō	bag′-ee-oh
	Sp. bä′-gyô	bah′-gyo
Bahan (Burma)	bə-hän′	buh-hahn′
Bahawalpur (India)	bə-hä′-wəl-po͝or′ *or* bä′-wəl-po͝or′	buh-hah′-wuhl-pur′ bah′-wuhl-pur′
Bahia (Brazil) *See Baía.*		
Bahrami (Per. leader)	bä-hrä-mē′	bah-hrah-mee′
Bahrein (Iran)	bä-hrān′	bah-hrayn′
Baía *or* Bahia (Brazil)	bä-ē′-ə *or* bə-ē′-ə	bah-ee′-uh *or* buh-ee′-uh
Officially called *São Salvador*, q.v.		
Baia Mare (Rum.)	bä′-yä mä′-rĕ	bah -yah mah′-reh
Hungarian *Nagybánya*, nŏd′(y)-bä-nyŏ [nod′(y)-bah-nyo].		

Baikal (Rus.)	bī-käl′	bai-kahl′
Baile Átha Cliath (Eire)	blô′ klē′-ĕ	blaw′ klee′-eh
	or bwäl′ ä klē′-ə	bwahl′ ah klee′-uh
English *Dublin*, q.v.		
Băileşti (Rum.)	bə-ē-lĕsht′	buh-ee-lesht′
Bailleul (Fr.)	bī-yûl′	bai-yœl′
Bairoko (Oc.)	bī-rô′-kô	bai-ro′-ko
Baja (Hung.)	bŏ′-yŏ	bo′-yo
Bajina Bašta (Yugosl.)	bä′-yĭ-nä bäsh′-tä	bah′-yi-nah bahsh′-tah
Bajmok (Yugosl.)	bī′-môk	bai′-mok
Bakar (Yugosl.)	bä′-kär	bah′-kahr
Italian *Buccari*, q.v.		
Bakarač (Yugosl.)	bä′-kä-räch	bah′-kah-rahch
Italian *Buccarizza*, q.v.		
Bakhatere (Oc.)	bä-k(h)ä′-tĕ-rĕ	bah-k(h)ah′-teh-reh
Bakhchisarai (Rus.)	bäk(h)′-chĭ-sä-rī′	bahk(h)′-chi-sah-rai′
Bakhireva (Rus.)	bä-hē′-rĕ-vä	bah-hee′-reh-vah
Bakhmach (Rus.)	bäk(h)-mäch′	bahk(h)-mahch′
Bakhtiari (Per. tribe)	băk(h)-tē-är-ē′	bak(h)-tee-ahr-ee′
Baku (Rus.)	bä-kōō′	bah-koo′
Balábac (P.I., str.)	bä-lä′-bäk	bah-lah′-bahk
Balabo (NEI)	bä-lä′-bô	bah-lah′-bo
Balaklava (Rus.)	*Eng.* băl′-ə-klä′-və	bal′-uh-klah′-vuh
	Rus. bä-lä-klä′-vä	bah-lah-klah′-vah
Balakleya (Rus.)	bä-lä-klĕ′-yä	bah-lah-kleh′-yah
Balanga (P.I.)	bä-läng′-gä	bah-lahng′-gah
Balashov (Rus.)	bä-lä-shôf′	bah-lah-shof′
Balasore (India)	băl′-ə-sōr′	bal′-uh-sohr′
Balassagyarmat (Hung.)	bŏ′-lŏ-shŏ-dyŏr′-mŏt	bo′-lo-sho-dyor′-mot
Balaton (Hung., lake)	bŏ′-lŏ-tôn	bo′-lo-ton
Balatonfüred (Hung.)	bŏ′-lŏ-tôn-fü′-rĕd	bo′-lo-ton-fü′-red
Balcic (Rum.)	bäl′-chēk′	bahl′-cheek′
Balearic Isls. (Sp.)	*Eng.* băl′-ĭ-ă′-rĭk	bal′-i-a′-rik
Spanish *Baleares*, bä-lĕ-ä′-rĕs [bah-leh-ah′-res].		
Baler (P.I.)	bä-lĕr′	bah-lehr′
Balestrand (Nor.)	bäl′-ə-strän	bahl′-uh-strahn
Balgai (New Guinea)	bäl-gī′	bahl-gai′
Bali (NEI)	bä′-lē	bah′-lee
Balıkesir (Turk.)	bä-lĭ-kĕ-sēr′	bah-li-keh-seer′
Balikpapan (NEI)	*Eng.* bä′-lēk-pä′-pän	bah′-leek-pah′-pahn
	Du. bä′-lē-pä′-pän	bah′-lee-pah′-pahn
Balintang (P.I.)	bä-lĭn-täng′	bah-lin-tahng′
Balki (Rus.)	bäl′-kĭ	bahl′-ki

Ballale (Oc.)	bäl-lä′-lĕ	bahl-lah′-leh
Ballia (India)	băl′-ĭ-ə	bal′-i-uh
Balsfjord (Nor.)	bäls′-fyōr	bahls′-fyohr
Balstad (Nor.)	bäl′-stä	bahl′-stah
Balta (Rus.)	bäl′-tä	bahl′-tah
Bălţi (Rum.)	bûlts′	buhlts′
Russian *Byeltsi*, bĕl′(y)-tsĭ [bel′(y)-tsi].		
Baltiski Port (Est.)	*Rus.* bäl-tē′-skĭ pôrt′	bahl-tee′-ski port′
Estonian *Paltiski*, q.v.		
Baluan (Oc.)	bä′-lo͞o-än	bah′-loo-ahn
Baluchistan (India)	bə-lo͞o′-chĭ-stän′	buh-loo′-chi-stahn′
Bambatana (Oc.)	bäm-bä-tä′-nä	bahm-bah-tah′-nah
Bambini (Gr.)	bäm-bē′-nē	bahm-bee′-nee
Banaczyk, Władysław (Pol. leader)	bä-nä′-chĭk, vlä-dĭ′-släf	bah-nah′-chik, vlah-di′-slahf
Banat (Rum., Yugosl.)	*Rum.* bä-nät′	bah-naht′
	S.-C. bä′-nät′	bah′-naht′
Banda (India; Oc., sea)	băn′-də *or* bän′-dä	ban′-duh *or* bahn′-dah
bandar	băn′-dər *or* bŭn′-dər	ban′-duhr *or* buhn′-duhr
An element, meaning *port*, in Persian and Indian place names.		
Bandar Abbas (Iran)	băn′-dər äb-bäs′	ban′-duhr ahb-bahs′
Bandar Pahlavi (Iran)	băn′-dər pä-lä-vē′	ban′-duhr pah-lah-vee′
Bandar Shah (Iran)	băn′-dər shä′	ban′-duhr shah′
Bandar Shapur (Iran)	băn′-dər shă-po͞or′	ban′-duhr sha-poor′
Bandırma (Turk.)	bän-dĭr-mä′	bahn-dihr-mah′
Also called *Panderma*, q.v.		
Bandjermasin (NEI)	bän′-jər-mä′-sĭn	bahn′-juhr-mah′-sin
Bandoeng *or* Bandung (NEI)	bän′-do͞ong	bahn′-doong
Bandon (Thai)	bän′-dôn	bahn′-dawn
Bandouvas, Christos (Gr. leader)	bä(n)-do͞o′-väs, hrē′-stôs	bah(n)-doo′-vahs, hree′-stos
Bandouvas, Manolis (Cretan leader)	bä(n)-do͞o′-väs, mä-nô′-lēs	bah(n)-doo′-vahs, mah-no′-lees
Bandung (NEI) See *Bandoeng*.		
Bangalore (India)	băng-gə-lōr′	bang-guh-lohr′
Bangatang (Oc.)	bäng′-ä-täng	bahng′-ah-tahng
Bangka (NEI)	*Eng.* băng′-kə	bang′-kuh
	Du. bäng′-kä	bahng′-kah
Bangkok (Thai)	băng′-kŏk′	bang′-kok′
Thai *Krungdheb*, kro͝ong-tāp′ [krung-tayp′].		
Bangued (P.I.)	bäng-gĕd′	bahng-ged′

Baniata (Oc.) bä-nē-ä′-tä bah-nee-ah′-tah
Banika (Oc.) bä-nē′-kä bah-nee′-kah
Banjak *or* Banyak (NEI) bän′-yäk bahn′-yahk
Banjaluka (Yugosl.) bä′-nyä-lōō′-kä bah′-nyah-loo′-kah
Banjani (Yugosl.) bä′-nyä-nĭ bah′-nyah-ni
Banjoewangi *or* Banyuwangi (NEI) bän-yōō-wäng′-ē bahn-yoo-wahng′-ee
banská (Cz.) bän′-skä bahn′-skah
A common element, meaning *springs* or *baths*, in Czech place names. It may be necessary to look up the other part of the name.
Banská Štiavnica (Cz.) bän′-skä shtyäv′-nĭ-tsä bahn′-skah shtyahv′-ni-tsah
Bansko (Bulg.) bän′-skŏ bahn′-sko
Bantam (NEI) *Eng.* băn′-təm ban′-tuhm
Du. bän-täm′ bahn-tahm′
Most Americans have an affection for the derivatives *bantam, bantie,* meaning small, slight.
bánya bän′-yŏ bahn′-yo
An element, meaning *mine*, in Hungarian place names.
Banyak (NEI) See *Banjak.*
Banyuwangi (NEI) See *Banjoewangi.*
Bao Dai (King of Annam) bou dī′ bau dai′
Baoe-baoe (NEI) bä′-ōō bä′-ōō bah′-oo bah′-oo
Bar (Yugosl.) bär′ bahr′
Italian *Antivari*, q.v.
Bar (Rus.) bär′ bahr′
Barahun (Oc.) bä-rä-hōōn′ bah-rah-hoon′
Baranof (Alaska, isl.) *Eng.* băr′-ə-nŏf behr′-uh-nof
Rus. bä-rä′-nŏf bah-rah′-nof
Baranowicze (Pol.) bä-rä-nô-vē′-chĕ bah-rah-no-vee′-cheh
Russian *Baranovichi*, bä-rä-nô′-vĭ-chĭ [bah-rah-no′-vi-chi].
Baranya (Hung., Yugosl.) *Hung.* bŏ′-rŏ-nyŏ bo′-ro-nyo
S.-C. bä′-rä-nyä bah′-rah-nyah
Barbarevo (Yugosl.) bär′-bä′-rĕ-vô bahr′-bah′-reh-vo
Barca (Libya) bär′-kä bahr′-kah
Barcelona (Sp.) *Eng.* bär′-sə-lō′-nə bahr′-suh-loh′-nuh
Sp. bär-thĕ-lô′-nä bahr-theh-lo′-nah
Bardejov (Cz.) bär′-dĕ-yôf bahr′-deh-yof
German *Bartfeld*, bärt′-fĕlt [bahrt′-felt].
Barden, Graham A. (U.S. representative) bär′-dən bahr′-duhn
Bardia (Libya) bär-dē′-ä *or* bär′-dĭ-ä bahr-dee′-ah *or* bahr′-di-ah
Bardo (Tun.) bär′-dō bahr′-doh
Also called *Le Bardo*, q.v.

Bardufoss (Nor.)	bär′-do͝o-fôs	bahr′-du-fos
Bareilly (India)	bə-rā′-lē	buh-ray′-lee
Barents Sea	*Eng.* băr′-ĕnts	behr′-ents
	Rus. bä-rĕnts′	bah-rents′
Barfleur (Fr., point)	bär-flûr′	bahr-flœr′
Barfrush (Iran)	bär-fro͞osh′	bahr-froosh′
Officially *Babol,* q.v.		
Barguzin (Rus.)	bär-go͞o-zēn′	bahr-goo-zeen′
Bari (It.)	bä′-rē	bah′-ree
Barič (Yugosl.)	bä′-rĭch	bah′-rĭch
Bariki (Oc.)	bä-rē′-kē	bah-ree′-kee
Barili (P.I.)	bä-rē′-lē	bah-ree′-lee
Barka (Libya)	bär′-kä	bahr′-kah
Also spelled *Barca,* q.v.		
Barköl (Ch., Sinkiang)	bär-kûl	bahr-kuhl
Also called *Chen-hsi,* q.v.		
Bârlad (Rum.)	bûr-läd′	buhr-lahd′
Barlee (Austral.)	bär′-lē′	bahr′-lee′
Barletta (It.)	bär-lĕt′-tä	bahr-let′-tah
Barnard College (N.Y.)	bär′-nərd kŏl′-ĭj	bahr′-nuhrd kol′-ij
Barnaul (Rus.)	bär-nä-o͞ol′	bahr-nah-ool′
Barneveld (Neth.)	bär′-nə-vĕlt	bahr′-nuh-velt
Bar Nicobar (India, isl.)	bär′ nĭk-ō-bär′	bahr′ nik-oh-bahr′
Baroda (India)	bə-rō′-də	buh-roh′-duh
Barola (Oc.)	bä-rô′-lä	bah-ro′-lah
Barrafranca (Sicily)	bär-rä-frän′-kä	bahr-rah-frahn′-kah
barrage	bə-räzh′ *or* bə-räj′	buh-rahzh′ *or* buh-rahj′
Also British băr′-äzh [behr′-ahzh].		
Barreiro (Port.)	bä-rā′-ro͝o	bah-ray′-ru
Bartfeld (Cz.) See *Bardejov.*		
Bartók, Béla (Hung. musician)	bŏr′-tôk, bā′-lŏ	bor′-tok, bay′-lo
Bartsch (Pol., riv.) See *Barycz.*		
Baruch, Bernard M.	bə-ro͞ok′	buh-rook′
Barvenkova (Rus.)	bär-vĕn′-kŏ-vä	bahr-ven′-ko-vah
Barwon (Austral.)	bär′-wən	bahr′-wuhn
Barycz (Pol., riv.)	bä′-rĭch	bah′-rich
German *Bartsch,* bärtsh′ [bahrtsh′].		
Barzas (Rus.)	bär-zäs′	bahr-zahs′
Basel (Switz.)	bä′-zel	bah′-zuhl
French *Basle* or *Bâle,* bäl′ [bahl′].		
bases (pl. of *base*)	bā′-sĭz	bay′-siz
This word is often confused with the next entry.		
bases (pl. of *basis*)	bā′-sēz	bay′-seez

Bashanta (Rus.)	bä-shän′-tä	bah-shahn′-tah
Bashi (P.I., channel)	bä′-shē	bah′-shee
Basilan (P.I.)	bä-sē′-län	bah-see′-lahn
Baška (Yugosl.)	bä′-shkä	bah′-shkah
Italian *Bescanuova*, q.v.		
Basra (Iraq)	bŭs′-rə *or* bäs′-rä	buhs′-ruh *or* bahs′-rah
Also English bă z′-rə [baz′-ruh].		
Bassac (Indo-Ch.)	bäs-säk′	bahs-sahk′
Bassano (It.)	bäs-sä′-nô	bahs-sah′-no
Bassein (Burma)	băs-sēn′	bas-seen′
Burman *Pathein.*		
Bastia (Corsica)	bä-stē′-ä	bah-stee′-ah
See *Terranova* and *Terravecchia.* Also English bäs′-chə [bahs′-chuh].		
Bataán (P.I.)	*Eng.* bă-tăn′	ba-tan′
	local bä-tä-än′	bah-tah-ahn′
Bátac (P.I.)	bä′-täk	bah′-tahk
Bataisk (Rus.)	bä-tīsk′	bah-taisk′
Batán (P.I.)	bä-tän′	bah-tahn′
Also called *Batanes,* bä-tä′-nĕs [bah-tah′-nes], and *Bashi,* bä′-shē [bah′-shee].		
Batang (Ch., Sikang)	bä-täng	bah-tahng
Batang (NEI)	bä′-täng	bah′-tahng
Batangas (P.I.)	bä-täng′-gäs	bah-tahng′-gahs
Batanja, Nova (Yugosl.)	bä′-tä-nyä, nô′-vä	bah′-tah-nyah, no′-vah
Batao (P.I.)	bä-tä′-ô	bah-tah′-o
Batavia (NEI)	*Eng.* bə-tā′-vyə	buh-tay′-vyuh
	Du. bä-tä′-vĭ-ä	bah-tah′-vi-ah
Bates Isl. (Oc.)	bāts′	bayts′
Batetsk (Rus.)	bä′-tĕtsk	bah′-tetsk
Batina (Yugosl.)	bä′-tĭ-nä	bah′-ti-nah
Batnfjordsoera *or* Batnfjordsöra (Nor.)	bät′n-fyōrs-û′-rä	baht′n-fyohrs-œ′-rah
Batjan (NEI)	bä-chän′	bah-chahn′
Batna (Alg.)	bät′-nä	baht′-nah
Batočina (Yugosl.)	bä′-tô′-chĭ-nä	bah′-to′-chi-nah
Batoe *or* Batu (NEI)	bä′-too͞	bah′-too
Batraki (Rus.)	bä-trä-kē′	bah-trah-kee′
Batschka (Yugosl.)	*Ger.* bäch′-kä	bahch′-kah
Serb-Croat *Bačka*, q.v.		
Battambang (Indo-Ch.)	bät′-əm-bäng	baht′-uhm-bahng
Thai *Phratabong,* prät′-ə-bông′ [praht′-uh-bong′].		
Batticaloa (Ceylon)	bät-tē-kä-lō′-ə	baht-tee-kah-loh′-uh
Battipaglia (It.)	bät-tē-pä′-lyä	baht-tee-pah′-lyah

Batu (NEI) See *Batoe.*		
Batum (Rus.)	bä-tŏŏm′	bah-tum′
Bauan (P.I.)	bä′-wän	bah′-wahn
Bauska (Latvia)	bous′-kä	baus′-kah
German *Bausk*, bousk′ [bausk′].		
Bavanište (Yugosl.)	bä′-vä-nĭ-shtĕ	bah′-vah-ni-shteh
Bavaria (Ger.)	*Eng.* bə-vĕr′-ĭ-ə	buh-vehr′-i-uh
German *Bayern*, q.v.		
Bawean (NEI)	bä′-vĕ-än	bah′-veh-ahn
Bayard, Fort (Ch., Kwangtung, Fr. colony)	*Eng.* bī′-ərd *or* bā′- *Fr.* bä-yär′	bai′-uhrd *or* bay′- bah-yahr′
Baybay (P.I.)	bī′-bī′	bai′-bai′
Bayern (Ger.)	bī′-ərn	bai′-uhrn
English *Bavaria*, q.v.		
Bayeux (Fr.)	bä-yû′	bah-yœ′
Bayonne (Fr.)	*Eng.* bā′-yōn′ *Fr.* bä-yôn′	bay′-yohn′ bah-yon′
Bayreuth (Ger.)	bī′-roit′	bai′-roit′
This name should be distinguished in pronunciation and spelling from *Beirut* or *Beyrouth* (Syria).		
Bazargic (Rum.)	bä′-zär′-jēk′	bah′-zahr′-jeek′
Also called *Dobrici*, q.v.		
Beall, J. Glenn (U.S. representative)	bĕl′	bel′
Beaufort (except in South Carolina)	bō′-fərt	boh′-fuhrt
Beaufort (S.C.)	bū′-fərt	byoo′-fuhrt
Beaufort bomber	bō′-fərt	boh′-fuhrt
Beauvais (Fr.)	*Eng.* bō-vā′ *Fr.* bō-vĕ′	boh-vay′ boh-veh′

because

We have received a letter from Fresno (frĕz′-nō) asking, "Why do announcers say 'be-cuz' for *because?*" The answer is probably—because most Americans do. However, dictionaries allow -kôz or -kŏz, and it is well not to give the vowel an emphatic ŭ value. Our correspondent would not like New York bĭ-kôs′ [bi-kaws′] or Texas bĭ-kŭ′ŭz [bi-kuh′uhz].

Bečej, Novi (Yugosl.)	bĕ′-chā, nô′-vĭ	beh′-chay, no′-vi
Bechateur (Tun.)	bĕ-shä-tûr′	beh-shah-tœr′
Bečkerek, Veliki (Yugosl.)	bĕch′-kĕ′-rĕk, vĕ′-lĭ-kĭ	bech′-keh′-rek, veh′-li-ki
Hungarian *Nagybecskerek*, nŏd′(y)-bĕch′-kĕ-rĕk (nod′(y)-bech′-keh-rek].		
Bédarieux (Fr.)	bĕ-dä-ryû′	beh-dah-ryœ′

Bednyakov (Rus. name)	bĕd-nyä-kôf′	bed-nyah-kof′
Będzin (Pol.)	băN′-jĭn	baN′-jin
Russian *Bendin*, bĕn′-dĭn [ben′-din]. German *Bendzin*, bĕn′-dzĭn [ben′-dzin].		
Beekbergen (Neth.)	bāk′-bĕr-k(h)ən	bayk′-behr-k(h)uhn
Beemster (Neth.)	bām′-stər	baym′-stuhr
Begaljica (Yugosl.)	bĕ′-gä′-lyĭ-tsä	beh′-gah′-lyi-tsah
Begej (Yugosl., riv.)	bĕ′-gā	beh′-gay
Bei el Chebir (Libya)	bā ĕl kə-bēr′	bay el kuh-beer′
Beilen (Neth.)	bī′-lən	bai′-luhn
Beirut (Syria)	bā′-rōōt′	bay′-root′
Also spelled *Beyrouth*. This name should be distinguished in pronunciation and spelling from *Bayreuth* (Ger.).		
Beiuş (Rum.)	bā-yŏŏsh′	bay-yush′
Hungarian *Belényes*, bĕ′-lā-nyĕsh [beh′-lay-nyesh].		
Beja (Tun.)	bĕ-zhä′	beh-zhah′
Békés (Hung.)	bā′-kāsh	bay′-kaysh
Békéscsaba (Hung.)	bā′-kāsh-chŏ-bŏ	bay′-kaysh-cho-bo
Bekkaria (Alg.)	bĕk-kə-rē′-ä	bek-kuh-ree′-ah
Bela (India)	bā′-lə	bay′-luh
Bela Crkva (Yugosl.)	bĕ′-lä tsər′-kvä	beh′-lah tsuhr′-kvah
German *Weisskirchen*.		
Belanovica (Yugosl.)	bĕ′-lä-nô′-vĭ-tsä	beh′-lah-no′-vi-tsah
Bela Palanka (Yugosl.)	bĕ′-lä pä′-län-kä	beh′-lah pah′-lahn-kah
Belasica planina (Balkan mts.)	bĕ′-lä′-sĭ-tsä plä′-nē′-nä	beh′-lah′-si-tsah plah′-nee′-nah
Greek *Kerkíne*, q.v.		
Belaya Glina (Rus.)	bĕ′-lä-yä glē′-nä	beh′-lah-yah glee′-nah
Also called *Byeloglina*, q.v.		
Belaya Tserkov (Rus.)	bĕ′-lä-yä tsĕr′-kŏf	beh′-lah-yah tsehr′-kof
Belbek (Rus.)	bĕl-bĕk′	bel-bek′
Bełchatów (Pol.)	bĕl-hä′-tŏŏf	bel-hah′-tuf
Russian *Belkhatov*, bĕl-hä′-tŏf [bel-hah′-tof].		
Belém (Port., Brazil)	bĕ-lĕN′	beh-leN′
Belém, Brazil, is also called *Pará*, q.v.		
Belényes (Rum.) See *Beiuş*.		
Belestinon (Gr.)	vĕ-lĕ-stē′-nô(n)	veh-leh-stee′-no(n)
Also called *Pherai*, q.v.		
Belev (Rus.)	bĕ′-lĕf	beh′-lef
Belgaum (India)	bĕl-goum′	bel-gaum′
Belgorod (Rus.)	*Eng.* bĕl′-gŏ-rŏd *Rus.* bĕl′-gŏ-rŏt	bel′-go-rod bel′-go-rot

Belgrade (Yugosl.)	*Eng.* bĕl′-grād′	bel′-grayd′
Serb-Croat *Beograd*, q.v.		
Beliao (Oc.)	bĕ-lē-ou′	beh-lee-au′
Belica (Yugosl.)	bĕ′-lĭ-tsä	beh′-li-tsah
Beli Drim (Balkan riv.)	*S.-C.* bĕ′-lĭ drēm′	beh′-li dreem′
Albanian *Drin i Bardhë*, q.v.		
Beli Krest (Rus.)	bĕ′-lĭ krĕst′	beh′-li krest′
Belisha, Hore- (Br. leader)	bə-lē′-shə, hōr	buh-lee′-shuh, hohr
The pronunciation to rhyme with *Elisha* is incorrect.		
Belitong (NEI)	bĕ-lē′-tŏng	beh-lee′-tong
Also called *Billiton*, q.v.		
Beljak (Austria) See *Villach.*		
Beljanica (Yugosl., mts.)	bĕ′-lyä′-nĭ-tsä	beh′-lyah′-ni-tsah
Bellary (India)	bĕ-lä′-rē	beh-lah′-ree
Belloc, Hilary *or* Hilaire (Brit. author)	bĕl′-ŏk, hĭl′-ə-rĭ *or* hĭ-lăr′	bel′-ok, hil′-uh-ri *or* hi-lehr′
Bellona (Oc.)	bĕl-lō′-nä	bel-loh′-nah
Belluno (It.)	bĕl-lo͞o′-nô	bel-loo′-no
Beloe (Rus., lake)	bĕ′-lŏ-yĕ	beh′-lo-yeh
Belo Horizonte (Brazil)	bĕ′-lŏ-rē-zôn′-tĭ	beh′-lo-ree-zon′-ti
Belopole (Rus.)	bĕ-lŏ-pô′-lyĕ	beh-lo-po′-lyeh
Beloretsk (Rus.)	bĕ-lŏ-rĕtsk′	beh-lo-retsk′
Belorussia (Rus., repub.)	bĕ′-lô-ro͞o′-sĭ-yä	beh′-lo-roo′-si-yah
White Russian Soviet Republic. It should not be confused with the "White Russian" army that fought against the "Red Russians" in 1919-1920.		
Beloshitsi (Rus.)	bĕ-lô′-shĭ-tsĭ	beh-lo′-shi-tsi
Belotince (Yugosl.)	bĕ′-lô′-tĭn-tsĕ	beh′-lo′-tin-tseh
Belozersk (Rus.)	bĕl-ŏ-zĕrsk′	bel-o-zehrsk′
Beltramí, Raúl Morales (Chilean leader)	bĕl-trä-mē′, rä-o͞ol′ mô-rä′-lĕs	bel-trah-mee′, rah-ool′ mo-rah′-les
Belušić (Yugosl.)	bĕ′-lo͞o′-shĭch	beh′-loo′-shich
Belyi (Rus.)	bĕ′-lĭ	beh′-li
Bełz (Pol.)	bĕls′	bels′
Bena Bena (Oc.)	bĕ′-nä bĕ′-nä	beh′-nah beh′-nah
Benares (India)	bə-nä′-rĭz	buh-nah′-riz
	native bə-nä′-rəs	buh-nah′-ruhs
bender An alternative spelling of *bandar*, q.v.		
Bender (Rum.) See *Tighina.*		
Bendigo (Austral.)	bĕn′-dĭ-gō	ben′-di-goh
Bendin, Bendzin (Pol.) See *Będzin.*		
Beneš, Eduard (Cz. leader)	bĕ′-nĕsh	beh′-nesh
Benešov (Cz.)	bĕ′-nĕ-shôf	beh′-neh-shof
Benevento (It.)	bĕ-nĕ-vĕn′-tô	beh-neh-ven′-to

Bengal (India)	bĕng′-gôl′	beng′-gol′
Ben Gardane (Tun.)	bĕn gär-dăn′	ben gahr-dan′
Bengasi *or* Benghazi (Libya)	bĕn-gä′-zē	ben-gah′-zee
Bengkalis (NEI)	bĕng-kä′-lēs	beng-kah′-lees
Benguet (P.I.)	bĕng-gĕt′	beng-get′
Benha (Egypt)	bĕn′-hä	ben′-hah
Beni Suef (Egypt)	bĕ′-nē swāf′	beh′-nee swayf′
Beni Ulid (Libya)	bĕ′-nē o͞o′-lĭd	beh′-nee oo′-lid
Benkoelen *or* Benkulen (NEI)	bĕn-ko͞o′-lĕn	ben-koo′-len
Benkovac (Yugosl.)	bĕn′-kô-väts	ben′-ko-vahts
Bennebroek (Neth.)	bĕn′-ə-bro͞ok	ben′-uh-brook
Benthuizen (Neth.)	bĕnt′-hûĭ-zən	bent′-hœi-zuhn
Beograd (Yugosl.)	bĕ′-ô′-gräd	beh′-o′-grahd

The English form, probably more suitable for American radio, is *Belgrade*, bĕl′-grād′ [bel′-grayd′].

Beogradska (Yugosl.)	bĕ′-ô′-gräd-skä	beh′-o′-grahd-skah
Berane (Yugosl.)	bĕ′-rä-nĕ	beh′-rah-neh
Berat (Alb., town, riv.)	bĕ′-rät	beh′-raht

The town is also called *Berati* and *Beligrad*. The river is part of the *Seman*, q.v., and is the ancient *Apsos*, q.v.

Berchem (Belg.)	bĕr′-k(h)əm	behr′-k(h)uhm
Berchtesgaden (Ger.)	bĕrk(h)′-təs-gä′-dən	behrk(h)′-tuhs-gah′-duhn
Berck (Fr.)	bĕrk′	behrk′
Berdichev (Rus.)	bĕr-dē′-chĕf	behr-dee′-chef
Berdyansk (Rus.)	bĕr-dyänsk′	behr-dyahnsk′
Berehovo (Cz.)	bĕ′-rĕ-hô-vô	beh′-reh-ho-vo

Hungarian *Beregszász*, bĕ′-rĕk-säs [beh′-rek-sahs].

Beresovka (Rus.)	bĕ-ryô′-sŏf-kä	beh-ryo′-sof-kah
Berettyó (Hung., riv.)	bĕ′-rĕt-tyô	beh′-ret-tyo
Bereza Kartuska (Pol.)	bĕ-rĕ′-zä kär-to͝o′-skä	beh-reh′-zah kahr-tu′-skah

Russian *Kartuzskaya Bereza*, kär-to͞oz′-skä-yä bĕ-ryô′-zä [kahr-tooz′-skah-yah beh-ryo′-zah].

Berezina (Pol., riv.) See *Berezyna*.

Berezyna (Pol., riv.)	bĕ-rĕ-zē′-nä	beh-reh-zee′-nah

Russian *Berezina*, bĕ-rĕ-zĭ-nä′ [beh-reh-zi-nah′].

Bergambacht (Neth.)	bĕrk(h)-äm′-bäk(h)t	behrk(h)-ahm′-bahk(h)t
Bergamo (It.)	bĕr′-gä-mô	behr′-gah-mo
Bergen (Nor.)	*Eng.* bûr′-gən *Nor.* bĕr′-gən	buhr′-guhn behr′-guhn
Bergen op Zoom (Neth.)	bĕr′-k(h)ən ôp zōm′	behr′-k(h)uhn op zohm′

Berggrav, Eivind (Bishop of Oslo, Nor.)	bĕrg′-gräv, ā′-vĭn	behrg′-grahv, ay′-vin
Bergolo (It.)	bĕr′-gô-lô	behr′-go-lo
Bergues (Fr.)	bĕrg′	behrg′
Berhampore (India)	bûr′-əm-pōr′	buhr′-uhm-pohr′
Berhampur (India)	bûr′-əm-po͝or′	buhr′-uhm-pur′
Beria, Lavrentii P. (Rus. leader)	bĕ′-rĭ-yä, lä-vrĕn′-tĭ	beh′-ri-yah, lah-vren′-ti
Bering Sea	bĕr′-ĭng *or* bĭr′-ĭng	behr′-ing *or* bihr′-ing
Berislav (Rus.)	bĕ-rĭ-släf′	beh-ri-slahf′
Berkaak (Nor.)	bĕrk′-ôk	behrk′-ok
Berkovitsa (Bulg.)	bĕr′-kŏ-vĭ-tsä	behr′-ko-vi-tsah
Berle, Adolph Augustus (Ass't Secy. of State)	bûr′-lĭ	buhr′-li
Berlevaag (Nor.)	bĕr′-lə-vôg	behr′-luh-vog
Berlin (Ger.)	*Eng.* bər-lĭn′	buhr-lin′
	Ger. bĕr-lēn′	behr-leen′
Bermeo (Sp.)	bĕr-mĕ′-ô	behr-meh′-o
Bernburg (Ger.)	*Eng.* bĕrn′-bûrg	behrn′-buhrg
	Ger. bĕrn′-bo͝ork(h)	behrn′-burk(h)
Berneval (Fr.)	bĕr-nə-väl′	behr-nuh-vahl′
Bern *or* Berne (Switz.)	*Eng.* bûrn′	buhrn′
	Fr. bĕrn′	behrn′
Beroun (Cz.)	bĕ′-rōn	beh′-rohn
Berovo (Yugosl.)	bĕ′-rô-vô	beh′-ro-vo
Besançon (Fr.)	bə-zäN-sôN′	buh-zahN-soN′
Bescanuova (Yugosl.) Serb-Croat *Baška*, q.v.	*It.* bĕ-skä-nwô′-vä	beh-skah-nwo′-vah
Bështriq (Balkan mt.) More correctly called *Pushtrik*, q.v.	*Alb.* bəsh′-trēk(y)	buhsh′-treek(y)
Beskid Mountains (Pol., Cz.)	bĕ′-skĭd *or* bĕs-kēd′	beh′-skid bes-keed′
Bessarabia (Rum.)	*Eng.* bĕs′-ə-rā′-byə	bes′-uh-ray′-byuh
	Rus. bĕ-sä-rä′-bĭ-yä	beh-sah-rah′-bi-yah
Rumanian *Basarabea*, bä-sä-rä′-byä [bah-sah-rah′-byah].		
Bessheim (Nor.)	bĕs′-hām	bes′-haym
Beszterce (Rum.) See *Bistriţa.*		
Béthune (Fr.)	bĕ-tün′	beh-tün′
Betio	bē′-shē-ō	bee′-shee-oh
Missionaries prefer bĕ′-chē-ô [beh′-chee-o]; some newsmen, bē′-shô [bee′-sho]. Cp. *Tarawa.*		
Beuthen (Ger.)	boi′-tən	boi′-tuhn
Beveland (Neth.)	bā′-və-länt	bay′-vuh-lahnt
Beverwijk (Neth.)	bā′-vər-wīk	bay′-vuhr-waik
Beyrouth (Syria) See *Beirut.*		

Bezdan (Yugosl.)	bĕz′-dän	bez′-dahn
Bezhetsk (Rus.)	bĕ′-zhĕtsk	beh′-zhetsk
Béziers (Fr.)	bĕ-zyĕ′	beh-zyeh′
Bezwada (India)	bĕz-wä′-də	bez-wah′-duh
Bhadhalung (Thai)	pät′-ə-lo͝ong′	paht′-uh-lung′
Bhagalpur (India)	bä′-gəl-po͝or′	bah′-guhl-pur′
Bhamo (Burma)	bä′-mō	bah′-moh
Burman *Bamaw.*		
Bhangnga (Thai)	päng′-(ng)ä′	pahng′-(ng)ah′
Bhaunagar (India)	bou-nŭg′-ər	bau-nuhg′-uhr
Bhejburi (Thai)	pĕt-bo͝o-rē′	pet-bu-ree′
	or pĕch′-ə-bo͝o-rē′	pech′-uh-bu-ree′
Bhisanulok (Thai)	pĭt′-sə-no͝o-lōk′	pit′-suh-nu-lohk′
Also spelled *Bisnulok.*		
Bhopal (India)	bō′-päl′	boh′-pahl′
Bhusaval (India)	bo͞o-sä′-vəl	boo-sah′-vuhl
Bhutan (India)	bo͞o′-tän′	boo′-tahn′
Biała Podlaska (Pol.)	byä′-lä pô-dlä′-skä	byah′-lah po-dlah′-skah
Russian *Byela,* bĕ′-lä [beh′-lah].		
Białowieża (Pol.)	byä-lô-vyĕ′-zhä	byah-lo-vyeh′-zhah
Russian *Byelovyezh,* bĕ-lŏ-vĕzh′ [beh-lo-vezh′].		
Białystok (Pol.)	byä-lĭ′-stôk	byah-li′-stok
Russian *Byelostok,* bĕ-lŏ-stôk′ [beh-lo-stok′].		
Biancavilla (Sicily)	byän-kä-vēl′-lä	byahn-kah-veel′-lah
Bielefeld (Ger.)	bē′-lə-fĕlt	bee′-luh-felt
Bielsko (Pol.)	byĕl′-skô	byel′-sko
German *Bielitz,* bē′-lĭts [bee′-lits].		
Biferno (It., riv.)	bē-fĕr′-nô	bee-fehr′-no
Bigej (Oc.)	bē′-gĕj	bee′-gej
Biggerann (Oc.)	bĭg′-gĕ-rän	big′-geh-rahn
Bihać (Yugosl.)	bē′-häch	bee′-hahch
Bihaćska (Yugosl.)	bē′-häch-skä	bee′-hahch-skah
Bihar (India)	bē-här′	bee-hahr′
Bihar (Rum.) See *Bihor.*		
Bihor (Rum.)	bē-hôr′	bee-hor′
Hungarian *Bihar,* bē′-hŏr [bee′-hor].		
Bihorului (Rum., mts.)	bē-hô′-ro͞o-lwē	bee-ho′-ru-lwee
Bijeljina (Yugosl.)	bĭ′-yĕ′-lyĭ-nä	bi′-yeh′-lyi-nah
Bijelo Polje (Yugosl.)	bĭ′-yĕ′-lô pô′-lyĕ	bi′-yeh′-lo po′-lyeh
Bikaj (Alb.)	bē′-kī	bee′-kai
Bikaner (India)	bē′-kə-nēr′	bee′-kuh-neer′
Bikar (Oc.)	bē′-kär	bee′-kahr
Bikin (Rus.)	bē-kēn′	bee-keen′

Bikini (Oc.)	bē-kē′-nē	bee-kee′-nee
Bilaspur (India)	bē-läs-po͝or′	bee-lahs-pur′
Bilbao (Sp.)	*Eng.* bĭl-bou′	bil-bau′
	Sp. bēl-bä′-ô	beel-bah′-o
Bilbo, Theodore G. (U.S. senator)	bĭl′-bō	bil′-boh
Bileća (Yugosl.)	bē′-lĕ-chä	bee′-leh-chah
Biłgoraj (Pol.)	bĭl-gô′-rī	bil-go′-rai
Russian *Byelgorai*, bĕl′-gŏ-rī [bel′-go-rai].		
Bilin (Burma, riv.)	bē′-lĭn	bee′-lin
Bilisht (Alb.)	bē′-lēsht	bee′-leesht
Bilishti (Alb.) See *Bilisht.*		
Billancourt (Fr.)	bē-yän-ko͞or′	bee-yahn-koor′
Billiton *or* Belitong (NEI)	bēl′-lē-tŏn	beel′-lee-ton
	or bĕ-lē′-tŏng	beh-lee′-tong
Bilt, de (Neth.)	bĭlt′, də	bilt′, duh
Bima (NEI)	bē′-mä	bee′-mah
Binačka Morava (Yugosl., riv.)	bē′-näch-kä mô′-rä′-vä	bee′-nahch-kah mo′-rah′-vah
Binhdinh (Indo-Ch.)	bĭn-dĭn′	bin-din′
Binnigem (Oc.)	bĭn-nē-gĕm′	bin-nee-gem′
Bio (Oc.)	bē′-ô	bee′-o
Bioč (Yugosl., mt.)	bē′-ôch	bee′-och
Biograd (Yugosl.)	bē′-ô′-gräd	bee′-o′-grahd
Italian *Zaravecchia*, q.v.		
bir	bēr′	beer′
In Arabic names an element, sometimes omitted, meaning *well* or *spring.*		
Bira (Rus.)	bē′-rä	bee′-rah
Birdum (Austral.)	bûr′-dəm	buhr′-duhm
Bir el Gobi (Libya)	bēr ĕl gō′-bē	beer el goh′-bee
Bires Sof (Tun.)	bēr′-ĕs sôf′	beer′-es sof′
Bir Hacheim (Libya)	bēr hə-kā′-yĭm	beer huh-kay′-yim
Biriukov (Rus.)	bĭ-rū-kôf′	bi-ryoo-kof′
Birjand (Iran)	bēr-jănd′	beer-jand′
Bir Mcherga (Tun.)	bēr mə-shĕr′-gä	beer muh-shehr′-gah
Bir Mrabbott (Tun., pass)	bēr mə-räb′-bŭt	beer muh-rahb′-buht
Birnbaum (Pol.) See *Międzychód.*		
Bir Tebeul (Tun.)	bēr tə-bûl′	beer tuh-bœl′
Birzula (Rus.)	bēr′-zo͞o-lä	beer′-zu-lah
Bisayas (P.I.)	bē-sä′-yäs	bee-sah′-yahs
Also called *Visayan* (Islands), q.v.		
Biscari (Sicily)	bē′-skä-rē	bee′-skah-ree

Biscaya (Sp., prov.)	bēs-kä′-yä	bees-kah′-yah
Also called *Vizcaya*, q.v. English *Biscay*, bĭs′-kā [bis′-kay].		
Bisceglie (It.)	bē-shĕ′-lyĕ	bee-sheh′-lyeh
Biševo (Yugosl., isl.)	bē′-shĕ-vô	bee′-sheh-vo
Italian *Busi*, q.v.		
bisht (Alb.)	bēsht′	beesht′
An element, meaning *cape* (literally *tail*), in Albanian place names. Look up the other part of the name.		
Bisk (Rus.)	bēsk′	beesk′
Biskra (Alg.)	bĭs′-krä	bis′-krah
Bistra planina (Yugosl., mts.)	bē′-strä plä′-nē′-nä	bee′-strah plah′-nee′-nah
Bistrica (Yugosl., riv.)	bē′-strĭ-tsä	bee′-stri-tsah
Bistriţa (Rum.)	bē′-strē-tsä	bee′-stree-tsah
Hungarian *Beszterce*, bĕs′-tĕr-tsĕ [bes′-tehr-tseh].		
Bitoi (Oc., riv.)	bē′-toi	bee′-toi
Bitolj (Yugosl.)	bē′-tôl(y)	bee′-tol(y)
Old Turkish *Monastir*, q.v. Greek *Monastérion*. Local Macedonian pronunciation almost bē′-toi [bee′-toi], as Rebecca West reports.		
Bitoljsko Polje (Yugosl.)	bē′-tôl(y)-skô pô′-lyĕ	bee′-tol(y)-sko po′-lyeh
bituminous	bĭ-tū′-mə-nəs	bi-tyoo′-muh-nuhs
Bityuk (Rus., riv.)	bē-tūk′	bee-tyook′
Bivona (Sicily)	bē-vô′-nä	bee-vo′-nah
Biwako (Jap.)	bē-wä-kô	bee-wah-ko
Bizerta (Tun.)	bĭ-zĕr′-tä	bi-zehr′-tah
French *Bizerte*, bē-zĕrt′ [bee-zehrt′]. English bĭ-zûr′-tə [bi-zuhr′-tuh], is in the making.		
Bjelasica (Yugosl., mts.)	byĕ′-lä′-sĭ-tsä	byeh′-lah′-si-tsah
Bjelica (Yugosl., riv.)	byĕ′-lĭ-tsä	byeh′-li-tsah
Bjelostock (Pol.) See *Białystok*.		
Bjelovar (Yugosl.)	byĕ′-lô-vär	byeh′-lo-vahr
Bjoernevatn *or* Björnevatn (Nor.)	byûr′-nə-vätn	byœr′-nuh-vahtn
Bjorli (Nor.)	byōr′-lē	byohr′-lee
Björneborg (Fin.) See *Pori*.		
Blace (Yugosl.)	blä′-tsĕ	blah′-tseh
Blagodarnoe (Rus.)	blä-gŏ-där′-nŏ-yĕ	blah-go-dahr′-no-yeh
Blagoveshchensk (Rus.)	blä-gŏ-vĕ′-shchĕnsk	blah-go-veh′-shchensk
Blaguša planina (Yugosl., mts.)	blä′-gōō-shä plä′-nē′-nä	blah′-goo-shah plah′-nee′-nah
Blajnica (Yugosl., mts.)	blī′-nĭ-tsä	blai′-ni-tsah
Blanc (Tun., cape) See *Cap Blanc*.		
Blashki (Pol.) See *Błaszki*.		

Blašica (Yugosl., riv.)	blä′-shĭ-tsä	blah′-shi-tsah
Błaszki (Pol.)	bläsh′-kĭ	blahsh′-ki
Russian *Blashki*, blä′-shkĭ [blah′-shki].		
Blatec (Yugosl.)	blä′-tĕts	blah′-tets
Blato (Yugosl.)	blä′-tô	blah′-to
Blatta (Yugosl.)	*It.* blät′-tä	blaht′-tah
Serb-Croat *Blato*, q.v.		
Bleiburg (Austria)	blī′-bo͝ork(h)	blai′-burk(h)
Blenheim	*Eng.* blĕn′-əm	blen′-uhm
Blida (Alg.)	blē′-dä	blee′-dah
Blinisht (Alb.)	blē′-nēsht	blee′-neesht
Blinishti (Alb.) See *Blinisht.*		
Bloemendaal (Neth.)	blo͞o′-mən-däl	bloo′-muhn-dahl
Blois (Fr.)	blwä′	blwah′
Błonie (Pol.)	blô′-nyĕ	blo′-nyeh
Russian *Blone*, blô′-nĕ [blo′-neh].		
Blora (NEI)	blô′-rä	blo′-rah
Bluie	blo͝o′-ĭ	blu′-i
Army air bases in Greenland are named *Bluie East 1, 2,* and so on, and *Bluie West, 1, 2,* and so on.		
Blupblup (Oc.)	blo͞op-blo͞op′	bloop-bloop′
Bö (Nor.)	bû′	bœ′
Boac (P.I.)	bwäk′	bwahk′
Bobduri (Oc.)	bôb-do͞o′-rē	bob-doo′-ree
Bobovište (Yugosl.)	bô′-bô-vĭ-shtĕ	bo′-bo-vi-shteh
Bobrinets (Rus.)	bŏ-brĭ-nĕts′	bo-bri-nets′
Bobruisk (Rus.)	bŏ-bro͝oĭsk′	boh-bru′-isk
Bocca di Falco (Sard.)	bôk′-kä dē fäl′-kô	bok′-kah dee fahl′-ko
Boccea (It.)	bôt-chĕ′-ä	bot-cheh′-ah
Bocche di Cattaro (Yugosl., gulf)	*It.* bôk′-kĕ dē kät′-tä-rô	bok′-keh dee kaht′-tah-ro
Serb-Croat *Boka Kotorska*, q.v.		
Bochkarevo (Rus.)	bŏch-kä-ryô′-vŏ	boch-kah-ryo′-vo
Bochnia (Pol.)	bôk(h)′-nyä	bok(h)′-nyah
Bochum (Ger.)	bō′-k(h)o͝om *or* bôk(h)′-o͝om	boh′-k(h)um bok(h)′-um
Bodena (Gr.)	vô-*th*ĕ-nä′	vo-*th*eh-nah′
Bodenbach (Cz.) See *Podmokly.*		
Bodjanegara (NEI)	bô-jŏ-nə-gŏ′-rŏ	bo-jo-nuh-go′-ro
In this neighborhood *a* is pronounced ŏ.		
Bodoe *or* Bodö (Nor.)	bō′-dû	boh′-dœ
Boe (Nor.)	bû′	bœ′
Boehmer Wald (Ger., Cz.) See *Böhmer Wald.*		
Boeing (U.S. manufacturer)	bō′-ĭng	boh′-ing

Boemlafjord (Nor.)	bûm'-lä-fyōr	bœm'-lah-fyohr
Boeo (Sicily, cape)	bô-ĕ'-ô	bo-eh'-o
Also called *Lilebeo*, q.v.		
Boeroe *or* Buru (NEI)	bōō'-rōō	boo'-roo
Boeton *or* Buton (NEI)	bōō'-tôn	boo'-ton
Also called *Boetoeng*, bōō'-tōōng [boo'-toong].		
Bogadyim (New Guinea)	bô-gä'-jĭm	bo-gah'-jim
Bogadyim (Oc.)	bô-gä'-dyĭm	bo-gah'-dyim
Bogatić (Yugosl.)	bô'-gä-tĭch	bo'-gah-tich
Boğaziçi (Turk., strait)	See *Bosporus*.	
Bogdanci (Yugosl.)	bôg'-dän-tsĭ	bog'-dahn-tsi
Boggeric (Oc.)	bôg'-gə-rēk	bog'-guh-reek
Bogia (New Guinea)	bô-gē'-ä	bo-gee'-ah
Bogićevica (Yugosl.)	bô'-gē'-chĕ-vĭ-tsä	bo'-gee'-cheh-vi-tsah
Bogodukhov (Rus.)	bŏ-gŏ-dōō'-hŏf	bo-go-doo'-hof
Bogojevo (Yugosl.)	bô'-gô'-yĕ-vô	bo'-go'-yeh-vo
Bogomila (Yugosl.)	bô'-gô'-mĭ-lä	bo'-go'-mi-lah
Bogoroditsk (Rus.)	bŏ-gŏ-rô'-dĭtsk	bo-go-ro'-ditsk
Bogoslof (Alaska, isl.)	bō'-gə-slôf	boh'-guh-slof
Bogotu (Oc.) See *Bugotu*.		
Bogoyavlensk (Rus.)	bŏ-gŏ-yäv-lĕnsk'	bo-go-yahv-lensk'
Boguchar (Rus.)	bŏ-gōō-chär'	bo-goo-chahr'
Bohan (Yugosl.)	bô'-hän	bo'-hahn
Bohdanów (Pol.)	bôk(h)-dä'-nŏŏf	bok(h)-dah'-nuf
Bohemia (Cz.)	*Eng.* bō-hē'-myə	boh-hee'-myuh
Czech *Čechy*, q.v.		
Böhmer Wald (Ger., Cz.)	bû'-mər vält'	bœ'-muhr vahlt'
English *Bohemian Forest*.		
Bohol (P.I.)	bô-hôl'	bo-hol'
Boibeis (Gr., lake)	vē-vē-ēs'	vee-vee-ees'
Also called *Karla*, kär'-lä [kahr'-lah].		
Boisson, Pierre (Fr. leader)	bwä-sôN', pyĕr'	bwah-soN', pyehr'
Bojana (Balkan riv.)	*S.-C.* bô'-yä'-nä	bo'-yah'-nah
Albanian *Buna*, q.v.		
Bojeador (P.I., cape)	bô-hĕ-ä-dôr'	bo-heh-ah-dor'
Boka Kotorska (Yugosl., gulf)	bô'-kä kô'-tôr-skä	bo'-kah ko'-tor-skah
Italian *Bocche di Cattaro*, q.v.		
Bokhara *or* Bukhara (Rus.)	bō-kä'-rä *or* bŏŏ-hä'-rä	boh-kah'-rah bu-hah'-rah
Boknfjord (Nor.)	bŏŏk'n-fyōr	buk'n-fyohr
Bokovskaya (Rus.)	bŏ-kŏf-skä'-yä	bo-kof-skah'-yah
Bokstel (Neth.)	bôk'-stəl	bok'-stuhl

Bolbec (Fr.)	bôl-bĕk′	bol-bek′
Bolechów (Pol.)	bô-lĕ′-hŏŏf	bo-leh′-huf
Bolgrad (Rum.)	bôl′-gräd	bol′-grahd
Bolin Odzhal (Rus., lake)	bŏ-lēn′ ŏd-zhäl′	bo-leen′ od-zhahl′
Bolinao (P.I.)	bô-lē-nou′	bo-lee-nau′
Bolivar, Simón (Sp. hero)	bô-lē′-vär, sē-môn′	bo-lee′-vahr, see-mon′
Boljanići (Yugosl.)	bô′-lyä′-nĭ-chĭ	bo′-lyah′-ni-chi
Boljevac (Yugosl.)	bô′-lyĕ-väts	bo′-lyeh-vahts
Boljevići (Yugosl.)	bô′-lyĕ′-vĭ-chĭ	bo′-lyeh′-vi-chi
Bolkesjoe *or* Bolkesjö (Nor.)	bôl′-kə-shû	bol′-kuh-shœ
Bolkhov (Rus.)	bŏl-hôf′	bol-hof′
Bologna (It.)	*Eng.* bə-lōn′-yə	buh-lohn′-yuh
	It. bô-lô′-nyä	bo-lo′-nyah

There is also a popular English pronunciation, bə-lō′-nə [buh-loh′-nuh].

Bologoe (Rus.)	bŏ-lŏ-gô′-yĕ	bo-lo-go′-yeh
Bolshoy Tokmak (Rus.)	bŏl(y)-shoi′ tŏk-mäk′	bol(y)-shoi′ tok-mahk′
Bolzano (It.)	bôl-tsä′-nô	bol-tsah′-no

German *Bozen*, bō′-tsən [boh′-tsuhn].

Bomba (Libya)	bôm′-bä	bom′-bah
Bombala (Austral.)	bŏm-bä′-lə	bom-bah′-luh

There is a tendency to introduce an *r* into such words, making bŏm-bär′-lə [bom-bahr′-luh].

bombardier	bŏm′-bər-dĭr′	bom′-buhr-dihr′

For centuries an English word, there is no reason to pronounce it as French.

Bombay (India)	bŏm′-bā′	bom′-bay′
Bömlafjord (Nor.)	bûm′-lä-fyōr	bœm′-lah-fyohr

Bon (Alg., cape) See *Cap Bon.*

Bonchaung (Burma)	bōn′-choung′	bohn′-chaung′
Bondowoso (NEI)	bôn-dô-wô′-sô	bon-do-wo′-so
Bône (Alg.)	bōn′	bohn′
Bone *or* Boni (NEI)	bô′-nĕ *or* bô′-nē	bo′-neh *or* bo′-nee
Bonga (Oc.)	bông′-ä	bong′-ah
Bonifacio (Sard., Corsica, strait)	bô-nē-fä′-chô	bo-nee-fah′-cho
Bonin (Oc.)	bō′-nĭn	boh′-nin

Japanese *Ogasawara Jima*, q.v.

Bonin (Rus., isl.)	bô′-nēn	bo′-neen
Bonner, Herbert C. (U.S. representative)	bŏn′-ər	bon′-uhr
Bonnet, Georges (Fr. leader)	bô-nĕ′, zhôrzh′	bo-neh′, zhorzh′

Bontoc (P.I.)	*Eng.* bŏn-tŏk′	bon-tok′
	Sp. bôn-tôk′	bon-tok′
Bor (Rus., Yugosl.)	bôr′	bor′
Boranja (Yugosl.)	bô′-rä-nyä	bo′-rah-nyah
Bordeaux (Fr.)	bôr-dō′	bor-doh′
Bordj Bou Hamra (Tun.)	bôrj′ bōō häm′-rä	borj′ boo hahm′-rah
Also called *Bou Hamran.*		
Bordj le Boeuf (Tun.)	bôrj lə bûf′	borj luh bœf′
Boren, Lyle H. (U.S. representative)	bō′-rĕn	boh′-ren
Borgå (Fin.) See *Borgo.*		
Borgerhout (Belg.)	bôr′-k(h)ər-hout	bor′-k(h)uhr-haut
Borghese, Stefano (It. prince)	bôr-gĕ′-zĕ, stĕ′-fä-nô	bor-geh′-zeh, steh′-fah-no
Borgo (Fin.)	bôr′-gō	bor′-goh
Swedish spelling *Borgå.*		
Borgund (Nor.)	bôr′-go͝on	bor′-gun
Borisoglebsk (Rus.)	bŏ-rē′-sŏ-glĕpsk′	bo-ree′-so-glepsk′
Borisov (Rus.)	bŏ-rē′-sŏf	bo-ree′-sof
Borisovka (Rus.)	bŏ-rē′-sŏf-kä	bo-ree′-sof-kah
Borizzo (Sicily)	bô-rēt′-sô	bo-reet′-so
Borkum (Ger., isl.)	bôr′-ko͝om	bor′-kum
Borneo (NEI)	bôr′-nĭ-ō	bor′-ni-oh
Bornholm (Den.)	bôrn′-hôlm	born′-holm
Borodino (Rus.)	bŏ-rŏ-dĭ-nô′	bo-ro-di-no′
Borovichi (Rus.)	bŏ-rŏ-vĭ-chē′	bo-ro-vi-chee′
Borovsk (Rus.)	bô′-rŏfsk	bo′-rofsk
Borroloola (Austral.)	bôr′-ə-lōō′-lä	bor′-uh-loo′-lah
Borşa (Rum.)	bôr′-shä	bor′-shah
Borysław (Pol.)	bô-rĭ′-släf	bo-ri′-slahf
Borzna (Rus.)	bôrz′-nä	borz′-nah
bos *or* bosch	bôs′	bos′
A common element, meaning *wood* or *forest,* in Dutch place names.		
Bos, den (Neth.) See *Den Bos.*		
Bosa (Sard.)	bô′-sä	bo′-sah
Bosanska	bô-sän′-skä	bo-sahn′-skah
An element, meaning *Bosnian,* in Serb-Croat place names. It may be necessary to look up the other part of the name.		
Bosanska Dubica (Yugosl.)	bô′-sän-skä dōō′-bĭ-tsä	bo′-sahn-skah doo′-bi-tsah
Bosanska Gradiška (Yugosl.)	bô′-sän-skä grä′-dĭ-shkä	bo′-sahn-skah grah′-di-shkah
Bošava (Yugosl.)	bô′-shä-vä	bo′-shah-vah

Bose, Subash Chundra (Indian collab.)	bōs′, sōō-bäsh′ chŭn′-drə	bohs′, soo-bahsh′ chuhn′-druh
Bosiljgrad (Yugosl.)	bô′-sĭl(y)-gräd	bo′-sil(y)-grahd
Boskija (Yugosl., mt.)	bô′-skĭ-yä	bo′-ski-yah
Bosnia (Yugosl.)	*Eng.* bôz′-nĭ-ə	boz′-ni-uh
Serb-Croat *Bosna*, bôs′-nä [bos′-nah].		
Bosporus (Turk., strait)	*Eng.* bŏs′-pə-rəs	bos′-puh-ruhs
Turkish *Boğaziçi*, bô-äz′-ē-chē′ [bo-ahz′-ee-chee′], or *Karadeniz Boğazı*, q.v.		
Bossekopp (Nor.)	bôs′-sə-kôp	bos′-suh-kop
Bossoglina (Yugosl.)	*It.* bôs-sô-lyē′-nä	bos-so-lyee′-nah
Serb-Croat *Marina*, q.v.		
Botevgrad (Bulg.)	bô′-tĕf-grät	bo′-tef-graht
Botn (Nor.)	bôt′n	bot′n
Botoşani (Rum.)	bô-tô-shän′	bo-to-shahn′
Botsa (Oc.)	bôt-sä′	bot-sah′
Bou Arada (Tun.)	bōō ä-ră′-dä	boo ah-ra′-dah
Bou is the western Arabic form of *Abu*.		
Bou Chebka (Tun.)	bōō shĕb′-kä	boo sheb′-kah
Bou Chekka (Tun., Alg.)	bōō shĕk′-kä	boo shek′-kah
Bou Ficha (Tun.)	bōō fē′-shä	boo fee′-shah
Bougainville (Oc.)	*Eng.* bōō′-gĕn-vĭl *or* bō′-	boo′-gen-vil *or* boh′-
	Fr. bōō-găN-vēl′	boo-gaN-veel′
Bougie (Alg.)	bōō-zhē′	boo-zhee′
Bou Hamran (Tun.)	bōō häm-răn′	boo hahm-ran′
Bou Krin (Tun.)	bōō′ krēn′	boo′ kreen′
Boulia (Austral.)	bōōl′-yə	bool′-yuh
Boulogne (Fr.)	*Eng.* bŏŏ-lōn′	bu-lohn′
	or bŏŏ-loin′	bu-loin′
	Fr. bōō-lôn′(y)	boo-lon′(y)
Bourges (Fr.)	bōōrzh′	boorzh′
Bourget, le (Fr.)	bōōr-zhĕ′, lə	boor-zheh′, luh
Bou Saada (Alg.)	bōō sä′-dä	boo sah′-dah
Bou Thadi (Tun.)	bōō tä′-dē	boo tah′-dee
Bouza (Crete, cape) See *Vouxa*.		
Bou Znika (Mor.)	bōō zə-nē′-kə	boo zuh-nee′-kuh
Bou Zouita (Tun.)	bōō zōō-ē′-tä	boo zoo-ee′-tah
Bou Zoumit (Tun.)	bōō zōō′-mĭt	boo zoo′-mit
Bovalino (It.)	bô-vä-lē′-nô	bo-vah-lee′-no
Bozen (It.) See *Bolzano*.		
Boževac (Yugosl.)	bô′-zhĕ-väts	bo′-zheh-vahts
Bozhilov, Dobri (Bulg. leader)	bô′-zhĭ-lôf, dô′-brĭ	bo′-zhi-lof, do′-bri
Božička (Yugosl.)	**bô′-zhĭch-kä**	**bo′-zhich-kah**

Brabant (Neth., Belg.)	brä′-bänt	brah′-bahnt
English brə-bănt′ [bruh-bant′], brä′-bənt [brah′-buhnt], and brăb′-ənt [brab′-uhnt].		
Brač (Yugosl., isl.)	bräch′	brahch′
Italian *Brazza*, q.v.		
Braćevac (Yugosl.)	brä′-chĕ-väts	brah′-cheh-vahts
Brad (Rum.)	bräd′	brahd′
Braga (Port.)	brä′-gə	brah′-guh
Braga, Melo (Braz. general)	brä′-gə, mĕ′-lo͝o	brah′-guh, meh′-lu
Both names should be used, thus: *Melo Braga*, not *Braga* alone.		
Bragança (Port., Brazil)	brä-gän′-sə	brah-gahn′-suh
Brahmaputra (India, riv.)	brä-mə-po͞o′-trə	brah-muh-poo′-truh
Brăila (Rum.)	brə-ē′-lä	bruh-ee′-lah
Braljina (Yugosl.)	brä′-lyĭ-nä	brah′-lyi-nah
Brandenburg (Ger.)	*Eng.* brăn′-dən-bûrg	bran′-duhn-buhrg
	Ger. brän′-dən-bo͝ork(h)	brahn′-duhn-burk(h)
Braničevo (Yugosl.)	brä′-nē′-chĕ-vô	brah′-nee′-cheh-vo
Branjin Vrh (Yugosl.)	brä′-nyĭn vərk(h)′	brah′-nyin vuhrk(h)′
Braşov (Rum.)	brä-shôv′	brah-shov′
Hungarian *Brassó*, brŏsh′-shô [brosh′-sho].		
Bratislava (Cz.)	brä′-tĭ-slä-vä	brah′-ti-slah-vah
German *Pressburg*, prĕs′-bo͝ork(h) [pres′-burk(h)]. Hungarian *Pozsony*, pô′-zhôn(y) [po′-zhon(y)].		
Bratland (Nor.)	brät′-län	braht′-lahn
Braunschweig (Ger.)	broun′-shvīk(h)	braun′-shvaik(h)
English *Brunswick*, q.v.		
Brazza (Yugosl., isl.)	*It.* brät′-sä	braht′-sah
Serb-Croat *Brač*, q.v.		
Brazzaville (Afr.)	brä-zä-vēl′	brah-zah-veel′
Brčko (Yugosl.)	bərch′-kô	buhrch′-ko
Brda (Pol., riv.)	bər′-dä	buhr′-dah
German *Brada.*		
Brda (Yugosl.)	bər′-dä	buhr′-dah
Břeclav (Cz.)	brzhĕts′-läf	brzhets′-lahf
Breda (It.)	brĕ′-dä	breh′-dah
Breda (Neth.)	brā-dä′	bray-dah′
Brega (Libya)	brā′-gä	bray′-gah
Also called *Mers el Brega*, mĕrs [mehrs].		
Bregalnica (Yugosl., riv.)	brĕ′-gäl′-nĭ-tsä	breh′-gahl′-ni-tsah
Bregenz (Austria)	brā′-gĕnts	bray′-gents
Brehm, Walter E. (U.S. representative)	brēm′	breem′

Breifonn (Nor.)	brā′-fôn	bray′-fon
Bremen (Ger.)	*Eng.* brĕm′-ən	brem′-uhn
	Ger. brā′-mən	bray′-muhn
Bremerhaven (Ger.)	*Eng.* brĕm′-ər-hā′-vən	brem′-uhr-hay′-vuhn
	Ger. brā′-mər-hä′-fən	bray′-muhr-hah′-fuhn
Brenner Pass	brĕn′-ər	bren′-uhr

The pronunciation brā′-nər (bray′-nuhr) is hyper-correct.

Brescia (It.)	brĕ′-shä	breh′-shah
Breskens (Neth.)	brĕs′-kəns	bres′-kuhns
Breslau (Ger.)	*Eng.* brĕz′-lou	brez′-lau
	Ger. brĕs′-lou	bres′-lau
Breslavl (Rus.)	brĕ-släv′l	breh-slahv′l
Bressanone (It.)	brĕs-sä-nô′-nĕ	bres-sah-no′-neh

Brest (Pol.) See *Brześć Kujawski.*

Brest Litovsk (Pol.)	*Rus.* brĕst′ lĭ-tôfsk′	brest′ li-tofsk′

Polish *Brześć nad Bugiem*, q.v.

Brestovac (Yugosl.)	brĕ′-stô-väts	breh′-sto-vahts
brevet	brĕv′-ĭt	brev′-it
	or brə-vĕt′	bruh-vet′

The first is military usage for noun and verb.

Brevik (Nor.)	brā′-vēk	bray′-veek
Brežice (Yugosl.)	brĕ′-zhĭ-tsĕ	breh′-zhi-tseh

German *Rann.*

Briatico (It.)	bryä′-tē-kô	bryah′-tee-ko
Brieg (Ger.)	brēk(h)′	breek(h)′
Briel, den (Neth.)	brēl′, dən	breel′, duhn

Also called *Brielle*, q.v.

Brielle (Neth.	*Du.* brē′-lə	bree′-luh
	Eng. brē-ĕl′	bree-el′

Also called *Den Briel,* dən brēl′ [duhn breel′]. English *The Bril,* brĭl [bril].

Brindisi (It.)	brēn′-dē-zē	breen′-dee-zee

English speakers often stress the second syllable.

Brinje (Yugosl.)	brē′-nyĕ	bree′-nyeh
Brinon, Fernand de (Fr. leader)	brē-nôN′, fĕr-näN′ də	bree-noN′, fehr-nahN′ duh
Brixham (Eng.)	brĭk′-səm	brik′-suhm
Brno (Cz.)	bər′-nô	buhr′-no

German *Brünn,* brün′ [brün′].

Brod (Yugosl.)	brôd′	brawd′
Brodarevo (Yugosl.)	brô′-dä′-rĕ-vô	bro′-dah′-reh-vo
Brodnica (Pol.)	brôd-nē′-tsä	brod-nee′-tsah

Brody (Pol.)	brô′-dĭ	bro′-di
Broennoeysund (Nor.)	brûn′-nûĭ-so͝on	brœn′-nœi-sun
Bromberg (Pol.)	*Eng.* brŏm′-bûrg	brom′-buhrg
	Ger. brôm′-bĕrk(h)	brom′-behrk(h)
Polish *Bydgoszcz*, q.v.		
Bronnitsi (Rus.)	brŏn′-nĭ-tsĭ	bron′-ni-tsi
Brönnöysund (Nor.)	brûn′-nûĭ-so͝on	brœn′-nœi-sun
Bronte (Sicily)	brôn′-tĕ	bron′-teh
Brontë, Charlotte	brŏn′-tĭ	bron′-ti
Broome (Austral.)	bro͞om′	broom′
Brouwershaven (Neth.)	brou-wərs-hä′-vən	brau-wuhrs-hah′-vuhn
Broz, Josip (Yugosl. leader)	brôz′, yô′-sĭp	broz′, yo′-sip
Nicknamed *Marshall Tito.*		
Bruenn (Cz.) See *Brno.*		
Bruges (Belg.)	*Eng.* bro͞ozh′	broozh′
Flemish *Brugge*, q.v.		
brugge	brûk(h)′-ə	brœk(h)′-uh
A common element, meaning *bridge*, in Dutch place names.		
Brugge (Belg.)	brûk(h)′-ə	brœk(h)′-uh
English *Bruges*, q.v. French *Bruges*, brüzh′.		
Bruinisse (Neth.)	brûĭ-nĭs′-ə	brœi-nis′-uh
Brunei (Borneo)	*Eng.* bro͝o-nī′	bru-nai′
	Du. bro͞o′-nā′	broo′-nay′
Brünn (Cz.) See *Brno.*		
Brunsbuettel *or* Brunsbüttel (Ger.)	bro͝ons′-büt-əl	bruns′-büt-uhl
Brunsum (Neth.)	brûn′-səm	brœn′-suhm
Brunswick (Ger.)	*Eng.* brŭnz′-wĭk	bruhnz′-wik
German *Braunschweig*, q.v.		
Brus (Yugosl.)	bro͞os′	broos′
Brusnik (Yugosl.)	bro͞o′-snĭk	broo′-snik
Brussels (Belg.)	*Eng.* brŭs′-əlz	bruhs′-uhlz
Flemish *Brussel*, brûs′-əl [brœs′-uhl]. French *Bruxelles*, brük-sĕl′ [brük-sel′] *and* brü-sĕl′ [brü-sel′].		
Brüster Ort (Ger., point)	brüs′-tər ôrt′	brüs′-tuhr ort′
Brüx (Cz.) See *Most.*		
Bryansk (Rus.)	*Eng.* brĭ-änsk′	bri-ahnsk′
	Rus. bryänsk′	bryahnsk′
Brynkovsk (Rus.)	brĭn′-kŏfsk	brin′-kofsk
Bryn Mawr (Pa.)	brĭn′ mär′	brin′ mahr′
	or brĭn′ môr′	brin′ mor′
Brynmawr (Wales)	brĭn-mour′	brin-maur′

Brzan (Yugosl.)	bər′-zän	buhr′-zahn
Brza Palanka (Yugosl.)	bər′-zä pä′-län-kä	buhr′-zah pah′-lahn-kah
Brześć Kujawski (Pol.)	bzhĕshch′ ko͝o-yäf′-skĭ	bzheshch′ ku-yahf′-ski
Russian *Brest*, brĕst′ [brest′].		
Brześć nad Bugiem (Pol.)	bzhĕshch′ näd bo͝o′-gyĕm	bzheshch′ nahd bu′-gyem
Russian *Brest Litovsk*, q.v.		
Brzeżany (Pol.)	bzhĕ-zhä′-nĭ	bzheh-zhah′-ni
Bua (Yugosl., isl.)	*It.* bo͞o′-ä	boo′-ah
Serb-Croat *Čiovo*, q.v.		
Buccari (Yugosl.)	*It.* bo͞ok′-kä-rē	book′-kah-ree
Serb-Croat *Bakar*, q.v.		
Buccarizza (Yugosl.)	*It.* bo͞ok-kä-rēt′-sä	book-kah-reet′-sah
Serb-Croat *Bakarač*, q.v.		
Bucharest (Rum.)	*Eng.* bo͞o′-kə-rĕst′	boo′-kuh-rest′
	or bū′-kə-rĕst′	byoo′-kuh-rest′
Rumanian *Bucureşti*, bo͝o-ko͝o-rĕsht′ [bu-ku-resht′].		
Bucovina (Rum.)	bo͝o-kô-vē′-nä	bu-ko-vee′-nah
Bucureşti (Rum.) See *Bucharest*.		
Buczacz (Pol.)	bo͝o′-chäch	bu′-chahch
Bud (Nor.)	bo͞od′	bood′
Budapest (Hung.)	*Eng.* bo͞o′-də-pĕst′	boo′-duh-pest′
	Hung. bo͝o′-dŏ-pĕsht′	bu′-do-pesht′
Budějovice (Cz.)	bo͞o′-dyĕ-yô-vĭ-tsĕ	boo′-dyeh-yo-vi-tseh
German *Budweis*, bo͝ot′-vīs [but′-vais].		
Budennovsk (Rus.)	bo͞o-dyô′-nŏfsk	boo-dyo′-nofsk
Budenny, Semyon (Rus. marshal)	bo͝o-dyô′-nĭ, sĕm-yôn′	bu-dyo′-ni, sem-yon′
There is also an English pronunciation, bo͞o-dĕn′-ĭ [boo-den′-i].		
Budrum (Turk.)	bo͝od′-ro͝om′	bud′-rum′
Budua (Yugosl.)	*It.* bo͞o′-dwä	boo′-dwah
Serb-Croat *Budva*, q.v.		
Budva (Yugosl.)	bo͞od′-vä	bood′-vah
Budweis (Cz.)	*Ger.* bo͝ot′-vīs	but′-vais
Czech *Budějovice*, q.v.		
Bue Marino (Pantelleria, point)	bwĕ′ mä-rē′-nô	bweh′ mah-ree′-no
Buerat el Hsun (Libya)	bo͞o-ĕ-răt′ ĕl hə-so͞on′	boo-eh-rat′ el huh-soon′
Bug (Pol., riv.)	bo͞og′ *or* bo͞ok′	bug′ *or* buk′
Bug (Rus., riv.)	bo͞og′	boog′

Bugaz (Rum.)	bo͝o-gäz′	bu-gahz′
Bugojno (Yugosl.)	bo͞o′-goi′-nô	boo′-goi′-no
Bugotu (Oc.)	bo͞o-gô′-to͞o	boo-go′-too
Also spelled *Bogotu.*		
Bui (Rus.)	bo͞o′(y) *or* bo͞o′ĭ	boo′(y) *or* boo′i
Buin (Oc.)	bo͞o′-ēn	boo′-een
Buitenzorg (NEI)	bûĭ′-tən-zôrk(h)	bœi′-tuhn-zork(h)
Bujanovce (Yugosl.)	bo͞o′-yä′-nôv-tsĕ	boo′-yah′-nov-tseh
Bujnurd (Iran)	bo͝oj-no͞ord′	buj-noord′
Buka (Oc.)	bo͞o′-kä	boo′-kah
Bukhara (Rus.) See *Bokhara.*		
Bukorovce (Yugosl.)	bo͞o′-kô′-rôv-tsĕ	boo′-ko′-rov-tseh
Bukovče (Yugosl.)	bo͞o′-kôv-chĕ	boo′-kov-cheh
Bukovik (Yugosl., mts.)	bo͞o′-kô-vĭk	boo′-ko-vik
Bukovina See *Bucovina.*		
Bukulja (Yugosl., mt.)	bo͞o′-ko͞o-lyä	boo′-koo-lyah
Bulačane (Yugosl.)	bo͞o′-lä′-chä-nĕ	boo′-lah′-chah-neh
Bulken (Nor.)	bo͝ol′-kən	bul′-kuhn
Bulwinkle, Alfred L. (U.S. representative)	bo͝ol′-wĭng-kəl	bul′-wing-kuhl
Buna (New Guinea)	bo͞o′-nä	boo′-nah
buna	*Eng.* bū′-nə	byoo′-nuh
	Ger. bo͞o′-nä	boo′-nah

Probably in American usage the English will supplant the German pronunciation.

Buna (Balkan riv.) See *Bunë.*		
Bunë (Balkan riv.)	*Alb.* bo͞o′-nə	boo′-nuh
Serb-Croat *Bojana,* q.v.		
Bungana (Oc.)	bo͞ong-ä′-nä	boong-ah′-nah
Buninga (Oc.)	bo͞o-nĭng′-ä	boo-ning′-ah
Bunschoten (Neth.)	bûn′-sk(h)ō-tən	bœn′-sk(h)oh-tuhn
Bunzlau (Ger.)	bo͝onts′-lou	bunts′-lau
Buqbuq (Egypt)	bo͝ok′-bo͝ok′	buk′-buk′
Buraku (Oc.)	bo͞o-rä′-ko͞o	boo-rah′-koo
Burenj (Yugosl., mts.)	bo͞o′-rĕn(y)	boo′-ren(y)
Burg, den (Neth.)	bûrk(h)′, dən	bœrk(h)′, duhn
Burg el Arab (Egypt)	bo͝org ĕl ăr′-əb	burg el ehr′-uhb
Burgajet (Alb.)	bo͞or-gä′-yĕt	boor-gah′-yet
Burgajeti (Alb.) See *Burgajet.*		
Burgas (Bulg.)	bo͝or-gäs′	bur-gahs′
Burgin, W. O. (U.S. representative)	bûr′-gĭn	buhr′-gin
Burgos (Sp.)	bo͞or′-gôs	boor′-gos

Burias (P.I.)	bo͞o′-ryäs	boo′-ryahs
Burnie (Austral.)	bûr′-nĭ	buhr′-ni
Burrel (Alb.)	bo͞or′-rĕl	boor′-rel
Burreli (Alb.) See *Burrel.*		
Burrinjuck (Austral.)	bûr′-ĭn-jŭk	buhr′-in-juhk
Buru (NEI) See *Boeroe.*		
Burujird (Iran)	bo͝o-ro͞o-jērd′	bu-roo-jeerd′
Bushire (Iran)	*Eng.* bo͞o-shēr′	boo-sheer′
	Per. bo͞o′-shăr′	boo′-shehr′
Busi (Yugosl.)	*It.* bo͞o′-sē	boo′-see
Serb-Croat *Biševo*, q.v.		
Busko (Pol.)	bo͝o′-skô	bu′-sko
Russian *Busk*, bo͞osk′ [boosk′].		
Busse (Rus.)	bo͝os′-sĕ	bus′-seh
Bussum (Neth.)	bûs′-əm	bœs′-uhm
Busto Arsizio (It.)	bo͞o′-stô är-sē′-tsyô	boo′-sto ahr-see′-tsyo
Buštranje (Yugosl.)	bo͞o′-shträ-nyĕ	boo′-shtrah-nyeh
Busuanga (P.I.)	bo͞os-wäng′-gä	boos-wahng′-gah
butadiene	bū′-tə-dī′-ēn	byoo′-tuh-dai′-een
Buthidaung (Burma)	bo͞o′-*th*ē-doung′	boo′-*th*ee-daung′
Buton (NEI) See *Boeton.*		
Butrint (Alb., town, lake)	bo͞o′-trĭnt	boo′-trint
Italian *Butrinto*, bo͞o-trēn′-tô [boo-treen′-to].		
Butrinti (Alb., town, lake) See *Butrint.*		
Butuan (P.I.)	bo͞o-to͞o′-än	boo-too′-ahn
butyl	bū′-tĭl	byoo′-til
butylene	bū′-tĭ-lēn′	byoo′-ti-leen′
Buzău (Rum.)	bo͝o-zû′-o͝o	bu-zuh′-u
Buzuluk (Rus.)	bo͞o-zo͞o-lo͞ok′	boo-zoo-look′
Bydgoszcz (Pol.)	bĭd′-gôshch	bid′-goshch
German *Bromberg*, q.v.		
Byela (Pol.) See *Biała Podlaska.*		
Byelgorai (Pol.) See *Biłgoraj.*		
Byeloglina (Rus.)	bĕ-lŏ-glē′-nä	beh-lo-glee′-nah
Also called *Belaya Glina*, q.v.		
Byelostok (Pol.) See *Białystok.*		
Byelovyezh (Pol.) See *Białowieża.*		
Byeltsi (Rum.) See *Bălţi.*		
Bygdin (Nor.)	büg′-dĭn	büg′-din
Byglandsfjord (Nor.)	büg′-läns-fyōr	büg′-lahns-fyohr
Bykhov (Rus.)	bwē′-hŏf	bwee′-hof
Bystrica (Cz., riv.)	bĭ′-strĭ-tsä	bi′-stri-tsah
Bzura (Pol., riv.)	bzo͝o′-rä	bzu′-rah

c and *k* are interchangeable in Greek and other languages. It may be necessary to look up both spellings. In Greek *k* is officially preferred.

Cabanatuan (P.I.)	kä′-bä-nä-tōō′-än	kah′-bah-nah-too′-ahn
Čabar (Yugosl.)	chä′-bär	chah′-bahr
cabo	kä′-bô	kah′-bo

An element, meaning *cape*, in Spanish place names. Look up the other part of the name.

Čačak (Yugosl.)	chä′-chäk	chah′-chahk
Caccia (Sard., cape)	kät′-chä	kaht′-chah
Cáceres (Sp.)	kä′-thĕ-rĕs *or* -sĕ-	kah′-theh-res *or* -seh-
Cádiz (Sp.)	*Eng.* kā′-dĭz *or* kə-dĭz′	kay′-diz *or* kuh-diz′
	Sp. kä′-*th*ēth	kah′-*th*eeth
	or kä′-*th*ēs	kah′-*th*ees
Cadogan (Brit. name)	kə-dŭg′-ən	kuh-duhg′-uhn
cadre	*Eng.* kăd′-rĭ	kad′-ri
	Fr. käd′r	kahd′r
Cadzand (Neth.)	kät-sänt′	kaht-sahnt′
Caen (Fr.)	käN′	kahN′
Caernarvon (Wales)	kär-när′-vŏn	kahr-nahr′-von
Cagayán (P.I.)	kä-gä-yän′	kah-gah-yahn′

Often Anglicized to kä-gä′-yən [kah-gah′-yuhn].

Cagli (It.)	kä′-lyē	kah′-lyee
Cagliari (Sard.)	kä′-lyä-rē	kah′-lyah-ree
Cahul (Rum.)	kä-hŏŏl′	kah-hul′

Russian *Kagul*, kä-gōōl′ [kah-gool′].

Caiazzo (It.)	kä-yät′-sô	kah-yaht′-so
Caibarién (Cuba)	kī-bär-yĕn′	kai-bahr-yen′
Caievola (It., mt.)	kä-yĕ′-vô-lä	kah-yeh′-vo-lah
Cairns (Austral.)	kărnz′	kehrnz′
Čajetina (Yugosl.)	chä′-yĕ′-tĭ-nä	chah′-yeh′-ti-nah
Čajniče (Yugosl.)	chī′-nĭ-chĕ	chai′-ni-cheh
Çakmak, Fevzi (Turk. general)	chäk-mäk′, fĕv-zē′	chahk-mahk′, fev-zee′
Čakovec (Yugosl.)	chä′-kô-vĕts	chah′-ko-vets
Calabria (It.)	*Eng.* kə-lā′-brĭ-ə	kuh-lay′-bri-uh
	It. kä-lä′-bryä	kah-lah′-bryah

The English pronunciation is preferable for American speakers, especially as the Italian kä-lä′-bryä [kah-lah′-bryah] degenerates with English speakers to kə-lăb′-rĭ-ə [kuh-lab′-ri-uh].

Calafat (Rum.)	kä-lä-fät′	kah-lah-faht′
Calais	*Eng.* kăl′-ā *or* kăl′-ĭs	kal′-ay *or* kal′-is
	Fr. kä-lĕ′	kah-leh′

For the French town the French pronunciation is probably the most common among American radio speakers. *Calais*, Maine, is pronounced kăl′-ĭs [kal′-is].

Calamián (P.I.)	kä-lä-myän′	kah-lah-myahn′
Calamotta (Yugosl., isl.)	*It.* kä-lä-môt′-tä	kah-lah-mot′-tah
Serb-Croat *Koločen*, q.v.		
Calapán (P.I.)	kä-lä-pän′	kah-lah-pahn′
Călăraşi (Rum.)	kə-lə-räsh′	kuh-luh-rahsh′
Hungarian *Harasztos*, hŏ′-rŏs-tôsh [ho′-ros-tosh].		
Calbayog (P.I.)	käl-bä′-yôg	kahl-bah′-yog
Calchi (Dodec.)	*It.* käl′-kē	kahl′-kee
Greek *Khalke*, q.v.		
Calcutta (India)	kăl-kŭt′-ə	kal-kuht′-uh
Caleta (Cuba)	kä-lĕ′-tä	kah-leh′-tah
Caliacra (Rum.)	kä-lyä′-krä	kah-lyah′-krah
Calicut (India)	kăl′-ĭ-kŭt	kal′-i-kuht
Calimere (India, cape)	kăl-ĭ-mĭr′	kal-i-mihr′
Calino (Dodec.) See *Kalymnos.*		
Callantsoog (Neth.)	kä′-länt-sōk(h)′	kah′-lahnt-sohk(h)′
Calle, la (Alg.)	käl′, lä	kahl′, lah
Calore (It., riv.)	kä-lô′-rĕ	kah-lo′-reh
Caltagirone (Sicily)	käl′-tä-jē-rô′-nĕ	kahl′-tah-jee-ro′-neh
Caltanissetta (Sicily)	käl′-tä-nēs-sĕt′-tä	kahl′-tah-nees-set′-tah
Calvados (Fr.)	käl-vä-dōs′	kahl-vah-dohs′
Calvi (It., Corsica)	käl′-vē	kahl′-vee
Camacho See *Ávila Camacho.*		
Camao *or* Camau (Indo-Ch.)	kä-mä′-ô *or* kä-mou′	kah-mah′-o *or* kah-mau′
Camargue, la (Fr., isl.)	kä-märg′, lä	kah-mahrg′, lah
Cambay (India)	kăm-bā′	kam-bay′
Cambodia (Indo-Ch.)	*Eng.* kăm-bō′-dĭ-ə	kam-boh′-di-uh
Indonesian *Caomien*, kou′-myĕn [kau′-myen].		
Cambrai (Belg.)	*Eng.* kăm-brā′	kam-bray′
	Fr. käN-brĕ′	kahN-breh′
Cameroons (Afr.)	kăm-ə-rōōnz′	kam-uh-roonz′
Camiguín (P. I.)	kä-mē-gēn′	kah-mee-geen′
Camooweal (Austral.)	kăm′-ŏŏ-wēl′	kam′-u-weel′
Campha (Indo-Ch.)	käm-fä′	kahm-fah′
Câmpina (Rum.)	kûm′-pē-nä	kuhm′-pee-nah
Campobasso (It.)	käm-pô-bäs′-sô	kahm-po-bahs′-so
Campofelice (Sicily)	käm′-pô-fĕ-lē′-chĕ	kahm′-po-feh-lee′-cheh
Campos, Francisco (Braz. leader)	käm′-pŏŏs, frän-sēs′-kŏŏ	kahm′-pus, frahn-sees′-ku

Câmpulung (Rum.)	kûm-po͞o-lo͞ong′	kuhm-pu-lung′
Also called *Kimpolung*, kĭm-pô-lo͞ong′ [kim-po-lung′].		
Câmpulung pe Tisa (Rum.)	kûm-po͞o-lo͞ong′ pĕ tē′-sä	kuhm-pu-lung′ peh tee′-sah
Camranh (Indo-Ch., bay)	käm′-rän′ *or* kăm′-răng′	kahm′-rahn′ kam′-rang′
Also spelled *Kamrang*. French käm-räN′ [kahm-rahN′]. Indonesian käm-rän′(y) [kahm-rahn′(y)].		
Çanakkale Boğazı (Turk., strait)	See *Dardanelles*.	
Canberra (Austral.)	kăn′-bĕr-ə	kan′-behr-uh
There is a story that government employees who receive more than £500 yearly pronounce the name of the capital kăn′-bə-rə; and those who receive less say kăn-bĕr′-ə.		
Cancello (It.)	kän-chĕl′-lô	kahn-chel′-lo
Canche (Fr.)	käNsh′	kahNsh′
Candia (Crete)	*Eng.* kăn′-dĭ-ə	kan′-di-uh
Greek *Herakleion*, q.v.		
Canea (Crete)	*Eng.* kä-nē′-ä	kah-nee′-ah
	Gr. hän-yä′	hahn-yah′
Also spelled *Khania*, q.v.		
Canicatti (Sicily)	kä-nē-kät′-tē	kah-nee-kaht′-tee
Cannes (Fr.)	*Eng.* kănz′	kanz′
	Fr. kän′	kahn′
Cannosa (Yugosl.)	*It.* kän-nô′-sä	kahn-no′-sah
Serb-Croat *Trsteno*, q.v.		
Canobie (Austral.)	kă-nō′-bĭ	ka-noh′-bi
Čantavir (Yugosl.)	chän′-tä-vēr	chahn′-tah-veer
Cantigny (Fr.)	käN-tē-nyē′	kahN-tee-nyee′
Canton (Ch., Kwangtung)	*Eng.* kăn′-tŏn′	kan′-ton′
cantonment	kăn′-tən-mənt *or* kăn-tŏn′-mənt	kan′-tuhn-muhnt kan-ton′-muhnt
The first seems to be more common in military usage. There is also a British pronunciation kăn-to͞on′-mənt [kan-toon′-muhnt].		
Caolanh (Indo-Ch.)	kou′-län′	kau′-lahn′
Cap St. Jaques (Indo-Ch.)	käp säN zhäk′	kahp sahN zhahk′
Capanema, Gustavo (Braz. leader)	kä-pə-nĕ′-mə, go͞os-tä′-vo͝o	kah-puh-neh′-muh, goos-tah′-vu
Capari (Yugosl.)	tsä′-pä-rĭ	tsah′-pah-ri
Cap Blanc (Tun.)	käp bläN′	kahp blahN′
English *Cape Blanc*, kāp blängk [kayp blahngk].		
Cap Bon (Tun.)	käp bôN′	kahp boN′
English *Cape Bon*, kāp′ bŏn′ [kayp′ bon′].		

cape	kāp′	kayp′
Cape is often ignored in the alphabetical listing. It may be necessary to look up the other part of the name.		
Capelle (Neth.)	kä-pĕl′-ə	kah-pel′-uh
Also spelled *Kapelle*, q.v.		
Cape Verde (Port., isls.)	*Eng.* vûrd′	vuhrd′
Portuguese *Cabo Verde*, kä′-bo͝o vĕr′-dĭ [kah′-bu vehr′-di]. French *Cap Vert*, käp vĕr′ [kahp vehr′].		
Cape Zebib (Tun.)	zə-bēb′	zuh-beeb′
Cap Gris Nez (Fr.)	käp grē nĕ′	kahp gree neh′
Capiz (P.I.)	kä′-pēth *or* -pēs	kah′-peeth *or* -pees
capo (It.)	kä′-pô	kah′-po
An element, meaning *cape*, in Italian place names. It may be necessary to look up the other part of the name.		
Capocesto (Yugosl.)	*It.* kä-pô-chĕ′-stô	kah-po-cheh′-sto
Serb-Croat *Primošten*, q.v.		
Capo di Chino (It., airfield)	kä′-pô dē kē′-nô	kah′-po dee kee′-no
An English pronunciation, chē′-nō [chee′-noh], may or may not be inevitable. It would be confused with *Cappuccino*.		
Capoterra (Sard.)	kä-pô-tĕr′-rä	kah-po-tehr′-rah
Capozzoli, Louis J. (U.S. representative)	kä-pō-zō′-lĭ	kah-poh-zoh′-li
Capraia (It., isls.)	kä-prī′-ä	kah-prai′-ah
Caprara (Sard., cape)	kä-prä′-rä	kah-prah′-rah
Capri (It., isl.)	kä′-prē	kah′-pree
The pronunciation kä′-prē [kah′-pree] is preferable to kə-prē′ [kuh-pree′].		
Capri (Yugosl.)	*It.* kä′-prē	kah′-pree
Serb-Croat *Kaprije*, q.v.		
Cap Serrat (Tun.)	käp sĕr-rä′	kahp sehr-rah′
English *Cape Serrat*, kāp sə-răt′ [kayp suh-rat′].		
Capua (It.)	*Eng.* kăp′-yo͞o-ə *It.* kä′-pwä	kap′-yu-uh kah′-pwah
Capuzzo, Fort (Libya)	kä-po͞ot′-tsō	kah-poot′-tsoh
Caracal (Rum.)	kä-rä-käl′	kah-rah-kahl′
Caraga (P.I.)	kä-rä′-gä	kah-rah′-gah
Caransebeş (Rum.)	kä-rän-sĕ′-bĕsh	kah-rahn-seh′-besh
Hungarian *Karansebes*, kä′-rän-shĕ-bĕsh [kah′-rahn-sheh-besh].		
Carapanayotis, Byron (Gr. leader)	kä-rä-pä-nä-yô′-tēs, *Eng.* bī′-rən, *Gr.* vē′-rôn	kah-rah-pah-nah-yo′-tees, *Eng.* bai′-ruhn, *Gr.* vee′-ron
Caraway, Hattie W. (U.S. senator)	kăr′-ə-wā	kehr′-uh-way

Carbaix (Fr.)	kär-bĕ′	kahr-beh′
Carbonara (Sard., cape)	kär-bô-nä′-rä	kahr-bo-nah′-rah
Carbonia (Sard.)	kär-bô-nē′-ä	kahr-bo-nee′-ah
carburetor	kär′-byə-rā′-tər	kahr′-byuh-ray′-tuhr

Dictionaries, except Thorndike-Century, give only kär′-bū-rĕt′-ər [kahr′-byoo-ret′-uhr] and kär′-bū-rĕsh′-ən [kahr′-byoo-resh′-uhn]. But these pronunciations would seem fantastic to almost every American.

Carcassonne (Fr.)	kär-kä-sôn′	kahr-kah-son′
Cárdenas, Lázaro (Mex. leader)	kär′-dĕ-näs, lä′-zä-rô	kahr′-deh-nahs, lah′-zah-ro
Carei (Rum.)	kä-rā′	kah-ray′

Hungarian *Nagykároly*, nät′(y)-kä-roi [naht′(y)-kah-roi].

Carevac (Yugosl.)	tsä′-rĕ-väts	tsah′-reh-vahts
Carevo Selo (Yugosl.)	tsä′-rĕ-vô sĕ′-lô	tsah′-reh-vo seh′-lo
Caribbean	kăr′-ĭ-bē′-ən	kehr′-i-bee′-uhn

The pronunciation kə-rĭb′-ĭ-ən [kuh-rib′-i-uhn] is a variation mysterious in origin. It has a "British" quality to American ears, and to the British it sounds like an American invention. (*See penicillin.*) "A competent phonetically trained observer in the Caribbean region tells me that repeated inquiries elicit the information that Caribbéan is almost universally recognized as the old established pronunciation but that many informants 'have recently heard Carib′bean and supposed it must be right'. I find no evidence that the neophony issues from England but some evidence that it may have spread from New York City. [John S. Kenyon, *Am. Sp.*, vol. 17, p. 284.]" Prof. H. M. Ayres suggests that Carib′bean may be based on the old form Carib′-bee and on the analogy of Európean, the popular 18th-century pronunciation of *European* [Walker, 1791, 1794, English eds.].

Caribrod (Yugosl.)	tsä′-rĭ-brôd	tsah′-ri-brod
Carini (Sicily)	kä-rē′-nē	kah-ree′-nee
Carinola (It.)	kä-rē′-nô-lä	kah-ree′-no-lah
Cârlibaba (Rum.)	kûr-lē-bä′-bä	kuhr-lee-bah′-bah
Carloforte (Sard.)	kär-lô-fôr′-tĕ	kahr-lo-for′-teh
Carlsbad	*Eng.* kärlz′-băd	kahrlz′-bad
	Ger. kärls′-bät	kahrls′-baht

Czech *Karlovy Vary*, kär′-lô-vĭ vä′-rĭ [kahr′-lo-vi vah′-ri].

Carnarvon (Austral., U. of S.A.)	kär-när′-vən	kahr-nahr′-vuhn
Carpathos (Dodec.)	kär′-pä-thô(s)	kahr′-pah-tho(s)

For variants see *Karpathos.*

Carpentaria (Austral., gulf)	kär-pən-tăr′-ĭ-ə	kahr-puhn-tehr′-i-uh
Carrara (It.)	kär-rä′-rä	kahr-rah′-rah
Carroceto (It.)	kär-rô-chĕ′-tô	kahr-ro-cheh′-to
Carsoli (It.)	**kär′-sô-lē**	**kahr′-so-lee**

Carstenz (NEI)	kär′-stənz	kahr′-stuhnz
Cartagena (Sp.)	*Eng.* kär′-tə-jē′-nə	kahr′-tuh-jee′-nuh
	Sp. kär-tä-hĕ′-nä	kahr-tah-heh′-nah
Car Vrh (Yugosl., mt.)	tsär′ vərk(h)′	tsahr′ vuhrk(h)′
Casablanca (Mor.)	kä-sä-bläng′-kä	kah-sah-blahng′-kah
Casano (It.)	kä-sä′-nô	kah′-sah′-no
Cascina (It.)	kä′-shē-nä	kah′-shee-nah
Caserta (It.)	kä-zĕr′-tä	kah-zehr′-tah

Casey
It is said that in Australia the usual pronunciation is kā′-zĭ [kay′-zi] rather than kā′-sĭ [kay′-si].

Caso (Dodec.) See *Kasos.*

Casola, -e, -i (It.)	kä′-sô-lä, -ĕ, -ē	kah′-so-lah, -eh, -ee
Casona, -e, -i (It.)	kä-sô′-nä, -ĕ, -ē	kah-so′-nah, -eh, -ee
Caspian Sea	*Eng.* kăs′-pĭ-ən	kas′-pi-uhn

Cassel (Ger.) See *Kassel.*

Cassino (It.)	käs-sē′-nô	kahs-see′-no

Casson (Yugosl.) See *Kason.*

Castel Benito (Libya)	käs-tĕl′ bĕ-nē′-tô	kahs-tel′ beh-nee′-to
Castelbottaccio (It.)	kä-stĕl′-bôt-tät′-chô	kah-stel′-bot-taht′-cho
Castel di Stabia (It.)	kä-stĕl′ dē stä′-byä	kah-stel′ dee stah′-byah
Castel di Velia (It.)	kä-stĕl′ dē vĕ′-lyä	kah-stel′ dee veh′-lyah
Castel Gandolfo (It.)	kä-stĕl′ gän-dôl′-fô	kah-stel′ gahn-dol′-fo
Castellabate (It.)	käs-tĕl′-lä-bä′-tĕ	kahs-tel′-lah-bah′-teh
Castellammare (It.)	kä-stĕl′-läm-mä′-rĕ	kah-stel′-lahm-mah′-reh
Castellón (Sp.)	käs-tĕ-lyôn′ *or* -yôn′	kahs-teh-lyon′ *or* -yon′
Castelluccio (It.)	kä-stĕl′-lōōt′-chô	kah-stel′-loot′-cho
Castelnuovo (Yugosl.)	*It.* kä-stĕl′-nwô′-vô	kah-stel′-nwo′-vo

Serb-Croat *Ercegnovi*, q.v.

Castelrosso (Dodec.)	*It.* kä-stĕl′-rôs′-sô	kah-stel′-ros′-so

Greek *Kastelorizon*, q.v.

Castel Sant' Angelo (It.)	kä-stĕl′ sän tän′-jĕ-lô	kah-stel′ sahn tahn′-jeh-lo
Casteltermini (Sicily)	kä-stĕl′-tĕr′-mē-nē	kah-stel′-tehr′-mee-nee
Castelvetrano (Sicily)	kä-stĕl′-vĕ-trä′-nô	kah-stel′-veh-trah′-no
Castiglione (It.)	kä-stē-lyô′-nĕ	kah-stee-lyo′-neh
Castilla (Sp.)	käs-tē′-lyä	kahs-tee′-lyah

English *Castile*, kăs-tēl′ [kas-teel′].

Castillo, Ramón (Sp., leader)	käs-tē′-lyô *or* -yô, rä-môn′	kahs-tee′-lyo *or* -yo, rah-mon′

Castres (Fr.)	käs′tr	kahs′tr
Castroreale (Sicily)	kä′-strô-rĕ-ä′-lĕ	kah′-stro-reh-ah′-leh
Çatalca (Turk.)	chä-täl′-jä	chah-tahl′-jah
Catanduanes (P.I.)	kä-tän-dwä′-nĕs	kah-tahn-dwah′-nes
Catania (Sicily)	kä-tän′-yä	kah-tahn′-yah
Catanzaro (It.)	kä-tän-dzä′-rô	kah-tahn-dzah′-ro
Catbalogan (P.I.)	kät′-bä-lô′-gän	kaht′-bah-lo′-gahn
Catel Viejo (P.I.)	kä-tĕl′ vyĕ′-hô	kah-tel′ vyeh′-ho
Catene, le (Yugosl., It., strait)	*It.* kä-tĕ′-nĕ, lĕ	kah-teh′-neh, leh
Serb-Croat *Verige*, q.v.		
Catroux, Georges (Fr. general)	kä-trōō′, zhôrzh	kah-troo′, zhorzh
Cattaro (Yugosl.)	*It.* kät′-tä-rô	kaht′-tah-ro
Serb-Croat *Kotor*, q.v.		
Caudillo, el (Sp.)	kou-dē′-lyô, ĕl *or* kou-dē′-yô, ĕl	kau-dee′-lyo, el kau-dee′-yo, el
Spanish for *the leader*. Cf. *il Duce* and *der Fuehrer*.		
Caulonia (It.)	kou-lô′-nyä	kau-lo′-nyah
Caucasian	kô-kā′-zhən	kaw-kay′-zhuhn
Other acceptable pronunciations are given in the dictionaries, but this is the most common in good American usage.		
Čaušli (Yugosl.)	chou′-shlĭ	chau′-shli
Cauvery (India, riv.)	kô′-və-rĭ	ko′-vuh-ri
Cavaia (Alb.)	*It.* kä-vä′-yä	kah-vah′-yah
Albanian *Kavajë*, q.v.		
Caviglia (It.)	kä-vē′-lyä	kah-vee′-lyah
Cavite (P.I.)	kä-vē′-tĕ	kah-vee′-teh
Čavka (Yugosl., mt.)	chäv′-kä	chahv′-kah
Cavtat (Yugosl.)	tsäv′-tät	tsahv′-taht
Cawnpore (India)	kôn′-pôr′	kawn′-por′
Also called *Cawnpur*, kôn′-pŏŏr′ [kawn′-pur′].		
Cazin (Yugosl.)	tsä′-zĭn	tsah′-zin
Čazma (Yugosl.)	chäz′-mä	chahz′-mah
Cazza (It., isl.)	kät′-sä	kaht′-sah
Serb-Croat *Sušac*, sōō′-shäts [soo′-shahts].		
Ceará (Brazil)	sĕ-ä-rä′	seh-ah-rah′
Cebú (P.I.)	sĕ-bōō′	seh-boo′
Cecchino (It.)	chĕ-kē′-nô	cheh-kee′-no
Čechy (Cz.)	chĕ′-hĭ	cheh′-hi
English *Bohemia*, q.v.		
Cecina (It.)	chĕ′-chē-nä	cheh′-chee-nah
Cecina near Verona, chĕ-chē′-nä [cheh-chee′-nah].		
Cedro (It., mt.)	chĕ′-drô	cheh′-dro

Ceduna (Austral.)	sə-do͞o′-nə	suh-doo′-nuh
	or kĕ-do͞o′-nə	keh-doo′-nuh
Cefalù (Sicily)	chĕ-fä-lo͞o′	cheh-fah-loo′
Cegléd (Hung.)	tsĕg′-lād	tseg′-layd
Cekhira (Tun.)	sə-kē′-rä	suh-kee′-rah
Also spelled *Skhirra*, q.v.		
Celebes (NEI)	*Eng.* sĕl′-ə-bēz	sel′-uh-beez
	Du. sĕ-lā′-bĕs	seh-lay′-bes
Celje (Yugosl.)	tsĕ′-lyĕ	tseh′-lyeh
Celler, Emanuel (U.S. representative)	sĕl′-ər	sel′-uhr
Čemerna planina (Yugosl., mts.)	chĕ′-mĕr-nä plä′-nē′-nä	cheh′-mehr-nah plah′-nee′-nah
Čemernik (Yugosl., mt.)	chĕ′-mĕr-nĭk	cheh′-mehr-nik
Cemi (Balkan riv.)	*Alb.* tsĕ′-mē	tseh′-mee
Serb-Croat *Cijevna*, q.v.		
Cenis, Mont (Fr., It., mt.)	sə-nē′, môN	suh-nee′, moN
Čenta (Yugosl.)	chĕn′-tä	chen′-tah
Centocelle (It.)	chĕn-tô-chĕl′-lĕ	chen-to-chel′-leh
Centrache (It.)	chĕn′-trä-kĕ	chen′-trah-keh
Centuripe (Sicily)	chĕn-to͞o′-rē-pĕ	chen-too′-ree-peh
Ceos (Gr., isl.) See *Keos.*		
Ćeotina (Yugosl., riv.)	chĕ′-ô′-tĭ-nä	cheh′-o′-ti-nah
Cephalonia (Gr., isl.)	*Eng.* sĕf-ə-lōn′-yə	sef-uh-lohn′-yuh
Greek *Kephalenia*, q.v.		
Cer (Yugosl.)	tsĕr′	tsehr′
Ceram (NEI)	*Eng.* sē-răm′	see-ram′
	Du. sā′-räm	say′-rahm
Cerami (Sicily)	chĕ-rä′-mē	cheh-rah′-mee
Ceraunia (Alb.)	*Eng.* sĭ-rô′-nĭ-ə	si-ro′-ni-uh
Albanian *Karaburun*, q.v.		
Ceremuşul (Pol., Rum., riv.) See *Czeremosz.*		
Çerevoda (Alb.) See *Çerevodë.*		
Çerevodë (Alb.)	chĕ-rĕ-vô′-də	cheh-reh-vo′-duh
Cerigo (Gr., isl.)	*It.* chĕ′-rē-gô	cheh′-ree-go
Greek *Kythera*, q.v. English *Cythera.*		
Cerknica (Yugosl.)	tsĕrk′-nĭ-tsä	tsehrk′-ni-tsah
Cerna (Rum., riv.)	chĕr′-nä	chehr′-nah
Cernăuţi (Rum.)	chĕr-nə-o͝ots′	chehr-nuh-uts′
Polish *Czernowitz*, q.v.		
Cerna Vodă (Rum.)	chĕr′-nä vô′-də	chehr′-nah vo′-duh
Černište (Yugosl.)	chĕr′-nĭ-shtĕ	chehr′-ni-shteh
Certosa (It.)	chĕr-tô′-zä	chehr-to′-zah

Cervaro (It., riv.)	chĕr-vä′-rô	chehr-vah′-ro
Cervino (Sicily)	chĕr-vē′-nô	chehr-vee′-no
Cesana (It.)	chĕ-sä′-nä	cheh-sah′-nah
Cesaro (It.)	chĕ′-zä-rô	cheh′-zah-ro
Cesarò (Sicily)	chĕ-zä-rô′	cheh-zah-ro′
Cesena (It.)	chĕ-zĕ′-nä	cheh-zeh′-nah
Cesima (It., mt.)	chĕ′-sē-mä	cheh′-see-mah
Cēsis (Latvia)	tsā′-sēs *or* -zēz	tsay′-sees *or* -zeez-

Also spelled *Tseziz* and *Zehsis*. German *Wenden*, q.v.

Český See *Czech.*

Češljeva Bara (Yugosl.)	chĕsh′-lyĕ-vä bä′-rä	chesh′-lyeh-vah bah′-rah
Cessnock (Austral.)	sĕs′-nŏk	ses′-nok
Cetatea Albă (Rum.)	chĕ-tä′-tyä äl′-bə	cheh-tah′-tyah ahl′-buh

Russian *Akkerman*, äk′-ər-män [ahk′-uhr-mahn].

Cetinje (Yugosl.)	tsĕ′-tĭ-nyĕ	tseh′-ti-nyeh
Četnik (Yugosl. guerrilla)	chĕt′-nĭk	chet′-nik
Cetraro (It.)	chĕ-trä′-rô	cheh-trah′-ro
Cette (Fr.)	sĕt′	set′

Now officially spelled *Sète*, q.v.

Ceuta (Mor.)	*Eng.* sū′-tə	syoo′-tuh
	Sp. thĕ-ōō′-tä *or* sĕ-	theh-oo′-tah *or* seh-
Cévennes (Fr.)	sĕ-vĕn′	seh-ven′
Čevo (Yugosl.)	chĕ′-vô	cheh′-vo

ch, *kh*, and often *h* are variant spellings in Greek. It may be necessary to look up all three.

Ch is an Anglicized spelling of Yugoslav č. It may be necessary to look up both spellings.

Ceylon (India, isl.)	sĭ-lŏn′	si-lon′
Chad (Afr., lake)	chăd′	chad′
Chahar (Ch., prov.)	chä-här	chah-hahr
Chagodoshcha (Rus.)	chä-gŏ-dô′-shchä	chah-go-do′-shchah
Chagos (India, isls.)	chä′-gōs	chah′-gohs
Chahbar (Iran)	shä-bär′	shah-bahr′
Chalcidice (Gr., pen.)	*Eng.* kăl-sĭd′-ĭ-sĭ	kal-sid′-i-si

Greek *Khalkidike*, q.v.

Chalkis *or* Chalcis (Gr.) See *Khalkis.*

Châlons sur Marne (Fr.)	shä-lôN′ sür märn′	shah-loN′ sür mahrn′
Chalon sur Saône (Fr.)	shä-lôN′ sür sōn′	shah-loN′ sür sohn′
Chalus (Iran)	chä-lōōs′	chah-loos′
Chambal (India)	chŭm′-bəl	chuhm′-buhl
Chambéry (Fr.)	shäN-bĕ-rē′	shahN-beh-ree′

Chamorros	chä-mô′-rôs	chah-mo′-ros
The people of the Marianas or Ladrone Isls. (Oc.)		
Chandalar (Alaska)	shăn-də-lär′	shan-duh-lahr′
Chandra Buri (Thai)	chän′-tə bə-rē′	chahn′-tuh buh-ree′
Chandernagor (India)	chŭn-dər-nə-gôr′	chuhn-duhr-nuh-gor′
Ch'ang-an (Ch., Shansi)	chäng-än	chahng-ahn
Also called *Si-an*, q.v.		
Ch'ang-chih (Ch., Shansi)	chäng-jû	chahng-juh
Ch'ang-chow (Ch., Kiangsu)	*Eng.* chăng-chou *Ch.* chäng-jō	chang-chau chahng-joh
Also called *Wu-chin*, q.v.		
Ch'ang-ch'un (Manchu.)	chäng-cho͞on	chahng-chun
Ch'ang Ch'un (Ch. leader)	chäng cho͞on	chahng chun
Ch'ang Hsüeh-liang (Ch. leader)	chäng shüĕ-lyäng	chahng shüeh-lyahng
Also called the *Young Marshall.*		
Ch'ang-hua (Ch., Chekiang)	chäng-whä	chahng-whah
Ch'ang-mên (Ch., Fukien)	chäng-mŭn	chahng-muhn
Ch'ang-sha (Ch., Hunan)	chäng-shä	chahng-shah
Ch'ang-shan (Ch., Chekiang)	chäng-shän	chahng-shahn
Ch'ang-tê *or* -teh (Ch., Hunan)	chäng-dŭ	chahng-duh
Ch'ang-tsu (Ch., Shansi)	chäng-dzə	chahng-dzuh
Ch'ang-yang (Ch., Hupeh)	chäng-yäng	chahng-yahng
Chantilly (Fr.)	*Eng.* shăn-tĭl′-ĭ *Fr.* shäN-tē-yē′	shan-til′-i shahN-tee-yee′
Chao-an (Ch., Fukien)	jou-än	jau-ahn
Ch'ao-an (Ch., Kwangtung)	chou-än	chau-ahn
Also called *Ch'ao-chou*, q.v.		
Ch'ao-chou (Ch., Kwangtung)	chou-jō	chau-joh
Chaouach (Tun.)	shä-wäsh′	shah-wahsh′
Ch'ao-yang (Ch., Kwangtung)	chou-yäng	chau-yahng
Ch'ao-yang (Manchu.)	chou-yäng	chau-yahng
Chapaev (Rus.)	chä-pä′-yĕf	chah-pah′-yef
Chaplinka (Rus.)	chäp′-lĭn-kä	chahp′-lin-kah

Chaplino (Rus.)	chäp′-lĭ-nŏ	chahp′-li-no
Charkhari (India)	chər-kä′-rē	chuhr-kah′-ree
charlatan	shär′-lə-tən	shahr′-luh-tuhn
Charleroi (Belg.)	shär-lə-rwä′	shahr-luh-rwah′
Charleville (Austral.)	chärl′-vĭl	chahrl′-vil
Charlottenburg (Ger.)	*Eng.* shär-lŏt′-ən-bûrg	shahr-lot′-uhn-buhrg
	Ger. shär-lŏt′-ən-bŏŏrk(h)	shahr-lot′-uhn-burk(h)
Chartres (Fr.)	shär′tr	shahr′tr
Charybdis (It.)	*Eng.* kə-rĭb′-dĭs	kuh-rib′-dis
Chasovaya (Rus.)	chä-sŏ-vä′-yä	chah-so-vah′-yah
Chatalja (Turk.)	chä-täl′-jä	chah-tahl′-jah
Turkish spelling *Çatalca*, q.v.		
Château Thierry (Fr.)	*Eng.* shă-tō′ tē′-ə-rē	sha-toh′ tee′-uh-ree
	Fr. shä-tō′ tyĕ-rē′	shah-toh′ tyeh-ree′
Chatham	chăt′-əm	chat′-uhm
	or chăt′-hăm	chat′-ham
Especially on Cape Cod, chăt′-hăm [chat′-ham].		
Chauk (Burma)	chouk′	chauk′
Chautauqua (N.Y.)	shə-tô′-kwə	shuh-taw′-kwuh
Chavez, Dennis (U.S. senator)	chä′-vĕs	chah′-ves
Cheb (Cz.)	hĕb′ *or* hĕp′	heb′ *or* hep′
German *Eger*, ā′-gər [ay′-guhr].		
Chebba (Tun.)	shĕb′-bä	sheb′-bah
Chebir (Libya)	kə-bēr′	kuh-beer′
Cf. *Kebir*.		
Cheboksari (Rus.)	chĕ-bŏk-sä′-rĭ	cheh-bok-sah′-ri
Chechen (Rus. district)	chĕ′-chĕn′	cheh′-chen′
Also called *Chechna*, chĕch-nyä′ [chech-nyah′].		
Chê-chiang (Ch., prov.)	jŭ-jyäng	juh-jyahng
Anglicized as *Chekiang*, q.v.		
Chęciny (Pol.)	hăN-tsē′-nĭ	haN-tsee′-ni
Russian *Khentsini*, hĕn-tsē′-nĭ [hen-tsee′-ni].		
Cheduba (Burma, isl.)	chĕ-dōō′-bə	cheh-doo′-buh
	or chĕ′-dŏŏ-bə	cheh′-du-buh
Chefoo (Ch., Shantung)	*Eng.* chē-fōō	chee-foo
Chinese *Chih-fu* and *Chih-fow*, q.v.		
Cheguimi (Tun.)	shĕ-gē′-mĭ	sheh-gee′-mi
Chekchagirskoe (Rus., lake)	chĕk-chä-gēr′-skŏ-yĕ	chek-chah-geer′-sko-yeh
Chekiang (Ch., prov.)	*Eng.* chĕ-kyăng	cheh-kyang
Chinese *Chê-chiang*, q.v.		

Chelles (Fr.)	shĕl′	shel′
Chełm (Pol.)	hĕlm′	helm′
Russian *Kholm*, hôlm′ [holm′].		
Chełmno (Pol.)	hĕlm′-nô	helm′-no
German *Kulm*, ko͝olm′ [kulm′].		
Chełmża (Pol.)	hĕlm′-zhä	helm′-zhah
German *Kulmsee*, ko͝olm′-zā [kulm′-zay].		
Chelyabinsk (Rus.)	chĕ-lyä′-bĭnsk	cheh-lyah′-binsk
Chelyadz (Pol.) See *Czeladź*.		
Chemulpo (Korea)	chĕ-mo͞ol-pô	cheh-mool-po
Chenango (N.Y.)	shə-năng′-gō	shuh-nang′-goh
Chên-chiang (Ch., Kiangsu)	jŭn-jyäng	juhn-jyahng
Variant of *Chin-kiang*, q.v.		
Ch'ên-chow (Ch., Hunan)	chŭn-jō	chuhn-joh
Also called *Yuan-ling*, q.v.		
Chêng-chia-tun (Manchu.)	jŭng-jyä-do͝on	juhng-jyah-dun
Chêng-chow (Ch., Honan)	jŭng-jō	juhng-joh
Chêng-hai (Ch., Kwangtung)	jŭng-hī	juhng-hai
Ch'êng-hsien (Ch., Chekiang)	chŭng-shyĕn	chuhng-shyen
Ch'êng-teh (Manchu.)	chŭng-dŭ	chuhng-duh
Also called *Jehol*, q.v.		
Ch'êng-tu (Ch., Szechwan)	chŭng-do͞o	chuhng-doo
Chên-hsi (Ch., Sinkiang)	jŭn-shē	juhn-shee
Also called *Barkol*, q.v.		
Ch'ên K'uo-fu (Ch. leader)	chŭn kwô-fo͞o	chuhn kwo-foo
Ch'ên Li-fu (Ch. leader)	chŭn lē-fo͞o	chuhn lee-foo
Chên-nan (Ch., pass, Kwangsi; town, Yünnan)	jŭn-nän	juhn-nahn
Chennault, Claire (U.S. general)	*Eng.* shə-nôlt′	shuh-nolt′
Chenoweth, J. Edgar (U.S. representative)	chĕn′-ə-wĕth	chen′-uh-weth
Ch'ên P'u-lei (Ch. leader)	chŭn po͞o lā	chuhn poo lay
Chenstokhov (Pol.) See *Częstochowa*.		
Chên-yüan (Ch., Kansu, Kweichow, Yünnan)	jŭn-yüän	juhn-yü-ahn

Cheops (Egyptian Pharaoh)	kē′-ŏps	kee′-ops
Cher (Fr., riv.)	shĕr′	shehr′
Cherbourg (Fr.)	*Eng.* shĕr′-bo͝org *Fr.* shĕr-bo͞or′	shehr′-burg shehr-boor′
Cherchen (Ch., Sinkiang)	chĕr-chĕn	chehr-chen
Cheremkhovo (Rus.)	chĕ-rĕm-hô′-vŏ	cheh-rem-ho′-vo
Cherepanovo (Rus.)	chĕ-rĕ-pä′-nŏ-vŏ	cheh-reh-pah′-no-vo
Cherepovets (Rus.)	chĕ-rĕ-pŏ-vĕts′	cheh-reh-po-vets′
Cheribon (NEI)	*Eng.* chĕr-ĭ-bŏn′	chehr-i-bon′
Cherkasi (Rus.)	chĕr-kä′-sĭ	chehr-kah′-si
Cherkessk (Rus.)	chĕr-kĕsk′	chehr-kesk′
Chern (Rus.)	chĕrn′(y)	chehrn′(y)
Chernaya (Pol., riv.)	See *Czarna.*	
Chernigov (Rus.)	chĕr-nē′-gŏf	chehr-nee′-gof
Chernyaevo (Rus.)	chĕr-nyä′-yĕ-vŏ	chehr-nyah′-yeh-vo
Cherny Rynok (Rus.)	chôr′-nĭ rwē′-nŏk	chor′-ni rwee′-nok
Cherny Yar (Rus.)	chôr′-nĭ yär′	chor′-ni yahr′
Chernyshevsk (Rus.)	chĕr-nĭ-shĕfsk′	chehr-ni-shefsk′
Cherso (It., isl) Serb-Croat *Cres,* q.v.	kĕr′-sô	kehr′-so
Chersonese (Turk., pen.)	*Eng.* kûr′-sə-nēz	kuhr′-suh-neez
Also called *Gallipoli,* q.v. Greek *Khersonesos,* q.v.		
Chertkovo (Rus.)	chĕrt-kô′-vŏ	chehrt-ko′-vo
Cheshkaya (Rus., bay)	chĕsh′-kä-yä	chesh′-kah-yah
Chetnik (Yugosl. guerrilla)	chĕt′-nĭk	chet′-nik
Chevigné, Pierre de (Fr. officer)	shə-vē-nyĕ′, pyĕr′ də	shuh-vee-nyeh′, pyehr′ duh
Cheylus (Tun.)	shā-lüs′	shay-lüs′
Chiaia *or* Chiaja (It., mt.)	kyä′-yä	kyah′-yah
Chia-mu-ssu, -seh (Manchu.)	jyä-mo͞o-sə	jyah-moo-suh
Chi-an (Ch., Kiangsi, Manchu.)	jē-än	jee-ahn
chiang *or* kiang	jyäng *or* kyäng	jyahng *or* kyahng
Chinese word meaning *river.*		
Chiang-chin (Ch., Szechwan)	jyäng-jĭn	jyahng-jin
Chiang Kai-shek (Ch. generalissimo)	*Eng.* chyäng kī-shĕk *Ch.* jyäng jyĕ-shû	chyahng kai-shek jyahng jyeh-shuh

Above is the accepted English spelling and pronunciation. If the name is spelled according to the usual system of Romanization, it is *Chiang Chieh-shih.* The Mandarin pronunciation is jyäng jyĕ-shû [jyahng jyeh-shuh]. This "Chinese" pronunciation is not so appropriate for American radio as is the English pronunciation.

Chiang Kai-shek is a "courtesy name" or nickname, the Generalissimo's real name being *Chiang Chung-chêng*, jyäng jo͝ong-jŭng [jyahng jung-juhng.] Though put first in Chinese, *Chiang* corresponds in use to an English "last name."

Chiang Kee-yen *or* Ch'ee- (Ch. general)	jyäng chē-yĕn	jyahng chee-yen
Chiang-ling (Ch., Hupeh)	jyäng-lĭng	jyahng-ling
Chiangmai (Thai)	chyäng-mī	chyahng-mai
For an English pronunciation, see *Chiengmai.* Also called *Kiang-mai,* q.v.		
Chiangrai (Thai)	chyäng-rī′	chyahng-rai′
Chiang-shan (Ch., Chekiang)	jyäng-shän	jyahng-shahn
Ch'ang-shan and *Chiang-shan* are neighboring cities and should be distinguished.		
Chianjur (NEI)	chyän′-jo͞or	chyahn′-joor
Also spelled *Tjiandjoer,* q.v.		
Chiasso (It.)	kyäs′-sô	kyahs′-so
Chicacole (India)	chĭk-ə-kōl′	chik-uh-kohl′
Chichagof (Alaska, isl.)	*Eng.* chĭch′-ə-gŏf	chich′-uh-gof
	Rus. chĭ-chä′-gŏf	chi-chah′-gof
Chichi Jima (Jap.)	chē-chē jē-mä	chee-chee jee-mah
Chieh-yäng (Ch., Kwangtung)	jyĕ-yäng	jyeh-yahng
Ch'ien-chiang (Ch., Kwangsi, Szechwan)	chyĕn-jyäng	chyen-jyahng
Variant of *Chien-kiang,* q.v.		
Chiengmai (Thai)	*Eng.* chyĕng-mī	chyeng-mai
Officially *Chiangmai,* q.v.		
Chien-kiang (Ch., Kwangsi, Szechwan)	*Eng.* chyĕn-kyăng	chyen-kyang
Variant of *Ch'ien-chiang,* q.v.		
Chien-li (Ch., Hupeh)	jyĕn-lē	jyen-lee
Ch'ien-nan (Ch., Kiangsi)	chyĕn-nän	chyen-nahn
Chien-ow (Ch., Fukien)	jyĕn-ō	jyen-oh
Ch'ien-shan (Ch., Kiangsi)	chyĕn-shän	chyen-shahn
Ch'ien-t'ang (Ch., riv.)	chyĕn-täng	chyen-tahng
Chien-tê *or* -teh (Ch., Chekiang)	jyĕn-dŭ	jyen-duh
Also spelled *Kien-teh.*		

Chiete (It.)	kyĕ′-tĕ	kyeh′-teh
Chieti (It.)	kyĕ′-tē	kyeh′-tee
Chigi (It.)	kē′-jē	kee′-jee
Chigirin (Rus.)	chĭ-gē′-rĭn	chi-gee′-rin
Chih-chiang (Ch., Hupeh)	jû-jyäng	juh-jyahng
Ch'ih-fêng (Manchu.)	chû-fŭng	chuh-fuhng
Chih-fu *or* Chih-fow (Ch., Shantung)	jû-fo͞o *or* jû-fō	juh-foo *or* juh-foh
Anglicized as *Chefoo*, q.v. Also called *Yen-t'ai*, q.v.		
Chihuahua (Mex.)	chē-wä′-wä	chee-wah′-wah
Chile (S.A.)	*Eng.* chĭl′-ĭ	chil′-i
	Sp. chē′-lĕ	chee′-leh
Chilia Nouă (Rum.)	kē-lē′-ä nô′-wə	kee-lee′-ah no′-wuh
Russian *Kilia*, kē′-lĭ-yä [kee′-li-yah].		
Chilivani (Sard.)	kē-lē-vä′-nē	kee-lee-vah′-nee
Chimara (Alb.)	*It.* kē-mä′-rä	kee-mah′-rah
Albanian *Himarë*, q.v.		
China	*Eng.* chī′-nə	chai′-nuh
Chinese *Ch'ung-hua Min-k'uo*, cho͝ong-whä mĭn-kwô [chung-whah min-kwo], Republic of China.		
Chi-nan (Ch., Shantung)	jē-nän	jee-nahn
Also spelled *Tsi-nan*. Also called *Li-cheng*, q.v.		
Chin-ch'êng (Ch., Shansi)	jĭn-chŭng	jin-chuhng
Chin-ch'i (Ch., Kiangsi)	jĭn-chē	jin-chee
Chindwin (Burma)	chĭn′-dwĭn	chin′-dwin
Chinese	chī-nēz′ *or* -nēs′	chai-neez′ *or* -nees′
The pronunciation chī-nēz′ [chai-neez′] is preferable. See *Japanese*.		
Ching-an (Ch., Kiangsi)	jĭng-än	jing-ahn
Ch'ing-chiang (Ch., Kiangsi)	chĭng-jyäng	ching-jyahng
Ch'ing-hai (Ch., prov.)	chĭng-hī	ching-hai
Also called *Koko Nor*, q.v., and *Kuku Nor*.		
Ching-hai (Ch., Hopeh, Shantung)	jĭng-hī	jing-hai
Ching-mên (Ch., Hupeh)	jĭng-mŭn	jing-muhn
Chin Hills (Burma)	chĭn′	chin′
Chin-hsien (Ch., Kiangsi)	jĭn-shyĕn	jin-shyen
Chin-hwa (Ch., Chekiang)	jĭn-whä	jin-whah
Also spelled *Kin-hwa*, q.v.		
Ch'in-hwang-tao (Ch., Hopeh)	chĭn-whäng-dou	chin-whahng-dau
Chi-ning (Ch., Shantung, Suiyüan)	jē-nĭng	jee-ning

Ch'in-ju (Korea)	chĭn-rōō *or* -jōō	chin-roo *or* -joo
Ch'in-kai (Korea)	chĭn-kī	chin-kai
Chin-kiang (Ch., Kiangsu)	*Eng.* chĭn-kyăng	chin-kyang
Variant of *Chên-chiang*, q.v.		
Ch'in-nam-po (Korea)	chĭn-näm-pô	chin-nahm-po
Chioggia (It.)	kyôd′-jä	kyod′-jah
Chios (Gr.)	*Eng.* kī′-ŏs	kai′-os
	Gr. hē′-ôs	hee′-os
Chiperfield, Robert (U.S. representative)	chĭp′-ər-fēld	chip′-uhr-feeld
Chir (Rus., riv.)	chēr′	cheer′
Chirikof (Alaska, Attu)	chē′-rĭ-kŏf	chee′-ri-kof
Chirpan (Bulg.)	chĭr-pän′	chihr-pahn′
Chirskaya (Rus.)	chēr′-skä-yä	cheer′-skah-yah
Chishima (Jap., isls.)	chē-shē-mä	chee-shee-mah
Russian *Kuril*, q.v.		
Chi-shui (Ch., Kiangsi)	jē-shwā	jee-shway
Ch'i-shui (Ch., Hupeh)	chē-shwā	chee-shway
Chişinău (Rum.)	kē-shē-nû′-ŏŏ	kee-shee-nuh′-u
Russian *Kishinev*, q.v.		
Chita (Rus.)	chĭ-tä′	chi-tah′
Chitral (India)	chĭ-träl′	chi-trahl′
Chittagong (India)	chĭt′-ə-gŏng	chit′-uh-gong
Chiu-chiang (Ch., Kiangsi)	jyōō-jyäng	jyoo-jyahng
Also spelled *Kiu-kiang*, q.v.		
Chiunzi (It., pass)	kyōōn′-dzē	kyoon′-dzee
Chiusa (It.)	kyōō′-sä	kyoo′-sah
Chiusi (It.)	kyōō′-sē	kyoo′-see
Chkaloff (Rus.)	chkä′-lŏf	chkah′-lof
Chmielnik (Pol.)	k(h)myĕl′-nĭk	k(h)myel′-nik
Russian *Khmyelnik.*		
Chodzież (Pol.)	hô′-jĕsh	ho′-jesh
German *Kolmar*, q.v.		
Choiseul (Oc.)	shwä-zûl′	shwah-zœl′
Chojnice (Pol.)	hoi-nē′-tsĕ	hoi-nee′-tseh
Cholon (Indo-Ch.)	*Fr.* shô-lôN′	shaw-loN′
	Indo. chə-lûn′	chuh-luhn′
Chomudinza (Rus.)	chŏ-mŏŏ-dēn′-tsä	cho-mu-deen′-tsah
Chomůtov (Cz.)	hô′-mōō-tôf	ho′-moo-tof
Chorzów (Pol.)	hô′-zhŏŏf	ho′-zhuf
Chosen (Korea)	chō-sĕn	choh-sen
Choshi (Jap.)	chô-shē	cho-shee
Chott Djerid (Tun.)	shŏt jĕ-rēd′	shot jeh-reed′

Chott el Fedjadj (Tun.)	shŏt ĕl fə-jăj′	shot el fuh-jaj′
Chott Melghir (Tun.)	shŏt mĕl-gēr′	shot mel-geer′
Also called *Chott Melrir*, shŏt mĕl-rēr′ [shot mel-reer′].		
Chouigi (Tun.)	shwē′-gē	shwee′-gee
Christiansund (Nor.)	krĭs′-tyän-so͝on′	kris′-tyahn-sun′
Variant spelling of *Kristiansund*.		
Chrzanów (Pol.)	k(h)zhä′-no͝of	k(h)zhah′-nuf
Ch'uan-chow (Ch., Fukien)	chwän-jō	chwahn-joh
Chu-chi (Ch., Chekiang)	jo͞o-jē	joo-jee
Ch'ü-ching (Ch., Yünnan)	chü-jĭng	chü-jing
Ch'u-chow (Ch., Chekiang)	*Eng.* cho͞o-chou *Ch.* cho͞o-jō	choo-chau choo-joh
Chudovo (Rus.)	cho͞o′-dŏ-vŏ	choo′-do-vo
Chudskoye ozero (Rus., Est., lake)	*Rus.* cho͝od-skô′-yĕ ô′-zĕ-rŏ	chud-sko′-yeh o′-zeh-ro
Estonian *Peipsijärv*, q.v.		
Chuguchak (Ch., Sinkiang)	cho͞o′-go͞o-chäk′	choo′-goo-chahk′
Also called *Tahcheng*, q.v.		
Chuguev (Rus.)	cho͝o-go͞o′-yĕf	chu-goo′-yef
Ch'ü-hsien (Ch., Chekiang)	chü-shyĕn	chü-shyen
Chu-ki Variant of *Chu-chi*, q.v.		
Chukok (Burma)	cho͝o-kōk′	chu-kohk′
Chumphon (Thai)	cho͝om-pôn′	chum-pawn′
Chumukan (Rus.)	cho͞o-mo͞o-kän′	choo-moo-kahn′
Ch'ung-i (Ch., Kiangsi)	cho͝ong-ē	chung-ee
Ch'ung-jin (Korea)	cho͝ong-jĭn	chung-jin
Ch'ung-ju (Korea)	cho͝ong-ro͞o *or* -jo͞o	chung-roo *or* -joo
Chung-king (Ch., Szechwan, Yünnan)	*Eng.* cho͝ong-kĭng *Ch.* jo͝ong-chĭng	chung-king jung-ching
Chung-tien (Yünnan)	jŭng-dyĕn	juhng-dyen
Ch'ung-yang (Ch., Hupeh)	cho͝ong-yäng	chung-yahng
Chuniksak (Alaska, Attu)	cho͞o′-nĭk-săk′	choo′-nik-sak′
Ch'u Shih-ming (Ch. general)	cho͞o shû-mĭng	choo shuh-ming
Chust (Cz.)	ho͞ost′	hoost′
Hungarian spelling *Huszt*.		
Ch'wan-shih (Ch., Fukien, isl.)	chwän-shû	chwahn-shuh
Ciampino (It.)	chäm-pē′-nô	chahm-pee′-no

Ćićevac (Yugosl.)	chē′-chĕ-väts	chee′-cheh-vahts
Čičevica (Yugosl., mts.)	chē′-chĕ′-vĭ-tsä	chee′-cheh′-vi-tsah
Čičevo, Gornje *and* Dolnje (Yugosl.)	chē′-chĕ-vô, gôr′-nyĕ *and* dôl′-nyĕ	chee′-cheh-vo, gor′-nyeh *and* dol′-nyeh
Ciechanów (Pol.)	chĕ-hä′-no͝of	cheh-hah′-nuf
Russian *Tsyekhanov*, tsĕ-hä′-nŏf [tseh-hah′-nof].		
Ciechanowski, Jan (Pol. leader)	chĕ-hä-nôf′-skĭ, yän′	cheh-hah-nof′-ski, yahn′
Ciechocinek (Pol.)	chĕ-hô-chē′-nĕk	cheh-ho-chee′-nek
Russian *Tsyekhotsinsk*, tsĕ-hŏ-tsēnsk′ [tseh-ho-tseensk′].		
Cieszyn (Pol., Cz.)	*Pol.* chĕ′-shĭn	cheh′-shin
German *Teschen*, q.v.		
Čiflik (Yugosl.)	chē′-flĭk	chee′-flik
Cijevna (Balkan riv.)	*S.-C.* tsē′-yĕv-nä	tsee′-yev-nah
Albanian *Cemi*, q.v.		
Cilento (It.)	chē-lĕn′-tô	chee-len′-to
Cincinnati (Ohio)	sĭn′-sĭ-năt′-ĭ *or* -ə	sin′-si-nat′-i *or* -uh
See *Missouri.*		
Cinquefronde (It.)	chēn′-kwĕ-frôn′-dĕ	cheen′-kweh-fron′-deh
Cinto (Corsica, mt.)	chēn′-tô	cheen′-to
Ciotat, la (Fr.)	syô-tä′, lä	syo-tah′, lah
Čiovo (Yugosl.)	chē′-ô-vô	chee′-o-vo
Italian *Bua*, q.v.		
Circassia (Rus.)	*Eng.* sər-kăsh′-ə	suhr-kash′-uh
Circeo (It., mt.)	chēr-chĕ′-ô	cheer-cheh′-o
Cirene (Libya) See *Cyrene.*		
Cisterna (It.)	chēs-tĕr′-nä	chees-tehr′-nah
Čitluk (Yugosl.)	chēt′-lo͞ok	cheet′-look
Città (It.)	chēt-tä′	cheet-tah′
Città Vecchia (It., Yugosl.)	chēt-tä′ vĕk′-kyä	cheet-tah′ vek′-kyah
Ciudad Juárez (Mex.)	syo͞o-*thäth*′ hwä′-rĕs	syoo-*thahth*′ hwah′-res
Local English hwŏr′-ĭz [hwor′-iz].		
Ciudad Real (Sp.)	thyo͞o-*thäth*′ (*or* syo͞o-) rĕ-äl′	thyoo-*thahth*′ (*or* syoo-) reh-ahl′
Civitavecchia (It.)	chē′-vē-tä-vĕk′-kyä	chee′-vee-tah-vek′-kyah
Cizre (Turk.)	jĭz′-rĕ′	jiz′-reh′
Clason, Charles R. (U.S. representative)	klā′-sən	klay′-suhn

Clemenceau, Georges (Fr. leader)	klĕ-mäN-sō′, zhôrzh′	kleh-mahN-soh′, zhorzh′
Clercken (Belg.)	klĕr′-kən	klehr′-kuhn
Clevenger, Cliff (U.S. representative)	klĕv′-ən-jər	klev′-uhn-juhr
Cliveden (Eng.)	klĭv′-dən	kliv′-duhn

The first syllable has the vowel of the verb, to *live.*

Cloncurry (Austral.)	klŏn-kûr′-ĭ	klon-kuhr′-i
cloture	klō′-chər	kloh′-chuhr
Cluj (Rum.)	klo͝ozh′	kluzh′

Hungarian *Kolozsvár,* kô′-lôzh-vär [ko′-lozh-vahr]. German *Klausenburg,* klou′-zən-bo͝ork(h) [klau′-zuhn-burk(h)].

Coblenz (Ger.)	kō′-blĕnts	koh′-blents

Also spelled *Koblenz,* q.v.

Cobourg (Austral.)	kō′-bûrg	koh′-buhrg
Cocanada (India)	kō-kə-nä′-də	koh-kuh-nah′-duh
Cochin (India)	kō′-chĭn′	koh′-chin′
Cochin China (Indo-Ch.)	kō′-chĭn chī′-nə	koh′-chin chai′-nuh

French *Cochinchine,* kô-shăN-shēn′ [ko-shaN-sheen′].

Cocos (Ind. Oc.)	kō′-kōs	koh′-kohs

Also called *Keeling Isls.,* q.v.

Coesfeld (Ger.)	kōs′-fĕlt	kohs′-felt
Coimbra (Port.)	kwēm′-brə	kweem′-bruh
Colban, Erik (Nor. leader)	kōl′-bän	kohl′-bahn

Colli Euganei (It.) See *Euganean Hills.*

Colmar (Fr.)	*Fr.* kôl-mär′	kol-mahr′
	Ger. kôl′-mär	kol′-mahr
Cologne (Ger.)	*Eng.* kə-lōn′	kuh-lohn′
	Fr. kô-lôn′(y)	ko-lon′(y)

German *Koeln,* q.v.

Colomb Béchar (Alg.)	kô-lôNb′ bĕ-shär′	ko-loNb′ beh-shahr′
Colombia (S. A)	*Eng.* kə-lŭm′-bĭ-ə	kuh-luhm′-bi-uh
	Sp. kô-lôm′-byä	ko-lom′-byah
Colombo (Ceylon)	kə-lŭm′-bō	kuh-luhm′-boh

Colomea (Pol.) See *Kołomyja.*

Columbia	kə-lŭm′-bĭ-ə	kuh-luhm′-bi-uh

It is best to pronounce the *o* of the first syllable as schwa. The vowel should not disappear, leaving klŭm-bĭ-ə, nor should it be pronounced like the *o* of *go.* Acceptable variants of -bĭ-ə are -bĭ-yə and -byə.

column	kŏl′-əm	kol′-uhm

The pronunciation kŏl′-yəm (and the spelling *colyum*) should be reserved for a newspaper *column.* Both were once comic.

Comacchio (It.)	kô-mäk′-kyô	ko-mahk′-kyo

Combermere (Burma)	kŭm′-bər-mĭr	kuhm′-buhr-mihr
Comines (Fr.)	kô-mēn′	ko-meen′
Comintern (Rus.)	*Eng.* kŏm′-ĭn-tûrn′	kom′-in-tuhrn′

The first syllable should not be pronounced kōm- [kohm-].

Comiso (Sicily)	kô′-mē-zô	ko′-mee-zo
communique	*Eng.* kə-mū′-nĭ-kā′	kuh-myoo′-ni-kay′

The pronunciation kū-mū′-nĭ-kā′ [kyoo-myoo′-ni-kay′] tempts many Americans. Cf. *coupon.*

Comorin (India, cape)	kŏm′-ə-rĭn	kom′-uh-rin
Comoro Isls. (E. Afr.)	*Eng.* kŏm′-ə-rō	kom′-uh-roh
Compiegne (Fr.)	kôN-pyĕn′(y)	koN-pyen′(y)
Comrat (Rum.)	kôm-rät′	kom-raht′
Condobolin (Austral.)	kən-dō′-bə-lĭn	kuhn-doh′-buh-lin
condolence	kən-dō′-ləns	kuhn-doh′-luhns

A stress on the first syllable is not recommended.

conduit	kŏn′-do͝o-ĭt *or* kŏn′-dĭt	kon′-du-it *or* kon′-dit

The first is the pronunciation of engineers. An old-fashioned pronunciation is kŭn′-dĭt.

Conjeeveram (India)	kŏn-jē-və-rŭm′	kon-jee-vuh-ruhm′
Čonoplja (Yugosl.)	chô′-nôp-lyä	cho′-nop-lyah
Constance (Ger.)	*Eng.* kŏn′-stəns	kon′-stuhns

German *Konstanz,* q.v.

Constanţa (Rum.)	kôn-stän′-tsä	kon-stahn′-tsah
Constantine (Alg.)	*Eng.* kŏn′-stən-tēn′	kon′-stuhn-teen′
	Fr. kôN-stäN-tēn′	koN-stahN-teen′
Constantinople (Turk)	*Eng.* kŏn′-stăn-tĭ-nō′-pəl	kon′-stan-ti-noh′-puhl

Now officially known as *İstanbul,* q.v.

contact	kŏn′-tăkt	kon′-takt

As a verb meaning to get in touch with a person, this word was overused in the golden age of sales promotion. Though the word suggested interesting metaphors of engineering, it excited objections from purists and many ordinary speakers, probably because they heard it too often. Now the verb seems likely to disappear with other foibles and symbols of the Golden Era. It is best avoided in radio scripts except for established technical phrases, such as *to contact the enemy.*

controversial	kŏn′-trō-vûr′-shəl	kon′-troh-vuhr′-shuhl

The last syllables, *-sial,* should not be pronounced -sĭ-əl [-si-uhl], an unidiomatic pronunciation based upon the spelling. Such false refinements are often the result of bad instruction in stage and concert diction. Radio must have idiomatic American English, and no arty speech can take its place. Announcers must critically examine pronunciations which will leave them open to a charge of being pretentious, affected, and unreal. This -sĭ-əl [-si-uhl] pronunciation is not listed in any dictionary, and it is not characteristic of any variety of American speech. Cf. *issue*.

convoy — *noun* kŏn′-voi — kon′-voi
verb kŏn-voi′ — kon-voi′

A principal stress on the first syllable of the verb still sounds awkward to many listeners.

Coo (Dodec.) — *It.* kô′-ô — ko′-o

Greek *Kos*, q.v.

Cooma (Austral.) — ko͞o′-mä *or* -mə — koo′-mah *or* -muh

Cooper, Jere (U.S. representative) — ko͝op′-ər, jĕr′-ĭ — kup′-uhr, jehr′-i

Cootamundra (Austral.) — ko͞o′-tə-mŭn′-drə — koo′-tuh-muhn′-druh

Čop (Cz.) — chôp′ — chop′

Hungarian *Csap*, chŏp′ [chop′].

Copacabana (Braz., Bol., Col.) — *Port.* kô-pə-kə-bä′-nə — ko-puh-kuh-bah′-nuh
Sp. kô-pä-kä-bä′-nä — ko-pah-kah-bah′-nah

Not *Copacabanha* nor *Copacabaña*.

Copanello (It.) — kô-pä-nĕl′-lô — ko-pah-nel′-lo

Copenhagen (Den.) — *Eng.* kō-pən-hā′-gən — koh-puhn-hay′-guhn

Copenhagen is the English variant of the Danish *Köbenhavn*. It should be pronounced as English with long *a* as in *haven*. A broad "ah", as in *Harvard*, does not give the native pronunciation, for *Köbenhavn* is pronounced kûpn-houn′ [kœpn-haun′].

Corab (Balkan mts.) See *Korab*.

Corabia (Rum.) — kô-rä′-byä — ko-rah′-byah

Córdoba (Sp.) — kôr′-*th*ô-bä — kor′-*th*o-bah

English *Cordova*, kôr′-də-və [kor′-duh-vuh].

Corfù (Gr.) — *Eng.* kôr′-fū — kor′-fyoo
It. kôr-fo͞o′ — kor-foo′

Greek *Kerkyra*, q.v.

Cories (Attu, lake) — kôr′-ĭz — kor′-iz

Corigliano (It.) — kô-rē-lyä′-nô — ko-ree-lyah′-no

Corinth (Gr.) — *Eng.* kŏr′-ĭnth — kor′-inth

Greek *Korinthos*, kô′-rĭn-thôs [ko′-rin-thos]. The gulf is also called *Lepanto*, (Eng.) lĭ-păn′-tō [li-pan′-toh).

Corizza (Alb.) — *It.* kô-rēt′-sä — ko-reet′-sah

Albanian *Korrçë*, q.v.

Corleone (Sicily) — kôr-lĕ-ô′-nĕ — kor-leh-o′-neh

Çorlu (Turk.) — chôr′-lo͝o′ — chor′-lu′

Corneliussen, Elias (Nor. admiral) — kōr-nā′-lĭ-o͝os′n, ĕ-lē′-äs — kohr-nay′-li-us′n, eh-lee′-ahs

Corogna (Sicily) — kô-rô′-nyä — ko-ro′-nyah

Coromandel (India) — kŏr′-ō-măn′-dəl — kor′-oh-man′-duhl

Corrêa, Jonas (Braz. leader)	kô-rā′-ə, zhô′-nəs	ko-ray′-uh, zho′-nuhs
Corregidor (P.I.)	*Eng.* kə-rĕg′-ĭ-dōr′	kuh-reg′-i-dohr′
	Sp. kô-rĕ′-hē-dôr′	ko-reh′-hee-dor′

The first is favored by men who have served in the Philippines.

Correio da Manhã (Braz. newspaper)	kô-rā′-o͝o də mə-nyäN′	ko-ray′-u duh muh-nyahN′
Correnti (Sicily, cape)	kôr-rĕn′-tē	kor-ren′-tee
Corsica (Med., isl.)	*Eng.* kôr′-sĭ-kə	kor′-si-kuh
	It. kôr′-sē-kä	kor′-see-kah

French *Corse*, kôrs′ [kors′].

Corte (Corsica)	kôr′-tĕ	kor′-teh
Cortina d'Ampezzo (It.)	kôr-tē′-nä däm-pĕt′-sô	kor-tee′-nah dahm-pet′-so
Coruña (Sp.)	kô-ro͞o′-nyä	ko-roo′-nyah
Cos (Dodec.) See *Kos.*		
Cosenza (It.)	kô-zĕn′-tsä	ko-zen′-tsah
Costa, Fernando (Braz. leader)	kôs′-tə, fĕr-näN′-do͝o	kos′-tuh, fehr-nahN′-du

Fernando may approach fĕr-nĕN′-do͝o [fehr-neN′-du].

Costa, Sousa (Braz. leader)	kôs′-tə, sō′-zə	kos′-tuh, soh′-zuh

Both names should be used, thus: *Sousa Costa*, not *Costa* alone.

Costa, Zenóbio da (Braz. general)	kôs′-tə, zĕ-nôb′-yo͝o də	kos′-tuh, zeh-nob′-yu duh
Cotabato (P.I.)	kô-tä-bä′-tô	ko-tah-bah′-to
Côtes du Nord (Fr.)	kōt dü nôr′	koht dü nor′
Cottian Alps (Fr., Switz.)	kŏt′-ĭ-ən	kot′-i-uhn
coupon	ko͞o′-pŏn *or* kū′-pŏn	koo′-pon *or* kyoo′-pon

The pronunciation of *coupon* is hotly debated. The *Thorndike-Century Dictionary* (1941) lists ko͞o′-pŏn [koo′-pon] first and kū′-pŏn [kyoo′-pon] second. *Webster's* (1934, 1936) gives ko͞o′-pŏn and adds, "in U.S. often, incorrectly, kū′-pŏn." However, soap dramas usually prefer kū′-pŏn [kyoo′-pon], and we hear it also from some of our most eloquent and most intelligent speakers. In time it may even win first place, but at present it is probably second to ko͞o′-pŏn [koo′-pon].

Cournarie, Pierre Charles (Fr. general)	ko͞or-nä-rē′, pyĕr′ shärl′	koor-nah-ree′, pyehr′ shahrl′
Coursan (Fr.)	ko͞or-säN′	koor-sahN′
Courseulles (Fr.)	ko͞or-sûl′	koor-sœl′
Courtney, Wirt (U.S. representative)	kōrt′-nĭ, wûrt′	kohrt′-ni, wuhrt′
Courtrai (Belg.)	*Fr.* ko͞or-trĕ′	koor-treh′

Flemish *Kortrijk*, q.v.

Coutras (Fr.)	kōō-trä′	koo-trah′
Coventry (Eng., U.S.)	kŭv′-ən-trĭ *or* kŏv′-	kuhv′-uhn-tri *or* kov′-
The BBC prefers the latter, but the former, with its eighteenth-century flavor, is more common in the United States.		
Cowell (Austral.)	kou′-əl	kau′-uhl
Cozmeni (Rum.)	kôz-mĕn′	koz-men′
Cracow (Pol.)	*Eng.* krăk′-ou *or* krăk′-ō *or* krā′-kō	krak′-au *or* krak′-oh *or* kray′-koh
	Ger. krä′-kou	krah′-kau
Polish *Kraków*, krä′-kŏŏf [krah′-kuf]. Russian *Krakov*, krä′-kŏf [krah′-kof].		
Craiova (Rum.)	krä-yô′-vä	krah-yo′-vah
Cravens, Fadjo (U.S. representative)	krā′-vənz, făd′-jō	kray′-vuhnz, fad′-joh
Crécy en Ponthieu (Fr.)	krĕ-sē′ äN pôN-tyû′	kreh-see′ ahN poN-tyœ′
credence	krē′-dəns *or* krēd′ns	kree′-duhns *or* kreed′ns
Not krā′-dəns [kray′-duhns].		
credo	*Eng.* krē′-dō	kree′-doh
	Lat. krā′-dō	kray′-doh
Crema (It.)	krĕ′-mä	kreh′-mah
Cremona (It.)	krĕ-mô′-nä	kreh-mo′-nah
Crepaja (Yugosl.)	tsrĕ′-pä-yä	tsreh′-pah-yah
Cres (It., isl.)	*S.-C.* tsrĕs′	tsres′
Italian *Cherso*, q.v.		
Crest (Fr.)	krĕst′	krest′
Crete (Gr., isl.)	*Eng.* krēt′	kreet′
Greek *Krete*, krē′-tē [kree′-tee].		
Créteil (Fr.)	krĕ-tĕ′(y)	kreh-teh′(y)
Creteville (Tun.)	krĕt-vēl′	kret-veel′
Creuse (Fr., riv.)	krûz′	krœz′
Creusot, le (Fr.)	krû-zō′, lə	krœ-zoh′, luh
Crionero (Alb.)	*It.* krē-ô-nĕ′-rô	kree-o-neh′-ro
Albanian *Kaninë*, q.v.		
Criquetot l'Esneval (Fr.)	krēk-tō′ lĕs-nə-väl′ *or* lĕ-nə-väl′	kreek-toh′ les-nuh-vahl′ *or* leh-nuh-vahl′
Cristobal	*Eng.* krĭs-tō′-bəl	kris-toh′-buhl
	Sp. krēs-tô′-bäl	krees-to′-bahl
Crkvena planina (Yugosl., mt.)	tsər′-kvĕ-nä plä′-nē′-nä	tsuhr′-kveh-nah plah′-nee′-nah

Crkvenica (Yugosl.)	tsərk′-vĕ′-nĭ-tsä	tsuhrk′-veh′-ni-tsah
Crkvice (Yugosl.)	tsər′-kvĭ-tsĕ	tsuhr′-kvi-tseh
Crljenac (Yugosl.)	tsər′-lyĕ-näts	tsuhr′-lyeh-nahts
Crljeni, Veliki (Yugosl.)	tsər′-lyĕ-nĭ, vĕ′-lĭ-kĭ	tsuhr′-lyeh-ni, veh′-li-ki
Crna (Yugosl., riv.)	tsər′-nä	tsuhr′-nah
Crna Bara (Yugosl.)	tsər′-nä bä′-rä	tsuhr′-nah bah′-rah
Crna Gora (Yugosl., mts.)	tsər′-nä gô′-rä	tsuhr′-nah go′-rah
Italian *Montenegro*, q.v. Former kingdom.		
Crnajka (Yugosl.)	tsər′-nī-kä	tsuhr′-nai-kah
Crniće, Veliko *and* Malo (Yugosl.)	tsər′-nĭ-chĕ, vĕ′-lĭ-kô *and* mä′-lô	tsuhr′-ni-cheh, veh′-li-ko *and* mah′-lo
Crni Drim (Balkan riv.)	tsər′-nĭ drēm′	tsuhr′-ni dreem′
Albanian *Drin i zi*, q.v.		
Crni Rt (Yugosl.)	tsər′-nĭ ərt′	tsuhr′-ni uhrt′
Crni Rzav (Yugosl.)	tsər′-nĭ ər′-zäv	tsuhr′-ni uhr′-zahv
Crnoljeva planina (Yugosl., mts.)	tsər′-nô′-lyĕ-vä plä′-nē′-nä	tsuhr′-no′-lyeh-vah plah′-nee′-nah
Črnomelj (Yugosl.)	chər′-nô-mĕl′(y)	chuhr′-no-mel′(y)
Crnook (Yugosl., mt.)	tsər′-nô-ôk′	tsuhr′-no-ok′
Croat	krō′-ăt	kroh′-at
Avoid krōt [kroht]. Serb-Croat *Hrvat*, q.v.		
Croatia (Yugosl.)	*Eng.* krô-ā′-shə	kro-ay′-shuh
Serb-Croat *Hrvatska*, q.v.		
Croce (It.)	krô′-chĕ	kro′-cheh
Croce, Benedetto (It. leader)	krô′-chĕ, bĕ-nĕ-dĕt′-tô	kro′-cheh, beh-neh-det′-to
Croia (Alb.)	*It.* krô′-yä	kro′-yah
Albanian *Krujë*, q.v.		
Croton (N.Y.)	krōt′n	kroht′n
The analogy of *Groton* (q.v.) is misleading.		
Crotone (It.)	krô-tô′-nĕ	kro-to′-neh
Crvena Jabuka (Yugosl.)	tsər′-vĕ-nä yä′-bo͞o-kä	tsuhr′-veh-nah yah′-boo-kah
Crvena Reka (Yugosl.)	tsər′-vĕ-nä rĕ′-kä	tsuhr′-veh-nah reh′-kah
Crvenka (Yugosl.)	tsər′-vĕn-kä	tsuhr′-ven-kah
Cs- For Serb-Croat names beginning with *Cs-*, see *C-* (*Č-*).		
Csap (Cz.) See *Čop*.		
Csepel (Hung., isl.)	chĕ′-pĕl	cheh′-pel
Village on island may also be called *Ráczkeve*, q.v.		
Csongrád (Hung.)	chông′-gräd	chong′-grahd
Cuddalore (India)	kŭd-ə-lōr′	kuhd-uh-lohr′

Cuenca (Sp.)	kwĕng′-kä	kweng′-kah
Cuernavaca (Mex.)	kwĕr-nä-vä′-kä	kwehr-nah-vah′-kah
Cugat, Xavier (Am.)	ko͞o′-gät′, ĕk-sā′-vĭ-ər	koo′-gaht′, ek-say′-vi-uhr
Cuiabá (Brazil)	ko͞o-yə-bä′	koo-yuh-bah′
Čukarica (Yugosl.)	cho͞o′-kä′-rĭ-tsä	choo′-kah′-ri-tsah
Çukat (Alb., mt.) See *Tomor.*		
Cum Burnu (Dodec., Rh., point)	*Turk.* ko͝om bo͝or-no͝o′	kum bur-nu′
Greek *Zonari,* zô-nä′-rē [zo-nah′-ree]. Italian *Punta Molino,* po͞on′-tä mô-lē′-nô [poon′-tah mo-lee′-no], and *Capo della Sabbia,* kä′-pô dĕl′-lä säb′-byä [kah′-po del′-lah sahb′-byah].		
Cuneo (It.)	ko͞o′-nĕ-ô	koo′-neh-o
French *Coni,* kô-nē′ [ko-nee′].		
Cunnamulla (Austral.)	kŭn′-ə-mŭl′-ə	kuhn′-uh-muhl′-uh
Čupino Brdo (Yugosl., mts.)	cho͞o′-pĭ-nô bər′-dô	choo′-pi-no buhr′-do
Ćuprija (Yugosl.)	cho͞o′-prĭ-yä	choo′-pri-yah
Curaçao (Du. W. I.)	*Eng.* kū′-rə-sō′	kyoo′-ruh-soh′
	for. ko͞o-rä-sou′	koo-rah-sau′
Curie, Marja Skłodowska (Pol. scientist)	kü-rē′ (*Eng.* kū-rē′), mär′-yä sklŏ-dôf′-skä	kü-ree′ (*Eng.* kyoo-ree′), mahr′-yah sklo-dof′-skah
——, Ève (author)	——, ĕv′ (*Eng.* ēv′)	——, ev′ (*Eng.* eev′)
Curitiba (Brazil)	ko͞o-rē-tē′-bə	koo-ree-tee′-buh
curmudgeon	kər-mŭj′-ən	kuhr-muhj′-uhn
Curtici (Rum.)	ko͝or-tēch′	kur-teech′
Čurug (Yugosl.)	cho͞o′-ro͞og	choo′-roog
Curzola (Yugosl.)	*It.* ko͞or-tsô′-lä	koor-tso′-lah
Serb-Croat *Korčula,* q.v.		
Cutch (India)	kŭch	kuhch
Also spelled *Kutch.*		
Cuttack (India)	kŭ-tăk′	kuh-tak′
Cuxhaven (Ger.)	ko͝oks′-hä-fən	kuks′-hah-fuhn
Cuzgan (Rum.)	ko͝oz-gän′	kuz-gahn′
Cyclades (Gr., isls.)	*Eng.* sĭk′-lə-dēz	sik′-luh-deez
	Gr. kē-klä′-*th*ĕs	kee-klah′-*th*es
Cyllene (Gr., mt.) See *Kyllene.*		
Cyrenaica (Libya)	sĭ-rə-nā′-ĭ-kə	si-ruh-nay′-i-kuh
	or sī′-rə-nā′-ĭ-kə	sai′-ruh-nay′-i-kuh
Not sĭ-rə-nī′-ĭ-kə [si-ruh-nai′-i-kuh].		
Cyrene (Libya)	*Eng.* sī-rē′-nē	sai-ree′-nee
Italian *Cirene,* chē-rĕ′-nĕ [chee-reh′-neh].		
Cythera (Gr., isl.) See *Kythera.*		

Czarna (Pol., riv.) chär′-nä chahr′-nah
Russian *Chernaya*, chôr′-nä-yä [chor′-nah-yah].

Czech *Eng.* chĕk′ chek′
Czech is the Polish spelling for Czechish *Čech*, chĕk(h)′ [chek(h)′], "a Bohemian." The Bohemian language is *Český*, chĕs′-kē [ches′-kee].

Czeladź (Pol.) chĕ′-läj cheh′-lahj
German *Tscheliadz*, chĕl′-yädz [chel′-yahdz]. Russian spelling *Chelyadz.*

Czeremosz (Pol., Rum., riv.) chĕ-rĕ′-môsh cheh-reh′-mosh
Rumanian *Ceremuşul*, chĕ-rĕ′-mo͝o-sho͝ol [cheh-reh′-mu-shul].

Czernowitz (Rum.) *Pol.* chĕr′-nô-vĭts chehr′-no-vits
Rumanian *Cernăuţi*, q.v.

Czersk (Pol.) chĕrsk′ chehrsk′

Częstochowa (Pol.) chăN-stô-hô′-vä chaN-sto-ho′-vah
Russian *Chenstokhov*, chĕn-stô′-hŏf [chen-sto′-hof]. German *Tschenstochau*, chĕn-shtō′-k(h)ou [chen-shtoh′-k(h)au].

Czortków (Pol.) chôrt′-ko͝of chort′-kuf

D- For some Yugoslav names spelled with *D-*, it may be necessary to look under *Dj-*.

daal däl′ dahl′
An element, meaning *valley*, in Dutch place names.

Daba, el (Libya) däb′-ä, ĕd dahb′-ah, ed

Dabir Soula (Tun.) dă′-bēr so͞o′-lä da′-beer soo′-lah

Dąbrowa Górnicza (Pol.) dôN-brô′-vä go͝or-nē′-chä doN-bro′-vah gur-nee′-chah
Russian *Dombrova*, dŏm-brô′-vä [dom-bro′-vah].

Dąbrowica (Pol.) dôN-brô-vē′-tsä doN-bro-vee′-tsah
Russian *Dombrovitsa*, dŏm-brô′-vĭ-tsä [dom-bro′-vi-tsah].

Dacca (India) dăk′-ə dak′-uh

Dachau (Ger.) dä′-k(h)ou dah′-k(h)au

Daet (P.I.) dä′-ĕt dah′-et

Dafne (Gr.) *Eng.* dăf′-nĭ daf′-ni
Gr. *th*äf′-nē *th*ahf′-nee

Dafni (Gr.) *th*äf-nē′ thahf-nee′

Dage (Est., isl.) *Rus.* dä′-gĕ dah′-geh
Estonian *Hiiumaa*, q.v. German *Dagö*, q.v.

Daghestan (Rus.) dä-gĕ-stän′ dah-geh-stahn′

Dagö (Est., isl.) *Ger.* dä′-gû dah′-gœ
Estonian *Hiiumaa*, q.v. Russian *Dage*, q.v.

Dagoe (Est., isl.) *Ger.* dä′-gû dah′-gœ
Estonian *Hiiumaa*, q.v. Russian *Dage*, q.v.

Dagupan (P.I.)	dä-gōō′-pän	dah-goo′-pahn
dahlia	dăl′-yə *or* däl′-yə *or* dāl′-yə	dal′-yuh *or* dahl′-yuh *or* dayl′-yuh
Dail Eireann (Ir.)	dôl′ ā′-rôn	dol′ ay′-ron
Daiquirí (Cuba)	dī-kē-rē′	dai-kee-ree′
Dairen (Manchu.)	dī-rĕn	dai-ren
Also called *Ta-lien(-wan)*, q.v. Russian *Dalny*, däl′(y)-nĭ [dahl′(y)-ni].		
Dajt (Alb., mt.)	dīt′	dait′
Also called *Mal i Dajtit*.		
Đak (Yugosl., mt.)	dyäk′	dyahk′
Dakar (Afr.)	dä′-kär′	dah′-kahr′
Đakovica (Yugosl.)	dyä′-kô-vĭ-tsä	dyah′-ko-vi-tsah
dal *or* dalen	däl′ *or* dä′-lən	dahl′ *or* dah′-luhn
An element, meaning *valley*, in Norwegian place names.		
Dalaguete (P.I.)	dä-lä-gĕ′-tĕ	dah-lah-geh′-teh
Dalat (Indo-Ch.)	dä-lät′	dah-laht′
Dale (Nor.)	dä′-lə	dah′-luh
Dalen (Nor.)	dä′-lən	dah′-luhn
D'Alesandro, Thomas, Jr. (U.S. representative)	dăl′-ĭ-săn′-drō	dal′-i-san′-droh
Đalica (Alb., mt.) See *Gjalicë*.		
Dalmatia (Yugosl.)	*Eng.* dăl-mā′-shə	dal-may′-shuh
Serb-Croat *Dalmacija*, däl′-mä′-tsĭ-yä [dahl′-mah′-tsi-yah].		
Dalny (Manchu.) See *Dairen*.		
Daluege, Kurt (Ger.)	dä-lü′-gə, kŏŏrt′	dah-lü′-guh, kurt′
Daman *or* Damão (Port. India)	dä′-män′ *or* dä-mouN′	dah′-mahn′ dah-mauN′
Damanhur (Egypt)	dä-män-hŏŏr′	dah-mahn-hur′
Damba Gavan (Latvia)	*Rus.* däm′-bä gä′-vän(y)	dahm′-bah gah′-vahn(y)
Dâmbovița (Rum., riv.)	dûm′-bô-vē-tsä	duhm′-bo-vee-tsah
Damghan (Iran)	däm-gän′	dahm-gahn′
Damietta (Egypt)	dăm-ĭ-ĕt′-ə	dam-i-et′-uh
Also called *Dumyat*, q.v.		
Dampier (Austral.)	dăm′-pĭr	dam′-pihr
Danaher, John A. (U.S. senator)	dăn′-ə-hûr	dan′-uh-huhr
Danbi (Burma)	dən-bē′	duhn-bee′
Dangila (Ethiopia)	dän′-gû-lä	dahn′-guh-lah
Danilovgrad (Yugosl.)	dä′-nē′-lôf-gräd	dah′-nee′-lof-grahd
Dankov (Rus.)	dän′-kŏf	dahn′-kof
Dannemora (N. Y.)	dăn′-ĭ-mô′-rə	dan′-i-mo′-ruh
d'Annunzio (It. leader)	dän-nōōn′-tsyô	dahn-noon′-tsyo
Dansalan (P.I.)	dän-sä′-län	dahn-sah′-lahn

Danube (Europ. riv.) *Eng.* dăn′-ūb dan′-yoob
Fr. dä-nüb′ dah-nüb′

The variations of the name of this great river are indicative of the problem of finding a "correct" pronunciation of any ancient landmark in Central Europe. We are fortunate when there is an established English form, in this instance as in many others derived from the French. Bulgarian *Dunav*, dŏŏ′-näf [du′-nahf]. Czech and Polish *Dunaj*, dŏŏ′-nī [du′-nai]. Italian *Danubio*, dä-nōō′-byô [dah-noo′-byo]. German *Donau*, dō′-nou [doh′-nau]. Greek *Dounabis*, *th*ōō′-nä-vēs [*th*oo′-nah-vees]. Hungarian *Duna*, dŏŏ′-nŏ [du′-no]. Rumanian *Dunărea*, dŏŏ′-nə-ryä [du′-nuh-ryah]. Russian *Dunai*, dōō-nī′ [doo-nai′] Serb-Croat *Dunav*, dōō′-näv [doo′-nahv.] And the vowels here marked are, of course, polite fictions. There are two classical forms: Greek *Istros*, ē′-strôs [ee′-stros]; Latin *Danuvius*, dä-nōō′-wē-ōōs [dah-noo′-wee-oos] and *Ister* or *Hister*, (h)ē′-stĕr [(h)ee′-stehr].

Danzig *Eng.* dăn′-sĭg dan′-sig
Ger. dän′-tsĭk(h) dahn′-tsik(h)

Polish *Gdańsk*, gdän(y)sk′ [gdahn(y)sk′].

Dapitan (P.I.) dä-pē′-tän dah-pee′-tahn

Dar For Arabic names with *Dar*, see *Deir*.

Đaravica (Yugosl., mt.) dyä′-rä′-vĭ-tsä dyah′-rah′-vi-tsah

Darband (Iran) där-bănd′ dahr-band′

Darbėnai (Lith.) där-bā′-nī dahr-bay′-nai

Darda (Yugosl.) där′-dä dahr′-dah

Dardanelles (Turk., strait) *Eng.* där′-də-nĕlz′ dahr′-duh-nelz′

Turkish *Çanakkale Boğazı*, chä-näk′-kä-lĕ′ bô-ä′-zĭ [chah-nahk′-kah-leh′ bo-ah′-zi]. Also called the *Hellespont*, (Eng.) hĕl′-əs-pŏnt [hel′-uhs-pont].

Dardha (Alb.) See *Dardhë*.

Dardhë (Alb.) där′-*th*ə dahr′-*th*uh

Darial (Rus., pass) där-yäl′ dahr-yahl′

Darjeeling (India) där-jē′-lĭng dahr-jee′-ling

Darlan, Jean François (Fr. leader) där-läN′, zhäN′ fräN-swä′ dahr-lahN′, zhahN′ frahN-swah′

Darmstadt (Ger.) *Eng.* därm′-stăt dahrm′-stat
Ger. därm′-shtät dahrm′-shtaht

Daru (New Guinea) dä′-rōō dah′-roo

Daruvar (Yugosl.) dä′-rōō-vär dah′-roo-vahr

Daryal (Rus.) där-yäl′ dahr-yahl′

Also spelled *Darial*, q.v.

dasht däsht′ dahsht′

An element, meaning *desert*, in Persian place names.

Dasht-i-Kavir (Iran) däsht′-ē-kə-vēr′ dahsht′-ee-kuh-veer′

Dasht-i-Lut (Iran) däsht′-ē-lōōt′ dahsht′-ee-loot′

Datteln (Ger.)	dät′-əln	daht′-uhln
Daugava (Latvia, Rus., riv.)	dou′-gä-vä	dau′-gah-vah
Russian *Dvina*, q.v. German *Düna*, q.v.		
Daugavgrīva (Latvia)	dou′-gäf-grē-vä	dau′-gahf-gree-vah
German *Dünamünde*, q.v. Russian *Ust Dvinsk*, q.v.		
Daugavpils (Latvia)	dou′-gäf-pēls	dau′-gahf-peels
Russian *Dvinsk*, q.v. German *Dünaburg*, q.v.		
Dauphin, Port (Madag.)	*Eng.* dô′-fĭn	do′-fin
	Fr. dō-făN′	doh-faN′
Davao (P.I.)	*Eng.* dä-vou′	dah-vau′
	native dä′-vou	dah′-vau
Daventry (Eng.)	dăv′-ən-trĭ	dav′-uhn-tri
	or dān′-trĭ	dayn′-tri
David Gorodok (Pol.)	See *Dawidgródek*.	
Dávila (Sp.)	dä′-vē-lä	dah′-vee-lah
Dawidgródek (Pol.)	dä-vĭd-gro͝o′-dĕk	dah-vid-gru′-dek
Russian *David Gorodok*, dä-vēd′ gŏ-rŏ-dôk′ [dah-veed′ go-ro-dok′].		
Deakin, Arthur (Brit. leader)	dē′-kĭn	dee′-kin
Déat, Marcel (Fr. leader)	dĕ-ä′, mär-sĕl′	deh-ah′, mahr-sel′
Deauville (Fr.)	*Eng.* dō′-vĭl	doh′-vil
	Fr. dō-vēl′	doh-veel′
Debaltsevo (Rus.)	dĕ-bäl′(y)-tsĕ-vŏ	deh-bahl′(y)-tseh-vo
Debar (Yugosl.)	dĕ′-bär	deh′-bahr
Albanian *Dibër*, q.v.		
Debeljača (Yugosl.)	dĕ′-bĕ′-lyä-chä	deh′-beh′-lyah-chah
Dębica (Pol.)	dăN-bē′-tsä	daN-bee′-tsah
De Bilt (Neth.)	də bĭlt′	duh bilt′
Dęblin (Pol.)	dăN′-blĭn	daN′-blin
Russian *Ivangorod*, ē-vän′-gŏ-rŏt [ee-vahn′-go-rot].		
Debrc (Yugosl.)	dĕ′-bərts	deh′-buhrts
Debrecen (Hung.)	dĕ′-brĕ-tsĕn	deh′-breh-tsen
Debussy (Fr. composer)	də-bü-sē′	duh-bü-see′
Dictionaries do not list the usual American pronunciation, də-bū′-sē [duh-byoo′-see], although the French pronunciation (above) is very difficult, almost impossible, for us to say in the cadence of an American sentence. Most announcers compromise between the two in order to avoid fluffs. The first syllable should contain schwa (ə), not ā.		
debut *or* début	*Eng.* dā′-bū *or* dĕ-bū′	day′-byoo *or* deh-byoo′
	Fr. dĕ-bü′	deh-bü′
Dečani (Yugosl.)	dĕ′-chä-nĭ	deh′-chah-ni
Dečanska Bistrica (Yugosl.)	dĕ′-chän-skä bē′-strĭ-tsä	deh′-chahn-skah bee′-stri-tsah

De Chevigné, Pierre (Fr. officer)	də shə-vē-nyĕ′, pyĕr′	duh shuh-vee-nyeh′, pyehr′
Decies (Eng. baron)	dē′-shēz	dee′-sheez
Decimomannu (Sard.)	dĕ′-chē-mô-mä′-no͞o	deh′-chee-mo-mah′-noo
Děčín (Cz.)	dyĕ′-chēn	dyeh′-cheen
German *Tetschen*, q.v.		
Decoux, J. (Fr. admiral)	də-ko͞o′	duh-koo′
Dede Agach (Gr.) See *Alexandroupolis*.		
Dedeli (Yugosl.)	dĕ′-dĕ-lĭ	deh′-deh-li
De Gaulle, Charles (Fr. leader)	də gōl′, shärl′	duh gohl′, shahrl′
Dehibat, el (Tun.)	dĕ-hĭ-băt′, ĕd	deh-hi-bat′, ed
Deir el Munassib (Egypt)	dār′ ĕl mo͞o-năs′-sĭb	dayr′ el moo-nas′-sib
Deir el Rahil (Egypt)	dār′ ĕl ră′-hĭl	dayr′ el ra′-hil
Also spelled *Dar* and *Ragil*.		
Dej (Rum.)	dĕzh′	dezh′
Hungarian *Dés*, dāsh′ [daysh′].		
Delden (Neth.)	dĕl′-dən	del′-duhn
De Lemmer (Neth.)	də lĕm′-ər	duh lem′-uhr
Also called *Lemmer*, q.v.		
Delft (Neth.)	dĕlft′	delft′
Delfzijl (Neth.)	dĕlf-zīl′	delf-zail′
Delhi (India)	dĕl′-ĭ	del′-i
Our correspondents agree upon this pronunciation of the Indian city, *New Delhi*. In India, the English approximation "Dilly" is frequently heard. Of course the American place name is dĕl′-hī [del′-hai].		
De Lier (Neth.)	də lēr′	duh leer′
Deligrad (Yugosl.)	dĕ′-lĭ-gräd	deh′-li-grahd
Deli Jovan (Yugosl., mts.)	dĕ′-lĭ yô′-vän	deh′-li yo′-vahn
Dellys (Alg.)	dĕ-lēs′	deh-lees′
Delmenhorst (Ger.)	dĕl′-mən-hôrst′	del′-muhn-horst′
Delnice (Yugosl.)	dĕl′-nĭ-tsĕ	del′-ni-tseh
Delphi (Gr.)	*Eng.* dĕl′-fī	del′-fai
Greek *Delphoi*, *th*ĕl-fē′ [*th*el-fee′].		
Delvina (Alb.) See *Delvinë*.		
Delvinë (Alb.)	dĕl-vē′-nə	del-vee′-nuh
Italian *Delvino*.		
Demavend (Iran, mt.)	dĕ-mə-vĕnd′	deh-muh-vend′
Demetrakakis, Stylianos (Gr. leader)	*th*ē-mē-trä-kä′-kēs, stē-lyä-nôs′	*th*ee-mee-trah-kah′-kees, stee-lyah-nos′
Demir Hissar (Gr.)	*th*ĕ-mēr′ hē-sär′	*th*eh-meer′ hee-sahr′
The official name is *Siderokastron*, q.v.		

Demir Kapija (Yugosl.)	dĕ′-mĭr kä′-pĭ-yä	deh′-mihr kah′-pi-yah
Demotika (Gr.)	*th*ē-mô-tē-kä′	*th*ee-mo-tee-kah′
Officially called *Didymoteikhon,* q.v.		
Demta (NEI)	dĕm′-tä	dem′-tah
Demyansk (Rus.)	dĕm-yänsk′	dem-yahnsk′
Denali (Alaska)	dĭ-nä′-lĭ	di-nah′-li
	sometimes dĭ′-nä-lĭ	di′-nah-li
Den Bos (Neth.)	dən bôs′	duhn bos′
The full name is *'s Hertogenbosch,* q.v. French *Bois le Duc,* bwä lə dük′ [bwah luh dük′].		
Den Briel (Neth.)	dən brēl′	duhn breel′
Also called *Brielle,* q.v.		
Den Burg (Neth.)	dən bûrk(h)′	duhn bœrk(h)′
Den Haag (Neth.)	dən häk(h)′	duhn hahk(h)′
English *The Hague,* q.v. The full name is *'s Gravenhage,* q.v.		
Den Helder (Neth.)	dən hĕl′-dĕr	duhn hel′-dehr
Denia (Sp.)	dĕ′-nyä	deh′-nyah
Đenovići (Yugosl.)	dyĕ′-nô′-vĭ-chĭ	dyeh′-no′-vi-chi
Denpasar (NEI)	dĕn-pä′-sär	den-pah′-sahr
D'Entrecasteaux (Oc.)	däN-trə-käs-tō′	dahN-truh-kahs-toh′
deportation	dē′-pōr-tā′-shən	dee′-pohr-tay′-shuhn
Not dĕ′-pōr-tā′-shən [deh′-pohr-tay′-shuhn].		
depot	dĕp′-ō	dep′-oh
	or dē′-pō	dee′-poh
The first is military usage; the second is more common in civilian usage.		
depravity	dĭ-prăv′-ĭ-tĭ	di-prav′-i-ti
The second syllable should not have the ā of *deprave.*		
Dera Ismail Khan (India)	dā′-rä ĭs-mä-ēl′ kän′	day′-rah is-mah-eel′ kahn′
Derbent (Rus.)	dĕr-bĕnt′	dehr-bent′
Derby (Conn., Vt., and also Austral.)	dûr′-bĭ	duhr′-bi
Derby	*Am. race* dûr′-bĭ	duhr′-bi
	Eng. race där′-bĭ	dahr′-bi
Derbyshire (Eng.)	där′-bĭ-shĭr *or* dûr′-	dahr′-bi-shihr *or* duhr′-
Dereva (Rus.)	dĕ′-rĕ-vä	deh′-reh-vah
Derg (Libya)	dĕrg′	dehrg′
Đerlap (Yugosl., Rum., gorge) See *Iron Gates.*		
Derna (Libya)	dĕr′-nä	dehr′-nah
Derventa (Yugosl.)	dĕr′-vĕn-tä	dehr′-ven-tah
Dés (Rum.) See *Dej.*		
Dešat (Yugosl., mts.)	dĕ′-shät	deh′-shaht
Despoto planina (Balkan mts.) See *Rhodope.*		

Despotovac (Yugosl.)	dĕ′-spô′-tô-väts	deh′-spo′-to-vahts
Dessau (Ger.)	dĕs′-ou	des′-au
Dessie (Ethiopia)	dĕ′-syĕ	deh′-syeh
Desterro (Brazil)	dĕs-tĕ′-ro͞o	des-teh′-ru
Officially called *Florianópolis*, q.v.		
Detinja (Yugosl., riv.)	dĕ′-tĭ-nyä	deh′-ti-nyah
detonator	dĕt′-ō-nā′-tər	det′-oh-nay′-tuhr
Possible but uncommon is dē′-tō-nā′-tər [dee′-toh-nay′-tuhr].		
Detskoe Selo (Rus.)	dĕt′-skŏ-yĕ sĕ-lô′	det′-sko-yeh seh-lo′
Deva (Rum.)	dĕ′-vä	deh′-vah
Hungarian *Déva*, dā′-vŏ [day′-vo].		
De Valera, Eamon	dĕ vä-lĕr′-ə, ā′-mən	deh vah-lehr′-uh, ay′-muhn
	or Irish dĕ vä-lā′-rə	deh vah-lay′-ruh
There are other pronunciations but these are probably the best.		
Đevđelija (Yugosl.)	dyĕv′-dyĕ′-lĭ-yä	dyev′-dyeh′-li-yah
Deve Bajir (Yugosl., mt.)	dĕ′-vĕ bä′-yĭr	deh′-veh bah′-yihr
Deventer (Neth.)	dā′-vən-tər	day′-vuhn-tuhr
Devers, Jacob L. (U.S. general)	dĕv′-ərz	dev′-uhrz
Devica (Yugosl., mts.)	dĕ′-vĭ-tsä	deh′-vi-tsah
Devoll (Alb.)	dĕ′-vôl	deh′-vol
Devolli (Alb.) See *Devoll.*		
Dia (Crete, isl.)	*th*ē′-ä	*th*ee′-ah
Also called *Standia*, stän-dē′-ä [stahn-dee′-ah].		
Diamantina (Austral., riv.)	dī′-ə-mən-tē′-nə	dai′-uh-muhn-tee′-nuh
Diário da Noite (Braz. newspaper)	dē-är′-yo͝o də noi′-tĭ	dee-ahr′-yu duh noi′-ti
Diário de Noticias (Braz. newspaper)	dē-är′-yo͝o dĭ nŏ-tēs′-yəs	dee-ahr′-yu di no-tees′-yuhs
Dibër *or* Dibra (Alb., Yugosl.)	*Alb.* dē′-bər *or* dē′-brä	dee′-buhr *or* dee′-brah
Serb-Croat *Debar*, q.v.		
Dičina (Yugosl., riv.)	dē′-chĭ-nä	dee′-chi-nah
Diciosânmărtin (Rum.)	dē′-chô-sûn-mûr′-tĭn	dee′-cho-suhn-muhr′-tin
Also called *Târnava* (q.v.) *Sânmărtin.*		
Dickstein, Samuel (U.S. representative)	dĭk′-stēn *or* dĭk′-stīn	dik′-steen dik′-stain
dictionary	dĭk′-shən-ĕr′-ĭ	dik′-shuhn-ehr′-i

In American dictionaries the pronunciation dĭk′-shən-ər-ĭ [dik′-shuhn-uhr-i], if given at all, is an alternative and marked, *or especially British.* It is unsuitable for American radio.

Didymoteikhon (Gr.)	*th*ē-*th*ē-mô′-tē-hô(n)	*th*ee-*th*ee-mo′-tee-ho(n)

Commonly called *Demotika*, q.v.

Diego Suarez (Madag.)	dyĕ′-gô swä′-rĕs	dyeh′-go swah′-res
Diember (NEI)	jĕm-bûr′	jem-buhr′
Diepholz (Ger.)	dēp′-hôlts	deep′-holts
Dieppe (Fr.)	*Eng.* dĭ-ĕp′	di-ep′
	Fr. dyĕp′	dyep′
Dieren (Neth.)	dē′-rən	dee′-ruhn
Dies, Martin (U.S. representative)	dīz′	daiz′
Dilasac (P.I., bay)	dē-lä′-säk	dee-lah′-sahk
Dili *or* Dilli (Port. Timor)	dĭl′-ē	dil′-ee
Dilweg, LaVern R. (U.S. representative)	dĭl′-wĭg	dil′-wig
Dimitsana (Gr.)	*th*ē-mē-tsä′-nä	*th*ee-mee-tsah′-nah
Dimond, Antony J. (Alaskan Delegate)	dī′-mənd	dai′-muhnd
Dinagat (P.I.)	dē-nä′-gät	dee-nah′-gaht
Dinan (Fr.)	dē-näN′	dee-nahN′
Dinant (Belg.)	dē-näN′	dee-nahN′
Dinard (Fr.)	dē-när′	dee-nahr′
Dinaric Alps (Yugosl.)	*Eng.* dĭ-năr′-ĭk	di-nehr′-ik

Serb-Croat *Dinarske Planine*, dē′-när-skĕ plä′-nē′-nĕ [dee′-nahr-skeh plah′-nee′-neh].

Dingalan (P.I., bay)	dēng-(n)gä′-län	deeng-(n)gah′-lahn
Dingell, John D. (U.S. representative)	dĭng′-gĕl	ding′-gel
dinghy *or* dingy	dĭng′-gĭ *or* dĭng′-ĭ *sometimes* dēngk′-ĭ *or* dēnk′	ding′-gi *or* ding′-i deengk′-i *or* deenk′

This is another fighting word. The local yachtsmen seem to prefer the second pronunciation. Producers leave *dinghy* in the script at their own risk.

Diosgyőr (Hung.)	dĭ′-ôsh-dyûr	di′-osh-dyœr
Diphrys (Gr., mt.)	*th*ē′-frēs	*th*ee′-frees
Diredawa (Ethiopia)	dē′-rĕ-dä′-wä	dee′-reh-dah′-wah
Dirksen, Everett M. (U.S. representative)	dûrk′-sən	duhrk′-suhn
Dirschau (Pol.) See *Tczew.*		
Disenka (Pol., riv.) See *Dzisna.*	*Rus.* dĭ-syôn′-kä	di-syon′-kah
Disko (Greenl., isl.)	dĭs′-kō	dis′-koh
Disna (Pol., village, riv., lake) See *Dzisna.*		

Di Tremiti (It., isls.)	dē trĕ′-mē-tē	dee treh′-mee-tee
Dittaino (Sicily, riv.)	dēt-tī′-nô	deet-tai′-no
Diu (Port. India)	dē′-o͞o	dee′-u
Divnoe (Rus.)	dēv′-nŏ-yĕ	deev′-no-yeh
Dixmude (Belg.)	*Fr.* dēks-müd′	deeks-müd′

Flemish *Dixmuiden*, dēks-mûĭ′-də(n) [deeks-mœi′-duh(n)].

Dizful (Iran)	dĭz-fo͞ol′	diz-fool′

Dj- See also Đ, an alternative spelling in Yugoslav place names.

Djailolo (NEI)	jī-lô′-lô	jai-lo′-lo
Djakovica (Yugosl.)	dyä′-kô′-vĭ-tsä	dyah′-ko′-vi-tsah
Djakovo (Yugosl.)	*Alb.* dyä′-kô-vô	dyah′-ko-vo

Serb-Croat *Đakovica*, q.v.

Djambi *or* Dyambi (NEI)	jäm′-bē	jahm′-bee
Djanet (Alg.)	jă′-nĕt	ja′-net
djebel *or* jebel	jĕb′-əl	jeb′-uhl

These are alternative spellings for an element, meaning *hill*, in Arabic place names. The former is to be expected in French territory. It may be necessary to look up both.

Djebel Abiod (Tun.)	jĕb′-əl äb-yŏd′	jeb′-uhl ahb-yod′
Djebel Ainchouna (Tun.)	jĕb′-əl ān-sho͞o′-nä	jeb′-uhl ayn-shoo′-nah
Djebel Ajred (Tun.)	jĕb′-əl äzh′-rĕd	jeb′-uhl ahzh′-red
Djebel Antra (Tun.)	jĕb′-əl än′-trä	jeb′-uhl ahn′-trah
Djebel Artoug el Hanech (Tun.)	jĕb′-əl är-to͞og′ ĕl hä′-nĕsh	jeb′-uhl ahr-toog′ el hah′-nesh
Djebel Azag (Tun.)	jĕb′-əl ä′-zäg	jeb′-uhl ah′-zahg
Djebel Berda (Tun., mt.)	jĕb′-əl bĕr′-dä	jeb′-uhl behr′-dah
Djebel Bou Aoukaz (Tun.)	jĕb′-əl bo͞o′ ou-kăz′	jeb′-uhl boo′ au-kaz′
Djebel Bou Hadjar (Tun.)	jĕb′-əl bo͞o′ hä′-jär	jeb′-uhl boo′ hah′-jahr
Djebel Bou Kournine (Tun.)	jĕb′-əl bo͞o′ ko͝or-nēn′	jeb′-uhl boo′ kur-neen′
Djebel Bou Kril (Tun.)	jĕb′-əl bo͞o′ krēl′	jeb′-uhl boo′ kreel′
Djebel Chirich (Tun.)	jĕb′-əl shĭ-rēsh′	jeb′-uhl shi-reesh′
Djebel Dardyss (Tun.)	jĕb′-əl där-dēs′	jeb′-uhl dahr-dees′
Djebel Edjehaf (Tun.)	jĕb′-əl ĕd-jə-hăf′	jeb′-uhl ed-juh-haf′

Also spelled *El Djehaf*.

Djebel el Ahmera (Tun.)	jĕb′-əl ĕl ä′-mə-rä	jeb′-uhl el ah′-muh-rah

Also called *Long Stop Hill*.

Djebel el Ang (Tun.)	jĕb′-əl ĕl äng′	jeb′-uhl el ahng′
Djebel el Bacouala (Tun.)	jĕb′-əl ĕl bä-kwä′-lä	jeb′-uhl el bah-kwah′-lah

Djebel el Menassir (Tun.)	jĕb′-əl ĕl mə-năs′-sĭr	jeb′-uhl el muh-nas′-sihr
Djebel el Sema (Tun.)	jĕb′-əl ĕs sĕ′-mä	jeb′-uhl es seh′-mah
Djebel Garci (Tun.)	jĕb′-əl gär′-sē	jeb′-uhl gahr′-see
Djebel Kalaat el Senam (Tun.)	jĕb′-əl kä-lät′ ĕs sĕ-năm′	jeb′-uhl kah-laht′ es seh-nam′
Djebel Mansour (Tun.)	jĕb′-əl män-so͞or′	jeb′-uhl mahn-soor′
Djebel Menobab (Tun.)	jĕb′-əl mĕ-nô-băb′	jeb′-uhl meh-no-bab′
Djebel Mrata (Tun.)	jĕb′-əl mə-ră′-tä	jeb′-uhl muh-ra′-tah
Djebel Nechat el Maza (Tun.)	jĕb′-əl nə-shăt′ ĕl mä′-zä	jeb′-uhl nuh-shat′ el mah′-zah
Djebel Orbata (Tun., mt.)	jĕb′-əl ôr-bä′-tä	jeb′-uhl or-bah′-tah
Djebel Rmel (Tun.)	jĕb′-əl rə-māl′	jeb′-uhl ruh-mayl′
Djebel Sidi Meftah (Tun.)	jĕb′-əl sē′-dē məf-tä′	jeb′-uhl see′-dee muhf-tah′
Djebel Tahent (Tun.)	jĕb′-əl tä-hĕnt′	jeb′-uhl tah-hent′
Djebel Tangouch (Tun.)	jĕb′-əl tän-go͞osh′	jeb′-uhl tahn-goosh′
Also called *Tangoucha*, tän-go͞o′-shä [tahn-goo′-shah].		
Djebel Tobaga (Tun., mt.)	jĕb′-əl tô-bä′-gä	jeb′-uhl to-bah′-gah
Djebel Zaghouan (Tun.)	*Ar.* jĕb′-əl zäg-wăn′	jeb′-uhl zahg-wan′
	Fr. zäg-wäN′	zahg-wahN′
Djebibina (Tun.)	jĕ-bĭ-bē′-nä	jeh-bi-bee′-nah
Djebiniana (Tun.)	jĕ-bĭn-yă′-nä	jeh-bin-ya′-nah
Djedeida (Tun.)	jə-dā′-dä	juh-day′-dah
Djefna (Tun.)	jĕf′-nä	jef′-nah
Also spelled *Jefna*, q.v.		
Djem, el (Tun.)	jĕm′, ĕd	jem′, ed
Djeradou (Tun.)	jĕ-rä-do͞o′	jeh-rah-doo′
Djerba (Tun., isl.)	jĕr′-bä	jehr′-bah
Djibouti (Fr. Som.)	jē-bo͞o′-tē	jee-boo′-tee
Also spelled *Jibuti*. French jē-bo͞o-tē′ [jee-boo-tee′].		
Djidjelli (Alg.)	jē-jĕ-lē′	jee-jeh-lee′
Also spelled *Jijelli*.		
Djoumine (Tun., riv.)	jo͞o-mēn′	joo-meen′
Dmitrievsk (Rus.)	dmē′-trĭ-yĕfsk	dmee′-tri-yefsk
Dmitrov (Rus.)	dmē-trôf′	dmee-trof′
Dmitrovsk (Rus.)	dmē-trôfsk′	dmee-trofsk′
Dnepr (Rus., riv.)	*Eng.* nē′-pər	nee′-puhr
	Rus. dnĕ′-pər	dneh′-puhr
Dneprodzerzhinsk (Rus.)	dnĕ′-prŏ-jĕr-zĭnsk′	dneh′-pro-jehr-zinsk′
	or Eng. nē′-pər-	nee′-puhr-

Dnepropetrovsk (Rus.)	dnĕ′-prŏ-pĕ-trôfsk′	dneh′-pro-peh-trofsk′
	or Eng. nē′-pər-	nee′-puhr-
Dnestr (Europ. riv.) See *Dniester.*		
Dnieper (Rus., riv.)	*Eng.* nē′-pər	nee′-puhr
Russian *Dnepr*, q.v.		
Dniester (Europ. riv.)	*Eng.* nē′-stər	nee′-stuhr
Polish *Dniestr*, Russian *Dnestr*, dnĕ′str [dne′str]. Rumanian *Nistru*, nē′-stro͝o [nee′-stru].		
Dno (Rus.)	dnô′	dno′
Dnyeprovsko-Bugski, Kanal (Pol.) See *Królewski, Kanal.*		
Döbeln (Ger.)	dû′-bəln	dœ′-buhln
Dobodura (Oc.)	dô-bô-do͞o′-rä	do-bo-doo′-rah
Dobra (Yugosl.)	dô′-brä	do′-brah
Dobrič (Yugosl.)	dô′-brĭch	do′-brich
Dobrici (Rum.)	dô′-brēch′	do′-breech′
Also called *Bazargic*, q.v.		
Dobrogea (Rum.)	*Rum.* dô′-brô-jä	do′-bro-jah
English and Bulgarian *Dobruja*, q.v.		
Dobro Polje (Yugosl., mt.)	dô′-brô pô′-lyĕ	do′-bro po′-lyeh
Dobrostica (Yugosl., mt.)	dô′-brô′-stĭ-tsä	do′-bro′-sti-tsah
Dobruja (Rum.)	*Eng.* dō′-bro͞o-jə	doh′-broo-juh
	Bulg. dô′-bro͝o-jä	do′-bru-jah
Rumanian *Dobrogea*, q.v.		
Dobruševo (Yugosl.)	dô′-bro͞o′-shĕ-vô	do′-broo′-sheh-vo
Dodecanese (Aegean isls.)	*Eng.* dō-dĕk′-ə-nēs′	doh-dek′-uh-nees′
The second and last syllables should be accented, not the first and last. The adjective, however, is *Dodecanesian*—dō′-dĕk-ə-nē′-shən [doh′-dek-uh-nee′-shuhn]. Greek *Dodekanesos*, q.v., and *Dodekanesa*, *th*ô-*th*ĕ-kä′-nē-sä [*th*o-*th*eh-kah′-nee-sah].		
Dodekanesos (Aegean isls.)	*th*ô-*th*ĕ-kä′-nē-sô(s)	*th*o-*th*eh-kah′-nee-so(s)
Dodo Oninskoe (Rus.)	dō′-dō ŏ-nĭn′-skŏ-yĕ	doh′-doh o-nin′-sko-yeh
Dodsworth, Henrique (Braz. leader)	dädz′-wûrth, ĕN-rē′-kĭ	dahdz′-wuhrth, eN-ree′-ki
Doebeln (Ger.)	dû′-bəln	dœ′-buhln
Doenitz, Karl (Ger. admiral)	dû′-nĭts	dœ′-nits
Doerane (Balkan lake)	*Gr.* dô-ē-rä′-nē	do-ee-rah′-nee
Also called *Limne Doeranes*, lēm′-nē dô-ē-rä′-nēs [leem′-nee do-ee-rah′-nees]. Serb-Croat *Dojran*, q.v.		
Doganica (Yugosl., mts.)	dô′-gä′-nĭ-tsä	do′-gah′-ni-tsah

Dogra (India)	dō-grä′	doh-grah′
Dojran (Balkan lake)	*S.-C.* doi′-rän	doi′-rahn
Also called *Dojransko jezero,* doi′-rän-skô yĕ′-zĕ-rô [doi′-rahn-sko yeh′-zeh-ro]. Greek *Doerane,* q.v.		
Dokkum (Neth.)	dôk′-əm	dok′-uhm
Dolban (Rus.)	dōl′-bän(y)	dohl′-bahn(y)
Dôle (Fr.)	dōl′	dohl′
Dolenji Logatec (Yugosl.)	dô′-lĕ-nyĭ lô′-gä-tĕts	do′-leh-nyi lo′-gah-tets
Dolgintsevo (Rus.)	dŏl-gēn′-tsĕ-vŏ	dol-geen′-tseh-vo
Dolina (Pol.)	dô-lē′-nä	do-lee′-nah
Dolinovka (Rus.)	dŏ-lē′-nŏf-kä	do-lee′-nof-kah
Doljevac (Yugosl.)	dô′-lyĕ-väts	do′-lyeh-vahts
Dolon (Ch., Chahar)	*Eng.* dō′-lŏn′	doh′-lon′
Dolon Nor (Ch., Hopeh)	*Eng.* dō′-lŏn nôr′	doh′-lon nor′
Dolovo (Yugosl.)	dô′-lô-vô	do′-lo-vo
Dolya (Rus.)	dôl′-yä	dol′-yah
Dolzhik (Rus.)	dôl′-zhĭk	dol′-zhik
Domažlice (Cz.) German *Taus.*	dô′-mäzh-lĭ-tsĕ	do′-mahzh-li-tseh
Dombaas (Nor.)	do͝om′-bôs	dum′-bos
Dombrova (Pol.) See *Dąbrowa Górnicza.*		
Dombrovitsa (Pol.) See *Dąbrowica.*		
Domburg (Neth.)	dôm′-bûrk(h)	dom′-bœrk(h)
Domei (Jap. News Agency)	dō-mā	doh-may
Domengeaux, James (U.S. representative)	dō-mäN-zhō′	doh-mahN-zhoh′
Dommel (Neth., riv.)	dôm′-əl	dom′-uhl
Domodossola (It.)	dô-mô-dôs′-sô-lä	do-mo-dos′-so-lah
Domozhirov (Rus.)	dŏ-mŏ-zhĭ′-rŏf	do-mo-zhi′-rof
Don (Rus., riv.)	dôn′ *or Eng.*dŏn′	don′
Donau (Europ. riv.) See *Danube.*		
Donbaik (Burma)	dōn′-bīk′	dohn′-baik′
Dondero, George A. (U.S. representative)	dŏn-dĕr′-ō	don-dehr′-oh
Dondon (Rus., riv.)	dŏn-dôn′	don-don′
Donets (Rus., riv.)	dŏ-nĕts′	do-nets′
Dongara (Austral.)	dŏn-gä′-rə	don-gah′-ruh
Donggala (NEI)	dông-gä′-lä	dong-gah′-lah
Donghoi (Indo-Ch.)	dŏng-hoi′	dong-hoi′
Donja Lendava (Yugosl.) German *Unter-Limbach.*	dô′-nyä lĕn′-dä-vä	do′-nyah len′-dah-vah

Donji Lapac (Yugosl.)	dô′-nyĭ lä′-päts	do′-nyi lah′-pahts
Donji Vakuf (Yugosl.)	See *Vakuf, Donji.*	
Donskaya (Rus., riv.)	dŏn-skä′-yä	don-skah′-yah
Dordogne (Fr., riv.)	dôr-dôn′(y)	dor-don′(y)
Dordrecht (Neth.)	dôr′-drĕk(h)t	dor′-drek(h)t
English *Dort.*		
D'Orlando (Sicily, cape)	dôr-län′-dô	dor-lahn′-do
Dorlobos (Yugosl.)	dôr′-lô-bôs	dor′-lo-bos
Dorogobuzh (Pol.) See *Drohobycz.*		
Dorohoi (Rum.)	dô-rô-hoi′	do-ro-hoi′
Dorozsma (Hung.)	dô′-rôzh-mŏ	do′-rozh-mo
Also called *Kiskundorozsma,* q.v.		
Dorpat (Est.)	*Ger.* dôr′-pät	dor′-paht
Estonian *Tartu,* q.v. Russian *Jurjev,* q.v.		
Dortmund (Ger.)	*Eng.* dôrt′-mo͝ond	dort′-mund
	Ger. dôrt′-mo͝ont	dort′-munt
Došnica (Yugosl., riv.)	dô′-shnĭ-tsä	do′-shni-tsah
Dostoevski, Feodor Mikhailovich (Rus. author)	dŏ-stŏ-yĕf′-skĭ, fyô′-dŏr mĭ-hī′-lŏ-vĭch	do-sto-yef′-ski, fyo′-dor mi-hai′-lo-vich
Douai (Fr.)	*Eng.* do͞o-ā′	doo-ay′
	Fr. dwĕ′	dweh′
Douala (W. Afr.)	do͝o-ä′-lä	du-ah′-lah
Also spelled *Duala,* q.v.		
Douarnenez (Fr.)	dwär-nə-nĕz′ *or* -nĕ′	dwahr-nuh-nez′ *or* -neh′
Douaumont (Fr.)	dwō-môN′	dwoh-moN′
Doubs (Fr., riv.)	do͞o′	doo′
Doughton, Robert L. (U.S. representative)	dout′n	daut′n
Douirat (Tun.)	do͞o-ĭ-răt′	doo-i-rat′
Dounabis (Europ. riv.)	See *Danube.*	
Douro (Port., Sp., riv.)	*Port.* dō′-ro͝o	doh′-ru
Spanish *Duera,* q.v.		
Douz (Tun.)	do͞oz′	dooz′
Dovezence (Yugosl.)	dô′-vĕ′-zĕn-tsĕ	do′-veh′-zen-tseh
Dovrefjell (Nor., mts.)	dô′-vrə-fyĕl	do′-vruh-fyel
Downey, Sheridan (U.S. senator)	dou′-nĭ	dau′-ni
Dozulé (Fr.)	dô-zü-lĕ′	do-zü-leh′
Dračevo (Yugosl.)	drä′-chĕ-vô	drah′-cheh-vo
Draginac (Yugosl.)	drä′-gĭ-näts	drah′-gi-nahts
Drajinci (Yugosl.)	drä′-yĭn-tsĭ	drah′-yin-tsi

Drama (Gr.)	*th*rä′-mä	*th*rah′-mah
Drammen (Nor.)	dräm′-ən	drahm′-uhn
Dramonara (Crete, isl.)	*th*rä-mô-nä′-rä	*th*rah-mo-nah′-rah
Drangedal (Nor.)	dräng′-ə-däl	drahng′-uh-dahl
Drapani (Crete, point)	*th*rä-pä′-nē	*th*rah-pah′-nee
Drava (Yugosl., riv.)	drä′-vä	drah′-vah
German *Drau*.		
Dravina (Yugosl., riv.)	drä′-vĭ-nä	drah′-vi-nah
German *Drann*.		
Dravograd (Yugosl.)	drä′-vô-gräd	drah′-vo-grahd
Drawski Młyn (Pol.)	dräf′-skĭ mlĭn′	drahf′-ski mlin′
Dren (Yugosl.)	drĕn′	dren′
Drenica (Yugosl.)	drĕ′-nĭ-tsä	dreh′-ni-tsah
Drenova, Velika (Yugosl.)	drĕ′-nô-vä, vĕ′-lĭ-kä	dreh′-no-vah, veh′-li-kah
Drente (Neth.)	drĕn′-tə	dren′-tuh
Drepanon, Ak. (Crete, point)	*th*rĕ′-pä-nô(n)	*th*reh′-pah-no(n)
Dresden (Ger.)	*Eng.* drĕz′-dən	drez′-duhn
	Ger. drās′-dən	drays′-duhn
Drewenz (Pol., riv.) See *Drwęca*.		
Drewry, Patrick H. (U.S. representative)	drŏŏr′-ĭ	drur′-i
Drina (Yugosl., riv.)	drē′-nä	dree′-nah
Drini (Balkan rivs.) See *Drin*		
Drin i Bardhë (Balkan riv.)	*Alb.* drēn′ ē bär′-*th*ə	dreen′ ee bahr′-*th*uh
Serb-Croat *Beli Drim*, q.v. English *White Drin*, drēn′ [dreen′].		
Drin i Math (Alb., riv.)	drēn′ ē mäth′	dreen′ ee mahth′
Italian *Drinasa*, drē′-nä-sä [dree′-nah-sah].		
Drin i Zi (Balkan riv.)	*Alb.* drēn′ ē zē′	dreen′ ee zee′
Serb-Croat *Crni Drim*, q.v. English *Black Drin*, drēn′ [dreen′].		
Drinska (Yugosl.)	drēn′-skä	dreen′-skah
Drissa (Rus.)	drēs′-sä	drees′-sah
Drivyati (Pol., lake) See *Drywiaty*.		
Dröbak (Nor.)	drû′-bäk	drœ′-bahk
Drobnjaci (Yugosl.)	drôb′-nyä′-tsĭ	drob′-nyah′-tsi
Droebak (Nor.)	drû′-bäk	drœ′-bahk
Drogichin (Pol.) See *Drohiczyn*.		
Drohiczyn (Pol.)	drô-hē′-chĭn	dro-hee′-chin
Russian *Drogichin*, drŏ-gē′-chĭn [dro-gee′-chin].		
Drohobycz (Pol.)	drô-hô′-bĭch	dro-ho′-bich
Russian *Dorogobuzh*, dŏ-rŏ-gŏ-bōōsh′ [do-ro-go-boosh′].		

Drôme (Fr.)	drōm′	drohm′
Drottningholm (Sw.)	drŏt′-nĭng-hôlm′	drot′-ning-holm′
Druja (Pol.)	dro͝o′-yä	dru′-yah
Russian spelling *Druya.*		
Druskieniki (Pol.)	dro͝o-skyĕ-nē′-kĭ	dru-skyeh-nee′-ki
Russian spelling *Druskeniki.*		
Druya (Pol.) See *Druja.*		
Drvenik (Yugosl.)	dər′-vĕ-nĭk	duhr′-veh-nik
Italian *Zirona,* q.v.		
Drventsa (Pol., riv.) See *Drwęca.*		
Drwęca (Pol., riv.)	dər-văN′-tsä	duhr-vaN′-tsah
Russian *Drventsa,* drvĕn′-tsä [drven′-tsah]. German *Drewenz,* drā′-vĕnts [dray′-vents].		
Drywiaty (Pol., lake)	drĭ-vyä′-tĭ	dri-vyah′-ti
Russian spelling *Drivyati.*		
Duala (W. Afr.)	do͝o-ä′-lä	du-ah′-lah
Dubbo (Austral.)	dŭb′-ō	duhb′-oh
Dubiecko (Pol.)	do͝o-byĕ′-tskô	du-byeh′-tsko
Dublin (Eire)	dŭb′-lĭn	duhb′-lin
Gaelic *Baile Átha Cliath,* q.v.		
Dublje (Yugosl.)	do͞ob′-lyĕ	doob′-lyeh
Dubossary (Rus.)	do͞o-bŏ-sä′-rĭ	doo-bo-sah′-rĭ
Dubravica (Yugosl.)	do͞o′-brä′-vĭ-tsä	doo′-brah′-vi-tsah
Dubrovačka (Yugosl.)	do͞o′-brô-väch-kä	doo′-bro-vahch-kah
Dubrovnik (Yugosl.)	do͞o′-brôv-nĭk	doo′-brov-nik
Italian *Ragusa,* q.v.		
Duce, il (It.)	do͞o′-chĕ, ēl	doo′-cheh, eel
Italian for *the leader.* Cf. *der Fuehrer* and *el Caudillo.*		
Duda, el (Libya)	do͞o′-dä, ĕd	doo′-dah, ed
Dudica (Yugosl., Gr., mt.)	do͞o′-dĭ-tsä	doo′-di-tsah
Due (Rus.)	do͞o′-ĕ	doo′-eh
Duena *or* Düna (Rus., Latvia, riv.)	*Ger.* dü′-nä	dü′-nah
Russian *Dvina,* q.v. Latvian *Daugava,* q.v.		
Duenamuende (Latvia)	*Ger.* dü′-nä-mün′-də	dü′-nah-mün′-duh
Latvian *Daugavgrīva,* q.v.		
Duera (Sp., Port., riv.)	*Sp.* dwĕ′-rä	dweh′-rah
Dueren *or* Düren (Ger.)	dü′-rən	dü′-ruhn
Duesseldorf *or* Düsseldorf	*Eng.* do͝os′-əl-dôrf	dus′-uhl-dorf
	Ger. düs′-əl-dôrf	düs′-uhl-dorf
Dugi Otok (Yugosl., isl.)	do͞o′-gĭ ô′-tôk	doo′-gi o′-tok
Italian *Isola Lunga,* q.v., or *Isola Grossa.*		
Dugiri (Oc.)	do͞o-gē′-rē	doo-gee′-ree
Dugo Selo (Yugosl.)	do͞o′-gô sĕ′-lô	doo′-go seh′-lo

Duisburg (Ger.)	*Eng.* dūz′-bûrg	dyooz′-buhrg
	Ger. düs′-bo͝ork(h)	düs′-burk(h)
Duizend (NEI)	dûĭ′-zənt	dœi′-zuhnt
Dukat (Alb.)	dōō′-kät	doo′-kaht
Dukati (Alb.) See *Dukat.*		
Dukhovshchina (Rus.)	dōō-hŏf-shchē′-nä	doo-hof-shchee′-nah
Dulcigno (Yugosl.)	*It.* dōōl-chē′-nyô	dool-chee′-nyo
Serb-Croat *Ulcinj.*		
Đulica (Yugosl., mt.)	dū′-lĭ-tsä	dyoo′-li-tsah
Dulles (family name)	dŭl′-əs	duhl′-uhs
Dum Dum (India)	dŭm dŭm	duhm duhm
Dumaguete (P.I.)	dōō-mä-gĕ′-tĕ	doo-mah-geh′-teh
Dumyat (Egypt)	do͝om-yät′	dum-yaht′
Also spelled *Dumiat.* Also called *Damietta,* q.v.		
Duna (Europ. riv.) See *Danube.*		
Düna (Rus., Latvia, riv.)	*Ger.* dü′-nä	dü′-nah
Russian *Dvina,* q.v. Latvian *Daugava,* q.v.		
Dünaburg (Latvia)	*Ger.* dü′-nä-bo͝ork(h)	dü′-nah-burk(h)
Latvian *Daugavpils,* q.v. Russian *Dvinsk,* q.v.		
Dunaföldvár (Hung.)	do͝o′-nŏ-fûld′-vär	du′-no-fœld′-vahr
Dunai *and* Dunaj (Europ. riv.) See *Danube.*		
Dunajec (Pol., riv.)	do͝o-nä′-yĕts	du-nah′-yets
Dünamünde (Latvia)	*Ger.* dü′-nä-mün′-də	dü′-nah-mün′-duh
Latvian *Daugavgrīva,* q.v.		
Dunărea (Europ. riv.) See *Danube.*		
Dunav (Europ. riv.) See *Danube.*		
Dunavska (Yugosl.)	dōō′-näv-skä	doo′-nahv-skah
Dunedin (N.Z.)	dŭn-ē′-dĭn	duhn-ee′-din
Dungeness (Eng.)	dŭnj′-nĕs′	duhnj′-nes′
Đunis (Yugosl.)	dū′-nĭs	dyoo′-nis
Dunkerque (Fr.)	dûN-kĕrk′	dœN-kehrk′
English *Dunkirk,* dŭn′-kərk [duhn′-kuhrk].		
Dupnitsa (Bulg.)	do͝op′-nĭ-tsä	dup′-ni-tsah
Durakova (Rus.)	do͝o-rä-kô′-vä	du-rah-ko′-vah
Durazzo (Alb.)	*It.* dōō-rät′-sô	doo-raht′-so
Albanian *Durrës,* q.v.		
Durban (U. of S. Af.)	dûr′-bən	duhr′-buhn
Düren (Ger.)	dü′-rən	dü′-ruhn
Durfuli (Yugosl.)	dōōr′-fōō-lĭ	door′-foo-li
Durham, Carl T. (U.S. representative)	dûr′-əm	duhr′-uhm
Durham (N.C.)	dûr′-əm	duhr′-uhm
Not do͝or′-əm [dur′-uhm].		
Durmitor (Yugosl., mts.)	dōōr′-mĭ-tôr	door′-mi-tor
Durostor (Rum.)	do͝o-rô-stôr′	du-ro-stor′

Durovo (Rus.)	do͞o′-rŏ-vŏ	doo′-ro-vo
Durrës (Alb.)	do͞or′-rəs	door′-ruhs
Italian *Durazzo*, q.v.		
Durrësi (Alb.) See *Durrës.*		
Dušanovac (Yugosl.)	do͞o′-shä′-nô-väts	doo′-shah′-no-vahts
Düsseldorf (Ger.) See *Duesseldorf.*		
Dutra, Gaspar (Braz. general)	do͞o′-trə, gäs-pär′	doo′-truh, gahs-pahr′
Dvina (Rus., Latvia, riv.)	dvĭ-nä′	dvi-nah′
Latvian *Daugava*, q.v. German *Duena*, q.v.		
Dvinsk (Latvia)	*Rus.* dvēnsk′	dveensk′
Latvian *Daugavpils*, q.v. German *Dünaburg*, q.v.		
Dwedar (Libya)	do͝o′-ĕ-där′	du′-eh-dahr′
Dworshak, Henry C. (U.S. representative)	dwōr′-shăk	dwohr′-shak
Dy- See also *Dj-* and Đ, alternative spellings in Yugoslav place names.		
Dyambi (NEI) See *Djambi.*		
Dyatkovo (Rus.)	dyät-kô′-vŏ	dyaht-ko′-vo
Dyaul (Oc.)	joul′	jaul′
Džep (Yugosl.)	jĕp′	jep′
Dzhankoi (Rus.)	jän-koi′	jahn-koi′
Dzherzinsk (Rus.)	jĕr-zĭnsk′	jehr-zinsk′
Dzhida (Rus., riv.)	jē′-dä	jee′-dah
Dzhulfa (Rus.)	jo͝ol-fä′	jul-fah′
Działdówka (Pol., Ger., riv.)	jäl-do͝of′-kä	jahl-duf′-kah
German *Soldau*, q.v. Also called *Wkra*, q.v.		
Działdowo (Pol.)	jäl-dô′-vô	jahl-do′-vo
German *Soldau*, q.v.		
Działoszyce (Pol.)	jä-lô-shĭ′-tsĕ	jah-lo-shi′-tseh
Dzisna (Pol.)	jēs′-nä	jees′-nah
Russian *Disna*, dĭs-nä′ [dis-nah′]. See also *Disenka.*		
Džuma Obasi (Yugosl.)	jo͞o′-mä ô′-bä-sĭ	joo′-mah o′-bah-si
Dzungaria (Ch., Sinkiang)	*Eng.* zo͝on-găr′-ĭ-ə	zun-gehr′-i-uh
Also spelled *Sungaria* and *Zungaria.*		
Eaker, Ira C. (U.S. general)	ā′-kər	ay′-kuhr
Eauripik (Oc.)	ĕ-ou′-rē-pēk	eh-au′-ree-peek
Ebadon (Oc.)	ĕ′-bä-dôn	eh′-bah-don
Ebeye (Oc.)	ĕ′-bĕ-yĕ	eh′-beh-yeh
Eboli (It.)	ĕ′-bô-lē	eh′-bo-lee
Ebon (Oc.)	ĕ′-bôn	eh′-bon
Also called *Boston Isl.*		

Ebro (Sp., riv.)	ĕ′-brô	eh′-bro
Écija (Sp.)	ĕ′-thē-hä *or* -sē-	eh′-thee-hah *or* -see-
economics	ē′-kə-nŏ′-mĭks	ee′-kuh-no′-miks
	or ĕk′-ə-nŏ′-mĭks	ek′-uh-no′-miks

Of nine authoritative dictionaries, eight list the pronunciation with ē- before that with ĕk-. While the order of placement is not decisive, it suggests the pronunciation ē′-kə-nŏ′-mĭks [ee′-kuh-no′-miks] for a program where agreement on the pronunciation is called for.

Edam (Neth.)	*Eng.* ē′-dăm	ee′-dam
	Du. ā-däm′	ay-dahm′
Eddekhila (Tun.)	ĕd-dĕ-kē′-lä	ed-deh-kee′-lah

Also spelled *El Dekhila.*

Ede (Neth.)	ā′-də	ay′-duh
Eder (Ger., riv.)	ā′-dər	ay′-duhr
Edessa (Gr.)	ĕ′-*th*ĕ-sä	eh′-*th*eh-sah
Edinburgh (Scot.)	ĕd′-ĭn-bŭ′-rŭ	ed′-in-buh′-ruh

As an American place name, *Edinburg* is pronounced ĕd′-ĭn-bûrg [ed′-in-buhrg].

Edirne (Turk.)	ĕ-dēr′-nĕ	eh-deer′-neh

Also called *Adrianople,* q.v.

Edjehan (Tun.)	ĕd-jə-hăn′	ed-juh-han′

Also spelled *El Djehan,* q.v.

Eduskunta	ĕ′-dŏŏs-kŏŏn-tä	eh′-dus-kun-tah

Finnish parliament.

Eecloo (Belg.)	āk′-lō	ayk′-loh
Eem (Neth., riv.)	ām′	aym′
Efogi (Oc.)	ĕ-fō′-gē	eh-foh′-gee
Egadi, Isole (Sicily)	ĕ′-gä-dē, ē′-zô-lĕ	eh′-gah-dee, ee′-zo-leh

English the *Aegadian Isles,* ĭ-gā′-dĭ-ən [i-gay′-di-uhn], or the *Aegates,* ĭ-gā′-tēz [i-gay′-teez].

Eger (Ger., Cz., riv.; Cz., town)	*Ger.* ā′-gər	ay′-guhr

See *Ohře* and *Cheb.*

Eger (Hung.)	ĕ′-gĕr	eh′-gehr

German *Erlau,* ĕr′-lou [ehr′-lau].

Egersund (Nor.)	āg-ər-sŏŏn′	ayg-uhr-sun′
Eggedal (Nor.)	ĕg′-ə-däl	eg′-uh-dahl
Egmond Binnen (Neth.)	ĕk(h)′-mônt bĭn′-ən	ek(h)′-mont bin′-uhn
Ehrenburg, Ilya (Rus. writer)	ĕ-rĕn-bŏŏrk(h)′, ĭl-yä′	eh-ren-boork(h)′, il-yah′

ei

In Dutch *ei* is interchangeable with *ij* and *y,* though *y* is usually preferred when initial. A consultant may have to look for all three forms before he finds his word. Dutch and German *ei* is pronounced approximately ī [ai]. In other languages, including Arabic, the pronunciation ā [ay] is usually required or preferable.

Eidanger (Nor.)	ā-däng′-ər	ay-dahng′-uhr
Eide (Nor.)	ā′-də	ay′-duh
Eidsbugaren (Nor.)	āds-bōō-gä′-rən	ayds-boo-gah′-ruhn
Eidsfoss (Nor.)	āds′-fôs	ayds′-fos
Eidsoera *or* Eidsöra (Nor.)	āds′-û-rə	ayds′-œ-ruh
Eidsvold (Nor.)	āds′-vôl	ayds′-vol
Eikesdal (Nor.)	ā′-kəs-däl	ay′-kuhs-dahl
Eil Malk (Oc.)	āl′ mälk′	ayl′ mahlk′
Eina (Nor.)	ā′-nä	ay′-nah
Eindhoven (Neth.)	īnt′-hō-vən	aint′-hoh-vuhn
Eire (=Ireland)	ĕr′-ə	ehr′-uh
	or Irish ā′-rə	ay′-ruh

The analogy should be *Erin* not *Ireland*.

Eirene, Agia (Crete)	ē-rē′-nē, ī′-yä	ee-ree′-nee, ai′-yah
Eisernes Tor (Rum., Yugosl., gorge) See *Iron Gates.*		
Eisk (Rus.)	āsk′	aysk′
Ekimchan (Rus.)	ĕ-kĭm-chän′	eh-kim-chahn′
Ela (Burma, riv.)	ā′-lä	ay′-lah
El Adem (Libya)	ĕl ă′-dĕm	el a′-dem
El Agelat (Libya)	ĕl ä-gĕ-lăt′	el ah-geh-lat′
El Agheila (Libya)	ĕl ä-gā′-lä	el ah-gay′-lah
El Akarit (Tun.)	ĕl ä-kä-rēt′	el ah-kah-reet′
El Alamein (Egypt)	ĕl ä-lä-mān′	el ah-lah-mayn′
El Alia (Tun.)	ĕl ä′-lĭ-ä	el ah′-li-ah
El Amine, Sidi Mohammed (Arab leader)	ĕl ä-mēn′, sē′-dē mō-hăm′-ĕd	el ah-meen′, see′-dee moh-ham′-ed
El Aouana (Tun.)	ĕl ä-wă′-nä	el ah-wa′-nah
El Aouaria (Tun.)	ĕl ä-wä-rē′-yä	el ah-wah-ree′-yah
Elaphonesi (Crete, isl.)	ĕ-lä-fô-nē′-sē	eh-lah-fo-nee′-see
Elaphonesos (Gr., isl.)	ĕ-lä-fô′-nē-sôs	eh-lah-fo′-nee-sos
El Arima (Tun.)	ĕl ä-rē′-mä	el ah-ree′-mah
El Arish (Egypt)	ĕl ä-rēsh′	el ah-reesh′
El Aroussa (Tun.)	ĕl ä-rōō′-sä	el ah-roo′-sah
Elasa (Crete, isl.)	ĕ′-lä-sä	eh′-lah-sah
Elason (Gr.)	ĕ-lä-sôn′	eh-lah-son′
Elato (Oc.)	ĕ-lä′-tô	eh-lah′-to
El Azib (Tun.)	ĕl ä′-zĭb	el ah′-zib
El Azizia (Libya)	ĕl ă-zĭ-zē′-ä	el a-zi-zee′-ah
Elbasan (Alb.)	ĕl-bä-sän′	el-bah-sahn′

Elbasani (Alb.) See *Elbasan.*

Elbe (Europ. riv.)	*Ger.* ĕl′-bə	el′-buh
Czech *Labe*, lä′-bĕ [lah′-beh].		
Elborus (Rus., mt.)	ĕl-bŏ-ro͝os′	el-bo-rus′
English *Elbrus*, ĕl′-bro͝os [el′-brus], *or* āl′-bro͞os′ [ayl′-broos′].		
Elburg (Neth.)	ĕl′-bûrk(h)	el′-bœrk(h)
Elburz (Iran, mts.)	ăl′-bo͝orz′	al′-burz′
El Caudillo (Sp.)	ĕl kou-dē′-lyô *or* -yô	el kau-dee′-lyo *or* -yo
Spanish for *the leader*. Cf. *il Duce* and *der Fuehrer*.		
El Daba (Libya)	ĕd däb′-ä	ed dahb′-ah
El Dehibat (Tun.)	ĕd dĕ-hĭ-băt′	ed deh-hi-bat′
El Dekhila (Tun.) See *Eddekhila*.		
El Djehaf (Tun.) See *Djebel Edjehaf*.		
El Djehan (Tun.)	ĕd jə-hăn′	ed juh-han′
Also spelled *Edjehan*, q.v.		
El Djem (Tun.)	ĕd jĕm′	ed jem′
El Duda (Libya)	ĕd do͞o′-dä	ed doo′-dah
Elelo (Oc.)	ĕ-lĕ′-lô	eh-leh′-lo
Elena (Bulg.)	yĕ′-lĕ-nä	yeh′-leh-nah
El Erg (Alg., Tun.)	ĕl ĕrg′	el ehrg′
Eleusis (Gr.)	*Eng.* ē-lū′-sĭs	ee-lyoo′-sis
Greek *Elevsis*, ĕ-lĕf-sēs′ [eh-lef-sees′].		
El Faiyum (Egypt)	ĕl fī-yo͞om′	el fai-yoom′
El Faregh (Libya)	ĕl fä′-rĕg	el fah′-reg
El Ferrol (Sp.)	ĕl fĕ-rôl′	el feh-rol′
Elgar, Sir Edward	ĕl′-gər	el′-guhr
The pronunciation ĕl′-gär is inferior to ĕl′-gər.		
El Gazala (Libya)	ĕl gä-zä′-lä	el gah-zah′-lah
El Giza (Egypt)	ĕl gē′-zə	el gee′-zuh
Also spelled *Gizeh*.		
El Gubbi (Libya)	ĕl go͝o′-bē *or* kô′-bä	el gu′-bee *or* ko′-bah
El Guettar (Tun.)	ĕl gĕ-tär′	el geh-tahr′
El Gusbat (Libya)	ĕl go͝os-băt′	el gus-bat′
El Hamma (Tun.)	ĕl häm′-mä	el hahm′-mah
El Haouaria (Tun.)	ĕl hä-wä-rē′-ä	el hah-wah-ree′-ah
Elia (Gr.)	ĕ-lyä′	eh-lyah′
Elia (Essays of Elia)	ē′-lĭ-ə	ee′-li-uh
Pseudonym of Charles Lamb.		
Elika (Gr.)	ĕ-lē′-kä	eh-lee′-kah
El Imayid Station (Egypt)	ĕl ē-mă′-yĭd	el ee-ma′-yid
Elis (Gr.) See *Achaia and Elis*.		
Elisenvaara (Fin.)	ĕ′-lĭ-sĕn-vä′-rä	eh′-li-sen-vah′-rah
Elista (Rus.)	ĕ′-lĭs-tä	eh′-lis-tah
Elizalde, Joaquín M. (Fil. leader)	ĕ-lē-säl′-dĕ, hwä-kēn′	eh-lee-sahl′-deh, hwah-keen′

El Kharita (Egypt)	ĕl kä′-rē-tə	el kah′-ree-tuh
Elkhotovo (Rus.)	ĕl-hô′-tŏ-vŏ	el-ho′-to-vo
Elkhovo (Bulg.)	yĕl′-kŏ-vŏ	yel′-ko-vo
Ellenikon (Gr.)	ĕ-lē-nē-kô(n)′	eh-lee-nee-ko(n)′
Ellice (Oc.)	ĕl′-ĭs	el′-is
El Mabtouha (Tun.)	ĕl məb-tōō′-hə	el muhb-too′-huh
El Maou (Tun.)	ĕl mou′	el mau′
Elmas (Sard.)	ĕl′-mäs	el′-mahs
El Mekhili (Libya)	ĕl mĕ-kē′-lē	el meh-kee′-lee
El Miteiriya (Egypt)	ĕl mĭ-tā-rē′-yä	el mi-tay-ree′-yah
Elmshorn (Ger.)	ĕlms′-hôrn	elms′-horn
Elne (Fr.)	ĕln′	eln′
El Paso (Tex.)	ĕl păs′-ō	el pas′-oh
El Rharsa (Tun.)	ĕr rär′-sä	ehr rahr′-sah
Elsene (Belg.)	*Flem.* ĕl′-sə-nə	el′-suh-nuh
French *Ixelles*, ĭk-sĕl′ [ik-sel′].		
El Taqa (Egypt)	ĕt tä′-kä	et tah′-kah
Eltegen (Rus.)	ĕl-tĕ′-gĕn	el-teh′-gen
Eltonskaya (Rus.)	ĕl-tôn′-skä-yä	el-ton′-skah-yah
Elvedalen (Nor.)	ĕl′-və-dä-lən	el′-vuh-dah-luhn
Elverum (Nor.)	ĕl′-və-rŏŏm	el′-vuh-rum
Elveseter (Nor.)	ĕl′-və-sā-tər	el′-vuh-say-tuhr
Emba (Rus.)	ĕm′-bä	em′-bah
Emirau (Oc.)	ĕ-mē-rou′	eh-mee-rau′
Empedocle (It.)	ĕm-pĕ′-dô-klĕ	em-peh′-do-kleh
Also called *Porto Empedocle*, q.v.		
Empoli (It.)	ĕm′-pô-lē	em′-po-lee
Ems (Ger., riv.)	*Eng.* ĕmz′	emz′
	Ger. ĕms′	ems′
Enez (Turk.)	ĕ′-nĕz	eh′-nez
Greek *Ainos*, ĕ′-nôs [eh′-nos]. Bulgarian *Enos*, ĕ′-nŏs [eh′-nos].		
Enfidaville (Tun.)	ĕn-fē-dä-vēl′ *or*	en-fee-dah-veel′
	Fr. äN-fē-dä-vēl′	ahN-fee-dah-veel′
Engaño (P.I., cape)	ĕn-gä′-nyô	en-gah′-nyo
Engebi (Oc.)	ĕng′-gĕ′-bē	eng′-geh′-bee
Engelhardt, V. A. (Rus. scientist)	ĕn-gĕl-gärt′	en-gel-gahrt′
Engels (Pokrovsk) (Rus.)	ĕng′-gĕls (pŏk-rôfsk′)	eng′-gels (pok-rofsk′)
Enggano (NEI)	ĕng-gä′-nô	eng-gah′-no
Englebright, Harry L. (Late U. S. representative)	ĕng′-gəl-brīt	eng′-guhl-brait
Enguinegatte (Fr.)	äN-gēn-gät′	ahN-geen-gaht′
Eniwetok (Oc.)	ĕ′-nē′-wĕ-tôk	eh′-nee′-weh-tok
Enkhuizen (Neth.)	ĕnk-hûĭ′-zən	enk-hœi′-zuhn
Enna (Sicily)	**ĕn′-nä**	**en′-nah**

En Nofilia (Libya)	ĕn nô-fē′-lyä	en no-fee′-lyah
Enogai (Oc.)	ĕ-nô-gī′	eh-no-gai′
Enos (Turk.) See *Enez.*		
Enschede (Neth.)	ĕn′-sk(h)ə-dā′	en′-sk(h)uh-day′
ensemble	*Eng.* än-sŏm′-bəl	ahn-som′-buhl
	Fr. äN-säN′bl	ahN-sahN′bl

The English pronunciation is preferable for American radio because the final *l* of our French pronunciation is usually lost in transmission.

entire	ĕn-tīr′	en-tair′

For emphasis the accent may occasionally shift to the first syllable; normally it should be placed on the final syllable.

Enubuj (Oc.)	ĕ′-nōō-bōōj	eh′-noo-booj
envoy	ĕn′-voi	en′-voi

The first syllable should not be pronounced like the first syllable of French *enfant,* but like that of English *envy.*

Eolie, Isole (Sicily)	ĕ-ô′-lyĕ, ē′-zô-lĕ	eh-o′-lyeh, ee′-zo-leh

The *Aeolian Isls.*, usually called in English the *Lipari Isls,* q.v.

Épernay (Fr.)	ĕ-pĕr-nĕ′	eh-pehr-neh′
Épinal (Fr.)	ĕ-pē-näl′	eh-pee-nahl′
Epirus *or* Epiros (Gr.)	*Eng.* ē-pī′-rəs	ee-pai′-ruhs
	Gr. ē′-pē-rôs	ee′-pee-ros
Erakleion (Crete)	ē-rä′-klē-ô(n)	ee-rah′-klee-o(n)

Also spelled *Herakleion,* q.v.

Ercegnovi (Yugosl.)	ĕr′-tsĕg-nô′-vĭ	ehr′-tseg-no′-vi
Erciyas (Turk., mt.)	ĕr-jē′-äs	ehr-jee′-ahs

Also called *Erceyiş,* ĕr-jā′-ĭsh [ehr-jay′-ish].

Erdželija (Yugosl.)	ĕr′-jĕ-lē′-yä	ehr′-jeh-lee′-yah
Ereğli (Turk.)	ĕ-rā′-lē	eh-ray′-lee

Greek *Herakleia,* ē-rä′-klē-ä [ee-rah′-klee-ah].

Erenik (Yugosl., riv.)	ĕ′-rĕ-nĭk	eh′-reh-nik
Eretria (Gr.)	*Eng.* ĭ-rē′-trĭ-ə	i-ree′-tri-uh
Erg, el (Alg., Tun.)	ĕrg′, ĕl	ehrg′, el
Ericussa (Gr., isl.)	ĕ-rē-kōōs′-sä	eh-ree-koos′-sah

Also called *Merlera.*

Erikub (Oc.)	ĕ-rē-kōōb′	eh-ree-koob′
Eritrea (Ethiopia)	*It.* ĕ-rē-trĕ′-ä	eh-ree-treh′-ah
	Eng. ĕ-rĭ-trē′-ə	eh-ri-tree′-uh
Erivan (Rus.)	ĕ′-rĭ-vän′(y)	eh′-ri-vahn′(y)

Also called *Yerevan,* q.v.

Erlau (Hung.) See *Eger.*		
Erma (Balkan riv.)	*Bulg.* yĕr′-mä	yehr′-mah

Serb-Croat *Jerma,* q.v.

Eromanga (Austral.)	ĕr′-ō-măng′-gə	ehr′-oh-mang′-guh
Erseka (Alb.) See *Ersekë.*		

Ersekë (Alb.)	ĕr-sĕ′-kə	ehr-seh′-kuh
Érsekújvár (Cz.) See *Nové Zámky.*		
Erzen (Alb., riv.)	ĕr-zĕn′	ehr-zen′
Greek *Artzen.* Italian *Arzen.*		
Erzeni (Alb., riv.) See *Erzen.*		
Erzerum (Turk.)	ĕr′-zə-ro͝om	ehr′-zuh-rum
Esbjærg *or* Esbjerg (Den.)	ĕs′-byĕr	es′-byehr
Esel (Est., isl.)	*Rus.* ĕ′-zĕl(y)	eh′-zel(y)
Estonian *Saare,* q.v., or *Saaremaa.* German *Oesel,* q.v.		
Eskişehir (Turk.)	ĕs-kē′-shĕ-hēr	es-kee′-sheh-heer
Eso (Yugos., isl.)	*It.* ĕ′-sô	eh′-so
Serb-Croat *Iž,* q.v.		
España	ĕs-pä′-nyä	es-pah′-nyah
English *Spain.*		
Espedal (Nor., lake)	ĕs′-pə-däl	es′-puh-dahl
Esperance (Austral.)	ĕs′-pə-rəns	es′-puh-ruhns
Esperia (It.)	ĕs-pĕ′-ryä	es-peh′-ryah
Espínola, Eduardo (Braz. leader)	(ĭ)spē′-nô-lə, ĕ-dwär′-do͝o	(i)spee′-no-luh, eh-dwahr′-du
The initial *e* is practically silent.		
Espirito Santo (Brazil)	(ĭ)spē′-rē-to͝o sän′-to͝o	(i)spee′-ree-tu sahn′-tu
Essen (Ger.)	ĕs′-ən	es′-uhn
Estado de São Paulo, O (Braz. newspaper)	(ĭ)stä′-do͝o dĭ souN pou′-lo͝o, o͝o	(i)stah′-du di sauN pau′-lu, u
Estremadura (Sp., Port., prov.)	*Sp.* ĕs-trĕ-mä-*th*o͞o′-rä	es-treh-mah-*th*oo′-rah
	Port. ĕsh-trə-mə-do͞o′-rə	esh-truh-muh-doo′-ruh
Esztergom (Hung.)	ĕs′-tĕr-gôm	es′-tehr-gom
German *Gran,* grän′ [grahn′].		
Etal (Oc.)	ĕ-täl′	eh-tahl′
Étaples (Fr.)	ĕ-tä′pl	eh-tah′pl
Etchegoyen, Alcides (Braz. leader)	ĕ-chə-gô′-yən, äl-sē′-dĭs	eh-chuh-go′-yuhn, ahl-see′-dis
Eten (Oc.)	ĕ′-tĕn	eh′-ten
Etienne (Alaska, Attu)	ĕ-tyĕn′	eh-tyen′
Etna (Sicily)	*Eng.* ĕt′-nə	et′-nuh
	It. ĕt′-nä	et′-nah
Etna (Crete) is pronounced ĕt-nä′ [et-nah′].		
Étretat (Fr.)	ĕ-trə-tä′	eh-truh-tah′
Eu (Gr.)	û′	œ′
Euboea (Gr., isl.) See *Evvoia.*		
Eucla (Austral.)	ū′-klə	yoo′-kluh

Euganean Hills (It.) ū-gā′-nĭ-ən yoo-gay′-ni-uhn
Italian *Colli Euganei*, kôl′-lē ĕ-ōō-gä′-nā [kol′-lee eh-oo-gah′-nay].
Eugen, Prince (Ger.) oi-gān′ *or* oi′-gān oi-gayn′ *or* oi′-gayn
Speakers of German would be inclined to use the first and older pronunciation in the phrase *Prince Eugen*, although the modern family name is the latter. The usual radio pronunciation has been oi′-gĕn [oi′-gen].
Eupen (Belg.) oi′-pən oi′-puhn
Eure (Fr., riv.) ûr′ œr′
Eureka (Calif.) ū-rē′-kə yoo-ree′-kuh
Eutaw (Ala., S.C.) ū′-tô yoo′-taw
Eutin (Ger.) oi-tēn′ oi-teen′
evacuee ĭ-văk′-ū-ē′ i-vak′-yoo-ee′
Webster's (1934) gives only the French word and pronunciation, but the word has since been Englished.
Évora (Port.) ĕ′-vô-rə eh′-vo-ruh
Evoron (Rus., lake) ĕ′-vŏ-rŏn eh′-vo-ron
Evreux (Fr.) ĕ-vrû′ eh-vrœ′
Evripos (Gr., strait) ĕ′-vrē-pôs eh′-vree-pos
See *Khalkis*.
Evros (Balkan riv.) ĕ′-vrôs eh′-vros
Also called *Maritsa*, q.v.
Evrotas (Gr., riv.) ĕ-vrô′-täsē eh-vro′-tahs
Evstratios, Agios (Gr., isl.) ĕf-strä′-t -ôs, ī′-yôs ef-strah′-tee-os, ai′-yos
Commonly called *Aïstrates*, ī-strä′-tēs [ai-strah′-tees].
Evvoia (Gr., isl.) ĕ′-vē-ä eh′-vee-ah
English *Euboea*, ū-bē′-ə [yoo-bee′-uh].
evzone *Eng.* ĕv′-zōn ev′-zohn
Plural *evzones*, ĕv′-zōnz [ev′-zohnz]. Greek *evzonos*, ĕv′-zô-nôs [ev′-zo-nos]; plural *evzoni*, ĕv′-zô-nē [ev′-zo-nee].
Exintaris, Georgios (Gr. leader) ĕ-ksēn-dä′-rēs, yôr′-yôs eh-kseen-dah′-rees, yor′-yos
extremist ĕks-trēm′-ĭst eks-treem′-ist
Short *e* in the second syllable is a mistake. The analogy should be *extreme*, not *extremity*.
Eya (Burma) ā′-yä ay′-yah
Eya (Rus., riv.) ā′-yä ay′-yah
Also spelled *Yeya*, q.v.
Eydtkuhnen (Ger.) īt′-kōō-nən ait′-koo-nuhn
Eyre (Austral.) ĕr′ ehr′
Eziorka (Pol., riv.) See *Jezierna*.
Ez Zauia (Libya) ĕz zä′-wĭ-ä ez zah′-wi-ah
Ez Zuetina (Libya) ĕz zŏŏ-ĕ-tē′-nä ez zu-eh-tee′-nah

Faaberg (Nor.)	fô′-bĕr	fo′-behr
Faaborg (Den.)	fô′-bôr	fo′-bor
Fabbriche (It.)	fäb′-brē-kĕ	fahb′-bree-keh
Fabbricia (It.)	fäb-brē′-chä	fahb-bree′-chah
Fabriano (It.)	fä-bryä′-nô	fah-bryah′-no
Faenza (It.)	fä-ĕn′-tsä	fah-en′-tsah
Færoeerne *or* Færöerne (Den., isls.)	fĕr-û′-ər-nə	fehr-œ′-uhr-nuh
English the *Faeroes*, făr′-ōz [fehr′-ohz].		
Făgăraş (Rum.)	fə-gə-räsh′	fuh-guh-rahsh′
Hungarian *Fogaras*, fô′-gŏ-rŏsh [fo′-go-rosh].		
Fagernes (Nor.)	fä′-gər-nĕs	fah′-guhr-nes
Făget (Rum.)	fə-jĕt′	fuh-jet′
Faid (Tun., pass)	fä′-ēd	fah′-eed
Faifo (Indo-Ch.)	fā-fō′	fay-foh′
Fais (Oc.)	fīs′	fais′
Faisi (Oc.)	fä-ē′-sē	fah-ee′-see
Faiyum, el (Egypt)	fī-yōōm′, ĕl	fai-yoom′, el
Fakfak (NEI)	fäk′-fäk	fahk′-fahk
Falam (Burma)	fə-läm′	fuh-lahm′
Falange	*Eng.* fā′-lănj′	fay′-lanj′
	Sp. fä-län′-hĕ	fah-lahn′-heh
Spanish political party.		
falangist	*Eng.* fā-lăn′-jĭst	fay-lan′-jist
Falangista	*Sp.* fä-län-hēs′-tä	fah-lahn-hees′-tah
See *Falange.*		
Falster (Den., isl.)	fäl′-stər	fahl′-stuhr
Falsterbo (Sw.)	fäl′-stər-bōō	fahl′-stuhr-boo
Fălticeni (Rum.)	fəl-tē-chĕn′	fuhl-tee-chen′
Famagusta (Cyprus)	fä-mä-gōōs′-tä	fah-mah-goos′-tah
Fano (It.)	fä′-nô	fah′-no
Fanò (Gr., isl.)	*It.* fä-nô′	fah-no′
Also called *Othonoi*, ô′-thô-nē [o′-tho-nee].		
Fara (Oc.)	fä′-ra	fah′-rah
Farafra (Egypt)	fə-rä′-frä	fuh-rah′-frah
Farallon de Medinilla (Oc.)	*Sp.* fä-rä-lyôn′ dĕ mĕ-*th*ē-nē′-lyä	fah-rah-lyon′ deh meh-*th*ee-nee′-lyah
—— de Pájaros (Oc.)	—— dĕ pä′-hä-rôs	—— deh pah′-hah-ros
Faraulep (Oc.)	fä-rou′-lĕp	fah-rau′-lep
Faregh, el (Libya)	fä′-rĕg, ĕl	fah′-reg, el
Faria, Gustavo Cordeiro de (Braz. leader)	fə-rē′-ə, gōōs-tä′-vŏŏ kôr-dā′-rŏŏ dĭ	fuh-ree′-uh, goos-tah′-vu kor-day′-ru di

Faria, Oswaldo Cordeiro de (Braz. general)	fə-rē′-ə, ôz-väl′-do͝o kŏr-dā′-ro͝o dĭ	fuh-ree′-uh, oz-vahl′-du kor-day′-ru di
Farinacci, Roberto (It. fascist)	fä-rē-nät′-chē, rô-bĕr′-tô	fah-ree-naht′-chee, ro-behr′-to
Faro (Port.)	fä′-ro͝o	fah′-ru
Farouk (King of Egypt)	fä-ro͞ok′	fah-rook′
Farrington, Joseph (U.S. representative)	făr′-ĭng-tən	fehr′-ing-tuhn
Fars (Iran)	färs′	fahrs′
Farsund (Nor.)	fär′-so͝on	fahr′-sun
Fas (Mor.)	fäs′	fahs′
English *Fez*, q.v.		
fascismo (It.)	fä-shēs′-mô	fah-shees′-mo
fascist	*Eng.* făsh′-ĭst	fash′-ist
Italian *fascista*, *-i*, fä-shē′-stä, -ē [fah-shee′-stah, -ee].		
Fastov (Rus.)	fäs′-tŏf	fahs′-tof
Fatezh (Rus.)	fä′-tĕsh	fah′-tesh
Fauconnerie, la (Tun., airfield)	fō-kôn-rē′, lä	foh-kon-ree′, lah
Făurei (Rum.)	fə-o͝o-rā′	fuh-u-ray′
Fauro (Oc.)	fä-o͞o′-rô	fah-oo′-ro
Fauske (Nor.)	fou′-skə	fau′-skuh
Fauzieh (Queen of Iran)	fou-zē′-ə	fau-zee′-uh
Favignana (Sicily, isl.)	fä-vē-nyä′-nä	fah-vee-nyah′-nah
Fay, James H. (U.S. representative)	fā′	fay′
Fayal (Azores)	fä-yäl′	fah-yahl′
Fayu (Oc.)	fä′-yo͞o	fah′-yoo
Fécamp (Fr.)	fĕ-käN′	feh-kahN′
Fedhala (Mor.)	fə-dä′-lä	fuh-dah′-lah
Also spelled *Fdala*.		
Fedorovka (Rus.)	fyô′-dŏ-rŏf-kä	fyo′-do-rof-kah
Feighan, Michael A. (U.S. representative)	fē′-ăn	fee′-an
Félegyháza (Hung.)	fā′-lĕt(y)-hä′-zŏ	fay′-let(y)-hah′-zo
Also called *Kiskunfélegyháza*, q.v.		
Fellin (Est.)	*Rus.* fĕl′-lĭn	fel′-lin
Estonian *Viljandi*, q.v.		
Femund (Nor., lake)	fĕ′-mo͝on	feh′-mun
Fên (Ch., Shansi, riv.)	fŭn	fuhn
Fêng-ch'êng (Ch., Kiangsi, Manchu.)	fŭng-chŭng	fuhng-chuhng
Fêng-hsin (Ch., Kiangsi)	fŭng-shĭn	fuhng-shin

Fêng-shun (Ch., Kwangtung)	fŭng-sho͝on	fuhng-shun
Fêng-t'ien (Manchu., prov. and city)	fŭng-tyĕn	fuhng-tyen
Also called *Mukden*, q.v.		
Fên-i (Ch., Kiangsi)	fŭn-ē	fuhn-ee
Feni (Oc.)	fĕ'-nē	feh'-nee
Also called *Anir*, q.v.		
Fenny (India)	fĕn'-nĭ	fen'-ni
Fên-shui (Ch., Chekiang)	fŭn-shwā	fuhn-shway
Feodor (Alaska, Attu)	fyô'-dŏr	fyo'-dor
English *Theodore*, q.v.		
Feodosiya (Rus.)	fĕ-ŏ-dô'-sĭ-yä	feh-o-do'-si-yah
Feriana (Tun.)	fĕ-rĭ-ă'-nä	feh-ri-a'-nah
Ferigh (Libya)	fĕ-rēg'	feh-reeg'
Fernana (Tun.)	fĕr-nä'-nä	fehr-nah'-nah
Fernandez, Antonio M. (U.S. representative)	fĕr-nän'-dĕs, än-tô'-nyô	fehr-nahn'-des, ahn-to'-nyo
Ferrara (It.)	fĕr-rä'-rä	fehr-rah'-rah
Ferrol, el (Sp.)	fĕ-rôl', ĕl	feh-rol', el
Ferryville (Tun.)	fĕ-rē-vēl'	feh-ree-veel'
Named after the French leader.		
Feteşti (Rum.)	fĕ-tĕsht'	feh-tesht'
Fez (Mor.)	*Eng.* fĕz'	fez'
Arabic *Fas*, q.v.		
Fezzan (Libya)	fĕz-zăn'	fez-zan'
Fianarantsoa (Madag.)	fyə-nä'-rən-tsô'-ə	fyuh-nah'-ruhn-tso'-uh
Fier (Alb.)	fyĕr'	fyehr'
Figeac (Fr.)	fē-zhäk'	fee-zhahk'
Figueiredo, Assís de (Braz. leader)	fē-gĕ-rĕ'-do͞o, ä-sēs' dĭ	fee-geh-reh'-du, ah-sees' di
Both names should be used, thus: *Assís de Figueiredo*, not *Figueiredo* alone.		
Figueroa, Manuel Mora (Sp. leader). See *Mora Figueroa, Manuel.*		
Filatov (Rus. scientist)	fĭ-lä'-tŏf	fi-lah'-tof
Filefjell (Nor., mt.)	fē'-lə-fyĕl	fee'-luh-fyel
Filene's (Boston)	fī-lēnz'	fai-leenz'
filho	fē'-lyo͞o	fee'-lyu
An element, meaning *son* or *junior*, in Portuguese names. Look up the other part of the name.		
Filiaşi (Rum.)	fē-lyäsh'	fee-lyahsh'
Filicudi (It., isl.)	fē-lē-ko͞o'-dē	fee-lee-koo'-dee
Filyas (Turk.)	fēl'-yäs'	feel'-yahs'

Finale (Sicily)	fē-nä′-lĕ	fee-nah′-leh
Finistère (Fr.)	fē-nē-stĕr′	fee-nee-stehr′
Finisterre (Sp., point)	*Eng.* fĭn′-ĭs-tĕr′	fin′-is-tehr′
	Sp. fē-nēs-tĕ′-rĕ	fee-nees-teh′-reh
Finland	*Eng.* fĭn′-lənd	fin′-luhnd

Finnish *Suomi*, sŏŏ′-ô′-mē [su′-o′-mee].

Finschhafen (Oc.)	*Eng.* fĭnch′-hä-fən	finch′-hah-fuhn
	Ger. fĭnsh′-hä-fən	finsh′-hah-fuhn
Finse (Nor.)	fĭn′-sə	fin′-suh
Firdausi (Per. poet)	*Eng.* fər-dou′-sē	fuhr-dau′-see
	Pers. fər-dō-sē′	fuhr-doh-see′
Firenze (It.)	fē-rĕn′-dzĕ	fee-ren′-dzeh

English *Florence*, q.v.

Firuzkuh (Iran)	fē-rōōz′-kōō	fee-rooz′-koo
Fischsee (Pol., lake)	*Ger.* fĭsh′-zā	fish′-zay

Polish *Morskie Oko*, q.v.

Fiuggi (It.)	fyōōd′-jē	fyood′-jee
fiume	fyōō′-mĕ	fyoo′-meh

An element, meaning *river*, in Italian place names. It may be necessary to look up the other part of the name.

Fiume (It.)	fyōō′-mĕ	fyoo′-meh
Fiume Torto (Sicily)	fyōō′-mĕ tôr′-tô	fyoo′-meh tor′-to
Fjærland (Nor.)	fyăr′-län	fyehr′-lahn
fjell	fyĕl′	fyel′

An element, meaning *mountain*, in Norwegian place names.

Fjelstad, Anders (Nor. minister)	fyĕl′-stä, än′-ərs *or* än′-dərs	fyel′-stah, ahn′-uhrs *or* ahn′-duhrs
Fjerland (Nor.)	fyăr′-län	fyehr′-lahn
fjord (Nor.)	fyōr′ *or* fyŏŏr′	fyohr′ *or* fyur′

An element in Norwegian place names. The English variant is *fiord*, pronounced *fyôrd* [fyord].

Flaam (Nor.)	flôm′	flom′
Flaminian Way (It., road)	*Eng.* flə-mĭn′-ĭ-ən	fluh-min′-i-uhn
Flandin, Pierre Étienne	fläN-dăN′, pyĕr′ ĕ-tyĕn′	flahN-daN′, pyehr′ eh-tyen′
Flekkefjord (Nor.)	flĕk′-ə-fyōr	flek′-uh-fyohr
Flensburg (Ger.)	*Eng.* flĕnz′-bûrg	flenz′-buhrg
	Ger. flĕns′-bŏŏrk(h)	flens′-burk(h)
Flinders (Austral., bay and mts.)	flĭn′-dərz	flin′-duhrz
Florence (It.)	*Eng.* flŏr′-əns	flor′-uhns

Italian *Firenze*, q.v.

Flores (Azores)	flô′-rĭsh	flo′-rish

Flores (NEI)	flô′-rĕs	flo′-res
Florianópolis (Brazil)	flôr-yə-nô′-po͝o-lēs	flor-yuh-no′-pu-lees
Also called, unofficially, *Desterro*, q.v.		
Florina (Gr.) See *Phlorina*.		
Floroe *or* Florö *or* Floroey *or* Floröy (Nor.)	flō′-rû *or* flō′-rûĭ	floh′-rœ *or* floh′-rœi
flotsam	flŏt′-səm	flot′-suhm
Flushing (Neth.)	*Eng.* flŭsh′-ĭng	fluhsh′-ing
Dutch *Vlissingen*, q.v.		
Fly (New Guinea riv.)	flī′	flai′
Foča (Yugosl.)	fô′-chä	fo′-chah
Focke, Heinrich	fôk′-ə	fok′-uh
German designer of the airplane Focke-Wulf, fôk′-ə-vo͝olf′ [fok′-uh-vulf′].		
Focşani (Rum.)	fôk-shän′	fok-shahn′
Foerde (Nor.)	fûr′-də	fœr′-duh
Fogaras (Rum.) See *Făgăraş*.		
Foggia (It.)	fôd′-jä	fod′-jah
Foix (Fr.)	fwä′	fwah′
Fojnica (Yugosl.)	foi′-nĭ-tsä	foi′-ni-tsah
Folgefonnen (Nor.)	fôl′-gə-fôn-ən	fol′-guh-fon-uhn
A variant is *Folgefonna*.		
Fondouk el Aouareb (Tun.)	fŏn′-do͞ok ĕl ä-wă′-rĕb	fon′-dook el ah-wa′-reb
Foo-chow (Ch., Fukien)	*Eng.* fo͞o-chou	foo-chau
	Ch. fo͞o-jō	foo-joh
Also called *Min-how*, q.v.		
Foo-chow (Ch., Yünnan)	fo͞o-jō	foo-joh
Forand, Aime J. (U.S. representative)	fōr′-ănd′, ā′-mĭ	fohr′-and′, ay′-mi
Förde (Nor.)	fûr′-də	fœr′-duh
Fordon (Pol.)	fôr′-dôn	for′-don
Forlì (It.)	fôr-lē′	for-lee′
Formia (It.)	fôr′-myä	for′-myah
Formicola (It.)	fôr-mē′-kô-lä	for-mee′-ko-lah
formidable	fôr′-mĭ-də-bəl	for′-mi-duh-buhl
A stress on the second syllable is not recommended.		
Formigny (Fr.)	fôr-mē-nyē′	for-mee-nyee′
Formosa (isl.)	fôr-mō′-sə	for-moh′-suh
Chinese *T'ai-wan*, tī-wän [tai-wahn].		
Fornebu (Nor.)	fôr′-nə-bo͞o	for′-nuh-boo
Fortaleza (Brazil)	fŏr-tä-lĕ′-zə	for-tah-leh′-zuh
Also called *Ceará*, q.v.		
Fort Bayard (Ch., Kwangtung, Fr. colony) See *Bayard*.		
Fort Lamy (Fr. Eq. Afr.) See *Lamy*.		

Foscari (It.)	fô′-skä-rē	fo′-skah-ree
Fosna (Nor.)	fōs′-nä	fohs′-nah
foss	fôs′	fos′
An element, meaning *waterfall* or *rapids*, in Norwegian place names.		
Fossheim (Nor.)	fôs′-hām	fos′-haym
Fossli (Nor.)	fôs′-lē	fos′-lee
Fougères (Fr.)	fo͞o-zhĕr′	foo-zhehr′
Fou-liang (Ch., Kiangsi)	fō-lyäng	foh-lyahng
Foum Tatahouine (Tun.)	fo͞om tä-tä-hwēn′	foom tah-tah-hween′
Fouquières lès Lens (Fr.)	fo͞o-kyĕr′ lĕ läN′	foo-kyehr′ leh lahN′
Franeker (Neth.)	frä′-nə-kər	frah′-nuh-kuhr
Frankfort on Main; on Oder (Ger.)	*Eng.* frănk′-fərt ŏn mān; ŏn ō′-dər	frank′-fuhrt on mayn; on oh′-duhr
Frankfurt am Main; an der Oder (Ger.)	fränk′-fo͝ort äm mīn′; än dər ō′-dər	frahnk′-furt ahm main′; ahn duhr oh′-duhr
English *Frankfort*, q.v.		
Frascati (It.)	frä-skä′-tē	frah-skah′-tee
Frashër (Alb.)	frä′-shər	frah′-shuhr
Greek *Phrasare*, frä′-sä-rē [frah′-sah-ree].		
Frashëri (Alb.) See *Frashër*.		
Fredericia (Den.)	*Eng.* frĕd′-ə-rĭsh′-yə *Dan.* frĕ-*th*ə-rē′-tsĭ-ä	fred′-uh-rish′-yuh freh-*th*uh-ree′-tsi-ah
Frederikshaap (Greenl.)	frĕ*th*′-ĕ-rēks-hôp′	fre*th*′-eh-reeks-hop′
Frederikshavn (Den.)	frĕ*th*′-ə-rēks-houn′	fre*th*′-uh-reeks-haun′
Fredrikshamn (Fin.)	*Sw.* frā′-drēks-hämn′	fray′-dreeks-hahmn′
Finnish *Hamina*, q.v.		
Fredrikstad (Nor.)	frĕd′-rēk-stä	fred′-reek-stah
Freiberg (Ger.)	frī′-bĕrk(h)	frai′-behrk(h)
Freiburg (Ger.)	frī′-bo͝ork(h)	frai′-burk(h)
An English pronunciation of both *Freiberg* and *Freiburg* is frī′-bûrg [frai′-buhrg].		
Freistadt (Austria)	frī′-shtät	frai′-shtaht
Fréjus, Col de (Fr., mt.)	frĕ-zhüs′, kôl də	freh-zhüs′, kol duh
Fremantle (Austral.)	frē′-măn-tl	free′-man-tl
Friedenshütte (Pol.)	*Ger.* frē′-dəns-hüt′-ə	free′-duhns-hüt′-uh
Polish *Nowy Bytom*, q.v.		
Friedrichshafen (Ger.)	frē′-drĭk(h)s-hä′-fən	free′-drik(h)s-hah′-fuhn
Friedrichstadt (Latvia)	*Ger.* frē′-drĭk(h)-shtät	free′-drik(h)-shtaht
Latvian *Jaunjelgava*, q.v.		
Friesche Meeren (Neth.)	frē′-sə mā′-rən	free′-suh may′-ruhn

Friesland (Neth., prov.)	*Eng.* frēz′-lənd	freez′-luhnd
	Du. frēs′-länt	frees′-lahnt
Friezenveen (Neth.)	frē′-zən-vān′	free′-zuhn-vayn′
Frihagen, Anders (Nor. leader)	frē′-hä-gən, än′-ərs *or* än′-dərs	free′-hah-guhn, ahn′-uhrs *or* ahn′-duhrs
Frisches Haff (Ger., lagoon)	frĭsh′-əs häf′	frish′-uhs hahf′
Frome	*Austral.* frōm′	frohm′
	Eng. fro͞om′	froom′
Frosinone (It.)	frô-sē-nô′-nĕ	fro-see-no′-neh
Frunze (Rus.)	fro͞on′-zĕ	froon′-zeh
Fuad (Former King of Egypt)	fo͞o-ăd′	foo-ad′
Fucine (It.)	fo͞o-chē′-nĕ	foo-chee′-neh
Fucino (It.)	fo͞o′-chē-nô	foo′-chee-no
Fuehrer, der (Ger.)	fü′-rər, dər	fü′-ruhr, duhr

German for *the leader*. Cf. *il Duce* and *el Caudillo*.

Fuenen (Den., isl.) See *Fyn.*

Fuenterrabía (Sp.)	fwĕn-tĕ-rä-bē′-ä	fwen-teh-rah-bee′-ah
Fuerstenwalde (Ger.)	für′-stən-väl′-də	für′-stuhn-vahl′-duh

Note that the second syllable is -stən, not -shtən.

Fuka (Egypt)	fo͞o′-kä	foo′-kah
Fukien (Ch., prov.)	fo͞o-kyĕn	foo-kyen
Fukui (Jap.)	fo͞o-ko͞o-ē	foo-koo-ee
Fukuoka (Jap.)	fo͞o-ko͞o-ô-kä	foo-koo-o-kah
Fulbright, J. W. (U.S. representative)	fo͝ol′-brīt	ful′-brait
Fulda (Ger.)	fo͝ol′-dä	ful′-dah
Fulmer, Hampton P. (U.S. representative)	fo͝ol′-mər	ful′-muhr
Fu-min (Ch., Yünnan)	fo͞o-mĭn	foo-min

Fum Tatavin (Tun.) See *Foum Tatahouine.*

Funafuti (Oc.)	fo͞o-nä-fo͞o′-tē	foo-nah-foo′-tee
Furka (Yugosl.)	fo͞or′-kä	foor′-kah
Furlong, Grant (U.S. representative)	fûr-lông′	fuhr-long′
Furneaux (Austral., isls.)	fûr′-nō	fuhr′-noh
Furnes (Belg.)	*Fr.* fürn′	fürn′

Flemish *Veurne*, q.v. If *Furnes* comes into the news, it will probably be Anglicized to fûr′-nĭs [fuhr′-nis].

Fürstenfeld (Austria)	für′-stən-fĕlt	für′-stuhn-felt
Fürstenwalde (Ger.)	für′-stən-väl′-də	für′-stuhn-vahl′-duh

Note that the second syllable is -stən, not -shtən.

Fusan (Korea)	fo͞o-sän	foo-sahn

fusha (Alb.) See *fushë.*

fushë (Alb.)	fo͞o′-shə	foo′-shuh
An element, meaning *plain*, in Albanian place names. Look up the other part of the name.		
Futog (Yugosl.)	fo͞o′-tôg	foo′-tog
Fu-t'u (Ch., Fukien, isl.)	fo͞o-to͞o	foo-too
Fuyang (Ch., Chekiang)	fo͞o-yäng	foo-yahng
Fyn (Den., isl.)	fün′	fün′
German *Fünen*, fü′-nən [fü′-nuhn].		
Gabès (Tun.)	gä′-bĕs	gah′-bes
Gablonz (Cz.)	*Ger.* gä′-blônts	gah′-blonts
Czech *Jablonec*, q.v.		
Gabrovo (Bulg.)	gä′-brŏ-vŏ	gah′-bro-vo
Gacko (Yugosl.)	gäts′-kô	gahts′-ko
Gadames *or* Gedames (Libya) See *Ghadames*.		
Gadaronesi (Dodec.) See *Gaidaro*.		
Gadd el Ahmar (Libya)	gäd ĕl ä′-mär *or* äk(h)′-mär	gahd el ah′-mahr *or* ahk(h)′-mahr
Gaasterland (Neth.)	k(h)äs′-tər-länt	k(h)ahs′-tuhr-lahnt
Gadyach (Rus.)	gä′-dyäch	gah′-dyahch
Gaeta (It.)	gä-ĕ′-tä	gah-eh′-tah
Gaeta (Oc.)	gä′-ĕ-tä	gah′-eh-tah
Gaetano (Italian name)	gä-ĕ-tä′-nô	gah-eh-tah′-no
Gaferut (Oc.)	gä′-fĕ-ro͞ot	gah′-feh-root
Gafsa (Tun.)	găf′-sä	gaf′-sah
Gagliano (It.)	gä-lyä′-nô	gah-lyah′-no
Gagi (Oc.)	gä′-gē	gah′-gee
Both *g's* as in *get.*		
Gaidaro (Dodec.)	*It.* gī-dä′-rô	gai-dah′-ro
Greek *Gaïdouronesi*, gī-*th*o͞o-rô-nē′-sē [gai-*th*oo-ro-nee′-see]; *Gaïdaronesi*, gī-*th*ä-rô-nē′-sē [gai-*th*ah-ro-nee′-see], and *Gadaronesi*, gä-*th*ä-rô-nē′-sē [gah-*th*ah-ro-nee′-see].		
Gaïdaronesi (Crete, isl.)	gī-*th*ä-rô-nē′-sē	gai-*th*ah-ro-nee′-see
Gaïdouronesi (Gr., isl.; Dodec.) See *Gaidaro.*		
Gaillard (Am. name)	gĭl-yärd′	gil-yahrd′
Gainasch (Latvia)	*Rus.* gī′-näsh	gai′-nahsh
Latvian *Ainaži*, q.v.		
Gainovka (Pol.) See *Hajnówka.*		
Galaţi (Rum.)	gä-läts′	gah-lahts′
Also spelled *Galatz.*		
Galato (Dodec., Rh.)	gä-lä′-tô	gah-lah′-to
Galdhoepiggen *or* Galdhöpiggen (Nor., mt.)	gäl′-hû-pĭg-ən	gahl′-hœ-pig-uhn

Galicia (Pol., dist.)	*Eng.* gə-lĭsh′-yə	guh-lish′-yuh
	Rus. gä-lē′-tsĭ-yä	gah-lee′-tsi-yah
Polish *Galicja*, gä-lē′-chä [gah-lee′-chah].		
Galicia (Sp., dist.)	*Eng.* gə-lĭsh′-ə	guh-lish′-uh
	Sp. gä-lē′-thyä *or* -syä	gah-lee′-thyah *or* -syah
Galičica (Yugosl., mts.)	gä′-lē′-chĭ-tsä	gah′-lee′-chi-tsah
Galičnik (Yugosl.)	gä′-lĭch-nĭk	gah′-lich-nik
Galle (Ceylon)	gäl′	gahl′
Gallipoli (It.)	gäl-lē′-pô-lē	gahl-lee′-po-lee
Gallipoli (Turk., pen., town)	*Eng.* gə-lĭp′-ə-lĭ	guh-lip′-uh-li
Turkish *Gelibolu*, gə-lē′-bô-lo͞o [guh-lee′-bo-lu]. The peninsula is also called the *Chersonese*, q.v.		
Gallipolis (Ohio)	găl′-ĭ-pō-lēs′	gal′-i-poh-lees′
Gallo (Gr., cape) See *Akritas.*		
Gallo (Sicily, cape)	gäl′-lô	gahl′-lo
Gambier (Austral., mt.)	găm′-bĭ-ər	gam′-bi-uhr
Gambut (Libya)	gäm′-bo͞ot′	gahm′-but′
Gamvik (Nor.)	gäm′-vēk	gahm′-veek
Gandhi, Mahatma Mohandas Karamchand (Indian leader)	gän′-dē, mə-hät′-mə mō-hən-däs′ kə-rəm-chŭnd′	gahn′-dee, muh-haht′-muh moh-huhn-dahs′ kuh-ruhm-chuhnd′
Gangaro (Yugosl., isl.)	*It.* gäng′-gä-rô	gahng′-gah-ro
Serb-Croat *Kankar*, q.v.		
Ganges (India, riv.)	găn′-jēz	gan′-jeez
Sanscrit *Ganga*, gŭng′-gä [guhng′-gah].		
Gangi (Sicily)	gän′-jē	gahn′-jee
Ganjam (India)	gŭn-jäm′	guhn-jahm′
Ganongga (Oc.)	gä-nông′-gä	gah-nong′-gah
Gantsevichi (Pol.) See *Hancewicze.*		
Gap (Fr.)	gäp′	gahp′
Gapsal (Est.)	*Rus.* gäp′-säl(y)	gahp′-sahl(y)
Estonian *Haapsalu*, q.v.		
Garaet Achkel (Tun., lake)	gä-rä′-ət äsh′-kĕl	gah-rah′-uht ahsh′-kel
Garam (Hung., Cz., riv.)	*Hung.* gŏ′-rŏm	go′-rom
Czech *Hron*, q.v.		
Garand, John C.	găr′-ənd	gehr′-uhnd

The inventor of the Garand rifle writes: "I have given different pronunciations of my name at various times but, right or wrong, I must live with it." These include gə-rănd′ [guh-rand′] and gä-räN′ [gah-rahN′], but găr′-ənd [gehr′-uhnd] is the pronunciation he prefers.

Gardemoen (Nor.)	gär′-də-mōn	gahr′-duh-mohn
Garešnica (Yugosl.)	gä′-rĕsh′-nĭ-tsä	gah′-resh′-ni-tsah
Gargaliani (*or* -noi) (Gr.)	gär-gä-lyä′-nē	gahr-gah-lyah′-nee
Garian (Libya)	gä-rē-yăn′	gah-ree-yan′
Garigliano (It.)	gä-rē-lyä′-nô	gah-ree-lyah′-no
Garitsa (Corfu)	gä-rē′-tsä	gah-ree′-tsah
Garnes (Nor.)	gär′-nĕs	gahr′-nes
Garonne (Fr., riv.)	gä-rôn′	gah-ron′
Garove (Oc.)	gä-rô′-vĕ	gah-ro′-veh
Gartok (India)	gär-tŏk′	gahr-tok′
Garwolin (Pol.)	gär-vô′-lĭn	gahr-vo′-lin
Russian spelling *Garvolin.*		
Gasenpot (Latvia)	*Rus.* gä′-zĕn-pŏt	gah′-zen-pot
Latvian *Aizpute*, q.v. German *Hasenpoth*, q.v.		
Gasmata (Oc.)	gäs-mä′-tä	gahs-mah′-tah
Gasr	gäsr′	gahsr′
An element, meaning *castle*, in Arabic place names.		
Gastein (Austria)	gä′-stīn	gah′-stain
Gastouni (Gr.)	gä-sto͞o′-nē	gah-stoo′-nee
Gathings, E. C. (U.S. representative)	găth′-ĭngz	gath′-ingz
Gatnya (Rus.)	gät′-nyä	gaht′-nyah
Gatukai (Oc.)	gä-to͞o-kī′	gah-too-kai′
Gauhati (India)	gou-hä′-tē	gau-hah′-tee
Gauja (Latvia, riv.)	gou′-yä	gau′-yah
Gaulle, Charles de (Fr. leader)	gōl′, shärl′ də	gohl′, shahrl′ duh
Gausta (Nor., mt.)	gou′-stä	gau′-stah
Gavagan, Joseph A. (Former U.S. representative)	găv′-ə-gĕn	gav′-uh-gen
Gavdos (Crete, isl.)	gäv′-*th*ô(s)	gahv′-*tho*(s)
Gavin, L. H. (U.S. representative)	găv′-ĭn	gav′-in
Gävle (Sw.)	yĕv′-lə	yev′-luh
Gavrilovo (Rus.)	gä-vrē′-lŏ-vŏ	gah-vree′-lo-vo
Gavrilovski Posad (Rus.)	gä-vrē′-lŏf-skĭ pŏ-säd′	gah-vree′-lof-ski po-sahd′
Gavutu (Oc.)	gä-vo͞o′-to͞o	gah-voo′-too
Gaya (India)	gī′-ə	gai′-uh
Gazala, el (Libya)	gä-zä′-lä, ĕl	gah-zah′-lah, el
Gazi (Crete)	gä′-zē	gah′-zee

Gaziköy (Turk.)	gä-zē′-kûĭ	gah-zee′-kœi
Gaziman (Rus., riv.)	gä-zē-män′	gah-zee-mahn′
Gdańsk See *Danzig*.		
Gdov (Rus.)	gdôf′	gdof′
Gdynia (Pol.)	gdĭ′-nyä	gdi′-nyah
Gearhart, Bertrand W. (U.S. representative)	gĭr′-härt	gihr′-hahrt

Mr. Gearhart writes, "With a hard G and an e-a-r as in 'ear' . . . In other words, Gear is pronounced like the gears you shift in your automobile."

Gedames (Libya) See *Ghadames*.		
Geelong (Austral.)	jĭ-lông′	ji-long′
Geelvink (NEI)	k(h)āl′-vĭngk	k(h)ayl′-vingk
Geg (Alb.)	*Eng.* gĕg′	geg′

North Albanian. Albanian *Gegë*, gĕ′-gə [geh′-guh], and *Gega*.

Geilo (Nor.)	yā′-lō	yay′-loh
Geiranger (Nor.)	gā′-räng-ər	gay′-rahng-uhr
Gela (Sicily)	*It.* jĕ′-lä	jeh′-lah
	Eng. jē′-lə	jee′-luh
Gelati (Sicily)	jĕ-lä′-tē	jeh-lah′-tee
Gelderland (Neth., prov.)	*Eng.* gĕl′-dər-lănd	gel′-duhr-land
	Du. k(h)ĕl′-dər-länt	k(h)el′-duhr-lahnt
Geldermalsen (Neth.)	k(h)ĕl′-dər-mäl′-sən	k(h)el′-duhr-mahl′-suhn
Geleen (Neth.)	k(h)ə-lān′	k(h)uh-layn′
Gelendzhik (Rus.)	gĕ-lĕn-jĭk′	geh-len-jik′
Gelibolu (Turk., pen., town) See *Gallipoli*.		
Gelsenkirchen (Ger.)	gĕl′-zən-kĭr′-k(h)ən	gel′-zuhn-kihr′-k(h)uhn
Genichesk (Rus.)	gĕ-nĭ-chĕsk′	geh-ni-chesk′
Genitsa *or* Gianitsa (Gr.)	yĕ-nē-tsä′	yeh-nee-tsah′
	or yä-nē-tsä′	yah-nee-tsah′

Serb-Croat *Janica*, yä′-nĭ-tsä [yah′-ni-tsah].

Gennargentu (Sard., mts.)	jĕn′-när-jĕn′-to͞o	jen′-nahr-jen′-too
Gennep (Neth.)	k(h)ĕn′-əp	k(h)en′-uhp
Genoa (It.)	*Eng.* jĕn′-ō-ə	jen′-oh-uh
Genova (It.)	jĕ′-nô-vä	jeh′-no-vah

English *Genoa*, q.v.

Gensan (Korea)	gĕn-sän	gen-sahn
Genusus (Alb., riv.) See *Shkumbi*.		
Genzano (It.)	jĕn-tsä′-nô	jen-tsah′-no
Georgatos (Gr. collab.)	yôr-gä′-tôs	yor-gah′-tos

George, Alphonse Joseph (Fr. general)	zhôrzh′, äl-fôNs′ zhô-zĕf′	zhorzh′, ahl-foNs′ zho-zef′
Georgioupolis (Crete)	yôr-yōō′-pô-lē(s)	yor-yoo′-po-lee(s)

Also called *Almyros*, äl-mē-rôs′ [ahl-mee-ros′] *or* är-mē-rôs′ [ahr-mee-ros′].

Geographe (Austral., bay)	jĭ-ŏg′-rə-fĭ	ji-og′-ruh-fi

Pronounced as if spelled *geography*.

Georgievsk (Rus.)	gĕ-ôr′-gĭ-yĕfsk	geh-or′-gi-yefsk
Gerace (It.)	jĕ-rä′-chĕ	jeh-rah′-cheh
Gerbini (Sicily)	jĕr-bē′-nē	jehr-bee′-nee
Gerlach, Charles L. (U.S. representative)	gûr′-läk(h)′	guhr′-lahk(h)′
Gerona (Sp.)	hĕ-rô′-nä	heh-ro′-nah
Gerry, Peter G. (U.S. senator)	gĕr′-ĭ	gehr′-i
Gesso (Sicily)	jĕs′-sô	jes′-so
Gestapo	gə-stä′-pō *or* gə-shtä′-pō	guh-stah′-poh guh-shtah′-poh

Getulio Vargas See *Vargas, Getulio.*

Ghadames (Libya)	gə-dä′-mĕs	guh-dah′-mes

Also spelled *Gadames* and *Gedames.*

Ghardimaou (Tun.)	gär-dĭ-mă′-ōō	gahr-di-ma′-oo
ghat	gôt′ *or* gät′	gawt′ *or* gaht′
Ghats (India, mts.)	gôts′ *or* gäts′	gawts′ *or* gahts′
Ghazni (Afghan.)	gŭz′-nē	guhz′-nee
Gheel (Belg.)	k(h)āl′	k(h)ayl′
Ghent (Belg.)	*Eng.* gĕnt′	gent′

Flemish *Gent*, k(h)ĕnt′ [k(h)ent′]. French *Gand*, gäN′ [gahN′].

Gheorgheni (Rum.)	gyôr-gĕn′	gyor-gen′

Hungarian *Gyergyószentmiklós*, dyĕr′-dyô-sĕnt′-mĭk-lôsh [dyehr′-dyo-sent′-mik-losh].

Gherla (Rum.)	gĕr′-lä	gehr′-lah
Ghilan *or* Gilan (Iran)	gē-län′	gee-lahn′
Ghisonaccia (Corsica)	gē-sô-nät′-chä	gee-so-naht′-chah
Giacomo	jä′-kô-mô	jah′-ko-mo

Italian form of *Jacob* and *James.* It should not be stressed on the second syllable.

Giadalla (Libya)	jä-däl′-lä	jah-dahl′-lah
Gialam (Indo-Ch.)	zhä-lŭm′	zhah-luhm′
Gialo (Libya)	jä′-lō	jah′-loh
Gialomonokhoron (Crete)	yä-lô-mô-nô′-hô-rô(n)	yah-lo-mo-no′-ho-ro(n)
Giannesada (Crete, isl.)	yä-nē-sä′-*th*ä	yah-nee-sah′-*th*ah

Giarabub (Libya)	jä′-rä-bo͞ob′	jah′-rah-boob′
Also spelled *Jarabub.*		
Giarre (Sicily)	jär′-rĕ	jahr′-reh
gibber	jĭb′-ər	jib′-uhr
An Australian word meaning *rock* or *stone.*		
Gibostad (Nor.)	gē′-bō-stä	gee′-boh-stah
Giglio (It., isls.)	jē′-lyô	jee′-lyo
Gijón (Sp.)	hē-hôn′	hee-hon′
Gijunabena (Oc.)	gē-jo͞o-nä-bĕ′-nä	gee-joo-nah-beh′-nah
Gilan *or* Ghilan (Iran)	gē-län′	gee-lahn′
Gilgit (India)	gĭl′-gĭt	gil′-git
Giljevo (Yugosl.)	gē′-lyĕ-vô	gee′-lyeh-vo
Gillette, Guy M. (U.S. senator)	jĭ-lĕt′	ji-let′
Gillie, George W. (U.S. representative)	gĭl′-ĭ	gil′-i
Gilze en Reijen (Neth.)	k(h)ĭl′-zə ĕn rī′-ən	k(h)il′-zuh en rai′-uhn
Ginneken (Neth.)	k(h)ĭn′-ə-kən	k(h)in′-uh-kuhn
Ginza (Jap.)	gĭn-zä	gin-zah
Gioia di Tauro (It.)	jô′-yä dē tou′-rô	jo′-yah dee tau′-ro
Gioiosa Ionica *or* Jonica (It.)	jô-yô′-sä yô′-nē-kä	jo-yo′-sah yo′-nee-kah
Gioja (It.)	jô′-yä	jo′-yah
Giojosa (It.)	jô-yô′-zä	jo-yo′-zah
Gioumoultzina (Gr.) See *Komotine.*		
Gioura (Gr., isl.)	yo͞o′-rä	yoo′-rah
giovanezza (It.)	jô-vä-nĕt′-sä	jo-vah-net′-sah
Giraud, Henri Honoré (Fr. general)	zhē-rō′, äN-rē′ ô-nô-rĕ′	zhee-roh′, ahN-ree′ o-no-reh′
Girgenti (It.)	jēr-jĕn′-tē	jeer-jen′-tee
Officially *Agrigento,* q.v.		
Gissi (It.)	jēs′-sē	jees′-see
Giupana (Yugosl., isl.)	*It.* jo͞o-pä′-nä	joo-pah′-nah
Serb-Croat *Šipan,* q.v.		
Giurgiu (Rum.)	jo͝or′-jo͝o	jur′-ju
Giza, el (Egypt)	gē′-zə, ĕl	gee′-zuh, el
Also spelled *Gizeh.*		
gizmo	gĭz′-mō	giz′-moh
A word meaning *gadget,* used in the Navy air force; perhaps derived from the Arabic *gism,* gĭsm′ [gism′], meaning *body, stature, strength.*		
Gizo (Oc.)	gē′-zô	gee′-zo
Gj- For names of Yugoslavia in *Gj-,* see also *D-, Đ,* and *Dj-.*		
Gjalica (Alb., mt.) See *Gjalicë.*		

Gjalicë (Alb., mt.)	gyä′-lē-tsə	gyah′-lee-tsuh

Also called *Mal i Gjalicës.* Serb-Croat *Đalica,* dyä′-lĭ-tsä [dyah′-li-tsah].

Gjendesheim (Nor.)	yĕn′-dəs-hām	yen′-duhs-haym
Gjinokastër (Alb.)	gyē-nô-kä′-stər	gyee-no-kah′-stuhr

Italian *Argirocastro,* är-jē-rô-kä′-strô [ahr-jee-ro-kah′-stro]. Greek *Argyrokastron,* q.v.

Gjinokastra (Alb.) See *Gjinokastër.*

Gjoevik *or* Gjövik (Nor.)	yû′-vēk	yœ′-veek

Gjuhëzës, Kep i (Alb., cape) English *Glossa,* q.v.

Gjurgjevac (Yugosl.)	dūr′-dyĕ-väts	dyoor′-dyeh-vahts
Gjusevo (Bulg.)	gū′-sĕ-vŏ	gyoo′-seh-vo
Gladbach-Rheydt (Ger.)	glät′-bäk(h)-rīt′	glaht′-bahk(h)-rait′
Glamoč (Yugosl.)	glä′-môch	glah′-moch
Glasgow (Scot.)	*Am.* glăs′-gō *or* -kō	glas′-goh *or* -koh
	Scot. gläs′-gō *or* -kō	glahs′-goh *or* -koh
Głębokie (Pol.)	glăN-bô′-kyĕ	glaN-bo′-kyeh

Russian *Glubokoe,* gl͝oo-bô′-kŏ-yĕ [glu-bo′-ko-yeh].

Gledićske planine (Yugosl., mts.)	glĕ′-dĭch-skĕ plä′-nē′-nĕ	gleh′-dich-skeh plah′-nee′-neh
Gleiwitz (Ger.)	glī′-vĭts	glai′-vits
Glibovac (Yugosl.)	glē′-bô-väts	glee′-bo-vahts
Glière, Reinhold (Rus. composer)	glĭ-yĕr′, rān′-gŏlt	gli-yehr′, rayn′-golt
Glittertind (Nor.)	glĭt′-ər-tĭn	glit′-uhr-tin
Globo, O (Braz. newspaper)	glô′-b͝oo, ͝oo	glo′-bu, u
Glomfjord (Nor.)	glôm′-fyōr	glom′-fyohr
Glomma (Nor., riv.)	glôm′-ä	glom′-ah
Gloška (Yugosl., mt.)	glôsh′-kä	glosh′-kah
Glossa (Alb., cape)	*Eng.* glôs′-ə	glos′-uh

Albanian *Kep i Gjuhëzës,* kĕp′ ē gū-hə′-zəs [kep′ ee gyoo-huh′-zuhs], and *Karaburun,* q.v.

Gloucester	glŏs′-tər	glos′-tuhr
	or glôs′-tər	glos′-tuhr
Glusk (Rus.)	gl͞oosk′	gloosk′
Glukhov (Rus.)	gl͞oo′-hŏf	gloo′-hof
Gneisenau (Ger.)	gnī′-zə-nou	gnai′-zuh-nau
Gniew (Pol.)	gnyĕf′	gnyef′
Gniezna (Pol., riv.)	gnyĕz′-nä	gnyez′-nah
Gniezno (Pol.)	gnyĕz′-nô	gnyez′-no
Gnjilane (Yugosl.)	gnyē′-lä-nĕ	gnyee′-lah-neh
Gnome et Rhône (Fr., Le Mans)	gnōm ĕ rōn′	gnohm eh rohn′
Goa *or* Gôa (Port. India)	gō′-ə	goh′-uh
Godavari (India, riv.)	**gō-dä′-və-rē**	**goh-dah′-vuh-ree**

Godhavn (Greenl.)	gô*th*′-houn	go*th*′-haun
Godolesh (Alb.)	gô-dô′-lĕsh	go-do′-lesh
Godoleshi (Alb.) See *Godolesh.*		
Gödöllő (Hung.)	gû′-dûl-lû	gœ′-dœl-lœ
Godthaab (Greenl.)	gôt′-hôp′	got′-hop′
Goedereede (Neth., isl.)	k(h)o͞o′-də-rā′-də	k(h)oo′-duh-ray′-duh
The island is divided into *Goeree,* q.v., and *Overflakkee,* q.v.		
Goeding (Cz.) See *Hodonín.*		
Goeree (Neth., isl.) See *Goedereede.*	k(h)o͞o′-rā′	k(h)oo′-ray′
Goerlitz (Ger.)	gûr′-lĭts	gœr′-lits
Gogra (India, riv.)	gō′-grä	goh′-grah
Goiânia (Brazil)	gô-yä′-nyə	go-yah′-nyuh
Goiaz (Brazil)	gô-yäs′	go-yahs′
Gokteik (Burma)	gōk′-tāk′	gohk′-tayk′
Gol (Nor.)	gōl′	gohl′
Goldingen (Latvia)	*Ger.* gôl′-dĭng-ən *Rus.* gôl(y)′-dĭn-gĕn	gol′-ding-uhn gol(y)′-din-gen
Latvian *Kuldiga,* q.v.		
Golema Rudina (Balkan mt.)	gô′-lĕ-mä ro͞o′-dĭ-nä	go′-leh-mah roo′-di-nah
Goleš (Yugosl., mt.)	gô′-lĕsh	go′-lesh
Golešnica (Yugosl.)	gô′-lĕsh′-nĭ-tsä	go′-lesh′-ni-tsah
golfo (It.) *Golfo* or *gulf* is often ignored in the alphabetical listing. Look for the name itself.		
Golija (Yugosl., mts.)	gô′-lĭ-yä	go′-li-yah
Golikov, Filip (Rus. general)	gô′-lĭ-kŏf, fĭ-lēp′	go′-li-kof, fi-leep′
Goljak planina (Yugosl., mts.)	gô′-lyäk plä′-nē′-nä	go′-lyahk plah′-nee′-nah
Golova (Rus.)	gŏ-lŏ-vä′	go-lo-vah′
Goltva (Rus.)	gôl′-tvä	gol′-tvah
Golub (Pol.)	gô′-lo͝op	go′-lup
Golubac (Yugosl.)	gô′-lo͞o′-bäts	go′-loo′-bahts
Gomel (Rus.)	gô′-mĕl(y)	go′-mel(y)
Gómes, Eduardo (Braz. general)	gô′-mĭs, ĕ-dwär′-do͝o	go′-mis, eh-dwahr′-du
Gómez de Jordana (Sp. leader)	gô′-mĕth (*or* -mĕs) dĕ hôr-dä′-nä	go′-meth (*or* -mes) deh hor-dah′-nah
Gómez Pérez, Blas (Sp. leader)	gô′-mĕth (*or* -mĕs) pĕ′-rĕth (*or* -rĕs), bläs′	go′-meth (*or* -mes) peh′-reth (*or* -res), blahs′
Gona (New Guinea)	gō′-nä	goh′-nah
Goodenough (Oc.)	go͝od′-ĭ-nŭf	gud′-i-nuhf
An English family name.		

Gopło (Pol., lake)	gô′-plô	go′-plo
Gora (Rus., mt.)	gŏ-rä′	go-rah′
Góra Kalwarja (Pol.)	go͝o′-rä käl-vär′-yä	gu′-rah kahl-vahr′-yah
Russian *Gora Kalvaria*, gŏ-rä′ käl(y)-vä′-rĭ-yä [go-rah′ kahl(y)-vah′-ri-yah].		
Goransko (Yugosl.)	gô′-rän-skô	go′-rahn-sko
Goražde (Yugosl.)	gô′-räzh-dĕ	go′-rahzh-deh
Gorbachovo (Rus.)	gŏr-bä-chô′-vŏ	gor-bah-cho′-vo
Gorbatov (Rus.)	gŏr-bä′-tŏf	gor-bah′-tof
Gorbitsa (Rus.)	gôr′-bĭ-tsä	gor′-bi-tsah
Goreloe (Rus.)	gŏ-rĕ′-lŏ-yĕ	go-reh′-lo-yeh
Gorgany (Pol., mts.)	gôr-gä′-nĭ	gor-gah′-ni
Gorgona (It., isl.)	gôr-gô′-nä	gor-go′-nah
Gori (Rus.)	gô′-rē	go′-ree
Gorica (Alb.) See *Goricë.*		
Gorica, Velika (Yugosl.)	gô′-rĭ-tsä, vĕ′-lĭ-kä	go′-ri-tsah, veh′-li-kah
Goricë (Alb.)	gô-rē′-tsə	go-ree′-tsuh
Gorin (Pol., riv.) See *Horyń.*		
Gorinchem (Neth.)	k(h)ō′-rĭ-kəm	k(h)oh′-ri-kuhm
Another form and the usual pronunciation is *Gorkum*, q.v.		
Gorizia (It.)	gô-rē′-tsyä	go-ree′-tsyah
Gorjanci (Yugosl., mts.)	gôr′-yän-tsĭ	gor′-yahn-tsi
Gorki (Rus.)	gôr′-kĭ	gor′-ki
Gorkum (Neth.)	k(h)ôr′-kəm	k(h)or′-kuhm
Another form is *Gorinchem*, q.v.		
Görlitz (Ger.)	gûr′-lĭts	gœr′-lits
Gorna Dzhumaya (Bulg.)	gôr′-nä jo͝o′-mä-yä′	gor′-nah ju′-mah-yah′
Gorna Orehovitsa (Bulg.)	gôr′-nä ŏ-rĕ-hô′-vĭ-tsä	gor′-nah o-reh-ho′-vi-tsah
Gorodlo (Pol.) See *Horodło.*		
Gorodnitsa (Rus.)	gŏ-rŏd-nē′-tsä	go-rod-nee′-tsah
Gorodno (Pol.) See *Horodno.*		
Gorontalo (NEI)	gô-rôn-tä′-lô	go-ron-tah′-lo
Gospić (Yugosl.)	gô′-spĭch	go′-spich
Gossett, Ed (U.S. representative)	gŏs′-ĭt	gos′-it
Gostivar (Yugosl.)	gô′-stĭ-vär	gô′-sti-vahr
Gostyń (Pol.)	gô′-stĭn(y)	go′-stin(y)
Gostynin (Pol.)	gô-stĭ′-nĭn	go-sti′-nin
Russian *Gostinin*, gŏ-stē′-nĭn [go-stee′-nin].		
Göteborg (Sw.)	yû′-tə-bôr′(y)	yœ′-tuh-bor′(y)
Often Englished as *Gothenburg*, q.v., especially in radio usage.		
Gotha (Ger.)	gō′-tä	goh′-tah

Gothenburg (Sw.)	*Eng.* gŏt′-ən-bûrg′	got′-n-buhrg′
Swedish *Göteborg*, q.v.		
Gotnya (Rus.)	gôt′-nyä	got′-nyah
Gotovuše (Yugosl.)	gô′-tô′-vo͞o-shĕ	go′-to′-voo-sheh
Got(t)land (Sw., isl.)	gŏt′-länd	got′-lahnd
Goubellat (Tun.)	go͞o-bəl-lăt′	goo-buhl-lat′
Gouda (Neth.)	k(h)ou′-dä	k(h)au′-dah
Goulburn (Austral.)	gōl′-bərn	gohl′-buhrn
Goulette, la (Tun.)	go͞o-lĕt′, lä	goo-let′, lah
Goumenitsa (Gr.)	go͞o-mĕ′-nē-tsä	goo-meh′-nee-tsah
Goumiers	go͞o-myĕ′	goo-myeh′
French Moroccan troops organized into units of 160 men called a *goum*, go͞om [goom], Arabic meaning *tribe* or *family*.		
Goura (Gr.)	go͞o′-rä	goo′-rah
gourd	gōrd′ *or* go͝ord′	gohrd′ *or* gurd′
Goussev, Fedor (Rus. leader)	go͞o′-sĕf, fyô′-dŏr	goo′-sef, fyo′-dor
Gouvais (Crete)	go͞o′-vĕs	goo′-ves
Govarljevo (Yugosl.)	gô′-vär′-lyĕ-vô	go′-vahr′-lyeh-vo
Govorov, Leonid (Rus. general)	gô′-vŏ-rŏf, lĕ-ŏ-nēd′	go′-vo-rof, leh-o-need′
Grabovica (Yugosl.)	grä′-bô-vĭ-tsä	grah′-bo-vi-tsah
Grabovnica (Yugosl.)	grä′-bôv-nĭ-tsä	grah′-bov-ni-tsah
Grabski, Stanislaw (Pol. leader)	gräp′-skĭ, stä-nē′-släf	grahp′-ski, stah-nee′-slahf
Gračac (Yugosl.)	grä′-chäts	grah′-chahts
Gračanica (Yugosl.)	grä′-chä′-nĭ-tsä	grah′-chah′-ni-tsah
Gračanka (Yugosl., riv.)	grä′-chän-kä	grah′-chahn-kah
Grad (Yugosl.)	gräd′	grahd′
Gradačac (Yugusl.)	grä′-dä′-chäts	grah′-dah′-chahts
Gradec (Yugosl.)	grä′-dĕts	grah′-dets
Gradešnica (Yugosl.)	grä′-dĕsh′-nĭ-tsä	grah′-desh′-ni-tsah
Gradiška, Stara (Yugosl.)	grä′-dĭ-shkä, stä′-rä	grah′-di-shkah, stah′-rah
Gradište (Yugosl.)	grä′-dĭ-shtĕ	grah′-di-shteh
Gradizhsk (Rus.)	grä-dĭshk′	grah-dishk′
Graevo (Pol.) See *Grajewo*.		
Graham, Louis E. (U.S. representative)	grā′-əm	greh′-uhm
Grahovo (Yugosl.)	grä′-hô-vô	grah′-ho-vo
Graiba (Tun.)	grä-ē′-bä	grah-ee′-bah
Graivoron (Rus.)	grī′-vŏ-rŏn	grai′-vo-ron
Grajewo (Pol.)	grä-yĕ′-vô	grah-yeh′-vo
Russian *Graevo*, grä′-yĕ-vŏ [grah′-yeh-vo].		

Gramada (Yugosl.)	grä′-mä-dä	grah′-mah-dah
Grambouza (Crete, isl.)	gräm-bo͞o′-zä	grahm-boo′-zah
Gramsh (Alb.)	grämsh′	grahmsh′
Gramshi (Alb.) See *Gramsh.*		
Gran (Hung.) See *Esztergom.*		
Granada (Sp.)	*Eng.* grə-nä′-də *or* -nā′-	gruh-nah′-duh *or* -nay′-
	Sp. grä-nä′-*th*ä	grah-nah′-*th*ah
Grand Dorsal (Tun., mts.)	*Eng.* grănd dôr′-səl	grand dor′-suhl
	Fr. gräN dôr-säl′	grahN dor-sahl′
Grandjean (Fr. leader)	gräN-zhäN′	grahN-zhahN′
Granitola (Sicily, cape)	grä-nē′-tô-lä	grah-nee′-to-lah
Granvin (Nor.)	grän′-vĭn	grahn′-vin
Gratang (Nor.)	grä′-täng	grah′-tahng
Gratangen (Nor.)	grä′-täng-ən	grah′-tahng-uhn
Graudenz (Pol.) See *Grudziądz.*		
Gravehals (Nor., tunnel)	grä′-və-häls	grah′-vuh-hahls
Gravelines (Fr.)	gräv-lēn′	grahv-leen′
’s Gravenhage (Neth.)	sk(h)rä′-vən-hä′-k(h)ə	sk(h)rah′-vuhn-hah′-k(h)uh

An abbreviated form and the common pronunciation is *Den Haag*, dən häk(h)′ [duhn hahk(h)′]. English The *Hague*, q.v.

Graz (Austria)	gräts′	grahts′
Graziani, Rodolfo (It. general)	grä-tsyä′-nē, rô-dôl′-fô	grah-tsyah′-nee, ro-dol′-fo
Grazzanise (It.)	grät-sä-nē′-zĕ	graht-sah-nee′-zeh
Grbalj (Yugosl.)	gər′-bäl(y)	guhr′-bahl(y)
Grčište (Yugosl.)	gər′-chĭ-shtĕ	guhr′-chi-shteh
Grdelica (Yugosl.)	gər′-dĕ′-lĭ-tsä	guhr′-deh′-li-tsah
Greben, Veliki (Yugosl., mts.)	grĕ′-bĕn, vĕ′-lĭ-kĭ	greh′-ben, veh′-li-ki
Grefsen (Nor.)	grĕfs′n	grefs′n
Grejač (Yugosl.)	grĕ′-yäch	greh′-yahch
Grenaa (Den.)	grĕn′-ô	gren′-o
Grenoble (Fr.)	*Eng.* grə-nō′-bəl	gruh-noh′-buhl
	Fr. grə-nô′bl	gruh-no′bl
Gretchaninoff (Rus. composer)	grĕ-chä-nē′-nŏf	greh-chah-nee′-nof
Grevena (Gr.)	grĕ-vĕ-nä′	greh-veh-nah′
Gridino (Rus.)	grē′-dĭ-nŏ	gree′-di-no
grievous	grēv′-əs	greev′-uhs

There is no such word as *grievious.* Cf. the erroneous forms *mischievious* for *mischievous, portentious* for *portentous, tremendious* for *tremendous.*

Grigoriopol (Rus.)	grĭ-gŏ-rĭ-ô′-pŏl(y)	gri-go-ri-o′-pol(y)
grimace	grĭ-mās′	gri-mays′
	or grĭm′-ĭs	grim′-is

If this somewhat literary word is uttered, the second pronunciation, though without dictionary authority, occurs more often than the first

Grimstad (Nor.)	grĭm′-stä	grim′-stah
Grini (Nor.)	grē′-nē	gree′-nee
Gris Nez (Fr., cape)	grē nĕ′	gree neh′
Grīva (Latvia)	grē′-vä	gree′-vah

Russian *Kalkuny*, q.v.

Grljan (Yugosl.)	gər′-lyän	guhr′-lyahn
Grocka (Yugosl.)	gər′-ô-tskä	guhr′-o-tskah
Gródek Jagielloński (Pol.)	grŏŏ′-dĕk yä-gyĕl-lôn′(y)-skĭ	gru′-dek yah-gyel-lon′(y)-ski
Grodisk (Pol.) See *Grodzisk*.		
Grodno (Pol.)	grôd′-nô	grod′-no

Russian *Grodna*, grôd′-nä [grod′-nah].

Grodzisk (Pol.)	grô′-jĭsk	gro′-jisk

Russian *Grodisk*, grô′-dĭsk [gro′-disk].

Grodzyanka (Rus.)	grŏd-zyän′-kä	grod-zyahn′-kah
Groenoey (Nor.)	grûn′-ûĭ	grœn′-œi
Groitsi (Pol.) See *Grójec*.		
Grójec (Pol.)	grŏŏ′-yĕts	gru′-yets

Russian *Groitsi*, groi′-tsĭ [groi′-tsi].

Grombalia (Tun.)	grŏm-bä′-lĭ-ä	grom-bah′-li-ah
Grong (Nor.)	grông′	grong′
Groningen (Neth.)	*Eng.* grō′-nĭng-ən	groh′-ning-uhn
	Du. k(h)rō′-nĭng-ən	k(h)roh′-ning-uhn
Groningen Diep (Neth.)	*Eng.* grō′-nĭng-ən dēp′	groh′-ning-uhn deep′
	Du. k(h)rō′-nĭng-ən dēp′	k(h)roh′-ning-uhn deep′

Also called *Reit Diep*, q.v.

Grönöy (Nor.)	grûn′-ûĭ	grœn′-œi
Groote Eylandt (Austral.)	grōōt ī′-lənd	groot ai′-luhnd

The earlier pronunciation was grō′-tə ī′-länt [groh′-tuh ai′-lahnt], but the name has been Englished.

Grosny (Rus.)	grôz′-nĭ	groz′-ni
Grosseto (It.)	grôs-sĕ′-tô	gros-seh′-to

This name (among others) strains the phonetic system, for the *e* is close. However it should not be pronounced a diphthong.

Grotli (Nor.)	grōt′-lē	groht′-lee

Groton (Mass., school)	grŏt′-ən	grot′-uhn

The analogy of *Croton* is misleading. However, *Groton*, Conn., is often pronounced grōt′n [groht′n].

Grottaglie (It.)	grôt-tä′-lyĕ	grot-tah′-lyeh
Grotteria (It., Calab.)	grôt-tĕ-rē′-ä	grot-teh-ree′-ah
Grubeshov (Pol.) See	*Hrubieszów.*	
Grubišno Polje (Yugosl.)	gro͞o′-bĭsh-nô pôl′-yĕ	groo′-bish-no pol′-yeh
Grudziądz (Pol.)	gro͝o′-jôNts	gru′-joNts

German *Graudenz*, grou′-dĕnts [grau′-dents].

Grunau (Rus.)	gro͞o′-nou	groo′-nau
Gruž (Yugosl.)	gro͞ozh′	groozh′
Gruža (Yugosl.)	gro͞o′-zhä	groo′-zhah
Gryazi (Rus.)	gryä′-zē	gryah′-zee
Grytviken (So. Georgia isl.)	grüt′-vēk-ən	grüt′-veek-uhn
Guadalajara (Sp., Mex.)	gwä-*th*ä-lä-hä′-rä	gwah-*th*ah-lah-hah′-rah
Guadalcanal (Oc.)	gwä-däl-kä-näl′	gwah-dahl-kah-nahl′

According to the Royal Geographical Society pamphlets the local pronunciation is kä-lä-kä′-nä [kah-lah-kah′-nah]. Another form is *Guadalcanar.*

Guadalquivir (Sp., riv.)	gwä-*th*äl-kē-vēr′	gwah-*th*ahl-kee-veer′
Guadalupe	*Sp.* gwä-*th*ä-lo͞o′-pĕ	gwah-*th*ah-loo′-peh
	Eng. gwä′-də-lo͞op′	gwah′-duh-loop′
	or gô′-də-lo͞op′	go′-duh-loop′
Guadarrama (Sp., mts.)	gwä-*th*ä-rä′-mä	gwah-*th*ah-rah′-mah
Guadeloupe	*Eng.* gô′-də-lo͞op′	go′-duh-loop′
(Fr. W. Indies)	*Fr.* gwä-də-lo͞op′	gwah-duh-loop′
Guadiana (Port., Sp.,	*Port.* gwä-dyä′-nə	gwah-dyah′-nuh
riv.)	*Sp.* gwä-*th*yä′-nä	gwah-*th*yah′-nah
Guadix (Sp.)	gwä′-*th*ēsh	gwah′-*th*eesh
Guam (Oc.)	gwäm′	gwahm′
Guanahuato (Mex.)	gwä-nä-hwä′-tô	gwah-nah-hwah′-to
Guani, Alberto (Urug. leader)	gwä′-nē, äl-bĕr′-tô	gwah′-nee, ahl-behr′-to
Guarcino (It.)	gwär-chē′-nô	gwahr-chee′-no
Guariglia, Raffaele (It. leader)	gwä-rē′-lyä, räf-fä-ĕ′-lĕ	gwah-ree′-lyah, rahf-fah-eh′-leh
guayule (Sp.)	gwä-yo͞o′-lĕ	gwah-yoo′-leh
Gubbi, el (Libya)	go͝o′-bē *or* kô′-bä, ĕl	gu′-bee *or* ko′-bah, el
Gubbio (It.)	go͞o′-byô	goo′-byo
Guča (Yugosl.)	go͞o′-chä	goo′-chah
Gudbrandsdalen (Nor.)	go͝od′-bräns-däln	gud′-brahns-dahln

Gudermes (Rus.)	go͞o-dĕr-mĕs′	goo-dehr-mes′
Gudjakovo (Yugosl.)	go͞o′-dyä′-kô-vô	goo′-dyah′-ko-vo
Gudvangen (Nor.)	go͝od′-väng-ən	gud′-vahng-uhn
Guebwiller (Fr.)	gĕb-vē-lĕr′	geb-vee-lehr′
Guelman (Alg.)	gĕl-măn′	gel-man′
Guernica (Sp.)	gĕr-nē′-kä	gehr-nee′-kah
Guetaria Pass (Tun.)	gĕ-tä-rē′-ä	geh-tah-ree′-ah
Guettar, el (Tun.)	gĕ-tär′, ĕl	geh-tahr′, el
Guglionesi (It.)	go͞o-lyô-nĕ′-zē	goo-lyo-neh′-zee
Guguan (Oc.)	go͞o-gwän′	goo-gwahn′
Guidonia (It.)	gwē-dô′-nyä	gwee-do′-nyah
Guilhem, Aristides (Braz. admiral)	gē′-lyəm ä-rēs-tē′-dĭs	gee′-lyuhm ah-rees-tee′-dis
Guiñazú, Enrique Ruiz (Arg. leader)	gē-nyä-so͞o′, ĕn-rē′-kĕ ro͞o-ēs′	gee-nyah-soo′, en-ree′-keh roo-ees′
Correctly *Ruiz Guiñazú* rather than simply *Guiñazú*. However the latter has been the usage of our radio and press.		
Guînes (Fr.)	gēn′	geen′
Guingamp (Fr.)	găN-gäN′	gaN-gahN′
Guipúzcoa (Sp., prov.)	gē-po͞oth′-kô-ä *or* -po͞os′-	gee-pooth′-ko-ah *or* -poos′-
Guixols (Sp.) See *San Feliú de Guixols*.		
Gulbene (Latvia)	go͝ol′-bĕ-nĕ	gul′-beh-neh
German *Schwanenburg*, q.v.		
Gulijanska planina (Yugosl., mts.)	go͞o′-lē′-yän-skä plä′-nē′-nä	goo′-lee′-yahn-skah plah′-nee′-nah
Gulsvik (Nor.)	go͝ols′-vēk	guls′-veek
Gulyui (Rus.)	go͝o-lū′ĭ	gu-lyoo′i
Gumbinnen (Ger.)	go͝om′-bĭn-ən	gum′-bin-uhn
Gümüljene (Gr.)	*Turk.* gü-mül′-jə-nĕ	gü-mül′-juh-neh
Greek *Komotine*, q.v.		
Gümüşhane (Turk.)	gü-müsh′-hä′-nĕ	gü-müsh′-hah′-neh
Gura Humorului (Rum.)	go͝o′-rä ho͝o-mô′-ro͝o-lwĭ	gu′-rah hu-mo′-ru-lwi
Gurev (Rus.)	go͞or′-yĕf	goor′-yef
Gurevsk (Rus.)	go͞or′-yĕfsk	goor′-yefsk
Gurgan (Iran)	go͞or-gän′	goor-gahn′
Formerly *Asterabad*, äs-tə-rä-bäd′ [ahs-tuh-rah-bahd′].		
Gurkha (India)	go͝or′-kä	gur′-kah
Gurney, Chan (U.S. senator)	gûr′-nē	guhr′-nee
Gus (Rus.)	go͞os′	goos′
Gusbat, el (Libya)	go͝os-băt′, ĕl	gus-bat′, el

Gusiatyn (Rus.)	go͞o-syä′-tĭn	goo-syah′-tin
Gusinje (Yugosl.)	go͞o′-sē′-nyĕ	goo′-see′-nyeh
Gussev, Fedor (Rus. leader)	go͞o′-sĕf, fyô′-dŏr	goo′-sef, fyo′-dor
Guštanj (Yugosl.)	go͞o′-shtän(y)	goo′-shtahn(y)
Guyer, U.S. (Late U.S. representative)	gī′-ər	gai′-uhr
Guyos (P.I.)	go͞o′-yôs	goo′-yos
Gwa (Burma)	gwä′	gwah′
Gwadar (Baluch.)	gwä′-dər	gwah′-duhr
Gyaing (Burma)	jīng′	jaing′
Gyergyószentmiklós (Rum.) See *Gheorgheni.*		
Gympie (Austral.)	gĭm′-pĭ	gim′-pi
Gyöngyös (Hung.)	dyûn′-dyûsh	dyœn′-dyœsh
Győr′ (Hung.)	dyûr′	dyœr′
Gytheion (Gr.)	yē′-thē-ô(n)	yee′-thee-o(n)
Gyula (Hung.)	dyo͝o′-lŏ	dyu′-lo
Gyulafehérvár (Rum.) See *Alba Julia.*		
Gzhatsk (Rus.)	gzhätsk′	gzhahtsk′

H- In Greek names initial *H-* is often omitted from the spelling. For example, it might be necessary to look up *Erakleion* instead of *Herakleion.* Also, instead of *H-*, one may find *Kh-* or *Ch-*.

Häädemeeste (Est.)	hă′-dĕ-mĕs-tĕ	ha′-deh-mes-teh
Haag, den (Neth.)	dən häk(h)′	duhn hahk(h)′
English *The Hague*, q.v. The full name is *'s Gravenhage*, q.v.		
Haakon VII (King of Norway)	hô′-ko͝on	ho′-kun
Haamstede (Neth.)	häm′-stā-də	hahm′-stay-duh
Haapasaari (Fin., isl.)	hä′-pä-sä-rē	hah′-pah-sah-ree
Haapsalu (Est.)	häp′-sä-lo͞o	hahp′-sah-loo
Russian *Gapsal*, q.v.		
Haarlem (Neth.)	här′-ləm	hahr′-luhm
Habanero, -a (Sp.)	ä-bä-nĕ′-rô, -ä	ah-bah-neh′-ro, -ah
Adjective of *Habana.* Not *Habañero.*		
Habanniya (Iraq)	hă-bă-nē′-yä	ha-ba-nee′-yah
Hacha, Emil (Czechosl. leader)	hä′-hä, ĕ′-mĭl	hah′-hah, eh′-mil
A possible Englishing is hä′-chä [hah′-chah].		
Hachinohe (Jap.)	hä-chē-nô-hĕ	hah-chee-no-heh
Hadeland (Nor.)	hä′-də-län	hah′-duh-lahn
Hadjeb el Aioun (Tun.)	hä′-jĕb ĕl ī-yo͞on′	hah′-jeb el ai-yoon′
Hadjes el Aiouth (Tun.)	hä′-jĕz ĕl ä-yo͞ot′	hah′-jez el ah-yoot′

Haft Kel (Iran)	hăft′ kĕl′	haft′ kel′
Hagen (Ger.)	hä′-gən	hah′-guhn
Hagen, Harold C. (U.S. representative)	hā′-gən	hay′-guhn
hagios, hagioi (Gr.)	ī′-yôs, ī′-yē	ai′-yos, ai′-yee
An element, meaning *saint(s)*, in Greek place names. Look up the other part of the name.		
Hagnides (Gr. leader)	ä-gnē′-*th*ēs	ah-gnee′-*th*ees
Hague, la (Fr., cape)	äg′, lä	ahg′, lah
Hague, The (Neth.)	*Eng.* hāg′	hayg′
Dutch *'s Gravenhage*, q.v., commonly abbreviated to *Den Haag*, q.v.		
Haguenau (Fr.)	äg-nō′	ahg-noh′
Hai-fêng (Ch., Kwangtung)	hī-fŭng	hai-fuhng
Hailar (Manchu.)	hī-lär	hai-lahr
Hailuoto (Fin., isl.)	hī′-lo͝o-ô-tô	hai′-lu-o-to
Swedish *Karloe*, kärl′-û′ [kahrl′-œ′].		
Hai-mên (Ch., Kwangtung, bay)	hī-mŭn	hai-muhn
Hainan (Ch. Kwangtung, isl.)	hī-nän	hai-nahn
Hainburg (Austria)	hīn′-bo͝ork(h)	hain′-burk(h)
Haiphong (Indo-Ch.)	*Eng.* hī-fŏng′	hai-fong′
Chinese *Hai-fang*.		
Haiti	hā′-tĭ	hay′-ti
Haitian	hā′-shən *or* hā′-tĭ-ən	hay′-shuhn hay′-ti-uhn
Hajdúböszörmény (Hung.)	hoi′-do͝o-bû′-sûr-mān(y)	hoi′-du-bœ′-sœr-mayn(y)
Hajdunánás (Hung.)	hoi′-do͝o-nä′-näsh	hoi′-du-nah′-nahsh
Hajduszoboszló (Hung.)	hoi′-do͝o-sô′-bôs-lô	hoi′-du-so′-bos-lo
Hajla (Yugosl., mts.)	hī′-lä	hai′-lah
Hajnówka (Pol.)	hī-no͝of′-kä	hai-nuf′-kah
Russian *Gainovka*, gī-nôf′-kä [gai-nof′-kah].		
Hakadal (Nor.)	hä′-kä-däl	hah′-kah-dahl
Hakodate (Jap.)	hä-kô-dä-tĕ	hah-ko-dah-teh
Halas (Hung.)	hŏ′-lŏsh	ho′-losh
Also called *Kiskunhalas*, q.v.		
Halberstadt (Ger.)	häl′-bər-shtät	hahl′-buhr-shtaht
Halden (Nor.)	häld′n	hahld′n
Halfaya (Libya)	häl-fä′-yä	hahl-fah′-yah
Halicz (Pol.)	hä′-lĭch	hah′-lich
Hallein (Austria)	häl′-īn	hahl′-ain
Hallingdal (Nor.)	häl′-lĭng-däl	hahl′-ling-dahl

Hallouf (Tun.)	häl-lo͞of′	hahl-loof′
Hallugh (Libya)	häl-lo͞og′	hahl-loog′
Halluin (Fr.)	äl-wăN′	ahl-waN′
Halmahera (NEI)	häl-mä-hĕ′-rä	hahl-mah-heh′-rah
Also called *Djailolo*, q.v.		
Halovo (Yugosl., mts.)	hä′-lô-vô	hah′-lo-vo
Hälsingborg (Sw.)	hĕl′-sĭng-bôr′(y)	hel′-sing-bor′(y)
Hamadan (Iran)	*Per.* hă-mə-dän′	ha-muh-dahn′
	Eng. hăm′-ə-dăn	ham′-uh-dan
Hamamatsu (Jap.)	hä-mä-mä-tso͞o	hah-mah-mah-tsoo
Hamar (Nor.)	hä′-mär	hah′-mahr
Hamaröy *or* Hamaroey (Nor.)	hä′-mär-ûĭ	hah′-mahr-œi
Hamborn (Ger.)	häm′-bôrn	hahm′-born
Hambro, Carl (Nor. leader)	*Nor.* häm′-bro͝o	hahm′-bru
	Eng. häm′-brō	hahm′-broh
Hamburg (Ger.)	*Eng.* hăm′-bûrg	ham′-buhrg
	Ger. häm′-bo͝ork(h)	hahm′-burk(h)
Hämeenlinna (Fin.)	hă′-mān-lĭn-nä	ha′-mayn-lin-nah
Ha-mi (Ch., Sinkiang)	hä-mē	hah-mee
Hamila (Tun.)	hä-mē′-lä	hah-mee′-lah
Hamina (Fin.)	hä′-mē-nä	hah′-mee-nah
Swedish *Fredrikshamn*, frā′-drēks-hämn′ [fray′-dreeks-hahmn′]. *Hamina* is an element, meaning *harbor* or *haven*, in Finnish place names.		
Hamm (Ger.)	häm′	hahm′
Hamma, el (Tun.)	häm′-mä, ĕl	hahm′-mah, el
Hammam (Egypt) See *Al Hammam.*		
Hammamet (Tun.)	häm-mä-mĕt′	hahm-mah-met′
Hammam Lif (Tun.)	häm-măm′ lēf′	hahm-mam′ leef′
Hammerfest (Nor.)	hä′-mər-fĕst	hah′-muhr-fest
Hancewicze (Pol.)	hän-tsĕ-vē′-chĕ	hahn-tseh-vee′-cheh
Russian *Gantsevichi*, gän-tsĕ′-vĭ-chĭ [gahn-tseh′-vi-chi].		
Hang-chow (Ch., Chekiang)	*Eng.* hăng-chou	hang-chau
	Ch. häng-jō	hahng-joh
Hangö (Fin.)	*Sw.* häng′-û	hahng′-œ
Finnish *Hanko*, q.v.		
Hanko (Fin.)	häng′-kô	hahng′-ko
Hankoe *or* Hankö (Nor.)	häng′-kû	hahng′-kœ
Han-kow (Ch., Hupeh)	*Eng.* hăn-kou	han-kau
	Ch. hän-kō	hahn-koh
Hannover (Ger.)	hän-ō′-vər	hahn-oh′-vuhr
	or hän-ō′-fər	hahn-oh′-fuhr
English *Hanover*, q.v.		
Hanoï (Indo-Ch.)	hä′-noi′	hah′-noi′

Hanover (Ger.)	*Eng.* hăn'-ō-vər	han'-oh-vuhr
German *Hannover*, q.v.		
Hansteen, Wilhelm (Nor. general)	hän'-stān, vĭl'-hĕlm	hahn'-stayn, vil'-helm
Hanthawaddy (Burma, riv.)	hăn-thə-wŏd'-ĭ	han-thuh-wod'-i
Han-yang (Ch., Hupeh)	hän-yäng	hahn-yahng
Han-yüan (Ch., Sikang)	hän-yüän	hahn-yü-ahn
Haouaria, el (Tun.)	hä-wä-rē'-ä, ĕl	hah-wah-ree'-ah, el
hara-kiri	hä'-rä-kē'-rĭ	hah'-rah-kee'-ri
Variants are *hari-kari* and *hara-kari.*		
Harald (Nor. prince)	hä'-räl	hah'-rahl
English *Harold.*		
Harar (Ethiopia)	hä'-rər	hah'-ruhr
Harasztos (Rum.) See *Călăraşi.*		
Harbin (Manchu.)	här'-bēn' *or* här'-bĭn	hahr'-been' *or* hahr'-bin
Hardanger (Nor.)	här-däng'-ər	hahr-dahng'-uhr
Hardangerfjord (Nor.)	här-däng'-ər-fyōr	hahr-dahng'-uhr-fyohr
Hardangerjoeklen *or* Hardangerjöklen (Nor.)	här-däng'-ər-yûk-lən	hahr-dahng'-uhr-yœk-luhn
Hardangervidda (Nor.)	här-däng'-ər-vĭd-dä	hahr-dahng'-uhr-vid-dah
Hardelot (Fr.)	ärd-lō'	ahrd-loh'
Harderwijk (Neth.)	här'-dər-wīk	hahr'-duhr-waik
Harewood (Eng. earl)	här'-wo͝od	hahr'-wud
Harfleur (Fr.)	är-flûr'	ahr-flœr'
Harijan (Gandhi's newspaper)	hŭ'-rĭ-jən	huh'-ri-juhn
Hari Rud (India, riv.)	hŭ'-rĭ ro͞od'	huh'-ri rood'
Hârlău (Rum.)	hûr'-lû'-o͞o	huhr'-luh'-u
Harlingen (Neth.)	här'-lĭng-ən	hahr'-ling-uhn
Harpefoss (Nor.)	här'-pə-fôs	hahr'-puh-fos
Hârşova (Rum.)	hûr'-shô-vä	huhr'-sho-vah
Harstad (Nor.)	här'-stä *or* häsh'-tä	hahr'-stah *or* hahsh'-tah
Hartman, Paul (Nor. minister)	härt'-män, poul'	hahrt'-mahn, paul'
Hasani (Gr.)	hä-sä'-nē	hah-sah'-nee
Hasanli (Yugosl.)	hä'-sän-lē	hah'-sahn-lee
Hasenpoth (Latvia)	*Ger.* hä'-zən-pôt	hah'-zuhn-pot
Latvian *Aizpute*, q.v. Russian *Gasenpot*, q.v.		
Hasselt (Belg.)	häs'-əlt	hahs'-uhlt

Hatvan (Hung.)	hŏt′-vŏn	hot′-von
Haubourdin (Fr.)	ō-bo͞or-dăN′	oh-boor-daN′
Haugastoel *or* Haugastöl (Nor.)	hou′-gä-stûl	hau′-gah-stœl
Haugesund (Nor.)	hou′-gə-so͝on	hau′-guh-sun
Haukeliseter (Nor.)	hou′-kə-lē-sā-tər	hau′-kuh-lee-say-tuhr
Hauketo (Nor.)	hou′-kə-tō	hau′-kuh-toh
Haute Saône (Fr., dept.)	ōt sōn′	oht sohn′
Haute Savoie (Fr., dept.)	ōt sä-vwä′	oht sah-vwah′
Hautmont (Fr.)	ō-môN′	oh-moN′
Haut Rhin (Fr., dept.)	ō răN′	oh raN′
Havre, le (Fr.)	*Eng.* hävr′, lə	hahvr′, luh
	Fr. ävr′, lə	ahvr′, luh
Haye, Henry- (Fr. ambassador)	ĕ′, äN-rē′	eh′, ahN-ree′
Hazebrouck (Fr.)	äz-bro͞ok′	ahz-brook′
Hebert, F. Edward (U.S. representative)	ā-bĕr′	ay-behr′
The word *ay* (long ā) plus the word *bear*.		
Hedmark (Nor.)	hĕd′-märk	hed′-mahrk
Heemstede (Neth.)	hām′-stā-də	haym′-stay-duh
Heerde (Neth.)	hār′-də	hayr′-duh
Heerenveen (Neth.)	hā′-rən-vān′	hay′-ruhn-vayn′
Heerlen (Neth.)	hār′-lən	hayr′-luhn
Heffernan, James J. (U.S. representative)	hĕf′-ər-năn	hef′-uhr-nan
Hegoumenitsa (Gr.)	ē-go͞o-mĕ-nē′-tsä	ee-goo-meh-nee′-tsah
Heho (Burma)	hā′-hō′	hay′-hoh′
Hei-an (Korea)	hā-än	hay-ahn
Heide (Ger.)	hī′-də	hai′-duh
Heidinger, J. V. (U.S. representative)	hī′-dĭng-ər	hai′-ding-uhr
Heidous (Tun.)	hā-do͞os′	hay-doos′
Hei-jo (Korea)	hā-jô *or* -rô	hay-jo *or* -ro
Hei-lung-kiang (Manchu., prov.)	hā-lo͝ong-jyäng	hay-lung-jyahng
Also called *Amur*, q.v.		
Heinkel (Ger.)	hīng′-kəl	haing′-kuhl
Hejaz (Arabia)	hē-jăz′	hee-jaz′
Hekmat (Per. leader)	hĕk′-măt′	hek′-mat′
Hel (Pol.)	hĕl′	hel′
Helder, den (Neth.)	*Eng.* hĕl′-dər, dən	hel′-duhr, duhn
	Du. hĕl′-dər, dən	hel′-duhr, duhn

Helena *Ark., Mont.* hĕl′-ə-nə hel′-uh-nuh
Ohio hĕ-lē′-nə heh-lee′-nuh

As a personal name *Helena* is usually stressed on the first syllable.

Helgoland (Ger.) hĕl′-gô-länt hel′-go-lahnt

English *Heligoland*, q.v.

helicopter hĕl′-ĭ-kŏp′-tər hel′-i-kop′-tuhr
or hē′-lĭ-kŏp′-tər hee′-li-kop′-tuhr

The second pronunciation, though without dictionary authority, is favored by aeronautical engineers. (Avoid *heliocopter*. *Helio-* [the sun] has no part in this word, which is made from *helico-pter*[*on*], spiral-wing.) So with many compounds of *helic*(*o*)-, meaning *spiral-*. Except perhaps in *helical*, engineers prefer hē′-lĭ- [hee′-li-], the dictionary recommendation to the contrary notwithstanding. In technical copy the engineers' preference should probably be followed. Although the *e* of Greek *helic-* is short, there is warrant for lengthening in an English stressed open syllable. In long words one expects short vowels (compare *penal*, *penalty*; *holy*, *holiday*); nevertheless long words are often pronounced as if they were two or more short words. Compare the several correct pronunciations of *genealogy*, *hegemony*, *hemoglobin*, *ideology*, *bivalent*, *dictionary*, *necessary*.

Heligoland (Ger.) *Eng.* hĕl′-ĭ-gō-lănd′ hel′-i-goh-land′

Hell (Nor.) hĕl′ hel′

Hellenikon (Gr.) See *Ellenikon.*

Hellespont (Turk., strait) See *Dardanelles.*

Hellesylt (Nor.) hĕl′-ə-sült hel′-uh-sült

Hellevoetsluis (Neth.) hĕl′-ə-vo͞ot-slûĭs′ hel′-uh-voot-slœis′

Helmand (India, riv.) hĕl′-mənd hel′-muhnd

Helmond (Neth.) hĕl′-mônt hel′-mont

Helsingfors (Fin.) *Eng.* hĕl′-sĭng-fôrz hel′-sing-forz
Sw. hĕl′-sĭng-fôrs′ hel′-sing-fors′

Finnish *Helsinki*, q.v.

Helsingoer *or* Helsingör (Den.) hĕl′-sĭng-ûr′ hel′-sing-œr′

English *Elsinore*, ĕl′-sĭ-nôr′ [el′-si-nor′].

Helsinki (Fin.) hĕl′-sĭng-kē hel′-sing-kee

Hemsedal (Nor.) hĕm′-sə-däl hem′-suh-dahl

Hencha, la (Tun.) hĕn′-shä, lä hen′-shah, lah

Hengeloo (Neth.) hĕng′-ə-lō heng′-uh-loh

Hêng-fêng (Ch., Kiangsi) hŭng-fŭng huhng-fuhng

Hêng-shan (Ch., Hunan) hŭng-shän huhng-shahn

Hêng-yang (Ch., Hunan) hŭng-yäng huhng-yahng

Henpan (Oc.) hĕn′-pän hen′-pahn

Henry-Haye (Fr. Ambassador) See Haye, Henry-.

Henzada (Burma) hĕn′-zə-dä′ hen′-zuh-dah′

Herakleia (Turk.) See *Ereğli.*

Herakleion (Crete)	ē-rä′-klē-ô(n)	ee-rah′-klee-o(n)

In English usually called *Candia*, q.v.; in Greek *Megalo Kastro*, q.v., or *Khandax*, hän′-däks [hahn′-dahks].

Herald Tribune (N.Y.) See *Tribune*.

Herat (Afghan.)	hĕr-ät′	hehr-aht′
Hérault (Fr., dept.)	ĕ-rō′	eh-roh′
Hercegovina (Yugosl.)	*Eng.* hĕr′-tsĭ-gō-vē′-nə	hehr′-tsi-goh-vee′-nuh
	S.-C. hĕr′-tsĕ-gô′-vĭ-nä	hehr′-tseh-go′-vi-nah

English *Herzegovina*.

Herefoss (Nor.)	hĕr′-ə-fôs	hehr′-uh-fos
Hergla (Tun.)	hĕr′-glä	hehr′-glah
Hermoupolis (Gr., Syros)	ĕr-mōō′-pô-lē(s)	ehr-moo′-po-lee(s)
Herne (Ger.)	hĕr′-nə	hehr′-nuh
Herning (Den.)	hĕr′-nĭng	hehr′-ning
Heroeya *or* Heröya (Nor.)	hĕr′-û-yä	hehr′-œ-yah
Herrera (Sp.)	ĕ-rĕ′-rä	eh-reh′-rah
Hersin Coupigny (Fr.)	ĕr-săN kōō-pē-nyē′	ehr-saN koo-pee-nyee′
Herter, Christian A. (U.S. representative)	hûr′-tər	huhr′-tuhr
’s Hertogenbosch (Neth.)	sĕr′-tō-k(h)ən-bôs′	sehr′-toh-k(h)uhn-bos′

A common abbreviated form is *Den Bos*, dən bôs′ [duhn bos′]. French *Bois le Duc*, bwä lə dük′ [bwah luh dük′].

Herzegovina (Yugosl.)	hĕr′-tsĭ-gō-vē′-nə	hehr′-tsi-goh-vee′-nuh

Serb-Croat *Hercegovina*, q.v.

Hesse (Ger.)	*Eng.* hĕs′	hes′
Hessen (Ger.)	hĕs′-ən	hes′-uhn

English *Hesse*, q.v.

Hestmannen (Nor., isls.)	hĕst′-män-ən	hest′-mahn-uhn
Het Loo (Neth.)	hĕt lō′	het loh′
Heydrich, Reinhard (Ger. leader)	hī′-drĭk(h), rīn′-härt	hai′-drik(h), rain′-hahrt
Heye Foundation (N.Y.)	hī′	hai′
Hieralimen (Gr.)	yĕ-rä-lē-mēn′	yeh-rah-lee-meen′
Hierapetra (Crete)	yĕ-rä′-pĕ-trä *or* ē-ĕ-rä′-pĕ-trä	yeh-rah′-peh-trah ee-eh-rah′-peh-trah

Also called *Kastelli*, kä-stĕ′-lē [kah-steh′-lee].

Hieropotamos (Crete)	yĕ-rô-pô′-tä-mô(s) *or* ē-ĕ-rô-pô′-tä-mô(s)	yeh-ro-po′-tah-mo(s) ee-eh-ro-po′-tah-mo(s)

Hiitola (Fin.)	hē′-tô-lä	hee′-to-lah
Hiiu *or* Hiiumaa	hē′-o͞o	hee′-oo
(Est., isl.)	*or* hē′-o͞o-mä	hee′-oo-mah
Russian *Dage*, q.v. German *Dagö*, q.v.		
Hilleroed *or* Hilleröd	hĭl′-ə-rûth	hil′-uh-rœ*th*
(Den.)		
Hilversum (Neth.)	hĭl′-vər-səm	hil′-vuhr-suhm
Himalaya(s) (Asia, mts.)	hĭ-mä′-lə-yə	hi-mah′-luh-yuh
	or hĭm-ə-lā′-yə	him-uh-lay′-yuh
Himara (Alb.) See *Himarë.*		
Himarë (Alb.)	hē-mä′-rə	hee-mah′-ruh
Italian *Chimara*, q.v. Greek *Kheimara*, hē-mä′-rä [hee-mah′-rah].		
Himeimat (Egypt)	hĭ-mā-măt′	hi-may-mat′
See *Qaret el Himeimat.*		
Hindahl, Olav	hĭn′-däl, ō′-läv	hin′-dahl, oh′-lahv
(Nor. minister)		
Hindeloopen (Neth.)	hĭn′-də-lō′-pən	hin′-duh-loh′-puhn
Hindenburg, von	*Eng.* hĭn′-dən-bûrg, vŏn	hin′-duhn-buhrg, von
	Ger. hĭn′-dən-bo͝ork(h), fôn	hin′-duhn-burk(h), fon
Hindu Kush (India, mts.)	hĭn′-do͞o ko͝osh′	hin′-doo kush′
Hirohito (Jap. emperor)	hē-rô-hē-tô	hee-ro-hee-to
Hirson (Fr.)	ēr-sôN′	eer-soN′
Hirtshals (Den.)	hĭrts′-häls	hihrts′-hahls
Hister *or* Ister (Europ. riv.) See *Danube.*		
Hitler, Adolph (Ger. leader)	hĭt′-lər, ăd′-ŏlf	hit′-luhr, ad′-olf
	Ger. ä′-dôlf	ah′-dolf
Called *der Schickelgruber*, dər shĭk′-əl-gro͞o′-bər [duhr shik′-uhl-groo′-buhr].		
Hitra (Nor.)	hĭt′-rä	hit′-rah
Hiw (Oc.)	hē′o͝o	hee′u
Hjelle (Nor.)	yĕl′-ə	yel′-uh
Hjelmtveit, Nils	yĕlm′-tvāt, nĭls′	yelm′-tvayt, nils′
(Nor. leader)		
Hjerkinn (Nor.)	yĕr′-kĭn	yehr′-kin
Hjoerring *or* Hjörring (Den.)	yûr′-ĭng	yœr′-ing
Hjukseboe *or* Hjuksebö (Nor.)	yo͝ok′-sə-bû	yuk′-suh-bœ
Ho (Chinese word	*Eng.* hō	hoh
meaning *river*)	*Ch.* hŭ	huh

Hoboken (N.J.)	hō′-bō′-kən	hoh′-boh′-kuhn
Hoch, Daniel K. (U.S. representative)	hōk(h)′	hohk(h)′
Ho-chiang (Ch., Szechwan) Also spelled *Ho-kiang*.	hŭ-jyäng	huh-jyahng
Ho-ch'ih (Ch., Kwangsi)	hŭ-chû	huh-chuh
Hódmezővásárhely (Hung.)	hôd′-mĕ-zû-vä′-shär-hā	hod′-meh-zœ-vah′-shahr-hay
Hodonín (Cz.) German *Göding*, gû′-dĭng [gœ′-ding].	hô′-dô-nēn	ho′-do-neen
Hoduciszki (Pol.)	hô-do͝o-tsē′-shkĭ	ho-du-tsee′-shki
Hoenefoss (Nor.)	hû′-nə-fôs	hœ′-nuh-fos
Hoerde (Ger.)	hûr′-də	hœr′-duh
Hoeven, Charles B. (U.S. representative)	ho͞o′-vən	hoo′-vuhn
Ho-fei (Ch., Anhwei) Also called *Lu-chow*, q.v.	hŭ-fā	huh-fay
Hogolu (Oc.)	hô′-gô-lo͞o	ho′-go-loo
Hohensalza (Pol.) See *Inowrocław*.		
Hohe Tauern (Austria, mts.)	hō′-ə tou′-ərn	hoh′-uh tau′-uhrn
Hokiang Variant of *Ho-chiang*, q.v.		
Hokkaido (Jap.)	hôk-kī-dô	hok-kai-do
Hokksund (Nor.)	hôk′-so͝on	hok′-sun
Hoko Gunto (Jap., isls.) See *Pescadores*.		
Hoko Ret (Jap., isls.) See *Pescadores*.		
Hoko To (Jap., isls.) See *Pescadores*.		
Ho-kow (Ch., Yünnan)	*Eng.* hō-kou	hoh-kau
	Ch. hŭ-kō	huh-koh
Holbæk (Den.)	hôl′-bĕk	hol′-bek
Holifield, Chet (U.S. representative)	hŏl′-ĭ-fēld′, chĕt′	hol′-i-feeld′, chet′
Hollandia (NEI)	hôl-län′-dĭ-ä	hol-lahn′-di-ah
Hollington K. Tong (Ch. leader)	hŏl′-ĭng-tən tông′	hol′-ing-tuhn tong′
Holmenkollen (Nor.)	hôlm′n-kôl-ən	holm′n-kol-uhn
Holmestrand (Nor.)	hôl′-mə-strän	hol′-muh-strahn
holocaust	hŏl′-ə-kôst	hol′-uh-kost
Holstebro (Den.)	hôl′-stə-brō′	hol′-stuh-broh′
Holsteinsborg (Greenl.)	hôl′-stīns-bôr	hol′-stains-bor
Holtz (Alaska, Attu)	hôlts′	holts′
Holyoke (Mass.)	hōl′-yōk	hohl′-yohk
Homolje (Yugosl.)	hô′-mô-lyĕ	ho′-mo-lyeh

Homorod (Rum., riv.)	hô′-mô-rôd′	ho′-mo-rod′
Homs (Libya)	hôms′	homs′
Ho-nan (Ch., prov.)	*Eng.* hō-năn	hoh-nan
	Ch. hŭ-nän	huh-nahn
Ho-nan-fu (Ch., Honan)	*Eng.* hō-năn-fo͞o	hoh-nan-foo
	Ch. hŭ-nän-fo͞o	huh-nahn-foo
Also called *Lo-yang*, q.v.		
Hönefoss (Nor.)	hû′-nə-fôs	hœ′-nuh-fos
Honfleur (Fr.)	ôN-flûr′	oN-flœr′
Hongay (Indo-Ch.)	hông-gī′	hong-gai′
Hong Kong (Ch., Kwangtung)	*Eng.* hŏng kŏng	hong kong
Honningsvaag (Nor.)	hôn′-ĭngs-vôg	hon′-ings-vog
Honshu (Jap.)	hôn-sho͞o	hon-shoo
Hoofdplaat (Neth.)	hōft′-plät	hohft′-plaht
Hoogezand (Neth.)	hō-k(h)ə-zänt′	hoh-k(h)uh-zahnt′
Hooghly *or* Hugli (India)	ho͞og′-lē	hoog′-lee
Hoorn (Neth.)	hōrn′	hohrn′
Hopeh (Ch., prov.)	*Eng.* hō-pā	hoh-pay
	Ch. hŭ-bā	huh-bay
Hopong (Burma)	hō′-pŏng′	hoh′-pong′
Hoppenot, Henri Etienne (Fr. leader)	ôp-nō′, äN-rē′ ĕ-tyĕn′	op-noh′, ahN-ree′ eh-tyen′
Hörde (Ger.)	hûr′-də	hœr′-duh
Hornád (Cz., riv.)	hôr′-nät	hor′-naht
Horodenka (Pol.)	hô-rô-dĕn′-kä	ho-ro-den′-kah
Horodło (Pol.)	hô-rôd′-lô	ho-rod′-lo
Russian *Gorodlo*, gŏ-rôd′-lŏ [go-rod′-lo].		
Horodno (Pol.)	hô-rôd′-nô	ho-rod′-no
Russian *Gorodno*, gŏ-rôd′-nŏ [go-rod′-no].		
Horsens (Den.)	hôr′-səns	hor′-suhns
Horta (Azores)	ôr′-tə	or′-tuh
Horten (Nor.)	hôrt′n	hort′n
Horthy, Miklós (Hung. leader)	hôr′-tĭ, mĭk′-lôsh	hor′-ti, mik′-losh
Horyń (Pol., riv.)	hô′-rĭn(y)	ho′-rin(y)
Russian *Gorin*, gô′-rĭn(y) [go′-rin(y)].		
Hoti (Yugosl., Alb.)	*S.-C.* hô′-tē	ho′-tee
Ho-t'ien (Ch., Kwangtung)	hŭ-tyĕn	huh-tyen
Hotin (Rum.)	hô′-tĭn	ho′-tin
Russian spelling *Khotin.*		
Houmt Souk (Tun.)	ho͞o′-mət so͝ok′	hoo′-muht sook′
Houplines (Fr.)	o͞o-plēn′	oo-pleen′

Hova (Madag.)	hŭ′-və	huh′-vuh
Hovden (Nor.)	hôvd′n	hovd′n
Howrah (India)	hou′-rä	hau′-rah
Ho Ying-chin (Ch.)	hŭ yĭng-jĭn	huh ying-jin

The chief of the Chinese general staff. Usually Anglicized to hō yĭng-chĭn [hoh ying-chin].

Hradec Králové (Cz.)	hrä′-dĕts krä′-lô-vĕ	hrah′-dets krah′-lo-veh
Hrubieszów (Pol.)	hrŏŏ-byĕ′-shŏŏf	hru-byeh′-shuf

Russian *Grubeshov*, grŏŏ-bĕ′-shŏf [gru-beh′-shof].

Hrvat (Croat)	hər′-vät	huhr′-vaht

Hrvatski, -a, hər′-vät′-ski, -ä [huhr′-vaht′-ski, -ah], adj., means *Croatian*.

Hrvatska (Yugosl.)	hər′-vät′-skä	huhr′-vaht′-skah

English *Croatia*, q.v.

Hs- See also names in *S*-.

Hsenwi (Burma)	shĕn′-wē′	shen′-wee′
Hsia-chiang (Ch., Kiangsi, Kweichow)	shyä-jyäng	shyah-jyahng
Hsia-kwan (Ch., Yünnan)	shyä-gwän	shyah-gwahn
Hsiang Chiang *or* River (Ch., Hunan)	shyäng	shyahng
Hsiang-yang (Ch., Hupeh)	shyäng-yäng	shyahng-yahng
Hsiang-yün (Ch., Yünnan)	shyäng-yün	shyahng-yün
Hsiao-fêng (Ch., Chekiang)	shyou-fŭng	shyau-fuhng
Hsiao-lin (Ch., Kiangsi)	shyou-lĭn	shyau-lin
Hsiao-shan (Ch., Chekiang)	shou-shän	shau-shahn
Hsi-ch'ang (Ch., Sikang)	shē-chäng	shee-chahng
Hsieh-mu-shan (Ch., Kwangtung)	shyĕ-mōō-shän	shyeh-moo-shahn
Hsien-ning (Ch., Kiangsi)	shyĕn-nĭng	shyen-ning
Hsin (Ch., Kiangsi, riv.)	shĭn	shin

Hsin-ching Variant spelling of *Hsin-king*, q.v.

Hsin-fêng (Ch., Kiangsi)	shĭn-fŭng	shin-fuhng
Hsing-hsan-chên (Manchu.)	shĭng-shän-jŭn	shing-shahn-juhn
Hsing-kwo (Ch., Kiangsi)	shĭng-gwô	shing-gwo

Also called *Nan-kang*, q.v.

Hsing-tzŭ (Ch., Kiangsi)	shĭng-dzə	shing-dzuh
Hsin-king (Manchu.)	shĭn-jĭng	shin-jing
Also spelled *Hsin-ching*.		
Hsin-têng (Ch., Chekiang)	shĭn-dŭng	shin-duhng
Hsin-ti (Ch., Hupeh)	shĭn-dē	shin-dee
Hsin-wu (Ch., Kiangsi)	shĭn-wōō	shin-woo
Hsin-yü (Ch., Kiangsi)	shĭn-yü	shin-yü
Hsipaw (Burma)	sē′-pô′	see′-paw′
Hsi-ts'ang (Ch. dependency) See *Si-ts'ang* and *Tibet*.		
Hsiung Shih-hui (Ch. leader)	shyŏŏng shû-whā	shyung shuh-whay
Hsiu-shui (Ch., Kiangsi)	shyōō-shwā	shyoo-shway
Hsü-ch'ang (Ch., Honan)	shü-chäng	shü-chahng
Hsü-chow (Ch., Szechwan)	shü-jō	shü-joh
Also called *I-p'in*, q.v.		
Hsueh Yüeh (Ch. general)	shü-ĕ yü-ĕ	shü-eh yü-eh
Htizwe (Burma)	tē′-zwĕ′	tee′-zweh′
Hua-yang (Ch., Anhwei)	whä-yäng	whah-yahng
Hua-yung (Ch., Hunan)	whä-yŏŏng	whah-yung
Hubli (India)	hŏŏ′-blĭ	hu′-bli
Hu-chow (Ch., Chekiang)	*Eng.* hōō-chou *Ch.* hōō-jō	hoo-chau hoo-joh
Hué (Indo-Ch.)	hwĕ′	hweh′
Huedin (Rum.)	k(h)wĕ-dēn′	k(h)weh-deen′
Huels (Ger.)	hüls′	hüls′
Huelva (Sp.)	wĕl′-vä	wel′-vah
Huesca (Sp., prov.)	wĕs′-kä	wes′-kah
Hughenden (Austral.)	hū′-ĭn-dən	hyoo′-in-duhn
Hugli (India) See *Hooghly*.		
Hui-ch'ang (Ch., Kiangsi)	whā-chäng	whay-chahng
Hui-lai (Ch., Kwangtung)	whā-lī	whay-lai
Huili (Ch., Sikang)	whā-lē	whay-lee
Also spelled *Hweili*.		
Huisduinen (Neth.)	hûĭs-dûĭ′-nən	hœis-dœi′-nuhn
Huizen (Neth.)	hûĭ′-zən	hœi′-zuhn
Hukawng (Burma, valley)	hōō′-kông′	hoo′-kawng′
Hukong (Burma)	hōō′-kông′	hoo′-kawng′
Also spelled *Hukawng*, q.v.		
Hu-k'ou (Ch., Kiangsi)	hōō-kō	hoo-koh

Hu-lin (Manchu.)	hōō-lĭn	hoo-lin
Hüls (Ger.)	hüls′	hüls′
Hu-lu-t'ao (Manchu.)	hōō-lōō-tou	hoo-loo-tau
Hu-ma (Manchu.)	hōō-mä	hoo-mah
Hun (Libya)	hōōn′	hoon′
Hu-nan (Ch., prov.)	hōō-nän	hoo-nahn
Hun-ch'un (Manchu.)	hŏŏn-chŏŏn	hun-chun
hunda (Alb.) See *hundë.*		
hundë (Alb.)	hōōn′-də	hoon′-duh
An element, meaning *cape,* in Albanian place names. Look up the other part of the name.		
Hunder (Nor.)	hŏŏn′-ər	hun′-uhr
Hundorp (Nor.)	hŏŏn′-dôrp	hun′-dorp
Hunedoara (Rum.)	hŏŏ-nĕ-dwä′-rä	hu-neh-dwah′-rah
Hungarian *Hunyad,* hŏŏ′-nyŏd [hu′-nyod], and *Vajdahunyad,* voi′-dŏ- [voi′-do-].		
Hungary	*Eng.* hŭng′-gə-rĭ	huhng′-guh-ri
Hungarian *Magyarország,* mŏ′-dyŏr-ôr′-säg [mo′-dyor-or′-sahg].		
Hunyad (Rum.) See *Hunedoara.*		
Hunze (Neth., riv.)	hûn′-zə	hœn′-zuh
Huon (Oc., pen.)	*Eng.* hū′-ŏn	hyoo′-on
Hu-peh (Ch., prov.)	*Eng.* hōō-pā	hoo-pay
	Ch. hōō-bĕ	hoo-beh
Huşi (Rum.)	hŏŏsh′	hush′
Husiatyn (Pol.)	hŏŏ-shä′-tĭn	hu-shah′-tin
Hussein Sirry (Egyptian leader)	hŏŏs-sān′ sĭr′-rĭ	hus-sayn′ sihr′-ri
Husum (Ger., Schles.-Hol.)	hōō′-zŏŏm	hoo′-zum
Husum (Nor.)	hōōs′-ŏŏm	hoos′-um
Huszt (Cz.) See *Chust.*		
Hvar (Yugosl.)	hvär′	hvahr′
Italian *Lesina,* q.v.		
Hvittingfoss (Nor.)	vĭt′-ĭng-fôs	vit′-ing-fos
Hwang Ho *or* River (Ch.)	whäng	whahng
Also called the *Yellow River.*		
Hwang-k'ang (Ch., Hupeh)	whäng-käng	whahng-kahng
Hwang-peh (Ch., Hupeh)	whäng-bĕ	whahng-beh
Hwa-yung (Ch., Hunan)	whä-yŏŏng	whah-yung
Hwei-chow (Ch., Anhwei)	*Eng.* whā-chou	whay-chau
	Ch. whā-jō	whay-joh
Hweili (Ch.) See *Huili.*		

Hyderabad (India)	hī-drə-băd′ *or* -bäd′	hai-druh-bad′ *or* -bahd′
Hydra (Gr., isl.)	ē′-*th*rä	ee′-*th*rah
Hyères (Fr.)	yĕr′	yehr′
Hyrynsalmi (Fin.)	hü′-rün-säl-mē	hü′-rün-sahl-mee
Hyvinkää (Fin.)	hü′-vĭng-kă	hü′-ving-ka
Ialomiţa (Rum., riv.)	yä′-lô-mē′-tsä	yah′-lo-mee′-tsah
Ianina (Gr.) See *Ioannina*.		
Iaşi (Rum.)	yäsh′	yahsh′
Also called *Jassy*, q.v.		
Ibar (Yugosl., riv.)	ē′-bär	ee′-bahr
Ibn Saud (King of Saudi Arabia)	ĭb′-ən sä-o͞od′	ib′-uhn sah-ood′
Icaria (Gr., isl.) See *Ikaria*.		
Içel (Turk.)	ē′-chĕl	ee′-chel
I-ch'ang (Ch., Hupeh)	ē-chäng	ee-chahng
Ichnya (Rus.)	ĭch-nyä′	ich-nyah′
I-chun (Ch., Kiangsi)	ē-jo͝on	ee-jun
Ickes, Harold L.	ĭk′-əs *or* ĭk′-ĭz	ik′-uhs *or* ik′-iz
Ide Oros (Crete, mt.)	ē′-*th*ē ô′-rôs	ee′-*th*ee o′-ros
English *Mt. Ida*, ī′-də [ai′-duh]. Also called *Ypseloreites*, ē-psē-lô-rē′-tēs [ee-psee-lo-ree′-tees].		
Iditerod (Alaska)	ī-dĭt′-ə-räd	ai-dit′-uh-rahd
Idritsa (Rus.)	ē′-drĭ-tsä	ee′-dri-tsah
Ieperen (Belg.)	ē′-pə-rən	ee′-puh-ruhn
French *Ypres*, q.v.		
Ieriki (Latvia)	ē′-ĕ′-rē-kē	ee′-eh′-ree-kee
Iesi (It.)	yĕ′-zē	yeh′-zee
Iewe (Est.)	*Rus.* yĕ′-vĕ	yeh′-veh
Estonian *Jõhvi*, q.v.		
Ifalik (Oc.)	ē′-fä-lēk	ee′-fah-leek
I-fêng (Ch., Kiangsi)	ē-fŭng	ee-fuhng
Ifni (Mor.)	ēf′-nē	eef′-nee
Iglau (Cz., riv., town) See *Jihlava*.		
Iglawa (Cz., riv., town) See *Jihlava*.		
Iglesias (Sard.)	ē-glĕ′-sĭ-äs	ee-gleh′-si-ahs
İğneada (Turk.)	ē-nĕ′-ä-dä	ee-neh′-ah-dah
I-hwang (Ch., Kiangsi)	ē-whäng	ee-whahng
Also spelled *Yi-hwang*.		
Iijärvi (Fin., lakes)	ē′-jăr-vē	ee′-jehr-vee

Iisalmi (Fin.)	ē′-säl-mē	ee′-sahl-mee

ij

In Dutch *ij* is interchangeable with *ei* and *y*, though *y* is usually preferred when initial. A consultant may have to look for all three forms before he finds his word.

IJmuiden (Neth.)	*Eng.* ī′-moi-dən	ai′-moi-duhn
	Du. ī′-mûĭ-dən	ai′-mœi-duhn
Ikaria (Gr., isl.)	*Eng.* ē-kăr′-ĭ-ə	ee-kehr′-i-uh
	Gr. ē-kä-rē′-ä	ee-kah-ree′-ah

Also called *Nicaria*, nē-kär-yä′ [nee-kahr-yah′].

Ikhthys (Gr., point)	ēk(h)-thēs′	eek(h)-thees′

The point of *Katakolon*, q.v.

Iles d'Hyères (Fr.)	ēl dyĕr′	eel dyehr′
Ilandža (Yugosl.)	ē′-län-jä	ee′-lahn-jah
Ilich (Rus.)	ĭl-yēch′	il-yeech′
Iligan (P.I.)	ē-lē′-gän	ee-lee′-gahn
Iliisk (Rus.)	ē-lēsk′	ee-leesk′
Ilijina Glava (Balkan mt.)	ē′-lē′-yĭ-nä glä′-vä	ee′-lee′-yi-nah glah′-vah
Ilja (Pol.) See *Iłża*.		
Illana (P.I., bay)	ē-lyä′-nä *or* -yä′-	ee-lyah′-nah *or* -yah′-
Illovaiskaya (Rus.)	ĭl-lŏ-vī′-skä-yä	il-lo-vai′-skah-yah
Ilmen (Rus., lake)	ēl′(y)-mĕn(y)	eel′(y)-men(y)
Iloilo (P.I.)	ē′-lô-ē′-lô	ee′-lo-ee′-lo
Ilok (Yugosl.)	ē′-lôk	ee′-lok
Iłowo (Pol.)	ĭ-lô′-vô	i-lo′-vo
Iłża (Pol.)	ēl′-zhä	eel′-zhah

Russian *Ilja*, ē-lyä′ [ee-lyah′].

Im (Rus.)	ēm′	eem′
Iman (Rus.)	ĭ-män′	i-mahn′
Imatra (Fin.)	ē′-mät-rä	ee′-maht-rah
Imbros (Turk., isl.)	*Gr.* ēm′-brôs	eem′-bros

Turkish *İmroz*, ēm′-rôz′ [eem′-roz′].

Imola (It.)	ē′-mô-lä	ee′-mo-lah
Imotski (Yugosl.)	ē′-môt-skĭ	ee′-mot-ski
Imphal (India)	ĭmp′-hŭl′	imp′-huhl′
İmroz (Turk., isl.)	ēm′-rôz′	eem′-roz′

Greek *Imbros*, q.v.

Inari (Fin., lake)	ē′-nä-rē	ee′-nah-ree
Incoronata (Yugosl., isl.)	*It.* ēn-kô-rô-nä′-tä	een-ko-ro-nah′-tah

Serb-Croat *Kornat*, q.v.

Indainggyi (Burma)	ĭn-dīng-jē′	in-daing-jee′
Inđija (Yugosl.)	ēn′-dyĭ-yä	een′-dyi-yah

Indore (India)	ĭn-dôr′	in-dor′
Indramajoe *or* Indramayu (NEI)	ĭn-drä-mä′-yōō	in-drah-mah′-yoo
Indre (Fr., riv.)	ăN′dr	aN′dr
Indus (India, riv.)	ĭn′-dəs	in′-duhs
Ineu (Rum.)	ē-nĕ′-ŏŏ	ee-neh′-u
Ingul (Rus., riv.)	ĭn-gŏŏl′	in-gul′
Ingulets (Rus., riv.)	ĭn-gŏŏ′-lĕts	in-gu′-lets
Ingyin (Burma)	ĭn-jĭn′	in-jin′
Inkerman (Rus.)	ĭng′-kər-män	ing′-kuhr-mahn
Innisfail (Austral.)	ĭn′-ĭs-fāl	in′-is-fayl
Innokentievka (Rus.)	ĭn-nŏ-kĕn′-tyĕf-kä	in-no-ken′-tyef-kah
Innsbruck (Austria)	*Eng.* ĭnz′-brŏŏk	inz′-bruk
	Ger. ĭns′-brŏŏk	ins′-bruk
Inogošte (Yugosl.)	ē′-nô-gô′-shtĕ	ee′-no-go′-shteh
İnönü, İsmet (President of Turkey)	ē′-nö-nü, ĭs-mĕt′	ee′-nö-nü, is-met′
Inowrocław (Pol.)	ĭ-nô-vrô′-tsläf	i-no-vro′-tslahf

German *Hohensalza*, hō′-ən-zäl-tsä [hoh′-uhn-zahl-tsah].

inquiry	ĭn-kwī′-rĭ	in-kwai′-ri
	or ĭn′-kwĭ-rĭ	in′-kwi-ri

Both pronunciations are acceptable although the second is recognized only in recent editions of American dictionaries. Presumably ĭn′-kwī-rĭ [in′-kwai-ri] is inferior to both.

Insterburg (Ger.)	*Eng.* ĭn′-stər-bûrg	in′-stuhr-buhrg
	Ger. ĭn′-stər-bŏŏrk(h)	in′-stuhr-burk(h)
interesting	ĭn′-tər-ĕs-tĭng	in′-tuhr-es-ting
	or ĭn′-trəs-tĭng	in′-truhs-ting

The alternative pronunciation of *interesting* has better standing in America than the similar pronunciations of *dictionary*, q.v., and *necessary*, q.v. The second vowel of *interest* is often lost, and this syncopation gives a native analogy, whereas the "British" pronunciations of *dictionary* and *necessary* sound alien to American ears.

Inza (Rus.)	ēn′-zä	een′-zah
Inzecca (Corsica)	ēn-dzĕk′-kä	een-dzek′-kah
Ioannes, Agios (Crete)	yô-ä′-nēs, ī′-yôs	yo-ah′-nees, ai′-yos
Ioannina (Gr.)	yô-ä′-nē-nä	yo-ah′-nee-nah
	or yä′-nē-nä	yah′-nee-nah

Serb-Croat *Janina*, yä′-nē-nä [yah′-nee-nah].

Ionia (Turk.)	*Eng.* ī-ō′-nyə	ai-oh′-nyuh
Ios (Gr., isl.)	ē′-ô(s)	ee′-o(s)
I-p'in (Ch., Szechwan)	ē-pĭn	ee-pin

Also called *Hsü-chow*, q.v.

Ipoh (Malaya)	ē′-pō	ee′-poh
Iput (Rus., riv.)	ē′-po͝ot	ee′-put
Iran	*Per.* ē-rän′	ee-rahn′
	Eng. ĭ-răn′	i-ran′
Iranian	ī-rā′-nĭ-ən	ai-ray′-ni-uhn
’Iraq	*Per.* ē-räk′	ee-rahk′
	Eng. ĭ-răk′	i-rak′
Irig (Yugosl.)	ē′-rĭg	ee′-rig
Irkutsk (Rus.)	ĭr-ko͞otsk′	ihr-kootsk′
Iron Gates (Yugosl., Rum., gorge)	ī′-ərn gāts′	ai′-uhrn gayts′

Serb-Croat *Đerlap*, dyĕr′-läp [dyehr′-lahp]. Rumanian *Porţile de Fier*, pôr-tsē′-lĕ dĕ fyĕr′ [por-tsee′-leh deh fyehr′]. German *Eisernes Tor*, ī′-zər-nəs tōr′ [ai′-zuhr-nuhs tohr′]. Hungarian *Vaskapu*, vŏsh′-kŏ-po͞o [vosh′-ko-poo].

Irrawaddy (Burma, riv.)	ĭr-ə-wŏd′-ĭ	ihr-uh-wod′-i
Irún (Sp.)	ē-ro͞on′	ee-roon′
Isarco (It.)	ē-sär′-kô	ee-sahr′-ko
Isarog (P.I., mt.)	ē-sä-rôg′	ee-sah-rog′
Ischia (It., isl.)	ē′-skyä	ee′-skyah
Ise (Jap.)	ē-sĕ	ee-seh
Isefjord (Den.)	ē′-sə-fyōrd	ee′-suh-fyohrd
Iseghem (Belg.)	ĭz′-ə-k(h)ĕm	iz′-uh-k(h)em
Isère (Fr., riv.)	ē-zĕr′	ee-zehr′
Isernia (It.)	ē-sĕr′-nyä	ee-sehr′-nyah
Isfahan (Iran)	ĭs-fə-hän′	is-fuh-hahn′
Ishim (Rus.)	ĭsh-ēm′	ish-eem′
Ishui (Ch., Shantung)	ē-shwā	ee-shway
Isigny (Fr.)	ē-zē-nyē′	ee-zee-nyee′
Isili (Sard.)	ē′-sē-lē	ee′-see-lee
İskenderun (Turk.)	ĭs-kĕn′-də-ro͞on	is-ken′-duh-roon

Also spelled *Iskanderon*. English *Alexandretta*, q.v.

Isker *or* Iskr (Bulg., riv.)	ĭs′-kər	is′-kuhr
Ismail (Rum.)	ēz-mä-ēl′	eez-mah-eel′

Russian *Tuchkof*, to͞och-kôf′ [tooch-kof′].

Ismailia (Egypt)	ēs′-mä-ĭ-lē′-yä	ees′-mah-i-lee′-yah
isola	ē′-zô-lä *or* ē′-sô-lä	ee′-zo-lah *or* ee′-so-lah

An element, meaning *island*, in Italian place names. It may be necessary to look up the other part of the name.

Isola Lunga *or* Isola Grossa (Yugosl.)	*It.* ē′-zô-lä lo͞on′-gä *or* grôs′-sä	ee′-zo-lah loon′-gah *or* gros′-sah

Serb-Croat *Dugi Otok*, q.v.

Isonzo (It., riv.)	ē-zôn′-tsô	ee-zon′-tso

Ispahan (Iran) See *Isfahan*.

Ispica (Sicily)	ēs′-pē-kä	ees′-pee-kah
Issayeff, Feodor (Rus.)	ĭ-sä′-yĕf, fyô′-dŏr	i-sah′-yef, fyo′-dor
Issei	ēs-sā	ees-say
Japanese subjects who have come to the United States and are living here. They are not eligible for citizenship. See *Kibei* and *Nisei*.		
issue	ĭsh′-ū *or* ĭsh′-o͞o	ish′-yoo *or* ish′-oo
There is no dictionary authority for the pronunciation of "s" instead of "sh" in this word. The pronunciation with "s" is probably not dialect but an overrefinement, technically called a hyperurbanism.		
Ist (Yugosl)	ēst′	eest′
İstanbul (Turk.)	*Eng.* ĭs′-tăn-bo͞ol′	is′-tan-bool′
	Turk. ĭs-täm′-bo͝ol	is-tahm′-bul
Formerly *Constantinople* and also *Byzantium.*		
Istok (Yugosl.)	ē′-stôk	ee′-stok
Istranca Dağları (Turk., mts.)	ĭs-trän′-jä dä′-lä-rĭ	is-trahn′-jah dah′-lah-ri
Istres (Fr.)	ē′str	ee′str
Istros (Europ. riv.) See *Danube.*		
Ithaca (Gr., isl.)	*Eng.* ĭth′-ə-kə	ith′-uh-kuh
Greek *Ithake*, ē-thä′-kē [ee-thah′-kee], or *Theaki*, thē-ä′-kē [thee-ah′-kee].		
I-tu (Ch., Hupeh)	ē-do͞o	ee-doo
Itzehoe (Ger.)	ĭt′-sə-hō	it′-suh-hoh
Ivailovgrad (Bulg.)	ē-vī′-lŏf-grät	ee-vai′-lof-graht
Ivanča, Mala (Yugosl.)	ē′-vän-chä, mä′-lä	ee′-vahn-chah, mah′-lah
Ivančica (Yugosl., mts.)	ē′-vän′-chĭ-tsä	ee′-vahn′-chi-tsah
Ivanec (Yugosl.)	ē′-vä-nĕts	ee′-vah-nets
Ivangorod (Pol.) See *Dęblin.*		
Ivanjica (Yugosl.)	ē′-vä′-nyĭ-tsä	ee′-vah′-nyi-tsah
Ivankovci (Yugosl.)	ē′-vän′-kôv-tsĭ	ee′-vahn′-kov-tsi
Ivanovka (Rus.)	ĭ-vä′-nŏf-kä	i-vah′-nof-kah
Ivanovo (Rus.)	ĭ-vä′-nŏ-vŏ	i-vah′-no-vo
Ivat (Rus.)	ĭ-vät′	i-vaht′
Ivatsevichi (Pol.) See *Iwacewicze.*		
Ivry (Fr.)	ē-vrē′	ee-vree′
Iwacewicze (Pol.)	ĭ-vä-tsĕ-vē′-chĕ	i-vah-tseh-vee′-cheh
Russian *Ivatsevichi*, ĭ-vä-tsĕ′-vĭ-chĭ [i-vah-tseh′-vi-chi].		
I-wu (Ch., Chekiang)	ē-wo͞o	ee-woo
Also spelled *Yi-wu.*		
Ixelles (Belg.) See *Elsene.*		
I-yang (Ch., Kiangsi)	ē-yäng	ee-yahng
Also spelled *Yi-yang.*		
Iž (Yugosl., isl.)	ēzh′	eezh′
Italian *Eso*, q.v.		

Izac, Ed. V. (U.S. representative)	ē′-zăk′	ee′-zak′
Izbor (Yugosl.)	ēz′-bôr	eez′-bor
Izhevsk (Rus.)	ĭ-zhĕfsk′	i-zhefsk′
İzmir (Turk.) English *Smyrna*, q.v.	ĭz′-mĭr	iz′-mihr
Izvestia (Rus. newspaper)	ĭz-vĕs′-tĭ-yä	iz-ves′-ti-yah
Izyaslav (Rus.)	ĭz-yä-släf′	iz-yah-slahf′
Izyum (Rus.)	ĭ-zyōōm′	i-zyoom′
Jablanac (Yugosl.)	yä′-blä-näts	yah′-blah-nahts
Jablanica (Yugosl., mts., riv.)	yä′-blä-nĭ-tsä	yah′-blah-ni-tsah
Jablanov Vrh (Yugosl., mt.)	yä′-blä-nôv vərk(h)′	yah′-blah-nov vuhrk(h)′
Jablonec (Cz.)	yä′-blô-nĕts	yah′-blo-nets
Jabłonowo (Pol.)	yä-blô-nô′-vô	yah-blo-no′-vo
Jabolčište (Yugosl.)	yä′-bôl′-chĭ-shtĕ	yah′-bol′-chi-shteh
Jabukovac (Yugosl.)	yä′-bōō-kô-väts	yah′-boo-ko-vahts
Jabwot (Oc.)	jäb′-wôt	jahb′-wot
Jaca (Sp.)	hä′-kä	hah′-kah
Jacomy, Henri Paul (Fr. general)	zhä-kô-mē′, äN-rē′ pôl′	zhah-ko-mee′, ahN-ree′ pol′
Jacquinot (Oc., bay)	zhä-kē-nō′	zhah-kee-noh′
Jadar (Yugosl., riv.)	yä′-där	yah′-dahr
Jadovnik (Yugosl., mts.)	yä′-dôv-nĭk	yah′-dov-nik
Jadre (Yugosl., isl.) Italian *Peschiera*, q.v.	yä′-drĕ	yah′-dreh
Jaeckle, Edwin F. (Repub. leader)	jĕk′-əl	jek′-uhl
Jaeger (Ger.)	yā′-gər	yay′-guhr
Jaén (Sp.)	hä-ĕn′	hah-en′
Jaeren (Nor.)	yăr′-ən	yehr′-uhn
Jaffna (Ceylon)	jăf′-nə	jaf′-nuh
Jagdführer *or* -fuehrer German *fighter-commander*.	yäkt′-fü′-rər	yahkt′-fü′-ruhr
Jägerndorf (Cz.) See *Krnov*.		
Jagodina (Yugosl.)	yä′-gô-dĭ-nä	yah′-go-di-nah
Jagodnja (Yugosl., mts.)	yä′-gôd-nyä	yah′-god-nyah
jaguar Often pronounced jăg′-wər [jag′-wuhr].	jăg′-wär	jag′-wahr
Jaipur (India)	jī′-pŏŏr′	jai′-pur′
Jajce (Yugosl.)	yī′-tsĕ	yai′-tseh

Jakobstad (Fin.)	*Sw.* yä′-kôp-städ′	yah′-kop-stahd′
Jakobstadt (Latvia)	*Ger.* yä′-kôp-shtät	yah′-kop-shtaht
Latvian *Jēkabpils*, q.v.		
Jalalabad (Afghan.)	jə-lä-lä-bäd′	juh-lah-lah-bahd′
Jaluit (Oc.)	jä′-lo͝o-ĭt	jah′-lu-it
Jamaja (Est., isl.)	yä′-mä-yä	yah′-mah-yah
Jamalpur (India)	jə-mäl′-po͝or′	juh-mahl′-pur′
Jamkhandi (India)	jŭm′-k(h)ŭn-dē	juhm′-k(h)uhn-dee
Jammerbugt (Den.)	yäm′-ər-bo͝okt	yahm′-uhr-bukt
Jammu (India)	jŭm′-o͞o	juhm′-oo
Jamnagar (India)	jăm-nŭg′-ər	jam-nuhg′-uhr
Also called *Navanagar*, q.v.		
Jamshedpur (India)	jăm-shĕd-po͝or′	jam-shed-pur′
Janakpur (Nepal)	jŭ′-nək-po͝or′	juh′-nuhk-pur′
Janica (Gr.) See *Genitsa.*		
Janina (Gr.) See *Ioánnina.*		
Jänisjärvi (Fin., dist.)	yă′-nĭs-yăr-vē	ya′-nis-yehr-vee
Janjevo (Yugosl.)	yä′-nyĕ-vô	yah′-nyeh-vo
Janjira (India)	jŭn′-jē-rä	juhn′-jee-rah
Jankoi (Rus.)	jän-koi′	jahn-koi′
Janov (Lith.)	*Rus.* yä′-nŏf	yah′-nof
Lithuanian *Jonava*, q.v.		
Janów (Pol.)	yä′-no͝of	yah′-nuf
Russian *Yanov*, yä′-nŏf [yah′-nof].		
Janów Podlaski (Pol.)	yä′-no͝of pôd-lä′-skĭ	yah′-nuf pod-lah′-ski
Russian *Yanov*, yä′-nŏf [yah′-nof].		
Jao-p'ing (Ch., Kwangtung)	jou-pĭng *or* rou-pĭng	jau-ping *or* rau-ping
Japanese	jăp′-ə-nēz′ *or* -nēs′	jap′-uh-neez′ *or* -nees′

In names like *Japanese* and *Chinese*, either "-nēz" or "-nēs" is correct. Of the two, *-nēz* is preferred by most speakers and by most dictionaries. Certainly no announcer who naturally says *-nēz* should affect *-nēs* as an elegance. For information on this and 1,100 other debatable pronunciations, see the famous Section 277 of Webster's (p. lix). There is a similar section in the *New Standard Dictionary.*

Japara (NEI)	jä-pä′-rä	jah-pah′-rah
Jarabub (Libia)	jä′-rä-bo͞ob′	jah′-rah-boob′
Jarkovac (Yugosl.)	yär′-kô-väts	yahr′-ko-vahts
Jarman, Pete (U.S. representative)	jär′-măn	jahr′-man
Jarocin (Pol.)	yä-rô′-chĭn	yah-ro′-chin
Jarosław (Pol.)	yä-rô′-släf	yah-ro′-slahf
Russian *Yaroslav*, yä-rŏ-släf′ [yah-ro-slahf′]		

järvi	yăr′-vē	yehr′-vee

An element, meaning *lake*, in Finnish place names.

Jasenica (Yugosl., riv.)	yä′-sĕ′-nĭ-tsä	yah′-seh′-ni-tsah
Jasenovac (Yugosl.)	yä′-sĕ′-nô-väts	yah′-seh′-no-vahts
Jasiňa (Cz.)	yä′-sĭ-nyä	yah′-si-nyah

Hungarian *Körösmező*, kû′-rûsh-mĕ′-zû [kœ′-rœsh-meh′-zœ].

Jasiolda (Pol., riv.)	yä-syôl′-dä	yah-syol′-dah

Russian *Yaselda*, yä-syôl′(y)-dä [yah-syol′(y)-dah].

Jask (Iran)	jäsk′	jahsk′
Jasło (Pol.)	yä′-slô	yah′-slo
Jassy (Rum.)	*Ger.* yäs′-ē	yahs′-ee

Rumanian *Iaşi*, q.v.

Jastrebac (Yugosl.)	yä′-strĕ-bäts	yah′-streh-bahts
Jastrebarsko (Yugosl.)	yä′-strĕ-bär-skô	yah′-streh-bahr-sko

Magyar *Jaska.*

Jászapáti (Hung.)	yäs′-ŏ′-pä-tĭ	yahs′-o′-pah-ti
Jászberény (Hung.)	yäs′-bĕ′-rān(y)	yahs′-beh′-rayn(y)
Jaunjelgava (Latvia)	youn′-yĕl′-gä-vä	yaun′-yel′-gah-vah

German *Friedrichstadt*, q.v.

Jaunlatgale (Latvia)	youn′-lät-gä-lĕ	yaun′-laht-gah-leh

Russian *Pytalovo*, q.v.

Java (NEI)	jä′-və	jah′-vuh
Javor (Yugosl., mts.)	yä′-vôr	yah′-vor
Javorište (Yugosl.)	yä′-vô′-rĭsh-tĕ	yah′-vo′-rish-teh
Jaz (Yugosl.)	yäz′	yahz′
jebel *or* djebel	jĕb′-əl	jeb′-uhl

These are alternative spellings for an element, meaning *hill*, in Arabic place names. The latter is to be expected in French territory. It may be necessary to look up both.

Jebel Ishkel (Tun.)	jĕb′-əl ĭsh′-kĕl	jeb′-uhl ish′-kel
Jebel Kalakh (Egypt)	jĕb′-əl kă-lăk′	jeb′-uhl ka-lak′
Jebel Khirag (Egypt)	jĕb′-əl kĭ-răg′	jeb′-uhl ki-rag′
Jedda (Saudi Arabia)	jĕd′-də	jed′-duh
Jędrzejów (Pol.)	yăN-jĕ′-yŏŏf	yaN-jeh′-yuf

Russian *Andreev*, än-drĕ′-yĕf [ahn-dreh′-yef].

Jefna (Tun.)	jĕf′-nä	jef′-nah

Also spelled *Djefna*, q.v.

Jehol (Manchu., prov., town)	*Eng.* jə-hŏl′	juh-hol′

It seems sensible to Anglicize this Jesuit spelling of a Chinese name that is unpronounceable in English sounds. Our dictionaries usually give rĕ-hō or rā-hō; BBC gives jə-hŏl′. The city is also called *Ch'êng-teh*, q.v.

Jēkabpils (Latvia) German *Jakobstadt*, q.v.	yā′-käb-pēls *or* yă′-	yay′-kahb-peels *or* ya′-
Jelgava (Latvia)	yĕl′-gä-vä	yel′-gah-vah
Russian *Mitava*, q.v. German *Mitau*, mē′-tou [mee′-tau].		
Jelica (Yugosl., mts.)	yĕ′-lĭ-tsä	yeh′-li-tsah
Jelova (Yugosl., mts.)	yĕ′-lô-vä	yeh′-lo-vah
Jemo (Oc.)	jĕ′-mô	jeh′-mo
Jena (Ger.)	yā′-nä	yay′-nah
Jensen, Ben F. (U.S. representative)	jĕn′-sən	jen′-suhn
Jeren (Nor.)	yăr′-ən	yehr′-uhn
Jerez (Sp.)	hĕ-rĕth′ *or* -rĕs′	heh-reth′ *or* -res′
Formerly *Xeres*, shĕ′-rĕs [sheh′-res].		
Jerma (Balkan riv.)	*S.-C.* yĕr′-mä	yehr′-mah
Bulgarian spelling *Erma*.		
Jesenice (Yugosl.)	yĕ′-sĕ′-nĭ-tsĕ	yeh′-seh′-ni-tseh
Jesselton (Brit. Borneo)	jĕs′-əl-tən	jes′-uhl-tuhn
jetsam	jĕt′-səm	jet′-suhm
Jette (Belg.)	zhĕt′	zhet′
Jezierna (Pol., riv.)	yĕ-zhĕr′-nä	yeh-zhehr′-nah
Russian *Eziorka*, yĕ-zĭ-ôr′-kä [yeh-zi-or′-kah].		
jezioro (Pol.)	yĕ-zhô′-rô	yeh-zho′-ro
A common element, meaning *lake*, in Polish place names. Look up the other part of the name.		
Jhansi (India)	jän′-sē	jahn′-see
Jhelum (India, riv.)	jā′-ləm	jay′-luhm
Jibuti (Fr. Som.)	jē-bo͞o′-tē	jee-boo′-tee
Also spelled *Djibouti*. French jē-bo͞o-tē′ [jee-boo-tee′].		
Jihlava (Cz., riv., town)	yē′-k(h)lä-vä	yee′-k(h)lah-vah
German *Iglawa* (river), ĭg′-lä-vä [ig′-lah-vah]; *Iglau* (town), ĭg′-lou [ig′-lau].		
Jijelli (Alg.)	jē-jĕ-lē′	jee-jeh-lee′
Also spelled *Djidjelli*.		
Jijona (Sp.)	hē-hô′-nä	hee-ho′-nah
Jiloca (Sp., riv.)	hē-lô′-kä	hee-lo′-kah
Jimbolea (Rum.)	zhēm-bô′-lyä	zheem-bo′-lyah
Serb-Croat *Žombolj*, q.v. Hungarian *Zsombolya*, zhôm′-bô-yŏ [zhom′-bo-yo].		
Jinatuan (P.I.)	hē-nä-to͞o′-än	hee-nah-too′-ahn
Jinnah, Mohamed Ali (Indian leader)	jĭn′-ə, mō-hăm′-ĭd ä′-lē	jin′-uh, moh-ham′-id ah′-lee
Jinsen (Korea)	jĭn-sĕn	jin-sen

Jiu (Rum., riv.)	zhē′-o͝o	zhee′-u
João (Port.)	zhô-ouN′	zho-auN′
	or zho͝o-ouN′	zhu-auN′
To an American ear, this name (*John*) often sounds like one syllable, zhouN′ [zhauN′], or even zhôN′ [zhoN′].		
João Pessoa (Brazil)	zho͝o-ouN′ pĕ-sô′-ə	zhu-auN′ peh-so′-uh
Also called, unofficially, *Paraíba* or *Parahiba*, q.v.		
Joaquin (Sp.)	hwä-kēn′	hwah-keen′
Jodhpur (India)	jōd′-po͝or	johd′-pur
Joelster (Nor.)	yûl′-stər	yœl′-stuhr
Joenkoeping (Sw.)	yûn′-chû-pĭng	yœn′-chœ-ping
Joensuu (Fin.)	yô′-ĕn′-so͞o	yo′-en′-soo
Jõgeva (Est.)	yû′-gĕ-vä	yuh′-geh-vah
Jogjakarta *or* Jogyakarta (NEI)	jōg-yä-kär′-tä	johg-yah-kahr′-tah
Johore (Malaya)	jə-hôr′	juh-hor′
Jõhvi (Est.)	yûk(h)′-vĭ	yuhk(h)′-vi
Russian *Iewe*, q.v.		
joki	yô′-kē	yo′-kee
An element, meaning *river* or *stream*, in Finnish place names.		
Jokonga (Rus.)	yŏ-kôn′-gä	yo-kon′-gah
Joló (P.I.)	*Eng.* hô′-lô	ho′-lo
	native hô-lô′	ho-lo′
Jölster (Nor.)	yûl′-stər	yœl′-stuhr
Jonava (Lith.)	yô′-nä-vä	yo′-nah-vah
Russian *Janov*, q.v.		
Joniškis (Lith.)	yô′-nĭsh-kĭs	yo′-nish-kis
Jonkman, Bartel J. (U.S. representative)	yŏngk′-män, bär-tĕl′	yongk′-mahn, bahr-tel′
Jönköping (Sw.)	yûn′-chû-pĭng	yœn′-chœ-ping
Jornal, O (Braz. newspaper)	zhôr-näl′, o͝o	zhor-nahl′, u
Jornal do Brasil (Braz. newspaper)	zhôr-näl′ do͝o brä-zēl′	zhor-nahl′ du brah-zeel′
Jornal do Comércio (Braz. newspaper)	zhôr-näl′ do͝o kô-mĕr′-syo͝o	zhor-nahl′ du ko-mehr′-syu
José (Sp.)	*Eng.* hō-zā′	hoh-zay′
	Sp. hô-sĕ′	ho-seh′

In Webster's Unabridged and in the College Standard dictionaries the common European variants of Christian names are listed with pronunciations under the English entry. For *José*, see *Joseph;* for *Jorge*, see *George;* and so on. This feature can be very helpful to radio speakers, not all of whom are aware of the extraordinary resources of our magnificent American dictionaries.

Jostedal (Nor.)	yôs′-tə-däl	yos′-tuh-dahl
Jostedals-Breen (Nor.)	yôs′-tə-däls-brā′-ən	yos′-tuh-dahls-bray′-uhn
Jotunheimen (Nor., mt. region)	yō′-tŏŏn-hā-mən	yoh′-tun-hay-muhn
Jovac (Yugosl.)	yô′-väts	yo′-vahts
Jovanovac (Yugosl.)	yô′-vä′-nô-väts	yo′-vah′-no-vahts
Juárez, Benito (Mex. hero)	hwä′-rĕs, bĕ-nē′-tô	hwah′-res, beh-nee′-to
Jubbulpore (India)	jŭb-əl-pôr′	juhb-uhl-por′
Juhor (Yugosl., mts.)	yōō′-hôr	yoo′-hor
Jui-an (Ch., Chekiang)	rwā-än	rway-ahn
Jui-ch'ang (Ch., Kiangsi)	rwā-chäng	rway-chahng
Jui-chin (Ch., Kiangsi)	rwā-jĭn	rway-jin
Jui-hung (Ch., Kiangsi)	rwā-hŏŏng	rway-hung
Juin, Alphonse (Fr. general)	zhwăN′, äl-fôNs′	zhwaN′, ahl-foNs′
Julfa (Iran)	jŏŏl′-fä	jul′-fah
Julianehaap (Greenl.)	yōō-lĭ-ä′-nə-hôp′	yoo-li-ah′-nuh-hop′
Jumet (Belg.)	zhü-mĕ′	zhü-meh′
Jumna (India)	jŭm′-nə	juhm′-nuh
Juneau (Alaska)	jōō′-nō	joo′-noh
Junik (Yugosl.)	yōō′-nĭk	yoo′-nik
Junker (Ger. aristocrat)	*Ger.* yŏŏng′-kər *Eng.* jŭngk′-ər	yung′-kuhr juhngk′-uhr
Junkovci (Yugosl.)	yōōn′-kôv-tsĭ	yoon′-kov-tsi
Jurjev *or* Yurev (Est.)	*Rus.* yōōr′-yĕf	yoor′-yef
Estonian *Tartu*, q.v. German *Dorpat*, q.v.		
Jurukluk (Yugosl.)	yōō′-rōōk-lōōk	yoo′-rook-look
Jutfaas (Neth.)	yût′-fäs	yœt′-fahs
Jutland (Den.)	*Eng.* jŭt′-lənd	juht′-luhnd
Danish *Jylland*, yül′-län [yül′-lahn].		
Južna Morava (Yugosl., riv.)	yōōzh′-nä mô′-rä-vä	yoozh′-nah mo′-rah-vah
Jylland (Den.) See *Jutland.*		
Jyväskylä (Fin.)	yü′-văs-kü-lă	yü′-vas-kü-la

k and *c* are interchangeable in Greek and other languages. It may be necessary to look up both spellings. In Greek *k* is officially preferred.

Kaala Djerda (Tun.)	kä′-ä-lä jĕr′-dä	kah′-ah-lah jehr′-dah
Kaballa (Gr.) See *Kavalla.*		
Kabanskoe (Rus.)	kä-bän′-skŏ-yĕ	kah-bahn′-sko-yeh
Kabardinka (Rus.)	kä-bär-dēn′-kä	kah-bahr-deen′-kah

Kabaw (Burma, valley)	kə-bô′	kuh-baw′
kabo (Gr.)	kä′-vô	kah′-vo

An element, meaning *cape*, in Greek place names. Look up the other part of the name.

Kabul (Afghan.)	kä′-bo͝ol	kah′-bul
Kabyu (Burma)	kə-bū′	kuh-byoo′
Kać (Yugosl.)	käch′	kahch′
Kačanik (Yugosl.)	kä′-chä-nĭk	kah′-chah-nik
Kačer (Yugosl., riv.)	kä′-chĕr	kah′-chehr
Kachalino (Rus.)	kä-chä′-lĭ-nŏ	kah-chah′-li-no
Kachanovka (Rus.)	kä-chä-nŏf′-kä	kah-chah-nof′-kah
Kachin (Burma, hills)	kə-chĭn′	kuh-chin′
Kack Mały (Pol.)	kätsk′ mä′-lĭ	kahtsk′ mah′-li
Kaczynski, Zygmunt (Pol. leader)	kä-chĭn′-skĭ, zĭg′-mo͝ont	kah-chin′-ski, zig′-munt
Kadijica (Balkan mt.)	*S.-C.* kä′-dĭ-yĭ-tsä	kah′-di-yi-tsah
Kadina (Yugosl., riv.)	kä′-dĭ-nä	kah′-di-nah
Kadnikov (Rus.)	käd′-nĭ-kŏf	kahd′-ni-kof
Kadovar (Oc.)	kä-dô-vär′	kah-do-vahr′
Kagalnitskaya (Rus.)	kä-gäl′(y)-nĭt-skä-yä	kah-gahl′(y)-nit-skah-yah
Kaganovich, Lazar M. (Rus. leader)	kä-gä-nô′-vĭch, lä′-zär	kah-gah-no′-vich, lah′-zahr
Kaggi (Sicily)	käd′-jē	kahd′-jee
Kagoshima (Jap.)	kä-gô-shē-mä	kah-go-shee-mah
Kagul (Rum.) See *Cahul.*		
Kahili (Oc.)	kä-hē′-lĭ	kah-hee′-li
Kai (NEI)	kī′	kai′
K'ai-fêng (Ch., Honan)	kī-fŭng	kai-fuhng
K'ai-lu (Manchu.)	kī-lo͞o	kai-loo
Kaimana (Oc.)	kī-mä′-nä	kai-mah′-nah
Kairiru (Oc.)	kī-rē-ro͞o′	kai-ree-roo′
Kairouan (Tun.)	*Fr.* kĕr-wäN′	kehr-wahN′

Arabic *Qairwan*, q.v.

Kaišiadorys (Lith.)	kī-shyä-dô-rēs′	kai-shyah-do-rees′

Russian *Koshedary*, q.v.

Kajaani (Fin.)	kä′-yä-nē	kah′-yah-nee
Kajali (Yugosl.)	kä′-yä-lĭ	kah′-yah-li
Kajmakčalan (Balkan mt.)	kī′-mäk-chä′-län	kai′-mahk-chah′-lahn
Kakavia (Dodec., Rh.)	kä-kä-vyä′	kah-kah-vyah′
Kake Skala (Crete, coast)	kä-kē′ skä′-lä	kah-kee′ skah′-lah
Kakhovka (Rus.)	kä-hôf′-kä	kah-hof′-kah

Käkisalmi (Fin.)	kă′-kē-säl-mē	ka′-kee-sahl-mee
Swedish *Kexholm*, chĕks′-hôlm′ [cheks′-holm′]. Russian *Keksholm*, kĕks′-hŏl(y)m [keks′-hol(y)m].		
Kalabak (Yugosl., Alb., mt.)	*S.-C.* kä′-lä-bäk	kah′-lah-bahk
Kalach (Rus.)	kä-läch′	kah-lahch′
Kaladan (Burma, riv.)	kə-lə-dăn′ *or* kə-lə-dŭn′	kuh-luh-dan′ kuh-luh-duhn′
Kalamai (Gr.)	kä-lä′-mĕ	kah-lah′-meh
Also called *Kalamata*, kä-lä-mä′-tä [kah-lah-mah′-tah].		
Kalamaki (Gr.)	kä-lä-mä′-kē	kah-lah-mah′-kee
Kalambaka (Gr.)	kä-lä-bä′-kä	kah-lah-bah′-kah
Kalamos (Gr., isl.)	kä′-lä-mô(s)	kah′-lah-mo(s)
Kalat *or* Khelat (Baluch.)	kə-lät′	kuh-laht′
Kalathos (Dodec., Rh.)	kä′-lä-thôs	kah′-lah-thos
Kalavryta (Gr.)	kä-lä′-vrē-tä	kah-lah′-vree-tah
Kalaw (Burma)	kə-lô′	kuh-law′
Kale (Burma, valley)	kə-lā′	kuh-lay′
Kalemyo (Burma)	kə-lā′-myō	kuh-lay′-myoh
Kalenić (Yugosl.)	kä′-lĕ-nĭch	kah′-leh-nich
Kaleničska (Yugosl., riv.)	kä′-lĕ′-nĭch-skä	kah′-leh′-nich-skah
Kalgachinskaya (Rus.)	käl-gä′-chĭn-skä-yä	kahl-gah′-chin-skah-yah
Kalgan (Ch., Chahar)	käl-gän	kahl-gahn
Kalgoorlie (Austral.)	kăl-gōōr′-lĭ	kal-goor′-li
Kalidjati (NEI)	kä-lē-jä′-tē	kah-lee-jah′-tee
Kalinga (P.I.)	kä-lĭng′-gä	kah-ling′-gah
Kalinin, Mikhail (Rus. leader)	kä-lē′-nĭn, mĭ-hä-ēl′	kah-lee′-nin, mi-hah-eel′
Kalinkovichi (Rus.)	kä-lĭn-kô′-vĭ-chĭ	kah-lin-ko′-vi-chi
Kalisz (Pol.)	kä′-lĭsh	kah′-lish
Russian spelling *Kalish*.		
Kalitva (Rus., riv.)	kä-lĭt-vä′	kah-lit-vah′
Kalitvenskaya (Rus.)	kä-lēt′-vĕn-skä-yä	kah-leet′-ven-skah-yah
Kalkuny (Latvia)	*Rus.* käl-kōō′-nĭ	kahl-koo′-ni
Latvian *Grīva*, q.v.		
Kallmet (Alb.)	käl′-mĕt	kahl′-met
Kallmeti (Alb.) See *Kallmet*.		
Kallone (Gr., Lesbos)	kä-lô-nē′	kah-lo-nee′
Kalmius (Rus., riv.)	käl′(y)-mē-ōōs	kahl′(y)-mee-oos
Kalmuck (Rus.)	kăl′-mŭk	kal′-muhk
Kalocsa (Hung.)	kŏ′-lô-chŏ	ko′-lo-cho

Kalogeri (Crete)	kä-lô-yĕ′-rē	kah-lo-yeh′-ree
Kaluga (Rus.)	kä-lo͞o′-gä	kah-loo′-gah
Kalundborg (Den.)	kä-lo͝on-bôr′	kah-lun-bor′
Kałuszyn (Pol.)	kä-lo͝o′-shĭn	kah-lu′-shin
Russian spelling *Kalushin.*		
Kalvarija (Lith.)	*Lith.* käl-vä-rē′-yä	kahl-vah-ree′-yah
	Rus. käl-vä′-rĭ-yä	kahl-vah′-ri-yah
Kalyazin (Rus.)	kä-lyä′-zĭn	kah-lyah′-zin
Kalymnos (Dodec.)	kä′-lēm-nô(s)	kah′-leem-no(s)
Italian *Calino*, kä-lē′-nô [kah-lee′-no]. The town is called *Kalymnos* or *Pothea*, pô′-thĕ-ä [po′-theh-ah].		
Kalyvas, N. (Gr. collab.)	kä-lē′-väs	kah-lee′-vahs
Kamaing (Burma)	kä-mīng′	kah-maing′
Kamâl Atatürk (Former President of Turkey)	See *Kemal Atatürk.*	
Kamara (Crete)	kä-mä′-rä	kah-mah′-rah
Kämärä (Fin.)	kă′-mă-ră	ka′-ma-ra
Kamauk (Burma)	kə-mouk′	kuh-mauk′
Kambeira (Oc.)	käm-bā′-rä	kahm-bay′-rah
Kambotorosh (Oc.)	käm-bô-tô-rôsh′	kahm-bo-to-rosh′
Kamchatka (Rus.)	*Eng.* kăm-chăt′-kə	kam-chat′-kuh
	Rus. käm-chät′-kä	kahm-chaht′-kah
Kamchia (Bulg., riv.)	käm′-chĭ-yä	kahm′-chi-yah
Kamen (Rus.)	kä′-mĕn(y)	kah′-men(y)
Kamendol (Yugosl.)	kä′-mĕn-dôl′	kah′-men-dol′
Kamenets Podolsk (Rus.)	kä-mĕ-nĕts′ pŏ-dôlsk′	kah-meh-nets′ po-dolsk′
Kamenica (Yugosl.)	kä′-mĕ-nĭ-tsä	kah′-meh-ni-tsah
Kamen Kashirski (Pol.)	See *Kamień Koszyrski.*	
Kamennaya (Pol., riv.)	See *Kamienna.*	
Kamensk (Rus.)	kä′-mĕnsk	kah′-mensk
Kamień Koszyrski (Pol.)	kä′-myĕn(y) kô-shĭr′-skĭ	kah′-myen(y) ko-shihr′-ski
Russian *Kamen Kashirski*, kä′-mĕn(y) kä-shĭr′-skĭ [kah′-men(y) kah-shihr′-ski].		
Kamienna (Pol., riv.)	kä-myĕn′-nä	kah-myen′-nah
Russian *Kamennaya*, kä′-mĕn-nä-yä [kah′-men-nah-yah].		
Kampanou (Crete)	kä(m)-bä-no͞o′	kah(m)-bah-noo′
Kampen (Neth.)	käm′-pən	kahm′-puhn
Kamperduin (Neth.)	käm′-pər-dûĭn′	kahm′-puhr-dœin′
Kampot (Indo-Ch.)	käm-pôt′	kahm-pot′
Kamptee (India)	kämp-tē′	kahmp-tee′
Kamrang (Indo-Ch., bay)	See *Camranh.*	
Kamyshevatsk (Rus.)	kä-mĭ-shĕ-vätsk′	kah-mi-sheh-vahtsk′

Kamyshin (Rus.)	kä-mwē′-shĭn	kah-mwee′-shin
Kanaka (Oc. people)	kə-năk′-ə *or* kăn′-ə-kə	kuh-nak′-uh kan′-uh-kuh
Kanali (Gr.)	kä-nä′-lē	kah-nah′-lee
Kanaung (Burma)	kăn-oung′	kan-aung′
Kanazawa (Jap.)	kä-nä-zä-wä	kah-nah-zah-wah
Kanbalu (Burma)	kăn-bə-lo͞o′	kan-buh-loo′
Kanburi (Thai)	kän′-bo͝o-rē′	kahn′-bu-ree′
Kan Chiang *or* River (Ch., Kiangsi)	gän	gahn
Kan-chow (Ch., Kiangsi)	gän-jō	gahn-joh
Kandahar (Afghan.)	kən-də-här′	kuhn-duh-hahr′
Kandalaksha (Rus.)	kän-dä-läk′-shä	kahn-dah-lahk′-shah
Kandalakskaya Guba (Rus.)	kän-dä-läk′-skä-yä go͞o-bä′	kahn-dah-lahk′-skah-yah goo-bah′
Kandy (Ceylon)	kăn′-dĭ	kan′-di
Kanelopoulos, Panagiotes (Gr. leader)	kä-nĕ-lô′-po͞o-lôs, pä-nä-yô′-tēs	kah-neh-lo′-poo-los, pah-nah-yo′-tees
Kangaung (Burma)	kăn-goung′	kan-gaung′
Kangean (NEI)	käng′-ĕ-än	kahng′-eh-ahn
K'ang-ting (Ch., Sikang)	käng-dĭng	kahng-ding
Kan-hsien (Ch., Kiangsi)	gän-shyĕn	gahn-shyen
Kaniet (Oc.)	kä-nē′-ĕt	kah-nee′-et
Kanina (Alb.) See *Kaninë*.		
Kaninë (Alb.) Italian *Crionero*, q.v.	kä-nē′-nə	kah-nee′-nuh
Kanjiža, Stara (Yugosl.)	kä′-nyĭ-zhä, stä′-rä	kah′-nyi-zhah, stah′-rah
Kankar (Yugosl.) Italian *Gangaro*, q.v.	kän′-kär	kahn′-kahr
Kan-ko (Korea)	käng-kô	kahng-ko
Kansk (Rus.)	känsk′	kahnsk′
Kan-su (Ch., prov.)	*Eng.* kăn-so͞o *Ch.* gän-so͞o	kan-soo gahn-soo
Kantang (Thai)	kän′-täng′	kahn′-tahng′
Kantanos (Crete)	kän′-dä-nôs	kahn′-dah-nos
Kantemirovka (Rus.)	kän-tĕ-mē′-rŏf-kä	kahn-teh-mee′-rof-kah
Kao-an (Ch., Kiangsi)	gou-än	gau-ahn
Kao-lan (Ch., Kangsu) Also called *Lan-chow*, q.v.	gou-län	gau-lahn
Kao-p'ing (Ch., Shansi)	gou-pĭng	gau-ping
Kao-t'ai (Ch., Kansu)	gou-tī	gau-tai

Kapela (Gr., Yugosl.)	kä-pĕ′-lä	kah-peh′-lah
Kapelle (Neth.)	kä-pĕl′-ə	kah-pel′-uh
Also spelled *Capelle*, q.v.		
Kapherevs (Gr., Euboea, point)	kä-fē-rĕfs′	kah-fee-refs′
Commonly called *Kabontoros*, kä-vô-dô′-rôs [kah-vo-do′-ros].		
Kapingamarangi (Oc.)	kä-pĭng′-ä-mä-räng′-ē	kah-ping′-ah-mah-rahng′-ee
Kapitza, Peter L. (Rus. scientist)	kä′-pĭ-tsä	kah′-pi-tsah
Kapos (Hung., riv.)	kŏ′-pôsh	ko′-posh
Kaposvár (Hung.)	kŏ′-pôsh-vär	ko′-posh-vahr
Kaprije (Yugosl.)	kä′-prĭ-yĕ	kah′-pri-yeh
Italian *Capri*, q.v.		
Kapsalion (Gr.) See *Kythera.*		
Karaburun (Alb., pen.)	kä-rä-bo͞o′-ro͞on	kah-rah-boo′-roon
English *Acroceraunia*, q.v., and (the point) Cape *Glossa*, q.v.		
Karaburuni (Alb., pen.) See *Karaburun.*		
Karachev (Rus.)	kä-rä-chôf′	kah-rah-chof′
Karachi (India)	kə-rä′-chē	kuh-rah′-chee
Karadeniz Boğazı (Turk., strait)	kä-rä′-dĕ-nēz bô-ä′-zĭ	kah-rah′-deh-neez bo-ah′-zi
English Bosporus, q.v.		
Karadžica planina (Yugosl., mts.)	kä′-rä′-jĭ-tsä plä′-nē′-nä	kah′-rah′-ji-tsah plah′-nee′-nah
Karafuto (Jap.)	kä-rä-fo͞o-tô	kah-rah-foo-to
Karahisar (Turk.)	kä′-rə′-hĭ-sär	kah′-ruh′-hi-sahr
Also called *Afyon Karahisar*, q.v.		
Karaj (Iran)	kă-rĕj′	ka-rej′
Karakoram (India, mts.)	kä-rä-kō′-rəm	kah-rah-koh′-ruhm
Karantaon (Gr., mt.)	kä-rän-dä′-ô(n)	kah-rahn-dah′-o(n)
Karapanayotis, Byron (Gr. leader) See *Carapanayotis.*		
Karaš (Yugosl., riv.)	kä′-räsh	kah′-rahsh
Kara Sou (Balkan riv.) See *Struma.*		
Kara Ular (Yugosl.)	kä′-rä o͞o′-lär	kah′-rah oo′-lahr
Karavasta (Alb., lake)	kä-rä-vä′-stä	kah-rah-vah′-stah
Also called *Knetë e Karavastas.*		
Karavoutas (Crete, point)	kä-rä-vo͞o′-täs	kah-rah-voo′-tahs
Also called *Khersonesos*, hĕr-sô′-nē-sôs [hehr-so′-nee-sos]. See also *Chersonese.*		
Karcag (Hung.)	kŏr′-tsŏg	kor′-tsog
Karczew (Pol.)	kär′-chĕf	kahr′-chef
Russian spelling *Karchev.*		
Kardamyli (Gr.)	kär-*th*ä-mē′-lē	kahr-*th*ah-mee′-lee

Karditsa (Gr.)	kär-*th*ē′-tsä	kahr-*th*ee′-tsah
Kärdla (Est.)	kărd′-lä	kehrd′-lah
Karelia (Rus., Fin.)	*Eng.* kə-rēl′-yə	kuh-reel′-yuh
	Rus. kä-rĕ′-lĭ-yä	kah-reh′-li-yah
Finnish *Karjala*, q.v.		
Karelian Isthmus (Fin.)	*Eng.* kə-rēl′-yən	kuh-reel′-yuhn
Karelskaya (Rus.)	kä-rĕl′(y)-skä-yä	kah-rel′(y)-skah-yah
Karikal (Fr. India)	kä-rē-käl′	kah-ree-kahl′
Karimata (NEI)	kä-rĭ-mä′-tä	kah-ri-mah′-tah
Karjala (Fin., Rus.)	kär′-yä-lä	kahr′-yah-lah
English and Russian *Karelia*, q.v.		
Karkar (New Guinea, isl.)	kär′-kär	kahr′-kahr
Karkinit (Rus., bay)	kär-kĭ-nēt′	kahr-ki-neet′
Karkinitski Zaliv (Rus.)	kär-kĭ-nēt′-skĭ zä-lēf′	kahr-ki-neet′-ski zah-leef′
Karla (Gr., lake) See *Boïbeis.*		
Karlobag (Yugosl.)	kär′-lô-bäg	kahr′-lo-bahg
Karloe *or* Karlö (Fin., isl.) See *Hailuoto.*		
Karlovac (Yugosl.)	kär′-lô-väts	kahr′-lo-vahts
Karlovci Sremski (Yugosl.)	kär′-lôv-tsĭ srĕm′-skĭ	kahr′-lov-tsi srem′-ski
Karlovka (Rus.)	kär′-lŏf-kä	kahr′-lof-kah
Karlovo (Bulg.)	kär′-lŏ-vŏ	kahr′-lo-vo
Karlovo Selo (Yugosl.)	kär′-lô-vô sĕ′-lô	kahr′-lo-vo seh′-lo
Karlovy Vary (Cz.) See *Carlsbad.*		
Karlsbad (Cz.) See *Carlsbad.*		
Karlsruhe (Ger.)	*Eng.* kärlz′-rōō-ə	kahrlz′-roo-uh
	Ger. kärls′-rōō-ə	kahrls′-roo-uh
Karmoey *or* Karmöy (Nor.)	kär′-mûĭ	kahr′-mœj
Karnabat (Bulg.)	kär′-nä-bät	kahr′-nah-baht
Karobka, Y. L. (Rus. leader)	kä-rôb′-kä	kah-rob′-kah
Károlyi, Michael, Count (Hung. leader)	kä′-rô-lyĭ *or* kä′-rô-yĭ	kah′-ro-lyi kah′-ro-yi
Karouva (Crete)	kä-rōō′-vä	kah-roo′-vah
Karpathos (Dodec.)	kär′-pä-thô(s)	kahr′-pah-tho(s)
Also called *Skarpatho*, skär′-pä-thô [skahr′-pah-tho]. Italian *Scarpanto.*		
Karpenesion (Gr.)	kär-pĕ-nē′-sē(-ôn)	kahr-peh-nee′-see(-on)
Kārsava (Latvia)	kär′-sä-vä	kahr′-sah-vah
Karteros (Crete)	kär-tĕ-rôs′	kahr-teh-ros′
Kartuzskaya Bereza (Pol.) See *Bereza Kartuska.*		

Kartuzy (Pol.)	kär-to͝o′-zĭ	kahr-tu′-zi
Karumba (Austral.)	kä-rŭm′-bə	kah-ruhm′-buh
Karun (Iran, riv.)	kä-ro͞on′	kah-roon′
Karuscia (Pantelleria, point)	kä-ro͞o′-shä	kah-roo′-shah
Karvasaras (Gr.)	kär-vä-sä-räs′	kahr-vah-sah-rahs′
Karydi (Crete)	kä-rē′-*th*ē	kah-ree′-*th*ee
Karystos (Gr.)	kä′-rē-stôs	kah′-ree-stos
Kashan (Iran)	kä-shän′	kah-shahn′
Kashgai (Per. tribe)	kăsh-gī′	kash-gai′
Kashgar (Ch., Sinkiang, riv. and town)	*Eng.* kăsh-gär	kash-gahr
Town also called *Sḥu-fu*, q.v.		
Kashin (Rus.)	kä′-shĭn	kah′-shin
Kashino (Rus.)	kä′-shĭ-nŏ	kah′-shi-no
Kashira (Rus.)	kä-shĭ′-rä	kah-shi′-rah
Kashkina (Rus.)	käsh′-kĭ-nä	kahsh′-ki-nah
Kashmir (India)	kăsh-mĭr′	kash-mihr′
Kasimov (Rus.)	kä-sē′-mŏf	kah-see′-mof
Kaskinen (Fin.)	käs′-kē-nĕn	kahs′-kee-nen
Swedish *Kaskoe*, käsk′-û [kahsk′-œ].		
Kaskoe *or* Kaskö (Fin.) See *Kaskinen*.		
Kason (Yugosl., mt.)	kä′-sôn	kah′-son
Kasos (Dodec.)	kä′-sô(s)	kah′-so(s)
Kassa (Cz.) See *Košice*.		
Kassandra (Gr.)	kä-sän′-drä	kah-sahn′-drah
Kassel (Ger.)	käs′-əl	kahs′-uhl
Also spelled *Cassel*.		
Kasserine (Tun.)	käs-sĕ-rēn′	kahs-seh-reen′
Kastelia (Gr.)	kä-stĕ′-lyä	kah-steh′-lyah
Kastelli (Crete)	kä-stĕ′-lē	kah-steh′-lee
Also called *Kastelli Pediadas* or *-os*, pĕ-*th*ē-ä′-*th*äs *or* -ôs [peh-*th*ee-ah′-*th*ahs *or* -os].		
Kastelli Pediadas *or* -os (Crete)	käs-tĕ′-lē pĕ-*th*ē-ä′-*th*äs *or* -ôs	kahs-teh′-lee peh-*th*ee-ah′-*th*ahs *or* -os
Kastelorizon (Dodec.)	käs-tĕl-ô′-rē-zô(n)	kahs-tel-o′-ree-zo(n)
Also called *Megiste*, mĕ-yē′-stē [meh-yee′-stee]. Italian *Castelrosso*, q.v.		
Kastoria (Gr.)	kä-stô-rē′-ä	kah-sto-ree′-ah
Kastornaya (Rus.)	käs-tôr′-nä-yä	kahs-tor′-nah-yah
Kastos (Gr., isl.)	kä-stôs′	kah-stos′
Kastron (Gr.)	kä′-strô(n)	kah′-stro(n)
Kastrosikia (Gr.)	kä-strô-sē-kyä′	kah-stro-see-kyah′

Kasvin (Iran)	kăz-vēn′	kaz-veen′
Also spelled *Kazvin* and *Qazvin*.		
Katakolon (Gr.)	kä-tä′-kô-lô(n)	kah-tah′-ko-lo(n)
Katanning (Austral.)	kə-tăn′-ĭng	kuh-tan′-ing
Katerine (Gr.)	kä-tĕ-rē′-nē	kah-teh-ree′-nee
Also called *Aikaterine*, ĕ-kä-tĕ-rē′-nē [eh-kah-teh-ree′-nee].		
Katha (Burma)	kə-thä′	kuh-thah′
Kathiawar (India)	kä-tĭ-ä-wär′	kah-ti-ah-wahr′
Katmandu (Nepal)	kät-män-do͞o′	kaht-mahn-doo′
Kato Akhaia (Gr.)	kä′-tô ä-hī′-ä	kah′-to ah-hai′-ah
See *Achaia* and *Elis*.		
Katoomba (Austral.)	kə-to͞om′-bə	kuh-toom′-buh
Katowice (Pol.)	kä-tô-vē′-tsĕ	kah-to-vee′-tseh
Kattegat (Den., Sw., sea)	*Eng.* kăt′-ĭ-găt	kat′-i-gat
Kattendijke (Neth.)	kät′-ən-dī′-kə	kaht′-uhn-dai′-kuh
Katwijk aan Zee (Neth.)	kät′-wīk än zā′	kaht′-waik ahn zay′
Katyn (Rus., forest)	kä-tēn′(y)	kah-teen′(y)
Kaunas (Lith.)	kou′-näs	kau′-nahs
Russian *Kovno*, q.v.		
kaupunki	kou′-po͝ong-kē	kau′-pung-kee
An element, meaning *town* or *borough*, in Finnish place names.		
Kautokeino (Nor.)	kou-tō-kā′-nō	kau-toh-kay′-noh
Kavadarci (Yugosl.)	kä′-vä′-där-tsĭ	kah′-vah′-dahr-tsi
Kavaja (Alb.) See *Kavajë*.		
Kavajë (Alb.)	kä-vä′-yə	kah-vah′-yuh
Italian *Cavaia*, q.v.		
Kavak (Turk.)	kä′-väk′	kah′-vahk′
Kavalla (Gr.)	kä-vä′-lä	kah-vah′-lah
Kavam (Per. leader)	kä-väm′	kah-vahm′
Kavieng (Oc.)	kĕ-vĭ-ĕng′	keh-vi-eng′
Kavkazskaya (Rus.)	käf-käz′-skä-yä	kahf-kahz′-skah-yah
Kavomalias (Gr., cape)	kä-vô-mä-lyä(s)′	kah-vo-mah-lyah(s)′
Also called *Maleas*, q.v.		
Kavontoros (Gr., Euboea, point) See *Kapherevs*.		
Kavousi (Crete)	kä-vo͞o′-sē	kah-voo′-see
Kawanishi (Jap.)	kä-wä-nē-shē	kah-wah-nee-shee
Kawlin (Burma)	kô′-lĭn′	kaw′-lin′
Kayangel (Oc.)	kä-yäng′-ĕl	kah-yahng′-el
Kazak (Rus.)	kä-zäk′	kah-zahk′
Kazan (Rus.)	kä-zän′(y)	kah-zahn′(y)
Kazanlik (Bulg.)	kä′-zän-lĭk′	kah′-zahn-lik′
Kazatin (Rus.)	kä-zä′-tĭn	kah-zah′-tin
Kazbek (Rus., mt.)	käz-bĕk′	kahz-bek′
Kazemi (Per. leader)	kä-zə-mē′	kah-zuh-mee′

Kazvin *or* Kasvin	kăz-vēn′	kaz-veen′
or Qazvin (Iran)		
Kearney, Bernard W.	kär′-nĭ, bûr′-nûrd′	kahr′-ni, buhr′-nuhrd′
(U.S. representative)		
Kebili (Tun.)	kə-bē′-lē	kuh-bee′-lee
Kebir (Alg.)	kə-bēr′	kuh-beer′
An abbreviation of *Mers el Kebir*, q.v.		
Kecskemét (Hung.)	kĕch′-kĕ-māt	kech′-keh-mayt
Kedah (Malaya)	kā′-dä	kay′-dah
Kėdainiai (Lith.)	kā-dī′-nyī *or* -nĕ	kay-dai′-nyai *or* -neh
Russian *Keidany*, q.v.		
Kediri (NEI)	kĕ-dē′-rē	keh-dee′-ree
Keeling Isls. (Ind. Oc.)	kē′-lĭng	kee′-ling
Also called *Cocos*, q.v.		
Kef, le (Tun.)	kāf′, lə	kayf′, luh
Kefauver, Estes	kē′-fô-vər, ĕs′-tĕs	kee′-faw-vuhr, es′-tes
(U.S. representative)		
Kef el Goraa (Tun.)	kāf′ ĕl gŭ-rä′	kayf′ el guh-rah′
Kef Touro (Tun.)	kāf′ to͞o′-rō	kayf′ too′-roh
Kegel (Est.)	*Rus.* kĕ′-gĕl(y)	keh′-gel(y)
	Ger. kā′-gəl	kay′-guhl
Estonian *Keila*, q.v.		
Kei (NEI)	kī′	kai′
Also spelled *Kai*, q.v.		
Keidany (Lith.)	*Rus.* kā-dä′-nĭ	kay-dah′-ni
Lithuanian *Kėdainiai*, q.v.		
K'ei-jo (Korea)	kā-rô *or* -jô	kay-ro *or* -jo
Also called *Seoul*, q.v.		
Keila (Est.)	kā′-lä	kay′-lah
Russian *Kegel*, q.v.		
Keksholm (Fin.) See *Käkisalmi*.		
Kelaua (Oc.)	kĕ-lou′-ä	keh-lau′-ah
Këlcyra (Alb.) See *Këlcyrë*.		
Këlcyrë (Alb.)	kəl-tsü′-rə	kuhl-tsü′-ruh
Greek *Kleisoura*, klē-so͞o′-rä [klee-soo′-rah].		
Kelibia (Tun.)	kə-lē′-bĭ-ä	kuh-lee′-bi-ah
Kem (Rus.)	kām′(y)	kaym′(y)
Kemal Atatürk	kə-mäl′ ä-tä-türk′	kuh-mahl′ ah-tah-türk′
(Turkish leader)		
Formerly called *Mustapha Kemal Pasha*, mo͞os′-tä-fä kə-mäl′ pä′-shä′ [mus′-tah-fah kuh-mahl′ pah′-shah′].		
Kemerovo (Rus.)	kĕ′-mĕ-rŏ-vŏ	keh′-meh-ro-vo
Kemi (Fin.)	kĕ′-mē	keh′-mee
Kemijärvi (Fin.)	kĕ′-mē-yăr-vē	keh′-mee-yehr-vee

Kemmel (Belg.)	kĕm′-əl	kem′-uhl
Kemozersk (Rus.)	kām′-ŏ-zûrsk′	kaym′-o-zuhrsk′
Kempen (Pol.) See *Kępno.*		
Kenali (Yugosl.)	kĕ′-nä-lĭ	keh′-nah-li
Kenayis (Egypt)	kĕ-nă′-yĭs	keh-na′-yis
Kendari (NEI)	kĕn-dä′-rē	ken-dah′-ree
Kengtung (Burma)	kāng′-tŏŏng′	kayng′-tung′
Also called *Chêng-tung,* jŭng-dŏŏng [juhng-dung].		
Kenya	kēn′-yä *or* kĕn′-yä	keen′-yah *or* ken′-yah
The more correct (and the BBC) pronunciation is kēn′-yä (keen′-yah). Our efforts to inculcate this pronunciation at WABC were enfeebled when Prime Minister Churchill himself said "kĕn′-yä."		
Keogh, Eugene J. (U.S. representative)	kē′-ō	kee′-oh
Keos *or* Kea (Gr., isl.)	kĕ′-ôs *or* kĕ′-ä	keh′-os *or* keh′-ah
English *Ceos,* sē′-ŏs [see′-os]. Also called *Tzia,* dzē-ä′ [dzee-ah′] *or* jä′ [jah′], and *Zea,* q.v.		
kep (Alb.)	kĕp′	kep′
An element, meaning *cape,* in Albanian place names. Look up the other part of the name.		
Kephalas (Crete)	kĕ-fä-läs′	keh-fah-lahs′
Kephalenia (Gr., isl.)	kĕ-fä-lē-nē′-ä	keh-fah-lee-nee′-ah
Also called *Kephalonia,* kĕ-fä-lô-nyä′ [keh-fah-lo-nyah′]. English *Cephalonia,* q.v.		
Kephisia (Gr.)	kē-fē-syä′	kee-fee-syah′
kepi (Alb.) See *kep.*		
Kępno (Pol.)	kăNp′-nô	kaNp′-no
German *Kempen,* kĕm′-pən [kem′-puhn].		
Ker, Stari (Yugosl.)	kĕr′, stä′-rĭ	kehr′, stah′-ri
Kerch (Rus.)	kĕrch′	kehrch′
Kerchenski (Rus., straits)	kĕr′-chĕn-skĭ	kehr′-chen-ski
Kerensk (Rus.)	kĕ-rĕnsk′	keh-rensk′
Kereny (Yugosl.)	*Mag.* kĕ′-rĕn(y)	keh′-ren(y)
Serb-Croat *Krnjaja,* q.v.		
Kerintji (NEI)	kə-rĭn′-chē	kuh-rin′-chee
Kerkennah (Tun., isl.)	kər-kĕn′-nä	kuhr-ken′-nah
Kerkine (Balkan mts.)	*Gr.* kĕr-kē′-nē	kehr-kee′-nee
Serb-Croat *Belasica planina,* q.v.		
Kerkrade (Neth.)	kĕrk′-rä-də	kehrk′-rah-duh
Kerkyra (Gr.)	kĕr′-kē-rä	kehr′-kee-rah
Italian *Corfù,* q.v.		
Kermadek Isls. (N.Z.)	kər-măd′-ĕk	kuhr-mad′-ek
Kerman (Iran)	kĕr-män′	ehr-mahn′

Kermanshah (Iran)	kĕr-män-shä′	kehr-mahn-shah′
Kerr, John H. (U.S. representative)	kär′	kahr′
Kersa (Libya)	kĕr′-sä	kehr′-sah
Kerulen (Mongolia, Rus., riv.; Mongol town)	kĕr′-ōō-lĕn	kehr′-oo-len
Keszthely (Hung.)	kĕst′-hā	kest′-hay
Ketchikan (Alaska)	kĕch′-ĭ-kăn	kech′-i-kan
Kexholm (Fin.) See *Käkisalmi.*		
Keynes, John Maynard (Eng. economist)	kānz′, mā′-närd	kaynz′, may′-nahrd

kh, ch, and often *h* are variant spellings in Greek. The consultant may have to look for all three.

Khabarovsk (Rus.)	hä-bä′-rŏfsk	hah-bah′-rofsk
khaki	kăk′-ĭ *or* kä′-ki	kak′-i *or* kah′-ki
The first is the general American and Army pronunciation.		
Khalepa (Crete)	hä-lĕ′-pä	hah-leh′-pah
Khalke (Dodec.)	häl′-kē	hahl′-kee
Also called *Khalkia,* häl-kyä′ [hahl-kyah′], and *Kharkia,* här-kyä′ [hahr-kyah′]. Italian *Calchi,* q.v.		
Khalkidike (Gr., pen.)	häl-kē-*th*ē′-kē	hahl-kee-*th*ee′-kee
English *Chalcidice,* kăl-sĭd′-ĭ-sĭ [kal-sid′-i-si].		
Khalkis *or* Chalcis (Gr.)	*Eng.* kăl′-sĭs	kal′-sis
	Gr. häl-kēs′	hahl-kees′
Also called *Evripos,* ĕ′-vrē-pôs [eh′-vree-pos].		
Khanaqin (Iraq)	*Per.* hä-nə-kēn′	hah-nuh-keen′
	Eng. kăn′-ə-kĭn	kan′-uh-kin
Khandax (Crete)	hän′-däks	hahn′-dahks
Also called *Herakleion,* q.v.		
Khania (Crete)	*Eng.* kä-nē′-ä	kah-nee′-ah
	Gr. hän-yä′	hahn-yah′
Also spelled *Canea,* q.v.		
Khanka (Rus., lake)	hän′-kä	hahn′-kah
Khantrinou (Gr.)	hän-drē-nōō′	hahn-dree-noo′
Kharita, el (Egypt)	kä′-rē-tə, ĕl	kah′-ree-tuh, el
Kharitonov (Rus. general)	hä-rĭ-tô′-nŏf	hah-ri-to′-nof
Kharkia (Dodec.) See *Khalke.*		
Kharkov (Rus.)	*Eng.* kär′-kŏf *or* -kŏv	kahr′-kof *or* -kov
	Rus. här′-kŏf	hahr′-kof
The name acquired its English pronunciation centuries ago.		
Kharokopeon (Gr.)	hä-rô-kô-pē-ô(n)′	hah-ro-ko-pee-o(n)′
Khasia (Gr., mt.)	hä-syä′	hah-syah′

Khaskovo (Bulg.)	häs′-kŏ-vŏ	hahs′-ko-vo
Khassan (Rus., lake)	häs-sän′	hahs-sahn′
Kheimara (Alb.) See *Himarë.*		
Khelat (Baluch.) See *Kalat.*		
Khenchela (Alg.)	kĕn-shā′-lä	ken-shay′-lah
Kherson (Rus.)	hĕr-sôn′	hehr-son′
Khersonesos (Crete, cape; Turk., pen.)	hĕr-sô′-nē-sôs	hehr-so′-nee-sos
English *Chersonese,* q.v.		
Khiliodromia (Gr., isl.) See *Alonesos.*		
Khilok (Rus., riv.)	hĭ-lôk′	hi-lok′
Khios (Gr., isl.)	*Eng.* kī′-ŏs	kai′-os
	Gr. hē′-ô(s)	hee′-o(s)
Khlebnikof (Alaska, Attu)	klĕb′-nĭ-kŏf	kleb′-ni-kof
Khlebnikov (Rus. officer)	k(h)lĕb′-nĭ-kŏf	k(h)leb′-ni-kof
Khmelnik (Rus.)	k(h)mĕl′(y)-nĭk	k(h)mel′(y)-nik
Khmyelnik (Pol.) See *Chmielnik.*		
Khodorkov (Rus.)	hŏ-dŏr-kôf′	ho-dor-kof′
Khohn Khen (Thai)	kôn′-kăn	kawn′-kan
Khoi (Iran)	k(h)oi′	k(h)oi′
Kholm (Pol.) See *Chełm.*		
Kholm (Rus.)	hôlm′	holm′
Khondron (Crete, point)	hôn-drô(n)′	hon-dro(n)′
Khong (Indo-Ch.)	kŭm′	kuhm′
It would probably be Englished as kŏng′ [kong′].		
Khoper (Rus., riv.)	hŏ-pyôr′	ho-pyor′
Khor (Rus., riv.)	hôr′	hor′
Khora Sphakion (Crete)	hô′-rä sfä-kē′-ô(n)	ho′-rah sfah-kee′-o(n)
Also called *Sphakia,* q.v.		
Khorog (Rus.)	hô′-rŏg	ho′-rog
Khorol (Rus.)	hŏ-rôl′	ho-rol′
Khotin (Rum.) See *Hotin.*		
Khotynets (Rus.)	hŏ-twē′-nĕts	ho-twee′-nets
Khurasan (Iran)	k(h)ŏŏ-rä-sän′	k(h)u-rah-sahn′
Khurramabad (Iran)	k(h)ŏŏr-räm′-ə-bäd′	k(h)ur-rahm′-uh-bahd′
Khurramshahr (Iran)	k(h)ŏŏr-räm′-shär′	k(h)ur-rahm′-shahr′
Formerly called *Mohammereh,* q.v.		
Khyber (India, pass)	kī′-bər	kai′-buhr
Kiakhta (Rus.)	kyä′-k(h)tä	kyah′-k(h)tah
Ki-an (Ch., Kiangsi) Variant spelling of *Chi-an,* q.v.		
kiang Chinese word meaning *river.* See *chiang.*		

Kiangmai (Thai)	kyäng-mī′	kyahng-mai′
Officially *Chiangmai*, q.v.		
Kiang-shan (Ch., Chekiang) Variant of *Chiang-shan*, q.v.		
Kiang-si (Ch., prov.)	*Eng.* kyăng-sē	kyang-see
	Ch. jyäng-sē	jyahng-see
Kiang-su (Ch., prov.)	*Eng.* kyăng-so͞o	kyang-soo
	Ch. jyäng-so͞o	jyahng-soo
Kiao-chow (Ch., Shantung)	*Eng.* kyou-chou	kyau-chau
	Ch. jyou-jō	jyau-joh
Kibei	kē-bā	kee-bay
U.S. citizens of Japanese ancestry, who visited Japan and returned to this country. See *Issei* and *Nisei*.		
Kičevo (Yugosl.)	kē′-chĕ-vô	kee′-cheh-vo
Kiel (Ger.)	kēl′	keel′
Kielce (Pol.)	kyĕl′-tsĕ	kyel′-tseh
Kien-ow (Ch., Fukien) Variant spelling of *Chien-ow*, q.v.		
Kien-teh Variant spelling of *Chien-teh*, q.v.		
Kieta (Oc.)	kē-ĕ′-tä	kee-eh′-tah
Kiev (Rus.)	kē′-yĕf	kee′-yef
Kihnu (Est., isl.)	kēk(h)′-no͞o	keek(h)′-noo
Russian *Kuno*, q.v.		
Kijkduin (Neth.)	kīk-dûĭn′	kaik-dœin′
Kikinda, Velika (Yugosl.)	kē′-kĭn-dä, vĕ′-lĭ-kä	kee′-kin-dah, veh′-li-kah
Hungarian *Nagykikinda*, nŏt′(y)-kĭ′-kĭn-dŏ [not′(y)-ki′-kin-do].		
Kikori (New Guinea)	kē′-kô′-rē	kee′-ko′-ree
Kilday, Paul J. (U.S. representative)	kĭl-dā′	kil-day′
Kildin (Rus.)	kēl′-dĭn	keel′-din
Kili (Oc.)	kē′-lē	kee′-lee
Kilia (Rum.) See *Chilia Nouă*.		
Kilinailau (Oc.)	kē′-lē-nī′-lou	kee′-lee-nai′-lau
Kilkis (Gr.)	kēl-kēs′	keel-kees′
Kimba (Austral.)	kĭm′-bə	kim′-buh
Kimkan (Rus.)	kĭm-kän′	kim-kahn′
Kimpolung (Rum.) See *Câmpulung*.		
Kimry (Rus.)	kēm′-rĭ	keem′-ri
Kin (Burma)	kĭn′	kin′
Kinabalu (NEI)	kĭn-ä-bä′-lo͞o	kin-ah-bah′-loo
Kindat (Burma)	kĭn-dăt′	kin-dat′
Kingisepp (Rus.)	kĭng′-gĭ-sĕp	king′-gi-sep
Kin-hwa (Ch., Chekiang)	jĭn-whä	jin-whah
Also spelled *Chin-hwa*, q.v.		
Kin-ki (Ch., Kiangsi) Variant spelling of *Chin-ch'i*, q.v.		

Kintore (Austral., mt.)	kĭn′-tôr	kin′-tor
Kinu (Burma)	kĭn-o͞o′	kin-oo′
Kinzer, J. Roland (U.S. representative)	kĭn′-zər	kin′-zuhr
Kir (Alb., riv.)	kēr′	keer′
Kirghiz (Rus.)	kĭr-gēz′	kihr-geez′
Kiri (Alb., riv.) See *Kir*.		
Kirin (Manchu., prov., town)	kē-rĭn	kee-rin
Kirkenes (Nor.)	chēr′-kə-nĕs	cheer′-kuh-nes
Kırklareli (Turk.)	kĭrk-lä′-rĕ-lē	kihrk-lah′-reh-lee
Kirov, Sergei (Rus. leader)	kē′-rŏf, sĕr-gā′	kee′-rof, sehr-gay′
Kirovabad (Rus.)	kē′-rŏ-vä-bät′	kee′-ro-vah-baht′
Kirovo (Rus.)	kē′-rŏ-vŏ	kee′-ro-vo
Kirovsk (Rus.)	kē′-rŏfsk	kee′-rofsk
Kirsanov (Rus.)	kĭr-sä′-nŏf	kihr-sah′-nof
Kirwan, Michael J. (U.S. representative)	kûr′-wän	kuhr′-wahn
Kisamos (Crete)	kē′-sä-môs	kee′-sah-mos
Kishinev (Rum.)	*Rus.* kĭ-shĭ-nyôf′	ki-shi-nyof′
	Eng. kĭ-shĭ-nyĕf′	ki-shi-nyef′
Rumanian *Chişinău*, q.v.		
Kishm (Iran, isl.)	kĭsh′m	kish′m
Kisiljevo (Yugosl.)	kē′-sē′-lyĕ-vô	kee′-see′-lyeh-vo
Kiska (Alaska, isl.)	kĭs′-kə	kis′-kuh
Kiskundorozsma (Hung.)	kĭsh′-ko͝on-dô′-rôzh-mŏ	kish′-kun-do′-rozh-mo
Kiskunfélegyháza (Hung.)	kĭsh′-ko͝on-fā′-lĕt(y)-hä′-zŏ	kish′-kun-fay′-let(y)-hah′-zo
Kiskunhalas (Hung.)	kĭsh′-ko͝on-hŏ′-lŏsh	kish′-kun-ho′-losh
Kissavos (Gr., mt.)	kē′-sä-vôs	kee′-sah-vos
Kistna (India, riv.)	kĭst′-nə	kist′-nuh
Kitzbühel (Austria)	kĭts′-bül	kits′-bül
Kiu-kiang (Ch., Kiangsi)	*Eng.* kyo͞o-kyăng	kyoo-kyang
	Ch. jyo͞o-jyäng	jyoo-jyahng
Also spelled *Chiu-chiang*, q.v.		
Kiung-shan (Hainan)	kyo͝ong-shän	kyung-shahn
Kizlar (Rus.)	kĭz-lyär′	kiz-lyahr′
Kjeller (Nor.)	kyĕl′-lər	kyel′-luhr
Kjoellefjord *or* Kjöllefjord (Nor.)	kyûl′-ə-fyōr	kyœl′-uh-fyohr
Kladanj (Yugosl.)	klä′-dän(y)	klah′-dahn(y)

Kladno (Cz.)	kläd′-nô	klahd′-no
Kladovo (Yugosl.)	klä′-dô-vô	klah′-do-vo
Klagenfurt (Austria)	klä′-gən-fo͝ort	klah′-guhn-furt
Klaipėda (Lith.)	klī′-pĕ-dä	klai′-peh-dah
German *Memel*, q.v.		
Klamath Falls (Oregon)	klăm′-əth	klam′-uhth
Klanjec (Yugosl.)	klä′-nyĕts	klah′-nyets
Klatovy (Cz.)	klä′-tô-vĭ	klah′-to-vi
German *Klattau.*		
Klausenburg (Rum.) See *Cluj.*		
Kleberg, R. M. (U.S. representative)	klā′-bûrg	klay′-buhrg
Kledia (Tun.)	klā′-dyä	klay′-dyah
Kletskaya (Rus.)	klĕt′-skä-yä	klet′-skah-yah
Kleisoura (Alb.) See *Këlcyrë.*		
Klenike (Yugosl.)	klĕ′-nĭ-kĕ	kleh′-ni-keh
Klenje (Yugosl.)	klĕ′-nyĕ	kleh′-nyeh
Kletnya (Rus.)	klĕt′-nyä	klet′-nyah
Klevan (Pol.) See *Klewań.*		
Klewań (Pol.)	klĕ′-vän(y)	kleh′-vahn(y)
Russian spelling *Klevan.*		
Kličevac (Yugosl.)	klē′-chĕ-väts	klee′-cheh-vahts
Klin (Rus.)	klēn′	kleen′
Klina (Yugosl., riv.)	klē′-nä	klee′-nah
Klinci (Yugosl.)	klēn′-tsĭ	kleen′-tsi
Klintsy (Rus.)	klĭn-tsĭ′	klin-tsi′
Ključ (Yugosl.)	klūch′	klyooch′
Kłodawa (Pol.)	klô-dä′-vä	klo-dah′-vah
Klukhor(ski) (Rus., pass)	klo͞o-hôr′(-skĭ)	kloo-hor′(-ski)
Klyazma (Rus., riv.)	klyäz′-mä	klyahz′-mah
Klyuchi (Rus.)	klū-chē′	klyoo-chee′
Knaben (Nor.)	knäb′n	knahb′n
kneta (Alb.) See *knetë.*		
knetë (Alb.)	knĕ′-tə	kneh′-tuh

An element, meaning *lagoon* or *lake*, in Albanian place names. Look up the other part of the name.

Knić (Yugosl.)	knēch′	kneech′
Knightsbridge (Libya)	nīts′-brĭj	naits′-brij
Knishin (Pol.) See *Knyszyn.*		
Knjaževac (Yugosl.)	knyä′-zhĕ-väts	knyah′-zheh-vahts
Knocke (Belg.)	knôk(h)′-ə	knok(h)′-uh
Knutson, Harold (U.S. representative)	kno͞ot′-sən	knoot′-suhn

Knyaz (Rus.)	knyäz′	knyahz′
Knyszyn (Pol.)	knĭ′-shĭn	kni′-shin
Russian spelling *Knishin.*		
Kobe (Jap.)	kô-bĕ	ko-beh
Kobelyaki (Rus.)	kŏ-bĕ-lyä′-kĭ	ko-beh-lyah′-ki
Köbenhavn (Den.) See *Copenhagen.*		
Kobilica (Yugosl., mt.)	kô′-bē′-lĭ-tsä	ko′-bee′-li-tsah
Kobišnica (Yugosl.)	kô′-bĭsh-nĭ-tsä	ko′-bish-ni-tsah
Koblenz (Ger.)	kō′-blĕnts	koh′-blents
Also spelled *Coblenz,* q.v.		
Kobrin (Pol.) See *Kobryń.*		
Kobryń (Pol.)	kô′-brĭn(y)	ko′-brin(y)
Russian spelling *Kobrin.*		
Kočane (Yugosl.)	kô′-chä-nĕ	ko′-chah-neh
Koceljeva (Yugosl.)	kô′-tsĕ′-lyĕ-vä	ko′-tseh′-lyeh-vah
Kočevje (Yugosl.)	kô′-chĕ-vyĕ	ko′-cheh-vyeh
Kochalino (Rus.)	kŏ-chä′-lĭ-nŏ	ko-chah′-li-no
Kochanskoe (Rus.)	kŏ-chän′-skŏ-yĕ	ko-chahn′-sko-yeh
Kock (Pol.)	kôtsk′	kotsk′
Russian spelling *Kotsk.*		
Kodály, Zoltán (Hung. musician)	kô′-dī, zôl′-tän	ko′-dai, zol′-tahn
Kodiak (Alaska, isl.)	kō′-dĭ-ăk	koh′-di-ak
Kodža Balkan (Yugosl., mts.)	kô′-jä bäl′-kän	ko′-jah bahl′-kahn
Kodžadžik (Yugosl.)	kô′-jä-jĭk	ko′-jah-jik
Koedoes (NEI)	kōō′-dōōs	koo′-doos
Koege (Den.)	kû′-gə	kœ′-guh
Koekelberg (Belg.)	kōō′-kəl-bĕrk(h)	koo′-kuhl-behrk(h)
Koeln (Ger.)	kûln′	kœln′
English *Cologne,* q.v.		
Koenigsberg (Ger.)	*Eng.* kû′-nĭgz-bûrg	kœ′-nigz-buhrg
	Ger. kû′-nĭk(h)s-bĕrk(h)	kœ′-nik(h)s-behrk(h)
Koenigstein (Ger.)	kû′-nĭk(h)-shtīn	kœ′-nik(h)-shtain
Koepang *or* Kupang (NEI)	kōō′-päng	koo′-pahng
Koesfeld (Ger.) See Coesfeld.		
Koeslin (Ger.)	kûs-lēn′	kœs-leen′
Koeta Radja *or* Kuta Radya (NEI)	kōō′-tä rä′-jä	koo′-tah rah′-jah
Koethen (Ger.)	kû′-tən	kœ′-tuhn
Köge (Den.)	kû′-gə	kœ′-guh
Koitere (Fin., dist.)	koi′-tĕ-rĕ	koi′-teh-reh

Koivisto (Fin.)	koi′-vĭs-tô	koi′-vis-to
Kokkola (Fin.)	kôk′-kô-lä	kok′-ko-lah
Kokoda (Oc.)	kô-kô′-dä	ko-ko′-dah
Kokombona (Oc.)	kô-kôm-bô′-nä	ko-kom-bo′-nah
Koko Nor (Ch., prov., lake)	kō-kō nôr	koh-koh nor

Also called *Kuku Nor*, kōō-kōō. Prov. also called *Ch'ing-hai*, q.v.

Kokopo (Oc.)	kô′-kô-pô	ko′-ko-po
Kokra (Yugosl., riv.)	kô′-krä	ko′-krah
Kola (Rus., pen.)	kô′-lä	ko′-lah
Kolari (Yugosl.)	kô′-lä-rĭ	ko′-lah-ri
Kolašin (Yugosl.)	kô′-lä′-shĭn	ko′-lah′-shin
Kolding (Den.)	kôl′-dĭng	kol′-ding
Kolhapur (India)	kōl′-hä-pŏŏr′	kohl′-hah-pur′
Kolín (Cz.)	kô′-lēn	ko′-leen
Kolkas Rags (Latvia, cape)	kŏl′-käs rägs′	kol′-kahs rahgs′
Kolmar (Pol.)	*Ger.* kôl′-mär	kol′-mahr

Polish *Chodzież*, q.v.

Köln (Ger.)	kûln′	kœln′

English *Cologne*, q.v.

Koło (Pol.)	kô′-lô	ko′-lo

Russian *Kola*, kô′-lä [ko′-lah].

Koločen (Yugosl., isl.)	kô′-lô-chĕn	ko′-lo-chen

Italian *Calamotta*, q.v.

Kolombangara (Oc.)	kô-lôm-bäng′-ä-rä	ko-lom-bahng′-ah-rah
Kolomea (Pol.) See *Kołomyja.*		
Kolomna (Rus.)	kŏ-lôm′-nä	ko-lom′-nah
Kołomyja (Pol.)	kô-lô-mĭ′-yä	ko-lo-mi′-yah

Russian spelling *Kolomia*. Rumanian *Colomea*, kô-lô-mĕ′-ä [ko-lo-meh′-ah]. German *Kolomea.*

Kolosovka (Rus.)	kŏ-lŏ-sôf′-kä	ko-lo-sof′-kah
Kolozsvár (Rum.) See *Cluj.*		
Kolpino (Rus.)	kôl′-pĭ-nŏ	kol′-pi-no
kolpos	kôl′-pôs	kol′-pos

An element, meaning *gulf*, in Greek place names. Look up the other part of the name.

Kolskaya Guba (Rus.)	kôl′(y)-skä-yä gōō-bä′	kol′(y)-skah-yah goo-bah′
Kolubara (Yugosl., riv.)	kô-lōō′-bä-rä	ko-loo′-bah-rah
Koluszki (Pol.)	kô-lŏŏsh′-kĭ	ko-lush′-ki
Kolymbari (Crete)	kô-lēm-bä′-rē	ko-leem-bah′-ree
Komandorskie (Rus., isls.)	kŏ-män-dôr′-skĭ-yĕ	ko-mahn-dor′-ski-yeh

Komarnicki, Wacław (Pol. leader)	kô-mär-nē′-tskĭ, vä′-tsläf	ko-mahr-nee′-tski, vah′-tslahf
Komárno (Cz.)	kô′-mär′-nô	ko′-mahr′-no
Hungarian *Komárom*, kô′-mä-rôm [ko′-mah-rom].		
Komárom (Cz.) See *Komárno*.		
Komarów (Pol.)	kô-mä′-ro͝of	ko-mah′-ruf
Komiatum (Oc.)	kô-mē-ä′-to͞om	ko-mee-ah′-toom
Komiža (Yugosl.)	kô′-mĭ-zhä	ko′-mi-zhah
Kommunari (Rus.)	kŏm-mo͞o-nä′-rĭ	kom-moo-nah′-ri
Komolova (Rus.)	kŏ-mô′-lŏ-vä	ko-mo′-lo-vah
Komotine (Gr.)	kô-mô-tē-nē′	ko-mo-tee-nee′
Also called *Gioumoultzina*, gyo͞o-mo͞ol-dzē′-nä [gyoo-mool-dzee′-nah]; and *Gümüljene*, q.v.		
Komovi (Yugosl., mts.)	kô′-mô-vĭ	ko′-mo-vi
Kompong Cham (Indo-Ch.)	kŏm-pŏng′ chäm′	kom-pong′ chahm′
Komsomolsk (Rus.)	kŏm-sŏ-mŏlsk′	kom-so-molsk′
Konev, Ivan (Rus. general)	kô′-nĕf, ē-vän′	ko′-nef, ee-vahn′
Kongsberg (Nor.)	kôngs′-bĕrg *or* -bĕr	kongs′-behrg *or* -behr
Kongsvinger (Nor.)	kôngs′-vĭng-ər	kongs′-ving-uhr
Königsberg (Ger.)	*Eng.* kû′-nĭgz-bûrg	kœ′-nigz-buhrg
	Ger. kû′-nĭk(h)s-bĕrk(h)	kœ′-nik(h)s-behrk(h)
Königstein (Ger.)	kû′-nĭk(h)-shtīn	kœ′-nik(h)-shtain
Konin (Pol.)	kô′-nĭn	ko′-nin
Konispol (Alb.)	kô-nēs′-pôl	ko-nees′-pol
Konispoli (Alb.) See *Konispol*.		
Konitsa (Gr.)	kô′-nē-tsä	ko′-nee-tsah
Konjic (Yugosl.)	kô′-nyĭts	ko′-nyits
Konjice (Yugosl.)	kô′-nyĭ-tsĕ	ko′-nyi-tseh
Konjska (Yugosl., riv.)	kôn(y)′-skä	kon(y)′-skah
Konotop (Rus.)	kŏ-nŏ-tôp′	ko-no-top′
Końskie (Pol.)	kôn′(y)-skyĕ	kon′(y)-skyeh
Russian *Konsk*, kônsk′ [konsk′].		
Konstantinovka Dimitrievka (Rus.)	kŏn′-stän-tē′-nŏf-kä dĭ-mē′-trĭ-yĕf-kä	kon′-stahn-tee′-nof-kah di-mee′-tri-yef-kah
Konstantynów (Pol.)	kôn-stän-tĭ′-no͝of	kon-stahn-ti′-nuf
Konstanz (Ger.)	kōn′-shtänts	kohn′-shtahnts
English *Constance*, q.v.		
Konya (Turk.)	kôn′-yä	kon′-yah
Kopač (Yugosl.)	kô′-päch	ko′-pahch
Kopanica (Pol.)	kô-pä-nē′-tsä	ko-pah-nee′-tsah

Kopanovka (Rus.)	kŏ-pä′-nŏf-kä	ko-pah′-nof-kah
Kopaonik (Yugosl., mts.)	kô′-pä′-ô-nĭk	ko′-pah′-o-nik
Kopervik (Nor.)	kō′-pər-vēk	koh′-puhr-veek
Koppang (Nor.)	kôp′-päng	kop′-pahng
Koprena (Gr.)	kô′-prĕ-nä	ko′-preh-nah
Koprivnica (Yugosl.)	kô′-prĭv′-nĭ-tsä	ko′-priv′-ni-tsah
Koprivnik (Yugosl., mt.)	kô′-prĭv-nĭk	ko′-priv-nik
Korab (Balkan mt.)	*Eng.* kô′-răb	ko′-rab
Albanian *Mal i Korabit.* Serb-Croat *Korab.*		
Korat (Thai)	kō-rät′	koh-raht′
Korba (Tun.)	kôr′-bä	kor′-bah
Korbous (Tun.)	kôr-bo͞os′	kor-boos′
Korcha (Alb.)	kôr′-chə	kor′-chuh
Albanian spelling *Korrçë,* q.v.		
Korčula (Yugosl.)	kôr′-cho͞o-lä	kor′-choo-lah
Italian *Curzola,* q.v.		
Korenevo (Rus.)	kô′-rĕ-nĕ-vŏ	ko′-reh-neh-vo
Korenica (Yugosl.)	kô′-rĕ′-nĭ-tsä	ko′-reh′-ni-tsah
Korijen (Yugosl., mts.)	kô′-rĭ-yĕn	ko′-ri-yen
Korinthos (Gr.) See *Corinth.*		
Koritnik (Balkan mt.)	*S.-C.* kô′-rĭt-nĭk	ko′-rit-nik
Kornat (Yugosl., isl.)	kôr′-nät	kor′-naht
Italian *Incoronata,* q.v.		
Kórnik (Pol.)	ko͝or′-nĭk	kur′-nik
German spelling *Kurnik.*		
Kornsjoe *or* Kornsjö (Nor.)	kōrn′-shû	kohrn′-shœ
Korocha (Rus.)	kŏ-rô′-chä	ko-ro′-chah
Korone (Gr.)	kô-rô′-nē	ko-ro′-nee
Also called *Asine,* ä-sē′-nē [ah-see′-nee].		
Korop (Rus.)	kô′-rŏp	ko′-rop
Koror (Oc.)	kô′-rôr	ko′-ror
Kőrös (Hung., riv.)	kû′-rûsh	kœ′-rœsh
Kőrösmező (Cz.) See *Jasiňa.*		
Korosten (Rus.)	kŏ-rŏ-stĕn′(y)	ko-ro-sten′(y)
Korotoyak (Rus.)	kŏ-rŏ-tŏ-yäk′	ko-ro-to-yahk′
Korrça (Alb.) See *Korrçë.*		
Korrçë (Alb.)	kôr′-chə	kor′-chuh
Italian *Corizza,* q.v. Greek *Korytsa,* q.v. English *Korcha,* q.v.		
Korsoer *or* Korsör (Den.)	kôrs-ûr′	kors-œr′
Korsun (Rus.)	kŏr-so͞on′(y)	kor-soon′(y)
Kortgene (Neth.)	kôrt′-k(h)ā′-nə	kort′-k(h)ay′-nuh
Kortrijk (Belg.)	*Flem.* kôrt′-rīk	kort′-raik
French *Courtrai,* q.v.		

Korytsa (Alb.) — *Gr.* kô-rē-tsä′ — ko-ree-tsah′
Albanian *Korrçë,* q.v.
Koryukovka (Rus.) — kŏr-ū-kôf′-kä — kor-yoo-kof′-kah
Kos (Dodec.) — *Eng.* kŏs′ — kos′
Gr. kô(s)′ — ko(s)′
Italian *Coo,* kô′-ô [ko′-o].
Kosančić (Yugosl.) — kô′-sän-chĭch — ko′-sahn-chich
Kosanica (Yugosl., riv.) — kô′-sä′-nĭ-tsä — ko′-sah′-ni-tsah
Kościan (Pol.) — kô′-shchän — ko′-shchahn
German *Kosten,* kôs′-tən [kos′-tuhn].
Kościerzyna (Pol.) — kô-shchĕ-zhĭ′-nä — ko-shcheh-zhi′-nah
Kosciusko (Austral., mt.) — kŏz′-ĭ-ŭs′-kō — koz′-i-uhs′-koh
Kościuszko, Tadeusz (Pol. hero) — *Eng.* kŏs′-ĭ-ŭs′-kō — kos′-i-uhs′-koh
Pol. kô-shchyo͝o′-shkô — ko-shchyu′-shko
English *Thaddeus,* thăd′-ĭ-əs [thad′-i-uhs]. Polish *Tadeusz,* tä-dĕ′-o͝osh [tah-deh′-ush].
Koshchagil (Rus.) — kŏ-shchä-gĭl′ — ko-shchah-gil′
Koshedary (Lith.) — *Rus.* kô′-shĕ-dä′-rĭ — ko′-sheh-dah′-ri
Lithuanian *Kaišiadorys,* q.v.
Košice (Cz.) — kô′-shĭ-tsĕ — ko′-shi-tseh
Hungarian *Kassa,* kŏsh′-shŏ [kosh′-sho].
Košíře (Cz.) — kô′-shē-rzhĕ — ko′-shee-rzheh
Kosjerići (Yugosl.) — kôs′-yĕ′-rĭ-chĭ — kos′-yeh′-ri-chi
Köslin (Ger.) — kûs-lēn′ — kœs-leen′
Kosmaj (Yugosl., hill) — kôs′-mī — kos′-mai
Kosovo Polje (Yugosl.) — kô′-sô-vô pô′-lyĕ — ko′-so-vo po′-lyeh
Kosów (Pol.) — kô′-so͝of — ko′-suf
Kossuth, Lajos (Hung. hero) — kô′-sho͝ot, lŏ′-yôsh — ko′-shut, lo′-yosh
English kŏs-so͞oth′ [kos-sooth′].
Kostajnica (Yugosl.) — kô′-stī′-nĭ-tsä — ko′-stai′-ni-tsah
Kosten (Pol.) See *Kościan.*
Kostolac (Yugosl.) — kô′-stô-läts — ko′-sto-lahts
Kostroma (Rus.) — kŏ-strŏ-mä′ — ko-stro-mah′
Kostrzyń (Pol.) — kôst′-zhĭn(y) — kost′-zhin(y)
Kosturino (Yugosl.) — kô′-sto͞o′-rĭ-nô — ko′-stoo′-ri-no
Kota Baroe *or* Baru (Malaya) — kô′-tä bä′-ro͞o — kaw′-tah bah′-roo
Kotel (Bulg.) — kô′-tĕl — ko′-tel
Kotelnikov (Rus.) — kŏ-tĕl(y)′-nĭ-kŏf — ko-tel(y)′-ni-kof
Köthen (Ger.) — kû′-tən — kœ′-tuhn
Kotikovo (Rus.) — kô′-tĭ-kŏ-vŏ — ko′-ti-ko-vo
Kotka (Fin.) — kôt′-kä — kot′-kah
Kotlas (Rus.) — kôt′-läs — kot′-lahs

Kotlenik (Yugosl., mts.)	kôt′-lĕ-nĭk	kot′-leh-nik
Kotor (Yugosl.)	kô′-tôr	ko′-tor
Italian *Cattaro*, q.v.		
Kotor Varoš (Yugosl.)	kô′-tôr vä′-rôsh	ko′-tor vah′-rosh
Kotronas (Gr.)	kô′-trô-näs	ko′-tro-nahs
Kotsk (Pol.) See *Kock.*		
Koudekerke (Neth.)	kou′-də-kĕr′-kə	kau′-duh-kehr′-kuh
Kouloure (Gr., isl.) See *Salamis.*		
Kouphonesi (Crete, isl.)	ko͞o-fô-nē′-sē	koo-fo-nee′-see
Also called *Lefke*, lĕf′-kē [lef′-kee].		
Koussevitzky, Sergei (Am. musician)	ko͞o′-sə-vĭt′-skĭ, sĕr-gā′	koo′-suh-vit′-ski, sehr-gay′
Sergei is sometimes Gallicized to *Serge*, sĕrzh′ [sehrzh′], or Englished as sûrj′ [suhrj′].		
Koutoulos (Crete, point)	ko͞o′-to͞o-lôs	koo′-too-los
Koutri (Crete, point)	ko͞o′-trē	koo′-tree
Kov (Rus., riv.)	kôf′	kof′
Kovačevac (Yugosl.)	kô′-vä′-chĕ-väts	ko′-vah′-cheh-vahts
Kovačica (Yugosl.)	kô′-vä′-chĭ-tsä	ko′-vah′-chi-tsah
Kovács, Ferenc (Hung. leader)	kô′-väch, fĕ′-rĕnts	ko′-vahch, feh′-rents
Kovda (Rus.)	kôv′-dä	kov′-dah
Koviljača (Yugosl.)	kô′-vĭ-lyä-chä	ko′-vi-lyah-chah
Kovin (Yugosl.)	kô′-vĭn	ko′-vin
Kovno (Lith.)	*Rus.* kôv′-nŏ	kov′-no
Lithuanian *Kaunas*, q.v.		
Kovrov (Rus.)	kŏv-rôf′	kov-rof′
Kovzha (Rus.)	kôv′-zhä	kov′-zhah
Kowel (Pol.)	kô′-vĕl	ko′-vel
Russian *Kovel*, kô′-vĕl(y) [ko′-vel(y)].		
Kozane (Gr.)	kô-zä′-nē	ko-zah′-nee
Kozelsk (Rus.)	kŏ-zĕlsk′	ko-zelsk′
Kozenitse (Pol.) See *Kozienice.*		
Kozienice (Pol.)	kô-zhĕ-nē′-tsĕ	ko-zheh-nee′-tseh
Russian *Kozenitse*, kŏ-zĕ-nē′-tsĕ [ko-zeh-nee′-tseh).		
Kozjak (Yugosl., mt.)	kôz′-yäk	koz′-yahk
Kozlov (Rus.)	kŏz-lôf′	koz-lof′
Koźmin (Pol.)	kôzh′-mĭn	kozh′-min
Kožuf (Balkan mts.)	*S.-C.* kô′-zho͞of	ko′-zhoof
Kra (Thai, isthmus)	krä′	krah′
Krageroe *or* Kragerö (Nor.)	krä′-gĕr-û	krah′-gehr-œ
Kragujevac (Yugosl.)	krä′-go͞o′-yĕ-väts	krah′-goo′-yeh-vahts
Krajina (Yugosl.)	krä′-yĭ-nä	krah′-yi-nah

Krajište (Yugosl.)	krä′-yĭ-shtĕ	krah′-yi-shteh
Krakatau (NEI)	krä-kä-tou′	krah-kah-tau′
Krakov *or* Kraków (Pol.)	See *Cracow.*	
Kralje (Yugosl.)	krä′-lyĕ	krah′-lyeh
Kraljevica (Yugosl.)	krä′-lyĕ′-vĭ-tsä	krah′-lyeh′-vi-tsah
Kraljevo (Yugosl.)	krä′-lyĕ-vô	krah′-lyeh-vo
Kramatorsk (Rus.)	krä-mä-tôrsk′	krah-mah-torsk′
Kranj (Yugosl.)	krän′(y)	krahn′(y)
Krapina (Yugosl.)	krä′-pĭ-nä	krah′-pi-nah
Krāslava (Latvia)	kräs′-lä-vä	krahs′-lah-vah
Kraśnik (Pol.)	kräsh′-nĭk	krahsh′-nik
Russian *Krasnik,* kräs′-nĭk [krahs′-nik].		
Krasnoarmeisk (Rus.)	kräs′-nŏ-är-māsk′	krahs′-no-ahr-maysk′
Krasnodar (Rus.)	kräs-nŏ-där′	krahs-no-dahr′
Krasnograd (Rus.)	kräs-nŏ-grät′	krahs-no-graht′
Krasnogvardeisk (Rus.)	kräs-nŏ-gvär-dāsk′	krahs-no-gvahr-daysk′
Krasnovodsk (Rus.)	kräs-nŏ-vôdsk′	krahs-no-vodsk′
Krasnoyarsk (Rus.)	kräs-nŏ-yärsk′	krahs-no-yahrsk′
Krasnoye (Rus.)	kräs′-nŏ-yĕ	krahs′-no-yeh
Krasny Kholm (Rus.)	kräs′-nĭ hôlm′	krahs′-ni holm′
Krasny Liman (Rus.)	kräs′-nĭ lĭ-män′	krahs′-ni li-mahn′
Krasnystaw (Pol.)	kräs′-nĭ-stäf	krahs′-ni-stahf
Russian *Krasnostav,* kräs-nŏ-stäf′ [krahs-no-stahf′].		
Kraste (Yugosl., hills)	krä′-stĕ	krah′-steh
Kratié (Indo-Ch.)	krä-tyĕ′	krah-tyeh′
Kratovo (Yugosl.)	krä′-tô-vô	krah′-to-vo
Krawang (NEI)	krä-wäng′	krah-wahng′
Krčin, Donji (Yugosl.)	kər′-chĭn, dôn′-yĭ	kuhr′-chin, don′-yĭ
Krefeld (Ger.)	*Eng.* krā′-fĕld	kray′-feld
	Ger. krā′-fĕlt	kray′-felt
Kremenchug (Rus.)	krĕ-mĕn-cho͝ok′	kreh-men-chuk′
Kremenets (Pol.) See *Krzemieniec.*		
Krepoljin (Yugosl.)	krĕ′-pô′-lyĭn	kreh′-po′-lyin
Kreševo (Yugosl.)	krĕ′-shĕ-vô	kreh′-sheh-vo
Kresta (Alaska, Attu)	krĕs′-tä	kres′-tah
Kresttsi (Rus.)	krĕst-tsĭ′	krest-tsi′
Krete (Gr., isl.) See *Crete.*		
Kretinga (Lith.)	krĕ′-tĭng-gä	kreh′-ting-gah
Kreutzburg (Latvia)	*Ger.* kroits′-bo͝ork(h)	kroits′-burk(h)
	Rus. krāts′-bo͝ork	krayts′-burk
Latvian *Krustpils,* q.v.		
Kreuznach (Ger.)	kroits′-näk(h)	kroits′-nahk(h)
Kriba (Tun.)	krē′-bə	kree′-buh

Krichev (Rus.)	krē′-chĕf	kree′-chef
Krim (Rus.)	krĭm′	krim′
Krimpen (Neth.)	krĭm′-pən	krim′-puhn
Krios (Crete, point)	krē-ôs′	kree-os′
Kriou Metopon (Crete, point)	krē-o͞o′ mĕ′-tô-pô(n)	kree-oo′ meh′-to-po(n)
Also called *Krios*, q.v.		
Kristiansand (Nor.)	krĭs-tyän-sän′	kris-tyahn-sahn′
Kristiansund (Nor.)	krĭs-tyän-so͝on′	kris-tyahn-sun′
Kristinestad (Fin.)	*Sw.* krĭs-tē′-nə-städ′	kris-tee′-nuh-stahd′
Finnish *Kristiinankaupunki*, krĭs′-tē-nän-kou′-po͝ong-kē [kris′-tee-nahn-kau′-pung-kee].		
Kritsa (Crete)	krē-tsä′	kree-tsah′
Kriva (Yugosl., riv.)	krē′-vä	kree′-vah
Kriva Lakavica (Yugosl., riv.)	krē′-vä lä′-kä-vĭ-tsä	kree′-vah lah′-kah-vi-tsah
Kriva Palanka (Yugosl.)	krē′-vä pä′-län-kä	kree′-vah pah′-lahn-kah
Krivelj (Yugosl.)	krē′-vĕl(y)	kree′-vel(y)
Krivogaštani (Yugosl.)	krē′-vô-gä′-shtä-nĭ	kree′-vo-gah′-shtah-ni
Krivoi Rog (Rus.)	krĭ-voi′ rôg′	kri-voi′ rog′
Krivolak (Yugosl.)	krē′-vô-läk	kree′-vo-lahk
Krivomuzginskaya (Rus.)	krĭ-vŏ-mo͞oz′-gĭn-skä-yä	kri-vo-mooz′-gin-skä-yä
Krivorozhe (Rus.)	krĭ-vŏ-rôzh′-yĕ	kri-vo-rozh′-yeh
Kriz (Tun.)	krēz′	kreez′
Križevci (Yugosl.)	krē′-zhĕv-tsĭ	kree′-zhev-tsi
Krk (Yugosl.)	kərk′	kuhrk′
Italian *Veglia*, q.v.		
Krka (Yugosl., rivs.)	kər′-kä	kuhr′-kah
Krnjaja (Yugosl.)	kər′-nyä-yä	kuhr′-nyah-yah
Krnov (Cz.)	kər′-nôf	kuhr′-nof
Kroederen *or* Kröderen (Nor.)	krû′-də-rən	krœ′-duh-ruhn
Krokowo (Pol.)	krô-kô′-vô	kro-ko′-vo
Krolevets (Rus.)	krŏ-lĕ′-vĕts	kro-leh′-vets
Królewska Huta (Pol.)	kro͝o-lĕf′-skä ho͝o′-tä	kru-lef′-skah hu′-tah
Królewski, Kanal (Pol.)	kro͝o-lĕf′-skĭ, kä′-näl	kru-lef′-ski, kah′-nahl
Russian *Dnyeprovsko-Bugski Kanal*, dnĕ-prôf′-skŏ-bo͞og′-skĭ kä-näl′ [dneh-prof′-sko-boog′-ski kah-nahl′].		
Kroměříž (Cz.)	krô′-myĕ-rzhēzh	kro′-myeh-rzheezh
Kromi (Rus.)	krô′-mĭ	kro′-mi
Kronstadt (Rus.)	krŏn-shtät′	kron-shtaht′

Kropotkin (Rus.)	krŏ-pôt′-kĭn	kro-pot′-kin
Krośniewice (Pol.)	krôsh-nyĕ-vē′-tsĕ	krosh-nyeh-vee′-tseh
Krotoszyn (Pol.)	krô-tô′-shĭn	kro-to′-shin
Krraba (Alb., pass) See *Krrabë.*		
Krrabë (Alb., pass)	krä′-bə	krah′-buh
Also called *Qafe e Krrabës.*		
Krš, Veliki *and* Mali (Yugosl., mts.)	kərsh′, vĕ′-lĭ-kĭ *and* mä′-lĭ	kuhrsh′, veh′-li-ki *and* mah′-li
Krševica (Yugosl.)	kər′-shĕ′-vĭ-tsä	kuhr′-sheh′-vi-tsah
Krško (Yugosl.)	kərsh′-kô	kuhrsh′-ko
Krsna, Velika *and* Mala (Yugosl.)	kərs′-nä, vĕ′-lĭ-kä *and* mä′-lä	kuhrs′-nah, veh′-li-kah *and* mah′-lah
Krtole (Yugosl.)	kər′-tô-lĕ	kuhr′-to-leh
Kruif, Paul de	krûĭf′	krœif′
Kruja (Alb.) See *Krujë.*		
Krujë (Alb.)	kro͞o′-yə	kroo′-yuh
Italian *Croia,* q.v. Formerly (Turkish) *Akçehisar.*		
Krungdheb (Thai) See *Bangkok.*		
Krupanj (Yugosl.)	kro͞o′-pän(y)	kroo′-pahn(y)
Krupp (Ger.)	*Eng.* krŭp′	kruhp′
	Ger. kro͝op′	krup′
Kruščica (Yugosl., mts.)	kro͞osh′-chĭ-tsä	kroosh′-chi-tsah
Kruševac (Yugosl.)	kro͞o′-shĕ-väts	kroo′-sheh-vahts
Kruševica (Yugosl.)	kro͞o′-shĕ′-vĭ-tsä	kroo′-sheh′-vi-tsah
Kruševo (Yugosl.)	kro͞o′-shĕ-vô	kroo′-sheh-vo
Krustpils (Latvia)	kro͝ost′-pēls	krust′-peels
Russian and German *Kreutzburg,* q.v.		
Kruszwica (Pol.)	kro͝osh-vē′-tsä	krush-vee′-tsah
Krvavi Kamik (Balkan mt.)	*S.-C.* kər′-vä-vĭ kä′-mĭk	kuhr′-vah-vi kah′-mik
Krylov, A. N. (Rus. scientist)	krĭ-lôf′	kri-lof′
Krymskaya (Rus.)	krĭm′-skä-yä	krim′-skah-yah
Krynica (Pol.)	krĭ-nē′-tsä	kri-nee′-tsah
Kryoneri (Gr.)	krē-ô-nĕ′-rē	kree-o-neh′-ree
Krzemieniec (Pol.)	kzhĕ-myĕ′-nyĕts	kzheh-myeh′-nyets
Russian *Kremenets,* krĕ-mĕ-nĕts′ [kreh-meh-nets′].		
Ksar (Tun.)	kə-sär′	kuh-sahr′
Ksar Rhilane (Tun.)	kə-sär′ rĭ-lăn′	kuh-sahr′ ri-lan′
Ksar Tyr (Tun.)	kə-sär′ tēr′	kuh-sahr′ teer′
Ksenievskaya (Rus.)	ksĕ′-nĭ-yĕf-skä-yä	kseh′-ni-yef-skah-yah
Książ (Pol.)	kshôNsh′	kshoNsh′
Ksour Essaf (Tun.)	kə-so͞or′ ĕs-săf′	kuh-soor′ es-saf′

Kuala Lumpur (Malaya)	kwä′-lə lo͝om′-po͝or′	kwah′-luh lum′-pur′
Kuaua (Oc.)	ko͞o-ä-o͞o′-ä	koo-ah-oo′-ah
Kuba (Rus.)	ko͞o′-bä	koo′-bah
Kuban (Rus., riv.)	ko͝o-bän′(y)	ku-bahn′(y)
Kuberle (Rus.)	ko͞o-bĕr-lĕ′	koo-behr-leh′
Kubršnica (Yugosl., riv.)	ko͞o′-bərsh′-nĭ-tsä	koo′-buhrsh′-ni-tsah
Kubuleti (Rus.)	ko͞o-bo͞o-lĕ′-tĭ	koo-boo-leh′-ti
Kuç (Alb.)	ko͞och′	kooch′
Kučaj (Yugosl.)	ko͞o′-chī	koo′-chai
Kučajna (Yugosl.)	ko͞o′-chī-nä	koo′-chai-nah
Kučevo (Yugosl.)	ko͞o′-chĕ-vô	koo′-cheh-vo
Kuchan *or* Quchan (Iran)	ko͞o-chän′	koo-chahn′
Kuching (Sarawac)	ko͞o′-chĭng	koo′-ching
Kučkovo (Yugosl.)	ko͞och′-kô-vô	kooch′-ko-vo
Kuçova (Alb.) See *Kuçovë.*		
Kuçovë (Alb.)	ko͞o-chô′-və	koo-cho′-vuh
Also called *Vajguras*, q.v. Italian *Petrolia*, q.v.		
Kudat (Brit. Borneo)	ko͞o-dät′	koo-daht′
Kuenga (Rus.)	ko͞o-ĕn-gä′	koo-en-gah′
Kuibyshev (Rus.)	*Eng.* kwē′-bĭ-shĕf	kwee′-bi-shef
	Rus. ko͞o′ĭ-bwē-shĕf	koo′i-bwee-shef
	or ko͝oĭ-bwē′-shĕf	kui-bwee′-shef
Kuilenburg (Neth.)	kûĭ′-lən-bûrk(h)	kœi′-luhn-bœrk(h)
Kukës (Alb.)	ko͞o′-kəs	koo′-kuhs
Kukësi (Alb.) See *Kukës.*		
Kukiel, Marian (Pol. general)	ko͝o′-kyĕl, mär′-yän	ku′-kyel, mahr′-yahn
Kuku Nor (Ch., prov., lake) See *Koko Nor.*		
Kukui (Rus.)	ko͝o-ko͞o′ĭ	ku-koo′i
Kukum (Oc.)	ko͞o′-ko͞om	koo′-koom
Kula (Yugosl.)	ko͞o′-lä	koo′-lah
Kula (Oc., gulf)	ko͞o′-lä	koo′-lah
Kulamadau (Oc.)	ko͞o-lä-mä′-dou	koo-lah-mah′-dau
Kuldiga (Latvia)	ko͝ol′-dē-gä	kul′-dee-gah
Russian and German *Goldingen*, q.v.		
Kuliviu (Oc.)	ko͞o-lē′-vē-o͞o	koo-lee′-vee-oo
Kulm (Pol.) See *Chełmno.*		
Kulmsee (Pol.) See *Chełmża.*		
Kum *or* Qum (Iran)	ko͝om′	kum′
Kuma (Rus., riv.)	ko͞o′-mä	koo′-mah
Kumamoto (Jap.)	ko͞o-mä-mô-tô	koo-mah-mo-to
Kumaničevo (Yugosl.)	ko͞o′-mä-nē′-chĕ-vô	koo′-mah-nee′-cheh-vo

Kumanovo (Yugosl.)	ko͞o′-mä-nô-vô	koo′-mah-no-vo
Kumanovska (Yugosl., riv.)	ko͞o′-mä-nôf-skä	koo′-mah-nof-skah
Kumbur (Yugosl.)	ko͞om′-bo͞or	koom′-boor
Kumodraž (Yugosl.)	ko͞o′-mô-dräzh	koo′-mo-drahzh
Kumusi (Oc., riv.)	ko͞o-mo͞o′-sē	koo-moo′-see
Kunda (Est.)	ko͞on′-dä	koon′-dah
K'ung, Dr. Hsiang Hsi (Chinese leader)	ko͝ong, shyäng shē	kung, shyahng shee
Kung-an (Ch., Hupeh)	go͝ong-än	gung-ahn
Kungur (Rus.)	ko͝on-go͝or′	kun-gur′
Kunkel, John C. (U.S. representative)	ko͝ong′-kĕl′	kung′-kel′
Kunlong (Burma)	ko͝on-lŏng′	kun-long′
K'un-lun (Ch., Sinkiang, mts.)	ko͝on-lo͝on	kun-lun
K'un-ming (Ch., Yünnan) Also called *Yün-nan-fu*, q.v.	ko͝on-mĭng	kun-ming
Kuno (Est., isl.) Estonian *Kihnu*, q.v.	*Rus.* ko͞o′-nŏ	koo′-no
Kunora (Alb., mt.) See *Kunorë*.		
Kunorë (Alb., mt.)	ko͞o-nô′-rə	koo-no′-ruh
Kuomintang (Ch. political party)	*Eng.* kwō-mĭn-tăng *Ch.* gwō-mĭn-däng	kwoh-min-tahng gwoh-min-dahng
Kuop (Oc.)	ko͞o′-ôp	koo′-op
Kuopio (Fin.)	ko͝o′-ô′-pē-ô	ku′-o′-pee-o
Kupa (Yugosl., riv.) German *Kulpa*.	ko͞o′-pä	koo′-pah
Kupci (Yugosl.)	ko͞op′-tsĭ	koop′-tsi
Kupekow (Ch., Hopeh)	go͞o-bā-kō	goo-bay-koh
Kupyansk (Rus.)	ko͞o′-pyänsk	koo′-pyahnsk
Kur (Rus., riv.)	ko͞or′	koor′
Kura (Rus., riv.)	ko͞o-rä′	koo-rah′
Kurd (Per. tribe)	*Eng.* kûrd′ *Pers.* ko͞ord′	kuhrd′ koord′
Kurdistan (Iran)	*Per.* ko͞or-dĭs-tän′ *Eng.* kûr′-dĭs-tăn	koor-dis-tahn′ kuhr′-dis-tan
Kure (Jap.)	ko͞o-rĕ	koo-reh
Kuressaare (Est.)	ko͞o′-rĕs-sä′-rĕ	koo′-res-sah′-reh

Also called *Kuresaari*, ko͞o-rĕ-sä′-rĭ [koo-reh-sah′-ri]. German *Arensburg*, q.v.

Kurgan (Rus.)	ko͝or-gän′	kur-gahn′

Kurgannaya (Rus.)	ko͝or-gän′-nä-yä	kur-gahn′-nah-yah
Kuria (Oc.)	ko͞o′-rē-ä	koo′-ree-ah
Kuril (Rus., str.; Jap., isls.)	ko͞o-rēl′ *or* ko͞o′-rĭl	koo-reel′ koo′-ril
Japanese *Chishima*, chē-shē-mä [chee-shee-mah].		
Kurishi (Rus.)	ko͞o′-rĭ-shĭ	koo′-ri-shi
Kurjače (Yugosl.)	ko͞or′-yä-chĕ	koor′-yah-cheh
Kurnik (Pol.) See *Kórnik*.		
Kursk (Rus.)	ko͞orsk′	koorsk′
Kuršumlija (Yugosl.)	ko͞or′-sho͞om′-lĭ-yä	koor′-shoom′-li-yah
Kusadak (Yugosl.)	ko͞o′-sä-däk	koo′-sah-dahk
Kusaie (Oc.)	ko͞o-sī′-ĕ	koo-sai′-eh
Kush (India, mts.) See *Hindu Kush*.		
Kushchevka (Rus.)	ko͞o-shchôf′-kä	koo-shchof′-kah
Kušiljevo (Yugosl.)	ko͞o′-shē′-lyĕ-vô	koo′-shee′-lyeh-vo
Kustanai (Rus.)	ko͞o-stä-nī′	koo-stah-nai′
Kutais (Rus.)	ko͞o-tä-ēs′	koo-tah-ees′
Kutch (India) See *Cutch*.		
Kutina (Yugosl., riv.)	ko͞o′-tĭ-nä	koo′-ti-nah
Kutkai (Burma)	ko͝ot-kī′	kut-kai′
Kutná Hora (Cz.)	ko͞ot′-nä hô′-rä	koot′-nah ho′-rah
Kutno (Pol.)	ko͝ot′-nô	kut′-no
Kuty (Pol.)	ko͝o′-tĭ	ku′-ti
Kuusamo (Rus.)	ko͞o′-sä-mō	koo′-sah-moh
Kuvshinovo (Rus.)	ko͞of-shĭ′-nŏ-vŏ	koof-shi′-no-vo
Kuznetsk (Rus.)	ko͞oz-nĕtsk′	kooz-netsk′
Kuznetsova (Rus.)	ko͞oz-nĕ-tsô′-vä	kooz-neh-tso′-vah
Kvam (Nor.)	kväm′	kvahm′
Kvanne (Nor.)	kvän′-nə	kvahn′-nuh
Kvaroey *or* Kvaröy (Nor.)	kvär′-ûĭ	kvahr′-œi
Kvėdarna (Lith.)	kvā′-där-nä	kvay′-dahr-nah
Kvesmenes (Nor.)	kvĕs′-mə-nĕs	kves′-muh-nes
Kvisvik (Nor.)	kvĭs′-vēk	kvis′-veek
Kviteseid (Nor.)	kvĭt′-sā *or* kvĭt′-ə-sād	kvit′-say kvit′-uh-sayd
Kwajalein (Oc.)	kwä′-jä-lān	kwah′-jah-layn
Kwakea (Oc.)	kwä-kĕ′-ä	kwah-keh′-ah
Kwang-ch'ang (Ch., Kiangsi)	gwäng-chäng	gwahng-chahng
Kwang Chow Wan (Ch., Kwangtung, Fr. colony)	gwäng jō wän	gwahng joh wahn
Kwang-fêng (Ch., Kiangsi)	gwäng-fŭng	gwahng-fuhng

Kwang-si (Ch., prov.)	*Eng.* kwăng-sē	kwang-see
	Ch. gwäng-sē	gwahng-see
Kwang-tung (Ch., prov.)	*Eng.* kwăng-to͝ong	kwang-tung
	Ch. gwäng-do͝ong	gwahng-dung
K'wan-t'o (Manchu.) See *Kwantung.*		
Kwan-tung (Manchu.)	*Eng.* kwăn-to͝ong	kwan-tung
	Ch. gwän-do͝ong	gwahn-dung
Also called *K'wan-t'o,* kwän-tô [kwahn-to].		
Kwapinski, Jan (Pol. leader)	kvä-pēn'-skĭ, yän'	kvah-peen'-ski, yahn'
Kwa-tsa (Ch., Yünnan)	gwä-dzä	gwah-dzah
Kwazon (Burma)	kwä-zōn'	kwah-zohn'
Kwei-ch'i (Ch., Kiangsi)	gwā-chē	gway-chee
Also spelled *Kwei-ki.*		
K'wei-ch'ieh (Burma)	kwā-chyĕ	kway-chyeh
Kwei-chow (Ch., prov.)	*Eng.* kwā-chou	kway-chau
	Ch. gwā-jō	gway-joh
Kwei-hwa (Ch., Suiyüan)	gwā-whä	gway-whah
Kwei-hwa Sui-yüan (Ch., prov.)	gwā-whä swā-yüän	gway-whah sway-yüahn
Also called *Sui-yüan,* q.v.		
Kwei-ki (Ch.) Variant spelling of *Kwei-ch'i,* q.v.		
Kwei-lin (Ch., Kiangsi)	gwā-lĭn	gway-lin
Kwei-sui (Ch., Suiyüan)	gwā-swā	gway-sway
Kwei-yang (Ch., Kweichow)	gwā-yäng	gway-yahng
Kyaikkami (Burma)	chīk'-kə-mē'	chaik'-kuh-mee'
Kyaikthin (Burma)	chīk'-thĭn'	chaik'-thin'
Kyamon (Crete, point) See *Melekhas.*		
Kyangin (Burma)	chăn'-gĭn'	chan'-gin'
Kyaukkyi (Burma)	chouk'-chē'	chauk'-chee'
Kyaukpadaung (Burma)	chouk'-pə-doung'	chauk'-puh-daung'
Kyaukpyu (Burma)	chouk'-pū'	chauk'-pyoo'
Kyaukse (Burma)	chouk'-sĕ'	chauk'-seh'
Kyauktaw (Burma)	chouk'-tô'	chauk'-taw'
Kybartai (Lith.)	kē-bär'-tī	kee-bahr'-tai
Kyelce (Pol.) See *Kielce.*		
Kyklades (Gr., isls.) See *Cyclades.*		
Kyllene (Gr.)	kē-lē'-nē	kee-lee'-nee
Also called *Zyria* or *Zerea,* zē'-rē-ä [zee'-ree-ah]. English *Cyllene,* sĭ-lē'-nē [si-lee'-nee].		
Kyme (Gr.)	kē'-mē *or* ko͞o'-mē	kee'-mee *or* koo'-mee
Kyoto (Jap.)	kyô-tô	kyo-to

Kyparisi (Gr.) kē-pä-rē′-sē kee-pah-ree′-see

Kyparissia (Gr.) kē-pä-rē-sē′-ä kee-pah-ree-see′-ah

Also some villages of this name accent the last syllable, and some the antepenult. For the noun (*cypress tree*) the accent is on the antepenult.

Kythera (Gr., isl., town) kē′-thē-rä kee′-thee-rah

English *Cythera*, sĭ-thē′-rä [si-thee′-rah]. The island is also called *Tserigo*, tsĕ-rē′-gô [tseh-ree′-go]; the town, *Kapsali(on)*, kä-psä′-lē [kah-psah′-lee].

Kythnos (Gr., isl.) kēth′-nô(s) keeth′-no(s)

English *Cythnus*, sĭth′-nəs [sĭth′-nuhs].

Kyukok (Burma) See *Chukok*.

Kyungon (Burma) cho͝on′-gōn′ chun′-gohn′

Kyushu (Jap.) kū-sho͞o kyoo-shoo

Kyustendil (Bulg.) kū′-stĕn-dĭl′ kyoo′-sten-dil′

Laagendal (Nor.) lô′-gən-däl lo′-guhn-dahl

Laaland (Den., isl.) lô′-län lo′-lahn

Laatefoss (Nor.) lô′-tə-fôs lo′-tuh-fos

Laba (Rus., riv.) lä′-bä lah′-bah

Lababia (Oc.) lä-bä′-bē-ä lah-bah′-bee-ah

Labe (Europ. riv.) See *Elbe*.

Labinskaya (Rus.) lä-bēn′-skä-yä lah-been′-skah-yah

Laboeha *or* Labuha (NEI) lä-bo͞o′-hä lah-boo′-hah

Labuan (Br. Borneo) lä-bo͝o-än′ lah-bu-ahn′

Labuha (NEI) See *Laboeha*.

La Calle (Alg.) lä käl′ lah kahl′

La Camargue (Fr., isl.) lä kä-märg′ lah kah-mahrg′

Laccadive (India, isls.) lăk′-ə-dīv lak′-uh-daiv

La Ciotat (Fr.) lä syô-tä′ lah syo-tah′

Laconia (Gr.) *Eng.* lə-kōn′-yə luh-kohn′-yuh
Ger. lä-kô-nē′-ä lah-ko-nee′-ah

Lacroma (Yugosl., isl.) *It.* lä-krô′-mä lah-kro′-mah

Serb-Croat *Lokrum*, q.v.

Ladoga (Indiana) lə-dō′-gə luh-doh′-guh

Ladoga (Rus., lake) lä′-dŏ-gä lah′-do-gah

Ladrone (Oc.) *Eng.* lə-drōn′ luh-drohn′

Spanish *Ladrones*, lä-*th*rô′-nĕs [lah-*th*ro′-nes]. Also called the *Marianas*, q.v.

Lae (New Guinea) lä′-ĕ *or* lī′ lah′-eh *or* lai′

Laeken (Belg.) lä′-kən lah′-kuhn

Lærdal (Nor.) lĕr′-däl lehr′-dahl

Læsoe *or* Læsö (Den., isl.) lĕs′-û les′-œ

La Fauconnerie (Tun., airfield) lä fō-kôn-rē′ lah foh-kon-ree′

La Follette, Robert M., Jr. (U. S. senator) la fŏl′-ĭt luh fol′-it

lago	lä′-gô	lah′-go
An element, meaning *lake*, in Italian place names. It may be necessary to look up the other part of the name.		
Lagonoy (P.I.)	lä-gô′-noi	lah-go′-noi
Lagos (Port.)	lä′-go͝osh	lah′-gush
Lagosta (It., isl.)	lä-gô′-stä	lah-go′-stah
Serb-Croat *Lastovo*, lä′-stô-vô [lah′-sto-vo].		
La Goulette (Tun.)	lä go͞o-lĕt′	lah goo-let′
La Guardia (Am. mayor)	*Eng.* lə gwär′-dĭ-ə	luh gwahr′-di-uh
	or lə gär′-dĭ-ə	luh gahr′-di-uh
	It. lä gwär′-dyä	lah gwahr′-dyah
The first of these pronunciations is the most comfortable for CBS speakers. The Mayor, moreover, before broadcasting from a WABC studio on October 20, 1942, said that he had pronounced his name lə gwär′-dĭ-ə [luh gwahr′-di-uh] for over fifty years and saw no reason to change it. This evidence contradicts that on which we based the recommendation in the Bulletin of September 30, 1942 (Vol. II, No. 3).		
La Hague (Fr., cape)	*Eng.* lä häg′	lah hahg′
	Fr. lä äg′	lah ahg′
Lahdenpohja (Fin.)	läk(h)′-dĕn-pô-yä	lahk(h)′-den-po-yah
La Hencha (Tun.)	lä hĕn′-shä	lah hen′-shah
Lahore (India)	lə-hôr′	luh-hor′
Lahti (Fin.)	lä′-tē	lah′-tee
Laibach (Yugosl.)	*Ger.* lī′-bäk(h)	lai′-bahk(h)
Serb-Croat *Llubljana*, q.v., and *Ljubljanica*, q.v.		
Laika (Oc.)	lä-ē′-kä	lah-ee′-kah
Lajkovac (Yugosl.)	lī′-kô-väts	lai′-ko-vahts
Lakchang (Burma)	lăk-chăng′	lak-chang′
Lake Achkel (Tun.)	äsh′-kĕl	ahsh′-kel
Also called *Garaet Achkel*, q.v.		
Lakonikos Kolpos (Gr., gulf)	lä-kô-nē-kôs′ kôl′-pôs	lah-ko-nee-kos′ kol′-pos
English Gulf of *Laconia*, q.v.		
La Línea (Sp.)	lä lē′-nĕ-ä	lah lee′-neh-ah
Lallemand, Fort (Alg.)	läl-mäN′	lahl-mahN′
La Maddalena (Sard., isl.)	lä mä-dä-lĕ′-nä	lah mah-dah-leh′-nah
La Marsa (Tun.)	lä mär′-sä	lah mahr′-sah
Lamballe (Fr.)	läN-bäl′	lahN-bahl′
Lambon (Oc.)	läm-bôm′	lahm-bom′
Lamensk (Rus.)	lä′-mĕnsk	lah′-mensk
Lamia (Gr.)	lä-mē′-ä	lah-mee′-ah
Lamotrec (Oc.)	lä′-mô-trĕk	lah′-mo-trek
Lampedusa (It., isl.)	läm′-pĕ-do͞o′-zä	lahm′-peh-doo′-zah
Lampione (It., isl.)	läm-pyô′-nĕ	lahm-pyo′-neh

Lamy, Fort (Fr. Eq. Afr.)	*Fr.* lä-mē′	lah-mee′
	Eng. lā′-mĭ	lay′-mi
Lan-ch'i (Ch., Chekiang)	län-chē	lahn-chee
Lan-chow (Ch., Kangsu)	län-jō	lahn-joh
Also called *Kao-lan*, q.v.		
Lanciano (It.)	län-chä′-nô	lahn-chah′-no
Łańcut (Pol.)	län′(y)-tso͝ot	lahn′(y)-tsut
-land	-lənd *or* -lănd	-luhnd *or* -land

In short compounds such as *Iceland*, *Greenland*, *Finland* the vowel of *land* should be schwa, not short *a*. This is generally recognized for *England* and *Poland*, but often an overemphatic radio pronunciation is īs′-lănd′, grēn′-lănd′; īs′-lənd, grēn′-lənd are preferable, for they suggest speech instead of reading. In long compounds, such as Somaliland, Newfoundland, *-land* has a stress and the correct vowel is short *a*.

Landerneau (Fr.)	läN-dĕr-nō′	lahN-dehr-noh′
Landes (Fr., dept.)	läNd′	lahNd′
Landskrona (Sw.)	läns-kro͞o′-nä	lahns-kroo′-nah
Landwarów (Pol.)	län-dvä′-ro͝of	lahn-dvah′-ruf
Russian *Landvarovo*, län-dvä′-rŏ-vŏ [lahn-dvah′-ro-vo].		
Langeland (Den., isl.)	läng′-ə-län	lahng′-uh-lahn
Langer, William (U.S. senator)	lăng′-ər	lang′-uhr
Langesund (Nor.)	läng′-ə-so͝on	lahng′-uh-sun
Langgoer *or* Langgur (Oc.)	läng′-go͞or	lahng′-goor
Langson (Indo-Ch.)	läng-sŭn′	lahng-suhn′
French läN-sôN′ [lahN-soN′]. English lăng′-sŭn′ [lang′-suhn′].		
Lanham, Fritz G. (U.S. representative)	lăn′-əm	lan′-uhm
Lanište (Yugosl.)	lä′-nĭ-shtĕ	lah′-ni-shteh
Lankada (Gr.)	läng-gä′-*th*ä	lahng-gah′-*th*ah
Lankadas (Gr.)	läng-gä-*th*äs′	lahng-gah-*th*ahs′
Lan-ki (Ch., Chekiang)	län-chē	lahn-chee
Also spelled *Lan-ch'i*, q.v.		
Lannion (Fr.)	lä-nyôN′	lah-nyoN′
Lan-tsang (S.E. Asia, riv.)	län′-tsäng′	lahn′-tsahng′
Also called the *Mekong*, q.v.		
Lanusei (Sard.)	lä-no͞o-sā′	lah-noo-say′
Lanuvio (It.)	lä-no͞o′-vyô	lah-noo′-vyo
Lanvéoc Poulmic (Fr.)	läN-vĕ-ôk′ po͞ol-mēk′	lahN-veh-ok′ pool-meek′
Laoag (P.I.)	lä-wäg′	lah-wahg′
Laokay (Indo-Ch.)	lou-kī′	lau-kai′

Laole (Yugosl.)	lä′-ô-lĕ	lah′-o-leh
Laon (Fr.)	läN′	lahN′
Laos (Indo-Ch.)	*Eng.* lā′-ŏs	lay′-os
	Fr. lä-ôs′	lah-os′
Lao-shan (Ch., bay)	lou-shän	lau-shahn
Lao-yao (Ch., Kiangsu)	lou-you	lau-yau
La Pallice (Fr.)	lä pä-lēs′	lah pah-lees′
Laparán (P.I.)	lä-pä-rän′	lah-pah-rahn′
Also called *Paragua*, pä-rä′-gwə [pah-rah′-gwuh].		
La Paz (Bolivia)	lä päs′	lah pahs′
La Perouse (Rus., Jap., str.)	lä pĕ-rōōz′	lah peh-rooz′
Lapovo (Yugosl.)	lä′-pô-vô	lah′-po-vo
Lappeenranta (Fin.)	läp′-pān-rän-tä	lahp′-payn-rahn-tah
Swedish *Villmanstrand*, vĭl′-män-stränd′ [vil′-mahn-strahnd′].		
Łapy (Pol.)	lä′-pĭ	lah′-pi
Russian spelling *Lapi.*		
Larcade, Henry D. (U.S. representative)	lär-kād′	lahr-kayd′
Laren (Neth.)	lä′-rən	lah′-ruhn
Larisa *or* Larissa (Gr.)	lä′-rē-sä	lah′-ree-sah
There is also an English pronunciation lə-rĭs′-ə [luh-ris′-uh].		
Larkana (India)	lär-kä′-nə	lahr-kah′-nuh
Larnaca (Cyprus)	lär′-nä-kä	lahr′-nah-kah
Larvik (Nor.)	lär′-vēk	lahr′-veek
Lašče, Velike (Yugosl.)	läsh′-chĕ, vĕ′-lĭ-kĕ	lahsh′-cheh, veh′-li-keh
La Sebala (Tun.)	lä sə-bă′-lä	lah suh-ba′-lah
La Senia (Alg.)	lä sā′-nyä	lah say′-nyah
Lasethion (Crete)	lä-sē′-thē(-ôn)	lah-see′-thee(-on)
Also called *Nikolaos, Agios*, q.v.		
La Seyne sur Mer (Fr.)	lä sĕn′ sür mĕr′	lah sen′ sür mehr′
Lashio (Burma)	lăsh′-yō	lash′-yoh
	or lə′-shyō′	luh′-shyoh′
Lashkar (India)	lŭsh′-kər	luhsh′-kuhr
Łask (Pol.)	läsk′	lahsk′
La Skhirra (Tun.)	lä sə-kĭr′-rä	lah suh-kihr′-rah
Often spelled *Cekhira*, q.v.		
Laško (Yugosl.)	läsh′-kô	lahsh′-ko
Lasovačka planina (Yugos., mts.)	lä′-sô-väch-kä plä′-nē′-nä	lah′-so-vahch-kah plah′-nee′-nah
La Spezia (It.)	lä spĕ′-tsyä	lah speh′-tsyah
Lastovo (It., isl.)	*S.-C.* lä′-stô-vô	lah′-sto-vo
Italian *Lagosta*, q.v.		

Latimodjong (NEI)	lä-tē-mô′-jŏng	lah-tee-mo′-jong
Latronico (It.)	lä-trô′-nē-kô	lah-tro′-nee-ko
Laudara (Yugosl., isl.)	*It.* lou-dä′-rä	lau-dah′-rah
Serb-Croat *Lavdara*, q.v.		
Launceston (Austral.)	lŏn′-sĕs-tən	lon′-ses-tuhn
Laurel, José P. (Fil. leader)	lou-rĕl′, hô-sĕ′	lau-rel′, ho-seh′
Lauria (It.)	lou-rē′-ä	lau-ree′-ah
Lauritsala (Fin.)	lou′-rĭt-sä-lä	lau′-rit-sah-lah
Lausanne (Switz.)	*Eng.* lō-zăn′	loh-zan′
	Fr. lō-zän′	loh-zahn′
Lausche, F. J. (Am. mayor)	lou-shē′	lau-shee′
Laut (NEI)	lout′	laut′
Lauta (Ger.)	lou′-tä	lau′-tah
Laval, Pierre (Fr. collab.)	lä-väl′, pyĕr′	lah-vahl′, pyehr′
The French *broad a* is rather like that of New England. It is between the *a* of *father* and the *a* of *fat.*		
Lavansaari (Fin., isl.)	lä′-vän-sä-rē	lah′-vahn-sah-ree
Lavdara (Yugosl., isl.)	läv′-dä-rä	lahv′-dah-rah
Laverton (Austral.)	lăv′-ər-tən	lav′-uhr-tuhn
Lavongai (Oc.)	lä-vông′-ī	lah-vong′-ai
Also called *New Hanover.*		
Lavrion (Gr.)	lä′-vrē-ô(n)	lah′-vree-o(n)
English *Laurium*, lô′-rĭ-əm [lo′-ri-uhm].		
Lawolai (Oc.)	lä′-wô-lī	lah′-wo-lai
Lazarevac (Yugosl.)	lä′-zä′-rĕ-väts	lah′-zah′-reh-vahts
Leathers, Lord (Br. leader)	lĕ*th*′-ərz	le*th*′-uhrz
Lebadeia (Gr., isl.)	lĕ-vä′-*th*yä	leh-vah′-*th*yah
	or lē-vä-*th*yä′	lee-vah-*th*yah′
Lebane (Yugosl.)	lĕ′-bä-nĕ	leh′-bah-neh
Lebanon (Syria)	*Eng.* lĕb′-ə-nən	leb′-uh-nuhn
Also called *Lebanese Republic*, lĕb′-ə-nēz′ *or* -nēs′ [leb′-uh-neez′ *or* -nees′]. French *République Libanaise*, rĕ-pü-blēk′ lē-bä-nĕz′ [reh-pü-bleek′ lee-bah-nez′]. Arabic *Libnan*, lēb-năn′ [leeb-nan′].		
Le Bardo (Tun.)	lə bär′-dō	luh bahr′-doh
Lebedev, Ivan (Rus. official)	lĕ′-bĕ-dĕf, ē-vän′	leh′-beh-def, ee-vahn′
Lebedin (Rus.)	lĕ-bĕ-dēn′	leh-beh-deen′
Lebedyan (Rus.)	lĕ-bĕ-dyän′(y)	leh-beh-dyahn′(y)
Lebrun, Albert (Fr. leader)	lə-brûN′, äl-bĕr′	luh-brœN′, ahl-behr′

Le Catene (Yugosl., It., str.)	*It.* lĕ kä-tĕ′-nĕ	leh kah-teh′-neh
Serb-Croat *Verige*, q.v.		
Lecce (It.)	lĕt′-chĕ	let′-cheh
Lecco (It.)	lĕk′-kô	lek′-ko
LeClerc, Jacques (Fr. general)	lə klĕr′, zhäk′	luh klehr′, zhahk′
Le Compte, Karl M. (U.S. representative)	lə kount′	luh kaunt′
Le Creusot (Fr.)	lə krû-zō′	luh krœ-zoh′
Łęczyca (Pol.)	lăN-chĭ′-tsä	laN-chi′-tsah
Russian *Lenchitsa*, lĕn-chē′-tsä [len-chee′-tsah].		
Ledo (India)	lē′-dō′	lee′-doh′
	or lā′-dō′	lay′-doh′
Leerdam (Neth.)	lār′-däm′	layr′-dahm′
Leeuwarden (Neth.)	lā′-ōō-wär′-dən	lay′-oo-wahr′-duhn
Leeuwin (Austral., cape)	lōō′-ĭn	loo′-in
Le Fevre, Jay (U.S. representative)	lə fē′-vər	luh fee′-vuhr
Lefke (Crete, isl.) See *Kouphonesi*.		
Legaspi (P.I.)	lĕ-gäs′-pĭ	leh-gahs′-pi
Leghorn (It.)	lĕg′-hôrn	leg′-horn
Italian *Livorno*, q.v.		
Leh (India)	lā′	lay′
Le Havre (Fr.)	*Eng.* lə hävr′	luh hahvr′
	Fr. lə ävr′	luh ahvr′
A pronunciation lə ärv′ [luh ahrv′] should be avoided.		
Lehman, Herbert H. (Am. leader)	lē′-mən	lee′-muhn
Lei Chiang *or* Lei River (Ch., Hunan, riv.)	lā′	lay′
Leiden (Neth.)	lī′-dən	lai′-duhn
Leili (Oc.)	lā′-lē	lay′-lee
Leïmona (Gr.)	lā′-mô-nä	lay′-mo-nah
Leipzig (Ger.)	*Eng.* līp′-sĭg	laip′-sig
	Ger. līp′-tsĭk(h)	laip′-tsik(h)
leisure	lē′-zhər *or* lĕzh′-ər	lee′-zhuhr *or* lezh′-uhr
"But the best is lā′-zhər [lay′-zhuhr]," the Irishman said.		
Leitha (Austria, riv.)	lī′-tä	lai′-tah
Leitmeritz (Cz.)	līt′-mĕ-rĭts	lait′-meh-rits
Czech *Litoměřice*, q.v.		
Lei-yang (Ch., Hunan)	lā-yäng	lay-yahng
Lek (Neth., riv.)	lĕk′	lek′
Le Kef (Tun.)	lə kāf′	luh kayf′

Lekhena (Gr.)	lĕ′-hĕ-nä	leh′-heh-nah
Lele (Oc.)	lə-lŭ′	luh-luh′
Lelle (Est.)	lĕl′-lĕ	lel′-leh
Lelova (Gr.)	lĕ′-lô-vä	leh′-lo-vah
Lelushenko (Rus. general)	lĕ-lū-shĕn′-kŏ	leh-lyoo-shen′-ko
Le Mans (Fr.)	lə mäN′	luh mahN′
Lemberg (Pol.) See *Lwów*.		
Lemmer (Neth.)	lĕm′-ər	lem′-uhr
Also called *De Lemmer*, q.v.		
Lemnos (Gr., isl.)	*Eng.* lĕm′-nŏs	lem′-nos
	Gr. lēm′-nô(s)	leem′-no(s)
Lemvig (Den.)	lĕm′-vēk(h)	lem′-veek(h)
Lenchitsa (Pol.) See *Łęczyca*.		
Lengyel, Menyhért (Hung. writer)	lĕn′-dyĕl, mĕn′(y)-hārt	len′-dyel, men′(y)-hayrt
Lenin (Rus. leader)	lĕ′-nĭn	leh′-nin
Real name *Vladimir Ilyich Ulyanov*, vlä-dē′-mĭr ĭl-yēch′ o͞ol-yä′-nŏf [vlah-dee′-mihr il-yeech′ ool-yah′-nof].		
Leninakan (Rus.)	lĕ′-nĭ-nä-kän′	leh′-ni-nah-kahn′
Leningrad (Rus.)	*Eng.* lĕn′-ĭn-grăd	len′-in-grad
	Rus. lĕ′-nĭn-grät′	leh′-nin-graht′
Leninsk (Rus.)	lĕ′-nĭnsk	leh′-ninsk
Leninsk Kuznetskii (Rus.)	— ko͝oz-nĕt′-skĭ	— kuz-net′-ski
Lenola (It.)	lĕ′-nô-lä	leh′-no-lah
Lens (Fr.)	läNs′	lahNs′
Lentini (Sicily)	lĕn-tē′-nē	len-tee′-nee
Leoben (Austria)	lĕ-ō′-bən	leh-oh′-buhn
León (Sp., prov.)	lĕ-ôn′	leh-on′
Leone (Pantelleria)	lĕ-ô′-nĕ	leh-o′-neh
Leonideion (Gr.)	lĕ-ô-nē′-*th*ē(-ôn)	leh-o-nee′-*th*ee(-on)
Leova (Rum.)	lĕ-ô′-vä	leh-o′-vah
Lepanto (Gr., gulf)	*Eng.* lĭ-păn′-tō	li-pan′-toh
	It. lĕ′-pän-tô	leh′-pahn-to
Also called the Gulf of *Corinth*, q.v.		
Lepel (Rus.)	lĕ′-pĕl(y)	leh′-pel(y)
Lepenac (Yugosl., riv.)	lĕ′-pĕ′-näts	leh′-peh′-nahts
Lepenica (Yugosl.)	lĕ′-pĕ′-nĭ-tsä	leh′-peh′-ni-tsah
Lepini (It., mt.)	lĕ-pē′-nē	leh-pee′-nee
Le Pollet (Fr.)	lə pô-lĕ′	luh po-leh′
Lercara (Sicily)	lĕr-kä′-rä	lehr-kah′-rah
Lérida (Sp.)	lĕ′-rē-*th*ä	leh′-ree-*th*ah
Leros (Dodec.)	lĕ′-rô(s)	leh′-ro(s)

Lesbos (Gr., isl.)	*Eng.* lĕz′-bŏs	lez′-bos
	Gr. lĕz′-vô(s)	lez′-vo(s)
Usually called *Mytilene*, q.v.		
Lešće (Yugosl.)	lĕsh′-chĕ	lesh′-cheh
Lesh (Alb.)	lĕsh′	lesh′
Italian *Alessio*, q.v.		
Leshi (Alb.) See *Lesh.*		
Lesina (Yugosl.)	*It.* lĕ′-sĭ-nä	leh′-si-nah
Serb-Croat *Hvar*, q.v.		
Lesinski, John (U.S. representative)	lĕ-sĭn′-skĭ	leh-sin′-ski
Lesja (Nor.)	lĕsh′-ä	lesh′-ah
Leskovac (Yugosl.)	lĕs′-kô-väts	les′-ko-vahts
Leskovik (Alb.)	lĕ-skô-vēk′	leh-sko-veek′
Leskoviku (Alb.) See *Leskovik.*		
Lešnica (Yugosl.)	lĕsh′-nĭ-tsä	lesh′-ni-tsah
Les Sables d'Olonne (Fr.)	lĕ sä′bl dô-lôn′	leh sah′bl do-lon′
	or Eng. sä′-bəl	sah′-buhl
Les Salines (Tun.)	lĕ sä-lēn′	leh sah-leen′
Leszno (Pol.)	lĕsh′-nô	lesh′-no
Letarf (Alg.)	lə-tärf′	luh-tahrf′
lethal	lē′-thəl	lee′-thuhl
Avoid lē′-thôl [lee′-thol].		
Letpadan (Burma)	lĕp′-pə-dän′	lep′-puh-dahn′
Le Tréport (Fr.)	lə trĕ-pôr′	luh treh-por′
Leuca (It.)	lĕ′-o͝o-kä	leh′-u-kah
Leucate (Fr.)	lû-kät′	lœ-kaht′
Leukas (Gr.) See *Levkas.*		
Leuna Odendorf (Ger.)	loi′-nä ō′-dən-dôrf	loi′-nah oh′-duhn-dorf
Leuven (Belg.)	*Flem.* lû′-vən	lœ′-vuhn
French *Louvain*, q.v.		
Léva (Cz.) See *Levice.*		
Levač (Yugosl.)	lĕ′-väch	leh′-vahch
Levan (Alb.)	lĕ′-vän	leh′-vahn
Levanger (Nor.)	lĕ-väng′-ər	leh-vahng′-uhr
Levani (Alb.) See *Levan.*		
Levant	lə-vănt′	luh-vant′
Levanzo (It., isl.)	lĕ′-vän-tsô	leh′-vahn-tso
Leverano (It.)	lĕ-vĕ-rä′-nô	leh-veh-rah′-no
Leverkusen (Ger.)	lā′-vər-ko͞o′-zən	lay′-vuhr-koo′-zuhn
Levice (Cz.)	lĕ′-vĭ-tsĕ	leh′-vi-tseh
Hungarian *Léva*, lā′-vŏ [lay′-vo].		
Levitha (Dodec.)	lĕ-vē′-thä	leh-vee′-thah

Levkas (Gr.)	lĕf-käs′	lef-kahs′
English *Leucas*, lū′-kəs [lyoo′-kuhs].		
Levoča (Cz.)	lĕ′-vô-chä	leh′-vo-chah
Lewes (Del.)	lo͞o′-ĭs	loo′-is
A variant spelling of *Lewis*. A family name and the name of a town.		
Ley, Robert (Ger. leader)	lī′	lai′
Leye (Fr., Belg., riv.) See *Lys*.		
Leyte (P.I.)	lā′-tĕ	lay′-teh
Ležaky (Cz.)	lĕ′-zhä-kĭ	leh′-zhah-ki
Lgov (Rus.)	lgôf (lə-gôf′)	lgof (luh-gof′)
Lhasa (Tibet)	*Eng.* lă′-sə *or* lä′-sä	la′-suh *or* lah′-sah
Li (Ch., Hunan)	lē	lee
Liadromia (Gr., isl.) See *Alonesos*.		
Liakoura (Gr., mt.) See *Parnassus*.		
Liang-chow (Ch., Kansu)	lyäng-jō	lyahng-joh
Liano (Crete, point)	lyä-nô′	lyah-no′
Lianokladi (Gr.)	lē-ä-nô-klä′-*th*ē	lee-ah-no-klah′-*th*ee
Liao-ning (Manchu., prov.)	lyou-nĭng	lyau-ning
Lib (Oc.)	lēb′	leeb′
Liban (Syria) See *Lebanon*.		
Libau (Latvia)	*Ger.* lē′-bou	lee′-bau
Latvian *Liepāja*, q.v. Russian *Libava*, q.v.		
Libava (Latvia)	*Rus.* lĭ-bä′-vä	li-bah′-vah
Latvian *Liepāja*, q.v. German *Libau*, q.v.		
Liberec (Cz.)	lē′-bĕ-rĕts	lee′-beh-rets
Libnan (Syria) See *Lebanon*.		
Libohova (Alb.) See *Libohovë*.		
Libohovë (Alb.)	lē-bô′-hô-və	lee-bo′-ho-vuh
Greek *Limpokhovon*, lē-bô′-hô-vô(n) [lee-bo′-ho-vo(n)].		
Librazhd (Alb.)	lē′-bräzhd	lee′-brahzhd
Librazhdi (Alb.) See *Librazhd*.		
Licata (Sicily)	lē-kä′-tä	lee-kah′-tah
Li-ch'êng (Ch., Shantung)	lē-chŭng	lee-chuhng
Lichtenfels (Greenl.)	lĭk(h)′-tən-fĕls	lik(h)′-tuhn-fels
Li-ch'wan (Ch., Kiangsi)	lē-chwän	lee-chwahn
Licosa (It., cape)	lē-kô′-zä	lee-ko′-zah
Lida (Pol.)	lē′-dä	lee′-dah
Lidice (Cz.)	lē′-dĭ-tsĕ	lee′-di-tseh
Lido di Roma (It.)	lē′-dô dē rô′-mä	lee′-do dee ro′-mah
Near the ancient *Ostia*, q.v.		
Lie, Trygve (Nor. minister)	lē, trüg′-və	lee, trüg′-vuh

Liebeslied	lē′-bəs-lēt′	lee′-buhs-leet′

German meaning *love song*. *Lied*, song, must be distinguished from *Leid*, līt′ [lait′], sorrow.

Liechtenstein (principality)	*Eng.* lĭk′-tən-stīn *Ger.* lēk(h)′-tən-shtīn	lik′-tuhn-stain leek(h)′-tuhn-shtain
Lied, *pl.* Lieder (Ger.)	lēt′, lē′-dər	leet′, lee′-duhr

See *Liebeslied.*

Liége (Belg.)	*Fr.* lyĕzh′ *Eng.* lĭ-āzh′	lyezh′ li-ayzh′

Flemish *Luik*, lûĭk′ [lœik′].

Liegnitz (Ger.)	lēg′-nĭts	leeg′-nits
Lieksa (Fin.)	lē′-ĕk′-sä	lee′-ek′-sah
Lielupe (Latvia, riv.)	lē′-ĕ′-lo͝o-pĕ	lee′-eh′-lu-peh
Lien-hua (Ch., Kiangsi)	lyĕn-whä	lyen-whah
Lienz (Austria)	lĭ-ĕnts′	li-ents′
Liepāja (Latvia)	lē′-ĕ′-pä-yä	lee′-eh′-pah-yah

Russian *Libava*, q.v. German *Libau*, q.v.

Lier (Belg.)	lēr′	leer′

French *Lierre*, lyĕr′ [lyehr′].

Lier (Nor.)	lē′-ər	lee′-uhr
Lier, de (Neth.)	lēr′, də	leer′, duh
Liévin (Fr.)	lyĕ-văN′	lyeh-vaN′
Liffey (Ire., riv.)	lĭf′-ĭ	lif′-ĭ
Ligurian Sea	lĭ-gū′-rĭ-ən	li-gyoo′-ri-uhn
Lihir (Oc.)	lē′-hēr	lee′-heer
Liinahamari (Fin.)	lē′-nä-hä′-mä-rē	lee′-nah-hah′-mah-ree
Lijeva Rijeka (Yugosl.)	lē′-yĕ-vä rĭ-yĕ′-kä	lee′-yeh-vah ri-yeh′-kah
Likhaya (Rus.)	lĭ-hä′-yä	li-hah′-yah
Likhoslavl (Rus.)	lĭ-hŏ-slävl′(y)	li-ho-slahvl′(y)
Likhvin (Rus.)	lēk(h)′-vĭn	leek(h)′-vin
Likiep (Oc.)	lē′-kē-ĕp	lee′-kee-ep
Lilibeo (Sicily, cape)	lē-lē-bĕ′-ô	lee-lee-beh′-o

Also called *Boeo*, q.v.

Lille (Fr.)	lēl′	leel′
Lillebaelt (Den., sound)	lĭl′-ə-bĕlt	lil′-uh-belt
Lillehammer (Nor.)	lĭl′-ə-hä-mər	lil′-uh-hah-muhr
Lillesand (Nor.)	lĭl′-ə-sän	lil′-uh-sahn
Lillestroem *or* Lilleström (Nor.)	lĭl′-ə-strûm	lil′-uh-strœm
Lim (Yugosl., riv.)	lēm′	leem′
Lima, Mendonça (Braz. leader)	lē′-mə, mĕn-dôn′-sə	lee′-muh, men-don′-suh

Both names should be used, thus: *Mendonça Lima*, not *Lima* alone.

Limburg (Neth., prov.)	*Eng.* lĭm′-bûrg	lim′-buhrg
	Du. lĭm′-bûrk(h)	lim′-bœrk(h)
limen (Gr.)	lē-mēn′	lee-meen′

A common element, meaning *harbor*, in Greek place names.

Limen Setias (Crete)	lē-mēn′ sē-tē′-äs	lee-meen′ see-tee′-ahs
Lim Fjord (Den.)	lēm′	leem′
Limljani (Yugosl.)	lēm′-lyä-nĭ	leem′-lyah-ni
Limne (Gr., Euboea)	lēm′-nē	leem′-nee

A common element, meaning *lake*, in Greek place names.

Limoges (Fr.)	*Eng.* lĭ-mōzh′	li-mohzh′
	Fr. lē-môzh′	lee-mozh′
Limoux (Fr.)	lē-mo͞o′	lee-moo′
Lin-an (Ch., Chekiang)	lĭn-än	lin-ahn
Línao (P.I.)	lē′-nou	lee′-nau
Linares (Sp., Chile)	lē-nä′-rĕs	lee-nah′-res
Lin-ch'wan (Ch., Kiangsi)	lĭn-chwän	lin-chwahn
Lindesnes (Nor.)	lĭn′-dəs-nĕs	lin′-duhs-nes

Also called The *Naze*, nāz [nayz].

Línea, la (Sp.)	lē′-nĕ-ä, lä	lee′-neh-ah, lah
Lineinoye (Rus.)	lĭ-nā′-nŏ-yĕ	li-nay′-no-yeh
Lingayén (P.I.)	lĭng-gä-yĕn′	ling-gah-yen′
Ling-ch'uan (Ch., Shansi)	lĭng-chwän	ling-chwahn
Lingeh (Iran)	lĭng′-gĕ′	ling′-geh′
Linguaglossa (Sicily)	lēn-gwä-glôs′-sä	leen-gwah-glos′-sah
Linguetta, Capo (Alb. cape)	*It.* lĭn-gwĕt′-tä	lin-gwet′-tah

English *Glossa*, q.v. Albanian *Kep i Gjuhëzës* and *Karaburum*, q.v.

Lin-hsiang (Ch., Hunan)	lĭn-shyäng	lin-shyahng
Lin-hsien (Ch., Hopeh)	lĭn-shyĕn	lin-shyen
Linkomies, Edwin (Fin. leader)	lĭng′-kô-mē-ĕs, ĕd′-vĭn	ling′-ko-mee-es, ed′-vin
Linlithgow (Scot.)	lĭn-lĭth′-gō	lin-lith′-goh
linna	lĭn′-nä	lin′-nah

An element, meaning *fort* or *castle*, in Finnish place names.

Linosa (It., isl.)	lē-nô′-zä	lee-no′-zah
Lin Sên (Late Ch. Pres.)	lĭn sŭn	lin suhn
Linz (Austria)	lĭnts′	lints′
Liot (Oc.)	lē′-ôt	lee′-ot

Lious (Gr., isl.) See *Aigila*.

Lipá (P.I.)	lĭ-pä′	li-pah′
Lipari (Sicily, isls.)	*Eng.* lĭp′-ə-rē	lip′-uh-ree
	It. lē′-pä-rē	lee′-pah-ree

Italian *Isole Eolie*, q.v. A local pronunciation is reported, lĭ′-pä-rē [li′-pah-ree].

Lipcani (Rum.)	lēp-kän′	leep-kahn′
Russian *Lipkany*, lĭp-kä′-nĭ [lip-kah′-ni].		
Lipec (Yugosl.)	lē′-pĕts	lee′-pets
Lipljan (Yugosl.)	lēp′-lyän	leep′-lyahn
Lipolist (Yugosl.)	lē′-pô-lēst′	lee′-po-leest′
Lippe (Ger., riv.)	lĭp′-ə	lip′-uh
Lipsi (Dodec.) See *Lipsos*.		
Lipso(s) (Dodec.)	*Eng.* lĭp′-sō *or* lĭp′-sŏs	lip′-soh *or* lip′-sos
	Gr. lē-psô(s)′	lee-pso(s)′
Also called *Lisso*, lĭs′-sō [lis′-soh].		
liqen (Alb.)	lē-kyĕn′	lee-kyen′
An element, meaning *lake*, in Albanian place names. Look up the other part of the name.		
liqeni (Alb.) See *liqen*.		
Lisac (Yugosl., mt.)	lē′-säts	lee′-sahts
Lisboa (Port.)	lēzh-bô′-ə	leezh-bo′-uh
English *Lisbon*, q.v.		
Lisbon (Port., U.S.)	*Eng.* lĭz′-bən	liz′-buhn
Li-shih (Ch., Shansi)	lē-shû	lee-shuh
Li-shui (Ch., Chekiang)	lē-shwā	lee-shway
Lisichansk (Rus.)	lĭ-sĭ-chänsk′	li-si-chahnsk′
Lisieux (Fr.)	lē-zyü′	lee-zyœ′
Lisinj (Yugosl., mt.)	lē′-sĭn(y)	lee′-sin(y)
Liski (Rus.)	lēs′-kĭ	lees′-ki
Lismore (Austral.)	lĭz′-môr	liz′-mor
Lissa (Yugosl., isl.)	*It.* lēs′-sä	lees′-sah
Serb-Croat *Vis*, q.v.		
Lisso (Dodec.) See *Lipso*.		
Literno (It.)	lē-tĕr′-nô	lee-tehr′-no
Lithgow (Austral.)	lĭth′-gō	lith′-goh
Litija (Yugosl.)	lē′-tĭ-yä	lee′-ti-yah
Litoměřice (Cz.)	lē′-tô-myĕ′-rzhĭ-tsĕ	lee′-to-myeh′-rzhi-tseh
German *Leitmeritz*, q.v.		
Littoria (It.)	lēt-tô′-ryä	leet-to′-ryah
Litvinov, Maxim (Rus. leader)	lĭt-vē′-nŏf, mäk-sēm′	lit-vee′-nof, mahk-seem′
Liu-chow (Ch., Kwangsi)	lū-jō	lyoo-joh
Liu-wang-lou (Ch., Kiangsu)	lyō-wäng-lō	lyoh-wahng-loh
Livno (Yugosl.)	lēv′-nô	leev′-no
Livorno (It.)	lē-vôr′-nô	lee-vor′-no
English *Leghorn*, q.v.		

Livny (Rus.)	lēv′-nĭ	leev′-ni
Livry (Rus.)	lē′-vrĭ	lee′-vri
Ljig (Yugosl.)	lyēg′	lyeeg′
Ljubičevac (Yugosl.)	lū′-bē′-chĕ-väts	lyoo′-bee′-cheh-vahts
Ljubljana (Yugosl.)	lū′-blyä′-nä	lyoo′-blyah′-nah
German *Laibach*, q.v.		
Ljubljanica (Yugosl., riv.)	lū′-blyä′-nĭ-tsä	lyoo′-blyah′-ni-tsah
German *Laibach*, q.v.		
Ljubljanska (Yugosl.)	lū′-blyän′-skä	lyoo′-blyahn′-skah
Ljuboten (Yugosl., mt.)	lū′-bô-tĕn	lyoo′-bo-ten
Ljubovija (Yugosl.)	lū′-bô′-vĭ-yä	lyoo′-bo′-vi-yah
Ljubuški (Yugosl.)	lū′-bo͞o-shkĭ	lyoo′-boo-shki
Ljutomer (Yugosl.)	lū′-tô-mĕr	lyoo′-to-mehr
Llanafan (Wales)	län-ä′-vän	lahn-ah′-vahn
In Welsh *ll* is pronounced as a *voiceless l*, similar to a final *l* sound in French or to *hl*.		
Llandaff (Wales)	län′-däf	lahn′-dahf
Llanelly (Wales)	län-ĕ′-lĭ	lahn-eh′-li
Llanfaethlu (Anglesey)	län-vīth′-lĭ	lahn-vaith′-li
Llano (Tex.)	lăn′-ō	lan′-oh
Llixha (Alb.) See *Llixhë.*		
Llixhë (Alb.)	lē′-jə	lee′-juh
Lo-an (Ch., Kiangsi)	lô-än	lo-ahn
Lochem (Neth.)	lôk(h)′-əm	lok(h)′-uhm
Loches (Fr.)	lôsh′	losh′
Lo-chia-tu (Ch., Kwangtung)	lô-jyä-do͞o	lo-jyah-doo
Lodeinoe Pole (Rus.)	lŏ-dā′-nŏ-yĕ pô′-lĕ	lo-day′-no-yeh po′-leh
Lödingen (Nor.)	lû′-dĭng-ən	lœ′-ding-uhn
Łódź (Pol.)	lo͝odzh′	ludzh′
Russian *Lodz*, lôdz′ (lodz′].		
Loedingen (Nor.)	lû′-dĭng-ən	lœ′-ding-uhn
Loekken (Nor.)	lŭk′-kən	luhk′-kuhn
Loen (Nor.)	lō′-ən	loh′-uhn
Lofoten (Nor., isls.)	lō′-fo͝otn	loh′-futn
Lofthus (Nor.)	lôft′-ho͞os	loft′-hoos
Logothetopoulos, Constantinos (Gr. collab.)	lô-gô-thĕ-tô′-po͞o-lôs, kô(n)-stä(n)-dē′-nôs	lo-go-theh-to′-poo-los, ko(n)-stah(n)-dee′-nos
Logroño (Sp.)	lô-grô′-nyô	lo-gro′-nyo
Lohja (Fin.)	lô′-yä	lo′-yah
Lo-ho (Ch., Anhwei)	lô-hô	lo-ho
Loikaw (Burma)	loi′-kô′	loi′-kaw′
Loilem (Burma)	loi′-lĕm′	loi′-lem′

Loire (Fr., riv.)	lwär′	lwahr′
Lokeren (Belg.)	lō′-kə-rən	loh′-kuh-ruhn
Lokhvitsa (Rus.)	lôk(h)′-vĭ-tsä	lok(h)′-vi-tsah
Lökken (Nor.)	lŭk′-kən	luhk′-kuhn
Lokrum (Yugosl., isl.)	lô′-kro͞om	lo′-kroom
Italian *Lacroma*, q.v.		
Lolland (Den., isl. See *Laaland*.		
Lolobau (Oc.)	lô′-lô-bou	lo′-lo-bau
Lom (Bulg.)	lôm′	lom′
Lom (Nor.)	lo͞om′	lum′
Lombardo Toledano (Mex. leader)	lôm-bär′-dô tô-lĕ-dä′-nô	lom-bahr′-do to-leh-dah′-no
Lombok (NEI)	lŏm-bŏk′	lom-bok′
Łomża (Pol.)	lôm′-zhä	lom′-zhah
Russian spelling *Lomzha*.		
Lomzha (Pol.) See *Łomża*.		
Longa (Gr.)	lông-gä′	long-gah′
Longos (Gr., pen.)	lông′-gôs	long′-gos
Also called *Sithonia*, sē-thô-nē′-ä [see-tho-nee′-ah].		
Longwy (Fr.)	lôN-wē′	lawN-wee′
Longxuyen (Indo-Ch.)	lŭm-swĭn′	luhm-swin′
	Thai lôŭm-swēn′	lo-uhm-sween′
Loo, Het (Neth.)	lō′, hĕt	loh′, het
Loochoo (Jap.) See *Okinawa Gunto*.		
Loparskaya (Rus.)	lŏ-pär′-skä-yä	lo-pahr′-skah-yah
Lopatka (Rus., cape)	lŏ-pät′-kä	lo-paht′-kah
Lopburi (Thai)	lōp′-bo͞o-rē′	lohp′-bu-ree′
Lopes, Simões (Braz. leader)	lô′-pĭs, sē-moiNs′	lo′-pis, see-moiNs′
Both names should be used, thus: *Simões Lopes*, not *Lopes* alone.		
López, Alfonso (Col. leader)	lô′-pĕs, äl-fôn′-sô	lo′-pes, ahl-fon′-so
Lo-p'ing (Ch., Kiangsi)	lô-pĭng	lo-ping
Lopud (Yugosl., isl.)	lô′-po͞od	lo′-pood
Italian *Mezzo*, q.v.		
Lorca (Sp.)	lôr′-kä	lor′-kah
Lorient (Fr.)	lô-ryäN′	lo-ryahN′
Lorungau (Oc.)	lô-ro͞ong-ou′	lo-roong-au′
Also called *Lorengau*, lô-rĕng-ou′ [lo-reng-au′].		
Los Angeles (Calif.)	lŏs *or* lōs ăng′-gə-ləs	los *or* lohs ang′-guh-luhs
	or lŏs ăn′-jə-ləs	los an′-juh-luhs
	or -lēz	-leez

Thorndike Century (1941), Holt (1938), and the Columbia Encyclopedia (1935) prefer lŏs (*not* lōs) ăng′-gə-ləs; but Webster's (1934) prefers lōs. The Standard prefers lŏs ăn′-jə-lēz. The pronunciation in the city itself is far from settled. The Spanish is lôs äng′-hĕ-lĕs [los ahng′-heh-les].

Losap (Oc.)	lô′-säp	lo′-sahp
Lo-shan (Ch., Honan)	lô-shän	lo-shahn
Lošinj (It., isl.)	*S.-C.* lô′-shĭn(y)	lo′-shin(y)
Italian *Lussino*, q.v.		
Los Negros (Oc.)	lôs nĕ′-grôs	los neh′-gros
Losoncz (Cz.) See *Lučenec.*		
Los Reyes (Oc.)	lôs rĕ′-yĕs	los reh′-yes
Lot (Fr., riv.)	lôt′	lot′
Lou (Oc.)	lō′	loh′
Louisiade (Oc., isls.)	lo͞o-ē′-zĭ-ăd′	loo-ee′-zi-ad′
Lourenço Marques (Mozambique, Afr.)	*Eng.* lō-rĕn′-sō mär′-kĕs	loh-ren′-soh mahr′-kes
	Port. lô-rĕN′-so͝o mär′-kĕzh	lo-reN′-su mahr′-kezh
Louros (Gr.)	lo͞o′-rôs	loo′-ros
Loutra (Gr., Lesbos)	lo͞o-trä′	loo-trah′
A common element, meaning *baths*, in Greek place names.		
Loutron (Crete)	lo͞o-trô(n)′	loo-tro(n)′
Loutros (Gr.)	lo͞o-trôs′	loo-tros′
Loutsa (Gr.)	lo͞o′-tsä	loo′-tsah
Louvain (Belg.)	*Eng.* lo͞o-vān′	loo-vayn′
	Fr. lo͞o-văN′	loo-vaN′
Flemish *Leuven*, q.v.		
Louvaris (Gr. collab.)	lo͞o′-vä-rēs	loo′-vah-rees
Lovćen (Yugosl., mt.)	lôv′-chĕn	lov′-chen
Lovech (Bulg.)	lô′-vĕch	lo′-vech
Lovich (Pol.) See *Łowicz.*		
Lovisa *or* Loviisa (Fin.)	lô′-vē-sä	lo′-vee-sah
The length of the second vowel may give the effect of an accent.		
Lowestoft (Eng.)	lōs′-tŏft *or* lōs′-təf	lohs′-toft *or* lohs′-tuhf
Łowicz (Pol.)	lô′-vĭch	lo′-vich
Russian spelling *Lovich.*		
Lo-yang (Ch., Honan)	lô-yäng	lo-yahng
Also called *Honanfu*, q.v.		
Lož (Yugosl.)	lôzh′	lozh′
German *Laas.*		
Loznica (Yugosl.)	lôz′-nĭ-tsä	loz′-ni-tsah
Lozovaya (Rus.)	lŏ-zŏ-vä′-yä	lo-zo-vah′-yah
Lozovik (Yugosl.)	lô′-zô-vĭk	lo′-zo-vik
Lozovsky (Rus.)	lŏ-zôf′-skĭ	lo-zof′-ski

luang	lwäng′	lwahng′
A Thai title. Look up the other part of the name.		
Luang Prabang (Indo-Ch.)	lwäng′ prə-bäng′	lwahng′ pruh-bahng′
Lubānas (Latvia)	lo͝o-bä-näs	lu′-bah-nahs
Lubartów (Pol.)	lo͝o-bär′-to͝of	lu-bahr′-tuf
Russian *Lyubartov*, lū-bär′-tŏf [lyoo-bahr′-tof].		
Lübeck (Ger.) See *Luebeck*.		
Lubiana (Yugosl.)	*It.* lo͞o-bē-ä′-nä	loo-bee-ah′-nah
Serb-Croat *Ljubljana*, q.v.		
Lublin (Pol.)	lyo͝o′-blĭn	lyu′-blin
Russian *Lyublin*, lū′-blĭn [lyoo′-blin].		
Lubny (Rus.)	lo͞ob′-nĭ	loob′-ni
Luboml (Pol.)	lyo͝o-bôml′(y)	lyu-boml′(y)
Russian spelling *Lyuboml*.		
Lubuagan (P.I.)	lo͞o-bwä′-gän	loo-bwah′-gahn
Lucca (It.)	lo͞ok′-kä	look′-kah
Lucch (Libya)	lo͝ok(h)′	luk(h)′
Luce, Clare Boothe (U.S. representative)	lo͞os′	loos′
Lucena (P.I.)	lo͞o-thĕ′-nä- *or* -sĕ′-	loo-theh′-nah *or* -seh′-
Lučenec (Cz.)	lo͞o′-chĕ-nĕts	loo′-cheh-nets
Hungarian *Losoncz*, lô′-shônts [lo′-shonts].		
Lu-chow (Ch., Anhwei)	*Eng.* lo͞o-chou	loo-chau
	Ch. lo͞o-jō	loo-joh
Also called *Ho-fei*.		
Lucia (Sicily)	lo͞o-chē′-ä	loo-chee′-ah
Lučica (Yugosl.)	lo͞o′-chĭ-tsä	loo′-chi-tsah
Lucien (Fr.)	lü-syĕN′	lü-syeN′
Łuck (Pol.)	lo͞otsk′	lootsk′
Russian spelling *Lutsk*.		
Lucknow (India)	lŭk′-nou	luhk′-nau
Ludbreg (Yugosl.)	lo͞od′-brĕg	lood′-breg
Ludwigshafen (Ger.)	lo͝od′-vĭk(h)s-hä′-fən	lud′-vik(h)s-hah′-fuhn
Ludze (Latvia)	lo͝od′-zĕ	lud′-zeh
Russian *Luzen*, q.v.		
Luebeck *or* Lübeck (Ger.)	*Eng.* lū′-bĕk′	lyoo′-bek′
	Ger. lü′-bĕk	lü′-bek
Lu-fêng (Ch., Kwangtung)	lo͞o-fŭng	loo-fuhng
Luftwaffe	lo͝oft′-väf-ə	luft′-vahf-uh
German word meaning *air force*.		

Ług (Pol., riv.)	lo͞ok′	look′
Russian *Luga*, lo͞o′-gä [loo′-gah].		
Luga (Rus., riv.)	lo͞o′-gä	loo′-gah
Lugavčina (Yugosl.)	lo͞o′-gäv′-chĭ-nä	loo′-gahv′-chi-nah
Lugo (Sp.)	lo͞o′-gô	loo′-go
Lugoj (Rum.)	lo͝o′-gôzh	lu′-gozh
Hungarian *Lugos*, lo͝o′-gôsh [lu′-gosh].		
Lugomir (Yugosl., riv.)	lo͞o′-gô-mĭr	loo′-go-mihr
Luik (Belg.) See *Liége*.		
Luino (It.)	lwē′-nô	lwee′-no
Luizet, Charles (Fr. leader)	lwē-zĕ′, shärl′	lwee-zeh′, shahrl′
Lu-k'ou (Ch., Hunan)	lo͞o-kō	loo-koh
Lukovica (Balkan riv.)	*S.-C.* lo͞o′-kô-vĭ-tsä	loo′-ko-vi-tsah
Lukovo (Yugosl.)	lo͞o′-kô-vô	loo′-ko-vo
Łuków (Pol.)	lo͝o′-ko͝of	lu′-kuf
Russian *Lukov*, lo͞o′-kŏf [loo′-kof].		
Luleaa (Sw.)	lü′-lĕ-ō	lü′-leh-oh
Lüleburgaz (Turk.)	lü-lĕ′-bo͝or-gäz	lü-leh′-bur-gahz
lum (Alb.)	lo͞om′	loom′
An element, meaning *river*, in Albanian place names. Look up the other part of the name.		
Luma (Alb.) See *Lumë*.		
Lumë (Alb.)	lo͞o′-mə	loo′-muh
lumi (Alb.) See *lum*.		
Lund (Sw.)	lo͝ond′	lund′
Lunde (Nor.)	lo͝on′-də	lun′-duh
Lunel (Fr.)	lü-nĕl′	lü-nel′
Lunga (Oc., point)	lo͞ong′-ä	loong′-ah
Americanized as lo͞ong′-gä [loong′-gah].		
Lung-ch'i (Ch., Fukien)	lo͝ong-chē	lung-chee
Also called *Lung-ki*, q.v.		
Lung-chiang (Manchu.) See *Tsitsihar*.		
Lung-ch'üan (Ch., Chekiang)	lo͝ong-chüän	lung-chü-ahn
Lung-ki (Ch., Fukien)	lo͝ong-kē	lung-kee
Also called *Lung-ch'i*, q.v.		
Lung-kow (Ch., Shantung)	*Eng.* lo͝ong-kou *Ch.* lo͝ong-kō	lung-kau lung-koh
Lung-ling (Ch., Yünnan)	lo͝ong-lĭng	lung-ling
Lung-nan (Ch., Kiangsi)	lo͝ong-nän	lung-nahn
Lung-yu (Ch., Chekiang)	lo͝ong-yo͞o	lung-yoo
Łuniniec (Pol.)	lo͝o-nē′-nyĕts	lu-nee′-nyets

Lur (Per. tribe	lo͞or′	loor′
Lushnja (Alb.) See) *Lushnje.*		
Lushnje (Alb.)	lo͞osh′-nyĕ	loosh′-nyeh
Serb-Croat *Lušnje.*		
Lussino (It., isl.)	lo͞os-sē′-nô	loos-see′-no
Serb-Croat *Lošinj,* q.v.		
Luštica (Yugosl.)	lo͞o′-shtĭ-tsä	loo′-shti-tsah
Lutsk (Pol.) See *Łuck.*		
Lützen (Ger.)	lüt′-sən	lüt′-suhn
Luxembourg	*Fr.* lük-säN-bo͞or′	lük-sahN-boor′
English *Luxemburg,* q.v.		
Luxemburg	*Eng.* lŭk′-səm-bûrg	luhk′-suhm-buhrg
	Ger. lo͝ok′-səm-bo͝ork(h)	luk′-suhm-burk(h)
French *Luxembourg,* q.v.		
luxurious	lŭg-zho͝or′-rĭ-əs	luhg-zhur′-ri-uhs
	or lŭks-ū′-rĭ-əs	luhks-yoo′-ri-uhs
luxury	lŭk′-sho͝o-rĭ	luhk′-shu-ri
The pronunciation lŭg′-sho͝o-rĭ [luhg′-shu-ri] is not recommended.		
Lužane (Yugosl.)	lo͞o′-zhä-nĕ	loo′-zhah-neh
Luzen (Latvia)	*Rus.* lū′-tsĕn	lyoo′-tsen
Latvian *Ludze,* q.v.		
Luzón (P.I.)	*Eng.* lo͞o-zŏn′	loo-zon′
	Sp. lo͞o-sôn′	loo-son′
Lwów (Pol.)	lvo͞of′	lvoof′
Russian *Lvov,* lvôf′ [lvof′]. German *Lemberg,* (Eng.) lĕm′-bûrg [lem′-buhrg], (Ger.) lĕm′-bĕrk(h) [lem′-behrk(h)].		
Lyangra (Rus.)	lyän-grä′	lyahn-grah′
Lyautey (Mor.)	*Eng.* lē-ō-tā′	lee-oh-tay′
Named after the French marshal, lyō-tĕ′ [lyoh-teh′].		
Lyck (Ger.)	lĭk′	lik′
Lyon (Fr.)	lyôN′	lyoN′
English *Lyons,* q.v.		
Lyons (Fr.)	*Eng.* lī′-ənz	lai′-uhnz
For the French City, the French form *Lyon,* q.v., is more common even in English contexts. The English form occurs as an American name.		
Lys (Fr., Belg., riv.)	lēs′	lees′
Flemish *Leye,* lī′-ə [lai′-uh].		
Lysaker (Nor.)	lüs′-ä-kər	lüs′-ah-kuhr
Lysefjord (Nor.)	lü′-sə-fyōr	lü′-suh-fyohr
Lysekloster (Nor.)	lü′-sə-klôs-tər	lü′-suh-klos-tuhr
Lysenko (Rus. scientist)	lĭ-sĕn′-kŏ	li-sen′-ko

Lysk (Ger.)	lĭsk′	lisk′
Lyubartov (Pol.) See *Lubartów.*		
Lyublin (Pol.) See *Lublin.*		
Lyuboml (Pol.) See *Luboml.*		
Lyubytino (Rus.)	lū-bwē′-tĭ-nŏ	lyoo-bwee′-ti-no
Lyudinovo (Rus.)	lū-dē′-nŏ-vŏ	lyoo-dee′-no-vo
Maaloey *or* Maalöy (Nor.)	môl′-ûĭ	mol′-œi
Maarianhamina (Fin.)	mä′-rē-än-hä′-mē-nä	mah′-ree-ahn-hah′-mee-nah
Swedish *Mariehamn,* q.v.		
Maas (Europ. riv.)	*Du., Flem.* mäs′	mahs′
French *Meuse,* q.v. See also *Nieuwe Maas, Oude Maas,* and *Merwede.*		
Maas, Melvin J. (U.S. representative)	mäs′	mahs′
Maasälkä (Fin., isth.)	mä′-săl-kă	mah′-sel-keh
Maaten Bagush (Egypt)	mä′-tĕn bä-gōōsh′	mah′-ten bah-goosh′
Mabtouha, el (Tun.)	məb-tōō′-hə, ĕl	muhb-too′-huh, el
Macao (Ch., Kwangtung, Port. col.)	mə-kou′	muh-kau′
Macchia (It.)	mäk′-kyä	mahk′-kyah
Macedonia (Bulg., Gr., Yugosl.)	*Eng.* măs-ĭ-dō′-nyə	mas-i-doh′-nyuh
Bulgarian *Makedoniya,* mä-kĕ-dô′-nē-yä [mah-keh-do′-nee-yah]. Greek *Makedonea,* mä-kĕ-*th*ô-nē′-ä [mah-keh-*th*o-nee′-ah]. Serb-Croat *Maćedonija,* mä′-chĕ-dô′-nē-yä [mah′-cheh-do′-nee-yah].		
Maceió (Brazil)	mä-sā-ô′	mah-say-o′
Macerata (It.)	mä-chĕ-rä′-tä	mah-cheh-rah′-tah
Machichaco (Sp., cape)	mä-chē-chä′-kô	mah-chee-chah′-ko
machination	măk′-ĭ-nā′-shən	mak′-i-nay′-shuhn
Maciejowice (Pol.)	mä-chĕ-yô-vē′-tsĕ	mah-cheh-yo-vee′-tseh
Russian *Matseyevitse,* mä-tsĕ-yĕ′-vĭ-tsĕ [mah-tseh-yeh′-vi-tseh].		
Mâcon (Fr.)	mä-kôN′	mah-koN′
Mačva (Yugosl.)	mäch′-vä	mahch′-vah
Madagascar (Afr., isl.)	măd′-ə-găs′-kər	mad′-uh-gas′-kuhr
In English usage, though not in French, the final syllable is better -kər than -kär.		
madame	*Eng.* măd′-əm	mad′-uhm
	Fr. mä-däm′	mah-dahm′
In English contexts, the English pronunciation should be used. For the plural, however, even in English contexts, *madams* is probably less common than *mesdames,* pronounced mĕ-däm′ [meh-dahm′].		

Madang (New Guinea)	mä′-däng	mah′-dahng
Maddalena (Libya)	mäd-dä-lĕ′-nä	mahd-dah-leh′-nah
Maddalena, la (Sard.)	mä-dä-lĕ′-nä, lä	mah-dah-leh′-nah, lah
Madeira (Port., isl.)	*Eng.* mə-dĭr′-ə	muh-dihr′-uh
	Port. mä-dā′-rə	mah-day′-ruh
Madhe, Fand i (Alb., riv.)	mä′-*th*ĕ, fänd′ ē	mah′-*th*eh, fahnd′ ee
The larger tributary of the *Mat*, q.v.		
Madioen *or* Madyun (NEI)	mä′-jōōn′	mah′-joon′
Madjene *or* Madyene (NEI)	mä-jĕ′-nĕ	mah-jeh′-neh
Madoera *or* Madura (NEI)	mä-dōō′-rä	mah-doo′-rah
Madras (India)	mə-drăs′ *or* -dräs′	muh-dras′ *or* -drahs′
Madrid (Sp.)	*Eng.* mə-drĭd′	muh-drid′
	Sp. mä-*th*rē′	mah-*th*ree′
Madura (India)	mă′-jŏŏ-rə	ma′-ju-ruh
Madyene (NEI) See *Madjene.*		
Madyun (NEI) See *Madioen.*		
Mæl (Nor.)	măl′	mal′
Mærtha (Crown Princess of Norway) English *Martha.*	măr′-tä	mehr′-tah
Maganik (Yugosl., mts.)	mä′-gä-nĭk	mah′-gah-nik
Magdagachi (Rus.)	mäg-dä-gä′-chĭ	mahg-dah-gah′-chi
Magdeburg (Ger.)	*Eng.* măg′-də-bûrg	mag′-duh-buhrg
	Ger. mäg′-də-bŏŏrk(h)	mahg′-duh-burk(h)
Magelang (NEI)	mä-gə-läng′	mah-guh-lahng′
Maggiore (It.)	mäd-jô′-rĕ	mahd-jo′-reh
Magiadag (Gr.) See *Phanos.*		
Maglaj (Yugosl.)	mä′-glī	mah′-glai
Maglić (Yugosl., mts.)	mä′-glĭch	mah′-glich
Magnitogorsk (Rus.)	mäg-nĭ-tŏ-gôrsk′	mahg-ni-to-gorsk′
Magnor (Nor.)	mäng′-nōr	mahng′-nohr
Magnuson, Warren G. (U.S. representative)	măg′-nə-sən	mag′-nuh-suhn
Magoffin (Ky.)	mə-gŏf′-ĭn	muh-gof′-in
Magresina (Yugosl., isl.) Serb-Croat *Planik*, q.v.	*It.* mä-grĕ-sē′-nä	mah-greh-see′-nah
Magusaiai (Oc.)	mä-gōō-sī′-ī	mah-goo-sai′-ai
Magwe (Burma)	mə-gwā′	muh-gway′
Magyar	*Hung.* mŏ′-dyŏr	mo′-dyor
	Eng. măg′-yär	mag′-yahr

Magyaróvár (Hung.)	mŏ′-dyŏr-ô′-vär	mo′-dyor-o′-vahr
Mahan, Alfred Thayer (U.S. admiral)	mə-hăn′	muh-han′
Mahares (Tun.)	mə-hä-rĕs′	muh-hah-res′
Mahalla el Kubra (Egypt)	mə-häl′-lə ĕl kōō′-brə	muh-hahl′-luh el koo′-bruh
Mahanadi (India, riv.)	mə-hä′-nŭ′-dĭ	muh-hah′-nuh′-di
maharajah	*Eng.* mä′-hä-rä′-jə	mah′-hah-rah′-juh
	Sans. mə-hä′-rä′-jə	muh-hah′-rah′-juh
Mahdia (Tun.)	mä-dē′-yä	mah-dee′-yah
Also called *Mahedia*, mä-hə-dē′-yä [mah-huh-dee′-yah].		
Mahé (Fr. India)	mä-ĕ′	mah-eh′
Mahedia (Tun.) See *Mahdia.*		
Mahige (Oc.)	mä-hē′-gĕ	mah-hee′-geh
Mahon, George (U.S. representative)	mā′-hŏn′	may′-hon′
Mahouin (Tun.)	mä-whēn′	mah-wheen′
Mahur (Oc.)	mä-hōōr′	mah-hoor′
Maidan-i-Naftun (Iran)	mā-dän′-ē-năft′-ōōn	may-dahn′-ee-naft′-oon
Maikop (Rus.)	mī-kôp′	mai-kop′
Maintirano (Madag.)	mīn′-tē-rä′-nô	main′-tee-rah′-no
Mainz (Ger.)	mīnts′	maints′
An English pronunciation, mānts′ [maynts′], is not recommended.		
Maiori (It.)	mä-yô′-rē	mah-yo′-ree
Maipo (Chile)	mī′-pô	mai′-po
Also called *Maipu,* mī′-pōō [mai′-poo].		
Maipu (Arg.)	mī′-pōō	mai′-poo
Maisky, Ivan M. (Rus. leader)	mī′-skĭ, ē-vän′	mai′-ski, ee-vahn′
Maisi (Cuba)	mī′-sē	mai′-see
Maizuru (Jap.)	mī-zōō-rōō	mai-zoo-roo
Maja Streoc (Yugosl.)	mä′-yä strĕ′-ôts	mah′-yah streh′-ots
Majdanpek (Yugosl.)	mī′-dän-pĕk′	mai′-dahn-pek′
Majella (It., mts.)	mä-yĕl′-lä	mah-yel′-lah
Majilovac (Yugosl.)	mī′-yĭ′-lô-väts	mai′-yi′-lo-vahts
Majlis (Per. parliament)	məj-lĭs′	muhj-lis′
Majo (It., mt.)	mä′-yô	mah′-yo
Majorca (Sp.)	*Eng.* mə-jôr′-kə	muh-jor′-kuh
Spanish *Mallorca,* q.v.		
Majunga (Madag.)	mə-jŭng′-gä	muh-juhng′-gah
Majuro (Oc.)	mä-jōō′-rô	mah-joo′-ro
Makada (Oc.)	mä-kä-dä′	mah-kah-dah′

Makarovo (Rus.)	mä-kä′-rŏ-vŏ	mah-kah′-ro-vo
Makarska (Yugosl.)	mä′-kär-skä	mah′-kahr-skah
Makassar (NEI)	*Eng.* mə-kăs′-ər	muh-kas′-uhr
Makci (Yugosl.)	mäk′-tsĭ	mahk′-tsi
Makedonea (Gr.) See *Macedonia.*		
Makeevka (Rus.)	mä-kĕ′-yĕf-kä	mah-keh′-yef-kah
Makhach Kala (Rus.)	mä-häch′ kä-lä′	mah-hahch′ kah-lah′
Makin (Oc.)	mä′-kĭn	mah′-kin

This name could be English with the pronunciation mā′-kĭn [may′-kin]. The U.S. Board on Geographical Names has kindly informed me that it is probably a native name. Even so, it may still become known to English speakers as mā′-kĭn [may′-kin].

Makkum (Neth.)	mäk′-əm	mahk′-uhm
Maknassy (Tun.)	mək-näs′-sĭ	muhk-nahs′-si
Maknine (Tun.)	mək-nēn′	muhk-neen′
Makó (Hung.)	mŏ′-kô	mo′-ko
Makoshino (Rus.)	mä-kô′-shĭ-nŏ	mah-ko′-shi-no
Makou (Iran)	mä-ko͞o′	mah-koo′
Makovo (Rus.)	mä′-kŏ-vŏ	mah′-ko-vo
Makreteikhos (Crete)	mä-krē′-tē-hôs	mah-kree′-tee-hos
Makršane (Yugosl.)	mä′-kər′-shä-nĕ	mah′-kuhr′-shah-neh
Makrysgialos (Crete, bay)	mä-krēs′-yä-lôs′	mah-krees′-yah-los′
Maksatikha (Rus.)	mäk-sä-tē′-hä	mahk-sah-tee′-hah
Maktar (Tun.)	mŭk′-tär	muhk′-tahr
mal (Alb.)	mäl′	mahl′

An element, meaning *mountain*, in Albanian place names. Look up the other part of the name.

mala, -li, -lo	mä′-lä, -lĭ, -lô	mah′-lah, -li, -lo

An element, meaning *little*, in Slavic place names. It may be necessary to look up the other part of the name.

Malacca (Malay)	*Eng.* mə-lăk′-ə	muh-lak′-uh
Málaga (Sp.)	*Eng.* măl′-ə-gə	mal′-uh-guh
	Sp. mä′-lä-gä	mah′-lah-gah
Malagasy (Madag.)	*Eng.* măl′-ə-găs′-ĭ	mal′-uh-gas′-i
Malaita (Oc.)	mä-lĕ′-tä	mah-leh′-tah
Malakal (Oc.)	mä′-lä-käl	mah′-lah-kahl
Malang (NEI)	mä-läng′	mah-lahng′
Malapa (Oc.)	mä-lä′-pä	mah-lah′-pah
Malaya Vishera (Rus.)	mä′-lä-yä vē′-shĕ-rä	mah′-lah-yah vee′-sheh-rah
Malče (Yugosl.)	mäl′-chĕ	mahl′-cheh
Maldive (Ceylon, isls.)	măl′-dīv	mal′-daiv
Malea (Crete, gulf)	mä′-lē-ä	mah′-lee-ah

Maleas (Gr., cape)	mä-lĕ′-ä(s) *or* mä-lyä(s)′	mah-leh′-ah(s) mah-lyah(s)′
Also called *Kavomalias*, q.v.		
Maleme (Crete)	mä′-lĕ-mĕ	mah′-leh-meh
Maleš (Yugosl.)	mä′-lĕsh	mah′-lesh
Maletto (Sicily)	mä-lĕt′-tô	mah-let′-to
mali (Alb.) See *mal.*		
Mali Kvarner (Yugosl., It., channel)	mä′-lĭ kvär′-nĕr	mah′-li kvahr′-nehr
Italian *Quarnerolo*, q.v.		
Malin (Rus.)	mä′-lĭn	mah′-lin
Malindang (P.I.)	mä-lĭn-däng′	mah-lin-dahng′
Malines (Belg.)	*Fr.* mä-lēn′ *Eng.* mə-lēnz′	mah-leen′ muh-leenz′
Flemish *Mechelen*, q.v.		
Maliq (Alb., lake)	*Eng.* mä′-lēk	mah′-leek
Albanian *Liqen(i) i Maliqit*, lē-kyĕn′ ē mä-lē′-kyēt [lee-kyen′ ee mah-lee′-kyeet].		
Małkinia (Pol.)	mäl-kē′-nyä	mahl-kee′-nyah
Russian *Malkin*, mäl′-kĭn [mahl′-kin].		
Malko Tarnovo (Bulg.)	mäl′-kŏ tär′-nŏ-vŏ	mahl′-ko tahr′-no-vo
Mallawi (Egypt)	məl-lä′-wē	muhl-lah′-wee
Also spelled *Mellawi.*		
Mallorca (Sp.)	mä-lyôr′-kä *or* -yôr-	mah-lyor′-kah *or* -yor-
English *Majorca*, q.v.		
Malmédy (Belg.)	mäl-mĕ-dē′	mahl-meh-dee′
Malmoe *or* Malmö (Sw.)	*Eng.* măl′-mō *Sw.* mälm′-û′	mal′-moh mahlm′-œ′
Malmyzh (Rus.)	mäl-mwēsh′	mahl-mweesh′
Malo Arkhangelsk (Rus.)	mä′-lŏ är-hän′-gĕlsk	mah′-lo ahr-hahn′-gelsk
Maloelap (Oc.)	mä′-lô-ĕ-läp′	mah′-lo-eh-lahp′
Malolo (Oc.)	mä-lô′-lô	mah-lo′-lo
Malolos (P.I.)	mä-lô′-lôs	mah-lo′-los
Malona (Dodec., Rh.)	mä-lô′-nä	mah-lo′-nah
Maloney, Paul H. (U.S. representative)	mə-lō′-nĭ	muh-loh′-ni
Malošište (Yugosl.)	mä′-lô-shĭ-shtĕ	mah′-lo-shi-shteh
Malo Tymovsk (Rus.)	mä′-lŏ twē′-mŏfsk	mah′-lo twee′-mofsk
Maloyaroslavets (Rus.)	mä′-lŏ-yä-rŏ-slä′-vĕts	mah′-lo-yah-ro-slah′-vets
Malum (Oc.)	mä′-lo͞om	mah′-loom
Mamberamo (NEI)	mäm-bĕ-rä′-mô	mahm-beh-rah′-mo

Ma-mien-kwan (Ch., Yünnan)	mä-myĕn-gwän	mah-myen-gwahn
Mamison (Rus., pass)	mä-mĭ-sôn′	mah-mi-son′
Mammola (It.)	mäm′-mô-lä	mahm′-mo-lah
Ma-mo-i (Ch., Fukien)	mä-mô-ē	mah-mo-ee
Manado (NEI)	mä-nä′-dō	mah-nah′-doh
Manakara (Madag.)	mä′-nə-kä′-rə	mah′-nuh-kah′-ruh
Manakwari (NEI)	mä-nä-kwä′-rē	mah-nah-kwah′-ree
Manam (New Guinea, isl.)	mä′-näm	mah′-nahm
Mananjary (Madag.)	mä′-nän-zhä′-rē	mah′-nahn-zhah′-ree
Manaoba (Oc.)	mä-nä-ô′-bä	mah-nah-o′-bah
Manasco, Carter (U.S. representative)	mə-năs′-kō	muh-nas′-koh
Manastir (Yugosl.) See *Monastir*.		
Manastir Morački (Yugosl.)	mä′-nä-stĭr mô′-räch-kĭ	mah′-nah-stihr mo′-rahch-ki
Manaus *or* Manáos (Brazil)	mä-nous′	mah-naus′
Manay (P.I.)	mä-nī′	mah-nai′
Manche (Fr., prov.)	mäNsh′	mahNsh′
Man-chu-k'uo (Manchu state)	*Eng.* măn-chōō-kwō *Ch.* män-jō-kwô	man-choo-kwoh mahn-joh-kwo
Man-ch'u-li (Manchu.)	män-chōō-lē	mahn-choo-lee
Mandakas, Manolis (Gr. leader)	män′-dä-käs, mä-nô′-lēs	mahn′-dah-kahs, mah-no′-lees
Mandal (Nor.)	män′-däl	mahn′-dahl
Mandalay (Burma)	măn′-də-lā′	man′-duh-lay′
Mandoliana (Oc.)	män-dô-lē-ä′-nä	mahn-do-lee-ah′-nah
Manduria (It.)	män-dōō′-ryä	mahn-doo′-ryah
Manfredonia (It.)	män-frĕ-dô′-nyä	mahn-freh-do′-nyah
Mangalia (Rum.)	män-gä′-lyä	mahn-gah′-lyah
Mangareva (Oc.)	mäng′-ä-rĕ′-vä	mahng′-ah-reh′-vah
Maniadakis (Gr. name)	mä-nyä-*th*ä′-kēs	mah-nyah-*th*ah′-kees
Manila (P.I.)	*Eng.* mə-nĭl′-ə	muh-nil′-uh
Tagalog mī-nē′-lä [mai-nee′-lah]. Spanish mä-nē′-lä [mah-nee′-lah].		
Manisa (Turk.)	mä′-nĭ-sä	mah′-ni-sah
Mankovo (Rus.)	män′(y)-kŏ-vŏ	mahn′(y)-ko-vo
Mannar (India, gulf)	măn-när′ *or* mə-när′	man-nahr′ *or* muh-nahr′
Mannheim (Ger.)	män′-hīm	mahn′-haim
Manouba (Tun.)	mə-nōō′-bä	muh-noo′-bah
Mans, le (Fr.)	mäN′, lə	mahN′, luh

Mansura, el (Egypt)	män-so͞o′-rä, ĕl	mahn-soo′-rah, el
Mansur (Libya)	män-so͝or′	mahn-sur′
Mantova (It.) See *Mantua.*		
Mantsurov (Rus.)	män-tso͞o′-rŏf	mahn-tsoo′-rof
Mantua (It.)	*Eng.* măn′-tū-ə	man′-tyoo-uh
Italian *Mantova,* män′-tô-vä [mahn′-to-vah].		
Mantzavinos, Georgios (Gr. leader)	män-dzä-vē′-nôs, yôr′-yôs	mahn-dzah-vee′-nos, yor′-yos
Manu (Oc.)	mä′-no͞o	mah′-noo
Manus (Oc.)	mä′-no͞os	mah′-noos
Manych (Rus., riv.)	mä-nwēch′	mah-nweech′
Maori (N.Z.)	mou′-rĭ *or* mä′-ô-rē	mau′-ri *or* mah′-o-ree
Mao Tsê-tung (Ch. general)	mou dzŭ-do͝ong	mau dzuh-dung
Maou, el (Tun.)	mou′, ĕl	mau′, el
Mapia (NEI)	mä′-pĭ-ə	mah′-pi-uh
Maracaibo (Ven.)	mä-rä-kī′-bô	mah-rah-kai′-bo
Maraghi (Egypt. leader)	mä-rä′-gē	mah-rah′-gee
Marakei (Oc.)	mä-rä′-kā	mah-rah′-kay
Maramasike (Oc.)	mä-rä-mä-sē′-kĕ	mah-rah-mah-see′-keh
Maranajt (Alb., mt.)	mä-rä′-nīt	mah-rah′-nait
Maranhão (Brazil)	mä-rə-nyouN′	mah-ruh-nyauN′
Mărăşeşti (Rum.)	mə-rə-shĕsht′	muh-ruh-shesht′
Marathon (Gr.)	*Eng.* măr′-ə-thŏn	mehr′-uh-thon
	Gr. mä-rä-thôn′	mah-rah-thon′
Maraua (Libya)	mä′-rə-wä	mah′-ruh-wah
Marburg (Ger.)	*Eng.* mär′-bûrg	mahr′-buhrg
	Ger. mär′-bo͝ork(h)	mahr′-burk(h)
Marcantonio, Vito (U.S. representative)	märk-ăn-tō′-nĭ-ō, vē′-tō	mahrk-an-toh′-ni-oh, vee′-toh
March (Europ. riv.) See *Morava.*		
Marcondes, Filho (Braz. leader)	mär-kôn′-dĭs, fē′-lyo͝o	mahr-kon′-dis, fee′-lyu
Marcus (Jap., isl.)	mär′-kəs	mahr′-kuhs
Mareth (Tun.)	mă′-rĕt *or* mă′-rĕth	ma′-ret *or* ma′-reth
Marettimo (Sicily, isl.)	mä-rĕt′-tē-mô	mah-ret′-tee-mo
margarine	mär′-jə-rēn *or* -rĭn	mahr′-juh-reen *or* -rin
	or mär′-gə-rēn *or* -rĭn	mahr′-guh-reen *or* -rin
Margariti (Gr.)	mär-gä-rē′-tē	mahr-gah-ree′-tee
Margesson (Br. leader)	mär′-jə-sən	mahr′-juh-suhn
Mărghita (Rum.)	mər-gē′-tä	muhr-gee′-tah
Margitsziget (Hung., isl.)	mŏr′-gĭt-sĭ′-gĕt	mor′-git-si′-get

Mariampolė (Lith.)	mä-rĭ-äm-pô′-lĕ	mah-ri-ahm-po′-leh
Russian *Mariampol*, mä-rĭ-äm′-pŏl(y) [mah-ri-ahm′-pol(y)].		
Marianas (Oc.)	mä-rē-ä′-näs	mah-ree-ah′-nahs
Also called the *Ladrone*, q.v.		
Mariazell (Austria)	mä-rē′-ä-tsĕl′	mah-ree′-ah-tsel′
Maribo (Den.)	mä′-rē-bō	mah′-ree-boh
Maribor (Yugosl.)	mä′-rĭ-bôr	mah′-ri-bor
German *Marburg*.		
Mariehamn (Fin.)	*Sw.* mä-rē′-ə-hämn′	mah-ree′-uh-hahmn′
Finnish *Maarianhamina*, q.v.		
Marienburg (Ger.)	*Eng.* mä-rē′-ən-bûrg	mah-ree′-uhn-buhrg
	Ger. mä-rē′-ən-bo͝ork(h)	mah-ree′-uhn-burk(h)
Marienburg (Latvia)	*Ger.* mä-rē′-ən-bo͝ork(h)	mah-ree′-uhn-burk(h)
	Rus. mä-rē′-yĕn-bo͝ork	mah-ree′-yen-burk
Latvian *Alūksne*, q.v.		
Marien Harbor (Oc.)	mä-rē′-ən	mah-ree′-uhn
Marienwerder (Ger.)	mä-rē′-ən-vĕr′-dər	mah-ree′-uhn-vehr′-duhr
Marifjord (Nor.)	mä′-rē-fyōr	mah′-ree-fyohr
Mari(i)nsk (Rus.)	mä-rē′-yĭnsk	mah-ree′-yinsk
Marin, Luis Muñoz (Puerto Rican leader)	mä-rēn′, lo͞o-ēs′ mo͞o′-nyôs	mah-reen′, lu-ees′ moo′-nyos
Marina	*Eng.* mə-rē′-nə	muh-ree′-nuh
Marina (Yugosl.)	mä′-rĭ-nä	mah′-ri-nah
Marina di Catanzaro (It.)	mä-rē′-nä dē kä-tän-dzä′-rô	mah-ree′-nah dee kah-tahn-dzah′-ro
Marina di Paola (Sicily)	mä-rē′-nä dē pä′-ô-lä	mah-ree′-nah dee pah′-o-lah
Marinduque (P.I.)	mä-rĭn-do͞o′-kĕ	mah-rin-doo′-keh
Maristova (Nor.)	mä′-rē-stô-vä	mah′-ree-sto-vah
Maritsa (Balkan riv.)	*Bulg.* mä-rē′-tsä	mah-ree′-tsah
	S.-C. mä′-rē-tsä	mah′-ree-tsah
Turkish *Meriç*, mĕ′-rēch′ [meh′-reech′]. Greek *Evros*, q.v.		
Maritsa (Dodec., Rh.)	mä-rē-tsä′	mah-ree-tsah′
Mariupol (Rus.)	mä-rĭ-o͞o′-pŏl(y)	mah-ri-oo′-pol(y)
Mariveles (P.I.)	mä-rē-vĕ′-lĕs	mah-ree-veh′-les
Marken (Neth., isl.)	mär′-kən	mahr′-kuhn
Markham (Oc., valley)	mär′-kəm	mahr′-kuhm
Markovac (Yugosl.)	mär′-kô-väts	mahr′-ko-vahts
Marmagao *and* Marmagoa (Port. India) See *Mormugão*.		
Mármarossziget (Rum.) See *Sighet*.		

Marne (Fr., riv.)	märn′	mahrn′
Marosvásárhely (Rum.)	See *Târgul Mureş.*	
Marovo (Oc.)	mä-rô′-vô	mah-ro′-vo
Marovoa (Madag.)	mä′-rô-vô′-ə	mah′-ro-vo′-uh
Marquart, Edward J. (U.S. admiral)	mär′-kärt	mahr′-kahrt
marquess	mär′-kwĭs	mahr′-kwis
An English variant of *marquis.*		
marquis	*Eng.* mär′-kwĭs	mahr′-kwis
	Fr. mär-kē′	mahr-kee′
Marrakesh (Mor.)	mär-rä′-kĕsh	mahr-rah′-kesh
Also called *Morocco.*		
Marree (Austral.)	mə-rē′	muh-ree′
Marsa, la (Tun.)	mär′-sä, lä	mahr′-sah, lah
Marsala (Sicily)	mär-sä′-lä	mahr-sah′-lah
Marsa Matruh (Egypt)	See *Mersa Matruh.* Cf. *La Marsa* (Tun.)	
Marseillan (Fr.)	mär-sĕ-yäN′	mahr-seh-yahN′
Marseille (Fr.)	mär-sĕ′y	mahr-seh′y
Marseilles (Fr.)	*Eng.* mär-sālz′	mahr-saylz′
For the French city, the French form, *Marseille,* q.v., is more common even in English contexts. The English form occurs as an American place name.		
Maršić (Yugosl.)	mär′-shĭch	mahr′-shich
Marstein (Nor.)	mär′-stān	mahr′-stayn
	or mäsh′-tān	mahsh′-tayn
Martaban (Burma)	mär′-tə-băn′	mahr′-tuh-ban′
Martelon (Crete, point)	mär′-tĕ-lô(n)	mahr′-teh-lo(n)
Märtha (Crown Princess of Norway)	mĕr′-tä	mehr′-tah
English *Martha,* mär′-thə [mahr′-thuh].		
Martigues (Fr.)	mär-tēg′	mahr-teeg′
Martin, St. (Cz.)	See *Turčiansky Svätý Martin.*	
Martínez (Sp. name)	mär-tē′-nĕth *or* -nĕs	mahr-tee′-neth *or* -nes
Martinez (Calif.)	mär-tē′-nĭz	mahr-tee′-niz
Martuba (Libya)	mär′-to͞o′-bä	mahr′-too′-bah
Marty, André (Fr. leader)	mär-tē′, äN-drĕ′	mahr-tee′, ahN-dreh′
Marunouchi (Jap.)	mä-ro͞o-nô-o͞o-chē	mah-roo-no-oo-chee
Masahet (Oc.)	mä-sä-hĕt′	mah-sah-het′
Masbate (P.I.)	mäs-bä′-tĕ	mahs-bah′-teh
Mascalucia (Sicily)	mäs-kä-lo͞o-chē′-ä	mahs-kah-loo-chee′-ah
Masjid-i-Sulaiman (Iran)	măs-jēd′-ē-so͝o-lā-män′	mas-jeed′-ee-su-lay-mahn′

Maslinica (Yugosl.)	mä′-slē′-nĭ-tsä	mah′-slee′-ni-tsah
Massicault (Tun.)	mäs-sē-kō′	mahs-see-koh′
Massico (It., mt.)	mäs′-sē-kô	mahs′-see-ko
Mastanli (Bulg.) See *Momtchilovgrad.*		
Mastekhon, Ak. (Gr., Chios) See *Phanai.*		
Masulipatam (India)	mə-so͞o′-lĭ-pə-tăm′	muh-soo′-li-puh-tam′
Masuria (Ger., region)	*Eng.* mə-zo͝or′-ĭ-ə	muh-zur′-i-uh
German *Masuren,* mä-zo͞o′-rən [mah-zoo′-ruhn].		
Mat (Alb., riv.)	mät′	maht′
Also called *Mati* and *Matja,* mä′-tyä, and *Lum i Matit.* Greek *Mathis,* mä′-thēs [mah′-thees].		
Matanatamberam (Oc.)	mä-tä-nä-täm′-bĕ-räm	mah-tah-nah-tahm′-beh-rahm
Matanikau (Oc.)	mä-tä-nē-kou′	mah-tah-nee-kau′
Matapan (Gr., cape)	*Eng.* măt′-ə-păn	mat′-uh-pan
Greek *Matapas* or *Tainaron,* q.v.		
Matara (Ceylon)	mä′-tə-rə	mah′-tuh-ruh
Matejča (Yugosl.)	mä′-tā-chä	mah′-tay-chah
Matejevac (Yugosl.)	mä′-tĕ′-yĕ-väts	mah′-teh′-yeh-vahts
Matema (Oc.)	mä′-tĕ-mä	mah′-teh-mah
Matera (It.)	mä-tĕ′-rä	mah-teh′-rah
Mateševo (Yugosl.)	mä′-tĕ′-shĕ-vô	mah′-teh′-sheh-vo
Mateur (Tun.)	mä-tûr′	mah-tœr′
Mati (P.I.)	mä′-tē	mah′-tee
Matjë (Alb., riv.) See *Mat.*		
Matmata (Tun.)	mät-mä′-tä	maht-mah′-tah
Mato Grosso (Brazil)	mä′-to͝o grô′-so͝o	mah′-tu gro′-su
Matratin (Libya)	mă-trə-tēn′	ma-truh-teen′
Matruh (Egypt)	mä-tro͞o′	mah-troo′
Also called *Mersa Matruh,* q.v.		
Matsuye (Jap.)	mä-tso͞o-yĕ	mah-tsoo-yeh
Maubeuge (Fr.)	mō-bûzh′	moh-bœzh′
Maubin (Burma)	mə-o͞o′-bĭn′	muh-oo′-bin′
Maug (Oc.)	moug′	maug′
Maulmain (Burma) See *Moulmein.*		
Maungdaw (Burma)	moung′-dô′	maung′-daw′
Mauritius (Brit., isl.)	mô-rĭsh′-əs *or* mô-rĭsh′-ĭ-əs	mo-rish′-uhs mo-rish′-i-uhs
Mauvromati (Gr.)	mä-vrô-mä′-tē	mah-vro-mah′-tee
Mavia (Oc.)	mä-vē′-ä	mah-vee′-ah
Mavrovouni (Gr.)	mä-vrô-vo͞o′-nē	mah-vro-voo′-nee
Mawchi (Burma)	mô′-chē′	maw′-chee′
Mawlaik (Burma)	mô′-līk′	maw′-laik′
Mayavaram (India)	mä′-yŭv′-ə-rəm	mah′-yuhv′-uh-ruhm

Maymyo (Burma)	mā′-myō′	may′-myoh′
Named after the English General May. Burman *myo* means *town.*		
Mayotte (Comoro isls.)	mä-yôt′	mah-yot′
Mayu (Burma, riv.)	mə-yo͞o′	muh-yoo′
Mazagan (Mor.)	mä-zä-gän′	mah-zah-gahn′
Mazanderan (Iran, prov.)	mä-zăn′-də-rän′	mah-zan′-duh-rahn′
Mazaraki (Gr.)	mä-zä-rä′-kē	mah-zah-rah′-kee
Mažeikiai (Lith.)	mä-zhā′-kyī	mah-zhay′-kyai
Russian *Muravyevo*, q.v.		
Mazzara (Sicily)	mäd-zä′-rä	mahd-zah′-rah
Mbalu Mbalu (Oc.)	mbä′-lo͞o mbä′-lo͞o	mbah′-loo mbah′-loo
Mboli (Oc.)	mbô′-lē	mbo′-lee
Mbretit, Fushë e (Alb.)	mbrĕ′-tēt, fo͞o′-shə ĕ	mbreh′-teet, foo′-shuh eh
English *Plain of Elbesan.*		
Mbuke (Oc.)	mbo͞o′-kĕ	mboo′-keh
Mbulo (Oc.)	mbo͞o′-lô	mboo′-lo
McCowen, Edward O. (U.S. representative)	mə-kou′-ĕn	muh-kau′-en
McGehee, Dan R. (U.S. representative)	mə-gē′-hē	muh-gee′-hee
McGranery, James P. (Former U.S. representative)	mə-grăn′-ər-ĭ	muh-gran′-uhr-i
Méaulte (Fr.)	mĕ-ōlt′	meh-ohlt′
Meaux (Fr.)	mō′	moh′
Mechelen (Belg.)	*Flem.* mĕk(h)′-ə-lən	mek(h)′-uh-luhn
French *Malines*, q.v. English *Mechlin*, mĕk′-lĭn [mek′-lin].		
Mechetinskaya (Rus.)	mĕ-chĕ′-tĭn-skä-yä	meh-cheh′-tin-skah-yah
Mechili (Libya)	mĕ-kē′-lē	meh-kee′-lee
Mecklenburg (Ger.)	*Eng.* mĕk′-lən-bûrg	mek′-luhn-buhrg
	Ger. mĕk′-lən-bo͝ork(h)	mek′-luhn-burk(h)
——Schwerin (Ger.)	——shvĕ-rēn′	——shveh-reen′
——Strelitz (Ger.)	——shtrā′-lĭts	——shtray′-lits
Mečkujevci (Yugosl.)	mĕch′-ko͞o′-yĕv-tsĭ	mech′-koo′-yev-tsi
Medalie, George G. (U.S. lawyer)	mĭ-däl′-yə	mi-dahl′-yuh
Medan (NEI)	mĕ-dän′	meh-dahn′
Medeia (Turk.) See *Midye.*		
Medemblik (Neth.)	mā′-dəm-blĭk	may′-duhm-blik
Medenine (Tun.)	mĕ-dĕ-nēn′	meh-deh-neen′
Mediaş (Rum.)	mĕ-dyäsh′	meh-dyahsh′

Medina (Arabia)	mĕ-dē′-nä	meh-dee′-nah
Medina Angarita, Isaías (Ven. leader)	mĕ-dē′-nä äng-gä-rē′-tä, ē-sä-ē′-äs	meh-dee′-nah ahng-gah-ree′-tah, ee-sah-ee′-ahs

Both names should be used, thus: *Medina Angarita*, not *Angarita* alone.

Medjerda (Tun., riv.)	mə-jĕr′-dä	muh-jehr′-dah
Medjes el Bab (Tun.)	mĕ′-jĕz ĕl băb′	meh′-jez el bab′
Medjidia (Rum.)	mĕ-jē-dē′-ä	meh-jee-dee′-ah
Medouina (Mor.)	mĕd-wē′-nä	med-wee′-nah
Medvedovsk (Rus.)	mĕd-vĕ′-dŏfsk	med-veh′-dofsk
Medvegja (Yugosl.)	mĕd′-vĕ-dyä	med′-veh-dyah
Medvegje (Yugosl.)	mĕd′-vĕ-dyĕ	med′-veh-dyeh
Medvezhya Gora (Rus.)	mĕd-vĕzh′-yä gŏ-rä′	med-vezh′-yah go-rah′
Medyn (Rus.)	mĕ-dwēn′(y)	meh-dween′(y)
Meenen (Belg.)	*Flem.* mā′-nən	may′-nuhn

French *Menin*, mə-năN′ [muh-naN′].

Meekatharra (Austral.)	mē′-kə-thăr′-ə	mee′-kuh-thehr′-uh
meer	*Du.* mār′	mayr′
	Eng. mĭr′	mihr′

An element, meaning *lake*, in Dutch place names. Cf. *Harlem Meer* in Central Park.

Meerut (India)	mē′-rət	mee′-ruht
Megalo Kastro (Crete)	mĕ-gä′-lô käs′-trô	meh-gah′-lo kahs′-tro

English *Candia*, q.v. Also called *Herakleion*, q.v.

Megalopolis (Gr.)	mĕ-gä-lô′-pô-lē(s)	meh-gah-lo′-po-lee(s)
Meganesi (Gr.)	mĕ-gä-nē′-sē	meh-gah-nee′-see
Megara (Gr.)	mĕ′-gä-rä	meh′-gah-rah
Megiste (Dodec.) See *Kastelorizon.*		
Mehamn (Nor.)	mā′-hämn	may′-hahmn
Mehdia (Mor.)	mĕ-dē′-yä	meh-dee′-yah

Also called *Mehediya*, mĕ-hə-dē′-yä [meh-huh-dee′-yah].

Meiktila (Burma)	mēk′-tĭ-lə	meek′-ti-luh
Mei-ling (Ch., Kiangsi, Kwangtung, pass)	mā-lĭng	may-ling
Mei-ling Soong (Mme. Chiang Kai-shek)	mā-lĭng so͝ong	may-ling sung
Meissen (Ger.)	mī′-sən	mai′-suhn
Mejit (Oc.)	mĕ′-jēt	meh′-jeet
Mekhili, el (Libya)	mĕ-kē′-lē, ĕl	meh-kee′-lee, el
Mekhov (Pol.) See *Miechów.*		
Meklong (Thai, riv.)	mă-klông′	ma-klawng′

Meknes (Mor.)	mĕk′-nĕs	mek′-nes
Mekong (S.E. Asia, riv.)	*Eng.* mā′-kŏng′	may′-kong′
	Thai mă-kōng′	ma-kohng′
Chinese *Lan-ts'ang*, q.v.		
Melada (Yugosl.)	*It.* mĕ-lä′-dä	meh-lah′-dah
Serb-Croat *Mulat*, q.v.		
Melbourne (Austral.)	mĕl′-bərn	mel′-buhrn
The pronunciation mĕl′-bôrn [mel′-born] is not recommended.		
Melbu (Nor.)	mĕl′-bo͞o	mel′-boo
Meleda (Yugosl., isl.)	*It.* mĕ′-lĕ-dä	meh′-leh-dah
Serb-Croat *Mljet*, q.v.		
Melekhas (Crete, point)	mĕ-lĕ′-häs	meh-leh′-hahs
Also called *Kyamon*, kē′-ä-môn [kee′-ah-mon].		
Melenci (Yugosl.)	mĕ′-lĕn-tsĭ	meh′-len-tsi
Melfa (Libya)	mĕl′-fä	mel′-fah
Also called *Bir el Melfa.*		
Meli (Tun.)	mā′-lē	may′-lee
Meligala (Gr.)	mĕ-lē-gä-lä′	meh-lee-gah-lah′
Meliha (Libya)	mā-lē′-hä	may-lee′-hah
Melissa (Crete, point)	mĕ′-lē-sä	meh′-lee-sah
Also called *Psykhion*, psē′-hē-ôn [psee′-hee-on].		
Melito (It.)	mĕ-lē′-tô	meh-lee′-to
Melitopol (Rus.)	mĕ-lĭ-tô′-pŏl(y)	meh-li-to′-pol(y)
Meljine (Yugosl.)	mĕ′-lyĭ-nĕ	meh′-lyi-neh
Melk (Austria)	mĕlk′	melk′
Melnica (Yugosl.)	mĕl′-nĭ-tsä	mel′-ni-tsah
Melnik (Bulg.)	mĕl′-nĭk	mel′-nik
Mělník (Cz.)	myĕl′-nēk	myel′-neek
Melnik (Pol.) See *Mielnik.*		
Melos (Gr., isl.)	mē′-lô(s)	mee′-lo(s)
Memel (Lith., city, riv.)	*Ger.* mā′-məl	may′-muhl
	or Eng. mĕm′-əl	mem′-uhl
Lithuanian city, *Klaipėda*, q.v.; riv., *Nemunas*, q.v.		
Memešli (Yugosl.)	mĕ′-mĕsh-lĭ	meh′-mesh-li
Menai (Wales, str.)	mĕ′-nī	meh′-nai
menam	mă-näm′	ma-nahm′
Thai word meaning *river*. It may be necessary to look up the other part of the name.		
Menam Chao Phya (Thai, riv.)	mă-näm′ chou′ pyä′ *or* pē-ä′	ma-nahm′ chau′ pyah′ *or* pee-ah′
Menassir (Tun.) See *Djebel el Menassir.*		
Mendre (Yugosl.)	mĕn′-drĕ	men′-dreh
Menemencioğlu, Numan (Turk. leader)	mĕ-nĕ-mĕn-jĭ′-ô-lo͝o, no͝o′-män′	meh-neh-men-ji′-o-lu, nu′-mahn′
Menfi (Sicily)	mĕn′-fē	men′-fee

Mêng-ma (Ch., Yünnan)	mŭng-mä	muhng-mah
Mêng-shui (Ch., Kansu)	mŭng-shwā	muhng-shway
Mêng-t'ing (Ch., Yünnan)	mŭng-tĭng	muhng-ting
Mêng-tzŭ (Ch., Yünnan)	mŭng-dzə	muhng-dzuh
Menidi (Gr.)	mĕ-nē′-*th*ē	meh-nee′-*th*ee
Menin (Belg.) See *Meenen.*		
Mentawei (NEI)	mĕn-tä′-wā	men-tah′-way
Menton (Fr.)	*Eng.* mĕn-tōn′	men-tohn′
	Fr. mäN-tôN′	mahN-toN′

Italian *Mentone,* mĕn-tô′-nĕ [men-to′-neh], *or Eng.* mĕn-tō′-nĭ [men-toh′-ni].

Menzel Bou Zelfa (Tun.)	mĕn′-zĕl bōō zĕl′-fä	men′-zel boo-zel′-fah
Menzel Djemil (Tun.)	mĕn′-zĕl jə-mēl′	men′-zel juh-meel′
Menzel Temime (Tun.)	mĕn′-zĕl tə-mēm′	men′-zel tuh-meem′
Menzies (Scot. name)	*Austral.* mĕn′-zĭz	men′-ziz
	Brit. mĕng′-ĭz	meng′-iz
	or mĭng′-ĭs	*or* ming′-is
Meppel (Neth.)	mĕp′-əl	mep′-uhl
Merak (NEI)	mû′-räk	mœ′-rahk
Merauke (NEI)	mĕ-rou′-kĕ	meh-rau′-keh
Mercurea (Rum.)	mĕr′-kŏŏ-ryä	mehr′-ku-ryah
Meretskov, Kiryl (Rus. general)	mĕ-rĕts-kôf′, kĭ-rēl′	meh-rets-kof′, ki-reel′
Mergui (Burma)	mər-gwē′	muhr-gwee′
Mérida (Sp., Mex.)	mĕ′-rē-*th*ä	meh′-ree-*th*ah
Merrow, Chester E. (U.S. representative)	mĕr′-ō	mehr′-oh
Merseburg (Ger.)	*Eng.* mûr′-zə-bûrg	muhr′-zuh-buhrg
	Ger. mĕr′-zə-bŏŏrk(h)	mehr′-zuh-burk(h)
Mersa Matruh (Egypt)	mĕr′-sä mä-trōō′	mehr′-sah mah-troo′
Mers el Kebir (Alg.)	mĕrs′ ĕl kə-bēr′	mehrs′ el kuh-beer′
Mersin (Turk.)	mĕr′-sĭn′	mehr′-sin′

Also called *Mersina,* mĕr-sē′-nä [mehr-see′-nah].

Méru (Fr.)	mĕ-rü′	meh-rü′
Merwede (Neth., riv.)	mĕr′-wā-də	mehr′-way-duh
Merxem (Belg.)	mĕrk′-səm	mehrk′-suhm
Mesara (Crete)	mĕ-sä-rä′	meh-sah-rah′
Mesemvria (Bulg.) See *Nesebar.*		
Meševište (Yugosl.)	mĕ′-shĕ-vĭ-shtĕ	meh′-sheh-vi-shteh
Meshchersk (Rus.)	mĕ-shchĕrsk′	meh-shchehrsk′
Meshchovsk (Rus.)	mĕ-shchŏfsk′	meh-shchofsk′
Meshed (Iran)	*Per.* măsh-hăd′	mash-had′
	Eng. mĕsh′-hĕd	mesh′-hed
Mesolongion (Gr.)	mĕ-sô-lông′-gē(-ôn)	meh-so-long′-gee(-on)

Messe (Sard.)	mĕs′-sĕ	mes′-seh
Messene (Gr.)	mĕ-sē′-nē	meh-see′-nee
Messenia (Gr.)	mĕ-sē-nē′-ä	meh-see-nee′-ah
Messeniakos Kolpos (Gr., gulf)	mĕ-sē-nē-ä-kôs′ kôl′-pôs	meh-see-nee-ah-kos′ kol′-pos
English Gulf of *Messenia*, q.v.		
Messina (Sicily)	mĕs-sē′-nä	mes-see′-nah
Mesta (Balkan riv.)	*Bulg.* mĕ′-stä	meh′-stah
Greek *Nestos*, q.v.		
Mestre (It.)	mĕ′-strĕ	meh′-streh
Metamer (Tun.)	mĕ-tă′-mĕr	meh-ta′-mehr
Metaponto (It.)	mĕ-tä-pôn′-tô	meh-tah-pon′-to
Methone (Gr.)	mĕ-thô′-nē	meh-tho′-nee
Metković (Yugosl.)	mĕt′-kô-vĭch	met′-ko-vich
Metlaoui (Tun.)	mĕt-lä′-wē	met-lah′-wee
Metline (Tun.)	mĕt-lēn′	met-leen′
Metlire (Tun.)	mĕt-lēr′	met-leer′
Metohija (Yugosl.)	mĕ′-tô′-hĭ-yä	meh′-to′-hi-yah
Metsovon (Gr.)	mĕ′-tsô-vô(n)	meh′-tso-vo(n)
Mettarheni (Tun.)	mĕt-tär-hā′-nē	met-tahr-hay′-nee
Metz (Fr.)	*Eng.*, *Ger.* mĕts′	mets′
	Fr. mĕs′	mes′
Meudon (Fr.)	mû-dôN′	mœ-doN′
Meulaboh (NEI)	mû-lä′-bô	mœ-lah′-bo
Meulan les Mureaux (Fr.)	mû-läN′ lĕ mü-rō′	mœ-lahN′ leh mü-roh′
Meuse (Europ. riv.)	*Eng.* mūz′	myooz′
	Fr. mûz′	mœz′
Dutch and Flemish *Maas*, q.v.		
Mexia (Tex.)	*local* mə-hā′-ə	muh-hay′-uh
	Sp. mĕ-hē′-ä	meh-hee′-ah
Mèze (Fr.)	mĕz′	mez′
Mézidon (Fr.)	mĕ-zē-dôN′	meh-zee-doN′
Mézières (Fr.)	mĕ-zyĕr′	meh-zyehr′
Mezőberény (Hung.)	mĕ′-zû-bĕ′-rān(y)	meh′-zœ-beh′-rayn(y)
Mezőkövesd (Hung.)	mĕ′-zû-kû′-vĕzhd	meh′-zœ-kœ′-vezhd
Mezőtúr (Hung.)	mĕ′-zû-to͞or	meh′-zœ-toor
Mezzo (Yugosl., isl.)	*It.* mĕd′-zô	med′-zo
Serb-Croat *Lopud*, q.v.		
Mezzouna (Tun.)	mĕz-zo͞o′-nä	mez-zoo′-nah
Mga (Rus.)	mgä′	mgah′
Mglin (Rus.)	mglēn′	mgleen′
Mhow (India)	mou′	mau′
Miagao (P.I.)	myä-gou′	myah-gau′

Mianeh (Iran)	mē-ä-nĕ′	mee-ah-neh′
Miangas (Oc.) See *Palmas*.		
Miaskovsky, Nikolai (Rus. composer)	myäs-kôf′-skĭ, nĭ-kŏ-lī′	myahs-kof′-ski, ni-ko-lai′
Michener, Earl C. (U.S. representative)	mĭch′-ə-nər	mich′-uh-nuhr
Michoacán (Mex.)	mē-chô-ä-kän′	mee-cho-ah-kahn′
Michurin (Rus. scientist)	mē-cho͞o′-rĭn	mee-choo′-rin
Michurinsk (Rus.)	mē-cho͞o′-rĭnsk	mee-choo′-rinsk
Middelburg (Neth.)	*Eng.* mĭd′-əl-bûrg	mid′-uhl-buhrg
	Du. mĭd′-əl-bûrk(h)	mid′-uhl-bœrk(h)
Middlesbrough (Eng.)	mĭd′lz-brə	mid′lz-bruh
Midoun (Tun.)	mĭ-do͞on′	mi-doon′
Midye (Turk.)	mēd′-yĕ′	meed′-yeh′
Greek *Medeia*, mē′-dē-ä [mee′-dee-ah].		
Midžor (Balkan mt.)	mē′-jôr	mee′-jor
Miechów (Pol.)	myĕ′-ko͝of	myeh′-kuf
Russian *Mekhov*, mĕ′-hŏf [meh′-hof].		
Międzychód (Pol.)	myăN-zĭ′-ho͝od	myaN-zi′-hud
German *Birnbaum*, bĭrn′-boum [bihrn′-baum].		
Międzyrzec (Pol.)	myăN-jĭ′-zhĕts	myaN-ji′-zhets
Russian *Mezhireche*, mĕ-zhĭ-rĕ′-chyĕ [meh-zhi-reh′-chyeh].		
Mielec (Pol.)	myĕ′-lĕts	myeh′-lets
Mielnik (Pol.)	myĕl′-nĭk	myel′-nik
Russian *Melnik*, mĕl′(y)-nĭk [mel′(y)-nik].		
Mignano (It.)	mē-nyä′-nô	mee-nyah′-no
Migulinsk (Rus.)	mĭ-go͞o′-lĭnsk	mi-goo′-linsk
Migyaungye (Burma)	mē-joung-yĕ′	mee-jaung-yeh′
Mihajlovac (Yugosl.)	mē-hī′-lô-väts	mee-hai′-lo-vahts
Miholjac, Donji (Yugosl.)	mē′-hô-lyäts, dôn′-yĭ	mee′-ho-lyahts, don′-yi
Mijajlovica (Yugosl., mt.)	mē-yī′-lô-vĭ-tsä	mee-yai′-lo-vi-tsah
Mikashevichi (Pol.) See *Mikaszewicze*.		
Mikaszewicze (Pol.)	mĭ-kä-shĕ-vē′-chĕ	mi-kah-sheh-vee′-cheh
Russian *Mikashevichi*, mĭ-kä-shĕ-vē′-chĭ [mi-kah-sheh-vee′-chi].		
Mikhailo-Semenovskaya (Rus.)	mĭ-hī′-lŏ-sĕ-myô′-nŏf-skä-yä	mi-hai′-lo-seh-myo′-nof-skah-yah
Mikhailović, Draža (Yugosl. leader)	mĭ-hī′-lô-vĭch, drä′-zhä	mi-hai′-lo-vich, drah′-zhah

Also spelled *Mihailovitch*, *Draja*. The familiar *Draža* is short for *Dragoljub*, drä′-gô-lūb′ [drah′-go-lyoob′]. *Mihailovitch* (however spelled) as a Serbian name is stressed on the second syllable; as a

Polish name on the third syllable; as a Russian name on the second or the third syllable.

Mikhailovka (Rus.)	mĭ-hī′-lŏf-kä	mi-hai′-lof-kah
Mikhalopoulos, A. (Gr. leader)	mē-hä-lô′-po͞o-lôs	mee-hah-lo′-poo-los
Mikoian, Anastasi I. (Rus. leader)	mĭ-kŏ-yän′, ä-nä-stä′-sĭ	mi-ko-yahn′, ah-nah-stah′-si
Mikołajczyk, Stanislaw (Pol. Prime Minister)	mĭ-kô-lī′-chĭk, stä-nē′-släf	mi-ko-lai′-chik, stah-nee′-slahf
Mikoyan Shakhar (Rus.)	mĭ-kŏ-yän′ shä′-här′	mi-ko-yahn′ shah′-hahr′
Mikra Mantinea (Gr.)	mē-krä′ män-dē′-nē-ä	mee-krah′ mahn-dee′-nee-ah
Milan (It.)	*Eng.* mĭ-lăn′ *or* mĭl′-ən *It.* mē-lä′-nô	mi-lan′ mil′-uhn mee-lah′-no
Milan (Mich., Mo., Tenn.)	mī′-lən	mai′-luhn
Milanovac, Gornji (Yugosl.)	mē′-lä′-nô-väts, gôr′-nyĭ	mee′-lah′-no-vahts, gor′-nyi
Milatos (Crete)	mē′-lä-tôs	mee′-lah-tos
Milatovac (Yugosl.)	mē′-lä′-tô-väts	mee′-lah′-to-vahts
Milazzo (Sicily)	mē-lät′-sô	mee-laht′-so
Mileškovo (Yugosl.)	mē′-lĕ′-shkô-vô	mee′-leh′-shko-vo
Mili (Crete, isl.) See *Pontikonesi.*		
Mili (Oc.)	mē′-lē	mee′-lee
Miliana (Tun., riv.)	mĭl-yă′-nä	mil-ya′-nah
Miliane (Tun., riv.)	mĭl-yăn′	mil-yan′
Miljevska planina (Yugosl.)	mē′-lyĕv-skä plä′-nē′-nä	mee′-lyev-skah plah′-nee′-nah
Millerovo (Rus.)	mĭl′-lĕ-rŏ-vŏ	mil′-leh-ro-vo
Milne (Oc., bay)	mĭln′ *or* mĭl′	miln′ *or* mil′
Named after the English geographer.		
Milo (Sicily)	mē′-lô	mee′-lo
Miloševac (Yugosl.)	mē′-lô′-shĕ-väts	mee′-lo′-sheh-vahts
Miloševo (Yugosl.)	mē′-lô′-shĕ-vô	mee′-lo′-sheh-vo
Milošević, Sima (Yugosl. leader)	mĭ-lô′-shĕ-vĭch, sē′-mä	mi-lo′-sheh-vich, see′-mah
Milot (Alb.)	mē′-lôt	mee′-lot
Miloti (Alb.) See *Milot.*		
Milparinka (Austral.)	mĭl′-pər-ēngk′-ə	mil′-puhr-eengk′-uh
Minas Gerais (Brazil)	mē′-nəs zhĕ-rīs′	mee′-nuhs zheh-rais′
Minbu (Burma)	mĭm′-bo͞o	mim′-boo

Minbya (Burma)	mĭm-byä′	mim-byah′
Min Chiang *or* Min River (Ch., Fukien)	mĭn	min
Also called *Min-kong*, q.v.		
Mindanao (P.I.)	mĭn-dä-nou′	min-dah-nau′
Mindoro (P.I.)	mĭn-dô′-rô	min-do′-ro
Mineralnye Vody (Rus.)	mĭ-nĕ-räl′(y)-nĭ-yĕ vô′-dĭ	mi-neh-rahl′(y)-ni-yeh vo′-di
Mingaladon (Burma)	mĭng′-gə-lə-dōn′	ming′-guh-luh-dohn′
Minho (Port., Sp., riv.)	mē′-nyŏŏ	mee′-nyu
Spanish *Miño*, q.v.		
Min-how (Ch., Fukien)	mĭn-hō	min-hoh
Also called *Foo-chow*, q.v.		
Min-kong (Ch., Fukien, riv.)	mĭn-jŏng	min-jong
Also called *Min Chiang*, q.v.		
Miño (Sp., Port., riv.)	mē′-nyô	mee′-nyo
Portuguese *Minho*, q.v.		
Minsk (Rus.)	mēnsk′	meensk′
Mińsk Mazowiecki (Pol.)	mēn(y)sk′ mä-zô-vyĕ′-tskĭ	meen(y)sk′ mah-zo-vyeh′-tski
Russian *Novominsk*, nô′-vŏ-mēnsk′ [no′-vo-meensk′].		
Minusinsk (Rus.)	mĭ-nōō-sēnsk′	mi-noo-seensk′
Mioko (Oc.)	mē-ô′-kô	mee-o′-ko
Mionica (Yugosl.)	mē′-ô′-nĭ-tsä	mee′-o′-ni-tsah
Mirambello (Crete, gulf)	mē-rä(m)-bĕ′-lô	mee-rah(m)-beh′-lo
Miravci (Yugosl.)	mē′-räv-tsĭ	mee′-rahv-tsi
Mirdita (Alb.) See *Mirditë*.		
Mirditë (Alb.)	mēr-dē′-tə	meer-dee′-tuh
Mirgorod (Rus.)	mēr′-gŏ-rŏt	meer′-go-rot
Mirjaweh (Iran)	mēr-jä′-vĕ	meer-jah′-veh
Mirkovce (Yugosl.)	mēr′-kôv-tsĕ	meer′-kov-tseh
Mirna (Yugosl., riv.)	mēr′-nä	meer′-nah
Miros, Agios (Crete)	mē′-rôs, ī′-yôs	mee′-ros, ai′-yos
Miruša (Yugosl., riv.)	mē′-rōō-shä	mee′-roo-shah
Misamis (P.I.)	mē-sä′-mēs	mee-sah′-mees
mischievous See *grievous*.		
Misilmeri (Sicily)	mē-zēl-mĕ′-rē	mee-zeel-meh′-ree
Misima (Oc.)	mē-sē′-mä	mee-see′-mah
Miskolc (Hung.)	mĭsh′-kôlts	mish′-kolts
Mislinja (Yugosl., riv.)	mē′-slĭ-nyä	mee′-slĭ-nyah
Mišljenovac (Yugosl.)	mēsh′-lyĕ′-nô-väts	meesh′-lyeh′-no-vahts
Misoöl (NEI)	mē′-sō′-əl	mee′-soh′-uhl
Missolonghi (Gr.) See *Mesolongion*.		

Missouri — mə-zo͝or′-ĭ *or* -ə — muh-zur′-i *or* -uh

American Speech once printed an article of 17 pages on the historical disputes about the pronunciation of this name. My impression is that three out of four Missourians today favor mə-zo͝or′-ə [muh-zur′-uh], but that the fourth preferring mə-zo͝or′-ĭ [muh-zur′-i] regards it as socially superior. The -ĭ pronunciation is stronger in St. Louis than in Kansas City. If mĭ-zo͝o′-rĭ is more respectable than mĭ-zo͝or′-ə, this is contrary to the social standing of "Louisy" as compared with *Louisa*, "Marthy" with *Martha*, and even the familiar "Annie" as a variant of *Anna* and *Anne*. However, for *Cincinnati*, final ĭ is more conservative than ə [*uh*].

Misterbianco (Sicily) — mē-stĕr-byän′-kô — mee-stehr-byahn′-ko

Misurata (Libya) — mē-zo͞o-rä′-tä — mee-zoo-rah′-tah

Mitau (Latvia) — *Ger.* mē′-tou — mee′-tau

Latvian *Jelgava*, q.v. Russian *Mitava*, q.v.

Mitava (Latvia) — *Rus.* mĭ-tä′-vä — mi-tah′-vah

Latvian *Jelgava*, q.v. German *Mitau*, mē′-tou [mee′-tau].

Miteiriya, el (Egypt) — mĭ-tā-rē′-yä, ĕl — mi-tay-ree′-yah, el

Mitikas (Gr.) — mē′-tē-käs — mee′-tee-kahs

Mito (Jap.) — mē-tô — mee-to

Mitrovica (Yugosl.) — mē′-trô-vĭ-tsä — mee′-tro-vi-tsah

Mitsubishi (Jap.) — mĭ-tso͞o-bē-shē — mi-tsoo-bee-shee

Mi-tu (Ch., Yünnan) — mē-do͞o — mee-doo

Mius (Rus., riv.) — mē-o͞os′ — mee-oos′

Miye (Jap.) — mē-yĕ — mee-yeh

Mizda (Libya) — mĭz′-dä — miz′-dah

Mizil (Rum.) — mē-zēl′ — mee-zeel′

Mjoesa *or* Mjösa (Nor., lake) — myû′-sä — myœ′-sah

Mladá Boleslav (Cz.) — mlä′-dä bô′-lĕ-släf — mlah′-dah bo′-leh-slahf

Mladenovac (Yugosl.) — mlä′-dĕ′-nô-väts — mlah′-deh′-no-vahts

Mlava (Yugosl., riv.) — mlä′-vä — mlah′-vah

Mława (Pol.) — mlä′-vä — mlah′-vah

Russian spelling *Mlava*.

Mljet (Yugosl., isl.) — mlyĕt′ — mlyet′

Italian *Meleda*, q.v.

Mo (Nor.) — mō′ — moh′

The Norwegian is close to mo͝o [mu].

Moçambique (Afr.) See *Mozambique*.

Modane (Fr.) — mô-dän′ — mo-dahn′

Modena (It.) — mô′-dĕ-nä — mo′-deh-nah

Modica (Sicily) — mô′-dē-kä — mo′-dee-kah

Modion (Crete) — mô′-*th*ē(-ôn) — mo′-*th*ee(-on)

Modlin (Pol.)	mô′-dlĭn	mo′-dlin
Russian *Novogeorgievsk*, nô′-vŏ-gĕ-ôr′-gĭ-yĕfsk [no′-vo-geh-or′-gi-yefsk].		
Moedling *or* Mödling (Austria)	mûd′-lĭng	mœd′-ling
Moeen *or* Möen (Den., isl.)	mû′-ən	mœ′-uhn
Moehne (Ger., dam)	mû′-nə	mœ′-nuh
Moen (Oc.)	mô′-ĕn	mo′-en
Moesi *or* Musi (NEI)	mo͞o′-sē	moo′-see
Moeskroen (Belg.)	*Flem.* mo͞os′-kro͞on	moos′-kroon
French *Mouscron*, q.v.		
Moesvatn (Nor., dam)	mûs′-vätn	mœs′-vahtn
Mogador (Mor.)	mô-gä-dôr′	mo-gah-dor′
There is also an English pronunciation, mŏg′-ə-dôr′ [mog′-uh-dor′].		
Mogaung (Burma)	mō′-goung′	moh′-gaung′
Mogelnitsa (Pol.) See *Mogielnica.*		
Mogzon (Rus.)	mŏg-zôn′	mog-zon′
Moghrane (Tun.)	mŭg-răn′	muhg-ran′
Mogielnica (Pol.)	mô-gyĕl-nē′-tsä	mo-gyel-nee′-tsah
Russian *Mogelnitsa*, mŏ-gĕl′(y)-nĭ-tsä [mo-gel′(y)-ni-tsah].		
Mogila (Yugosl.)	mô′-gĭ-lä	mo′-gi-lah
Mogilev (Rus.)	mŏ-gĭ-lyôf′	mo-gi-lyof′
The name is Anglicized mō′-gĭ-lĕf′ [moh′-gi-lef′].		
Mogilev Podolski (Rus.)	mŏ-gĭ-lyôf′ pŏ-dôl′(y)-skĭ	mo-gi-lyof′ po-dol′(y)-ski
Mogilyani (Pol.) See *Mohylany.*		
Mohács (Hung.)	mô′-häch	mo′-hahch
Mohamedia (Tun.)	mô-hä-mə-dē′-ä	mo-hah-muh-dee′-ah
Mohammereh (Iran)	mə-häm′-mə-rə	muh-hahm′-muh-ruh
Now called *Khurramshahr*, q.v.		
Möhne (Ger., dam)	mû′-nə	mœ′-nuh
Mohylany (Pol.)	mô-hĭ-lä′-nĭ	mo-hi-lah′-ni
Russian *Mogilyani*, mŏ-gĭ-lyä′-nĭ [mo-gi-lyah′-ni].		
Moi (Nor.)	mō′-ē	moh′-ee
Moires (Crete)	mē′-rĕs	mee′-res
Mõisaküla (Est.)	mûĭ′-sä-kü′-lä	muh(y)′-sah-kü′-lah
Russian *Moisekul*, q.v.		
Moisekul (Est.)	*Rus.* moi′-zĕ-kūl(y)	moi′-zeh-kyool(y)
Estonian *Mõisaküla*, q.v.		
Mojan (Balkan mt.)	mô′-yän	mo′-yahn
Moji (Jap.)	mô-jē	mo-jee
Mokotów (Pol., airport)	mô-kô′-to͝of	mo-ko′-tuf
Mokpalin (Burma)	mōk′-pə-lĭn′	mohk′-puh-lin′

Mokpo (Korea)	môk-pô	mok-po
Mokranja (Yugosl.)	mô′-krä-nyä	mo′-krah-nyah
Mokrin (Yugosl.)	mô′-krĭn	mo′-krin
Mokshan (Rus.)	mŏk-shän′	mok-shahn′
Mol (Yugosl.)	môl′	mawl′
Molakobi (Oc.)	mô-lä-kô′-bē	mo-lah-ko′-bee
Moldau (Cz., riv.)	*Ger.* môl′-dou	mol′-dau
Czech *Vltava*, q.v.		
Moldava (Cz.)	môl′-dä-vä	mol′-dah-vah
Moldavia (Rum.)	*Eng.* mŏl-dā′-vyə	mol-day′-vyuh
Rumanian *Moldova*, q.v.		
Molde (Nor.)	môl′-də *or* môl′-lə	mol′-duh *or* mol′-luh
Moldova (Rum.)	môl-dô′-vä	mol-do′-vah
English *Moldavia*, q.v.		
Molenbeek (Belg.)	mō′-lən-bāk	moh′-luhn-bayk
Mołodeczno (Pol.)	mô-lô-dĕch′-nô	mo-lo-dech′-no
Russian spelling *Molodechno*.		
Mologa (Rus., riv.)	mŏ-lô′-gä	mo-lo′-gah
Molonta (Yugosl., pen.)	*It.* mô-lôn′-tä	mo-lon′-tah
Serb-Croat *Molunat*, q.v.		
Molotoff, Vyacheslaff (Rus.)	mô′-lŏ-tŏf, vyä-chĕ-släf′	mo′-lo-tof, vyah-cheh-slahf′
Molotovo (Rus.)	mô′-lŏ-tŏ-vŏ	mo′-lo-to-vo
Moluccas (NEI)	*Eng.* mō-lŭk′-əz	moh-luhk′-uhz
Molunat (Yugosl., pen.)	mô′-lo͞o-nät	mo′-loo-naht
Molyvos (Gr., Lesbos)	mô′-lē-vôs	mo′-lee-vos
Momein (Ch., Yünnan)	mô-mān	mo-mayn
Also called *T'êng-ch'ung*, q.v.		
Momote (Oc.)	mô-mô′-tĕ	mo-mo′-teh
Momtchilovgrad (Bulg.)	mŏm-chē′-lŏf-grät	mom-chee′-lof-graht
Also called *Mastanli*, mä′-stän-lē′ [mah′-stahn-lee′].		
Mon (Est., isl.)	*Rus.* môn′	mon′
	Ger. mōn′	mohn′
Estonian *Muhu*, q.v.		
Monaco (It.)	mô′-nä-kô	mo′-nah-ko
Monaco (principality)	mô′-nä-kô	mo′-nah-ko
There is no dictionary authority for the American pronunciation accenting the second syllable.		
Monasterace (It.)	mô-nä-stĕ-rä′-chĕ	mo-nah-steh-rah′-cheh
Monastir (Yugosl.)	*Turk.* mô-nä-stēr′	mo-nah-steer′
Yugoslav *Bitolj*, q.v. Greek *Monastḗri(on)*, mô-nä-stē′-rē(-ôn) [mo-nah-stee′-ree(-on)].		
Moncay (Indo-Ch.)	môn-kī′	mon-kai′

mond	mônt′	mont′

An element, meaning *river mouth*, in Dutch place names.

Mondego (Port., riv.)	môn-dĕ′-go͞o	mon-deh′-gu
Mondidier (Fr.)	môN-dē-dyĕ′	moN-dee-dyeh′
Mondragone (It.)	môn-drä-gô′-nĕ	mon-drah-go′-neh
Monemvasia (Gr.)	mô-nĕm-vä-sē′-ä	mo-nem-vah-see′-ah
Mongmau (Burma)	mŏng′-mou′	mong′-mau′
Mongolia	*Eng.* mŏng-gō′-lĭ-ə	mong-goh′-li-uh
Mongsit (Burma)	mŏng′-sĭt′	mong′-sit′
Monheim (Ger.)	môn′-hīm	mon′-haim
Monkiewicz, B. J. (U.S. representative)	mŭn′-kĕ-vēts′	muhn′-keh-veets′
Monnet, Jean (Fr. leader)	môn-nĕ′, zhäN′	mon-neh′, zhahN′
Mono (Oc.)	mô′-nô	mo′-no
Monopoli (It.)	mô-nô′-pô-lē	mo-no′-po-lee
Monoštor (Yugosl.)	mô′-nô-shtôr	mo′-no-shtor
Monroney, Mike (U.S. representative)	mən-rō′-nĭ	muhn-roh′-ni
Mons (Belg.)	*Eng.* mŏnz′ *Fr.* môNs′	monz′ moNs′
Mons en Baroeul (Fr.)	môN′ säN bä-rûl′	moN′ sahN bah-rœl′
Monserrato (It.)	môn-sĕr-rä′-tô	mon-sehr-rah′-to
Monster (Neth.)	môn′-stər	mon′-stuhr
Montargis (Fr.)	môN-tär-zhē′	moN-tahr-zhee′
Montauban (Fr.)	môN-tō-bäN′	moN-toh-bahN′
Montbéliard (Fr.)	môN-bĕ-lyär′	moN-beh-lyahr′
Mont Cenis (Fr., It., mt.)	môN sə-nē′	moN suh-nee′
Montchanin les Mines (Fr.)	môN-shä-năN′ lĕ mēn′	moN-shah-naN′ leh meen′
Mont de Marsan (Fr.)	môN′ də mär-säN′	moN′ duh mahr-sahN′
monte	môn′-tĕ	mon′-teh

An element, meaning *mount*, in Italian place names. It may be necessary to look up the other part of the name.

Monte Carlo (Mon.)	*Eng.* mŏn′-tĭ kär′-lō *It.* môn′-tĕ kär′-lô	mon′-ti kahr′-loh mon′-teh kahr′-lo
Montecilfone (It.)	môn-tĕ-chēl-fô′-nĕ	mon-teh-cheel-fo′-neh
Monteiro, Goes (Braz. general)	môn-tā′-ro͞o, gô′-ĭs	mon-tay′-ru, go′-is

Both names should be used, thus: *Goes Monteiro*, not *Monteiro* alone.

Montenegro (Yugosl.)	*Eng.* mŏn′-tĭ-nē′-grô *It.* môn′-tĕ-nĕ′-grô	mon′-ti-nee′-gro mon′-teh-neh′-gro

Serb-Croat *Crna Gora*, q.v.

Montgomery	mən(t)-gŭm′-(ə-)rĭ	muhn(t)-guhm′-(uh-)ri
	or mŏn(t)-gŭm′-(ə-)rĭ	mon(t)-guhm′-(uh-)ri

In America and England mən-gŭm′-rĭ [muhn-guhm′-ri] is both old-fashioned genteel and popular. As the most idiomatic pronunciation it is probably preferable for radio, although pronunciations according to the spelling are as common.

Montluçon (Fr.)	môN-lü-sôN′	moN-lü-soN′
Montpelier (Vt.)	mŏnt-pē′-lyər	mont-pee′-lyuhr
Montpellier (Fr.)	môN-pĕ-lyĕ′	moN-peh-lyeh′
Montreuil (Fr.)	môN-trû′(y)	moN-trœ′(y)
Monywa (Burma)	mōn-yo͝oä′	mohn-yu-ah′
Moppo (Korea)	môp-pô	mop-po
Morača (Yugosl., riv.)	mô′-rä-chä	mo′-rah-chah
Moradabad (India)	mō-rə-də-băd′	moh-ruh-duh-bad′
	or mō-rä-dä-bäd′	moh-rah-dah-bahd′
Mora Figueroa, Manuel (Sp. leader)	mô′-rä fē-gĕ-rô′-ä, mä-nwĕl′	mo′-rah fee-geh-ro′-ah, mah-nwel′
Morava (Europ. riv.)	*Cz.* mô′-rä-vä	mo′-rah-vah

German *March*, märk(h)′ [mahrk(h)′].

Morava (Yugosl., riv.)	mô′-rä′-vä	mo′-rah′-vah
Moravia (Cz., prov.)	*Eng.* mō-rā′-vĭ-ə	moh-ray′-vi-uh

Czech *Morava*, mô′-rä-vä [mo′-rah-vah]. German *Mähren*, mĕ′-rən [meh′-ruhn].

Moravica (Yugosl., riv.)	mô′-rä′-vĭ-tsä	mo′-rah′-vi-tsah
Moravice, Staro (Yugosl.)	mô′-rä′-vĭ-tsĕ, stä′-rô	mo′-rah′-vi-tseh, stah′-ro
Moravská, -é, -ý (Cz.)	mô′-räf-skä, -ĕ, -ĭ	mo′-rahf-skah, -eh, -i

A common element, meaning *Moravian*, in Czech place names. It may be necessary to look up the other part of the name.

Moravska (Yugosl.)	mô′-räv′-skä	mo′-rahv′-skah
Moravská Ostrava (Cz.)	mô′-räf-skä ô′-strä-vä	mo′-rahf-skah o′-strah-vah

German *Mährisch Ostrau*, mĕ′-rĭsh ôs′-trou [meh′-rish os′-trau].

Morbihan (Fr., dept.)	môr-bē-äN′	mor-bee-ahN′
Morea (Gr.)	*Eng.* mō-rē′-ə	moh-ree′-uh

Greek *Moreas*, mô-rĕ′-äs [mo-reh′-ahs] *or* môr-yäs′ [mor-yahs′]. See *Peloponnesos*.

Moree (Austral.)	mō-rē′	moh-ree′
Moreton (Austral., bay)	môrt′n	mort′n
Morgenstierne, Wilhelm (Nor. diplomat)	môr′-gən-styĕr′-nə, vĭl′-hĕlm	mor′-guhn-styehr′-nuh, vil′-helm
Morgenthau, Sec. Henry	môr′-gən-thô	mor′-guhn-thaw

Morínigo, Higinio (President of Paraguay)	mô-rē′-nē-gô, ē-hēn′-yô	mo-ree′-nee-go, ee-heen′-yo
Morinj (Yugosl.)	mô′-rĭn(y)	mo′-rin(y)
Morlacca Channel (Yugosl.)	*Eng.* môr-lăk′-ə *It.* môr-läk′-kä	mor-lak′-uh mor-lahk′-kah

Serb-Croat *Planinski Kanal,* q.v.

Morlaix (Fr.)	môr-lĕ′	mor-leh′
Mormanno (It.)	môr-män′-nô	mor-mahn′-no
Mormugão (Port. India)	môr-mōō-gouN′	mor-moo-gauN′

Also called *Marmagao,* mär-mə-gou′ [mahr-muh-gau′], and *Marmagoa,* mär-mə-gō′-ə [mahr-muh-goh′-uh].

Morobe (New Guinea)	mô-rô′-bĕ	mo-ro′-beh
Morombe (Madag.)	mô-rôm-bĕ′	mo-rom-beh′
Morotai (NEI)	mô-rô-tī′	mo-ro-tai′
Morova planina (Alb., mts.)	mô′-rô-vä plä′-nē′-nä	mo′-ro-vah plah′-nee′-nah
Morozovskaya (Rus.)	mŏ-rô′-zŏf-skä-yä	mo-ro′-zof-skah-yah
Morshansk (Rus.)	mŏr-shänsk′	mor-shahnsk′
Morskie Oko (Pol., lake)	môr′-skyĕ ô′-kô	mor′-skyeh o′-ko

German *Fischsee,* q.v.

Morsott (Alg.)	mŏr-sŏt′	mor-sot′
Mosalsk (Rus.)	mŏ-sälsk′	mo-sahlsk′
Moscow (Rus.)	mŏs′-kō	mos′-koh

This is the only pronunciation recorded in dictionaries, and radio speakers should therefore adopt it as probably the most convenient. However, a spelling pronunciation, mŏs′-kou [mos′-kau], is very common in the United States and deserves dictionary recognition. The Russian is *Moskva,* pronounced mŏs-kvä′ [mos-kvah′]. English derivatives are *Muscovy* and *Muscovite*—mŭs′-kō-vĭ [muhs′-koh-vi] and mŭs′-kō-vīt [muhs′-koh-vait].

Moselle (Fr., Ger., riv.)	mô-zĕl′	mo-zel′

German *Mosel,* mō′-zəl [moh′-zuhl].

Mosjoeen *or* Mosjöen (Nor.)	mō′-shû-ən	moh′-shœ-uhn
Moskenes (Nor., isl.)	mŏŏs′-kĕ-nĕs	mus′-keh-nes
Moskva (Rus., riv.)	mŏs-kvä′	mos-kvah′
Moslem	mŏz′-ləm *or* mŏs′-ləm	moz′-luhm *or* mos′-luhm
Mosoedji *or* Mosudyi (NEI)	mô-sōōd′-yē	mo-sood′-yee
Moson (Hung.)	mô′-shôn	mo′-shon
Moss (Nor.)	môs′	mos′
Most (Cz.)	môst′	most′

German *Brüx,* brüks′ [brüks′].

Mostaganem (Alg.)	môs-tä-gä-nĕm′	mos-tah-gah-nem′
Moštanica (Yugosl.)	mô′-shtä′-nĭ-tsä	mo′-shtah′-ni-tsah
Mostar (Yugosl.)	mô′-stär	mo′-stahr
Mösvatn (Nor., dam)	mûs′-vätn	mœs′-vahtn
Motovski Zaliv (Rus.)	mŏ-tôf′-skĭ zä-lēf′	mo-tof′-ski zah-leef′
Mouliana (Crete)	mo͞o-lyä-nä′	moo-lyah-nah′
Moulins (Fr.)	mo͞o-lăN′	moo-laN′
Moulmein (Burma)	mo͝ol-mān′	mul-mayn′
The first syllable is also pronounced *môl-* and *mōl-*. The native pronunciation is approximately mô′-lə-myīng′ [maw′-luh-myaing′].		
Mount Etna (Sicily)	*Eng.* ĕt′-nə	et′-nuh
Mouscron (Belg.)	mo͞o-skrôN′	moo-skroN′
Flemish *Moeskroen*, q.v.		
Mouzaki (Gr.)	mo͞o-zä′-kē	moo-zah′-kee
Mowinckel, Johan Ludwig (Nor. leader)	mō′-vĭng-kəl, yō-hän′ lo͝od′-vĭk	moh′-ving-kuhl, yoh-hahn′ lud′-vik
Mozambique (Afr.)	mō′-zəm-bēk′	moh′-zuhm-beek′
Portuguese *Moçambique*, mô′-səm-bē′-kə [mo′-suhm-bee′-kuh].		
Mozdok (Rus.)	mŏz-dŏk′	moz-dok′
Mozgovo (Yugosl.)	môz′-gô-vô	moz′-go-vo
Mozhaisk (Rus.)	mŏ-zhīsk′	mo-zhaisk′
Mozirje (Yugosl.)	mô′-zĭr-yĕ	mo′-zihr-yeh
Mozyr (Rus.)	mŏ-zwēr′	mo-zweer′
Mramorak (Yugosl.)	mrä′-mô-räk	mrah′-mo-rahk
Mrčajevci (Yugosl.)	mər′-chä′-yĕv-tsĭ	muhr′-chah′-yev-tsi
Mrkonjićgrad (Yugosl.)	mər′-kô′-nyĭch-gräd	muhr′-ko′-nyich-grahd
Mrsać (Yugosl.)	mər′-säch	muhr′-sahch
Mruk, Joseph (U.S. representative)	mə-rŭk′	muh-ruhk′
Mrzen (Yugosl.)	mər′-zĕn	muhr′-zen
Mrzenci (Yugosl.)	mər′-zĕn-tsĭ	muhr′-zen-tsi
Msaken (Tun.)	mə-să′-kĕn	muh-sa′-ken
Mshchonov (Pol.) See *Mszczonów*.		
Mshinskaya (Rus.)	mshĭn′-skä-yä	mshin′-skah-yah
Msta (Rus., riv.)	mstä′	mstah′
Msus (Libya)	mə-so͞os′	muh-soos′
Mszczonów (Pol.)	mshchô′-no͝of	mshcho′-nuf
Russian *Mshchonov*, mshchô′-nŏf [mshcho′-nof].		
Mtsensk (Rus.)	mtsĕnsk′	mtsensk′
Mubo (Oc.)	mo͞o′-bô	moo′-bo
Muelheim (Ger.)	mül′-hīm	mül′-haim
Muenchen (Ger.)	mün′-k(h)ən	mün′-k(h)uhn
English *Munich*, q.v.		

muende *or* münde	mün′-də	mün′-duh
An element, meaning *river mouth*, in German place names.		
Muenster (Ger.)	mün′-stər	mün′-stuhr
Mufta (Libya)	mo͝of′-tä	muf′-tah
Mugil (Oc.)	mo͞o′-gēl	moo′-geel
Muğla (Turk.)	mo͞o′-lä′	moo′-lah′
Muhlenberg (Am. name)	mū′-lən-bûrg	myoo′-luhn-buhrg
Muhu(maa) (Est., isl.)	mo͞o′-ho͞o(-mä)	moo′-hoo(-mah)
Russian and German *Mon*, q.v.		
Muka (Sarawak)	mo͞o′-kä	moo′-kah
Mukačevo (Cz.)	mo͞o′-kä-chô′-vŏ	moo′-kah-cho′-vo
	or mo͞o′-kä-chĕ′-vŏ	moo′-kah-cheh′-vo
Hungarian *Munkács*, mo͝ong′-käch [mung′-kahch].		
Mukden (Manchu., prov., city)	mo͝ok-dĕn *or* mo͞ok-dĕn	muk-den *or* mook-den
Also called *Fêng-t'ien*, q.v.		
Mulat (Yugosl.)	mo͞o′-lät	moo′-laht
Italian *Melada*, q.v.		
mulga (Australian tree)	mŭl′-gə	muhl′-guh
Mülheim (Ger.)	mül′-hīm	mül′-haim
Mulhouse (Fr.)	mü-lo͞oz′	mü-looz′
German *Mülhausen*, mül′-hou′-zən [mül′-hau′-zuhn].		
Multan (India)	mo͝ol-tän′	mul-tahn′
Munchar (Tun.)	mo͝on-shär′	mun-shahr′
München (Ger.)	mün′-k(h)ən	mün′-k(h)uhn
English *Munich*, q.v.		
München-Gladbach (Ger.)	mün′-k(h)ən-gläd′-bäk(h)	mün′-k(h)uhn-glahd′-bahk(h)
Munda (Oc.)	mo͞on′-dä	moon′-dah
Mundt, Karl (U.S. representative)	mŭnt′	muhnt′
Munich (Ger.)	*Eng.* mū′-nĭk	myoo′-nik
German *Muenchen*, q.v.		
Munkács (Cz.) See *Mukačevo.*		
Muñoz Marín, Luis (P. R. leader)	mo͞o-nyôs′ mä-rēn′, lwēs′	moo-nyos′ mah-reen′, lwees′
Münster (Ger.)	mün′-stər	mün′-stuhr
To be distinguished from *Munster*, Eire, mŭn′-stər [muhn′-stuhr].		
Muntenia (Rum.) See *Walachia.*		
Mur (Austria, Yugosl., riv.)	mo͞or′	moor′
Mura (Yugosl., riv.)	mo͞o′-rä	moo′-rah
Muraszombat (Yugosl.) See *Murska Sobota.*		
Muravyevo (Lith.)	*Rus.* mo͝o-rä-vyô′-vŏ	mu-rah-vyo′-vo
Lithuanian *Mažeikiai*, q.v.		

Murcia (Sp.)	*Eng.* mo͝or′-shə	mur′-shuh
	Sp. mo͞or′-thyä *or* -syä	moor′-thyah *or* -syah
Mureş (Rum., riv.)	mo͝o′-rĕsh	mu′-resh
Murilo (Oc.)	mo͞o-rē-lô′	moo-ree-lo′
Murmansk (Rus.)	mo͞or′-mänsk′	moor′-mahnsk′
Murom (Rus.)	mo͞o′-rŏm	moo′-rom
Murro di Porco *or* Porto (Sicily, cape)	mo͞or′-rô dē pôr′-kô *or* pôr′-tô	moor′-ro dee por′-ko *or* por′-to
Murska Sobota (Yugosl.)	mo͞or′-skä sô′-bô-tä	moor′-skah so′-bo-tah
Hungarian *Muraszombat*, mo͝o′-rŏ-sôm′-bŏt [mu′-ro-som′-bot]. German *Olsnitz.*		
Murua (Oc.)	mo͞o′-ro͞o-ä	moo′-roo-ah
Murzuch (Libya)	mo͞or′-zo͞ok	moor′-zook
Also spelled *Murzuq*, *Murzuk*, *Mourzouk.*		
Musacchia (Alb.)	*It.* mo͞o-säk′-kyä	moo-sahk′-kyah
Albanian *Myzeqe*, q.v.		
Muscel (Rum.)	mo͝os-chĕl′	mus-chel′
Mushu (New Guinea)	mo͞o-sho͞o′	moo-shoo′
Musi (NEI) See *Moesi.*		
Mussau (Oc.)	mo͞os-sou′	moos-sau′
Mussolini, Benito (It. leader)	mo͞os-sô-lē′-nē, bĕ-nē′-tô	moos-so-lee′-nee, beh-nee′-to
See *Duce.*		
Mussulman	mŭs′-əl-mən	muhs′-uhl-muhn
Mustapha Kemal Pasha (Turk.) See *Kemal Atatürk.*		
Mušutište (Yugosl.)	mo͞o′-sho͞o′-tĭ-shtĕ	moo′-shoo′-ti-shteh
Mutnica (Yugosl.)	mo͞ot′-nĭ-tsä	moot′-ni-tsah
Mutupina (Oc.)	mo͞o-to͞o-pē′-nä	moo-too-pee′-nah
Muzhëll (Alb.)	mo͞o′-zhəl	moo′-zhuhl
Muzhlli (Alb.) See *Muzhëll.*		
Myanaung (Burma)	myän-oung′	myahn-aung′
Myebon (Burma)	myĕ-bōn′	myeh-bohn′
Myingyan (Burma)	myĭn′-jän′	myin′-jahn′
Myitkyina (Burma)	myĭt′-chĭ-nä *or* myĭt-chē-nä′	myit′-chi-nah myit-chee-nah′
Myittha (Burma)	myĭt-thä′	myit-thah′
Mykonos (Gr., isl.)	mē′-kô-nô(s)	mee′-ko-no(s)
Myohaung (Burma)	myō-houng′	myoh-haung′
Myrdal (Nor.)	mür′-däl	mür′-dahl
Myrtos (Crete)	mēr′-tôs	meer′-tos
Mysen (Nor.)	müs′n	müs′n
Mysore (India)	mī-sōr′	mai-sohr′
Mysovaya (Rus.)	mĭ-sŏ-vä′-yä	mi-so-vah′-yah

Mytho (Indo-Ch.)	mē-tô′	mee-taw′
Mytilene (Gr., isl., city)	*Eng.* mĭt′-ĭ-lē′-nĭ	mit′-i-lee′-ni
	Gr. mē-tē-lē′-nē	mee-tee-lee′-nee
Also called *Lesbos*, q.v.		
Myzeqe (Alb.)	mü-zĕ′-kyĕ	mü-zeh′-kyeh
Italian *Musacchia*, q.v.		
Myzeqeja (Alb.) See *Myzeqe.*		
Naaldwijk (Neth.)	nält′-wīk	nahlt′-waik
Naarden (Neth.)	när′-dən	nahr′-duhn
Naba (Burma)	nə-bä′	nuh-bah′
Nabeul (Tun.)	nä-bûl′	nah-bœl′
Nabeur (Tun.)	nä-bûr′	nah-bœr′
Náchod (Cz.)	nä′-hôd	nah′-hod
Nădlac (Rum.)	nəd-läk′	nuhd-lahk′
Nadvoitsy (Rus.)	nä-dvoi′-tsĭ	nah-dvoi′-tsi
Nadwórna (Pol.)	nä-dwo͝or′-nä	nah-dwur′-nah
Næröfjord (Nor.)	năr′-û-fyōr	nehr′-œ-fyohr
Næstved (Den.)	nĕst′-vĕ*th*	nest′-ve*th*
Naft Safid (Iran)	năft′ să-fēd′	naft′ seh-feed′
Naga (P.I.)	nä′-gä	nah′-gah
Nagano (Jap.)	nä-gä-nô	nah-gah-no
Nagara Patom (Thai)	nə-kôn pə-tōm′	nuh-kawn puh-tohm′
Also spelled *Nakon Patom.*		
Nagara Svagara (Thai) See *Nagorn Sawarn.*		
Nagasaki (Jap.)	nä-gä-sä-kē	nah-gah-sah-kee
Nagorn Sawarn (Thai)	nə-kôn′ sə-wän′	nuh-kawn′ suh-wahn′
Also spelled *Nagara Svagara.*		
Nagorn Sridharmarat (Thai)	nə-kôn′ sē′-tŭm-ə-rät′	nuh-kawn′ see′-tuhm-uh-raht′
Nagornoe (Rus.)	nä-gôr′-nŏ-yĕ	nah-gor′-no-yeh
Nagoya (Jap.)	nä-gô-yä	nah-go-yah
Nagpur (India)	năg-po͝or′	nag-pur′
Nagy, Costa (Yugosl. leader)	nä′-gē, kôs′-tä	nah′-gee, kos′-tah
nagy (Hung.)	nŏd′(y) *or* nŏt′(y)	nod′(y) *or* not′(y)
An element, meaning *great* or *large*, in Hungarian place names. It may be necessary to look up the other part of the name.		
Nagybánya (Rum.) See *Baia Mare.*		
Nagybecskerek (Yugosl.) See *Bečkerek*, Veliki.		
Nagykanizsa (Hung.)	nŏt′(y)-kŏ′-nĭ-zhŏ	not′(y)-ko′-ni-zho
Nagykároly (Rum.) See *Carei.*		
Nagykikinda (Yugosl.) See *Kikinda, Velika.*		

Nagykőrös (Hung.)	nŏt′(y)-kû′-rûsh	not′(y)-kœ′-rœsh
Nagyszalonta (Rum.) See *Salonta.*		
Nagyszeben (Rum.) See *Sibiu.*		
Nagyvárad (Rum.) See *Oradea.*		
Nahas, Pasha Mustapha (Egypt. leader)	nä-häs′, pä′-shä mo͝os′-tä-fä	nah-hahs′, pah′-shah mus′-tah-fah
Nairobi (Kenya)	nī-rō′-bĭ	nai-roh′-bi
Naistenjärvi (Fin.)	nīs′-tĕn-yăr-vĭ	nais′-ten-yehr-vi
Nájera, Francisco Castillo (Mex. leader)	nä′-hĕ-rä, frän-sēs′-kô käs-tē′-yô	nah′-heh-rah, frahn-sees′-ko kahs-tee′-yo
Nakhichevan (Rus.)	nä-hĭ-chĕ-vän′(y)	nah-hi-cheh-vahn′(y)
Nakło (Pol.)	nä′-klô	nah′-klo
Nakon Patom (Thai) See *Nagara Patom.*		
Nakta (Tun.)	näk′-tä	nahk′-tah
Nalchik (Rus.)	näl′(y)-chĭk	nahl′(y)-chik
Nalut (Libya)	nä-lo͞ot′	nah-loot′
Nam, Menam (Thai, riv.)	näm′, mă-näm′	nahm′, ma-nahm′
Namdalen (Nor.)	näm′-dä-lən	nahm′-dah-luhn
Namdinh (Indo-Ch.)	näm-dĭn′	nahm-din′
Namoluk (Oc.)	nä′-mô-lo͞ok	nah′-mo-look
Namonuito (Oc.)	nä-mô-no͞o-ē′-tô	nah-mo-noo-ee′-to
Namorik (Oc.)	nä′-mô-rēk	nah′-mo-reek
Namsos (Nor.)	näm′-sōs	nahm′-sohs
Nam-t'ing (Ch., Yünnan)	näm-tĭng	nahm-ting
Namtu (Burma)	nəm-to͞o′	nuhm-too′
Namu (Oc.)	nä′-mo͞o	nah′-moo
Namur (Belg.)	*Eng.* nä-mo͞or′	nah-moor′
	Fr. nä-mür′	nah-mür′
Namur (Oc.)	nä′-mo͞or	nah′-moor
Nan (Thai)	nän′	nahn′
Nan-ch'ang (Ch., Kiangsi)	nän-chäng	nahn-chahng
Nan-ch'êng (Ch., Kiangsi)	nän-chŭng	nahn-chuhng
Nan-chêng (Ch., Shansi)	nän-jŭng	nahn-juhng
Nan-ch'i (Ch., Szechwan)	nän-chē	nahn-chee
Nan-ching (Ch., Fukien)	nän-jĭng	nahn-jing
Nancy (Fr.)	*Eng.* năn′-sĭ	nan′-si
	Fr. näN-sē′	nahN-see′
Nan-fêng (Ch., Kiangsi)	nän-fŭng	nahn-fuhng
Nan-hsien (Ch., Hunan)	nän-shyĕn	nahn-shyen
Nan-k'ang (Ch., Kiangsi)	nän-käng	nahn-kahng

Also called *Hsing-tzu,* q.v. This city is north of Lake Poyang.

Nan-k'ang (Ch., Kiangsi)	nän-chäng	nahn-chahng
A variant spelling of *Nan-ch'ang*, q.v. This city is south of Lake Poyang.		
Nan-king (Ch., Kiangsu)	*Eng.* năn-kĭng	nan-king
	Ch. nän-kĭng	nahn-king
Nan-ling (Ch., mt. range)	nän-lĭng	nahn-ling
Also called *Nan-shan*, q.v.		
Nan Lui (Ch., Yünnan, riv.)	nän lo͞o-ē	nahn loo-ee
Nan-ning (Ch., Kwangsi)	*Eng.* năn-nĭng	nan-ning
	Ch. nän-nĭng	nahn-ning
Nan-pên-chiang (Ch., Yünnan)	nän-pŭn-jyäng	nahn-puhn-jyahng
Nan-shan (Ch., mt. range)	nän-shän	nahn-shahn
Also called *Nan-ling*, q.v.		
Nantes (Fr.)	*Eng.* nănts'	nants'
	Fr. näNt'	nahNt'
Nanumanga (Oc.)	nä'-no͞o-mäng'-ä	nah'-noo-mahng'-ah
Nanumea (Oc.)	nä-no͞o-mĕ'-ä	nah-noo-meh'-ah
Nanyaseik (Burma)	nän'-yä-sāk'	nahn'-yah-sayk'
Naousa *or* Niaousta (Gr.)	nou'-sä *or* nyou'-stä	nau'-sah nyau'-stah
Naples (It.)	*Eng.* nā'-pəlz	nay'-puhlz
Napoli (It)	nä'-pô-lē	nah'-po-lee
English *Naples*, q.v.		
Nara (Jap.)	nä-rä	nah-rah
Narage (Oc.)	nä-rä'-gĕ	nah-rah'-geh
Narbada (India, riv.)	nər-bŭd'-ə	nuhr-buhd'-uh
Narbonne (Fr.)	när-bôn'	nahr-bon'
Narew (Pol.)	nä'-rĕf	nah'-ref
Russian spelling *Narev.*		
Narik (Oc.)	nä'-rēk	nah'-reek
Narocz (Pol.)	nä'-rôch	nah'-roch
Russian spelling *Naroch.*		
Narodichi (Rus.)	nä-rô'-dĭ-chĭ	nah-ro'-di-chi
Naro Fominsk (Rus.)	nä'-rŏ fŏ-mēnsk'	nah'-ro fo-meensk'
Narova (Est., riv.)	nä-rô'-vä	nah-ro'-vah
Narromine (Austral.)	năr'-ə-mīn'	nehr'-uh-main'
Nartë (Alb.) See *Arta.*		
Narva (Est.)	när'-vä	nahr'-vah
Narvik (Nor.)	*Eng.* när'-vĭk	nahr'-vik
	Nor. när'-vēk	nahr'-veek

The analogy of the English pronunciation of *Narvik* with "short *i*" will probably govern other place names with *-vik* if they come into the news.

Năsăud (Rum.) nə-sə-o͝od′ nuh-suh-ud′
  Hungarian *Naszod*, nŏ′-sôd [no′-sod].
Naselsk (Pol.) See *Nasielsk*.
Nashchi (Rus.) nä′-shchĭ nah′-shchi
Našice (Yugosl.) nä′-shĭ-tsĕ nah′-shi-tseh
Nasielsk (Pol.) nä′-syĕlsk nah′-syelsk
  Russian *Naselsk*, nä-sĕl(y)sk′ [nah-sel(y)sk′].
Nassa (Gr., Paros) nä′-sä nah′-sah
Nassau (Ger.) *Eng.* năs′-ô nas′-aw
  Ger. nä′-sou nah′-sau
Naszod (Rum.) See *Năsăud*.
Natal (Brazil) nä-täl′ nah-tahl′
  Almost nä-toul′ [nah-taul′] or nä-tôl′ [nah-tawl′].
Natal (U. of S. Afr.) nə-tăl′ nuh-tal′
Natalinci (Yugosl.) nä′-tä′-lĭn-tsĭ nah′-tah′-lin-tsi
Natmaw (Burma) nət′-mô′ nuht′-maw′
Natoena *or* Natuna (NEI) nä-to͞o′-nä nah-too′-nah
Naturaliste (Austral., cape) năt′-ū-rə-lĭst nat′-yoo-ruh-list
  Pronounced like *naturalist*.
Naumiestis (Lith.) nou′-myĕs-tĭs nau′-myes-tis
Nauna (Oc.) nä-o͞o′-nä nah-oo′-nah
Nauplia (Gr.) See *Navplion*.
Naura (Oc.) nä-o͞o′-rä nah-oo′-rah
Nauroz (Iran) nō-ro͞oz′ noh-rooz′
  The great spring holiday of Persia.
Nauru (Oc.) nä-o͞o′-ro͞o nah-oo′-roo
Navanagar (India) nŭv-ə-nŭg′-ər nuhv-uh-nuhg′-uhr
  Also spelled *Nawanagar*; also called *Jamnagar*, q.v.
Navarino (Gr.) *It.* nä-vä-rē′-nô nah-vah-ree′-no
  Gr. nä-vä-rē′-nô(n) nah-vah-ree′-no(n)
  The official name is *Pylos*, q.v.
Navarra (Sp.) nä-vä′-rä nah-vah′-rah
  English *Navarre*, nə-vär′ [nuh-vahr′].
Navlya (Rus.) näv′-lyä nahv′-lyah
Navpaktos (Gr.) näf′-pä-ktôs nahf′-pah-ktos
Navplion (Gr.) näf′-plē-ô(n) nahf′-plee-o(n)
  English *Nauplia*, nô′-plĭ-ə [naw′-pli-uh].
Nawanagar (India) See *Navanagar*.
Naxos (Gr.) *Eng.* năk′-sŏs nak′-sos
  Gr. nä′-ksô(s) nah′-kso(s)
Naze, the (Nor.) *Eng.* nāz′ nayz′
  Norwegian *Lindesnes*, q.v.

Nazi	nä′-tsĭ *or* năt′-sĭ *or* năz′-ĭ *or* nä′-zĭ	nah′-tsi *or* nat′-si naz′-i *or* nah′-zi

An abbreviation of German *Nationalsozialistische* Partei. The first pronunciation is probably the most common, but it may be displaced by the second or third.

Ndawara (Oc.)	ndä-wä′-rä	ndah-wah′-rah
Ndruval (Oc.)	ndrōō′-väl	ndroo′-vahl
Nduke (Oc.)	ndōō′-kĕ	ndoo′-keh
Neai Kalamai (Gr.)	nĕ′-ĕ kä-lä′-mĕ	neh′-eh kah-lah′-meh
Neapolis (Crete)	nĕ-ä′-pô-lēs	neh-ah′-po-lees
Nebeur (Tun.)	nĕ-bûr′	neh-bœr′
necessary	nĕs′-ə-sĕr′-ĭ	nes′-uh-sehr′-i

The pronunciation nĕs′-ə-sər-ĭ [nes′-uh-suhr-i] is listed (as an alternative marked *or, especially British*) by only one of five American dictionaries. It is not suited to American radio use.

Nedrigaylov (Rus.)	nĕ-drĭ-gī′-lŏf	neh-dri-gai′-lof
Neerpelt (Belg.)	nār′-pĕlt	nayr′-pelt
Nefta (Tun.)	nĕf′-tä	nef′-tah
Negapatam (India)	nĕ′-gə-pə-tăm′	neh′-guh-puh-tam′
Negoi (Rum., mt.)	nĕ-goi′	neh-goi′
Negotin (Yugosl.)	nĕ′-gô-tĭn	neh′-go-tin
Negrais (Burma)	nĕ-grā′-ĭs	neh-gray′-is
Negros (P.I.)	nĕ′-grôs	neh′-gros
Nehru, Pandit Jawaharlal (Indian leader)	nĕ′-rōō, pŭn′-dĭt jə-wə-hər-läl′	neh′-roo, puhn′-dit juh-wuh-huhr-lahl′
Neikban (Burma)	nāk′-băn′	nayk′-ban′
Neisse (Ger.)	nīs′-ə	nais′-uh
Nelidovo (Rus.)	nĕ-lē′-dŏ-vŏ	neh-lee′-do-vo
Nellore (India)	nĕl-lôr′	nel-lor′
Neman (Europ. riv.) See *Niemen.*		
Nemanjinci (Yugosl.)	nĕ′-mä′-nyĭn-tsĭ	neh′-mah′-nyin-tsi
Nemenikuće (Yugosl.)	nĕ′-mĕ-nē′-kōō-chĕ	neh′-meh-nee′-koo-cheh
Nemi (It., lake)	*Eng.* nā′-mĭ	nay′-mi
	It. nĕ′-mē	neh′-mee
Nemirov (Rus.)	nĕ-mē′-rŏf	neh-mee′-rof
Nemunas (Europ. riv.) See *Niemen.*	*Lith.* nyĕ′-mŏŏ-näs	nyeh′-mu-nahs
Nemuro (Jap.)	nĕ-mōō-rô	neh-moo-ro
Nenana (Alaska)	nĭ-năn′-ə	ni-nan′-uh
Nënerçka (Alb., mts.) See *Nënerçkë.*		
Nënerçkë (Alb., mts.)	nə-nĕrch′-kə	nuh-nehrch′-kuh
neoprene	nē′-ō-prēn′	nee′-oh-preen′
Nepal (Asia)	nə-pôl′	nuh-pawl′

Nercha (Rus., riv.)	nĕr′-chä	nehr′-chah
Nerchinsk (Rus.)	nĕr′-chĭnsk	nehr′-chinsk
Nerchinski Zavod (Rus.)	nĕr′-chĭn-skĭ zä-vôd′	nehr′-chin-ski zah-vod′
Neresnica (Yugosl.)	nĕ′-rĕs′-nĭ-tsä	neh′-res′-ni-tsah
Neretva (Yugosl.)	nĕ′-rĕ-tvä	neh′-reh-tvah
Italian *Narenta.*		
Nerodimka (Yugosl., riv.)	nĕ′-rô′-dĭm-kä	neh′-ro′-dim-kah
Neroefjord (Nor.)	nĕr′-û-fyōr	nehr′-œ-fyohr
nes	nĕs′	nes′
An element meaning *headland,* in Norwegian place names.		
Nesebar (Bulg.)	nĕ′-sĕ-bär	neh′-seh-bahr
Also called *Mesemvria,* mĕ-sĕm′-vrē-yä [meh-sem′-vree-yah].		
Nesflaten (Nor.)	nĕs′-flätn	nes′-flahtn
Neshava (Pol.) See *Nieszawa.*		
Nestos (Balkan riv.)	nĕ′-stôs	neh′-stos
Bulgarian *Mesta,* q.v.		
Nesvizh (Pol.) See *Nieśwież.*		
Nethe (Belg., riv.)	nā′-tə	nay′-tuh
Nettuno (It.)	nĕt-tōō′-nô	net-too′-no
Netze (Ger., Pol., riv.)	*Ger.* nĕt′-sə	net′-suh
Polish *Noteć,* q.v.		
Neubrandenburg (Ger.)	noi-brän′-dən-bo͝ork(h)	noi-brahn′-duhn-burk(h)
Neufbrisach (Fr.)	nûf-brē-zäsh′	nœf-bree-zahsh′
German *Neubreisach,* noi-brī′-zäk(h) [noi-brai′-zahk(h)].		
Neufchateau (Fr.)	nûf-shä-tō′	nœf-shah-toh′
Neuilly (Fr.)	nû-yē′	nœ-yee′
Neunkirchen (Austria)	noin′-kĭr′-k(h)ən	noin′-kihr′-k(h)uhn
Neusalz (Ger.)	noi′-zälts′	noi′-zahlts′
Neu Sandec (Pol.) See *Nowy Sącz.*		
Neuss (Ger.)	nois′	nois′
Neustadt (Ger.)	noi′-shtät	noi′-shtaht
Neuwied (Ger.)	noi′-vēt	noi′-veet
Neva (Rus., riv.)	*Eng.* nē′-və	nee′-vuh
	Rus. nĕ-vä′	neh-vah′
Nevel (Rus.)	nĕ′-vĕl(y)	neh′-vel(y)
Nevers (Fr.)	nə-vĕr′	nuh-vehr′
Nevesinje (Yugosl.)	nĕ′-vĕ′-sĭ-nyĕ	neh′-veh′-si-nyeh
Nevidiskof (Alaska, Attu)	nĕ-vē′-dĭs-kŏf	neh-vee′-dis-kof
Nevinnomyssk (Rus.)	nĕ-vĭn-nŏ-mwēsk′	neh-vin-no-mweesk′
Also called *Nevinnomysskaya,* nĕ-vĭn-nŏ-mwēs′-skä-yä [neh-vin-no-mwees′-skah-yah].		
Nevrokop (Bulg.)	nĕ′-vrŏ-kŏp	neh′-vro-kop

Newfoundland	nū′-fənd-lănd′	nyoo′-fuhnd-land′

Note that the second syllable is normally not stressed and has the vowel schwa. However, as an attribute in *Newfoundland dog*, the second syllable is stressed and is pronounced "found."

New Guinea (Oc.)	nū gĭn′-ĭ	nyoo gin′-i
New Orleans (La.)	nū ôr′-lyənz	nyoo or′-lyuhnz
	or nū ôr′-lĭ-ənz	nyoo or′-li-uhnz

Elsewhere in the South, the city is often called nū ôr′-lənz (nyoo or′-luhnz). The minstrel show pronunciation rhyming with *jeans*, nū′ ôr-lēnz′ [nyoo′ or-leenz′] should be avoided. Cf. *Orleans.*

Nezhin (Rus.)	nĕ′-zhĭn	neh′-zhin
Ngatik (Oc.)	ngä′-tēk	ngah′-teek
Nggela (Oc.)	nggĕ′-lä	nggeh′-lah
Ngulu (Oc.)	ngo͞o-lo͞o′	ngoo-loo′
Nguna (Oc.)	ngo͞o′-nä	ngoo′-nah
Nha Trang (Indo-Ch.)	nyä-träng′	nyah-trahng′
Niamţ (Rum.)	nyämts′	nyahmts′
Nias (NEI)	nē′-äs	nee′-ahs
Niau (Oc.)	nē-ou′	nee-au′
Nicaria (Gr., isl.) See *Ikaria.*		
Nicobar (India, isls.)	nĭk-ō-bär′	nik-oh-bahr′
Nicosia (Sicily)	nē-kô-zē′-ä	nee-ko-zee′-ah
Nida (Pol., riv.)	nē′-dä	nee′-dah
Nidaros (Nor.)	nē′-dä-rōs	nee′-dah-rohs

Officially called *Trondheim*, q.v.

Nidže (Balkan mt.)	nē′-jĕ	nee′-jeh
Niedere Tauern (Austria, mts.)	nē′-də-rə tou′-ərn	nee′-duh-ruh tau′-uhrn
Nielsen, Sven (Nor. minister)	nēl′-sən, svĕn′	neel′-suhn, sven′
Niemen (Europ. riv.)	*Eng.* nē′-mən	nee′-muhn
	Pol. nyĕ′-mĕn	nyeh′-men

Lithuanian *Nemunas*, q.v. Russian *Nyeman*, nĕ′-män [neh′-mahn]. German *Memel*, q.v.

niemi	nē′-ĕ′-mē	nee′-eh′-mee

An element, meaning *cape* or *point*, in Finnish place names.

Nienburg (Ger.)	nēn′-bo͝ork(h)	neen′-burk(h)
Nieśwież (Pol.)	nyĕsh′-vyĕsh	nyesh′-vyesh

Russian *Nesvizh*, nĕs′-vĭzh [nes′-vizh].

Nieszawa (Pol.)	nyĕ-shä′-vä	nyeh-shah′-vah

Russian *Neshava*, nĕ-shä′-vä [neh-shah′-vah].

Nietzsche, F. W.	nē′-chə	nee′-chuh

Nieuport (Belg.)	nē′-o͝o-pôrt	nee′-u-port
Inevitable English nū′-pôrt [nyoo′-port].		
Nieuwe Maas (Neth., riv.)	nē′-wə mäs′	nee′-wuh mahs′
Nigrita (Gr.)	nē-grē′-tä	nee-gree′-tah
Niigata (Jap.)	nyē-ē-gä-tä	nyee-ee-gah-tah
Nijmegen (Neth.)	*Eng.* nī′-mā-gən	nai′-may-guhn
	Du. nī′-mā-k(h)ən	nai′-may-k(h)uhn
For the usual Dutch pronunciation see *Nimwegen.* Cf. *Nimeguen.*		
Nikitinka (Rus.)	nĭ-kē′-tĭn-kä	ni-kee′-tin-kah
Nikitovka (Rus.)	nĭ-kē′-tŏf-kä	ni-kee′-tof-kah
Nikolaev (Rus.)	nĭ-kŏ-lä′-yĕf	ni-ko-lah′-yef
Nikolaeva, Klavdia I. (Rus. leader)	nĭ-kŏ-lä′-yĕ-vä, kläv′-dĭ-yä	ni-ko-lah′-yeh-vah, klahv′-di-yah
Nikolaevskaya (Rus.)	nĭ-kŏ-lä′-yĕf-skä-yä	ni-ko-lah′-yef-skah-yah
Nikolaos, Hagios (Gr., Crete)	nē-kô′-lä-ôs, ī′-yôs	nee-ko′-lah-os, ai′-yos
Also called *Lasethion,* lä-sē′-thē(-ôn) [lah-see′-thee(-on)].		
Nikolinci (Yugosl.)	nē′-kô′-lĭn-tsĭ	nee′-ko′-lin-tsi
Nikoloudes (Gr. leader)	nē-kô-lo͞o′-*th*ēs	nee-ko-loo′-*th*ees
Nikolsk Ussuriiski (Rus.)	nĭ-kôl(y)sk′ o͞os-so͞o-rē′-skĭ	ni-kol(y)sk′ oos-soo-ree′-ski
Nikopol (Bulg.)	nē′-kŏ-pŏl(y)	nee′-ko-pol(y)
Nikopol (Rus.)	nē′-kŏ-pŏl(y)	nee′-ko-pol(y)
Nikšić (Yugosl.)	nēk′-shĭch	neek′-shich
Nimeguen (Neth.)	nĭm′-ā-gən	nim′-ay-guhn
For an English pronunciation, see *Nijmegen.* For the usual Dutch pronunciation see *Nimwegen.*		
Nîmes (Fr.)	*Eng.* nēmz′	neemz′
	Fr. nēm′	neem′
Nimwegen (Neth.)	nĭm′-vā-k(h)ən	nim′-vay-k(h)uhn
This pronunciation is the most common in the Netherlands, however the name is spelled. Cf. *Nijmegen* and *Nimeguen.* For an English pronunciation see *Nijmegen.*		
Nin (Yugosl.)	nēn′	neen′
Ning-kang (Ch., Kiangsi)	nĭng-gäng	ning-gahng
Ning-p'o (Ch., Chekiang)	nĭng-pô	ning-po
Ning-sia (Ch., prov., town)	nĭng-shyä	ning-shyah
Also spelled *Ning-hsia.*		
Ning-tu (Ch., Kiangsi)	nĭng-do͞o	ning-doo
Ninigo (Oc.)	nē′-nē-gô	nee′-nee-go
Niokastro (Gr.) See *Pylos.*		

Niort (Fr.)	nyôr′	nyor′
Niš (Yugosl.)	nēsh′	neesh′
Nišava (Yugosl., riv.)	nē′-shä-vä	nee′-shah-vah
Niscemi (Sicily)	nē-shĕ′-mē	nee-sheh′-mee
Nisei	nē-sā	nee-say

U.S. citizens by birth, born of Japanese subjects living in this country. See *Issei* and *Kibei.*

Niseros (Dodec.) See *Nisyros.*

Niševac (Yugosl.)	nē′-shĕ-väts	nee′-sheh-vahts
Nishapur (Iran)	nē-shä-po͞or′ *or* nē-shä-bo͞or′	nee-shah-pur′ nee-shah-bur′
Niška Banja (Yugosl.)	nēsh′-kä bän′-yä	neesh′-kah bahn′-yah
Nissan (Oc.)	nĭs-sän′	nis-sahn′
Nisser (Nor., riv.)	nĭs′-ər	nis′-uhr

Nistru (Europ. riv.) See *Dniester.*

Nisyros (Dodec.)	nē′-sē-rô(s)	nee′-see-ro(s)
Niterói (Brazil)	nē-tĕ-roi′	nee-teh-roi′
Nitra (Cz.)	nē′-trä	nee′-trah
Niutao (Oc.)	nē-o͞o-tä′-ô *or* nū-tou′	nee-oo-tah′-o *or* nyoo-tau′
Nivelles (Belg.)	nē-vĕl′	nee-vel′
Nizhne Tambovskoe (Rus.)	nēzh′-nĕ täm-bôf′-skŏ-yĕ	neezh′-neh tahm-bof′-sko-yeh
Nizhneudinsk (Rus.)	nēzh′-nĕ-o͞o-dēnsk′	neezh′-neh-oo-deensk′
Nizhny Lomov (Rus.)	nēzh′-nĭ lô′-mŏf	neezh′-ni lo′-mof
Nizkovka (Rus.)	nēz′-kŏf-kä	neez′-kof-kah
Nizza (Sicily)	nēt′-sä	neet′-sah
Njeguši (Yugosl.)	nyĕ′-go͞o-shĭ	nyeh′-goo-shi
Nocera (It.)	nô-chĕ′-rä	no-cheh′-rah
Noe	*Am. name* nō′-ĭ *Fr. name* nô-ĕ′	noh′-i no-eh′
Noemfoor *or* Numfoor (NEI)	no͞om′-fōr	noom′-fohr

Nofilia (Libya) See *Zauta en Nofilia.*

Nogaisk (Rus.)	nŏ-gīsk′	no-gaisk′
Noginsk (Rus.)	nŏ-gēnsk′	no-geensk′
Noguès, Auguste (Fr. general)	nô-gĕs′, ō-güst′	no-ges′, oh-güst′
Nomwin (Oc.)	nôm′-wĭn	nom′-win
Non-ni (Manchu., riv.)	nŏn-nē	non-nee
Nonouti (Oc.)	nô-nô-o͞o′-tē	no-no-oo′-tee
Noon, Firozkhan (Indian leader)	no͞on′, fē-rôz-k(h)än′	noon′, fee-roz-k(h)ahn′
Noord Beveland (Neth.)	nōrt bā′-və-länt	nohrt bay′-vuh-lahnt

Noord Brabant (Neth.)	nōrt brä′-bänt	nohrt brah′-bahnt
For English pronunciations, see *Brabant*.		
Noord Holland (Neth., prov.)	nōrt hôl′-änt	nohrt hol′-ahnt
Noordwijk (Neth.)	nōrt′-wīk	nohrt′-waik
Nordagutu (Nor.)	nō′-rä-go͞o′-to͝o	noh′-rah-goo′-tu
Norden (Ger.)	nôr′-dən	nor′-duhn
Norderney (Ger., isl.)	nôr′-dər-nī′	nor′-duhr-nai′
Nordfjord (Nor.)	nōr′-fyōr	nohr′-fyohr
Nordhordland (Nor.)	nōr′-hôr-län	nohr′-hor-lahn
Nordkapp (Nor.)	nōr′-käp	nohr′-kahp
English *North Cape* is usually preferable for American radio.		
Nordmarka (Nor.)	nōr′-mär-kä	nohr′-mahr-kah
Nordmoere *or* Nordmöre (Nor.)	nōr′-mû-rə	nohr′-mœ-ruh
Nordreisa (Nor.)	nōr′-rā-sä	nohr′-ray-sah
Nore (Nor.)	nō′-rə	noh′-ruh
Noreanlegget (Nor.)	nō′-rə-än-lĕg-ə	noh′-ruh-ahn-leg-uh
Normanton (Austral.)	nôr′-mən-tən	nor′-muhn-tuhn
Norrell, W. F. (U.S. representative)	nôr′-əl	nor′-uhl
Northam (Austral.)	nôr′-thəm	nor′-thuhm
Norwich (Eng.)	nôr′-ĭch	nor′-ich
Noteć (Pol., Ger., riv.)	*Pol.* nô′-tĕch	no′-tech
German *Netze*, q.v.		
Noto (Sicily)	nô′-tô	no′-to
Notodden (Nor.)	nōt′-ôdn	noht′-odn
Notre Dame (Ind.)	*Eng.* nō′-trə dām′	noh′-truh daym′
In rapid speech often nōt′r dām′ [noht′r daym′]. French nō′tr däm′ [noh′tr dahm′].		
Nouméa (Oc.)	*Eng.* no͞o-mē′-ə	noo-mee′-uh
	Fr. no͞o-mĕ-ä′	noo-meh-ah′
Also spelled *Numea* and pronounced no͞o-mĕ′-ä [noo-meh′-ah]. There is some evidence to support *Noumea* pronounced nô-o͞o-mĕ′-ä [no-oo-meh′-ah].		
nová, -é, -ý (Cz.)	nô′-vä, -ĕ, -ĭ	no′-vah, -eh, -i
A common element, meaning *new*, in Czech place names. It may be necessary to look up the other part of the name.		
Nova Gradiška (Yugosl.)	nô′-vä grä′-dĭsh-kä	no′-vah grah′-dish-kah
Novalja (Yugosl.)	nô-vä′-lyä	no-vah′-lyah
Nová Ves (Cz.)	nô′-vä vĕs′	no′-vah ves′
Nova Zagora (Bulg.)	nô′-vä zä′-gŏ-rä	no′-vah zah′-go-rah
Nové Zámky (Cz.)	nô′-vĕ zäm′-kĭ	no′-veh zahm′-ki
Hungarian *Érsekújvár*, ār′-shĕk-o͞o′ĭ-vär [ayr′-shek-oo′(y)-vahr].		

Novgorod Severski (Rus.)	nôv′-gŏ-rŏt sĕ′-vĕr-skĭ	nov′-go-rot seh′-vehr-ski
Novi, Bosanski (Yugosl.)	nô′-vĭ, bô′-sän-skĭ	no′-vi, bo′-sahn-ski
Novikov, Alexander (Rus. general)	nô′-vĭ-kŏf, ä-lĕk-sän′-dər	no′-vi-kof, ah-lek-sahn′-duhr
Novi Pazar (Yugosl.)	nô′-vĭ pä′-zär	no′-vi pah′-zahr
Novi Sad (Yugosl.)	nô′-vĭ säd′	no′-vi sahd′
Hungarian *Újvidék,* o͞o′ĭ-vĭ-dāk [oo′(y)-vi-dayk].		
Novi Vileisk (Pol.) See *Nowa Wilejka.*		
Novoaleksandriya (Pol.) See *Puławy.*		
Novocherkassk (Rus.)	nô′-vŏ-chĕr-käsk′	no′-vo-chehr-kahsk′
Novodugino (Rus.)	nô′-vŏ-do͞o′-gĭ-nŏ	no′-vo-doo′-gi-no
Novogeorgievsk (Pol.) See *Modlin.*		
Novograd (Rus.)	nô′-vŏ-grät′	no′-vo-graht′
Novogrudok (Pol.) See *Nowogródek.*		
Novoierusalimskaya (Rus.)	nô′-vŏ-yĕ-ro͞o-sä-lēm′-skä-yä	no′-vo-yeh-roo-sah-leem′-skah-yah
Novominsk (Pol.) See *Mińsk Mazowiecki.*		
Novoradomsk (Pol.) See *Radomsko.*		
Novorossisk (Rus.)	nô′-vŏ-rŏ-sēsk′	no′-vo-ro-seesk′
Novorzhev (Rus.)	nô′-vŏ-rzhĕf′	no′-vo-rzhef′
Novo Selo (Yugosl.)	nô′-vô sĕ′-lô	no′-vo seh′-lo
Novosibirsk (Rus.)	nô′-vŏ-sĭ-bērsk′	no′-vo-si-beersk′
Novosil (Rus.)	nô′-vŏ-sēl′	no′-vo-seel′
Novosokolniki (Rus.)	nô′-vŏ-sŏ-kôl′(y)-nē-kĭ	no′-vo-so-kol′(y)-nee-ki
Novosvyentsyani (Pol.) See *Nowe Święciany.*		
Novoukrainka (Rus.)	nô′-vŏ-o͞o-krīn′-kä	no′-vo-oo-krain′-kah
Novozybkov (Rus.)	nô′-vŏ-zĭp′-kŏf	no′-vo-zip′-kof
Novy Bug (Rus.)	nô′-vĭ bo͝og′	no′-vi boog′
Novy Oskol (Rus.)	nô′-vĭ ŏs-kôl′	no′-vi os-kol′
Nowa Wilejka (Pol.)	nô′-vä vĭ-lā′-kä	no′-vah vi-lay′-kah
Russian *Novi Vileisk,* nô′-vĭ vĭ-lāsk′ [no′-vi vi-laysk′].		
Nowemiasto (Pol.)	nô′-vĕ-myä′-stô	no′-veh-myah′-sto
Nowe Święciany (Pol.)	nô′-vĕ shvyăN-chä′-nĭ	no′-veh shvyaN-chah′-ni
Russian *Novosventsyani,* nô′-vŏ-svĕn-tsyä′-nĭ [no′-vo-sven-tsyah′-ni].		
Nowgong (India)	nou-gŏng′	nau-gong′
Nowogródek (Pol.)	nô-vô-gro͝o′-dĕk	no-vo-gru′-dek
Russian *Novogrudok,* nô′-vŏ-gro͞o′-dŏk [no′-vo-groo′-dok].		
Nowy Bytom (Pol.)	nô′-vĭ bĭ′-tôm	no′-vi bi′-tom
German *Friedenshütte,* q.v.		
Nowy Sącz (Pol.)	nô′-vĭ sôNch′	no′-vi soNch′
German *Neu Sandec,* noi zän′-dĕts [noi zahn′-dets].		

Nowy Targ (Pol.)	nô′-vĭ tärk′	no′-vi tahrk′
Nowy Tomyśl (Pol.)	nô′-vĭ tô′-mĭshl	no′-vi to′-mishl
Noyon (Fr.)	nwä-yôN′	nwah-yoN′
Nsopzup (Burma)	nsôp-zo͝op′	nsawp-zup′
Nuan-shui-chieh (Ch., Hupeh)	nwän-shwā-jyĕ	nwahn-shway-jyeh
Nubia (Sicily)	no͞o′-byä	noo′-byah
Nuernberg *or* Nürnberg (Ger.) English *Nuremberg*, q.v.	nürn′-bĕrk(h)	nürn′-behrk(h)
Nueva Cáceres (P.I.)	nwĕ′-vä kä′-sĕ-rĕs	nweh′-vah kah′-seh-res
Nueva Écija (P.I., prov.)	nwĕ′-vä ĕ′-sē-hä	nweh′-vah eh′-see-hah
Nuevo Laredo (Mex.)	nwĕ′-vô lä-rĕ′-dô	nweh′-vo lah-reh′-do
Nuguria (Oc.)	no͞o-go͞o-rē′-ä	noo-goo-ree′-ah
Nui (Oc.)	no͞o′-ē	noo′-ee
Nukha (Rus.)	no͞o′-hä	noo′-hah
Nukufetau (Oc.)	no͞o′-ko͞o-fĕ-tou′	noo′-koo-feh-tau′
Nukulaelae (Oc.)	no͞o′-ko͞o-lä′-ĕ-lä′-ĕ	noo′-koo-lah′-eh-lah′-eh
Nukunau (Oc.)	no͞o′-ko͞o-nou′	noo′-koo-nau′
Nukuoro (Oc.)	no͞o-kwô′-rô	noo-kwo′-ro
Nullarbor (Austral.) An amusing Latinism, or so it is said.	nŭl′-ə-bōr′	nuhl′-uh-bohr′
Numea (Oc.) See *Nouméa.*		
Numedal (Nor.)	no͞o′-mə-däl	noo′-muh-dahl
Numfoor (NEI) See *Noemfoor.*		
nuncio	nŭn′-shĭ-ō	nuhn′-shi-oh
Nunivak (Alaska, isl.)	no͞o′-nĭ-văk	noo′-ni-vak
Nuremberg (Ger.) German *Nuernberg*, q.v.	*Eng.* nū′-rəm-bûrg	nyoo′-ruhm-buhrg
Nurmi, Paavo (Fin. athlete)	no͝or′-mē, pä′-vô	nur′-mee, pah′-vo
Nurri (Sard.)	no͞or′-rē	noor′-ree
Nyaungbinwun (Burma)	nyoung′-bĭn-wo͝on′	nyaung′bin-wun′
Nyaungywe (Burma) See *Yawnghwe.*		
Nyborg (Den.)	nü′-bôr	nü′-bor
Nyeman (Europ. riv.) See *Niemen.*		
Nygaardsvold, Johan (Nor. leader)	nü′-gôrs-vôl, yo͝o-hän′	nü′-gors-vol, yu-hahn′
Nyiregyháza (Hung.)	nyĭ′-rĕd(y)-hä′-zŏ	nyi′-red(y)-hah′-zo
Nykoebing *or* Nyköbing (Den.)	nü′-kû-bĭng	nü′-kœ-bing
Nymburk (Cz.)	nĭm′-bo͝ork	nim′-burk
Nystad (Fin.) See *Uusikaupunki.*		

Nystua (Nor.)	nü′-sto͞o-ä	nü′-stoo-ah
Nyukzha (Rus.)	nūk′-zhä′	nyook′-zhah′

ø is commonly used in Norwegian orthography for *ö* or *œ*. In this book spellings with both *ö* and *œ* are listed, for each may occur in the English spelling of Norwegian names. The use of ø did not seem important enough, from the English point of view, to justify the listing of a third spelling.

Ob (Rus., riv.)	ôp′	op′
Oberhausen (Ger.)	ō′-bər-hou′-zən	oh′-buhr-hau′-zuhn
Obilić (Yugosl.)	ô′-bĭ-lĭch	o′-bi-lich
Obot (Alb.)	ô′-bôt	o′-bot
Oboti (Alb.) See *Obot.*		
Oboyan (Rus.)	ŏ-bŏ-yän′(y)	o-bo-yahn′(y)
Obra (Pol., Ger., riv.)	ô′-brä	o′-brah
Obrenovac (Yugosl.)	ô′-brĕ′-nô-väts	o′-breh′-no-vahts
Obrež (Yugosl.)	ô′-brĕzh	o′-brezh
Obrovac (Yugosl.)	ô′-brô-väts	o′-bro-vahts
Obruchev, V. A. (Rus. scientist)	ô′-bro͞o-chĕf	o′-broo-chef
Ochakov (Rus.)	ŏ-chä′-kŏf	o-chah′-kof
Ochemchiri (Rus.)	ō-chĕm-chē′-rĭ	oh-chem-chee′-ri
Ochrida (Yugosl., city; Balkan lake) See *Ohrid.*		
Odda (Nor.)	ôd′-ä	od′-ah
Odense (Den.)	ō′-*th*ən-sĕ	oh′-*th*uhn-seh
Oder (Europ. riv.)	ō′-dər	oh′-duhr
Czech *Odra*, ô′-drä [o′-drah].		
Odessa (Rus.)	*Eng.* ō-dĕs′-ə	oh-des′-uh
	Rus. ŏ-dĕ′-sä	o-deh′-sah
Odnes (Nor.)	ôd′-nĕs	od′-nes
Odoevo (Rus.)	ŏ-dô′-yĕ-vŏ	o-do′-yeh-vo
Odomari (Jap.)	ô-dô-mä-rē	o-do-mah-ree
Odorhei (Rum.)	ô-dôr-hā′	o-dor-hay′
Hungarian *Székelyudvarhely*, sā′-kĕĭ-o͝od′-vŏr-hĕĭ [say′-kei-ud′-vor-hei].		
Odžaci (Yugosl.)	ô′-jä-tsĭ	o′-jah-tsi
Oedelem (Belg.)	o͞o′-də-lĕm	oo′-duh-lem
Oedenburg (Hung.) See *Sopron.*		
Oeksfjord (Nor.)	ûks′-fyōr	œks′-fyohr
Oeland (Sw., isl.)	û-länd′	œ-lahnd′
Oelen (Nor.)	û′-lən	œ′-luhn
Oema (Oc.)	ô-ĕ′-mä	o-eh′-mah
Oeresund (Sw., Den., sound)	û′-rə-so͝on	œ′-ruh-sun

Oerskog (Nor.)	ûr′-skōg or ûsh′-kōg	œr′-skohg œsh′-kohg
Oesel (Est., isl.)	*Ger.* û′-zəl	œ′-zuhl
Estonian *Saare*, q.v. Russian *Esel*, q.v.		
O Estado de São Paulo (Braz. newspaper) See *Estado de São Paulo, O.*		
Oesterdalen (Nor.)	ûs′-tər-dä′-lən	œs′-tuhr-dah′-luhn
Oestfold (Nor.)	ûst′-fôl	œst′-fol
Oestvaagoe (Nor., isl.)	ûst′-vôg-û′	œst′-vog-œ′
Oetzthal (Austria, mts.)	ûts′-täl	œts′-tahl
Oeye (Nor.)	ûĭ′-ə	œi′-uh
Oeyjord (Nor.)	ûĭ′-yōr	œi′-yohr
Ogaki (Jap.)	ô-gä-kē	o-gah-kee
Ogasawara Jima (Oc.)	ô-gä-sä-wä-rä jē-mä	o-gah-sah-wah-rah jee-mah
Also called *Bonin*, bō′-nĭn [boh′-nin].		
Ogińskiego, Kanał (Pol.)	ô-gĭn(y)-skyĕ′-gô, kä′-näl	o-gin(y)-skyeh′-go, kah′-nahl
Russian *Oginski Kanal*, ŏ-gĭn′-skĭ kä-näl′ [o-gin′-ski kah-nahl′].		
Ogliastro (It.)	ô-lyäs′-trô	o-lyahs′-tro
O Globo (Braz. newspaper) See *Globo, O.*		
Ogražden (Yugosl., mt.)	ô′-gräzh-dĕn	o′-grahzh-den
Ogulin (Yugosl.)	ô′-gōō-lĭn	o′-goo-lin
Oguni (Jap.)	ô-gōō-nē	o-goo-nee
Ohře (Cz., Ger., riv.)	*Cz.* ô′-rzhĕ	o′-rzheh
German *Eger*, ā′-gər [ay′-guhr].		
Ohri (Yugosl.)	*Alb.* ô′-hrē	o′-hree
Serb-Croat *Ohrid*, q.v.		
Ohrid (Yugosl., city; Balkan lake)	*Eng.* ô′-krĭd *S.-C.* ôk(h)′-rĭd	o′-krid ok(h)′-rid
The lake is called *Ohridsko Jezero*, ôk(h)′-rĭd-skô yĕ′-zĕ-rô [ok(h)′-rid-sko yeh′-zeh-ro]. Albanian *Liqen i Ohrit*, lē-kyĕn′ ē ô′-hrēt [lee-kyen′ ee o′-hreet]. Greek *Limne Achridos*, lēm′-nē äk(h)-rē′-dôs [leem′-nee ahk(h)-ree′-dos], or *Achris*, äk(h)-rēs′ [ahk(h)-rees′].		
Oirat Tula (Rus.)	oi-rät′ tōō′-lä	oi-raht′ too′-lah
Oise (Fr., riv.)	wäz′	wahz′
Oita (Jap.)	ô′-ē-tä	o′-ee-tah
Oivi (Oc.)	ô-ē′-vē	o-ee′-vee
O Jornal (Braz. newspaper) See *Jornal, O.*		
Oka (Rus., riv.)	ŏ-kä′	o-kah′
Okaba (NEI)	ô-kä′-bä	o-kah′-bah
Okayama (Jap.)	ô-kä-yä-mä	o-kah-yah-mah
Okhotsk (Rus., sea)	*Eng.* ō-kŏtsk′ *Rus.* ŏ-hôtsk′	oh-kotsk′ o-hotsk′
Okhrida (Yugosl., city; Balkan lake) See *Ohrid.*		

Okhtokanda (Rus.)	ŏk(h)-tŏ-kän′-dä	ok(h)-to-kahn′-dah
Okinawa Gunto (Jap.)	ô-kē-nä-wä go͞on-tô	o-kee-nah-wah goon-to

Also called *Ryukyu*, rū-kū [ryoo-kyoo]; and *Loochoo*, lo͞o-cho͞o [loo-choo].

Okol (Alb.)	ô-kôl′	o-kol′
O'Konski, Alvin E. (U.S. representative)	ō-kŏn′-skĭ	oh-kon′-ski
Öksfjord (Nor.)	ûks′-fyōr	œks′-fyohr
Okusi Ambeno (Port. Timor)	ô-ko͞o′-sē äm-bĕ′-nô	o-koo′-see ahm-beh′-no
Öland (Sw., isl.)	û-länd′	œ-lahnd′
Olav (Crown Prince of Norway)	ō′-läv	oh′-lahv
Olbia (Sard.)	ôl′-byä	ol′-byah

Also called *Terranova*, q.v.

Olden (Nor.)	ôl′-dən	ol′-duhn
Oldenburg (Ger.)	*Eng.* ōl′-dən-bûrg	ohl′-duhn-buhrg
	Ger. ōl′-dən-bo͝ork(h)	ohl′-duhn-burk(h)
Olekma (Rus., riv.)	ŏ-lĕk′-mä	o-lek′-mah
Ölen (Nor.)	û′-lən	œ′-luhn
Olenino (Rus.)	ŏ-lĕ′-nĭ-nŏ	o-leh′-ni-no
Olenya (Rus.)	ŏ-lĕ′-nyä	o-leh′-nyah
Olevsk (Rus.)	ŏ-lĕfsk′	o-lefsk′
Olevuga (Oc.)	ô-lĕ-vo͞o′-gä	o-leh-voo′-gah
Olga (Rus.)	ŏl(y)-gä′	ol(y)-gah′

Not the same as the girl's name *Olga*, which is pronounced ôl′-gä [ol′-gah].

Olgopol (Rus.)	ŏl(y)-gô′-pŏl(y)	ol(y)-go′-pol(y)
Olib (Yugosl.)	ô′-lĭb	o′-lib

Italian *Ulbo*, q.v.

Olika (Pol.) See *Olyka.*

Olimarao (Oc.)	ô-lē-mä-rou′	o-lee-mah-rau′
Olita (Lith.)	*Rus.* ŏ-lē′-tä	o-lee′-tah

Lithuanian *Alytus*, q.v.

Olkusz (Pol.)	ôl′-ko͝osh	ol′-kush

Olmütz (Cz.) See *Olomouc.*

Olomouc (Cz.)	ô′-lô-mōts	o′-lo-mohts

German *Olmütz*, ôl′-müts [ol′-müts].

Olonets (Rus.)	ŏ-lô′-nĕts	o-lo′-nets
Olongapo (P.I.)	ô-lông′-gä-pô′	o-long′-gah-po′
Olovyannaya (Rus.)	ŏ-lŏ-vyän′-nä-yä	o-lo-vyahn′-nah-yah

Olsau (Pol.) See *Olza.*

Olt (Rum., riv.)	ôlt′	olt′
Also called *Oltul*, q.v.		
Oltenia (Rum.)	ôl-tĕ′-nyä	ol-teh′-nyah
Oltenița (Rum.)	ôl-tĕ′-nē-tsä	ol-teh′-nee-tsah
Oltul (Rum., riv.)	ôl′-tŏŏl	ol′-tul
Also called *Oltu*, ôl′-tŏŏ [ol′-tu].		
Olu Malau (Oc.)	ô′-lōō mä-lou′	o′-loo mah-lau′
Ołyka (Pol.)	ô-lĭ′-kä	o-li′-kah
Russian spelling *Olika*.		
Olympia (Gr.)	*Eng.* ō lĭm′-pyə	oh-lim′-pyuh
	Gr. ô-lē(m)-bē′-ä	o-lee(m)-bee′-ah
Olympos (Gr., mt.)	*Eng.* ō-lĭm′-pəs	oh-lim′-puhs
	Gr. ô′-lēm-bôs	o′-leem-bos
Olza (Pol.)	ôl′-zä	ol′-zah
German *Olsau*, ôl′-zou [ol′-zau].		
O'Mahoney, Joseph C. (U.S. senator)	ō-mă′-hə-nĭ	oh-ma′-huh-ni

The *a* of the second syllable is properly pronounced between the usual *ä* of *father* and the *ă* of *fat*. The Senator's father described his name thus:

"Oh, the bleat of the lamb
And the fruit of the bee
Make the name of the man
Who's speaking to thee—
OH-MA′-HONEY."

Oman (Baluch.)	ō-män′	oh-mahn′
Ominato (Jap.)	ô-mē-nä-tô	o-mee-nah-to
Omiš (Yugosl.)	ô′-mĭsh	o′-mish
Omišalj (Yugosl.)	ô′-mĭ-shäl(y)	o′-mi-shahl(y)
Ommen (Neth.)	ôm′-ən	om′-uhn
Omoljica (Yugosl.)	ô′-mô′-lyĭ-tsä	o′-mo′-lyi-tsah
Omsk (Rus.)	ômsk′	omsk′
Onda (Rus., riv.)	ôn′-dä	on′-dah
Ondozero (Rus.)	ŏn-dô′-zĕ-rŏ	on-do′-zeh-ro
Onega (Rus., lake)	*Eng.* ō-nē′-gə	oh-nee′-guh
	Rus. ŏ-nĕ′-gä	o-neh′-gah
Onegin, Eugene (Tchaikovsky's opera)	ŏ-nĕ′-gĭn, ū-jēn′	o-neh′-gin, yoo-jeen′

In this title *Eugene* is commonly Anglicized. French *Eugène*, û-zhĕn′ [œ-zhen′]. Russian *Evgeni*, yĕv-gĕ′-nĭ [yev-geh′-ni]. As I remember, FPA in the old days took pains to point out that it was not "Eugene, one gin, and be quick about it."

Onezhskoe (Rus., lake)	ŏ-nĕsh′-skŏ-yĕ	o-nesh′-sko-yeh
Onomichi (Jap.)	ô-nô-mē-chē	o-no-mee-chee
Ontong Java (Oc.)	ôn′-tông jä′-vä	on′-tong jah′-vah

Onykhas (Crete, mt.)	ô′-nē-häs	o′-nee-hahs
Oodnadatta (Austral.)	ōōd′-nə-dăt′-ə	ood′-nuh-dat′-uh
Ooldea (Austral.)	ōōl-dē′-ə	ool-dee′-uh
oost *and* ooster	ōst′ *and* ōs′-tər	ohst′ *and* ohs′-tuhr

An element, meaning *east*, in Dutch place names. It may be necessary to look up the other part of the name.

Oostdongeradeel (Neth.)	ōst-dông′-ə-rä-dāl′	ohst-dong′-uh-rah-dayl′
Oosterbeek (Neth.)	ōs′-tər-bāk	ohs′-tuhr-bayk
Oosterhout (Neth.)	ōs′-tər-hout	ohs′-tuhr-haut
Oosterwijk (Neth.)	ōs′-tər-wīk	ohs′-tuhr-waik
Ooststellingwerf (Neth.)	ōst-stĕl′-ĭng-wĕrf′	ohst-stel′-ing-wehrf′
Ootacamund (India)	ōō′-tə-kə-mŭnd′	oo′-tuh-kuh-muhnd′
Opatów (Pol.)	ô-pä′-tŏŏf	o-pah′-tuf
Opava (Cz.)	ô′-pä-vä	o′-pah-vah

German *Troppau*, trôp′-ou [trop′-au].

Opdal (Nor.)	ôp′-däl	op′-dahl
Opochinskoe (Rus.)	ŏ-pô′-chĭn-skŏ-yĕ	o-po′-chin-sko-yeh
Opochka (Rus.)	ŏ-pôch′-kä	o-poch′-kah
Opoczno (Pol.)	ô-pôch′-nô	o-poch′-no

Russian spelling *Opochno.*

Oporto (Port.)	*Eng.* ō-pôr′-tō	oh-por′-toh

Portuguese *Porto*, q.v.

Oppido (It.)	ôp′-pē-dô	op′-pee-do
opus	ō′-pəs	oh′-puhs

The plural of *opus* is *opera*. The plural *opuses* is badly needed but not yet authorized by the dictionaries. Cp. *octopuses* alongside of *octopodes* and *octopi*—all plurals of *octopus.*

Opuzen (Yugosl.)	ô′-pōō-zĕn	o′-poo-zen
Oradea (Rum.)	ô-rä′-dyä	o-rah′-dyah

Hungarian *Nagyvárad*, nŏd′(y)-vä′-rŏd [nod′(y)-vah′-rod].

Orahovac (Yugosl.)	ô′-rä′-hô-väts	o′-rah′-ho-vahts
Orahovica (Yugosl.)	ô′-rä′-hô-vĭ-tsä	o′-rah′-ho-vi-tsah
Oran (Alg.)	*Eng.* ō′-răn′	oh′-ran′
	Fr. ô-räN′	o-rahN′
Oranienbaum (Rus.)	ŏ-rän′-yĕn-boum	o-rahn′-yen-baum
Orany (Pol.)	ô-rä′-nĭ	o-rah′-ni

Russian spelling *Orani.*

Orašac (Yugosl.)	ô′-rä′-shäts	o′-rah′-shahts
Orašje (Yugosl.)	ô′-räsh′-yĕ	o′-rahsh′-yeh
Orăştie (Rum.)	ô-rûsh′-tyĕ	o-ruhsh′-tyeh
Oraviţa (Rum.)	ô-rä′-vē-tsä	o-rah′-vee-tsah
Ord (Austral., riv.)	ôrd′	ord′
Ordos (Ch., Suiyuan)	*Eng.* ōr′-dŏs	ohr′-dos

Ordzhonikidzegrad (Rus.)	ŏr-jŏ-nĭ-kēd′-zĕ-grät	or-jo-ni-keed′-zeh-graht
Orebić (Yugosl.)	ô′-rĕ-bĭch	o′-reh-bich
Orekhovo (Bulg.)	ŏ-rĕ′-hŏ-vŏ	o-reh′-ho-vo
Orekhovo Zuevo (Rus.)	ŏ-rĕ′-hŏ-vŏ zo͞o′-yĕ-vŏ	o-reh′-ho-vo zoo′-yeh-vo
Orel (Rus.)	*Rus.* ŏr-yôl′	or-yol′
	Eng. ō-rĕl′	oh-rel′
Orenburg (Rus.)	ŏ-rĕn-bo͝ork′	o-ren-burk′
Orense (Sp.)	ô-rĕn′-sĕ	o-ren′-seh
Oreovica (Yugosl.)	ô′-rĕ′-ô-vĭ-tsä	o′-reh′-o-vi-tsah
Öresund (Sw., Den., sound)	û′-rə-so͝on	œ′-ruh-sun
English the *Sound*.		
Orgyeev (Rum.) See *Orhei*.		
Orhei (Rum.)	ôr-hā′	or-hay′
Russian *Orgyeev*, ŏr-gĕ′-yĕf [or-geh′-yef].		
Orissa (India)	ə-rĭs′-ə	uh-ris′-uh
Oristano (Sard.)	ô-rē-stä′-nô	o-ree-stah′-no
Orjen (Yugosl., mt.)	ôr′-yĕn	or′-yen
Orkdalsoeyra *or* Orkdalsöyra (Nor.)	ôrk′-däls-û′-rä	ork′-dahls-œ′-rah
D'Orlando (Sicily, cape)	dôr-län′-dô	dor-lahn′-do
Orléans, Orleans	*Fr.* ôr-lĕ-äN′	or-leh-ahN′
	Eng. ôr-lēNz′	or-leeNz′

For the French city the French pronunciation is probably the more common among American radio speakers. The American place name is pronounced ôr-lēnz′ [or-leenz′] except for *New Orleans*, Louisiana, where the pronunciation is ôr′-lyənz [or′-lyuhnz] *or* ôr′-lĭ-ənz [or′-li-uhnz].

Orlovka (Rus.)	ŏr-lôf′-kä	or-lof′-kah
Ormanli (Yugosl.)	ôr′-män-lĭ	or′-mahn-li
Ormoc (P.I.)	ôr-môk′	or-mok′
Ormož (Yugosl.)	ôr′-môzh	or′-mozh
Oro (Oc., bay)	ô′-rô	o′-ro
Oroluk (Oc.)	ô′-rô-lo͝ok	o′-ro-look
Oros, Agion (Gr., mt.) See *Athos*.		
Orosh (Alb.)	ô′-rôsh	o′-rosh
Orosháza (Hung.)	ô′-rôsh-hä′-zŏ	o′-rosh-hah′-zo
Oroshi (Alb.) See *Orosh*.		
Orsk (Rus.)	ôrsk′	orsk′
Örskog (Nor.)	ûr′-skōg *or* ûsh′-kōg	œr′-skohg *or* œsh′-kohg
Officially *Aurskog*, q.v.		

Orsogna (It.)	ôr-sô′-nyä	or-so′-nyah
Orşova (Rum.)	ôr′-shô-vä	or′-sho-vah
Hungarian *Orsova*, ôr′-shô-vŏ [or′-sho-vo].		
Orte (It.)	ôr′-tĕ	or′-teh
Ortega (Sp., cape)	ôr-tĕ′-gä	or-teh′-gah
Ortegal (Sp., cape)	ôr-tĕ-gäl′	or-teh-gahl′
Ortona (It.)	ôr-tô′-nä	or-to′-nah
Orvieto (It.)	ôr-vyĕ′-tô	or-vyeh′-to
Osaka (Jap.)	ô-sä-kä	o-sah-kah
Locally ô-zä-kä [o-zah-kah], sounding to American ears as if the first syllable had an accent.		
Oschersleben (Ger.)	ôsh′-ərs-lā′-bən *or* ōsh′-ərs-lā′-bən	osh′-uhrs-lay′-buhn ohsh′-uhrs-lay′-buhn
Osečina (Yugosl.)	ô′-sĕ′-chĭ-nä	o′-seh′-chi-nah
Ösel (Est., isl.)	*Ger.* û′-zəl	œ′-zuhl
Estonian *Saare*, q.v. Russian *Esel*, q.v.		
Osen (Nor.)	ō′-sən	oh′-suhn
Osh (Rus.)	ôsh′	osh′
Osias, Camilo (Fil. leader)	ô′-syäs *or* ô-sē′-yäs, kä-mē′-lô	o′-syahs *or* o-see′-yahs, kah-mee′-lo
Osoeyra *or* Osöyra (Nor.)	ōs′-ûĭ-rä	ohs′-œi-rah
Osiječka (Yugosl.)	ô′-sĭ-yĕch-kä	o′-si-yech-kah
Osijek (Yugosl.)	ô′-sĭ-yĕk	o′-si-yek
Osipaonica (Yugosl.)	ô′-sē-pä′-ô-nĭ-tsä	o′-see-pah′-o-ni-tsah
Osipovichi (Rus.)	ŏ-sĭ-pô′-vĭ-chĭ	o-si-po′-vi-chi
Oskol (Rus., riv.)	ŏs-kôl′	os-kol′
Oslo (Nor.)	*Eng.* ŏz′-lō *or* ōs′-lō *Nor.* o͝os′-lo͝o	oz′-loh *or* ohs′-loh us′-lu
Oslofjord (Nor.)	*Eng.* ŏz′-lō-fyōrd′ *or* ōs′-lō-fyōrd′ *Nor.* o͝os′-lo͝o-fyōr	oz′-loh-fyohrd′ ohs′-loh-fyohrd′ us′-lu-fyohr
Osma (Bulg., riv.)	ôs′-mä	os′-mah
Also called *Osam*, ô′-säm [o′-sahm].		
Osmeña, Sergio (Fil. leader)	ôs-mĕ′-nyä, sĕr′-hyô	os-meh′-nyah, sehr′-hyo
Osnabrueck *or* Osnabrück (Ger.)	*Eng.* ŏz′-nə-bro͝ok *Ger.* ôs-nä-brük′	oz′-nuh-bruk os-nah-brük′
Osogovska planina (Balkan mts.)	ô′-sô-gôv-skä plä′-nē′-nä	o′-so-gov-skah plah′-nee′-nah
Ossa (Gr., mt.)	*Eng.* ŏs′-ə *Gr.* ô′-sä	os′-uh o′-sah
Ossetia (Rus.)	ŏ-sĕt′-ĭ-ə	o-set′-i-uh
Ostashkov (Rus.)	ŏs-täsh′-kŏf	os-tahsh′-kof

Ostend (Belg.)	*Eng.* ŏst-ĕnd′	ost-end′
French *Ostende*, ôs′-tăNd′ [os′-tahNd′]. Flemish *Oostende*, ōst-ĕn′-də [ohst-en′-duh].		
Österdalen (Nor.)	ûs′-tər-dä′-lən	œs′-tuhr-dah′-luhn
Osterode (Ger.)	ôs′-tə-rō′-də	os′-tuh-roh′-duh
Östfold (Nor.)	ûst′-fôl	œst′-fol
Ostia (It.)	*Eng.* ŏs′-tĭ-ə	os′-ti-uh
	It. ô′-styä	o′-styah
Ostrau (Cz.) See *Moravská Ostrava.*		
Oštro Koplje (Yugosl., mt.)	ô′-shtrô kôp′-lyĕ	o′-shtro kop′-lyeh
Ostrogozhsk (Rus.)	ŏs-trŏ-gôshsk′	os-tro-goshsk′
Ostrołęka (Pol.)	ô-strô-lăN′-kä	o-stro-laN′-kah
Russian *Ostrolenka*, ŏ-strŏ-lĕn′-kä [o-stro-len′-kah].		
Ostrov (Rus.)	ô′-strŏf	o′-strof
Ostrów (Pol.)	ô′-stro͝of	o′-struf
Russian *Ostrov*, ô′-strŏf [o′-strof]. German *Ostrowo*, ôs-trō′-vō [os-troh′-voh].		
Ostrowiec (Pol.)	ô-strô′-vyĕts	o-stro′-vyets
Russian *Ostrovets*, ŏ-strô′-vĕts [o-stro′-vets].		
Ostrów Mazowiecki (Pol.)	ô′-stro͝of mä-zô-vyĕ′-tskĭ	o′-struf mah-zo-vyeh′-tski
Russian *Ostrov*, ô′-strŏf [o′-strof].		
Ostružnica (Yugosl.)	ô′-stro͞ozh′-nĭ-tsä	o′-stroozh′-ni-tsah
Ostrvo (Yugosl., isl.)	ô′-stər′-vô	o′-stuhr′-vo
Östvaagö (Nor., isl.)	ûst′-vôg-û′	œst′-vog-œ′
Oświęcim (Pol.)	ôsh-vyăN′-tsĭm	osh-vyaN′-tsim
Oszmiana (Pol.)	ôsh-myä′-nä	osh-myah′-nah
Russian *Oshmyana*, ŏsh-myä′-nä [osh-myah′-nah].		
Otaru (Jap.)	ô-tä-ro͞o	o-tah-roo
Othonoi (Gr., isl.). See *Fanò.*		
Otočac (Yugosl.)	ô′-tô-chäts	o′-to-chahts
Otórola, Oscar Escudero (Chilean general)	ô-tô′-rô-lä, ôs-kär′ ĕs-ko͞o-dĕ′-rô	o-to′-ro-lah, os-kahr′ es-koo-deh′-ro
Otra (Nor., riv.)	ōt′-rä	oht′-rah
Otranto (It., town, strait)	*Eng.* ō-trän′-tō	oh-trahn′-toh
	It. ô′-trän-tô	o′-trahn-to
Otsu (Jap.)	ô-tso͞o	o-tsoo
Otta (Nor.)	o͝ot′-ä	ut′-ah
Ötzthal (Austria, mts.)	ûts′-täl	œts′-tahl
Ou-ch'ih-k'ou (Ch., Hupeh)	ō-chû-kō	oh-chœ-koh
Oude Maas (Neth., riv.)	ou′-də mäs′	au′-duh mahs′

Oudref (Tun.)	o͞o′-drĕf	oo′-dref
Oued Zarga (Tun.)	wĕd zär′-gä	wed zahr′-gah
Ouessant (Fr., isl.)	wĕ-säN′	weh-sahN′
English *Ushant*, q.v.		
Oulu (Fin.)	ō′-lo͞o	oh′-lu
Swedish *Uleåborg*, ü′-lĕ-ō-bôr′(y) [ü′-leh-oh-bor′(y)].		
Ounas Selkä (Fin., mts.)	ō′-näs sĕl′-kă	oh′-nahs sel′-ka
Ousseltia (Tun.)	o͞o-sĕl′-tĭ-ä	oo-sel′-ti-ah
Outland, George E. (U.S. representative)	out′-lənd	aut′-luhnd
Ovau (Oc.)	ô-vou′	o-vau′
Ovče Polje (Yugosl.)	ôv′-chĕ pôl′-yĕ	ov′-cheh pol′-yeh
Overflakkee (Neth., isl.)	ō′-vər-flä-kā′	oh′-vuhr-flah-kay′
See *Goedereede*.		
Overysel (Neth.)	ō′-vər-ī′-səl	oh′-vuhr-ai′-suhl
Also spelled *Overyssel*.		
Ovidiopol (Rus.)	ŏ-vĭ-dĭ-ô′-pŏl(y)	o-vi-di-o′-pol(y)
Oviedo (Sp.)	ô-vyĕ′-*th*ô	o-vyeh′-*th*o
Ovinishche (Rus.)	ŏ-vē′-nĭ-shchĕ	o-vee′-ni-shcheh
Ovruch (Rus.)	ôv′-ro͞och	ov′-rooch
Oxia (Gr., isl.)	ô-ksē′-ä	o-ksee′-ah
Oxya (Gr., mt.)	ô-ksē-ä′	o-ksee-ah′
Öye (Nor.)	ûĭ′-ə	œi′-uh
Öyjord (Nor.)	ûĭ′-yōr	œi′-yohr
Oza (Gr., mt.) See *Parnes*.		
ozero (Rus.)	ô′-zĕ-rŏ	o′-zeh-ro
A common element, meaning *lake*, in Russian place names. Look up the other part of the name.		
Ozery (Rus.)	ŏ-zyô′-rĭ	o-zyo′-ri
Ozieri (Sard.)	ô-dzyĕ′-rē	o-dzyeh′-ree
Ozrinići (Yugosl.)	ôz′-rē′-nĭ-chĭ	oz′-ree′-ni-chi
Paama (Oc.)	pä-ä′-mä	pah-ah′-mah
Paan (Burma)	pä-än′	pah-ahn′
Paasikivi, Juho Kusti (Fin. leader)	pä′-sē-kē-vē, ū′-hô ko͞os′-tē	pah′-see-kee-vee, yoo′-ho kus′-tee
Pabjanice (Pol.)	pä-byä-nē′-tsĕ	pah-byah-nee′-tseh
Pachino (Sicily)	pä-kē′-nô	pah-kee′-no
Pacijan (Phil.)	pä-sē′-hän	pah-see′-hahn
Packard (Am. name)	păk′-ərd	pak′-uhrd
Occasional British error, pă-kärd′ [pa-kahrd′].		
Padang (NEI)	pä-däng′	pah-dahng′
Padina (Yugosl.)	pä′-dĭ-nä	pah′-di-nah
Padova (It.) See *Padua*.		

Padua (It.)	*Eng.* păd′-ū-ə	pad′-yoo-uh
Italian *Padova*, pä′-dô-vä [pah′-do-vah].		
Paestum (It.)	*Eng.* pĕs′-təm	pes′-tuhm
Also called *Pesto*, pĕ′-stô [peh′-sto].		
Pag (Yugosl.)	päg′	pahg′
Italian *Pago*, pä′-gô [pah′-go].		
Pagai (NEI)	pä′-gī	pah′-gai
Pagan, Bolivar (P. R. Resident Commissioner at Washington)	pä-gän′, bô-lē′-vär	pah-gahn′, bo-lee′-vahr
Pagan (Burma)	pə-gän′	puh-gahn′
Pagan (Oc.)	pä-gän′	pah-gahn′
Pagėgiai (Lith.)	pä-gā′-gyī	pah-gay′-gyai
Pago Pago (Oc.)	päng′-ô päng′-ô	pahng′-o pahng′-o
Also spelled *Pango Pango*. Also pronounced päng′-gō [pahng′-goh], pä′-gō [pah′-goh], and pā′-gō [pay′-goh].		
Pahlavi, Shah Muhammad (Ruler of Iran)	pä-lä-vē′, shä′ mə-häm′-məd	pah-lah-vee′, shah′ muh-hahm′-muhd
Pahlavi, Shah Riza (Former ruler of Iran)	pä-lä-vē′, shä′ rē′-zə	pah-lah-vee′, shah′ ree′-zuh
Paide (Est.)	pī′-dĕ	pai′-deh
Russian and German *Weissenstein*, q.v.		
P'ai-ling-miao (Ch., Suiyüan)	pī-lĭng-myou	pai-ling-myau
Paimpol (Fr.)	păN-pôl′	paN-pol′
Pai-sê (Ch., Kwangsi)	bī-sŭ	bai-suh
Also called *Po-seh*, q.v.		
Paita (Oc.)	pä-ē′-tä	pah-ee′-tah
Pakhoi (Ch., Kwangtung)	*Eng.* păk-hoi *Ch.* bäk-hoi	pak-hoi bahk-hoi
Pakin (Oc.)	pä′-kēn	pah′-keen
Paklay (Indo-Ch.)	päk-lī′	pahk-lai′
Pakleni Otoci (Yugosl.)	pä′-klĕ-nĭ ô′-tô-tsĭ	pah′-kleh-ni o′-to-tsi
Italian *Spalmadori*, q.v.		
Paknam (Thai)	päk-näm′ *or* păk-năm′	pahk-nahm′ pak-nam′
Paknampo (Thai)	päk-näm′-pō′	pahk-nahm′-poh′
Pakokku (Burma)	pə-kōk′-ko͞o′	puh-kohk′-koo′
Pakrac (Yugosl.)	pä′-kräts	pah′-krahts
Paks (Hung.)	pŏksh′	poksh′
Pakse (Indo-Ch.)	päk-sĕ′	pahk-seh′
Palagonia (Sicily)	pä-lä-gô-nē′-ä	pah-lah-go-nee′-ah
Palagruža (It., isl.)	*S.-C.* pä′-lä-gro͞o′-zhä	pah′-lah-groo′-zhah
Italian *Pelagosa*, q.v.		

Palanan (P.I., bay)	pä-lä′-nän	pah-lah′-nahn
Palanga (Lith.)	pä′-läng-gä	pah′-lahng-gah
Russian *Polangen*, q.v.		
Palanka (Yugosl.)	pä′-län-kä	pah′-lahn-kah
Palata (It.)	pä-lä′-tä	pah-lah′-tah
Palau (Oc.)	pä-lou′	pah-lau′
Also called *Pelew*, pē-lo͞o′ [pee-loo′].		
Palazzo (Sicily)	pä-lät′-sô	pah-laht′-so
Palazzolo (It.)	pä-lät-sô′-lô	pah-laht-so′-lo
Palembang (NEI)	pä-lĕm-bäng′	pah-lem-bahng′
Palencia (Sp.)	pä-lĕn′-thyä *or* -syä	pah-len′-thyah *or* -syah
Paleokhora (Crete) See *Selinon*.		
Palermo (Sicily)	*Eng.* pə-lûr′-mō	puh-luhr′-moh
	It. pä-lĕr′-mô	pah-lehr′-mo
Palermo (Alb.) Also called *Porto Palermo*. Albanian *Portë e Palermos*, q.v.		
Paletwa (Burma)	pə-lĕt′-wä′	puh-let′-wah′
Pali (Alb., cape)	*Eng.* pä′-lē	pah′-lee
Albanian *Kep i Palit.*		
Paliki (Rus.)	pä-lē′-kĭ	pah-lee′-ki
Palinuro (It., cape)	pä-lē-no͞o′-rô	pah-lee-noo′-ro
Paliros (Gr.)	pä′-lē-rôs	pah′-lee-ros
Palk (India, str.)	pôk′	pawk′
Pallene (Gr., point)	pä-lē′-nē	pah-lee′-nee
The point of *Kassandra*, q.v.		
Pallës, Bisht i *or* Hundë e (Alb.) Local names for *Pali* (cape), q.v.		
Palmas (Oc.)	päl′-mäs	pahl′-mahs
Also called *Miangas*, myäng′-gäs [myahng′-gahs].		
Palmi (It.)	päl′-mē	pahl′-mee
Palokastro, Nos (Bulg., cape)	pä-lŏ-kä′-strŏ, nôs′	pah-lo-kah′-stro, nos′
Palos (Sp.)	pä′-lôs	pah′-los
Paltiski (Est.)	päl′-tĭs-kĭ	pahl′-tis-ki
Russian *Baltiski Port*, q.v.		
Pameungpeuk (NEI)	pä-mûng′-pûk	pah-mœng′-pœk
Pana (Rus., riv.)	pä′-nä	pah′-nah
Panagyurishte (Bulg.)	pä′-nä-gū′-rĭ-shtĕ	pah′-nah-gyoo′-ri-shteh
Panaria (It., isl.)	pä-nä-rē′-ä	pah-nah-ree′-ah
Panaroekan (NEI)	pä-nä-ro͞o′-kän	pah-nah-roo′-kahn
Panay (P.I.)	pä-nī′	pah-nai′
Pančevo (Yugosl.)	pän′-chĕ-vô	pahn′-cheh-vo
Hungarian *Pancsova*, pŏn′-chô-vŏ [pon′-cho-vo].		

Panderma (Turk.)	pän-dĕr′-mä	pahn-dehr′-mah
Also called *Bandırma*, q.v.		
pandit *or* pundit	pŭn′-dĭt	puhn′-dit
Pandit and *pundit* are variants and should be pronounced alike. This is an example of the Indian "short *a*," which is close to schwa or "short *u*" (as in *but*), but which is often Angliziced to "short *a*" (as in *bat*). *Pandit* as an honorific tends to retain the more conservative pronunciation.		
Panevėžys (Lith.)	pä-nyĕ-vĕ-zhēs′	pah-nyeh-veh-zhees′
Russian *Ponevyezh*, q.v.		
Pangasinán (P.I.)	päng-gä-sĭ-nän′	pahng-gah-si-nahn′
Pangkal-pinang (NEI)	päng′-käl-pē′-näng	pahng′-kahl-pee′-nahng
	or Eng. pē-năng′	pee-nang′
Pango Pango (Oc.) See *Pago Pago*.		
Pangutarán (P.I.)	päng-gōō-tä-rän′	pahng-goo-tah-rahn′
Paniqui (P. I.)	pä-nē′-kē	pah-nee′-kee
Panjim (Port. India)	päN-zhēN′	pahN-zheeN′
Pannerden (Neth.)	pän′-ər-dən	pahn′-uhr-duhn
Panorm (Alb.)	pä′-nôrm	pah′-norm
Also called *Portë e Palermos*, q.v.		
Panormi (Alb.) See *Panorm*.		
Pantelimon, Agios (Crete)	pän-dĕ-lē′-môn, ī′-yôs	pahn-deh-lee′-mon, ai′-yos
Pantelleria (It., isl.)	pän-tĕl′-lĕ-rē′-ä	pahn-tel′-leh-ree′-ah
Pantocrator (Corfù, mt.)	pän-tô-krä′-tôr	pahn-to-krah′-tor
Pao-ch'i (Ch., Shensi)	bou-chē	bau-chee
Pao-ch'ing (Ch., Hunan)	bou-chĭng	bau-ching
Also called *Shao-yang*, q.v.		
Pao-shan (Ch., Yünnan)	bou-shän	bau-shahn
Also called *Yung-ch'ang*, q.v.		
Pao-t'ou (Ch., Suiyüan)	bou-tō	bau-toh
Papialou (Oc.)	pä-pē′-ä-lô′-ōō	pah-pee′-ah-lo′-oo
Papitalai (Oc.)	pä-pē-tä-lī′	pah-pee-tah-lai′
Papua (New Guinea)	*Eng.* păp′-ū-ə	pap′-yoo-uh
	foreign pä′-pōō-ə	pah′-poo-uh
Pará (Brazil)	pä-rä′	pah-rah′
Paracel (Fr., isls.)	pä-rä-sĕl′	pah-rah-sel′
Japanese *Hirata Gunto*, hē-rä-tä gōōn-tô [hee-rah-tah goon-to].		
Paraćin (Yugosl.)	pä′-rä-chĭn	pah′-rah-chin
Paragua (P.I.) See *Laparán*.		
Paraíba *or* Parahiba (Brazil)	pä-rə-ē′-bə	pah-ruh-ee′-buh
Officially *João Pessoa*, q.v.		

Paramushiro (Jap., isl.)	pä-rä-mo͞o-shē-rô	pah-rah-moo-shee-ro
Paramythia (Gr.)	pä-rä-mē-thē′-ä	pah-rah-mee-thee′-ah
Paraná (Brazil)	pä-rə-nä′	pah-ruh-nah′
Parandova (Rus.)	pä-rän′-dŏ-vä	pah-rahn′-do-vah
Pardubice (Cz.)	pär′-do͞o-bĭ-tsĕ	pahr′-doo-bi-tseh
Paredes, Quintín (Fil. leader)	pä-rĕ′-dĕs, kēn-tēn′	pah-reh′-des, keen-teen′
Parenzo (It.)	pä-rĕn′-tsô	pah-ren′-tso
Parga (Gr.)	pär′-gä	pahr′-gah
Parichi (Rus.)	pä′-rĭ-chĭ	pah′-ri-chi
Paricutín (Mex.)	pä-rē-ko͞o-tēn′	pah-ree-koo-teen′

This is the usual spelling and pronunciation in Mexico City. Perhaps nearer to the Tarascan is *Parícutin*, pä-rē′-ko͞o-tēn [pah-ree′-koo-teen]. Also called *Parácutin* and *Paracutín*, q.v.

Paris (Fr.)	*Eng.* păr′-ĭs	pehr′-is
	Fr. pä-rē′	pah-ree′
Parma (It.)	pär′-mä	pahr′-mah
Parnassus (Gr., mt.)	*Eng.* pär-năs′-əs	pahr-nas′-uhs

Greek *Parnasos*, pär-nä-sôs′ [pahr-nah-sos′]. Also called *Liakoura*, lyä′-ko͞o-rä [lyah′-koo-rah].

Parnes (Gr., mt.)	*Eng.* pär′-nēz	pahr′-neez
	Gr. pär′-nēs	pahr′-nees

Also called *Oza*, ô-zä′ [o-zah′].

Pärnu (Est.)	păr′-no͞o	pehr′-noo

Russian *Pernov*, q.v. German *Pernau*, q.v.

Paros (Gr., isl.)	pä′-rô(s)	pah′-ro(s)
Parpatsch (Rus.)	pär-päch′	pahr-pahch′
Parpeyev (Rus. officer)	pär-pĕ′-yĕf	pahr-peh′-yef
Parry (Oc.)	păr′-ĭ	pehr′-i
Partinico (Sicily)	pär-tē-nē′-kô	pahr-tee-nee′-ko
partisan *or* partizan	pär′-tĭ-zən	pahr′-ti-zuhn
	or pär′-tĭ-zăn′	pahr′-ti-zan′

The latter spelling and pronunciation is sometimes associated with the military sense of the word.

Paşcani (Rum.)	päsh-kän′	pahsh-kahn′
Pas de Calais (Fr.)	pä də kä-lĕ′	pah duh kah-leh′
Pasha (Rus., riv.)	pä′-shä	pah′-shah
pasha (title)	păsh′-ə *or* päsh′-ə	pash′-uh *or* pahsh′-uh
	Turk. pä′-shä′	pah′-shah′
Pashmakli (Bulg.) See *Smolian.*		
Pasig (P.I.)	pä′-sĭg	pah′-sig
Pasjača (Yugosl., mts.)	päs′-yä-chä	pahs′-yah-chah
Pasjane (Yugosl.)	päs′-yä-nĕ	pahs′-yah-neh
Pasley (Austral., cape)	pāz′-lĭ	payz′-li

Pašman (Yugosl.)	päsh′-män	pahsh′-mahn
Pasoeroean *or* Pasuruan (NEI)	pä-so͞o-ro͞o-än′	pah-soo-roo-ahn′
Passarowitz (Yugosl.) See *Požarevats.*		
Passero (Sicily, cape)	päs′-sĕ-rô	pahs′-seh-ro
Paštrik (Balkan mt.)	*S.-C.* päsh′-trĭk	pahsh′-trik
English *Pushtrik,* q.v.		
Patani (Thai)	pät′-ə-nē′	paht′-uh-nee′
Patarica (Yugosl., mt.)	pä′-tä-rĭ-tsä	pah′-tah-ri-tsah
Paterno	*Sicily* pä-tĕr-nô′	pah-tehr-no′
	Italy pä-tĕr′-nô	pah-tehr′-no
As a family name in America, usually Anglicized pə-tûr′-nō [puh-tuhr′-noh].		
Pathan (India)	pə-tän′	puh-tahn′
Patinos (Dodec.)	pä′-tē-nô(s)	pah′-tee-no(s)
Also called *Patmos,* q.v.		
Patjitan (NEI)	pä′-chē-tän	pah′-chee-tahn
Patmos (Dodec.)	pät′-mô(s)	paht′-mo(s)
Also called *Patinos,* q.v.		
Patna (India)	păt′-nə *or* pŭt′-nä′	pat′-nuh *or* puht′-nah′
Patrai (Gr.)	pä′-trĕ	pah′-treh
Patras (Gr.)	pä-träs′	pah-trahs′
Officially *Patrai,* q.v.		
Patron Kolpos (Gr., gulf)	pä-trôn′ kôl′-pôs	pah-tron′ kol′-pos
English Gulf of *Patras,* q.v.		
Patti (Sicily)	pät′-tē	paht′-tee
Pau (Fr.)	pō′	poh′
Paukkan (Burma)	pouk′-kän	pauk′-kahn
Paungde (Burma)	poung′-dĕ′	paung′-deh′
Pavelets (Rus.)	pä-vĕ-lĕts′	pah-veh-lets′
Pavelić, Ante (Serb-Croat leader)	pä′-vĕ-lĭch, än′-tĕ	pah′-veh-lich, ahn′-teh
Pavia (It.)	pä-vē′-ä	pah-vee′-ah
Pāvilosta (Latvia)	pä′-vē-lôs-tä	pah′-vee-los-tah
Pavlof (Alaska, volcano)	pä′-vlŏf	pah′-vlof
Pavlograd (Rus.)	pä-vlŏ-grät′	pah-vlo-graht′
Pavsk (Rus.)	päfsk′	pahfsk′
Pavuvu (Oc.)	pä-vo͞o′-vo͞o	pah-voo′-voo
Paximadi (Gr., Euboea, cape; Crete, isl.)	pä-ksē-mä′-*th*ē	pah-ksee-mah′-*th*ee
Paximadia (Crete, isls.)	pä-ksē-mä′-*th*yä	pah-ksee-mah′-*th*yah
Paxos *or* Paxoi (Gr.)	pä-ksôs′ *or* pä-ksē′	pah-ksos′ *or* pah-ksee′
Payagyi (Burma)	pə-yä-jē′	puh-yah-jee′
Pazova, Stara (Yugosl.)	pä′-zô-vä, stä′-rä	pah′-zo-vah, stah′-rah

Pčinja (Yugosl., riv.)	pchē′-nyä	pchee′-nyah
Peć (Yugosl.)	pĕch′	pech′
Formerly *Ipek*.		
Pečenjevce (Yugosl.)	pĕ′-chĕ′-nyĕv-tsĕ	peh′-cheh′-nyev-tseh
Pechory (Est.)	*Rus.* pĕ-chô′-rĭ	peh-cho′-ri
Estonian *Petseri*, q.v.		
Pecka (Yugosl.)	pĕts′-kä	pets′-kah
Pécs (Hung.)	pāch′	paych′
Pećska Bistrica	pĕch′-skä bē′-strĭ-tsä	pech′-skah bee′-stri-
(Yugosl., riv.)		tsah
Peenemuende *or*	pā′-nə-mün′-də	pay′-nuh-mün′-duh
Peenemünde (Ger.)		
Pege (Crete)	pē′-yē	pee′-yee
Pegu (Burma)	*Burman* pĕ-go͞o′	peh-goo′
	Eng. pē′-gū′	pee′-gyoo′
Pegu Yoma (Burma,	*Burman* pĕ-go͞o′	peh-goo′ yoh′-muh
mts.)	yō′-mə	
	Eng. pē′-gū′	pee′-gyoo′ yoh′-muh
	yō′-mə	
Pehčevo (Yugosl.)	pĕk(h)′-chĕ-vô	pek(h)′-cheh-vo
Pei Chiang *or* Pei River	bā	bay
(Ch., Kwangtung, riv.)		
Peine (Ger.)	pī′-nə	pai′-nuh
Pei-p'ing (Ch., Hopeh)	bā-pĭng	bay-ping
Formerly *Peking*, q.v.		
Peipsi järv (Est., Rus.,	pā′-psĭ jăry′	pay′-psi jehrv′
lake)		
Russian *Chudskoye ozero*, q.v. English Lake *Peipus*, q.v.		
Peipus (Est., Rus., lake)	*Eng.* pī′-pəs	pai′-puhs
	Ger. pī′-po͝os	pai′-pus
Estonian *Peipsi järv*, q.v. Russian *Chudskoye ozero*, q.v.		
Peiraievs (Gr.) See *Piraeus*.		
Peixoto, Amaral	pā-shô′-to͝o, ä-mə-räl′	pay-sho′-tu, ah-muh-
(Braz. leader)		rahl′
Both names should be used, thus: *Amaral Peixoto*, not *Peixoto* alone.		
Pek (Yugosl., riv.)	pĕk′	pek′
Pekalongan (NEI)	pĕ′-kä-lông′-gän	peh′-kah-long′-gahn
Peking (Ch., Hopeh)	*Eng.* pē-kĭng	pee-king
	Ch. bā-jĭng	bay-jing
Now officially *Pei-p'ing*, q.v.		
Pelagian (Sicily, isls.)	*Eng.* pə-lā′-jən	puh-lay′-juhn
Pelagonesi (Gr., isl.)	pĕ-lä-gô-nē′-sē	peh-lah-go-nee′-see
Pelagonia (Yugosl.)	*Gr.* pĕ-lä-gô-nē′-ä	peh-lah-go-nee′-ah
Serb-Croat *Bitoljsko Polje*, q.v.		

Pelagosa (It., isl.) pĕ-lä-gô′-sä peh-lah-go′-sah
Serb-Croat *Palagruža*, pä′-lä-grōō-zhä [pah′-lah-groo-zhah].
Peleliu (Oc.) pĕ′-lĕ-lū peh′-leh-lyoo
Pelew (Oc.) See *Palau*.
Pelion (Gr., mt.) *Eng.* pē′-lĭ-ən pee′-li-uhn
Gr. pē′-lē-ô(n) pee′-lee-o(n)
Pelješac (Yugosl., pen.) pĕ′-lyĕ-shäts peh′-lyeh-shahts
Italian *Sabbioncello*, q.v.
Pellaro (It.) pĕl′-lä-rô pel′-lah-ro
pellg (Alb.) pĕlg′ pelg′
An element, meaning *bay* or *gulf*, in Albanian place names. Look up the other part of the name.
pellgu (Alb.) See *pellg*.
Peloponnesos (Gr.) *Eng.* pĕl′-ō-pə-nē′-səs pel′-oh-puh-nee′-suhs
Gr. pĕ-lô-pô′-nē-sôs peh-lo-po′-nee-sos
Also called the *Morea*, q.v.
Pelusium (Egypt) *Eng.* pə-lū′-zĭ-əm puh-lyoo′-zi-uhm
Penang (Malaya) *Eng.* pē′-năng′ pee′-nang′
Malay *Pulau Pinang*.
Peñaranda, Enrique (Bolivian leader) pĕ-nyä-rän′-dä, ĕn-rē′-kĕ peh-nyah-rahn′-dah, en-ree′-keh
Peñas, de (Sp., cape) pĕ′-nyäs, dĕ peh′-nyahs, deh
Peneios (Gr., rivs.) *Eng.* pē-nē′-əs pee-nee′-uhs
Gr. pē-nē-ôs′ pee-nee-os′
The Thessalian *Peneus* is also called *Salambrias*, sä-läm-brē-äs′ [sah-lahm-bree-ahs′].
Penfoei (Oc.) pĕn-fōō′-ē pen-foo′-ee
Pêng-p'u (Ch., Anhwei) bŭng-pōō buhng-poo
P'êng-shih (Ch., Hupeh, riv.) pŭng-shû puhng-shuh
P'êng-tsê (Ch., Kiangsi) pŭng-dzŭ puhng-dzuh
penicillin pĕn′-ə-sĭl′-ən pen′-uh-sil′-uhn
or pĕn-ĭs′-ə-lən pen-is′-uh-luhn

The doctors have not yet agreed upon the pronunciation of their new remedy. One should expect the first because the source, a mold of the *Penicillium* genus, is always pronounced pĕn′-ĭ-sĭl′-ĭ-əm [pen′-i-sil′-i-uhm], and similarly *pénicíllate*, *pénicílliform*, *pénicíllum*, and *pénicíllus*. However, to the contrary is the analogy of *ínsulin*, *península*, *penínsulate*, and *penníferous*. The American Illustrated Medical Dictionary places the accent on the second syllable. Black's dictionary (British) has the word but has not a pronunciation. Steadman's (1942) does not list the word. The New York Academy of Medicine reports that the doctors seem evenly divided between the two pronunciations, perhaps those who work on molds preferring pĕn′-ə-sĭl′-ən [pen′-uh-sil′-uhn]. However, Dr. Chester S. Keefer, Chairman of the National Research Committee on Chemotherapeutics, writes, Dec. 7, 1943: "As is often the case with technical terms, and this is particularly true when something is introduced in England, the emphasis is frequently placed on the second syllable rather than the first. It is my understanding that the British pronounce *penicillin* as *penícillin*. By common usage in the U.S., the pronunciation has been *penicíllin*." A somewhat similar problem is *salicylate* pronounced săl′-ə-sĭl′-ĭt [sal′-uh-sil′-it] *or* sə-lĭs′-ə-lāt′ [suh-lis′-uh-layt′]. The pronunciations of *helicopter* and *depot* show that professional usage may depart from conventional expectations.—P.S. Mr. Edward Murrow cables from London, Dec. 20, 1943, that Mr. Alexander Fleming, the British doctor who originated the treatment, says pĕn′-ə-sĭl′-ən [pen′-uh-sil′-uhn]. Is this another instance when Americans consider an odd pronunciation "British" and the British think it "American"? Cf. *Caribbean.*

Penong (Austral.)	pē′-nông′	pee′-nong′
Penza (Rus.)	pĕn′-zä	pen′-zah
Pepys (Eng. name)	pĕp′-ĭs *or* pēps′	pep′-is *or* peeps′
The second is preferred for Samuel Pepys, the diarist.		
Peqin (Alb.)	pĕ′-kyēn	peh′-kyeen
Peqini (Alb.) See *Peqin.*		
Perak (Malaya)	*Eng.* pā′-răk′	pay′-rak′
	Malay pĕ′-rä	peh′-rah
Perama (Crete)	pĕ′-rä-mä	peh′-rah-mah
Përat (Alb.)	pər′-ät	puhr′-aht
Përati (Alb.) See *Përat.*		
Pereira, Orozimbo Martins (Braz. general)	pĕ-rā′-rə, ô-rô-zēm′-bo͝o mär-tēns′	peh-ray′-ruh, o-ro-zeem′-bu mahr-teens′
Perekop (Rus.)	pĕ-rĕ-kôp′	peh-reh-kop′
Perelazovsky (Rus.)	pĕ-rĕ-lä′-zŏf-skĭ	peh-reh-lah′-zof-ski
Peremishl (Pol.) See *Przemyśl.*		
Peremyshl (Rus.)	pĕ-rĕ-mwēshl′(y)	peh-reh-mweeshl′(y)
Pergola (It.)	pĕr′-gô-lä	pehr′-go-lah
Perguba (Rus.)	pĕr-go͞o-bä′	pehr-goo-bah′
Périgueux (Fr.)	pĕ-rē-gû′	peh-ree-gœ′
Peristeri (Gr., isl.)	pĕ-rē-stĕ′-rē	peh-ree-steh′-ree
Peristeri (Yugosl., mts.)	pĕ′-rĭ-stĕ-rĭ	peh′-ri-steh-ri
Perlez (Yugosl.)	pĕr′-lĕz	pehr′-lez
Perm (Rus.)	pĕrm′(y)	pehrm′(y)
Përmet (Alb.)	pər′-mĕt	puhr′-met
Also called *Prëmet*, prə′-mĕt [pruh′-met].		
Permeti (Alb.) See *Përmet.*		

Pernambuco (Brazil)	*Eng.* pûr′-nəm-bo͞o′-kō	puhr′-nuhm-boo′-koh
	Port. pĕr-nəm-bo͞o′-ko͝o	pehr-nuhm-boo′-ku
Officially *Recife*, q.v.		
Pernau (Est.)	*Ger.* pĕr′-nou	pehr′-nau
Estonian *Pärnu*, q.v. Russian *Pernov*, q.v.		
Pernov (Est.)	*Rus.* pĕr′-nŏf	pehr′-nof
Estonian *Pärnu*, q.v. German *Pernau*, q.v.		
Perón, Juan (Arg. leader)	pĕ-rôn′, whän′	peh-ron′, whahn′
Perouse, la (Rus., Jap., str.)	pĕ-ro͞oz′, lä	peh-rooz′, lah
Perpignan (Fr.)	pĕr-pē-nyäN′	pehr-pee-nyahN′
Perugia (It.)	pĕ-ro͞o′-jä	peh-roo′-jah
Perušić (Yugosl.)	pĕ′-ro͞o-shĭch	peh′-roo-shich
Pervicchio (Yugosl., isl.)	*It.* pĕr-vēk′-kyô	pehr-veek′-kyo
Serb-Croat *Prvić*, q.v.		
Pervomaisk (Rus.)	pĕr-vŏ-mīsk′	pehr-vo-maisk′
Pervozvanovka (Rus.)	pĕr-vŏ-zvä′-nŏf-kä	pehr-vo-zvah′-nof-kah
Pescadores (Jap., isls.)	pĕs-kä-dô′-rĕs	pes-kah-do′-res
Japanese *Hoko Gunto*, hô-kô go͞on-tô [ho-ko goon-to]; *Hoko Ret*, hô-kô rĕt [ho-ko ret]; *Hoko To*, hô-kô tô [ho-ko to]		
Pescara (It.)	pĕ-skä′-rä	peh-skah′-rah
Peschici (It.)	pĕ′-skē-chē	peh′-skee-chee
Peschiera (Yugosl., isl.)	*It.* pĕ-skyĕ′-rä	peh-skyeh′-rah
Serb-Croat *Jadre*, q.v.		
Peshawar (India)	pĕ-shä′-wər	peh-shah′-wuhr
Peshkopi (Alb.)	pĕ-shkô′-pē	peh-shko′-pee
Italian *Piscopeia*, q.v.		
Peshkopija (Alb.) See *Peshkopi*.		
Peshtera (Bulg.)	pĕ′-shtĕ-rä	peh′-shteh-rah
Pesjak (Yugosl., mts.)	pĕs′-yäk	pes′-yahk
Peski (Rus.)	pĕs-kē′	pes-kee′
Pesnica (Yugosl., riv.)	pĕs′-nĭ-tsä	pes′-ni-tsah
Pessoa, Alfredo (Braz. leader)	pĕ-sô′-ə, äl-frĕ′-do͝o	peh-so′-uh, ahl-freh′-du
Pešter (Yugosl.)	pĕsh′-tĕr	pesh′-tehr
Pesto (It.)	pĕ′-stô	peh′-sto
English *Pestum* (or *Paestum*), pĕs′-təm [pes′-tuhm].		
Petacciato (It.)	pĕ-tät-chä′-tô	peh-taht-chah′-to
Pétain, Henri Philippe (Fr. leader)	pĕ-tăN′, äN-rē′ fē-lēp′	peh-taN′, ahN-ree′ fee-leep′

Petalas (Gr., isl.)	pĕ-tä-läs′	peh-tah-lahs′
Petalidi (Gr.)	pĕ-tä-lē′-*th*ē	peh-tah-lee′-*th*ee
Petra Velikogo, Zaliv	See *Zaliv*. . . .	
Petrace (It., riv.)	pĕ-trä′-chĕ	peh-trah′-cheh
Petrich (Bulg.)	pĕ′-trĭch	peh′-trich
Petrinja (Yugosl.)	pĕ′-trĭ-nyä	peh′-tri-nyah
Petrograd	*Eng.* pĕt′-rō-grăd	pet′-roh-grad
	Rus. pĕ-trŏ-grät′	peh-tro-graht′
Officially *Leningrad*, q.v.		
Petrokov (Pol.) See *Piotrków*.		
Petrolia (Alb.)	*It.* pĕ-trô′-lyä	peh-tro′-lyah
Albanian *Vajguras*, q.v., and *Kuçovë*, q.v.		
Petropavlovsk Kamchatski (Rus.)	pĕ-trŏ-päv′-lŏfsk käm-chät′-skĭ	peh-tro-pahv′-lofsk kahm-chaht′-ski
Petroşani (Rum.)	pĕ-trô-shän′	peh-tro-shahn′
Hungarian *Petrozsény*, pĕt′-rŏ-zhān(y) [pet′-ro-zhayn(y)].		
Petrovac (Yugosl.)	pĕ′-trô-väts	peh′-tro-vahts
Petrovaradin (Yugosl.)	pĕ′-trô-vä-rä′-dĭn	peh′-tro-vah-rah′-din
Petrovo Selo (Yugosl.)	pĕ′-trô-vô sĕ′-lô	peh′-tro-vo seh′-lo
Petrovsk (Rus.)	pĕ-trôfsk′	peh-trofsk′
Petrovskoe (Rus.)	pĕ-trôf′-skŏ-yĕ	peh-trof′-sko-yeh
Petrozavodsk (Rus.)	pĕ′-trŏ-zä-vôdsk′	peh′-tro-zah-vodsk′
Petrozsény (Rum.) See *Petroşani*.		
Petsamo (Fin.)	pĕt′-sä-mô	pet′-sah-mo
Petseri (Est.)	pĕ′-tsĕ-rĭ	peh′-tseh-ri
Russian *Pechory*, q.v.		
Petten (Neth.)	pĕt′-ən	pet′-uhn
Pfeifer, Joseph L. (U.S. representative)	fī′-fər	fai′-fuhr
Phanai, Ak. (Gr., Chios)	fä′-nĕ	fah′-neh
Also called *Mastekhos*, mä′-stē-hôs [mah′-stee-hos], or *Mastikhis*, mä-stē′-hē(s) [mah-stee′-hee(s)].		
Phanos (Gr.)	fä-nôs′	fah-nos′
Also called *Magiadag*, mī-yä-*th*äg′ [mai-yah-*th*ahg′].		
Phanrang (Indo-Ch.)	fän-räng′	fahn-rahng′
Pharsala (Gr.)	fär′-sä-lä	fahr′-sah-lah
Also called *Phersala*, fĕr′-sä-lä [fehr′-sah-lah].		
Pherai (Gr.)	fĕ-rĕ′ *or* fĕ′-rĕ	feh-reh′ *or* feh′-reh
English *Pherae*, fē′-rē [fee′-ree]. Also called *Bęlestinon*, q.v.		
Pherrai (Gr.)	fĕ′-rĕ	feh′-reh
This Thracian town is distinguished from the Thessalian *Pherai*, q.v.		
Phersala (Gr.) See *Pharsala*.		
Philbin, Philip (U.S. representative)	fĭl′-bĭn	fil′-bin

Philiates (Gr.)	fē-lyä′-tĕs	fee-lyah′-tes
Philiatra (Gr.)	fē-lyä-trä′	fee-lyah-trah′
Philip, André (Fr. leader)	fē-lēp′, äN-drĕ′	fee-leep′, ahN-dreh′
Philipias (Gr.)	fē-lē-pyäs′	fee-lee-pyahs′
Phillipopolis (Bulg.) See *Plovdif.*		
Philippeville (Alg.)	*Eng.* fĭl′-ĭp-vĭl	fil′-ip-vil
	Fr. fē-lēp-vēl′	fee leep-veel′
Phlorina (Gr.)	flô′-rē-nä	flo′-ree-nah
Phnom Penh (Indo-Ch.)	See *Pnompenh.*	
Phodelai (Crete)	fô′-*th*ĕ-lĕ	fo′-*th*eh-leh
Phoenicia	fĭ-nĭsh′-ə	fi-nish′-uh
The pronunciation fĭ-nē′-shə [fi-nee′-shuh], though common, is not recommended by dictionaries.		
Phoinikias (Crete)	fē-nē-kyäs′	fee-nee-kyahs′
Pholegandros (Gr., isl.)	fô-lĕ′-gän-drô(s)	fo-leh′-gahn-dro(s)
Also called *Polykantro,* pô-lē′-kän-drô [po-lee′-kahn-dro].		
Phourni (Gr.)	fo͞or′-nē	foor′-nee
Phrae (Thai)	pră′	pra′
Phrankokastelli (Crete)	fräng-gô-kä-stĕ′-lē	frahng-go-kah-steh′-lee
Phrasare (Alb.) See *Frashër.*		
Phratabong (Indo-Ch.)	See *Battambang.*	
Phuquoc (Indo-Ch., isl.)	fo͞o-kwo͝ok′	foo-kwuk′
Also spelled *Phukok.*		
Piacenza (It.)	pyä-chĕn′-tsä	pyah-chen′-tsah
pianist	pĭ-ăn′-ĭst	pi-an′-ist
	or pē′-ə-nĭst	pee′-uh-nist
The first pronunciation is preferred for American usage.		
Pianosa (It., isls.)	pyä-nô′-sä	pyah-no′-sah
Piaseczno (Pol.)	pyä-sĕch′-nô	pyah-sech′-no
Russian spelling *Pyasechno.*		
Piatra Neamţ (Rum.)	pyä′-trä nyämts′	pyah′-trah nyahmts′
Piauí (Brazil)	pē-ə-wē′	pee-uh-wee′
Piave (It., riv.)	pyä′-vĕ	pyah′-veh
Pibul Songkram (Thai leader)	pē′-bo͝on sōng-kräm′	pee′-bun sohng-krahm′
Piccia (It.)	pēt′-chä	peet′-chah
Pi-chieh (Ch., Kweichow)	bē-jyĕ	bee-jyeh
Pichon (Tun.)	pē-shôN′	pee-shoN′
Piedimonte Etneo (Sicily)	pyĕ-dē-môn′-tĕ ĕt-nĕ′-ô	pyeh-dee-mon′-teh et-neh′-o
Pieksämäki (Fin.)	pē′-ĕk′-să-mă-kē	pee′-ek′-sa-ma-kee
Pielinin (Fin.) See *Pielisjärvi.*		

Pielisjärvi (Fin., lake)	pē′-ĕ′-lĭs-yăr-vē	pee′-eh′-lis-yehr-vee
Also called *Pielinin*, pē′-ĕ′-lē-nĭn [pee′-eh′-lee-nin].		
P'ien-mä (Ch., Yünnan)	pyĕn-mä	pyen-mah
Piešt'any (Cz.)	pyĕsh′-tyä-nĭ	pyesh′-tyah-ni
Pietà (It.)	pyĕ-tä′	pyeh-tah′
Pietarsaari (Fin.)	pē′-ĕ′-tär-sä-rē	pee′-eh′-tahr-sah-ree
Swedish *Jakobstad*, q.v.		
Pieve (It.)	pyĕ′-vĕ	pyeh′-veh
Pignataro (It.)	pē-nyä-tä′-rô	pee-nyah-tah′-ro
Pikela (Oc.)	pē′-kĕ-lä	pee′-keh-lah
Pikelot (Oc.)	pē′-kĕ-lôt	pee′-keh-lot
Pilatovica (Yugosl., mt.)	pē′-lä′-tô-vĭ-tsä	pee′-lah′-to-vi-tsah
Pilica *or* Pilitsa (Pol., riv.)	pĭ-lē′-tsä	pi-lee′-tsah
Pillau (Ger.)	pĭl′-ou	pil′-au
Pillauer Tief (Ger., Frisches Haff)	pĭl′-ou-ər tēf′	pil′-au-uhr teef′
Pilsen (Cz.)	*Ger.* pĭl′-zən	pil′-zuhn
Czech *Plzeň*, pəl′-zĕn(y) [puhl′-zen(y)].		
Pina (Pol., riv.)	*Pol.* pē′-nä	pee′-nah
	Rus. pĭ-nä′	pi-nah′
Pinapil (Oc.)	pē-nä-pēl′	pee-nah-peel′
Pin Chaung (Burma, riv.)	pĭn′ choung′	pin′ chaung′
Pińczów (Pol.)	pēn′(y)-cho͝of	peen′(y)-chuf
Russian *Pinchov*, pĭn-chôf′ [pin-chof′].		
Pindus (Gr., mts.)	*Eng.* pĭn′-dəs	pin′-duhs
Greek *Pindos*, pēn′-dôs [peen′-dos].		
Pingelap (Oc.)	pĭng′-ĕ-läp	ping′-eh-lahp
P'ing-hsiang (Ch., Kiangsi)	pĭng-shyäng	ping-shyahng
P'ing T'an (Ch., Fukien, isls.)	pĭng tän	ping tahn
P'ing-yang (Ch., Chekiang)	pĭng-yäng	ping-yahng
Pinlebu (Burma)	pĭn′-lĕ-bo͞o′	pin′-leh-boo′
Pińsk (Pol.)	pēn(y)sk′	peen(y)sk′
Russian *Pinsk*, pēnsk′ [peensk′].		
Piombino (It.)	pyôm-bē′-nô	pyom-bee′-no
Piotrków (Pol.)	pyô′tr-ko͝of	pyo′tr-kuf
Russian *Petrokov*, pĕ-trŏ-kôf′ [peh-tro-kof′].		
Piperi (Gr., isl.)	pē-pĕ′-rē	pee-peh′-ree
Piraeus (Gr.)	*Eng.* pī-rē′-əs	pai-ree′-uhs
Greek *Peiraievs*, pē-rĕ-ĕfs′ [pee-reh-efs′]. The English form should be preceded by the article *the*.		

Piraino (Sicily)	pē-rī′-nô	pee-rai′-no
Piroe *or* Piru (NEI)	pē′-rōō	pee′-roo
Pirot (Yugosl.)	pē′-rôt	pee′-rot
Piryatin (Rus.)	pĭ-ryä′-tĭn	pi-ryah′-tin
Pisa (It.)	*Eng.* pē′-zə	pee′-zuh
	It. pē′-sä	pee′-sah
Pisciotta (It.)	pē-shôt′-tä	pee-shot′-tah
Piscopeia (Alb.)	*It.* pē-skô′-pĕ-yä	pee-sko′-peh-yah
Albanian *Peshkopi*, q.v.		
Piscopi (Dodec.)	*It.* pē′-skô-pē	pee′-sko-pee
Greek *Tilos*, q.v.		
Písek (Cz.)	pē′-sĕk	pee′-sek
Pisida (Libya)	pē-sē′-dä	pee-see′-dah
Pistoia (It.)	pē-stô′-yä	pee-sto′-yah
Piteşti (Rum.)	pē-tĕsht′	pee-tesht′
Pittenger, Wm. A. (U.S. representative)	pĭt′n-jûr′	pit′n-juhr′
Pityilu (Oc.)	pē-tyē′-lōō	pee-tyee′-loo
Pizzo (It.)	pēt′-sô	peet′-so
Pješivci (Yugosl.)	pyĕ′-shĭv-tsĭ	pyeh′-shiv-tsi
Planik (Yugosl., isl.)	plä′-nĭk	plah′-nik
Italian *Magresina*, q.v.		
Planinica (Yugosl.)	plä′-nē′-nĭ-tsä	plah′-nee′-ni-tsah
Planinski Kanal (Yugosl.)	plä′-nēn′-skĭ kä′-näl	plah′-neen′-ski kah′-nahl
English and Italian *Morlacca* (Channel), q.v.		
Plastun (Rus., bay)	plä-stōōn′	plah-stoon′
Plata *or* Plate (S. A., estuary) See *Río de la Plata.*		
Platamon (Gr.)	plä-tä-môn′	plah-tah-mon′
Platamon, Rt (Yugosl.)	plä′-tä-môn, ərt′	plah′-tah-mon, uhrt′
Italian *Punta Platamone*, q.v.		
Plataria (Gr.)	plä-tär-yä′	plah-tahr-yah′
Platsa (Gr.)	plä′-tsä	plah′-tsah
Plauen (Ger.)	plou′-ən	plau′-uhn
Plavinas (Latvia)	plä′-vē-nyäs	plah′-vee-nyahs
German *Stockmanshof*, q.v.		
Plavnica (Yugosl.)	pläv′-nĭ-tsä	plahv′-ni-tsah
Plavnik (Yugosl., isl.)	pläv′-nĭk	plahv′-nik
Plavsko Blato (Yugosl., lake)	pläv′-skô blä′-tô	plahv′-sko blah′-to
Pless (Pol.) See *Pszczyna.*		
Pleven (Bulg.)	*Eng.* plĕv′-ĕn	plev′-en
	Bulg. plĕ′-vĕn(y)	pleh′-ven(y)
Also called *Plevna*, plĕv′-nä [plev′-nah].		

Pljačkovica (Yugosl., mts.)	plyäch′-kô′-vĭ-tsä	plyahch′-ko′-vi-tsah
Pljevlja (Yugosl.)	plyĕv′-lyä	plyev′-lyah
Ploče, Rt (Yugosl.)	plô′-chĕ, ərt′	plo′-cheh, uhrt′
Italian *Punta Planca*, q.v.		
Płock (Pol.)	plôtsk′	plotsk′
Russian spelling *Plotsk*.		
Ploeser, Walter C. (U.S. representative)	plā′-zər	play′-zuhr
Ploeşti (Rum.)	plô-yĕsht′	plo-yesht′
Płońsk (Pol.)	plôn(y)sk′	plon(y)sk′
Plonton, Jacques (Fr. leader)	plôN-tôN′, zhäk′	ploN-toN′, zhahk′
Plora (Crete)	plô′-rä	plo′-rah
Plotsk (Pol.) See *Płock*.		
Ploudalmézeau (Fr.)	plōō-däl-mĕ-zō′	ploo-dahl-meh-zoh′
Plougastel Daoulas (Fr.)	plōō-gä-stĕl′ dou-läs′	ploo-gah-stel′ dau-lahs′
Plouguerneau (Fr.)	plōō-gĕr-nō′	ploo-gehr-noh′
Plouhinec (Fr.)	plōō-ē-nĕk′	ploo-ee-nek′
Plovdiv (Bulg.)	plôv′-dĭf	plov′-dif
Greek *Phillipopolis*, (Eng.) fĭl′-ĭ-pŏp′-ə-lĭs [fil′-i-pop′-uh-lis].		
Plyusa (Rus.)	plū′-sä	plyoo′-sah
Plzeň (Cz.) See *Pilsen*.		
Pnompenh (Indo-Ch.)	*Eng.* nŏm′-pĕn′	nom′-pen′
	local pnŏŏm-pĕn′(y)	pnum-pen′(y)
Thai *Phnom Penh*, pnōm pĕn′ [pnohm pen′].		
Poage, W. R. (U.S. representative)	pōg′	pohg′
Pobijenik (Yugosl., mts.)	pô′-bĭ-yĕ′-nĭk	po′-bi-yeh′-nik
Počekovina (Yugosl.)	pô′-chĕ′-kô-vĭ-nä	po′-cheh′-ko-vi-nah
Pochep (Rus.)	pô′-chĕp	po′-chep
Pochinok (Rus.)	pŏ-chē′-nŏk	po-chee′-nok
Pöchlarn (Austria)	pûk(h)′-lärn	pœk(h)′-lahrn
Podareš (Yugosl.)	pô′-dä-rĕsh	po′-dah-resh
Podgorac (Yugosl.)	pôd′-gô-räts	pod′-go-rahts
Podgorica (Yugosl.)	pôd′-gô′-rĭ-tsä	pod′-go′-ri-tsah
Podhum (Yugosl.)	pôd′-hōōm	pod′-hoom
Podlec (Yugosl.)	pôd′-lĕts	pod′-lets
Podmokly (Cz.)	pôd′-mô-klĭ	pod′-mo-kli
Podolsk (Rus.)	pŏ-dôl(y)sk′	po-dol(y)sk′
Podujevo (Yugosl.)	pô′-dōō′-yĕ-vô	po′-doo′-yeh-vo
Podunavci (Yugosl.)	pô′-dōō′-näv-tsĭ	po′-doo′-nahv-tsi
Podunavska (Yugosl.)	pô′-dōō′-näv-skä	po′-doo′-nahv-skah

Podwołoczyska (Pol.)	pôd-vô-lô-chĭ′-skä	pod-vo-lo-chi′-skah
Poechlarn (Austria)	pûk(h)′-lärn	pœk(h)′-lahrn
Poelitz (Ger.)	pû′-lĭts	pœ′-lits
Poerwakarta (NEI)	po͞or-wä-kär′-tä	poor-wah-kahr′-tah
Poggiardo (It.)	pôd-jär′-dô	pod-jahr′-do
Poggibonsi (It.)	pôd-jē-bôn′-sē	pod-jee-bon′-see
Poggio (It.)	pôd′-jô	pod′-jo
Pogled (Yugosl., mt.)	pô′-glĕd	po′-gled
Pogodinsk (Rus.)	pŏ-gô′-dĭnsk	po-go′-dinsk
Pogoryeloye Gorodishche (Rus.)	pŏ-gŏ-rĕ′-lŏ-yĕ gŏ-rŏ-dē′-shchĕ	po-go-reh′-lo-yeh go-ro-dee′-shcheh
Pogradea (Alb.) See *Pogradec.*		
Pogradec (Alb.)	pô-grä′-dĕts	po-grah′-dets
Also called *Pogradea*, pô-grä′-dĕ-ä [po-grah′-deh-ah].		
Pogranichnaya (Rus.)	pŏ-grä-nēch′-nä-yä	po-grah-neech′-nah-yah
Pohorje (Yugosl., mts.)	pô′-hŏr-yĕ	po′-hor-yeh
Poitiers (Fr.)	pwä-tyĕ′	pwah-tyeh′
Poix (Fr.)	pwä′	pwah′
Pojan (Alb.)	pô′-yän	po′-yahn
Pojani (Alb.) See *Pojan.*		
Pokaakku (Oc.)	pô′-kä-äk′-ko͞o	po′-kah-ahk′-ko͞o
Also called *Taongi*, q.v.		
Pola (It.)	pô′-lä	po′-lah
Polangen (Lith.)	*Rus.* pŏ-län′-gĕn	po-lahn′-gen
Lithuanian *Palanga*, q.v.		
Polesia (Pol.)	*Eng.* pō-lē′-shə	poh-lee′-shuh
Polish *Polesie*, pô-lĕ′-syĕ [po-leh′-syeh].		
Po-li (Manchu.)	bô-lē	bo-lee
Poliçan (Alb.)	pô-lē′-chän	po-lee′-chahn
Poliçani (Alb.) See *Poliçan.*		
Policastro (It., gulf)	pôl-ē-kä′-strô	pol-ee-kah′-stro
Polillo (P.I.)	pô-lē′-lyô *or* -yô	po-lee′-lyo *or* -yo
Pölitz (Ger.)	pû′-lĭts	pœ′-lits
Poljana (Yugosl.)	pô′-lyä′-nä	po′-lyah′-nah
Poljčane (Yugosl.)	pôl(y)′-chä-nĕ	pol(y)′-chah-neh
Pollet, le (Fr.)	pô-lĕ′, lə	po-leh′, luh
Polnoe (Rus.)	pôl′-nŏ-yĕ	pol′-no-yeh
Pologi (Rus.)	pŏ-lô′-gĭ	po-lo′-gi
Polotsk (Rus.)	pô′-lŏtsk	po′-lotsk
Poltava (Rus.)	pŏl-tä′-vä	pol-tah′-vah
Poltavka (Rus.)	pŏl-täf′-kä	pol-tahf′-kah
Polygyros (Gr.)	pô-lē′-yē-rôs	po-lee′-yee-ros
Polykantro (Gr., isl.) See *Pholegandros.*		

Pombelaa (NEI)	pôm′-bĕ-lä′	pom′-beh-lah′
Pomerania (Ger., Pol.)	*Eng.* pŏm-ə-rā′-nyə	pom-uh-ray′-nyuh
Polish *Pomorze*, q.v. German *Pommern*, pôm′-ərn [pom′-uhrn].		
Pomigliano d'Arco (It.)	pô-mē-lyä′-nô där′-kô	po-mee-lyah′-no dahr′-ko
Pommern (Ger., Pol., provs.) See *Pomerania.*		
Pomorie (Bulg.)	pŏ-mô′-ryĕ	po-mo′-ryeh
Pomorze (Pol., Ger., provs.) See *Pomerania.*	pô-mô′-zhĕ	po-mo′-zheh
Ponape (Oc.)	pô′-nä-pĕ	po′-nah-peh
Ponchielli, Amilcare (It. composer)	pôn-kyĕl′-lē, ä-mēl′-kä-rĕ	pon-kyel′-lee, ah-meel′-kah-reh
Pondichéry (Fr. India)	*Eng.* pŏn′-dĭ-chĕr′-ĭ	pon′-di-chehr′-i
	Fr. pôN-dē-shĕ-rē′	poN-dee-sheh-ree′
Ponevyezh (Lith.)	*Rus.* pŏ-nĕ-vĕzh′	po-neh-vezh′
Lithuanian *Panevėžys*, q.v.		
Pongoma (Rus., riv.)	pŏn-gô′-mä	pon-go′-mah
Ponta Delgada (Azores)	pôn′-tə dĕl-gä′-də	pon′-tuh del-gah′-duh
Pontarlier (Fr.)	pôN-tär-lyĕ′	poN-tahr-lyeh′
Pont du Fahs (Tun.)	pôN′ dü fäs′	poN′ dü fahs′
Ponte Olivo (Sicily)	pôn′-tĕ ô-lē′-vô	pon′-teh o-lee′-vo
Pontevedra (Sp.)	pôn-tĕ-vĕ′-*th*rä	pon-teh-veh′-*th*rah
Pontianak (NEI)	pŏn-tē-ä′-näk	pon-tee-ah′-nahk
Pontikonesi (Crete, isl.)	pôn-dē-kô-nē′-sē	pon-dee-ko-nee′-see
Also called *Mili*, mē′-lē [mee′-lee].		
Pontine Marshes (It.)	*Eng.* pŏn′-tĭn *or* -tīn	pon′-tin *or* -tain
Pontivy (Fr.)	pôN-tē-vē′	poN-tee-vee′
pontoon	pŏn-tōōn′	pon-toon′
Military *ponton*, pŏnt′n [pont′n].		
Pontotoc (Miss.)	pŏn′-tə-tŏk′	pon′-tuh-tok′
Pontremoli (It.)	pôn-trĕ′-mô-lē	pon-treh′-mo-lee
Ponyri (Rus.)	pŏ-nû-rē′	po-nuh-ree′
Ponza (It., isl.)	pôn′-tsä	pon′-tsah
Ponziane (It., isls.)	pôn-tsyä′-nĕ	pon-tsyah′-neh
Poona (India)	pōō′-nə	poo′-nuh
Poperinghe (Belg.)	*Eng.* pŏp′-ər-ĭng	pop′-uhr-ing
	Flem. pō-pə-rĭng′-k(h)ə	poh-puh-ring′-k(h)uh
	Fr. pô-pə-răNg′	po-puh-raNg′
Popiel, Karol (Pol. leader)	pô′-pyĕl, kä′-rôl	po′-pyel, kah′-rol
Popoli (It.)	pô′-pô-lē	po′-po-lee
Popolo (It.)	pô′-pô-lô	po′-po-lo

Poporang (Oc.)	pô-pô-räng′	po-po-rahng′
Popovac (Yugosl.)	pô′-pô-väts	po′-po-vahts
Popović (Yugosl.)	pô′-pô-vĭch	po′-po-vich
Popovo (Bulg.)	pô′-pŏ-vŏ	po′-po-vo
Poprad (Cz.)	pô′-prät	po′-praht
Porbandar (India)	pôr-bŭn′-dər	por-buhn′-duhr
Porchia (It., mt.)	pôr′-kyä	por′-kyah
Porečka (Yugosl., riv.)	pô′-rĕch-kä	po′-rech-kah
Pori (Fin.)	pô′-rē	po′-ree
Swedish *Bjoerneborg*, byûr′-nə-bŏr′(y) [byœr′-nuh-bor′(y)].		
Porkhov (Rus.)	pôr′-hŏf	por′-hof
Porsgrunn (Nor.)	pôrs′-gro͝on *or* pôsh′-gro͝on	pors′-grun posh′-grun
Porta e Palermos (Alb.)	See *Portë e Palermos.*	
Port de Bouc (Fr.)	pôr′ də bo͞ok′	por′ duh book′
Portë e Palermos (Alb.)	pôr′-tə ĕ pä-lĕr′-môs	por′-tuh eh pah-lehr′-mos
Also called *Panorm,* q.v. Italian *Palermo,* q.v., or *Porto Palermo.*		
Portela (Port.)	pôr′-tĕ-lä	por′-teh-lah
portentous See *grievous.*		
Port Moresby (New Guinea)	*Eng.* mōrz′-bĭ	mohrz′-bi
Porto (Port.)	pôr′-to͝o	por′-tu
English *Oporto,* ō-pôr′-tō [oh-por′-toh].		
Porto Alegre (Brazil)	pôr′-to͝o ä-lĕ′-grĭ	por′-tu ah-leh′-gri
Porto Caldo (Yugosl.)	*It.* pôr′-tô käl′-dô	por′-to kahl′-do
Serb-Croat *Teplo Pristanište,* q.v.		
Porto da Praia (Port., C. Verde)	pôr′-to͝o də prī′-ə	por′-tu duh prai′-uh
Porto Edda (Alb.)	*It.* pôr′-tô ĕd′-dä	por′-to ed′-dah
Recent name for (Italian) *Santi Quaranta,* q.v., Albanian *Sarandë,* q.v.		
Porto Empedocle (Sicily)	pôr′-tô ĕm-pĕ′-dô-klĕ	por′-to em-peh′-do-kleh
Porto Farina (Tun.)	pôr′-tô fä-rē′-nä	por′-to fah-ree′-nah
Portoferraio (It.)	pôr′-tô-fĕr-rä′-yô	por′-to-fehr-rah′-yo
Porto Lago (Dodec., bay)	pôr′-tô lä′-gô	por′-to lah′-go
Porto Ponte Romano (It.)	pôr′-tô pôn′-tĕ rô-mä′-nô	por′-to pon′-teh ro-mah′-no
Porto Re (Yugosl.)	*It.* pôr′-tô rĕ′	por′-to reh′
Serb-Croat *Kraljevica,* q.v.		
Portoscuso (Sard.)	pôr′-tô-sko͞o′-zô	por′-to-skoo′-zo
Porto Torres (Sard.)	pôr′-tô tôr′-rĕs	por′-to tor′-res
Porto Vecchio (It. and Corsica)	pôr′-tô vĕk′-kyô	por′-to vek′-kyo

Port Said (Egypt)	sä-ēd′	sah-eed′
Portugal	*Eng.* pôr′-chə-gəl	por′-chuh-guhl
	Port. pôr-to͝o-gäl′	por-tu-gahl′
Port Vendres (Fr.)	pôr väN′dr	por vahN′dr
Porya (Rus.)	pōr′-yä	pohr′-yah
Posad (Rus.)	pŏ-säd′	po-sahd′
An element, meaning *settlement,* in Russian place names.		
Poschiavo (It.)	pô-skyä′-vô	po-skyah′-vo
Po-seh (Ch., Kwangsi)	bô-sŭ	bo-suh
Also called *Pai-seh,* q.v.		
Posen (Pol.)	*Ger.* pō′-zən	poh′-zuhn
Polish *Poznań,* pôz′-nän(y) [poz′-nahn(y)].		
Posillipo (It.)	pô-zēl′-lē-pô	po-zeel′-lee-po
Postumia (It.)	pô-sto͞o′-myä	po-stoo′-myah
Postyshevo (Rus.)	pŏs-twē′-shĕ-vŏ	pos-twee′-sheh-vo
Potamos (Gr.)	pô-tä-môs′	po-tah-mos′
Potemkinsk (Rus.)	pŏ-tyôm′-kĭnsk	po-tyom′-kinsk
Potenza (It.)	pô-tĕn′-tsä	po-ten′-tsah
Pothea (Dodec., Kalymnos) See *Kalymnos.*		
Poti (Rus.)	pô′-tē	po′-tee
Potinville (Tun.)	pô-tăN-vēl′	po-taN-veel′
Potomac	pə-tō′-mək	puh-toh′-muhk
The pronunciation pə-tō′-mĭk [puh-toh′-mik] should be avoided. Cf. *stomach.*		
Poulson, Norris (U.S. representative)	pōl′-sən	pohl′-suhn
Pournaras, D. (Gr. collab.)	po͞or-nä′-räs	poor-nah′-rahs
Povenets (Rus.)	pŏ-vĕ-nĕts′	po-veh-nets′
Povorino (Rus.)	pŏ-vô′-rĭ-nŏ	po-vo′-ri-no
P'o-yang (Ch., Kiangsi, lake)	pô-yäng	po-yahng
Požarevac (Yugosl.)	pô′-zhä′-rĕ-väts	po′-zhah′-reh-vahts
German *Passarowitz,* pä-sä′-rō-vĭts [pah-sah′-roh-vits].		
Požega (Yugosl.)	pô′-zhĕ-gä	po′-zheh-gah
Požežena (Yugosl.)	pô′-zhĕ′-zhĕ-nä	po′-zheh′-zheh-nah
Poznań (Pol.)	pôz′-nän(y)	poz′-nahn(y)
German *Posen,* pō′-zən [poh′-zuhn].		
Pozzallo (Sicily)	pôt-sä′-lô	pot-sah′-lo
Pozzuoli (It.)	pôt-swô′-lē	pot-swo′-lee
Pracht, C. Frederick (U.S. representative)	präkt′	prahkt′
Prachuap Giri Khan (Thai)	prä′-chwŭp′ kē-rē kän′	prah′-chwuhp′ kee-ree kahn′

Pradist Manudharm (Thai leader)	prə-dĭt′ mä-no͝o′-täm	pruh-dit′ mah-nu′-tahm
Prądnik (Pol., riv.)	prôNd′-nĭk	proNd′-nik

Russian *Prondnik*, prônd′-nĭk [prond′-nik].

Pragersko (Yugosl.)	prä′-gĕr-skô	prah′-gehr-sko
Prague (Cz.)	*Eng.* präg′	prahg′

This pronunciation has been adopted from the French. The older English pronunciation is prāg′ [prayg′]. Czech *Praha*, prä′-hä [prah′-hah]. German *Prag*, präk(h)′ [prahk(h)′].

Praha (Cz.) See *Prague.*

Prahovo (Yugosl.)	prä′-hô-vô	prah′-ho-vo
Prajadhipok (Former king of Siam)	prə-chä′-tĭ-pōk	pruh-chah′-ti-pohk

Prasonesi (Dodec., Rh., point) See *Prasso.*

Prasso (Dodec., Rh., point)	*It.* präs′-sô	prahs′-so

Greek *Prasonesi*, prä-sô-nē′-sē [prah-so-nee′-see].

Pratas (Ch., isls.)	prä′-täs	prah′-tahs
Pratica di Mare (It.)	prä′-tē-kä dē mä′-rĕ	prah′-tee-kah dee mah′-reh
Pratola (It.)	prä′-tô-lä	prah′-to-lah
Pravda (Rus. newspaper)	präv′-dä	prahv′-dah
Prčanj (Yugosl.)	pər′-chän(y)	puhr′-chahn(y)
Prčja Glava (Yugosl., mt.)	pər′-chyä glä′-vä	puhr′-chyah glah′-vah
Prdejci (Yugosl.)	pər′-dā-tsĭ	puhr′-day-tsi

Preca (Alb.) See *Precë.*

Precë (Alb.)	prĕ′-tsə	preh′-tsuh

Italian *Preza.*

precedence	prĭ-sēd′-əns	pri-seed′-uhns
precedent(s) (noun)	prĕs′-ĭ-dənt(s)	pres′-i-duhnt(s)

To be distinguished from *precedence*, q.v.

Predborzh (Pol.) See *Przedbórz.*

Predejane (Yugosl.)	prĕ′-dĕ-yä-nĕ	preh′-deh-yah-neh
Pregel (Ger., riv.)	prā′-gəl	pray′-guhl
Prekestolen (Nor.)	prā′-kə-stō-lən	pray′-kuh-stoh-luhn
Prekornica (Yugosl., mts.)	prĕ′-kôr′-nĭ-tsä	preh′-kor′-ni-tsah
Prekoruplje (Yugosl.)	prĕ′-kô-ro͞op′-lyĕ	preh′-ko-roop′-lyeh
Preljina (Yugosl.)	prĕ′-lyĭ-nä	preh′-lyi-nah
Prelog (Yugosl.)	prĕ′-lôg	preh′-log
prelude	*Eng.* prĕl′-ūd	prel′-yood
	or prē′-lūd	pree′-lyood
	Fr. prĕ-lüd′	preh-lüd′

One of the English pronunciations should be used except in French contexts. "The prĕ-lüd′ [preh-lüd′] to the battle" sounds curious to

English ears, though this pronunciation may be preferred when speaking of Chopin's compositions.

Prëmet (Alb.) See *Përmet.*

premier	prē′-mĭ-ər	pree′-mi-uhr
	or prĭ-mēr′	pri-meer′
	or prĕm′-yər	prem′-yuhr

Here is a wealth of choice. The word should not be confused with *premiere* prə-myĕr′ [pruh-myehr′].

Premuda (Yugosl.)	prĕ′-mo͞o-dä	preh′-moo-dah
Přerov (Cz.)	przhĕ′-rôf	przheh′-rof
presage (noun)	prĕs′-ĭj	pres′-ij
presage (verb)	prĭ-sāj′	pri-sayj′

Presaging is prĭ-sā′-jĭng [pri-say′-jing]. Avoid prĭ-sä′-jĭng [pri-sah′-jing].

Preševo (Yugosl.)	prĕ′-shĕ-vô	preh′-sheh-vo
Presicce (It.)	prĕ-sēt′-chĕ	preh-seet′-cheh
Preslav (Bulg.)	prĕ′-släf	preh′-slahf
Prešov (Cz.)	prĕ′-shôf	preh′-shof
Prespa (Balkan lake)	*Eng.* prĕs′-pə	pres′-puh
	S.-C. prĕs′-pä	pres′-pah

Also called *Prespansko jezero*, prĕs′-pän-skô yĕ′-zĕ-rô [pres′-pahn-sko yeh′-zeh-ro]. Albanian *Liqen i Presbës*, lē-kyĕn′ ē prĕs′-bəs [lee-kyen′ ee pres′-buhs]. Greek *Limne Prespa*, lēm′-nē prĕs′-pä [leem′-nee pres′-pah].

Pressburg (Cz.) See *Bratislava.*

Pretoria (U. of S. Afr.)	prĭ-tō′-rĭ-ə	pri-toh′-ri-uh
Preussen (Ger.)	proi′-sən	proi′-suhn

English *Prussia*, q.v.

Prevalje (Yugosl.)	prĕ′-vä-lyĕ	preh′-vah-lyeh
Preveza (Gr.)	prĕ′-vĕ-zä	preh′-veh-zah
Prevlaka (Yugosl.)	prĕ′-vlä′-kä	preh′-vlah′-kah

Preza (Alb.) See *Precë.*

Pribilci (Yugosl.)	prē′-bĭl-tsĭ	pree′-bil-tsi
Pribilof (Alaska, isl.)	prĭb′-ĭ-lŏf′	prib′i-lof′
Priboj (Yugosl.)	prē′-boi	pree′-boi
Příbor (Cz.)	przhē′-bôr	przhee′-bor
Přibram (Cz.)	przhē′-bräm	przhee′-brahm
Pričinović (Yugosl.)	prē′-chĭ′-nô-vĭch	pree′-chi′-no-vich
Prijedor (Yugosl.)	prē′-yĕ-dôr	pree′-yeh-dor
Prijepolje (Yugosl.)	prē′-yĕ-pô′-lyĕ	pree′-yeh-po′-lyeh
Prikubansky (Rus.)	prĭ-ko͞o-bän′-skĭ	pri-ku-bahn′-ski
Prilep (Yugosl.)	prē′-lĕp	pree′-lep
Priluki (Rus.)	prĭ-lo͞o′-kĭ	pri-loo′-ki
Prilužje (Yugosl.)	prē′-lo͞ozh-yĕ	pree′-loozh-yeh

Primorsko Akhtarskaya (Rus.)	prĭ-môr′-skŏ äk(h)-tär′-skä-yä	pri-mor′-sko ahk(h)-tahr′-skah-yah
Primorsko Krajiška (Yugosl.)	prē′-môr-skô krä′-yĭsh-kä	pree′-mor-sko krah′-yish-kah
Primošten (Yugosl.)	prē′-mô-shtĕn	pree′-mo-shten
Pripyat (Rus., Pol., riv.) Polish *Prypeć*, q.v.	*Rus.* prē′-pyät(y)	pree′-pyaht(y)
Přísečnice (Cz.)	przhē′-sĕch′-nĭ-tsĕ	przhee′-sech′-ni-tseh
Prishibskaya (Rus.)	prĭ-shĭp′-skä-yä	pri-ship′-skah-yah
Priština (Yugosl.)	prē′-shtĭ-nä	pree′-shti-nah
Prisukha (Pol.) See *Przysucha.*		
Přívoz (Cz.)	przhē′-vôs	przhee′-vos
Prizren (Yugosl.)	prē′-zrĕn	pree′-zren
Prnjavor (Yugosl., near *Banjaluka*)	pər′-nyä-vôr	puhr′-nyah-vor
Prnjavor (Yugosl., near *Sarajevo*)	pər-nyä′-vôr	puhr-nyah′-vor
Proastion (Gr.)	prô-ä′-stē(-ôn)	pro-ah′-stee(-on)
Procida (It., isl.)	prô′-chē-dä	pro′-chee-dah
program	prō′-grăm	proh′-gram

Announcers are asked to follow the dictionaries and say prō′-grăm [proh′-gram], but everyone else in radio says prō′-grəm [proh′-gruhm]. The spelling has been simplified from *programme* and the new pronunciation prō′-grəm [proh′-gruhm] has developed. It will probably be authorized by future dictionaries. (P.S. It is given as the second pronunciation in Kenyon and Knott, *A Pronouncing Dictionary* [1944].)

Prokhladnaya (Rus.) Also called *Prokhladnenski*, q.v.	prŏ-hläd′-nä-yä	pro-hlahd′-nah-yah
Prokhladnenski (Rus.) Also called *Prokhladnaya*, q.v.	prŏ-hläd′-nĕn-skĭ	pro-hlahd′-nen-ski
Prokletija (Yugosl., mts.)	prô′-klĕ′-tĭ-yä	pro′-kleh′-ti-yah
Prokofieff (Rus. composer)	prŏ-kô′-fyĕf	pro-ko′-fyef
Prokuplje (Yugosl.)	prô′-ko͞op′-lyĕ	pro′-koop′-lyeh
Proletarskaya (Rus.)	prŏ-lĕ-tär′-skä-yä	pro-leh-tahr′-skah-yah
Prome (Burma)	prōm′	prohm′

An English spelling; pronounce as one syllable, not two. Kipling rhymes *Prome* and *home*, as many will remember. The Burman is *Pyemyo*, pyā-myō′ [pyay-myoh′].

Prondnik (Pol., riv.) See *Prądnik.*		
Pronsk (Rus.)	prônsk′	pronsk′
Prosenikovo (Yugosl.)	prô′-sĕ-nē′-kô-vô	pro′-seh-nee′-ko-vo
Proskurov (Rus.)	prŏ-sko͞o′-rŏf	pro-skoo′-rof

Prostějov (Cz.)	prô′-styĕ-yôf	pro′-styeh-yof
German *Prossnitz*, prôs′-nĭts [pros′-nits].		
Proti (Gr., isl.)	prô′-tē	pro′-tee
Protville (Tun.)	prôt-vēl′	prot-veel′
Provence (Fr.)	prô-väNs′	pro-vahNs′
provost	prŏv′-əst	prov′-uhst
Military usage prō′-vō′ [proh′-voh′].		
Prozor (Yugosl.)	prô′-zôr	pro′-zor
Prsten (Yugosl.)	pər′-stĕn	puhr′-sten
Prussia (Ger.)	*Eng.* prŭsh′-ə	pruhsh′-uh
German *Preussen*, q.v.		
Pruszków (Pol.)	pro͝osh′-ko͝of	prush′-kuf
Russian *Prushkov*, pro͝osh-kôf′ [prush-kof′].		
Prut (Pol., Rum., riv.)	*Pol.* pro͝ot′	prut′
Russian *Prut*, prōōt′ [proot′]. Rumanian *Prutul*, pro͝o′-to͝ol [pru′-tul].		
Prvić (Yugosl., isl.)	pər′-vĭch	puhr′-vich
Italian *Pervicchio*, q.v.		
Prypeć (Pol., Rus., riv.)	*Pol.* prĭ′-pĕch	pri′-pech
Russian *Pripyat*, q.v.		
Przedbórz (Pol.)	pshĕd′-bo͝ozh	pshed′-buzh
Russian *Predborzh*, prĕd′-bŏrsh [pred′-borsh].		
Przemyśl (Pol.)	pshĕ′-mĭshl	psheh′-mishl
Russian *Peremyshl*, pĕ-rĕ-mwēshl′(y) [peh-reh-mweeshl′(y)].		
Przeworsk (Pol.)	pshĕ′-vôrsk	psheh′-vorsk
Przh- Also see *Př-*.		
Przysucha (Pol.)	pshĭ-so͝o′-hä	pshi-su′-hah
Russian *Prisukha*, prĭ-sōō′-hä [pri-soo′-hah].		
Psakon (Crete, pen.)	psä′-kô(n)	psah′-ko(n)
Also called *Rodopou*, q.v.		
Psara (Gr., isl.)	psä-rä′	psah-rah′
Psaros (Gr. leader)	psä-rôs′	psah-ros′
Psathoura (Gr.)	psä-thōō′-rä	psah-thoo′-rah
Psel (Rus., riv.)	psyôl′	psyol′
Psira (Crete, isl.)	psē′-rä	psee′-rah
Pskov (Rus.)	pskôf′	pskof′
Psykhion (Crete, point)	See *Melissa*.	
Pszczyna (Pol.)	pshchĭ′-nä	pshchi′-nah
German *Pless*, plĕs′ [ples′].		
Ptich (Rus., riv.)	ptēch′	pteech′
Ptuj (Yugosl.)	pto͞oy′ *or* ptōō′ĭ	ptooy′ *or* ptoo′i
P'u-ch'êng (Ch., Fukien)	pōō-chŭng	poo-chuhng
Pucheu, Pierre (Fr. leader)	pü-shû′, pyĕr′	pü-shœ′, pyehr′
P'u-chiang (Ch., Chekiang)	pōō-jyäng	poo-jyahng

Puck (Pol.)	po͝otsk′	putsk′
German *Putsig*, po͝ot′-sĭk(h) [put′-sik(h)].		
Pudozh (Rus.)	po͞o′-dŏsh	poo′-dosh
Puglia (It.)	po͞o′-lyä	poo′-lyah
English *Apulia*, q.v.		
Pühalepa (Est.)	pü′-hä-lĕ′-pä	pü′-hah-leh′-pah
Puka (Alb.) See *Pukë.*		
Pukë (Alb.)	po͞o′-kə	poo′-kuh
P'u-kiang (Ch., Chekiang) Variant of *P'u-chiang*, q.v.		
Pukovac (Yugosl.)	po͞o′-kô-väts	poo′-ko-vahts
P'u-k'ow (Ch., Kiangsu)	po͞o-kō	poo-koh
Pulap (Oc.)	po͞o′-läp	poo′-lahp
Also called *Tamatam*, q.v.		
Puławy (Pol.)	po͝o-lä′-vĭ	pu-lah′-vi
Russian *Novoaleksandriya*, nô′-vŏ-ä-lĕk-sän-drē′-yä [no′-vo-ah-lek-sahn-dree′-yah].		
Pulicat (India)	po͞o′-lĭ-kăt	poo′-li-kat
Pulitzer, Joseph	pū′-lĭt-sər	pyoo′-lit-suhr
Pulo Anna (Oc.)	po͞o′-lô än′-nä	poo′-lo ahn′-nah
Also called *Puru*, po͞o′-ro͞o [poo′-roo].		
Pulozero (Rus.)	po͝ol-ô′-zĕ-rŏ	pul-o′-zeh-ro
Pułtusk (Pol.)	po͝ol′-to͝osk	pul′-tusk
Pulusuk (Oc.)	po͞o-lo͞o-so͞ok′	poo-loo-sook′
Puluwat (Oc.)	po͞o-lo͞o-wät′	poo-loo-waht′
Punaka (Bhutan)	po͝o-nŭk′-ə	pu-nuhk′-uh
P'u-ning (Ch., Kwangtung)	po͞o-nĭng	poo-ning
Punjab (India)	pŭn′-jäb′	puhn′-jahb′
Punjabi (India)	pŭn-jä′-bē	puhn-jah′-bee
punta (It.) *Punta* or *Point* is often ignored in the alphabetical listing. Look up the other part of the name.		
Punta d'Arza (Yugosl.)	*It.* po͞on′-tä d'är′-tsä	poon′-tah d'ahr′-tsah
Serb-Croat Rt *Arca*, q.v.		
Punta di Stilo (It.)	po͞on′-tä dē stē′-lô	poon′-tah dee stee′-lo
Puntadura (Yugosl.)	*It.* po͞on-tä-do͞o′-rä	poon-tah-doo′-rah
Serb-Croat *Vir*, q.v.		
Punta Planca (Yugos.)	*It.* po͞on′-tä plän′-kä	poon′-tah plahn′-kah
Serb-Croat Rt *Ploče*, q.v.		
Punta Platamone (Yugosl.)	*It.* po͞on′-tä plä-tä-mô′-nĕ	poon′-tah plah-tah-mo′-neh
Serb-Croat Rt *Platamon*, q.v.		
Purcell, Henry (17th cent. Brit. composer)	pûr′-sĕl	puhr′-sel
As an American family name the last syllable is often accented.		

Puri (India)	po͞o′-rē′	poo′-ree′
Purič, Božidar (Yugosl. leader)	po͞o′-rĭch, bô′-zhĭ-där	poo′-rich, bo′-zhi-dahr
Purmerend (Neth.)	pûr-mə-rĕnt′	pœr-muh-rent′
Puru (Oc.) See *Pulo Anna.*		
Pushkino (Rus.)	po͞osh′-kĭ-nŏ	poosh′-ki-no
Pushtrik (Balkan mt.)	*Eng.* po͝osh′-trĭk	push′-trik

Albanian *Mal i Pushtrikut* or *Bështriq,* q.v. Serb-Croat *Paštrik,* q.v.

Pusta (Yugosl.)	po͞o′-stä	poo′-stah
P'u-t'ien (Ch., Fukien)	po͞o-tyĕn	poo-tyen
Putivl (Rus.)	po͞o-tēvl′(y)	poo-teevl′(y)
Putsig (Pol.) See *Puck.*		
Puy, le (Fr.)	pwē′, lə	pwee′, luh
Puy de Dôme (Fr.)	pwē də dōm′	pwee duh dohm′
Pyapon (Burma)	pyä′-pōn	pyah′-pohn
Pyasechno (Pol.) See *Piaseczno.*		
Pyatigorsk (Rus.)	pyä-tĭ-gôrsk′	pyah-ti-gorsk′
Pyawbwe (Burma)	pyô-bwĕ′	pyaw-bweh′
Pyinmana (Burma)	pyĭn′-mə-nä′	pyin′-muh-nah′
Pylos (Gr.)	*Eng.* pī′-lŏs	pai′-los
	Gr. pē′-lôs	pee′-los

Also called *Navarino,* q.v., and *Niokastro,* nyô′-kä-strô [nyo′-kah-stro].

Pyrgi (Gr.)	pēr′-yē	peer′-yee
Pyrgos (Gr., Crete)	pēr′-gôs	peer′-gos
Pytalovo (Latvia)	*Rus.* pĭ-tä′-lŏ-vŏ	pi-tah′-lo-vo

Latvian *Jaunlatgale,* q.v.

qafa (Alb.) See *qafë.*		
qafë (Alb.)	kyä′-fə	kyah′-fuh

An element, meaning *pass,* in Albanian place names. Look up the other part of the name.

Qairwan (Tun.)	kīr-wän′	kair-wahn′

French *Kairouan,* q.v.

Qaret el Himeimat (Egypt)	kă′-rĕt ĕl hĭ-mā-măt′	ka′-ret el hi-may-mat′
Qasr-i-Shirin (Iran)	kăzr′-ē-shē-rēn′	kazr′-ee-shee-reen′
Qatia (Egypt)	kä-tē′-ä	kah-tee′-ah
Qattara (Egypt)	kä-tä′-rä	kah-tah′-rah
Qazvin (Iran)	kăz-vēn′	kaz-veen′

Also spelled *Kasvin* or *Kazvin.*

Quai d'Orsay	*Eng.* kā′ dôr-sā′	kay′ dor-say′
	Fr. kĕ dôr-sĕ′	keh dor-seh′

Quangngai (Indo-Ch.)	*Eng.* kwäng-nī′	kwahng-nai′
	local kwäng-ngī′	kwahng-ngai′
Quarnerolo (Yugosl., It., channel)	*It.* kwär-nĕ-rô′-lô	kwahr-neh-ro′-lo
Serb-Croat *Mali Kvarner*, q.v.		
quay	*Eng.* kē′	kee′
	Fr. kĕ′	keh′
Modern French spelling *quai*.		
Quchan (Iran)	ko͞o-chän′	koo-chahn′
Also spelled *Kuchan*.		
Quejo (Sp., cape)	kĕ′-hô	keh′-ho
Quetta (-Pishin) (Baluch.)	kwĕt′-ä (pĭ-shēn′)	kwet′-ah (pi-sheen′)
Quezon, Manuel (Fil. leader)	*Eng.* kā′-zŏn′, măn′-ū-əl	kay′-zon′, man′-yoo-uhl
	Sp. kĕ′-sôn (*or* -thôn), mä-nwĕl′	keh′-son (*or* -thon), mah-nwel′

One might expect Spanish *Quezon* to bear an accent on the final syllable. In a broadcast in honor of President Quezon, President Ávila Camacho of Mexico so stressed it. However, this seems not to be the usage of the Philippines. The name is usually Anglicized by American speakers.

Quiberon (Fr.)	kē-brôN′	kee-broN′
quiescent	kwī-ĕs′-ənt	kwai-es′-uhnt
Quimper (Fr.)	kăN-pĕr′	kaN-pehr′
Quinhon (Indo-Ch.)	kwē-nyŭn′	kwee-nyuhn′
Quirinal (Rome)	*Eng.* kwĭr′-ĭ-nəl	kwihr′-i-nuhl
Italian *Quirinale*, kwē-rē-nä′-lĕ [kwee-ree-nah′-leh].		
Quisling, Vidkun Abraham (Nor. collab.)	*Eng.* kwĭz′-lĭng	kwiz′-ling
	Nor. kvĭs′-lĭng, vĭd′-ko͝on	kvis′-ling, vid′-kun
Quisquina (Sicily)	kwēs-kwē′-nä	kwees-kwee′-nah
Qum *or* Kum (Iran)	ko͝om′	kum′
Raab (Austria, Hung., riv.)	*Ger.* räp′	rahp′
Hungarian *Rába*, rä′-bŏ [rah′-bo].		
Raadhusplads (Den.)	rô*th*′-ho͞os-pläs	ro*th*′-hoos-plahs
Raahe (Fin.)	rä′-hĕ	rah′-heh
Rab (Yugosl.)	räb′	rahb′
Italian *Arbe*, q.v.		
Rába (Hung., Austria, riv.)	See *Raab*.	
Raba (Pol., riv.)	rä′-bä	rah′-bah

Rabat (Mor.)	rä-bät′	rah-baht′
Rabaul (Oc.)	rä-boul′ *or* rä′-boul	rah-baul′ *or* rah′-baul
See *Tahiti.*		
Rabaut, Louis C. (U.S. representative)	răb′-ō	rab′-oh
Rabrovo (Yugosl.)	rä′-brô-vô	rah′-bro-vo
Rača (Yugosl.)	rä′-chä	rah′-chah
Raccuja (Sicily)	räk-ko͞o′-yä	rahk-koo′-yah
Rachgia (Indo-Ch.)	rä-zhä′	rah-zhah′
Rachov (Cz.)	rä′-hôf	rah′-hof
Hungarian *Rahó,* rä′-hô [rah′-ho].		
Ráczkeve (Hung.)	räts′-kĕ-vĕ	rahts′-keh-veh
Also called *Csepel,* q.v.		
Raczkiewicz, Wladyslaw (President of Poland)	räch-kyĕ′-vĭch, vlä-dĭ′-släf	rahch-kyeh′-vich, vlah-di′-slahf
Radac (Oc.)	rä′-däk	rah′-dahk
radar	rā′-där	ray′-dahr
Rădăuţi (Rum.)	rə-də-o͝ots′	ruh-duh-uts′
German *Radautz,* rä′-douts [rah′-dauts].		
Rades (Tun.)	rä′-dĕs	rah′-des
Radin (Pol.) See *Radzyń.*		
Radłowo (Pol.)	rä-dlô′-vô	rah-dlo′-vo
Radočelo (Yugosl., mts.)	rä′-dô-chĕ-lô	rah′-do-cheh-lo
Radomir (Bulg.)	rä′-dŏ-mēr′	rah′-do-meer′
Radomka (Pol., riv.)	rä-dôm′-kä	rah-dom′-kah
Radomsko (Pol.)	rä-dôm′-skô	rah-dom′-sko
Russian *Novoradomsk,* nô′-vô-rä′-dŏmsk [no′-vo-rah′-domsk].		
Radomysl (Rus.)	rä-dŏ-mwēshl′(y)	rah-do-mweeshl′(y)
Radoštak (Yugosl., mt.)	rä′-dô-shtäk	rah′-do-shtahk
Radovište (Yugosl.)	rä′-dô′-vĭ-shtĕ	rah′-do′-vi-shteh
Radovljica (Yugosl.)	rä′-dôv′-lyĭ-tsä	rah′-dov′-lyi-tsah
Radujevac (Yugosl.)	rä′-do͞o′-yĕ-väts	rah′-doo′-yeh-vahts
Raduša (Yugosl.)	rä′-do͞o-shä	rah′-doo-shah
Radziwiłłów (Pol.)	rä-jĭ-vē′-lo͝of	rah-ji-vee′-luf
Russian *Radzivilov,* rä-dzĭ-vē′-lŏf [rah-dzi-vee′-lof].		
Radzyń (Pol.)	rä′-jĭn(y)	rah′-jin(y)
Russian *Radin,* rä′-dĭn [rah′-din].		
Ragnhild (Nor. princess)	rängn′-hĭl *or* rägn′-hĭl	rahngn′-hil rahgn′-hil
Ragusa (Sicily)	rä-go͞o′-zä	rah-goo′-zah
Ragusa (Yugosl.)	*It.* rä-go͞o′-zä	rah-goo′-zah
Serb-Croat *Dubrovnik,* q.v.		
Rahó (Cz.) See *Rachov.*		
Raiatea (Oc.)	rī-ä-tĕ′-ä	rai-ah-teh′-ah

Rainier (Wash., pk. and mt.)	rā-nĭr′ *or* rā′-nĭr	ray-nihr′ *or* ray′-nihr
Rainò (It.)	rī-nô′	rai-no′
Raipur (India)	rī′-po͝or′	rai′-pur′
Raivavae (Oc.)	rī′-vä-vä′-ĕ	rai′-vah-vah′-eh
Rajagopalachari, C. (Indian leader)	rä-jə-gô-pä-lə-chä′-rē	rah-juh-go-pah-luh-chah′-ree
Rajburi (Thai)	rät′-bo͝o-rē′ *or* räj′-ə-bo͝o-rē′	raht′-bu-ree′ rahj′-uh-bu-ree′
Rajistovac (Yugosl.)	rä′-yĭs-tô-väts	rah′-yis-to-vahts
Rajkot (India)	räj′-kōt	rahj′-koht
Rajpipla (India)	räj-pē′-plə	rahj-pee′-pluh
Rajput (India)	räj′-po͝ot	rahj′-put
Rajputana (India)	räj′-po͝o-tä′-nə	rahj′-pu-tah′-nuh
Rakinac (Yugosl.)	rä′-kĭ-näts	rah′-ki-nahts
Rakitno (Pol.) See *Rokitno.*		
Raków (Pol.)	rä′-ko͝of	rah′-kuf
Russian *Rakov*, rä′-kŏf [rah′-kof].		
Rakusha (Rus.)	rä′-ko͞o-shä	rah′-koo-shah
Rakvere (Est.)	räk′-vĕ-rĕ	rahk′-veh-reh
German *Wesenberg*, q.v.		
Ralik (Oc.)	rä′-lĭk	rah′-lik
Ralinna (Austral.)	rə-lĭn′-ə	ruh-lin′-uh
Ralja (Yugosl.)	rä′-lyä	rah′-lyah
Rallis, Joannes (Gr. collab.)	rä′-lēs, yô-ä′-nēs	rah′-lees, yo-ah′-nees
Rambutyo (Oc.)	räm-bo͞o′-tyô	rahm-boo′-tyo
Rameswaram *or* Ramisseram (India)	rä-mĕs′-wə-rŭm′ *or* rä-mĭs′-ə-räm′	rah-mes′-wuh-ruhm′ rah-mis′-uh-rahm′
Ramírez, Pedro (Arg. leader)	rä-mē′-rĕs, pĕ′-drô	rah-mee′-res, peh′-dro
Râmnicul Sărat (Rum.)	rûm′-nē-ko͝ol sə-rät′	ruhm′-nee-kul suh-raht′
Râmnicul Vâlcea (Rum.)	rûm′-nē-ko͝ol vûl′-chä	ruhm′-nee-kul vuhl′-chah
Ramón (Sp. name)	rä-môn′	rah-mon′
Ramon (Rus.)	rä-môn′(y)	rah-mon′(y)
Ramree (Burma)	răm-rē′	ram-ree′
Ramu (New Guinea, riv.)	rä′-mo͞o	rah′-moo
Rance (Fr., riv.)	räNs′	rahNs′
Ranchi (India)	rän′-chē′	rahn′-chee′
Randazzo (Sicily)	rän-dät′-sô	rahn-daht′-so
Randers (Den.)	rän′-ərs	rahn′-uhrs
Randsfjord (Nor.)	räns′-fyōr	rahns′-fyohr

Ranenburg (Rus.)	rä′-nĕn-bo͝ork	rah′-nen-burk
Rangoon (Burma)	răng-go͞on′	rang-goon′
Rann (Yugosl.) See *Brežice.*		
Ranohng (Thai)	rə-nông′	ruh-nawng′
ranta	rän′-tä	rahn′-tah
An element, meaning *shore* or *strand,* in Finnish place names.		
Rapido (It., riv.)	rä′-pē-dô	rah′-pee-do
Rarotonga (Oc.)	rä-rô-tông′-ä	rah-ro-tong′-ah
Ras Abu Laho (Egypt)	räs′ ä′-bo͞o lä′-hô	rahs′ ah′-boo lah′-ho
Ras Alam el Rum (Egypt)	räs′ ä-lăm′ ĕr ro͞om′	rahs′ ah-lam′ ehr room′
Rašče (Yugosl.)	räsh′-chĕ	rahsh′-cheh
Raseiniai (Lith.)	rä-syā′-nyī	rah-syay′-nyai
Russian *Rossieny,* q.v.		
Ras el Milh (Libya)	räs′ ĕl mĭl(kh)′	rahs′ el mil(kh)′
Rashid (Egypt)	rä-shēd′	rah-sheed′
Also called *Rosetta,* q.v.		
Rashin (Korea)	rä-shĭn	rah-shin
Rasht *or* Resht (Iran)	răsht′	rasht′
Rasina (Yugosl., riv.)	rä′-sĭ-nä	rah′-si-nah
Raška (Yugosl.)	rä′-shkä	rah′-shkah
Raspopinsk (Rus.)	räs-pô′-pĭnsk	rahs-po′-pinsk
Rass ben Sekka (Tun.)	räs′ bĕn sĕk′-kä	rahs′ ben sek′-kah
Rastenburg (Ger.)	*Eng.* räs′-tən-bûrg	rahs′-tuhn-buhrg
	Ger. räs′-tən-bo͝ork(h)	rahs′-tuhn-burk(h)
Rathedaung (Burma)	rə-thā′-doung′	ruh-thay′-daung′
ration (noun and verb)	răsh′-ən *or* rā′-shən	rash′-uhn *or* ray′-shuhn

Probably nine out of ten Americans in all walks of life use a pronunciation illustrated by *national* and *rational* rather than by *nation.* It is interesting that this general American usage is better reflected in British dictionaries, which are inclined to ignore rā′-shən [ray′-shuhn] than in American dictionaries, which list both pronunciations but place răsh′-ən [rash′-uhn] second. *Ration* is one of a number of instances where our dictionaries show a preference for a New England schoolmaster's pronunciation in contrast to an all-American usage. (However, it should be said that dictionary makers when they set down two pronunciations are required by two-dimensional space to place one either before or above the other and frequently mean nothing by the order. Fortunately, each new edition of our dictionaries shows a greater awareness of America west of the Connecticut River, though there are still corrections to be made.) There is no doubt that in military usage răsh′-ən [rash′-uhn] is preferred. It is likewise the pronunciation of President Roosevelt, Prime Minister Churchill, James F. Byrnes, Leon Henderson, Elmer Davis, and Eddie Rickenbacker. From the historical point of view, rӑsh′-ən [rash′-uhn] is the Englishing of a French pronunciation and corresponds nicely to *depot* pronounced dĕ′-pō [deh′-poh] in military circles. Both words in technical senses were borrowed by the English army from the French. On the other hand rā′-shən [ray′-shuhn] follows the rules of the English pronunciation of Latin. It is natural that officers should favor the first and schoolmasters the latter. See Prof. Kemp Malone's article, "Ration," *American Speech*, vol. 18, pp 128-30, April, 1943. Other romance words appear in English with "short *a*" before a single consonant: *palace, satire, salad, fashion.* P.S.: The pronunciation rӑsh′-ən [rash′-uhn] is placed first by Kenyon and Knott, *A Pronouncing Dictionary* (1944).

Ratisbon (Ger.)	*Eng.* rӑt′-ĭs-bŏn	rat′-is-bon
German *Regensburg*, q.v.		
Ratlam (India)	rət-läm′	ruht-lahm′
Ratmirovichi (Rus.)	rät-mē′-rŏ-vĭ-chĭ	raht-mee′-ro-vi-chi
Rauma (Fin.; Nor., riv.)	rou′-mä	rau′-mah
Ravenga (Oc.)	rä-vĕng′-ä	rah-veng′-ah
Ravenna (It.)	*Eng.* rə-vĕn′-ə	ruh-ven′-uh
	It. rä-vĕn′-nä	rah-ven′-nah
Raviscanina (It.)	rä-vē-skä-nē′-nä	rah-vee-skah-nee′-nah
Rawa (Pol.)	rä′-vä	rah′-vah
Russian spelling *Rava.*		
Rawalpindi (India)	rä-wəl-pĭn′-dē	rah-wuhl-pin′-dee
Rawa Ruska (Pol.)	rä′-vä rŏŏ′-skä	rah′-vah ru′-skah
Rawka (Pol., riv.)	räf′-kä	rahf′-kah
Russian spelling *Ravka.*		
Rawson, Arturo (Arg. general)	rou′-sôn, är-tōō′-rô	rau′-son, ahr-too′-ro
Rayohng (Thai)	rə-yông′	ruh-yawng′
Raz (Fr., point)	räz′	rahz′
Ražanj (Yugosl.)	rä′-zhän(y)	rah′-zhahn(y)
Razdelnaya (Rus.)	räz-dĕl′(y)-nä-yä	rahz-del′(y)-nah-yah
Razelm (Rum., lake)	rä′-zĕlm	rah′-zelm
Razgrad (Bulg.)	räs′-grät	rahs′-graht
Razliv (Rus.)	räz-lēf′	rahz-leef′
Ré (Fr., isl.)	rĕ′	reh′
Recebedon (Fr.)	rĕ-sĕ-bĕ-dôN′	reh-seh-beh-doN′
Rechitsa (Rus.)	rĕ′-chĭ-tsä	reh′-chi-tsah
Recife (Brazil)	rĕ-sē′-fĭ	reh-see′-fi
Also called, unofficially, *Pernambuco*, q.v.		
Reciţa (Rum.)	rĕ′-chē-tsä	reh′-chee-tsah

Hungarian *Resiczabánya*, rĕ′-shĭ-tsŏ-bä′-nyŏ [reh′-shi-tso-bah′-nyo].

Recklinghausen (Ger.)	rĕk′-lĭng-hou′-zən	rek′-ling-hau′-zuhn
Recto, Claro M. (Fil. leader)	rĕk′-tô, klä′-rô	rek′-to, klah′-ro
Redeyef (Tun.)	rə-dā′-yĕf	ruh-day′-yef
Regalbuto (Sicily)	rĕ-gäl-bo͞o′-tô	reh-gahl-boo′-to
Regensburg (Ger.)	*Eng.* rā′-gənz-bûrg	ray′-guhnz-buhrg
	Ger. rā′-gəns-bo͝ork(h)	ray′-guhns-burk(h)

English *Ratisbon*, q.v.

Regge (Neth., riv.)	rĕk(h)′-ə	rek(h)′-uh
Reggio Calabria (It.)	rĕd′-jô kä-lä′-brē-ä	red′-jo kah-lah′-bree-ah

American speakers may follow the example of Italians and call it simply *Reggio*, rĕd′-jô [red′-jo].

Reggio Emilia (It.)	rĕd′-jô ĕ-mē′-lyä	red′-jo eh-mee′-lyah
Reghin (Rum.)	rĕ-gēn′	reh-geen′
Reichstag	*Eng.* rīks′-täg	raiks′-tahg
	Ger. rīk(h)s′-täkh	raik(h)s′-tahkh

The pronunciation rīk′-shtäg [raik′-shtahg] is incorrect. The *s*, as a genitive inflection, belongs to the first syllable, not to the second.

Reims (Fr.)	*Eng.* rēmz′	reemz′
	Fr. răNs′	raNs′
Reinovo (Rus.)	rĕ′-ĭ-nŏ-vŏ	reh′-i-no-vo
Reiovets (Pol.) See *Rejowiec.*		
Reis, Coelho dos (Braz. leader)	rās′, kwĕ′-lyo͝o do͝os	rays′, kweh′-lyu dus

Both names should be used, thus: *Coelho dos Reis*, not *Reis* alone.

Reistad, Ole (Nor. colonel)	rā′-stä, ō′-lə	ray′-stah, oh′-luh
Reit Diep (Neth.)	rīt′ dēp′	rait′ deep′

Also called *Groningen Diep*, q.v.

Rejowiec (Pol.)	rĕ-yô′-vyĕts	reh-yo′-vyets

Russian spelling *Reiovets*.

Rekovac (Yugosl.)	rĕ′-kô-väts	reh′-ko-vahts
Remada (Tun.)	rə-mă′-dä	ruh-ma′-dah
Rembang (NEI)	rĕm′-bäng′	rem′-bahng′
Remscheid (Ger.)	rĕm′-shīt	rem′-shait
Rena (Nor.)	rā′-nä	ray′-nah
Renaix (Belg.) See *Ronse.*		
Renault (Fr.)	rə-nō′	ruh-noh′
Renault, Abgar (Braz. leader)	rĕ-nō′, äb-gär′	reh-noh′, ahb-gahr′
Rendova (Oc.)	rĕn-dô′-vä	ren-do′-vah
	or rĕn′-dô-vä	ren′-do-vah
Renesse (Neth.)	rə-nĕs′-ə	ruh-nes′-uh

Reni (Rum.)	rĕn′	ren′

Russian *Reni,* rĕ′-nĭ [reh′-ni].

Rennell (Oc.)	rĕn′-əl	ren′-uhl

Probably named after the English geographer.

Rennes (Fr.)	rĕn′	ren′
Reno (It., riv.)	rĕ′-nô	reh′-no
Resan (Yugosl.)	rĕ′-sän	reh′-sahn
Resava (Yugosl., riv.)	rĕ′-sä-vä	reh′-sah-vah
Reschenscheideck (Austria, It., pass)	rĕ-shən-shī′-dĕk	reh-shuhn-shai′-dek
research	rĭ-sûrch′ *or* rē′-sûrch	ri-suhrch′ *or* ree′-suhrch

A campus joke is that those who talk about it say rĭ-sûrch′ [ri-suhrch′]; those who do it, say rē′-sûrch [ree′-suhrch]. Though this isn't true, the usage of many if not most scientists has made the pronunciation rē′-sûrch [ree′-suhrch] acceptable. It was admitted by Webster's (1934) and the Thorndike Century (1941).

Reshidiya (Libya)	rĕ-shĭ-dē′-yä	reh-shi-dee′-yah
Reshitsa (Rus.)	rĕ′-shĭ-tsä	reh′-shi-tsah
Resht *or* Rasht (Iran)	răsht′	rasht′
Resiczabánya (Rum.)	See *Reciţa.*	
Restelica (Yugosl.)	rĕ′-stĕ′-lĭ-tsä	reh′-steh′-li-tsah
Rethymne (Crete)	rĕ-thēm′-nē	reh-theem′-nee
Rethymnon (Crete)	rĕ′-thēm-nô(n)	reh′-theem-no(n)

Also called *Rethymne,* q.v., and *Rethymnos,* rĕ′-thēm-nôs [reh′-theem-nos].

Retournemer (Fr.)	rə-tōōr-nə-mĕr′ *or* -mĕ′	ruh-toor-nuh-mehr′ *or* -meh′
Reval *or* Revel (Est.)	*Eng.* rĕv′-əl *Rus.* rĕ′-vĕl(y)	rev′-uhl reh′-vel(y)

Estonian *Tallinn,* q.v.

Revercomb, Chapman (U.S. senator)	rĕv′-ər-kōm, chăp′-mən	rev′-uhr-kohm, chap′-muhn
Reykjavik (Icel.)	rā′-kyə-vēk	ray′-kyuh-veek
Reza Shah Pahlevi (Iran)	See *Pahlevi, Shah Riza.*	
Rezayeh (Iran, lake)	See *Rizaiyeh.*	
Rēzekne (Latvia)	rā′-zĕk-nĕ	ray′-zek-neh

Russian *Ryezhitsa,* q.v. German *Rositten,* q.v.

Rezina (Rum.)	rĕ-zē′-nä	reh-zee′-nah
Rēznas (Latvia, lake)	rāz′-näs	rayz′-nahs
Rgotina (Yugosl.)	ər′-gô′-tĭ-nä	uhr′-go′-ti-nah
Rharsa, el (Tun.)	rär′-sä, ĕr	rahr′-sah, ehr
Rheydt (Ger.)	rīt′	rait′

Rhine (Europ. riv.)	*Eng.* rīn′	rain′
Dutch spelling *Rijn*. German spelling *Rhein*. French *Rhin*, răN′ [raN′].		
Rhio (NEI) Variant spelling of *Riouw*, q.v.		
Rhodes (Dodec.)	*Eng.* rōdz′	rohdz′
Greek *Rodos*, q.v. Italian *Rodi*, rô′-dē [ro′-dee].		
Rhodope (Balkan mts.)	*Eng.* rŏd′-ə-pĭ	rod′-uh-pi
	Gr. rô-*th*ô′-pē	ro-*th*o′-pee
Bulgarian *Despoto planina*, dĕ′-spŏ-tŏ plä′-nē′-nä [deh′-spo-to plah′-nee′-nah].		
Rhône (Fr., Switz., riv.)	rōn′	rohn′
Ribarci (Yugosl.)	rē′-bär-tsĭ	ree′-bahr-tsi
Ribe (Den.)	rē′-bə	ree′-buh
Ribera (Sicily)	rē-bĕ′-rä	ree-beh′-rah
Ribnica (Yugosl.)	rēb′-nĭ-tsä	reeb′-ni-tsah
Ricarte, Artemio (Fil. leader)	rē-kär′-tĕ, är-tĕ′-myô	ree-kahr′-teh, ahr-teh′-myo
Riesi (Sicily)	ryĕ′-zē	ryeh′-zee
Rieti (It.)	ryĕ′-tē	ryeh′-tee
Riga (Latvia)	rē′-gä	ree′-gah
Riiser-Larsen, Hjalmar (Nor. admiral)	rē-sər-lär′-sən, yäl′-mär	ree-suhr-lahr′-suhn, yahl′-mahr
Rijeka Crnojevića (Yugosl.)	rĭ-yĕ′-kä tsər′-nô′-yĕ-vĭ-chä	ri-yeh′-kah tsuhr′-no′-yeh-vi-chah
Rijssen (Neth.)	rīs′-ən	rais′-uhn
Rijswijk (Neth.)	rīs′-wīk	rais′-waik
English *Ryswick*, rĭz′-wĭk [riz′-wik].		
Riksdag	rēks′-däg	reeks′-dahg
Swedish parliament.		
Rila (Bulg., mts.)	rē′-lä	ree′-lah
Greek *Rilos*, rē′-lôs [ree′-los]. Turkish *Rilo*.		
Rimini (It.)	*Eng.* rĭm′-ĭ-nĭ	rim′-i-ni
	It. rē′-mē-nē	ree′-mee-nee
Rimske Toplice (Yugosl.)	rēm′-skĕ tôp′-lĭ-tsĕ	reem′-skeh top′-li-tseh
Rindjano (NEI)	rĭn-jä′-nô	rin-jah′-no
Ringebu (Nor.)	rĭng′-ə-bo͞o	ring′-uh-boo
Ringerike (Nor.)	rĭng′-ə-rē-kə	ring′-uh-ree-kuh
Ringkoebing *or* Ringköbing (Den.)	rĭng′-kû-bĭng	ring′-kœ-bing
Ringsaker (Nor.)	rĭng′-sä-kər	ring′-sah-kuhr
Ringsted (Den.)	rĭng′-stĕ*th*	ring′-ste*th*
Rio Branco (Brazil)	rē′-o͝o brăng′-ko͝o	ree′-u brahng′-ku

Rio de Janeiro (Brazil)	*Eng.* rē′-ō də zhə-nĕr′-ō	ree′-oh duh zhuh-nehr′-oh
	Port. rē′-o͝o dĭ zhə-nā′-ro͝o	ree′-u di zhuh-nay′-ru
Río de la Plata (S. A.)	rē′-ô dĕ lä plä′-tä	ree′-o deh lah plah′-tah
British *River Plate*, plāt′ [playt′].		
Rio Grande do Norte (Brazil)	rē′-o͝o grän′-dĭ do͝o nôr′-tĭ	ree′-u grahn′-di du nor′-ti
Rio Grande do Sul (Brazil)	rē′-o͝o grän′-dĭ do͝o so͞ol′	ree′-u grahn′-di du sool′
Riom (Fr.)	*Fr.* ryôN′	ryoN′
Rion (Rus., riv.)	rĭ-ōn′	ri-ohn′
Ríos, Juan Antonio (Chilean leader)	rē′-ôs, hwän′ än-tôn′-yô	ree′-os, hwahn′ ahn-ton′-yo
Riouw *or* Rhio (NEI)	rē′-ō	ree′-oh
Ripanj (Yugosl.)	rē′-pän(y)	ree′-pahn(y)
Risan (Yugosl.)	rē′-sän	ree′-sahn
Italian *Risano*, rē-sä′-nô [ree-sah′-no].		
Risoer (Nor.)	rē′-sûr	ree′-sœr
Risoeyhavn (Nor.)	rē′-sûĭ-hävn	ree′-sœi-hahvn
Risör (Nor.)	rē′-sûr	ree′-sœr
Risovon (Gr.)	rē′-sô-vô(n)	ree′-so-vo(n)
Risöyhavn (Nor.)	rē′-sûĭ-hävn	ree′-sœi-hahvn
Ristna (Est., Hiiu)	rĭst′-nä	rist′-nah
Risto Ryti (Fin. leader)	See *Ryti, Risto.*	
Rivadeo (Sp.)	rē-vä-*th*ĕ′-ô	ree-vah-*th*eh′-o
Rivers, L. Mendel (U.S. representative)	rĭv′-ərz, mĕn′-dəl	riv′-uhrz, men′-duhl
Rizaiyeh (Iran, lake)	rē′-zä-ē′-yə	ree′-zah-ee′-yuh
Formerly called *Urmiah*, (Eng.) o͞or′-mĭ-ä [oor′-mi-ah].		
Rizal, José (Fil. leader)	rē-säl′, hô-sĕ′	ree-sahl′, ho-seh′
Rizzuto (It., cape)	rēd-zo͞o′-tô	reed-zoo′-to
Rjukan (Nor.)	rū′-kän	ryoo′-kahn
Roa (Nor.)	rō′-ä	roh′-ah
Robsion, John M. (U.S. representative)	rŏb′-sĭ-ən	rob′-si-uhn
Roccella (It.)	rôt-chĕl′-lä	rot-chel′-lah
Rochefort (Fr.)	rôsh-fôr′	rosh-for′
Rodakinon (Gr.)	rô-*th*ä′-kē-nô(n)	ro-*th*ah′-kee-no(n)
Rödberg (Nor.)	rû′-bĕrg	rœ′-behrg
Rodi (Dodec.) See *Rhodes.*		
Rodimtsev (Rus. general)	rŏ-dēm′-tsĕf	ro-deem′-tsef

Rodoni (Alb., cape)	rô-dô′-nē	ro-do′-nee
Albanian *Kep i Rodonit.*		
Rodopou (Crete, pen., mt.)	rô-*th*ô-pōō′	ro-*th*o-poo′
Also called *Tityron*, tē′-tē-rôn [tee′-tee-ron]; *Spada*, spä′-*th*ä [spah′-*th*ah; and *Psakon*, q.v.		
Rodos (Dodec.)	rô′-thôs(s)	ro′-tho(s)
English *Rhodes*, rōdz′ [rohdz′].		
Rodosto (Turk.)	*It.* rô-dô′-stô	ro-do′-sto
Turkish *Tekirdağ*, q.v.		
Roebourne (Austral.)	rō′-bûrn′	roh′-buhrn′
Roedberg (Nor.)	rû′-bĕrg	rœ′-behrg
Roeldal (Nor.)	rûl′-däl	rœl′-dahl
Roem (Den., isl.)	rûm′	rœm′
Also called *Roemoe*, rûm′-û [rœm′-œ].		
Roemoe (Den., isl.) See *Roem.*		
Roermond (Neth.)	rōōr-mônt′	roor-mont′
Roeros (Nor.)	rû′-rōs	rœ′-rohs
Roervik (Nor.)	rûr′-vēk	rœr′-veek
Roesvann (Nor., lake)	rûs′-vän	rœs′-vahn
Roeykenvik (Nor.)	rûĭ′-kən-vēk	rœi′-kuhn-veek
Roeysheim (Nor.)	rûĭs′-hām	rœis′-haym
Rogachevsky (Rus. general)	rŏ-gä-chĕf′-skĭ	ro-gah-chef′-ski
Rogačica (Yugosl.)	rô′-gä′-chĭ-tsä	ro′-gah′-chi-tsah
Rogatica (Yugosl.)	rô′-gä′-tĭ-tsä	ro′-gah′-ti-tsah
Rognac (Fr.)	rô-nyäk′	ro-nyahk′
Rogozna (Yugosl., mts.)	rô′-gôz-nä	ro′-goz-nah
Rogoznica (Yugosl.)	rô′-gôz′-nĭ-tsä	ro′-goz′-ni-tsah
Rohrbough, Edward G. (U.S. representative)	rōr′-bô	rohr′-baw
Roi (Oc.)	rô′-ē *or* roi′	ro′-ee *or* roi′
Roi Et (Thai)	roi′ ĕt	roi′ et
Rokietnica (Pol.)	rô-kyĕt-nē′-tsä	ro-kyet-nee′-tsah
Rokiškis (Lith.)	rŏ′-kĭsh-kĭs	ro′-kish-kis
Rokitno (Pol.)	rô-kēt′-nô	ro-keet′-no
Russian *Rakitno*, rä-kēt′-nŏ [rah-keet′-no].		
Rokossovsky, K. (Rus. general)	rŏ-kŏs-sôf′-skĭ	ro-kos-sof′-ski
Röldal (Nor.)	rûl′-däl	rœl′-dahl
Rolph, Thomas (U.S. representative)	rŏlf′	rolf′
Röm (Den., isl.)	rûm′	rœm′
Also called *Römö*, rûm′-û [rœm′-œ].		

Roma (It.)	rô′-mä	ro′-mah
English *Rome*, q.v.		
Roman (Rum.)	rô′-män	ro′-mahn
Romȃnia	*Eng.* rō-mān′-yə	roh-mayn′-yuh
	Rum. rô-mû′-nyä	ro-muh′-nyah
The common English form is *Rumania*, rōō-mā′-nyə [roo-may′-nyuh].		
Romanov (Rus. name)	*Eng.* rō′-mä-nôf	roh′-mah-nof
	Rus. rŏ-mä′-nŏf	ro-mah′-nof
Romanovce (Yugosl.)	rô′-mä′-nôv-tsĕ	ro′-mah′-nov-tseh
Romanovka (Rus.)	rŏ-mä′-nŏf-kä	ro-mah′-nof-kah
Romay, Lina (singer)	rō-mī′, lē′-nə	roh-mai′, lee′-nuh
Romblón (P.I.)	rôm-blôn′	rom-blon′
Rome (It.)	rōm′	rohm′
Italian *Roma*, q.v.		
Romer, Tadeusz (Pol. leader)	rô′-mĕr, tä-dĕ′-o͝osh	ro′-mehr, tah-deh′-ush
Romerike (Nor.)	rō′-mə-rĭ-kə	roh′-muh-ri-kuh
Romilly sur Seine (Fr.)	rô-mē-yē′ sür sĕn′	ro-mee-yee′ sür sen′
Rommel (Ger. general)	rŭm′l *or* rôm′l	ruhm′l *or* rom′l
Romny (Rus.)	rôm′-nĭ	rom′-ni
Römö (Den., isl.) See *Roem.*		
Romsdal (Nor.)	ro͝oms′-däl	rums′-dahl
Romsdalsfjord (Nor.)	ro͝oms′-däls-fyōr	rums′-dahls-fyohr
Romsdalshorn (Nor., mt.)	ro͝oms′-däls-hōrn	rums′-dahls-hohrn
Rómulo, Carlos P. (Fil. leader)	rô′-mōō-lô, kär′-lôs	ro′-moo-lo, kahr′-los
Roncador (Oc.)	rôn-kä-dôr′	ron-kah-dor′
Rongelap (Oc.)	rông′-ĕ-läp	rong′-eh-lahp
Rongerik (Oc.)	rông′-ĕ-rĭk	rong′-eh-rik
Ronse (Belg.)	*Flem.* rôn′-sə	ron′-suh
French *Renaix*, rə-nĕ′ [ruh-neh′].		
Rook *or* Rooke (Oc.)	ro͝ok′	ruk′
Named for Sir George Rook. Also called *Umboi*, ōōm′-boi [oom′-boi].		
Roosenburg (Neth.)	rō′-zən-bûrk(h)	roh′-zuhn-bœrk(h)
Roosendaal (Neth.)	rō′-zən-däl	roh′-zuhn-dahl
Also spelled *Rozendaal*, q.v.		
Roosevelt	rō′-zə-vĕlt	roh′-zuh-velt

The pronunciation with *ō* has been preferred by the families of both Presidents, and it is the only pronunciation given in our dictionaries. However, a pronunciation rōō′-zə-vĕlt [roo′-zuh-velt] is also current. In certain stress patterns the name has two syllables—rōz′-vĕlt [rohz′-velt] or rōōs′-vĕlt. This same principle holds true of words like *president, governor, government, rationing.*)

Röros (Nor.)	rû′-rōs	rœ′-rohs
Rörvik (Nor.)	rûr′-vēk	rœr′-veek
Rosarno (It.)	rô-sär′-nô	ro-sahr′-no
Roscoff (Fr.)	rôs-kôf′	ros-kof′
Rosenborg (Den.)	rō′-sən-bôr	roh′-suhn-bor
Rosendal (Nor.)	rō′-sən-däl	roh′-suhn-dahl
Rosenovskaya (Latvia)	*Rus.* rô′-zĕ-nŏf-skä-yä	ro′-zeh-nof-skah-yah
Latvian *Zilupe*, q.v.		
Rosetta (Egypt)	*Eng.* rō-zĕt′-ə	roh-zet′-uh
Also called *Rashid*, q.v.		
Roşiorii de Vede (Rum.)	rô-shyô′-rē dĕ vĕ′-dĕ	ro-shyo′-ree deh veh′-deh
Rositten (Latvia)	*Ger.* rô-zĭt′-ən	ro-zit′-uhn
Latvian *Rēzekne*, q.v. Russian *Ryezhitsa*, q.v.		
Roskilde (Den.)	rôs′-kĭl-ə	ros′-kil-uh
Roslavl (Rus.)	rŏs-lävl′(y)	ros-lahvl′(y)
Rosolini (It.)	rô-sô-lē′-nē	ro-so-lee′-nee
Rossieny (Lith.)	*Rus.* rôs′-sĭ-yĕ-nĭ	ros′-si-yeh-ni
Lithuanian *Raseiniai*, q.v.		
Rossosh (Rus.)	rôs′-sŏsh	ros′-sosh
Rostock (Ger.)	*Eng.* rŏs′-tŏk	ros′-tok
	Ger. rôs′-tŏk	ros′-tok
Rostov (Rus.)	rŏ-stôf′	ro-stof′
Roşu (Rum., pass)	rô′-shōō	ro′-shu
Also called *Turnu Roşu*, tōōr′-nōō [tur′-nu]. German *Roten Turm.*		
Rösvann (Nor., lake)	rûs′-vän	rœs′-vahn
Rosyth (Scot.)	rō-sīth′	roh-saith′
Rota (Oc.)	rô′-tä	ro′-tah
Rothenburg (Ger.)	*Eng.* rō′-tən-bûrg	roh′-tuhn-buhrg
	Ger. rō′-tən-bōōrk(h)	roh′-tuhn-burk(h)
Rotterdam (Neth.)	*Eng.* rŏt′-ər-dăm	rot′-uhr-dam
	Du. rôt′-ər-däm′	rot′-uhr-dahm′
Rottumeroog (Neth., isl.)	rôt′-ə-mə-rōk(h)′	rot′-uh-muh-rohk(h)′
Roubaix (Fr.)	rōō-bĕ′	roo-beh′
Rouen (Fr.)	rwäN′	rwahN′
Roulers (Belg.) See *Rouselare.*		
Roumele, Agia (Crete)	rōō-mĕ′-lē, ä-yē′-ä	roo-meh′-lee, ah-yee′-ah
Rouselare (Belg.)	rōō′-sə-lär	roo′-suh-lahr
French *Roulers*, rōō-lĕrs′ [roo-lehrs′], *and* rōō-lĕr′ [roo-lehr′].		
Roussos, Georgios (Gr. leader)	rou′-sôs, yôr′-yôs	rau′-sos, yor′-yos

route

In military use and in all traffic departments, the pronunciation is "raut." This is also the popular, old-fashioned American pronunciation. Dictionaries and purists, however, prefer "root," a Gallicism. Certainly *en route* is a French phrase, the English equivalent being *in route*. Like *ration*, *route* is a fighting word.

Rov (Rus., riv.)	rôf′	rof′
Rovaniemi (Fin.)	rô′-vä-nē-ĕ-mē	ro′-vah-nee-eh-mee
Rovenki (Rus.)	rŏ-vĕn(y)-kē′	ro-ven(y)-kee′
Rovigno (It.)	rô-vē′-nyô	ro-vee′-nyo
Rovno (Pol.) See *Równe*.		
Rowan, Wm. A. (U.S. representative)	rō′-ən	roh′-uhn
Równe (Pol.)	ro͝ov′-nĕ	ruv′-neh
Russian *Rovno*, rôv′-nŏ [rov′-no].		
Roxas, Manuel A. (Fil. leader)	rô′-häs, mä-nwĕl′	ro′-hahs, mah-nwel′
Röykenvik (Nor.)	rûĭ′-kən-vēk	rœi′-kuhn-veek
Röysheim (Nor.)	rûĭs′-hām	rœis′-haym
Rožaj (Yugosl.)	rô′-zhī	ro′-zhai
Roze (Yugosl.)	rô′-zĕ	ro′-zeh
Rozendaal (Neth.)	rō′-zən-däl	roh′-zuhn-dahl
Also spelled *Roosendaal*, q.v.		
Rožňava (Cz.)	rôzh′-nyä-vä	rozh′-nyah-vah
Hungarian *Rozsnyó*, rôzh′-nyô [rozh′-nyo].		
Rozsnyó (Cz.) See *Rožňava*.		
Rozwadów (Pol.)	rô-zvä′-do͝of	ro-zvah′-duf
rt	ərt′	uhrt′

In the case of compounds with *rt*, such as *Rt Arca*, look up the other part of the name, e.g., *Arca*. *Rt* is Serb-Croat meaning *point* or *headland*.

Rtanj (Yugosl., mts.)	ər′-tän(y)	uhr′-tahn(y)
Rtkovo (Yugosl.)	ərt′-kô-vô	uhrt′-ko-vo
Rua Sura (Oc.)	ro͞o′-ä so͞o′-rä	roo′-ah soo′-rah
Rugozero (Rus.)	ro͞o-gô′-zĕ-rŏ	roo-go′-zeh-ro
Rubezhnoye (Rus.)	ro͞o-bĕzh′-nŏ-yĕ	roo-bezh′-no-yeh
Rublevka (Rus.)	ro͝ob-lyôf′-kä	rub-lyof′-kah
Ruddervoorde (Belg.)	rŭd′-ər-vōr′-də	ruhd′-uhr-vohr′-duh
Rudkoebing *or* Rudköbing (Den.)	ro͞o′-kû-bĭng	roo′-kœ-bing
Rudnitsa (Rus.)	ro͞od′-nĭ-tsä	rood′-ni-tsah
Ruhnu (Est., isl.)	ro͞ok(h)′-no͞o	rook(h)′-noo
Russian *Runo*, ro͞o′-nŏ [roo′-no].		
Ruhr (Ger., riv.)	ro͞or′	roor′

Ruj (Balkan mt.)	ro͞oy′ *or* ro͞o′ĭ	rooy′ *or* roo′i
Rujen (Balkan, mt.)	ro͞o′-yĕn	roo′-yen
Rukhlovo (Rus.)	ro͝ok(h)-lô′-vŏ	ruk(h)-lo′-vo
Rumania	*Eng.* ro͞o-mān′-yə	roo-mayn′-yuh
The English variant of *Romînia*, q.v.		
Rumija (Yugosl., mt.)	ro͞o′-mē-yä	roo′-mee-yah
Ruschuk (Bulg.)	ro͝os′-cho͝ok	rus′-chuk
Officially *Russe*, q.v.		
Russe *or* Ruse (Bulg.)	ro͝os′-sĕ	rus′-seh
Rutevce (Yugosl.)	ro͞o′-tĕv-tsĕ	roo′-tev-tseh
Ruweisat (Egypt)	ro͞o-wā-săt′	roo-way-sat′
Ruysbroek (Belg.)	rûĭs′-bro͞ok	rœis′-brook
Ruysselede (Belg.)	rûĭs′-ə-lā′-də	rœis′-uh-lay′-duh
Ruza (Rus.)	ro͞o′-zä	roo′-zah
Ruzaevka (Rus.)	ro͞o-zä′-yĕf-kä	roo-zah′-yef-kah
Ružomberok (Cz.)	ro͞o′-zhôm-bĕ-rôk	roo′-zhom-beh-rok
Ryashev (Pol.) See *Rzeszów*.		
Ryazan (Rus.)	ryä-zän′(y)	ryah-zahn′(y)
Ryazhsk (Rus.)	ryäshsk′	ryahshsk′
Rybachi (Rus.)	rĭ-bä′-chĭ	ri-bah′-chi
Rybinsk (Rus.)	rwē′-bĭnsk	rwee′-binsk
Rybnik (Pol.)	rĭb′-nĭk	rib′-nik
Rybnitsa (Rus.)	rĭb′-nĭ-tsä	rib′-ni-tsah
Ryes (Fr.)	rē′	ree′
Ryezhitsa (Latvia)	*Rus.* rĕ′-zhĭ-tsä	reh′-zhi-tsah
Latvian *Rēzekne*, q.v. German *Rositten*, q.v.		
Ryfylke (Nor.)	rü′-fül-kə	rü′-fül-kuh
Rylsk (Rus.)	rĭl(y)sk′	ril(y)sk′
Rynda (Rus.)	rĭn′-dä	rin′-dah
Ryswick (Neth.) See *Rijswijk*.		
Ryti, Risto (Fin. leader)	rü′-tē, rĭs′-tô	rü′-tee, rĭs′-to
	or Eng. rĭ′-tē	ri′-tee
Ryukyu (Jap.) See *Okinawa Gunto*.		
Rzeszów (Pol.)	zhĕ′-sho͝of	zheh′-shuf
Russian *Ryashev*, ryä′-shĕf [ryah′-shef].		
Rzhava (Rus.)	rzhä′-vä	rzhah′-vah
Rzhev (Rus.)	rzhĕf′	rzhef′

S—For Chinese names beginning in *S*- see also names in *Hs*-.

Saarbruecken *or* Saarbrücken (Ger.)	*Eng.* zär-bro͝ok′-ən *Ger.* zär-brük′-ən	zahr-bruk′-uhn zahr-brük′-uhn
Saare(maa) (Est., isl.)	sä′-rĕ(-mä)	sah′-reh(-mah)
Russian *Esel*, q.v. German *Oesel*, q.v.		

saari	sä′-rē	sah′-ree
An element, meaning *island*, in Finnish place names.		
Saari Selkä (Fin., mts.)	sä′-rē sĕl′-kă	sah′-ree sel′-ka
Šabac (Yugosl.)	shä′-bäts	shah′-bahts
Sabang (NEI)	sä′-bäng	sah′-bahng
Sabath, A. J. (U.S. representative)	săb′-əth	sab′-uhth
Sabaudia (It.)	sä-bou′-dyä	sah-bau′-dyah
A Pontine town and the old form of *Savoy*.		
Sabbia (Dodec., Rh., point) See *Cum Burnu*.		
Sabbia (It.)	säb′-byä	sahb′-byah
Sabbioncello (Yugosl.)	*It.* säb-byôn-chĕl′-lô	sahb-byon-chel′-lo
The Italian name of a Yugoslav town, *Orebić*, q.v., and the peninsula *Pelješac*, q.v.		
saboteur	săb-ō-tûr′	sab-oh-tœr′
This word keeps usually its French final syllable; the pronunciation săb-ə-tūr′ [sab-uh-tyoor′] is not recommended. In contrast *amateur* has been completely Englished, and Webster's (q.v.) allows -tûr or -tūr with accent on the final or the first syllable.		
Sabria (Tun.)	sä′-brĭ-ä	sah′-bri-ah
Sabsko (Rus.)	säp′-skŏ	sahp′-sko
Sabzawar (Iran)	săb-zə-vär′	sab-zuh-vahr′
Sachsen (Ger.)	zäk′-sən	zahk′-suhn
English *Saxony*, q.v.		
Sadaguia (Tun.)	să-dă-gē′-yä	sa-da-gee′-yah
Sadiya (India)	sə-dē′-yä′	suh-dee′-yah′
Sadowski, George G. (U.S. representative)	să-dŭs′-kĭ	sa-duhs′-ki
Sae (Oc.)	sä′-ĕ	sah′-eh
Sæby (Den.)	sĕ′-bü	seh′-bü
Safi (Mor.)	sä′-fē	sah′-fee
Also spelled *Saffi*.		
Safid Rud (Iran, riv.)	să-fēd′ rōōd′	seh-feed′ rood′
Safrana (Dodec.) See *Zafrana*.		
Sagaing (Burma)	sə-gīng′	suh-gaing′
Sagiada (Gr.)	sī-yä′-*th*ä	sai-yah′-*th*ah
Sagone (Corsica, gulf)	sä-gô′-nĕ	sah-go′-neh
Sagsag (Oc.)	säg′-säg′	sahg′-sahg′
Saharanpur (India)	sə-hä′-rən-pŏŏr′	suh-hah′-ruhn-pur′
Šahovići (Yugosl.)	shä′-hô-vĭ-chĭ	shah′-ho-vi-chi
Saida (Lebanon)	sä′-ē-dä	sah′-ee-dah
Also called *Sidon*, q.v.		
Saidor (Oc.)	sä-ē-dôr′	sah-ee-dor′

Saïgon (Indo-Ch.)	*Eng.* sī-gŏn′	sai-gon′
	Fr. sä-ē-gôN′	sah-ee-goN′
Saimaa (Fin., lake)	sī′-mä	sai′-mah
Saint André de l'Eure (Fr.)	săN täN-drĕ′ də lûr′	saN tahN-dreh′ duh lœr′
Saint Brieuc (Fr.)	săN brē-û′	saN bree-œ′
Saint Cyprien (Tun.)	*Eng.* sānt sĭp′-rĭ-ən	saynt sip′-ri-uhn
	Fr. săN sē-prē-ăN′	saN see-pree-aN′
Saint Denis (Fr.)	săN də-nē′	saN duh-nee′
Saint Dié (Fr.)	săN dyĕ′	saN dyeh′
Saint Dizier (Fr.)	săN dē-zyĕ′	saN dee-zyeh′
Saint Florent (Corsica)	săN flô-räN′	saN flo-rahN′
Saint Gilles (Belg.)	săN zhēl′	saN zheel′
Saint Gilles (Fr.)	săN zhēl′	saN zheel′
Saint Gotthard	sānt gŏt′-ərd	saynt got′-uhrd
Saint Hélier (Eng., Jersey)	sānt hĕl′-yər	saynt hel′-yuhr
	Fr. săN-tĕ-lyĕ′	saN-teh-lyeh′
Saint Laurent de la Salanque (Fr.)	săN lô-räN′ də lä sä-läNk′	saN lo-rahN′ duh lah sah-lahNk′
Saint Lô (Fr.)	săN lō′	saN loh′
Saint Lucia (W. Indies)	sānt lū′-shĭ-ə	saynt lyoo′-shi-uh
	or lo͞o-sē′-ə	loo-see′-uh
As a British colony the name has been Anglicized.		
Saint Malo (Fr.)	săN mä-lō′	saN mah-loh′
Saint Nazaire (Fr.)	săN nä-zăr′	saN nah-zehr′
Saint Omer (Fr.)	săN-tô-mĕr′	saN-to-mehr′
Saint Osyth (Essex, Eng.)	to͞o′-zĭ	too′-zi
Saint Poelten (Austria)	*Eng.* sānt pûl′-tən	saynt puhl′-tuhn
German *Sankt Poelten* or *Pölten*, zängkt pûl′-tən [zahngkt pœl′-tuhn].		
Saint Pol de Léon (Fr.)	săN pôl də lĕ-ôN′	saN pol duh leh-oN′
Saint Quai (Fr.)	săN kĕ′	saN keh′
Saint Quentin (Fr.)	*Eng.* sānt kwĕnt′n	saynt kwent′n
	Fr. săN käN-tăN′	saN kahN-taN′
Saint Rémy (Fr.)	săN rĕ-mē′	saN reh-mee′
Saint Servan (Fr.)	săN sĕr-väN′	saN sehr-vahN′
Saint Valéry (Fr.)	săN vä-lĕ-rē′	saN vah-leh-ree′
Saint Veit (Austria)	*Eng.* sānt vīt′	saynt vait′
German *Sankt Veit*, zängkt fīt′ [zahngkt fait′].		
Saint Vith (Belg.)	săN vēt′	saN veet′
Saipan (Oc.)	sī-pän′	sai-pahn′
Sajo (Cz., riv.) See *Slaná*.		
Sakai (Jap.)	sä-kī	sah-kai

Sakalava (Madag.)	sä′-kə-lä′-və	sah′-kuh-lah′-vuh
Sakar (New Guinea)	sä′-kär	sah′-kahr
Sakellariou, A. (Gr. leader)	sä-kĕ-lä′-rē-o͞o	sah-keh-lah′-ree-oo
Sakhalin (Rus.)	sä-hä-lēn′	sah-hah-leen′
Saki (Rus.)	sä′-kĭ	sah′-ki
Salakhora (Gr.)	sä-lä-hô′-rä	sah-lah-ho′-rah
Salamanca (Sp.)	sä-lä-mäng′-kä	sah-lah-mahng′-kah
Salamaua (New Guinea)	sä-lä-mou′-ä	sah-lah-mau′-ah

Salambrias (Gr., riv.) See *Peneios*.

Salamis (Gr., isl.)	*Eng.* săl′-ə-mĭs	sal′-uh-mis
	Gr. sä-lä-mēs′	sah-lah-mees′

Also called *Kouloure*, ko͞o′-lo͞o-rē [koo′-loo-ree].

Salangen (Nor.)	sä′-läng-ən	sah′-lahng-uhn
Salaš (Yugosl.)	sä′-läsh	sah′-lahsh
Salcha (Alaska)	sôl′-chə	sol′-chuh
Sale (Austral.)	sāl′	sayl′
Sale (Burma)	sə-lā′	suh-lay′
Saleh (Per. name)	sä′-lĕ	sah′-leh
Salerno (It.)	sä-lĕr′-nô	sah-lehr′-no
Sales, Apolônio (Braz. leader)	sä′-lĭs, ä-pô-lô′-nyo͝o	sah′-lis, ah-po-lo′-nyu
Salgado Filho (Braz. general)	səl-gä′-do͝o fē′-lyo͝o	suhl-gah′-du fee′-lyu
Salgótarján (Hung.)	shŏl′-gô-tŏr-yän	shol′-go-tor-yahn
salient	sā′-lĭ-ənt	say′-li-uhnt

The mispronunciation săl′-ĭ-ənt [sal′-i-uhnt] is sometimes carried over from childhood when the spelling of such words is more familiar than the sound.

Salikana (Oc.)	sä-lē-kä′-nä	sah-lee-kah′-nah
Salina (It., isl.)	sä-lē′-nä	sah-lee′-nah
Salla (Rus.)	säl′-lä	sahl′-lah
salmi	säl′-mē	sahl′-mee

An element, meaning *inlet* or *sound*, in Finnish place names.

Salome	*Eng.* sə-lō′-mĭ	suh-loh′-mi
	Fr. sä-lô-mĕ′	sah-lo-meh′
	Ger. zä′-lō-mĕ	zah′-loh-meh

There is no reason for avoiding the English pronunciation, although the foreign pronunciations are appropriate in foreign contexts.

Salomon (Crete, point)	sä-lô-môn′	sah-lo-mon′

Salona (Gr.) See *Amphissa*.

Salonica (Gr.) See *Saloniki*.

Saloniki (Gr.)	sä-lô-nē′-kē	sah-lo-nee′-kee

The common abbreviation of *Thessalonike*, q.v. English *Salonica*, commonly pronounced sä-lŏn′-ĭ-kə [sah-lon′-i-kuh], although dictionaries authorize only sä-lô-nē′-kä [sah-lo-nee′-kah].

Salonta (Rum.)	sä-lôn′-tä	sah-lon′-tah

Also called *Şalonta*, shä-lôn′-tä [shah-lon′-tah]. Hungarian *Nagyszalonta*, nŏt′(y)-sŏ′-lôn-tä [not′(y)-so′-lon-tah].

Salpaus Selkä (Fin., mts.)	säl′-pous sĕl′-kă	sahl′-paus sel′-ka
Salsette (India, isl.)	săl′-sĕt′	sal′-set′
Salsk (Rus.)	säl(y)sk′	sahl(y)sk′
Salso (Sicily)	säl′-sô	sahl′-so
Saltdal (Nor.)	sält′-däl	sahlt′-dahl
Sal(l)um *or* Sol(l)um (Egypt)	säl-lo͞om′	sahl-loom′
Salween (Burma, Ch., riv.)	săl′-wēn′	sal′-ween′
Salzach (Austria, riv.)	zäl′-tsäk(h)	zahl′-tsahk(h)
Salzburg (Austria)	*Eng.* sôlz′-bûrg	solz′-buhrg
	Ger. zälts′-bo͝ork(h)	zahlts′-burk(h)
Salzkammergut (Austria)	zälts′-käm′-ər-go͞ot′	zahlts′-kahm′-uhr-goot′
Šamac, Bosanski (Yugosl.)	shä′-mäts, bô′-sän-skĭ	shah′-mahts, bo′-sahn-ski
Samal (P.I.)	sä′-mäl	sah′-mahl
Samanjac (Yugosl., mts.)	sä′-mä-nyäts	sah′-mah-nyahts
Sámar (P.I.)	sä′-mär	sah′-mahr
Samara (Rus., riv.)	sä-mä′-rä	sah-mah′-rah
Samarai (New Guinea)	sä-mä-rī′	sah-mah-rai′
Samaritis, Myron (Gr. leader)	sä-mä-rē′-tēs, mē′-rôn	sah-mah-ree′-tees, mee′-ron
Samarkand (Rus.)	*Eng.* săm′-ər-kănd′	sam′-uhr-kand′
	Rus. sä′-mär-känt′	sah′-mahr-kahnt′
Sambor (Pol.)	säm′-bôr	sahm′-bor
Sambre (Fr., Belg., riv.)	säN′br	sahN′br
Samerinda (NEI)	sä-mĕ-rĭn′-dä	sah-meh-rin′-dah
Samikon (Gr.)	sä-mē-kô(n)′	sah-mee-ko(n)′
Samnan (Iran)	sĕm-nän′	sem-nahn′
Samobor (Yugosl.)	sä′-mô-bôr	sah′-mo-bor
Samokov (Bulg.)	sä′-mŏ-kŏf	sah′-mo-kof
Samonion (Crete, point)	sä-mô′-nē(-ôn)	sah-mo′-nee(-on)
Samos (Gr., isl.)	*Eng.* sā′-mŏs	say′-mos
	Gr. sä′-mô(s)	sah′-mo(s)
Samothrace (Gr., isl.)	*Eng.* săm′-ō-thrās′	sam′-oh-thrays′

Greek *Samothrake*, sä-mô-thrä′-kē [sah-mo-thrah′-kee].

Samsoe *or* Samsö (Den., isl.)	säms′-û	sahms′-œ
Sampang (NEI)	säm′-päng	sahm′-pahng
Samsun (Turk.)	säm′-so͝on′	sahm′-sun′
San (Pol., riv.)	sän′	sahn′
Sananánda (Oc.)	sä-nä-nän′-dä	sah-nah-nahn′-dah
Sanandaj (Iran)	sĕ-nən-däj′	seh-nuhn-dahj′
Also called *Sehneh*, q.v.		
San Cipriano (It.)	sän chē-prē-ä′-nô	sahn chee-pree-ah′-no
San Cosimo (It.)	sän kô′-sē-mô	sahn ko′-see-mo
San Cristobal (Oc. and elsewhere)	*Eng.* săn krĭs-tō′-bəl *Sp.* sän krēs-tô′-bäl	san kris-toh′-buhl sahn krees-to′-bahl
sand	sän′	sahn′
Norwegian meaning *sand* (often the delta sand at a river mouth); an element in place names.		
Sand (Nor.)	sän′	sahn′
Sandakan (Brit. Borneo)	săn-dä′-kən	san-dah′-kuhn
San Damyano (It.)	sän dä-myä′-nô	sahn dah-myah′-no
Sandane (Nor.)	sän′-ä-nə	sahn′-ah-nuh
Sandefjord (Nor.)	sän′-ə-fyōr	sahn′-uh-fyohr
Sandhaug (Nor.)	sän′-hou	sahn′-hau
Sandia (N. Mex., mts.)	*Eng.* săn-dē′-ə *Sp.* sän-dē′-ä	san-dee′-uh sahn-dee′-ah
Sandnes (Nor.)	sän′-nĕs	sahn′-nes
Sandnessjoeen *or* Sandnessjöen (Nor.)	sän′-nĕs-shû′-ən	sahn′-nes-shœ′-uhn
Sandomierz (Pol.)	sän-dô′-myĕzh	sahn-do′-myezh
Russian *Sandomir*, sän-dŏ-mēr′ [sahn-do-meer′].		
Sandoway (Burma)	săn′-dō-wā′	san′-doh-way′
Burman *Thandwe*, thən-dwĕ′ [thuhn-dweh′].		
Sandvika (Nor.)	sän′-vē-kä	sahn′-vee-kah
San Feliú de Guixols (Sp.)	sän fĕ-lyo͞o′ dĕ gē-shôls′	sahn feh-lyoo′ deh gee-shols′
San Fratello (Sicily)	sän frä-tĕl′-lô	sahn frah-tel′-lo
San Gaetano (It.)	sän gä-ĕ-tä′-nô	sahn gah-eh-tah′-no
San Giorgio (It.)	sän jôr′-jô	sahn jor′-jo
San Giovanni (It.)	sän jô-vän′-nē	sahn jo-vahn′-nee
San Giovanni di Medua (Alb.)	*It.* sän jô-vän′-nē dē mĕ′-do͞o-ä	sahn jo-vahn′-nee dee meh′-doo-ah
Albanian *Shëngjin*, q.v.		
San Giuliano (It.)	sän jū-lyä′-nô	sahn jyoo-lyah′-no
San Isidro (P.I.)	sän ē-sē′-drô	sahn ee-see′-dro
San Jorge (Oc.)	sän hôr′-hĕ	sahn hor′-heh

San José	*Eng.* săn′ ə-zā′	san′ uh-zay′
	Sp. sän′ hô-sĕ′	sahn′ ho-seh′
Sankovo (Rus.)	sän′-kŏ-vŏ	sahn′-ko-vo
Sankt Poelten *or* Pölten (Austria) See *Saint Poelten.*		
Sankt Veit (Austria) See *Saint Veit.*		
San Leonardo (Pantelleria, point)	sän lĕ-ô-när′-dô	sahn leh-o-nahr′-do
San Lorenzo fuori le Mura (Rome)	sän lô-rĕn′-tsô fwô′-rē lĕ mōō′-rä	sahn lo-ren′-tso fwo′-ree leh moo′-rah
San Marino (It.)	*Eng.* săn mə-rē′-nō	san muh-ree′-noh
	It. sän mä-rē′-nô	sahn-mah ree′-no
San Miguel (Sp.)	sän mē-gĕl′	sahn mee-gel′
San Niccolò (It.)	sän nēk-kô-lô′	sahn neek-ko-lo′
San Nicola (It.)	sän nē-kô′-lä	sahn nee-ko′-lah
San Nicolai (It.)	sän nē-kô-lī′	sahn nee-ko-lai′
San Nicolao (It.)	sän nē-kô-lou′	sahn nee-ko-lau′
San Nicolaus (It.)	sän nē-kô-lous′	sahn nee-ko-laus′
San Nicolò (It.)	sän nē-kô-lô′	sahn nee-ko-lo′
San Paolo (Sicily)	sän pä′-ô-lô	sahn pah′-o-lo
San Pietro (It.; Sard., isl.)	sän pyĕ′-trô	sahn pyeh′-tro
San Rafael	*Calif.* săn rə-fĕl′	san ruh-fel′
	Sp. sän rä-fä-ĕl′	sahn rah-fah-el′
San Sebastián (Sp.)	*Eng.* săn′ sə-băs′-chən	san′ suh-bas′-chuhn
	Sp. sän′ sĕ-bäs-tyän′	sahn′ seh-bahs-tyahn′
Sansego (It., isl.)	sän-sĕ′-gô	sahn-seh′-go
Serb-Croat *Sušak*, sōō′-shäk [soo′-shahk].		
San Severo (It.)	sän sĕ-vĕ′-rô	sahn seh-veh′-ro
San-shui (Ch., Kwantung)	sän-shwā	sahn-shway
San Stefano di Camastra (Sicily)	sän stĕ′-fä-nô dē kä-mäs′-trä	sahn steh′-fah-no dee kah-mahs′-′trah
Santa Croce (It.)	sän′-tä krô′-chĕ	sahn′-tah kro-′cheh
Santa Cruz	*Eng.* săn′-tə krōōz′	san′-tuh krooz
	Sp. sän′-tä krōōth′ *or* krōōs′	sahn′-tah krooth′ *or* kroos′
Sant' Agata di Militello (Sicily)	sän tä′-gä-tä dē mē-lē-tĕl′-lô	sahn tah′-gah-tah dee mee-lee-tel′-lo
Santa Isabel (Oc.)	sän′-tä ē-sä-bĕl′	sahn′-tah ee-sah-bel′
Santa Maria Maggiore (It., Rome)	sän′-tä mä-rē′-ä mäd-jô′-rĕ	sahn′-tah mah-ree′-ah mahd-jo′-reh

Santander (Sp.)	sän-tän-dĕr′	sahn-tahn-dehr′
Sant' Antioco (Sard., isl.)	sän′ tän-tē′-ô-kô	sahn′ tahn-tee′-o-ko
Santarém (Port.)	sän-tə-rĕN′	sahn-tuh-reN′
Sant' Elia (It.)	sän′-tä ĕ-lē′-ä	sahn′-tah eh-lee′-ah
Sant' Eufemia (It., gulf)	sän′ tĕ-ōō-fĕ′-myä	sahn′ teh-oo-feh′-myah
Santi Quaranta (Alb.)	*It.* sän′-tē kwä-rän′-tä	sahn′-tee kwah-rahn′-tah

Also called *Porto Edda*, q.v. Albanian *Sarandë*, q.v.

Santorini (Gr., isl.) See *Thera*.

San Vito (Sicily, cape)	sän vē′-tô	sahn vee′-to
San Vittorio (It.)	sän vēt-tô′-ryô	sahn veet-to′-ryo
São Jorge (Azores)	souN zhôr′-zhĭ	sauN zhor′-zhi
São Luiz do Maranhão (Brazil)	souN lwēs′ dŏŏ mä-rə-nyouN′	sauN lwees′ du mah-ruh-nyauN′
Saône (Fr., riv.)	sōn′	sohn′
São Paulo (Brazil)	souN pou′-lŏŏ	sauN pau′-lu
São Salvador (Brazil)	souN′ säl-və-dôr′	sauN′ sahl-vuh-dor′

Also called, unofficially, *Bahia* or *Baia*, q.v.

Sapientza (Gr., isl.)	sä-pyĕn′-dzä	sah-pyen′-dzah
Šapina (Yugosl.)	shä′-pĭ-nä	shah′-pi-nah
Sapoedi *or* Sapudi (NEI)	sä-pōō′-dē	sah-poo′-dee
Sapporo (Jap.)	sä-pô-rô	sah-po-ro
Sapri (It.)	sä′-prē	sah′-pree
Saqqiz (Iran)	säk-kĕz′	sahk-kez′

Sapudi (NEI) See *Sapoedi*.

Sarabuz (Rus.)	sä-rä′-bŏŏs	sah-rah′-bus
Saracoğlu, Şükrü (Turk. leader)	sä-rä′-jô-lŏŏ, shü′-krü′	sah-rah′-jo-lu, shü′-krü′
Sarafis (Gr. guerrilla)	sä-rä′-fēs	sah-rah′-fees
Saragossa (Sp.)	*Eng.* săr′-ə-gŏs′-ə	sehr′-uh-gos′-uh

Spanish *Zaragoza*, q.v.

Sarajevo (Yugosl.)	sä′-rä′-yĕ-vô	sah′-rah′-yeh-vo
Sarajevska (Yugosl.)	sä′-rä′-yĕf-skä	sah′-rah′-yef-skah
Sarakhs (Iran)	sä-räk(h)s′	sah-rahk(h)s′
Sarana (Alaska, Attu)	sä-rä′-nä	sah-rah′-nah
Šaranci (Yugosl.)	shä′-rän-tsĭ	shah′-rahn-tsi

Saranda (Alb.) See *Sarandë*.

Sarandë (Alb.)	sä-rän′-də	sah-rahn′-duh

Greek *Saranta*, sä-rän′-tä [sah-rahn′-tah].

Sarang (Oc.)	sä′-räng	sah′-rahng
Sarangani (P.I.)	sä-räng-gä′-nĭ	sah-rahng-gah′-ni
Saransk (Rus.)	sä-ränsk′	sah-rahnsk′

Saranta (Alb.) See *Sarandë*

Saraorci (Yugosl.)	sä′-rä′-ôr-tsĭ	sah′-rah′-or-tsi
Sarapul (Rus.)	sä-rä′-po͝ol	sah-rah′-pul
Sarapulskoe (Rus.)	sä-rä′-po͝ol(y)-skŏ-yĕ	sah-rah′-pul(y)-sko-yeh
Saratov (Rus.)	sä-rä′-tŏf	sah-rah′-tof
Sarawak (Borneo)	*Eng.* sə-rä′-wäk	suh-rah′-wahk
	native sə-rä′-wä	suh-rah′-wah
Šarbanovac (Yugosl.)	shär′-bä′-nô-väts	shahr′-bah′-no-vahts
Sardinia	*Eng.* sär-dĭn′-yə	sahr-din′-yuh

Italian *Sardegna*, sär-dĕ′-nyä [sahr-deh′-nyah].

Saria (Dodec.) See *Saros*.

Sariguan (Oc.)	sä-rē-gwän′	sah-ree-gwahn′
Sarmi (NEI)	sär′-mē	sahr′-mee
Sarny (Pol.)	sär′-nĭ	sahr′-ni

Russian spelling *Sarni*.

Saronic Gulf (Gr.)	*Eng.* sə-rô′-nĭk	suh-ro′-nik

Greek *Saronikos Kolpos*, sä-rô-nē-kôs′ kôl′-pôs [sah-ro-nee-kos′ kol′-pos].

Saros (Dodec.)	sä′-rô(s)	sah′-ro(s)

Also called *Saria*, sä-rē′-ä [sah-ree′-ah] and sär-yä′ [sahr-yah′].

Šar planina (Yugosl., mts.)	shär′ plä′-nē′-nä	shahr′ plah′-nee′-nah
Sarpsborg (Nor.)	särps′-bôr	sahrps′-bor
Sartène (Corsica)	sär-tĕn′	sahr-ten′
Sarthe (Fr.)	särt′	sahrt′
Sarych (Rus.)	sä-rĭch′	sah-rich′
Sarzana (It.)	sär-dzä′-nä	sahr-dzah′-nah
Sasebo (Jap.)	sä-sĕ-bô	sah-seh-bo
Saseno (It., isl.)	sä′-sĕ-nô	sah′-seh-no

Albanian *Sazan*, q.v. Greek *Sasson*, sä′-sôn [sah′-son].

Šasko Blato (Yugosl.)	shä′-skô blä′-tô	shah′-sko blah′-to
Sassari (Sard.)	säs′-sä-rē	sahs′-sah-ree
Sasscer, L. G. (U.S. representative)	săs′-ər	sas′-uhr
Sassenheim (Neth.)	säs′-ən-hīm	sahs′-uhn-haim
Sas van Gent (Neth.)	säs′ vän k(h)ĕnt′	sahs′ vahn k(h)ent′
Satara (India)	sä-tä′-rə	sah-tah′-ruh
Sataria (Pantelleria, bay)	sä-tä-rē′-ä	sah-tah-ree′-ah
Satawal (Oc.)	sä′-tä-wäl	sah′-tah-wahl
Satawan (Oc.)	sä′-tä-wän	sah′-tah-wahn
Sátoraljaujhely (Hung.)	shä′-tôr-oi-yŏ-o͞o′ĭ-hĕĭ	shah′-tor-oi-yo-u′(y)-hey
Šatornja, Donja (Yugosl.)	shä′-tôr-nyä, dô′-nyä	shah′-tor-nyah, do′-nyah

Satul (Rum., riv.)	sä′-to͝ol	sah′-tul
Satul Mare (Rum.)	sä′-to͝ol mä′-rĕ	sah′-tul mah′-reh
Satul Nou (Rum.)	sä′-to͝ol nō′	sah′-tul noh′
Sauda (Nor.)	sou′-dä	sau′-dah
Saudi (Arabia)	sä-o͞o′-dē	sah-oo′-dee
Saugor *or* Sagar (India)	sô-gōr′ *or* sä′-gər	so-gohr′ *or* sah′-guhr
Saumlakki (Oc.)	soum-läk′-kē	saum-lahk′-kee
Sauthoff, Harry (U.S. representative)	sôt′-hŭf	sawt′-huhf
Sava (Yugosl., riv.)	sä′-vä	sah′-vah
Savina (Yugosl., riv.)	sä′-vĭ-nä	sah′-vi-nah
Šavnik (Yugosl.)	shäv′-nĭk	shahv′-nik
Savo (Oc.)	sä′-vô	sah′-vo
Savoe *or* Savu (NEI)	See Sawoe *or* Sawu.	
Savona (It.)	sä-vô′-nä	sah-vo′-nah
Savonlinna (Fin.)	sä′-vôn-lĭn-nä	sah′-von-lin-nah
Savran (Rus.)	sä-vrän′(y)	sah-vrahn′(y)
Sawoe *or* Sawu; Savoe *or* Savu (NEI)	sä′-vo͞o	sah′-voo
Saxe-Coburg-Gotha (Ger.)	*Eng.* săks′ kō′-bûrg gō′-thə	saks′ koh′-buhrg goh′-thuh
German *Sachsen-Coburg und Gotha.*		
Saxony (Ger.)	*Eng.* săk′-sə-nĭ	sak′-suh-ni
German *Sachsen*, q.v.		
Sazan (It., isl.)	*Alb.* sä′-zän	sah′-zahn
Italian *Saseno*, q.v.		
Sazani (It., isl.)	See *Sazan.*	
Sbeitla (Tun.)	sbāt′-lä	sbayt′-lah
Sbiba (Tun.)	sbē′-bä	sbee′-bah
Scalea (It.)	skä-lĕ′-ä	skah-leh′-ah
Scanderbeg (Alb., mt.)	*Eng.* skăn′-dər-bĕg	skan′-duhr-beg
Albanian *Mal i Skanderbeut.* Named after an Albanian hero whose Turkish name was *Iskander Bey* (or *Beğ*).		
Scanlon, Thomas E. (U.S. representative)	skăn′-lŏn	skan′-lon
Scaramia (Sicily, cape)	skä-rä′-myä	skah-rah′-myah
Scarpanto (Dodec.)	*It.* skär′-pän-tô	skahr′-pahn-to
Greek *Karpathos*, q.v.		
Scavenius, Erik (Danish leader)	skä-vā′-nĭ-o͝os	skah-vay′-ni-us
Ščavnica (Yugosl., riv.)	shchäv′-nĭ-tsä	shchahv′-ni-tsah
Šćedro (Yugosl., isl.)	shchĕ′-drô *or* shtyĕ′-drô	shcheh′-dro shtyeh′-dro
Italian *Torcola*, q.v.		

Schaarsbergen (Neth.)	sk(h)ärs′-bĕr-k(h)ən	sk(h)ahrs′-behr-k(h)uhn
Schaerbeek (Belg.)	sk(h)är′-bāk	sk(h)ahr′-bayk
Schagen (Neth.)	sk(h)ä′-k(h)ən	sk(h)ah′-k(h)uhn
Scharendijke (Neth.)	sk(h)ä′-rən-dī′-kə	sk(h)ah′-ruhn-dai′-kuh
Scharnhorst (Ger.)	shärn′-hôrst	shahrn′-horst
Schaulen (Lith.)	*Ger.* shou′-lən	shau′-luhn
Lithuanian *Šiauliai*, q.v. Russian *Shavli*, q.v.		
Scheldt (Neth., Belg., riv.)	*Eng.* skĕlt′	skelt′
Dutch *Schelde*, sk(h)ĕl′-də [sk(h)el′-duh]. French *Escaut*, ĕs-kō′ [es-koh′].		
Schermerhorn (Neth.)	sk(h)ĕr′-mər-hôrn	sk(h)ehr′-muhr-horn
Scheveningen (Neth.)	sk(h)ā′-və-nĭng-ən	sk(h)ay′-vuh-ning-uhn
Schiavonia (Yugosl.)	*It.* skyä-vô′-nyä	skyah-vo′-nyah
English *Slavonia*, q.v.		
Schiedam (Neth.)	sk(h)ē-däm′	sk(h)ee-dahm′
Schiermonnikoog (Neth., isl.)	sk(h)ēr′-môn-ĭ-kōk(h)′	sk(h)eer′-mon-i-kohk(h)′
Schiffler, Andrew C. (U.S. representative)	shĭf′-lər	shif′-luhr
Schio (It.)	skē′-ô	skee′-o
Schiphol (Neth.)	sk(h)ĭp-hôl′	sk(h)ip-hol′
Schlesien (Ger., Pol., Cz.) See *Silesia*.		
Schleswig (Den., Ger.)	*Eng.* slĕs′-wĭk	sles′-wik
	Ger. shlās′-vĭk(h)	shlays′-vik(h)
Danish *Slesvig*, q.v.		
———Holstein (Ger.)	*Eng.* hōl′-stīn	hohl′-stain
	Ger. hôl′-shtīn	hol′-shtain
Schlok (Latvia)	*Ger.* shlôk′	shlok′
Latvian *Sloka*, q.v.		
Schlusselburg (Rus.)	shlēs′-sĕl-bŏŏrk′	shlees′-sel-burk′
German *Schluesselburg* or *Schlüsselburg*, shlüs′-əl-bŏŏrk(h) [shlüs′-uhl-burk(h)].		
Schneidemuehl *or* Schneidemühl (Ger.)	shnī′-də-mül′	shnai′-duh-mül′
Schouten (NEI)	sk(h)ou′-tən	sk(h)au′-tuhn
Schouwen (Neth., isl.)	sk(h)ou′-wən	sk(h)au′-wuhn
Schrimm (Pol.) See *Śrem*.		
Schroda (Pol.) See *Środa*.		
Schuetz, Leonard W. (Late U.S. representative)	shŏŏts′	shoots′

schwa

No matter how spelt, the vowels of unstressed syllables in English tend to become an obscured "uh" sound. Its phonetic symbol is ə. Its name is *schwa*, which seems a comical word to speakers of English but is very useful as the name of the commonest vowel in spoken English. This is the sound spelled *a* in *about* and *sofa*, *e* in *taken*, *i* in *evil*, *o* in *connect*, *u* in *circus*.

Schwabe, Max (U.S. representative)	swä'-bĕ	swah'-beh
Schwanenburg (Latvia)	*Ger.* shvä'-nən-bo͝ork(h)	shvah'-nuhn-burk(h)

Latvian *Gulbene*, q.v.

Schweidnitz (Ger.)	shvĭt'-nĭts	shvait'-nits
Schweinfurt (Ger.)	shvīn'-fo͝ort	shvain'-furt
Sciacca (Sicily)	shäk'-kä	shahk'-kah
Sciaccazze (Pantelleria, point)	shäk-kät'-sĕ	shahk-kaht'-seh
Scicli (Sicily)	shē'-klē	shee'-klee
Scido (It.)	shē'-dô	shee'-do
Scilla (It.)	shēl'-lä	sheel'-lah

English *Scylla*, sĭl'-ə [sil'-uh]. Probably the English pronunciation is preferable for American speakers.

Scoglitti (Sicily)	skô-lyē'-tē	sko-lyee'-tee
Scordia (Sicily)	skôr-dē'-ä	skor-dee'-ah
Scorza, Carlo (It. Fascist leader)	skôr'-dzä, kär'-lô	skor'-dzah, kahr'-lo
Scrugham, James C. (U.S. senator)	skrŭg'-hăm	skruhg'-ham
Scutari (Alb., city; Balkan lake)	*Eng.* sko͞o'-tä-rē	skoo'-tah-ree

Albanian *Shkodër*, shkô'-dər [shko'-duhr]. Serb-Croat *Skadar*, skä'-där [skah'-dahr]. English *Lake Scutari*. Albanian *Liqen i Shkodrës*, lē-kyĕn' ē shkô'-drəs [lee-kyen' ee shko'-druhs]. Serb-Croat *Skadarsko Jezero*, skä'-där-skô yĕ'-zĕ-rô [skah'-dahr-sko yeh'-zeh-ro]. Turkish *Üsküdar*, q.v.

Scylla (It.)	*Eng.* sĭl'-ə	sil'-uh

Italian *Scilla*, shēl'-lä [sheel'-lah]. The English pronunciation is preferable for American speakers, especially when speaking of *Scylla* and *Charybdis*, q.v.

Sebala, la (Tun.)	sə-bă'-lä, lä	suh-ba'-lah, lah

Sebastopol See *Sevastopol.*

Sebenico (Yugosl.)	*It.* sĕ-bĕ-nē'-kô	seh-beh-nee'-ko

Serb-Croat *Šibenik*, q.v.

Sebeşul (Rum.)	sĕ-bĕ′-sho͝ol	seh-beh′-shul
Sebezh (Rus.)	sĕ′-bĕsh	seh′-besh
Sebkra Sidi Khalifa (Tun.)	sĕb′-krä sē′-dē kä-lē′-fä	seb′-krah see′-dee kah-lee′-fah
Sebkret Djaber (Tun.)	sĕb′-krĕt jă′-bər	seb′-kret ja′-buhr
Sebkret el Kourzia (Tun.)	sĕb′-krĕt ĕl ko͝or-zē′-ä	seb′-kret el kur-zee′-ah
Seboekoe *or* Sebuku (NEI)	sā-bo͞o′-ko͞o	say-boo′-koo
Secunderabad (India)	sĭ-kŭn′-drə-băd′ *or* sē-kŭn′-drä-bäd′	si-kuhn′-druh-bad′ see-kuhn′-drah-bahd′
Sedan (Fr.)	*Eng.* sə-dăn′	suh-dan′
	Fr. sə-däN′	suh-dahN′
Sedes (Gr.)	sĕ′-*th*ĕs	seh′-*th*es
Sedjenane (Tun.)	sĕ-jĕ-năn′	seh-jeh-nan′
Sedjouna (Tun.)	sə-jo͞o′-nä	suh-joo′-nah
Šeduva (Lith.)	shĕ′-do͞o-vä	sheh′-doo-vah
Seg (Rus.)	sĕg′	seg′
Segesvár (Rum.) See *Sighişoara.*		
Segnali (Libya)	sā-nyä′-lē	say-nyah′-lee
Segovia (Sp.)	sĕ-gô′-vyä	seh-go′-vyah
Segré (Fr.)	sə-grĕ′	suh-greh′
Sehneh (Iran)	sĕ′-nĕ′	seh′-neh′
Also called *Sanandaj*, q.v.		
Seibersdorf (Pol.) See *Zebrzydowice.*		
Seim (Rus., riv.)	sām′	saym′
Seine (Fr., riv.)	*Eng.* sān′	sayn′
	Fr. sĕn′	sen′
Seishin (Korea)	sā-shĭn	say-shin
Seiskari (Fin.)	sās′-kä-rē	says′-kah-ree
Seitler (Rus.)	*Rus.* sāt′-lər	sayt′-luhr
	Ger. zīt′-lər	zait′-luhr
Sekeris, Evangelos (Gr. leader)	sĕ′-kĕ-rēs, ĕ-väng′-gĕ-lôs	seh′-keh-rees, eh-vahng′-geh-los
Sekurić (Yugosl.)	sĕ′-ko͞o-rĭch	seh′-koo-rich
Selapiu (Oc.)	sĕ-lä-pē′-o͞o	seh-lah-pee′-oo
Selaru (Oc.)	sĕ-lä′-ro͞o	seh-lah′-roo
Selbu (Nor.)	sĕl′-bo͞o	sel′-boo
Selce (Yugosl.)	sĕl′-tsĕ	sel′-tseh
Sele (It., riv.)	sĕ′-lĕ	seh′-leh
Selečka planina (Yugosl., mts.)	sĕ′-lĕch-kä plä′-nē′-nä	seh′-lech-kah plah′-nee′-nah
Selemdzha (Rus., riv.)	sĕ-lĕm-jä′	seh-lem-jah′

Selenga (Rus., riv.)	sĕ-lĕn-gä′	seh-len-gah′
Selenginskaya Duma (Rus.)	sĕ-lĕn-gĭn′-skä-yä doo′-mä	seh-len-gin′-skah-yah doo′-mah
Sélestat (Fr.)	sĕ-lĕs-tä′	seh-les-tah′
Selevac (Yugosl.)	sĕ′-lĕ-väts	seh′-leh-vahts
Seličevica (Yugosl., mts.)	sĕ-lē′-chĕ-vĭ-tsä	seh-lee′-cheh-vi-tsah
Seliger (Rus.)	sĕ′-lĭ-gĕr	seh′-li-gehr
Selinon (Crete)	sĕ′-lē-nô(n)	seh′-lee-no(n)
Also called *Paleokhora*, pä-lyô-hô′-rä [pah-lyo-ho′-rah].		
Selinou Kastelli (Crete, cape)	sĕ-lē′-noo kä-stĕ′-lē	seh-lee′-noo kah-steh′-lee
Selizharovo (Rus.)	sĕ-lĭ-zhä′-rŏ-vŏ	seh-li-zhah′-ro-vo
Seljestad (Nor.)	sĕl′-yə-stä	sel′-yuh-stah
Seljord (Nor.)	sĕl′-yōr	sel′-yohr
selkä	sĕl′-kă	sel′-ka
An element, meaning *ridge* or *range* of mountains, sometimes *bay* or *channel*, in Finnish place names.		
Selve (Yugosl.)	*It.* sĕl′-vĕ	sel′-veh
Serb-Croat *Silba*, q.v.		
Seman *or* Semen (Alb., riv., cape)	sĕ′-män	seh′-mahn
Semani *or* Semeni (Alb., riv., cape) See *Seman*.		
Semarang (NEI)	sə-mä′-räng	suh-mah′-rahng
Semeroe *or* Semeru (NEI)	sĕm′-ə-roo *or* smĕ′-roo	sem′-uh-roo smeh′-roo
Semidi (Alaska, isls.)	sĕ′-mĭ-dĭ	seh′-mi-di
Semijaj (Yugosl.)	sĕ′-mĭ-yī′	seh′-mi-yai′
Semiostrovskoe (Rus.)	sĕ-mĭ-ŏs′-trŏf-skŏ-yĕ	seh-mi-os′-trof-sko-yeh
Semipalatinsk (Rus.)	sĕ-mĭ-pä-lä′-tĭnsk	seh-mi-pah-lah′-tinsk
Semki (Rus.)	sĕm-kē′	sem-kee′
Sendai (Jap.)	sĕn-dī	sen-dai
Sened (Tun.)	sĕ′-nĕd	seh′-ned
Senia, la (Alg.)	sĕ′-nyä, lä	seh′-nyah, lah
Senigallia (It.)	sĕ-nē-gäl′-lyä	seh-nee-gahl′-lyah
Senj (Yugosl.)	sĕn′(y)	sen′(y)
Senja (Nor., isl.)	sĕn′-yä	sen′-yah
Senjski Rudnik (Yugosl.)	sĕn(y)′-skĭ rood′-nĭk	sen(y)′-ski rood′-nik
Senta (Yugosl.)	sĕn′-tä	sen′-tah
Hungarian *Zenta*, zĕn′-tŏ [zen′-to].		
Senyavin (Oc.)	sĕ-nyä′-vĭn	seh-nyah′-vin

Seoul (Korea)	*Eng.* sä-o͝ol	sah-ul
	Kor. syû-o͝ol	syœ-ul
Japanese *Keijo*, q.v.		
Sepic (Oc., riv.)	sĕ′-pēk	seh′-peek
Sepoy (India)	sē′-poi	see′-poi
Sepsiszentgyörgy (Rum.) See *Sfântul Gheorghe.*		
Serafimovich (Rus.)	sĕ-rä-fĭ-mô′-vĭch	seh-rah-fi-mo′-vich
Seraing (Belg.)	sə-răN′	suh-raN′
Serajevo (Yugosl.) See *Sarajevo.*		
Serang (NEI)	sĕ-räng′	seh-rahng′
Serbariu (Sard.)	sĕr-bä-rē′-o͞o	sehr-bah-ree′-oo
Serbia (Yugosl.)	*Eng.* sûr′-bĭ-ə	suhr′-bi-uh
Serb-Croat *Srbija*, sər′-bĭ-yä [suhr′-bi-yah].		
Serbino (Rus.)	sĕr′-bĭ-nŏ	sehr′-bi-no
Seret (Pol., riv.)	sĕ′-rĕt	seh′-ret
Sergiopol (Rus.)	sĕr-gĭ-ô′-pŏl(y)	sehr-gi-o′-pol(y)
Sergipe (Brazil)	sĕr-zhē′-pĭ	sehr-zhee′-pi
Sergo (Rus.)	sĕr′-gŏ	sehr′-go
Sergo Ivanovskaya (Rus.)	sĕr′-gô ē-vä′-nŏf-skä-yä	sehr′-go ee-vah′-nof-skah-yah
Seriphos (Gr., isl.)	sĕ′-rĭ-fô(s)	seh′-ri-fo(s)
Sermenin (Yugosl.)	sĕr′-mĕ-nĭn	sehr′-meh-nin
Serpets (Pol.) See *Sierpc.*		
Serpukhov (Rus.)	sĕr′-po͞o-hŏf	sehr′-poo-hof
Serrai (Gr.)	sĕ′-rĕ	seh′-reh
Also called *Serres*, sĕ′-rĕs [seh′-res].		
Serrano Suñer, Ramón (Sp. leader)	sĕ-rä′-nô so͞o-nyĕr′, rä-môn′	se-rah′-no soo-nyehr′, rah-mon′
Both names should be used, thus: *Serrano Suñer*, not *Suñer* alone.		
Serres (Gr.) See *Serrai.*		
Servech (Pol., riv.) See *Serwecz.*		
Serwecz (Pol., riv.)	sĕr′-vĕch	sehr′-vech
Russian spelling *Servech.*		
Sète (Fr.)	sĕt′	set′
Setesdal (Nor.)	sā′-təs-däl	say′-tuhs-dahl
Setia (Crete, town, gulf)	sē-tē′-ä	see-tee′-ah
Sétif (Alg.)	sĕ-tēf′	seh-teef′
Setúbal (Port.)	sĕ-to͞o′-bäl	seh-too′-bahl
Sevastopol (Rus.)	*Eng.* sĭ-väs′-tə-pōl	si-vahs′-tuh-pohl
	Rus. sĕ-väs-tô′-pŏl(y)	seh-vahs-to′-pol(y)
Sévérac (Fr.)	sĕ-vĕ-räk′	seh-veh-rahk′
Severnaya (Rus.)	sĕ′-vĕr-nä-yä	seh′-vehr-nah-yah

Severnaya Dvina (Rus., riv.)	sĕ′-vĕr-nä-yä dvĭ-nä′	seh′-vehr-nah-yah dvi-nah′
Sevilla (Sp.)	sĕ-vē′-lyä *or* -yä	seh-vee′-lyah *or* -yah

English *Seville*, sə-vĭl′ [suh-vil′] *or* sĕ′-vĭl [seh′-vil].

Sevlievo (Bulg.)	sĕ′-vlĭ-yĕ-vŏ	seh′-vli-yeh-vo
Sevsk (Rus.)	sĕfsk′	sefsk′
Sewanee (Tenn.)	sĭ-wô′-nĭ	si-wo′-ni
Seychelles (isls.)	sā-shĕl′ *or* sā-shĕlz′	say-shel′ *or* say-shelz′
Seyne, la (Fr.)	sĕn′, lä	sen′, lah
Sézanne (Fr.)	sĕ-zän′	seh-zahn′
Sezze (It.)	*near Rome* sĕt′-sĕ	set′-seh
	near Milan sĕt-sĕ′	set-seh′
Sfântul Gheorghe (Rum.)	sfûn′-to͝ol gyôr′-gĕ	sfuhn′-tul gyor′-geh

Hungarian *Sepsiszentgyörgy*, shĕp′-shĭ-sĕn′-dyûrd(y) [shep′-shi-sen′-dyœrd(y)].

Sfax (Tun.)	sfäks′	sfahks′
Sforza, Carlo (It. leader)	sfôr′-tsä, kär′-lô	sfor′-tsah, kahr′-lo
's Gravenhage (Neth.)	sk(h)rä′-vən-hä′-k(h)ə	sk(h)rah′-vuhn-hah′-k(h)uh

The common abbreviated form is *Den Haag*, dən häk(h)′ [duhn hahk(h)′]. English *The Hague*, q.v.

Shabelsk (Rus.)	shä-bĕl(y)sk′	shah-bel(y)sk′
Shahi (Iran)	shä′-hē′	shah′-hee′
Shah Muhammad Pahlavi (Ruler of Iran)	shä′ mə-häm′-məd pä-lä-vē′	shah′ muh-hahm′-muhd pah-lah-vee′
Shah Riza Pahlavi (Former ruler of Iran)	shä′ rē′-zə pä-lä-vē′	shah′ ree′-zuh pah-lah-vee′
Shahrud (Iran)	shä-hro͞od′	shah-hrood′
Shakhnovo (Rus.)	shäk(h)′-nŏ-vŏ	shahk(h)′-no-vo
Shakhty (Rus.)	shäk(h)′-tĭ	shahk(h)′-ti
Shan States (Burma)	shăn′ *or* shän′	shan′ *or* shahn′
Shang-hai (Ch., Kiangsu)	*Eng.* shăng-hī	shang-hai
	Ch. shäng-hī	shahng-hai
Shang-jao (Ch., Kiangsi)	shäng-rou	shahng-rau
Shang-kao (Ch., Kiangsi)	shäng-gou	shahng-gau
Shang-yü (Ch., Chekiang)	shäng-yü	shahng-yü
Shang-yu (Ch., Kiangsi)	shäng-yō	shahng-yoh
Shan-hsien (Ch., Shantung)	shän-shyĕn	shahn-shyen
Shan-si (Ch., prov.)	*Eng.* shăn-sē	shan-see
	Ch. shän-sē	shahn-see

Shan-t'ow (Ch., Kwangtung)	shän-tō	shahn-toh
Also called *Swatow*, q.v.		
Shan-tung (Ch., prov.)	*Eng.* shăn-to͞ong	shan-tung
	Ch. shän-do͞ong	shahn-dung
Shao-hsing *or* Shao-hing	shou-shĭng	shau-shing
(Ch., Chekiang)	*or* shou-hĭng	shau-hing
Shao-yang (Ch., Hunan)	shou-yäng	shau-yahng
Also called *Pao-ching*, q.v.		
Shaposhnikov, Boris (Rus. general)	shä′-pŏsh-nĭ-kŏf, bŏ-rēs′	shah′-posh-ni-kof, bo-rees′
Sha-shih (Ch., Hupeh)	shä-shû	shah-shœ
Sha-si *or* Sha-shih	*Eng.* shä-sē	shah-see
(Ch., Hupeh)	*Ch.* shä-shû	shah-shuh
Shatt al Arab (Iran, Iraq, riv.)	shăt′ əl ä′-räb	shat′ uhl ah′-rahb
Shavli (Lith.)	*Rus.* shäv′-lĭ	shahv′-li
Lithuanian *Šiauliai*, q.v.		
Sha-yang (Ch., Hupeh)	shä-yäng	shah-yahng
Shchara (Pol., riv.) See *Szczara.*		
Shcherbakov, Aleksei (Rus. leader)	shchĕr-bä-kŏf′, ä-lĕk-sā′	shchehr-bah-kof′, ah-lek-say′
Shchigry (Rus.)	shchē′-grĭ	shchee′-gri
Shchuchin (Pol.) See *Szczuczyn.*		
Shebekino (Rus.)	shĕ-bĕ′-kĭ-nŏ	sheh-beh′-ki-no
Shek-lung (Ch., Kwangtung)	shû-lo͞ong	shœ-lung
Also spelled *Shih-lung.*		
Shelikof (Alaska, str.)	shĕl′-ə-kŏf′	shel′-uh-kof′
Shelovsky (Rus. general)	shĕ-lôf′-skĭ	sheh-lof′-ski
Shëngjin (Alb.)	shən′-gyĭn	shuhn′-gyin
Italian *San Giovanni di Medua*, q.v.		
Shëngjini (Alb.) See *Shëngjin.*		
Shenjt, Mal i (Alb., mt.)	shĕn(y)t′, mäl′ ē	shen(y)t′, mahl′ ee
Shên-si (Ch., prov.)	*Eng.* shĕn-sē	shen-see
	Ch. shŭn-shē	shuhn-shee
Shên-yang (Manchu.)	shŭn-yäng	shuhn-yahng
Shepetovka (Rus.)	shĕ-pĕ-tôf′-kä	sheh-peh-tof′-kah
's Hertogenbosch (Neth.)	sĕr′-tō-k(h)ən-bôs′	sehr′-toh-k(h)uhn-bos′

The common abbreviated form is *Den Bos*, dən bôs′ [duhn bos′]. French *Bois le Duc*, bwä lə dük′ [bwah luh dük′].

Shibertui (Rus.)	shĭ-bĕr-to͞o′ĭ	shi-behr-too′i

Shibin el Kom (Egypt)	shĭ-bēn′ ĕl kôm′	shi-been′ el kom′
Shidlovets (Pol.) See *Szydłowiec.*		
Shiga (Jap.)	shē-gä	shee-gah
Shigatse (Tibet)	shē-gä′-tsĕ	shee-gah′-tseh
Shih-ch'êng (Ch., Kiangsi)	shû-chŭng	shuh-chuhng
Shih-chia-chwang (Ch., Hopeh) Also spelled *Shih-kia-chwang.*	shû-jyä-jwäng	shuh-jyah-jwahng
Shih-fêng (Manchu.)	shû-fŭng	shuh-fuhng
Shih-kia-chwang (Ch., Hopeh) See *Shih-chia-chwang.*		
Shih-li-miao (Ch., Honan)	shû-lē-myou	shuh-lee-myau
Shih-mên (Ch., Hunan)	shû-mŭn	shuh-muhn
Shih-p'ai (Ch., Hupeh)	shû-pī	shuh-pai
Shih-shou (Ch., Hupeh)	shû-shō	shuh-shoh
Shih-wei (Manchu.)	shû-wā	shuh-way
Shijak (Alb.)	shē′-yäk	shee′-yahk
Shijaku (Alb.) See *Shijak.*		
Shikapur (India)	shē-kä′-po͝or′	shee-kah′-pur′
Shikoku (Jap.)	shē-kô-ko͞o	shee-ko-koo
Shilka (Rus., riv.)	shĭl′-kä	shil′-kah
Shillong (India)	shĭl-lông′	shil-long′
Shimonoseki (Jap.)	*Eng.* shĭm′-ə-nə-săk′-ĭ	shim′-uh-nuh-sak′-i
	Jap. shē-mô-nô-sĕ-kē	shee-mo-no-seh-kee
Shimsk (Rus.)	shĭmsk′	shimsk′
Shingishu (Korea)	shĭn-gĭ-sho͞o	shin-gi-shoo
Shipka (Bulg., pass)	shĭp′-kä	ship′-kah
Shiraz (Iran)	shē-räz′	shee-rahz′
Shizuoka (Jap.)	shē-zo͞o-ô-kä	shee-zoo-o-kah
Shkodër *or* Shkodra (Alb., city; Balkan lake) See *Scutari.*		
Shklov (Rus.)	shklôf′	shklof′
Shkumbi (Alb., riv.) Latin *Genusus.*	shko͞om′-bē	shkoom′-bee
Shkumbini (Alb., riv.) See *Shkumbi.*		
Shkva (Pol., riv.) See *Szkwa.*		
Sholapur (India)	shō-lə-po͝or′	shoh-luh-pur′
Sholokhov, M. A. (Rus. writer)	shô′-lŏ-hŏf	sho′-lo-hof
Shostakovich, Dmitri Dmitriyevich (Rus. composer)	shŏ-stä-kô′-vĭch, dmē′-trē dmē′-trĭ-yĕ-vĭch	sho-stah-ko′-vich, dmee′-tree dmee′-tri-yeh-vich

Shqipni (Albania)	shkyēp′-nē	shkyeep′-nee
Also called *Shqipnija*, *Shqipri*, and *Shqiprija*. English *Albania*, q.v.		
Shu-fu (Ch., Sinkiang)	sho͞o-fo͞o	shoo-foo
Also called *Kashgar*, q.v.		
Shumagin (Alaska, isl.)	sho͞o′-mə-gĭn	shoo′-muh-gin
Shumen (Bulg.)	sho͝o′-mĕn(y)	shu′-men(y)
Shushica (Alb., riv.) See *Shushicë*.		
Shushicë (Alb., riv.)	sho͞o-shē′-tsə	shoo-shee′-tsuh
Shuya (Rus., riv.)	sho͞o′-yä	shoo′-yah
Shvernik, Nikolai M. (Rus. leader)	shvĕr′-nĭk, nē-kŏ-lī′	shvehr′-nik, nee-ko-lai′
Shwebo (Burma)	shwā′-bō′	shway′-boh′
Shwedaung (Burma)	shwā′-doung′	shway′-daung′
Shweli (Burma, riv.)	shwā′-lē′	shway′-lee′
Siagne (It., riv.)	syä′-nyĕ	syah′-nyeh
Sialkot (India)	sĭ-äl′-kōt′	si-ahl′-koht′
Siam *or* Thai	sī-ăm′ *or* tī′	sai-am′ *or* tai′
Si-an *or* Hsi-an (Ch., Shensi)	sē-än *or* shē-än	see-ahn *or* shee-ahn
Also called *Ch'ang-an*, q.v.		
Siatista (Gr.)	sē-ä′-tē-stä	see-ah′-tee-stah
Šiauliai (Lith.)	shyou′-lyī	shyau′-lyai
Russian *Shavli*, q.v. German *Schaulen*, shou′-lən [shau′-luhn].		
Sibari (It.)	sē′-bä-rē	see′-bah-ree
The ancient form is *Sybaris*, pronounced in *Eng.* sĭb′-ə-rĭs [sib′-uh-ris].		
Sibelius, Jean (Fin.)	sĭ-bā′-lyo͝os, zhäN′	si-bay′-lyus, zhahN′
Šibenik (Yugosl.)	shē′-bĕ′-nĭk	shee′-beh′-nik
Italian *Sebenico*, q.v.		
Siberut *or* Siberoet (NEI)	sē-bə-ro͞ot′	see-buh-root′
Sibiu (Rum.)	sē-byo͝o′	see-byu′
Hungarian *Szeben*, sĕ′-bĕn [seh′-ben], and *Nagyszeben*, nŏt′(y)- [not′(y)-].		
Sibnica (Yugosl.)	sēb′-nĭ-tsä	seeb′-ni-tsah
Sibolga (NEI)	sē-bôl′-gä	see-bol′-gah
Sibu (Sarawak)	sē′-bo͞o	see′-boo
Sibutu (P.I.)	sĭ-bo͞o′-to͞o	si-boo′-too
Sibuyán (P.I.)	*Eng.* sē-bo͞o′-yän	see-boo′-yahn
	native sē-bo͞o-yän′	see-boo-yahn′
Sićevo (Yugosl.)	sē′-chĕ-vô	see′-cheh-vo
Sicily (It., isl.)	*Eng.* sĭs′-ĭ-lĭ	sis′-i-li
Italian *Sicilia*, sē-chē′-lyä [see-chee′-lyah].		
Siculiania (Sicily)	sē-ko͞o-lyä′-nä	see-koo-lyah′-nah
Šid (Yugosl.)	shēd′	sheed′
Sidari (Corfù)	*It.* sē-dä′-rē	see-dah′-ree
	Gr. sē-*th*ä′-rē	see-*th*ah′-ree

Siderno Marina (It.)	sē-dĕr′-nô mä-rē′-nä	see-dehr′-no mah-ree′-nah
Siderokastron (Gr.)	sē-*th*ĕ-rô′-kä-strô(n)	see-*th*eh-ro′-kah-stro(n)
Also called *Demir Hissar*, q.v.		
Sideron (Crete, point)	sē′-*th*ē-rô(n)	see′-*th*ee-ro(n)
sidi	sē′-dē	see′-dee
In Arabic names an element, sometimes omitted, meaning *saint.*		
Sidi Abdallah *or* Abdullah (Tun.)	sē′-dē äb-dŭl′-lə	see′-dee ahb-duhl′-luh
Sidi Abu el Rahman (Egypt)	sē′-dē ä′-bo͞o ĕr ră-măn′	see′-dee ah′-boo ehr ra-man′
Sidi Ahmed (Tun.)	sē′-dē ä′-mĕd	see′-dee ah′-med
Sidi Atman (Tun.)	sē′-dē ät-măn′	see′-dee aht-man′
Sidi Barrani (Egypt)	sē′-dē bä-rä′-nē	see′-dee bah-rah′-nee
Sidi-bel-Abbès (Alg.)	sē′-dē-bĕl-ä-bĕs′	see′-dee-bel-ah-bes′
Sidi Belgasem (Libya)	sē′-dē bĕl-gä′-sĕm	see′-dee bel-gah′-sem
Sidi Bou Zid (Tun.)	sē′-dē bo͞o zēd′	see′-dee boo zeed′
Sidi Ferruch (Alg.)	sē′-dē fĕr-ro͞ok′	see′-dee fehr-rook′
Sidi Haneish (Egypt)	sē′-dē hä-nāsh′	see′-dee hah-naysh′
Sidi Mar(r)our (Tun.)	sē′-dē mä-ro͝or′	see′-dee mah-rur′
Sidi Nair (Tun.)	sē′-dē nä-ēr′	see′-dee nah-eer′
Sidi Nsir (Tun.)	sē′-dē nə-sēr′	see′-dee nuh-seer′
Sidi Omar (Libya)	sē′-dē ō′-mär	see′-dee oh′-mahr
Sidi Rezegh (Libya)	sē′-dē rĕ-zĕg′	see′-dee reh-zeg′
Sidon (Lebanon)	*Eng.* sīd′n	said′n
Also called *Saida*, q.v.		
Siedlce (Pol.)	shĕ′dl-tsĕ	she′dl-tseh
Russian *Sedlets*, sĕd′-lĕts [sed′-lets].		
Sidra (Libya)	sĭd′-rə	sid′-ruh
Also called *Sirte*, q.v.		
Siegen (Ger.)	zē′-gən	zee′-guhn
Siemreap (Indo-Ch.)	sē′-əm-rĭ′-əp	see′-uhm-ri′-uhp
Siena (It.)	*Eng.* sĭ-ĕn′-ə	si-en′-uh
	It. syĕ′-nä	syeh′-nah
Sieradz (Pol.)	shĕ′-räts	sheh′-rahts
Sieraków (Pol.)	shĕ-rä′-ko͝of	sheh-rah′-kuf
Sierpc (Pol.)	shĕrpts′	shehrpts′
Russian *Serpets*, sĕr′-pĕts [sehr′-pets].		
Sierra Morena (Sp., mts.)	syĕ′-rä mô-rĕ′-nä	syeh′-rah mo-reh′-nah
Sierra Nevada (Sp., U.S., mts.)	*Eng.* sĭ-ĕr′-ə nə-vä′-də	si-ehr′-uh nuh-vah′-duh
	Sp. syĕ′-rä nĕ-vä′-*th*ä	syeh′-rah neh-vah′-*th*ah

Sigale (Alg., cape)	sē-gäl′	see-gahl′
Sigdal (Nor.)	sĭg′-däl	sig′-dahl
Sighet (Rum.)	sē-gĕt′	see-get′
Hungarian *Mármarossziget*, mär′-mŏ-rôsh-sĭ′-gĕt [mahr′-mo-rosh-si′-get].		
Sighişoara (Rum.)	sē-gē-shwä′-rä	see-gee-shwah′-rah
Hungarian *Segesvár*, shĕ′-gĕsh-vär [sheh′-gesh-vahr].		
Sikaiana (Oc.)	sē-kī-ä′-nä	see-kai-ah′-nah
Si-kang *or* Hsi-kang (Ch., prov.)	*Eng.* sē-kăng *Ch.* shē-käng	see-kang shee-kahng
Sikes, Bob (U.S. representative)	sīks′	saiks′
Sikh (India)	sēk′	seek′
Sikinos (Gr.)	sē′-kē-nôs	see′-kee-nos
Sikirica (Yugosl.)	sē′-kĭ-rĭ-tsä	see′-ki-ri-tsah
Sikorsky, Wladislaw (Pol. leader)	sĭ-kôr′-skĭ, vlä-dĭs′-läf	si-kor′-ski, vlah-dis′-lahf
Silba (Yugosl.)	sēl′-bä	seel′-bah
Italian *Selve*, q.v.		
Silesia (Ger., Pol., Cz.)	*Eng.* sĭ-lē′-shə	si-lee′-shuh
German *Schlesien*, shlā′-zĭ-ən [shlay′-zi-uhn]. Polish *Śląnsk*, shlôNsk′ [shloNsk′]. Czech *Slezsko*, slĕs′-kô [sles′-ko].		
Siliana (Tun.)	sēl-yă′-nä	seel-ya′-nah
Silistra (Rum.)	*Eng.* sĭ-lĭs′-trə *Rum.* sē-lē′-strä	si-lis′-truh see-lee′-strah
Bulgarian *Silistria*, (Eng.) sĭ-lĭs′-trĭ-ə [si-lis′-tri-uh]; (Bulg.) sĭ-lē′-strĭ-yä [si-lee′-stri-yah].		
Silistria (Rum.) See *Silistra*.		
Silivri (Turk.)	sē-lēv′-rē′	see-leev′-ree′
Šiljegovac (Yugosl.)	shē′-lyĕ′-gô-väts	shee′-lyeh′-go-vahts
Šilutė (Lith.)	shē-lo͞o′-tĕ	shee-loo′-teh
Simberi (Oc.)	sĭm-bĕ′-rē	sim-beh′-ree
Simbirsk (Rus.)	sĭm-bērsk′	sim-beersk′
Simbo (Oc.)	sĭm′-bô	sim′-bo
Simeto (Sicily, riv.)	sē-mĕ′-tô	see-meh′-to
Simeuloee *or* Simeulue (NEI)	sē-mû-lo͞o′-ĕ	see-mœ-loo′-eh
Simferopol (Rus.)	sĭm-fĕ-rô′-pŏl(y)	sim-feh-ro′-pol(y)
Also called *Ak Mechet*, äk′ mĕ-chĕt′ [ahk′ meh-chet′].		
Simi (Dodec.) See *Syme*.		
Simla (India)	sĭm′-lə	sim′-luh
Simola (Fin.)	sē′-mô-lä	see′-mo-lah
Simrishamn (Sw.)	sēm′-rēs-hämn	seem′-rees-hahmn
Sinaia (Rum.)	sē-nī′-yä	see-nai′-yah

Sinauen (Libya)	sĭ-nä′-wĕn	si-nah′-wen
Sinbaungwe (Burma)	sĭn-boung-wĕ′	sin-baung-weh′
Sinelnikovo (Rus.)	sĭ-nĕl′(y)-nĭ-kŏ-vŏ	si-nel′(y)-ni-ko-vo
Singapore (Straits Settlements)	sĭng′-gə-pôr′	sing′-guh-por′

The pronunciation sĭng′-ə-pôr [sing′-uh-por] is common, though not authorized by the dictionaries. Malaysian sĭng-ä-po͞o′-rə [sing-ah-poo′-ruh].

Singaradja (NEI)	sĭng′-gä-rä′-jä	sing′-gah-rah′-jah
Singhalese (Ceylonese)	sĭng-gə-lēz′	sing-guh-leez′
Singora (Thai)	sĭng-gô′-rä	sing-gaw′-rah

Thai *Songkla*, sŏng-klä′ [song-klah′].

Sing-sing-sia *or* Hsing-hsing-hsia (Ch., Sinkiang-Kansu)	shĭng-shĭng-shyä	shing-shing-shyah
Singu (Burma)	sĭn-go͞o′	sin-goo′
Sining *or* Hsining) Ch., Chinghai)	shē-nĭng	shee-ning
Sinj (Yugosl.)	sēn′(y)	seen′(y)
Sinjajevina planina (Yugosl., mts.)	sē′-nyä′-yĕ-vĭ-nä plä′-nē′-nä	see′-nyah′-yeh-vi-nah plah′-nee′-nah
Sin-kiang *or* Hsin-kiang	*Eng.* sĭn-kyăng *Ch.* shĭn-jyäng	sin-kyang shin-jyahng
Sinopoli (It.)	sē-nô′-pô-lē	see-no′-po-lee
Sint Niklaas (Belg.)	sĭnt nē′-kläs	sint nee′-klahs
Sin-yang *or* Hsin-yang (Ch., Honan)	shĭn-yäng	shin-yahng
Siófok (Hung.)	shĭ′-ô-fôk	shi′-o-fok
Šipan (Yugosl.)	shē′-pän(y)	shee′-pahn(y)

Italian *Giupana*, q.v.

Siphnos (Gr., isl.)	sēf′-nô(s)	seef′-no(s)
Sira (Nor., riv.)	sē′-rä	see′-rah
Siracusa (Sicily)	sē-rä-ko͞o′-zä	see-rah-koo′-zah

American *Syracuse*, sĭr′-ə-kūs [sihr′-uh-kyoos] is preferable for American radio. British sī′-rə-kūz [sai′-ruh-kyooz].

Sirakovo (Yugosl.)	sē′-rä′-kô-vô	see′-rah′-ko-vo
Siredalen (Nor.)	sē′-rə-dä-lən	see′-ruh-dah-luhn
Siret (Rum.)	sĭ-rĕt′	si-ret′
Siretul (Rum., riv.)	sĭ-rĕ′-to͝ol	si-reh′-tul
Sirot (Oc.)	sē-rôt′	see-rot′
Sirte (Libya)	sĭr′-tĕ	sihr′-teh

Also called *Sidra*, q.v., and *Zaafran*, q.v.

Sisevac Vrčić (Yugosl.)	sē′-sĕ-väts vər′-chĭch	see′-seh-vahts vuhr′-chich

Sison, Teófilo (Fil. leader)	sē′-sôn, tyô′-fē-lô	see′-son, tyo′-fee-lo
Şiştov (Bulg.) See *Svishtov.*		
Sithonia (Gr., pen.) See *Longos.*		
Sitka (Alaska)	sĭt′-kə	sit′-kuh
Sitnica (Yugosl., riv.)	sēt′-nĭ-tsä	seet′-ni-tsah
Si-ts'ang (Ch. dependency)	sē-tsäng	see-tsahng
Also called *Hsi-ts'äng,* shē-tsäng [shee-tsahng]. English *Tibet,* q.v.		
Sittang (Burma, riv.)	sĭt′-tăng′	sit′-tang′
Sittard (Neth.)	sĭt′-ärt	sit′-ahrt
Sivac (Yugosl.)	sē′-väts	see′-vahts
Sivash (Rus., lagoons)	sĭ-väsh′	si-vahsh′
Also called the *Putrid Sea.*		
Siwa (Egypt)	sē′-wä	see′-wah
Sjaelland (Den., isl.) See *Zealand.*		
Sjenica (Yugosl.)	syĕ′-nĭ-tsä	syeh′-ni-tsah
Sjoa (Nor.)	shō′-ä	shoh′-ah
Skadar (Alb.) See *Scutari.*		
Skadovsk (Rus.)	skä-dôfsk′	skah-dofsk′
Skagen (Den., cape)	skä′-gən	skah′-guhn
English the *Skaw,* skô′ [skaw′].		
Skagerrak (Nor., Den., sea)	*Eng.* skăg′-ə-răk	skag′-uh-rak
Skalani (Crete)	skä-lä′-nē	skah-lah′-nee
Skanderbeut, Mal i (Alb., mt.) See *Scanderbeg.*		
Skantzoura (Gr., isl.)	skä′-dzōō-rä	skah′-dzoo-rah
Skaramangas (Gr.)	skä-rä-mä(ng)-gäs′	skah-rah-mah(ng)-gahs′
Škarda (Yugosl., isl.)	shkär′-dä	shkahr′-dah
Skarsfoss (Nor., dam)	skärs′-fôs *or* skäsh′-fôs	skahrs′-fos skahsh′-fos
Skarżysko (Pol.)	skär-zhĭ′-skô	skahr-zhi′-sko
Skaw, the (Den., cape) See *Skagen.*		
Skawa (Pol., riv.)	skä′-vä	skah′-vah
Skawina (Pol.)	skä-vē′-nä	skah-vee′-nah
Skei (Nor.)	shā′	shay′
Skerda (Yugosl., isl.)	skĕr′-dä	skehr′-dah
Skernevitsi (Pol.) See *Skierniewice.*		
Skhirra, la (Tun.)	sə-kĭr′-rä, lä	suh-kihr′-rah, lah
Often spelled *Cekhira.*		
ski	*Eng.* skē′ *Nor.* shē′	skee′ shee′
Skiathos (Gr., isl.)	skē′-ä-thô(s)	skee′-ah-tho(s)

Skidel (Pol.)	skē′-dĕl(y)	skee′-del(y)
Skien (Nor.)	shā′-ən	shay′-uhn
	or shē′-ən	shee′-uhn
Skierniewice (Pol.)	skyĕr-nyĕ-vē′-tsĕ	skyehr-nyeh-vee′-tseh
Russian *Skernevitsi*, skĕr-nĕ-vē′-tsĭ [skehr-neh-vee′-tsi].		
skijoring	*Eng.* skē-jôr′-ĭng	skee-jor′-ing
Skive (Den.)	skē′-və	skee′-vuh
Skiza (Gr., isl.)	skē′-zä	skee′-zah
Skjeggedalsfoss (Nor., lake)	shĕg′-ə-däls-fôs′	sheg′-uh-dahls-fos′
Skjervoei *or* Skjervöi (Nor.)	shĕrv′-ûĭ	shehrv′-œi
Skjoenstaa *or* Skjönstaa (Nor.)	shûn′-stô	shœn′-sto
Skjolden (Nor.)	shôl′-dən	shol′-duhn
Škofja Loka (Yugosl.)	shkô′-fyä lô′-kä	shko′-fyah lo′-kah
Skogfoss (Nor.)	skōg′-fôs	skohg′-fos
Skopelos (Gr., isl.)	skô′-pĕ-lô(s)	sko′-peh-lo(s)
Skopin (Rus.)	skŏ-pēn′	sko-peen′
Skoplje (Yugosl.)	skôp′-lyĕ	skop′-lyeh
Greek *Skopia*, skô′-pē-ä [sko′-pee-ah].		
Skoppum (Nor.)	skôp′-o͝om	skop′-um
Skoupitsa (Gr.)	sko͞o-pē′-tsä	skoo-pee′-tsah
Skrapež (Yugosl., riv.)	skrä′-pĕzh	skrah′-pezh
Skreia (Nor.)	skrā′-ä	skray′-ah
Skrwa (Pol., riv.)	skər-vä′	skuhr-vah′
Skudeneshavn (Nor.)	sko͞o′-də-nĕs-hävn′	skoo′-duh-nes-hahvn′
Skulerud (Nor.)	sko͞o′-lə-ro͞od′	skoo′-luh-rood′
Skvira (Rus.)	skvē′-rä	skvee′-rah
Skyros (Gr., isl.)	skē′-rô(s)	skee′-ro(s)
Slack (Fr., riv.)	släk′	slahk′
Slaná (Cz., riv.)	slä′-nä	slah′-nah
Hungarian *Sajó*, shŏ′-yô [sho′-yo].		
Slănic (Rum.)	slə-nēk′	sluh-neek′
Śląsk (Pol.) See *Silesia*.		
Slatina (Rum.)	slä′-tē-nä	slah′-tee-nah
Slatino (Rus.)	slä′-tĭ-nŏ	slah′-ti-no
Slavište (Yugosl.)	slä′-vĭsh-tĕ	slah′-vish-teh
Slavkov (Cz.) See *Austerlitz*.		
Slavnoe (Rus.)	släv′-nŏ-yĕ	slahv′-no-yeh
Slavonia (Yugosl.)	*Eng.* slə-vōn′-yə	sluh-vohn′-yuh
Serb-Croat *Slavonija*, slä-vô′-nĭ-yä [slah-vo′-ni-yah].		
Slavyanoserbsk (Rus.)	slä-vyä-nŏ-sĕrpsk′	slah-vyah-no-sehrpsk′
Slavyansk (Rus.)	slä′-vyänsk	slah′-vyahnsk

Slesvig (Den.)	*Dan.* slĕs′-vĭk(h)	sles′-vik(h)
German *Schleswig*, q.v.		
Slezsko (Ger., Pol., Cz.) See *Silesia*.		
Slidre (Nor.)	slē′-rə	slee′-ruh
Sliedrecht (Neth.)	slē′-drĕk(h)t	slee′-drek(h)t
Slišane (Yugosl.)	slē′-shä-nĕ	slee′-shah-neh
Sliven (Bulg.)	slē′-vĕn(y)	slee′-ven(y)
Also called *Slivno*, slēv′-nŏ [sleev′-no].		
Slivno (Bulg.) See *Sliven*.		
Sloka (Latvia)	slô′-kä *or* slwŏ′-	slo′-kah *or* slwo′-
German *Schlok*, q.v.		
Słomniki (Pol.)	slôm-nē′-kĭ	slom-nee′-ki
Słonim (Pol.)	slô′-nĭm	slo′-nim
Russian spelling *Slonim*.		
Slovakia (Cz.)	*Eng.* slō-vä′-kĭ-ə	sloh-vah′-ki-uh

Czech *Slovensko*, slô′-vĕn-skô [slo′-ven-sko]. The English pronunciation might well be slō-vā′-kĭ-ə [sloh-vay′-ki-uh] or slō-văk′-ĭ-ə [sloh-vak′-i-uh], but the seeming-foreign slō-vä′-kĭ-ə [sloh-vah′-ki-uh] is the most common. See *Copenhagen*.

Slovenia (Yugosl.)	*Eng.* slō-vēn′-yə	sloh-veen′-yuh
Serb-Croat *Slovenija*, slô-vĕ′-nĭ-yä [slo-veh′-ni-yah].		
Slovenjgradec (Yugosl.)	slô′-vĕn(y)-grä′-dĕts	slo′-ven(y)-grah′-dets
Słucz (Pol., riv.)	slo͞och′	slooch′
Russian spelling *Sluch*.		
Slyudyanka (Rus.)	slū-dyän′-kä	slyoo-dyahn′-kah
Sluiskil (Neth.)	slûĭs′-kĭl	slœis′-kil
Slunj (Yugosl.)	slo͞on′(y)	sloon′(y)
Słupca (Pol.)	slo͝op′-tsä	slup′-tsah
Russian *Sluptsi*, slo͞op′-tsĭ [sloop′-tsi].		
Sluptsi (Pol.) See *Słupca*.		
Smaalenene *or* Smålenene (Nor.)	smô′-lĕ-nə-nə	smo′-leh-nuh-nuh
Smederevo (Yugosl.)	smĕ′-dĕ-rĕ-vô	smeh′-deh-reh-vo
Smela (Rus.)	smĕ′-lä	smeh′-lah
Smilde (Neth., canal)	smĭl′-də	smil′-duh
Smiltene (Latvia)	smēl′-tĕ-nĕ	smeel′-teh-neh
Russian *Smilten*, smēl′(y)-tĕn [smeel′(y)-ten].		
Smindja (Tun.)	smĭn′-jä	smin′-jah
Smolensk (Rus.)	smŏ-lĕnsk′	smo-lensk′
Smolian (Bulg.)	smô′-lĭ-yän	smo′-li-yahn
Also called *Pashmakli*, päsh′-mä-klē′ [pahsh′-mah-klee′].		
Smoljinac (Yugosl.)	smô′-lyĭ-näts	smo′-lyi-nahts
Smorgonie (Pol.)	smôr-gô′-nyĕ	smor-go′-nyeh
Russian *Smorgon*, smŏr-gôn′(y) [smor-gon′(y)].		

Smuts, Jan C. (S. Afr. leader)	smŭts′, yän′	smuhts′, yahn′
Smyrna (Turk.)	*Eng.* smûr′-nə	smuhr′-nuh
Turkish *İzmir*, q.v.		
Sneek (Neth.)	snāk′	snayk′
Śniatyn (Pol.)	shnyä′-tĭn	shnyah′-tin
Snigirevka (Rus.)	snĭ-gĭ-ryôf′-kä	sni-gi-ryof′-kah
Snoehetta *or* Snöhetta (Nor., mt.)	snû′-hĕt-ä	snœ′-het-ah
Sobolev, Arcady (Rus. leader)	sô′-bŏ-lĕf, är-kä′-dē	so′-bo-lef, ahr-kah′-dee
Sochaczew (Pol.)	sô-hä′-chĕf	so-hah′-chef
Russian spelling *Sokhachev.*		
Sochi (Rus.)	sô′-chĭ	so′-chi
Socna (Libya)	sŏk′-nä	sok′-nah
Söderhamn (Sw.)	sû′-dər-hämn′	sœ′-duhr-hahmn′
Södertälje (Sw.)	sû′-dər-tĕl′-yĕ	sœ′-duhr-tel′-yeh
Sodražica (Yugosl.)	sô-drä′-zhĭ-tsä	so-drah′-zhi-tsah
Soebang *or* Subang (NEI)	so͞o′-bäng	soo′-bahng
Soederhamn (Sw.)	sû′-dər-hämn′	sœ′-duhr-hahmn′
Soedertälje (Sw.)	sû′-dər-tĕl′-yĕ	sœ′-duhr-tel′-yeh
Soekaboemi *or* Sukabumi (NEI)	so͞o-kä-bo͞o′-mē	soo-kah-boo′-mee
Soela *or* Sula (NEI)	so͞o′-lä	soo′-lah
Soemba *or* Sumba (NEI)	so͞om′-bä	soom′-bah
Soembawa *or* Sumbawa (NEI)	so͞om-bä′-wä	soom-bah′-wah
Soenda (NEI) See *Sunda.*		
Soerabaja *or* Surabaya (NEI)	so͞o-rä-bä′-yä	soo-rah-bah′-yah
Soerakarta *or* Surakarta (NEI)	so͞o-rä-kär′-tä	soo-rah-kahr′-tah
Soerfold (Nor.)	sûr′-fôl	sœr′-fol
Soerumsand (Nor.)	sû′-ro͝om-sän	sœ′-rum-sahn
Soervaranger (Nor.)	sûr′-vä-räng′-ər	sœr′-vah-rahng′-uhr
Soest (Ger.)	zōst′	zohst′
Soest (Neth.)	so͞ost′	soost′
Soesterberg (Neth.)	so͞os′-tər-bĕrk(h)	soos′-tuhr-behrk(h)
Sofia (Bulg.)	*Eng.* sō′-fĭ-ə	soh′-fi-uh
	Bulg. sô′-fĭ-yä	so′-fi-yah
Also spelled *Sofiya*. There is also an English pronunciation sō-fē′-ə [soh-fee′-uh]. Formerly called *Sredets*, srĕ′-dĕts [sreh′-dets].		
Sofiskoe (Rus.)	sŏ-fē′-skŏ-yĕ	so-fee′-sko-yeh

Sofoulis, Emmanuel (Gr. leader)	sô′-fo͞o′-lēs, ĕ-mä-no͞o-ēl′	so-foo′-lees, eh-mah-noo-eel′
Sogn (Nor.)	sông′n *local* sôg′-ən	song′n sog′-uhn
Sogndal (Nor.)	sông′n-däl	song′n-dahl
Sognefjord (Nor.)	sông′-nə-fyōr	song′-nuh-fyohr
Soheily (Per. leader)	sô-hā′-lē	so-hay′-lee
Soissons (Fr.)	swä-sôN′	swah-soN′
Sokhachev (Pol.) See *Sochaczew.*		
Soko Banja (Yugosl.)	sô′-kô bä′-nyä	so′-ko bah′-nyah
Sola (Nor.)	sō′-lä	soh′-lah
Soła (Pol., riv.)	sô′-lä	so′-lah
Soldau (Pol.)	*Ger.* zôl′-dou	zol′-dau
Polish *Działdówka* and *Działdówo,* q.v.		
Solenzara (Corsica)	sô-lĕn-tsä′-rä	so-len-tsah′-rah
Soliman (Tun.)	*Eng.* sŏl′-ə-mən *Fr.* sô-lē-mäN′	sol′-uh-muhn so-lee-mahN′
Solingen (Ger.)	zō′-lĭng-ən	zoh′-ling-uhn
Sol(l)um (Egypt) See *Sal(l)um.*		
Soloer *or* Solör (Nor.)	sō′-lûr	soh′-lœr
Solovets (Rus.)	sŏ-lŏ-vĕts′	so-lo-vets′
Solovetskie Ostrova (Rus.)	sŏ-lŏ-vĕt′-skĭ-yĕ ŏs-trŏ-vä′	so-lo-vet′-ski-yeh os-tro-vah′
Solovtsy (Rus.)	sŏ-lŏf-tsē′	so-lof-tsee′
Solsk (Rus.)	sôl(y)sk′	sol(y)sk′
Solstrand (Nor.)	sōl′-strän	sohl′-strahn
Solta (Yugosl., isl.)	*It.* sôl′-tä	sol′-tah
Serb-Croat *Sulet,* q.v.		
Soltsi (Rus.)	sŏl(y)-tsē′	sol(y)-tsee′
Soluch (Libya)	sô-lo͝ok′	so-luk′
So-lun (Manchu.)	sô-lo͝on	so-lun
Sombor (Yugosl.)	sôm′-bôr	som′-bor
Hungarian *Zombor,* zôm′-bôr [zom′-bor].		
Somers, Andrew L. (U.S. representative)	sŭm′-ərz	suhm′-uhrz
Somervell, Brehon (U.S. general)	sŭm′-ər-vəl, brā′-hŏn	suhm′-uhr-vuhl, bray′-hon
Someş (Rum.)	sô′-mĕsh	so′-mesh
Someşul (Rum., riv.)	sô-mĕ′-sho͝ol	so-meh′-shul
Somino (Rus.)	sô′-mĭ-nŏ	so′-mi-no
Somme (Fr.)	sôm′	som′
Šomrda (Yugosl., mts.)	shô′-mər′-dä	sho′-muhr′-dah
Son (India, riv.)	sōn′	sohn′
Songcau (Indo-Ch.)	sŏng′-kou′	song′-kau′
Songkla (Thai) See *Singora.*		

Sonsorol (Oc.)	sôn′-sô-rôl	son′-so-rol
Sontay (Indo-Ch.)	sŭn-tī′	suhn-tai′
Soo-chow (Ch., Kiangsu)	*Eng.* sōō-chou	soo-chau
	Ch. sōō-jō	soo-joh
Near Shanghai. Also spelled *Su-chow.*		
Soong Hsi-lien (Ch. general)	sŏŏng shē-lyĕn	sung shee-lyen
Sophali (Gr.) See *Souphli.*		
Sopot (Yugosl.)	sô′-pôt	so′-pot
Sopron (Hung.)	shôp′-rôn	shop′-ron
German *Oedenburg* or *Ödenburg,* û′-dən-bŏŏrk(h) [œ′-duhn-burk(h)].		
Sorau (Ger.)	zō′-rou	zoh′-rau
Sorba (Corsica)	sôr′-bä	sor′-bah
Sörfold (Nor.)	sûr′-fôl	sœr′-fol
Sorgenfri (Den.)	sôr′-gən-frē	sor′-guhn-free
Sorgono (Sard.)	sôr′-gô-nô	sor′-go-no
Soria (Sp.)	sô′-ryä	so′-ryah
Sormovo (Rus.)	sôr′-mŏ-vŏ	sor′-mo-vo
Soroca (Rum.)	sô-rô′-kä	so-ro′-kah
Russian *Soroki,* sŏ-rô′-kĭ [so-ro′-ki].		
Soroe *or* Sorö (Nor.)	sō′-rû	soh′-rœ
Soroka *or* Soroki (Rus.)	sŏ-rô′-kä, sŏ-rô′-kĭ	so-ro′-kah, so-ro′-ki
Sorol (Oc.)	sô′-rôl	so′-rol
Sorong (Oc.)	sô′-rông	so′-rong
Sorot (Rus., riv.)	sô′-rŏt	so′-rot
Sorsogón (P.I.)	sôr-sô-gôn′	sor-so-gon′
Sortavala (Fin.)	sôr′-tä-vä-lä	sor′-tah-vah-lah
Sortland (Nor.)	sŏŏrt′-län	surt′-lahn
Sörumsand (Nor.)	sû′-rŏŏm-sän	sœ′-rum-sahn
Sörvaranger (Nor.)	sûr′-vä-räng′-ər	sœr′-vah-rahng′-uhr
Sosnitsa (Rus.)	sŏs-nē′-tsä	sos-nee′-tsah
Sosnkowski, Kazimierz (Pol. general)	sôsn-kôf′-skĭ, kä-zē′-myĕzh	sosn-kof′-ski, kah-zee′-myezh
Sosnowiec (Pol.)	sô-snô′-vyĕts	so-sno′-vyets
Russian spelling *Sosnovets.*		
Šoštanj (Yugosl.)	shô′-shtän(y)	sho′-shtahn(y)
Sosunov (Rus., cape)	sŏ-sōō-nôf′	so-soo-nof′
Sosyka (Rus.)	sŏ-swē′-kä	so-swee′-kah
Sotteville (Fr.)	sôt-vēl′	sot-veel′
Souda (Crete)	*Eng.* sōō′-də	soo′-duh
	Gr. sōō′-*th*ä	soo′-*th*ah
Gulf of Souda, *Kolpos Soudas,* kôl′-pôs sōō′-*th*äs [kol′-pos soo′-*th*ahs].		
souk *or* suq *or* suk	sōōk′	sook′
In Arabic names an element, sometimes omitted, meaning *market.*		

Souk Ahras (Alg.)	so͞ok ă-hrăs′	sook a-hras′
Souk el Arba (Tun.)	so͞ok ĕl är′-bä	sook el ahr′-bah
Souk el Khemis (Tun.)	kə-mēs′	kuh-mees′
Souliasi (Gr.)	so͞o′-lyä-sē	soo′-lyah-see
Souphli (Gr.)	so͞o-flē′	soo-flee′
Also called *Sophali*, sô-fä-lē′ [so-fah-lee′].		
Souphlion (Gr.)	so͞o-flē′(-ôn)	soo-flee′(-on)
Sousse (Tun.)	*Fr.* so͞os′	soos′
Also called *Susa*, q.v.		
Soveria (It.)	sô-vĕ-rē′-ä	so-veh-ree′-ah
Sovetskaya Gavan (Rus.)	sŏ-vĕt′-skä-yä gä′-vän(y)	so-vet′-skah-yah gah′-vahn(y)
Soviet (Rus.)	*Eng.* sō′-vĭ-ĕt′	soh′-vi-et′
Russian *Sovet.*		
Sozh (Rus., riv.)	sôzh′	sozh′
Sozopol (Bulg.)	sô′-zŏ-pŏl(y)	so′-zo-pol(y)
Spaatz, Carl (U.S. general)	späts′	spahts′
Airforce headquarters in the Tunisian campaign had the nickname, according to *Time*, March 22, 1943, of *Souk el Spaatz*, so͞ok′ ĕl späts′ [sook′ el spahts′]. The General's nickname is *Tooey*, to͞o′-ĭ [too′-i].		
Spada (Crete, pen., mt.)	See *Rodopou.*	
Spadillo (Pantelleria, point)	spä-dēl′-lô	spah-deel′-lo
Spahi	spä′-hē	spah′-hee
Spain See *España.*		
Spalato (Yugosl.)	*It.* spä′-lä-tô	spah′-lah-to
Serb-Croat *Split*, q.v.		
Spalmadori (Yugosl., isls.)	*It.* späl-mä-dô′-rĭ	spahl-mah-do′-ri
Serb-Croat *Pakleni Otoci*, q.v.		
Spančevo (Yugosl.)	spän′-chĕ-vô	spahn′-cheh-vo
Sparanise (It.)	spä-rä-nē′-zĕ	spah-rah-nee′-zeh
Sparta (Gr.)	*Eng.* spär′-tə	spahr′-tuh
Greek *Sparte*, spär′-tē [spahr′-tee].		
Spartivento (It., Sard., cape)	spär-tē-vĕn′-tô	spahr-tee-ven′-to
Spas Demensk (Rus.)	späs′ dĕ-mĕnsk′	spahs′ deh-mensk′
Spassk (Rus.)	späsk′	spahsk′
Spatha (Crete, cape)	spä′-thä	spah′-thah
Also called *Psakon*, q.v.		
Spelea (Crete)	spē-lyä′	spee-lyah′
Speli (Crete)	spē′-lē	spee′-lee
Sperillen (Nor.)	spĕr′-ĭl-ən	spehr′-il-uhn
Spetsai (Gr., isl.)	spĕt′-sĕ	spet′-seh
Italian *Spezzia*, spĕt′-syä [spet′-syah].		

Speyer (Ger.)	shpī′-ər	shpai′-uhr
English *Spires*, spīrz′ [spairz′].		
Spezia, la (It.)	spĕ′-tsyä, lä	speh′-tsyah, lah
Spezzia (Gr., isl.) See *Spetsai*.		
Sphakia (Crete)	sfä-kyä′	sfah-kyah′
Also called *Khora Sphakion*, q.v.		
Sphakteria (Gr., isl.)	sfä-ktē-rē′-ä	sfah-ktee-ree′-ah
Sphenari (Crete)	sfē-nä′-rē	sfee-nah′-ree
Spič, Zaliv (Yugosl., bay)	spēch′, zä′-lĭv	speech′, zah′-liv
Italian *Valle Spizza*, väl′-lĕ spēt′-sä [vahl′-leh speet′-sah].		
Spielfeld (Austria)	shpēl′-fĕlt	shpeel′-felt
Spinalonga (Crete, point, isl.)	spē-nä-lông′-gä	spee-nah-long′-gah
Spinazzola (Italy)	spē-nät-sô′-lä	spee-naht-so′-lah
Spires (Ger.) See *Speyer*.		
Spirovo (Rus.)	spē′-rŏ-vŏ	spee′-ro-vo
Spiš (Cz.)	spēsh′	speesh′
Hungarian *Szepes*, sĕ′-pĕsh [seh′-pesh].		
Spišká, -é	spēsh′-kä, -ĕ	speesh′-kah, -eh
An element, meaning *of Spiš*, q.v., in Czech place names. Look up the other part of the name.		
Spital (Austria)	shpē′-täl	shpee′-tahl
Split (Yugosl.)	splēt′	spleet′
Italian *Spalato*, q.v.		
Spoleto (It.)	spô-lĕ′-tô	spo-leh′-to
Sporades (Gr., isls.)	*Eng.* spôr′-ə-dēz	spor′-uh-deez
	Gr. spô-rä′-*th*ĕs	spo-rah′-*th*es
Spratly (Jap., isl.)	sprăt′-lĭ	sprat′-li
Spuž (Yugosl.)	spōōzh′	spoozh′
sqep *or* sqepi (Alb.) See *kep*.		
Squillace (It., gulf)	skwēl-lä′-chĕ	skweel-lah′-cheh
Srbica (Yugosl.)	sər′-bĭ-tsä	suhr′-bi-tsah
Srbobran (Yugosl.)	sər′-bô-brän′	suhr′-bo-brahn′
Srebrenica (Yugosl.)	srĕ′-brĕ-nĭ-tsä	sreh′-breh-ni-tsah
Srebrna Glava (Yugosl., mt.)	srĕ′-bər-nä glä′-vä	sreh′-buhr-nah glah′-vah
Sredets (Bulg.) See *Sofia*.		
Srednjevo (Yugosl.)	srĕd′-nyĕ-vô	sred′-nyeh-vo
Śrem (Pol.)	shrĕm′	shrem′
German *Schrimm*, shrĭm′ [shrim′].		
Srem (Yugosl.) See *Syrmia*.		
Sremčica (Yugosl.)	srĕm′-chĭ-tsä	srem′-chi-tsah
Sretensk (Rus.)	srĕ′-tĕnsk	sreh′-tensk
Srinagar (India)	srē-nŭg′-ər	sree-nuhg′-uhr

Środa (Pol.)	shrô′-dä	shro′-dah
Srpska Crnja (Yugosl.)	sərp′-skä tsər′-nyä	suhrp′-skah tsuhr′-nyah
Srpski Elemir (Yugosl.)	sərp′-skĭ ĕ′-lĕ-mĭr	suhrp′-ski eh′-leh-mihr
Srpski Itebej (Yugosl.)	sərp′-skĭ ē′-tĕ-bā	suhrp′-ski ee′-teh-bay
Srpski Krstur (Yugosl.)	sərp′-skĭ kər′-sto͞or	suhrp′-ski kuhr′-stoor
St. . . . For compounds with *St.*, not listed here, see *Saint* . . .		
Stabekk (Nor.)	stä′-bĕk	stah′-bek
Stachouwer, Tjarda van Starkenborgh (Du. leader)	stä′-k(h)ou-ər, tyär′-dä vän stär′-kən-bôrk(h)	stah′-k(h)au-uhr, tyahr′-dah vahn stahr′-kuhn-bork(h)
stad	stät′	staht′
Dutch word meaning *city*; an element in place names.		
stad	stä′	stah′
Norwegian word meaning *place*; an element in place names.		
Stad (Nor.)	städ′	stahd′
Stagnone (Sicily, isl.)	stän-yô′-nĕ	stahn-yo′-neh
Staiti (It.)	stī′-tē	stai′-tee
Stalać (Yugosl.)	stä′-läch	stah′-lahch
Stalheim (Nor.)	stäl′-hām	stahl′-haym
Stalin (Rus. leader)	stä′-lĭn	stah′-lin
Real name is *Dzugashvili*, jo͞o-gäsh-vē′-lē [joo-gahsh-vee′-lee].		
Stalinabad (Rus.)	stä-lĭ-nä-bät′	stah-li-nah-baht′
Stalingrad (Rus.)	*Eng.* stä′-lĭn-grăd	stah′-lin-grad
	Rus. stä-lĭn-grät′	stah-lin-graht′
The analogy of the English pronunciation of *Petrograd* will probably govern all Russian names in *-grad* that enter the news.		
Stalino (Rus.)	stä′-lĭ-nŏ	stah′-li-no
Stalinsk (Rus.)	stä′-lĭnsk	stah′-linsk
Stampalia (Dodec.)	*It.* stäm-pä-lē′-ä	stahm-pah-lee′-ah
Greek *Astypalea*, q.v.		
Stamsund (Nor.)	stäm′-so͝on	stahm′-sun
Stańczyk, Jan (Pol. leader)	stän′(y)-chĭk, yän′	stahn′(y)-chik, yahn′
Standia (Crete, isl.) See *Dia.*		
Staničenje (Yugosl.)	stä′-nĭ-chĕ-nyĕ	stah′-ni-cheh-nyeh
Stanišić (Yugosl.)	stä′-nĭ-shĭch	stah′-ni-shich
Stanisławów (Pol.)	stä-nē-slä′-vo͝of	stah-nee-slah′-vuf
Russian *Stanislavov*, stä-nĭ-slä′-vŏf [stah-ni-slah′-vof].		
stara, -ri, -ro	stä′-rä, -rĭ, -rô	stah′-rah, -ri, -ro
An element, meaning *old*, in Yugoslav and Bulgarian place names. It may be necessary to look up the second part of the name.		

Stara planina (Balkan mts.)	stä′-rä plä′-nē′-nä	stah′-rah plah′-nee′-nah
Staraya Russa (Rus.)	stä′-rä-yä ro͞o′-sä	stah′-rah-yah roo′-sah
Stara Zagora (Bulg.)	stä′-rä zä′-gŏ-rä	stah′-rah zah′-go-rah
Starčevo (Yugosl.)	stär′-chĕ-vô	stahr′-cheh-vo
Stargard (Ger.)	shtär′-gärt	shtahr′-gahrt
Stari Grad (Yugosl.)	stä′-rĭ gräd′	stah′-ri grahd′

Italian *Citta Vecchia*, q.v.

Starii Oskol (Rus.)	stä′-rĭ ŏs-kôl′	stah′-ri os-kol′
Staritsa (Rus.)	stä′-rĭ-tsä	stah′-ri-tsah
Stari Vlah (Yugosl.)	stä′-rĭ vläk(h)′	stah′-ri vlahk(h)′
Starobelsk (Rus.)	stä-rŏ-bĕl(y)sk′	stah-ro-bel(y)sk′
Starodub (Rus.)	stä-rŏ-do͞op′	stah-ro-doop′
Starogard (Pol.)	stä-rô′-gärt	stah-ro′-gahrt
Starojineţ (Rum.)	stä-rô-zhē-nĕts′	stah-ro-zhee-nets′
Staro Konstantinov (Rus.)	stä′-rŏ kŏn-stän-tē′-nŏf	stah′-ro kon-stahn-tee′-nof
Staro Minskaya (Rus.)	stä′-rŏ mēn′-skä-yä	stah′-ro meen′-skah-yah
Staro Tsurukhaituevsk (Rus.)	stä′-rŏ tso͞o-ro͞o-hī-to͞o′-yĕfsk	stah′-ro tsoo-roo-hai-too′-yefsk
Stathelle (Nor.)	stät′-hĕl-ə	staht′-hel-uh
status	stā′-təs	stay′-tuhs

Many Americans say stăt′-əs [stat′-uhs] but radio speakers can play safe by following the dictionary recommendation, as above. Webster's (1934) allows short ă, as well as ā [*ay*], in *stratum*, *strata*, *apparatus*, probably because so many scientists have the *ă*-pronunciation. But *datum* and *data*, according to Webster's, should have ā [*ay*] or ä [*ah*]. Of course it would be reasonable to treat all such words alike and, I believe, to admit ā [*ay*] and ă for the group.

Stavanger (Nor.)	stä-väng′-ər	stah-vahng′-uhr
Stavern (Nor.)	stä′-vĕrn	stah′-vehrn
Staviski (Pol.) See *Stawiski*.		
Stavoren (Neth.)	stä′-və-rən	stah′-vuh-ruhn
Stavros (Gr., point)	stä-vrôs′	stah-vros′
Stawiski (Pol.)	stä-vē′-skĭ	stah-vee′-ski

Russian spelling *Staviski.*

Steagall, Henry B. (Late U.S. representative)	stē-gôl′	stee-gawl′
stede	stā′-də	stay′-duh

An element, meaning *place*, in Dutch place names.

Steenbergen (Neth.)	stān′-bĕr-k(h)ən	stayn′-behr-k(h)uhn
Stefan, Carl (U.S. representative)	stĕf′-ən	stef′-uhn

Stefano (It.)	stĕ′-fä-nô	steh′-fah-no
Steinkjer (Nor.)	stān′-chĕr	stayn′-chehr
Stepanakert (Rus.)	stĕ′-pä-nä-kĕrt′	steh′-pah-nah-kehrt′
Stepojevac (Yugosl.)	stĕ′-pô′-yĕ-väts	steh′-po′-yeh-vahts
Sterkrade (Ger.)	shtĕrk′-rä-də	shtehrk′-rah-duh
Sterlitamak (Rus.)	stĕr′-lĭ-tä-mäk′	stehr′-li-tah-mahk′
Sternes (Crete)	stĕr′-nĕs	stehr′-nes
Stettin (Ger.)	shtĕ-tēn′	shteh-teen′
Stettinius, Edward R. (U.S. leader)	stĕ-tĭn′-ĭ-əs	steh-tin′-i-uhs
Steyr (Austria)	shtīr′	shtair′
Štimlje (Yugosl.)	shtēm′-lyĕ	shteem′-lyeh
Stinica (Yugosl.)	stē′-nĭ-tsä	stee′-ni-tsah
Štip (Yugosl.)	shtēp′	shteep′
Stir (Pol., riv.) See *Styr.*		
Štirovica (Yugosl.)	shtē′-rô-vĭ-tsä	shtee′-ro-vi-tsah
St. Niklaas (Belg.) See *Sint Niklaas.*		
Sto (Yugosl., mt.)	stô′	staw′
Stochód (Pol., riv.)	stô′-ho͝ot	sto′-hut
Russian *Stokhod,* stŏ-hôt′ [sto-hot′].		
Stockerau (Austria)	shtôk′-ə-rou	shtok′-uh-rau
Stockholm (Sw.)	*Eng.* stŏk′-hōm	stok′-hohm
	Sw. stôk′-hôlm′	stok′-holm′
Stockmanshof (Latvia)	*Ger.* shtôk′-mäns-hôf	shtok′-mahns-hof
Latvian *Plaviņas,* q.v.		
Stoczek (Pol.)	stô′-chĕk	sto′-chek
Russian spelling *Stochek.*		
Stoeren (Nor.)	stû′-rən	stœ′-ruhn
Stoestad, Sverre (Nor. minister)	stû′-stä, svĕr′-ə	stœ′-stah, svehr′-uh
Stojakovo (Yugosl.)	stô′-yä′-kô-vô	sto′-yah′-ko-vo
Stojnik (Yugosl.)	stoi′-nĭk	stoi′-nik
Stokmarksnes (Nor.)	stôk′-märks-nĕs	stok′-mahrks-nes
Stolac (Yugosl.)	stô′-läts	sto′-lahts
Stolbtsi (Pol.) See *Stołpce.*		
Stolp (Ger.)	shtôlp′	shtolp′
Stołpce (Pol.)	stôlp′-tsĕ	stolp′-tseh
Russian *Stolbtsi,* stôlp′-tsĭ [stolp′-tsi].		
stomach	stŭm′-ək	stuhm′-uhk
The pronunciation stŭm′-ĭk [stuhm′-ik] is common, but it isn't recommended.		
Ston (Yugosl.)	stôn′	ston′
Stopanja (Yugosl.)	stô′-pä-nyä	sto′-pah-nyah
Stopnica (Pol.)	stôp-nē′-tsä	stop-nee′-tsah

Stord (Nor., isl.)	sto͝ord′	sturd′
Storebaelt (Den., sound]	stô′-rə-bĕlt	sto′-ruh-belt
Stören (Nor.)	stû′-rən	stœ′-ruhn
Storfjord (Nor.)	stōr′-fyōr	stohr′-fyohr
Storfosshei (Nor.)	stōr′-fôs-hā′	stohr′-fos-hay′
Storlien (Sw.)	stōr′-lē-ən	stohr′-lee-uhn
Storni, Ramón (Arg. leader)	stôr′-nē, rä-môn′	stor′-nee, rah-mon′
Stöstad, Sverre (Nor. leader)	stû′-stä, svĕr′-ə	stœ′-stah, svehr′-uh
Stožac (Yugosl., mt.)	stô′-zhäts	sto′-zhahts
Strabolgi, Lord (Eng. leader)	strə-bō′-gĭ	struh-boh′-gi
Stradiotti (Yugosl., isl.) Serb-Croat *Sveti Marko*, q.v.	*It.* strä-dē-ôt′-tē	strah-dee-ot′-tee
strafe, strafed, strafing	strāf′ *or* sträf′, -t, -ĭng	strayf′ *or* strahf′, -t, -ing

Because *strafe* is freely inflected as an English verb, the completely Anglicized pronunciation with ā [*ay*] is preferable to ä [*ah*] in all forms; sträf′ [strahf′] is not difficult to say, but to many people, sträft′ [strahft′] and sträf′-ĭng [strahf′-ing] seem unidiomatic. In contrast is *suave*, q.v., which as an adjective has only one form and more easily maintains an exotic pronunciation.

Stragari (Yugosl.)	strä′-gä-rĭ	strah′-gah-ri
Strait of Messina (Sicily)	mĕs-sē′-nä	mes-see′-nah
Strakonice (Cz.)	strä′-kô-nĭ-tsĕ	strah′-ko-ni-tseh
Strasbourg (Fr.)	*Eng.* sträz′-bo͝org	strahz′-burg
	Fr. sträz-bo͞or′	strahz-boor′

As an American place name, it is pronounced străs′-bûrg [stras′-buhrg]. German *Strassburg*, shträs′-bo͝orkh [shtrahs′-burkh].

Stratoni (Gr.)	strä-tô′-nē	strah-to′-nee
Štrba (Cz.)	shtər′-bä	shtuhr′-bah
Štrbac (Yugosl., mts.)	shtər′-bäts	shtuhr′-bahts
Strelac (Yugosl.)	strĕ′-läts	streh′-lahts

strengthen

The pronunciation strĕn′-thən [stren′-thuhn], probably an infantilism, is not uncommon. It should, of course, be avoided.

Streoci (Yugosl.)	strĕ′-ô-tsĭ	streh′-o-tsi
Strešer (Yugosl., mt.)	strĕ′-shĕr	streh′-shehr
Strezlecki (Austral., mts.)	strĕz-lĕk′-ĭ	strez-lek′-i
Stri (Pol.) See *Stryj*.		
Štrice (Yugosl.)	shtrē′-tsĕ	shtree′-tseh
Strojkovce (Yugosl.)	stroi′-kôv-tsĕ	stroi′-kov-tseh

Stromboli (It., isl.)	strôm′-bô-lē	strom′-bo-lee
Strophades (Gr., isls.)	*Eng.* strō′-fə-dēz	stroh′-fuh-deez
	Gr. strô-fä′-*th*ĕs	stro-fah′-*th*es
Struer (Den.)	stro͞o′-ər	stroo′-uhr
Struga (Yugosl.)	stro͞o′-gä	stroo′-gah
Strugi (Rus.)	stro͞o′-gĭ	stroo′-gi
Struma (Balkan riv.)	stro͞o′-mä	stroo′-mah
Greek *Strouma* and *Strymon*, strē-môn′ [stree-mon′]. Turkish *Kara Sou*, kä-rä′ so͞o′ [kah-rah′ soo′].		
Strumica (Yugosl.)	stro͞o′-mĭ-tsä	stroo′-mi-tsah
Stryj (Pol.)	strē′	stree′
Russian spelling *Stri*.		
Strzałkowo (Pol.)	stzhäl-kô′-vô	stzhahl-ko′-vo
Stubica (Yugosl.)	sto͞o′-bĭ-tsä	stoo′-bi-tsah
Štubik (Yugosl.)	shto͞o′-bĭk	shtoo′-bik
Studenica (Yugosl.)	sto͞o′-dĕ′-nĭ-tsä	stoo′-deh′-ni-tsah
Studeničane (Yugosl.)	sto͞o′-dĕ-nē′-chä-nĕ	stoo′-deh-nee′-chah-neh
Stuka (Ger. plane)	*Eng.* stū′-kə	styoo′-kuh
	Ger. shto͞o′-kä	shtoo′-kah
Šturac (Yugosl., mt.)	shto͞o′-räts	shtoo′-rahts
Stuttgart (Ger.)	*Eng.* stŭt′-gärt	stuht′-gahrt
	Ger. shto͝ot′-gärt	shtut′-gahrt
Styr (Pol., riv.)	stĭr′	stihr′
Russian spelling *Stir*.		
Styria (Austria)	stĭr′-ĭ-ə	stihr′-i-uh
German *Steiermark*, shtīr′-märk [shtair′-mahrk].		
suave	swäv′ *or* swāv′	swahv′ *or* swayv′
The pronunciation swäv′ [swahv′] is more common in America, swāv′ [swayv′] in England. Cf. *strafe*.		
Subiaco (It.)	so͞o-byä′-kô	soo-byah′-ko
Subotica (Yugosl.)	so͞o′-bô′-tĭ-tsä	soo′-bo′-ti-tsah
Hungarian *Szabadka*, sŏ′-bŏt-kŏ [so′-bot-ko].		
Subotinac (Yugosl.)	so͞o′-bô′-tĭ-näts	soo′-bo′-ti-nahts
Suceava (Rum.)	so͝o-chä′-vä	su-chah′-vah
Suchan (Rus.)	so͞o-chän′	soo-chahn′
Su-chow (Ch., Kansu)	so͞o-jō	soo-joh
Sü-chow (Ch., N. Kiangsu)	shü-jō	shü-joh
Also spelled *Hsü-chow*.		
Su-chow (Ch., Kiangsu, near Shanghai) See *Soo-chow*.		
Suda (Crete, bay)	so͞o′-*th*ä	soo′-*th*ah
Also spelled *Souda*, q.v.		

Sudak (Rus.)	sōō-däk′	soo-dahk′
Sudeten (Cz., Ger.)	*Eng.* sōō-dāt′n	soo-dayt′n
	Ger. zōō-dā′-tən	zoo-day′-tuhn
English *Sudetes* (noun), sŏŏ-dē′-tēz [su-dee′-teez], and *Sudetic* (adj.), sŏŏ-dĕt′-ĭk [su-det′-ik]. The noun *Sudetens* was coined in 1938. For the history of this interesting word see the article by Prof. Franz H. Mautner in *American Speech*, XVIII (October, 1943), 200-207.		
Sudzha (Rus.)	sŏŏ-jä′	su-jah′
Sui-an (Ch., Chekiang)	swē-än	swee-ahn
Sui-ch'ang (Ch., Chekiang)	swē-chäng	swee-chahng
Sui-ch'wan (Ch., Kiangsi)	swē-chwän	swee-chwahn
Sui-fên(-ho) (Manchu.)	swā-fŭn(-hŭ)	sway-fuhn(-huh)
Sui-fu (Ch., Szechwan)	swā-fōō	sway-foo
Sui-yüan (Ch., prov.)	swā-yüän	sway-yü-ahn
Webster's, soi′-ywän′; BBC, swā-yŏŏ-ăn′. This province is also known as *Kweihwa-Suiyuan*, q.v.		
Sukabumi (NEI)	sōō-kä-bōō′-mē	soo-kah-boo′-mee
Sukhinichi (Rus.)	sōō-hē′-nĭ-chĭ	soo-hee′-ni-chi
Sukhum (Rus.)	sōō-hōōm′	soo-hoom′
Sukkertoppen (Greenl.)	sŏŏk′-ər-tôp′n	suk′-uhr-top′n
Sukkur (India)	sŭk′-ər	suhk′-uhr
Sukošan (Yugosl.)	sōō′-kô-shän	soo′-ko-shahn
Sula (Rus., riv.)	sōō′-lä	soo′-lah
Suldal (Nor.)	sŏŏl′-däl	sul′-dahl
Suleev (Pol.) See *Sulejów*.		
Sulejów (Pol.)	sŏŏ-lĕ′-yŏŏf	su-leh′-yuf
Russian *Suleev*, sŏŏ-lĕ′-yĕf [su-leh′-yef].		
Sulet (Yugosl.)	sōō′-lĕt	soo′-let
Italian *Solta*, q.v.		
Sulina (Rum.)	sŏŏ-lē′-nä	su-lee′-nah
Sulitjelma (Nor.)	sŏŏl-ē-tyĕl′-mä	sul-ee-tyel′-mah
Sulmona (It.)	sōōl-mô′-nä	sool-mo′-nah
Sultanabad (Iran)	sŏŏl-tä′-nə-bäd′	sul-tah′-nuh-bahd′
Also called *'Iraq*, ē-räk′ [ee-rahk′].		
Sulu (P.I.)	sōō′-lōō	soo′-loo
Šumadija (Yugosl.)	shōō′-mä′-dĭ-yä	shoo′-mah′-di-yah
Sumatra (NEI)	sŏŏ-mä′-trə	su-mah′-truh
Sumba (NEI) See *Soemba*.		
Sumbawa (NEI) See *Soembawa*.		
Sumprabum (Burma)	sŏŏm′-prä-bŏŏm′	sum′-prah-bum′
Sumy (Rus.)	sōō′-mĭ	soo′-mi

sund	so͝on′	sun′
An element, meaning *strait*, in Norwegian place names.		
Sunda *or* Soenda (NEI)	*Eng.* sŭn′-də	suhn′-duh
	Du. so͞on′-dä	soon′-dah
Sundalsoeyra *or* Sundalsöyra (Nor.)	so͝on′-däls-ûĭ-rä	sun′-dahls-œi-rah
Sunde, Arne (Nor. minister)	so͝on′-də, är′-nə	sun′-duh, ahr′-nuh
Sundstrom, Frank L. (U.S. representative)	sŭnd′-strəm	suhnd′-struhm
Sundsvall (Sw.)	so͝ons′-väl	suns′-vahl
Sundvollen (Nor.)	so͝on′-vôl-ən	sun′-vol-uhn
Suñer, Ramón Serrano (Sp. leader) See *Serrano Suñer, Ramón.*		
Sungari (Manchu., riv.)	*Eng.* so͞ong′-gə-rē′	soong′-guh-ree′
Sungaria (Ch., Sinkiang) See *Dzungaria.*		
Sung-tzŭ (Ch., Hupeh)	so͝ong-dzə	sung-dzuh
Also spelled *Sung-tze.*		
Sung-yang (Ch., Chekiang)	so͝ong-yäng	sung-yahng
Sunnhordland (Nor.)	so͝on′-hôr-län	sun′-hor-lahn
Sunnmoere *or* Sunnmöre (Nor.)	so͝on′-mû-rə	sun′-mœ-ruh
Suojärvi (Fin.)	so͝o′-ô′-yăr-vē	su′-o′-yehr-vee
Suomenlinna (Fin.)	so͝o′-ô′-mĕn-lĭn-nä	su′-o′-men-lin-nah
Swedish *Sveaborg,* svĕ′-ä-bôr′(y) [sveh′-ah-bor′(y)].		
Suomi See *Finland.*		
Suomussalmi (Fin.)	so͝o′-ô′-mo͝os-säl-mē	su′-o′-mus-sahl-mee
Supetar (Yugosl.)	so͞o′-pĕ′-tär	soo′-peh′-tahr
Italian *San Pietro della Brazza.*		
Suphli (Gr.) See *Souphlion.*		
Sura (Rus., riv.)	so͞o-rä′	soo-rah′
Surabaya *or* Soerabaja (NEI)	so͞o-rä-bä′-yä	soo-rah-bah′-yah
Surakarta (NEI) See *Soerakarta.*		
Surat (India, riv.)	so͝o-răt′ *or* so͞o′-rət	su-rat′ *or* soo′-ruht
Surazh (Rus.)	so͞o-räzh′	soo-rahzh′
Surcouf (Fr.)	sür-ko͞of′	sür-koof′
Surdulica (Yugosl.)	so͞or′-do͞o′-lĭ-tsä	soor′-doo′-li-tsah
Surigao (P.I.)	so͞o-rĭ-gou′	soo-ri-gau′
Surovikino (Rus.)	so͝o-rŏ-vē′-kĭ-nŏ	su-ro-vee′-ki-no
Susa (Tun.)	so͞o′-sä	soo′-sah
French *Sousse,* q.v.		
Sušac (It., isl.)	*S.-C.* so͞o′-shäts	soo′-shahts
Italian *Cazza,* q.v.		

Sušak (It., isl.)	*S.-C.* sōō′-shăk	soo′-shahk
Italian *Sansego*, q.v.		
Sušak (Yugosl.)	sōō′-shăk	soo′-shahk
Susitna (Alaska)	sōō-sĭt′-nə	soo-sit′-nuh
Sutlej (India, riv.)	sŭt′-lĕj	suht′-lej
Suursaari (Fin.)	sōōr′-sä-rē	soor′-sah-ree
Suvo Rudište (Yugosl., mt.)	sōō′-vô rōō′-dĭ-shtĕ	soo′-vo roo′-di-shteh
Suwałki (Pol.)	sŏŏ-väl′-kĭ	su-vahl′-ki
Russian spelling *Suvalki*.		
Suzdal (Rus.)	sōōz′-däl(y)	sooz′-dahl(y)
Svalava (Cz.)	svä′-lyä-vä	svah′-lyah-vah
Hungarian *Szolyva*, sô′ĭ-vŏ [so′i-vo].		
Svanvik (Nor.)	svän′-vēk	svahn′-veek
Svartisen (Nor., glacier)	svärt′-ē-sən	svahrt′-ee-suhn
Sveaborg (Fin.) See *Suomenlinna*.		
Svecha (Rus.)	svĕ-chä′ (locally -tsä′)	sveh-chah′ (locally -tsah′)
Svelvik (Nor.)	svĕl′-vēk	svel′-veek
Svendborg (Den.)	svĕn′-bôr	sven′-bor
Svenska Dagbladet (Sw. newspaper)	svĕns′-kä däg′-blä′-dət	svens′-kah dahg′-blah′-duht
Šventoyi (Lith., riv.)	shvĕn-tô′-yē	shven-to′-yee
Sventsyani (Pol.) See *Swięciany*.		
Sverdlovsk (Rus.)	svĕrd-lôfsk′	svehrd-lofsk′
Sveti Grgur (Yugosl., isl.)	svĕ′-tĭ gər′-gōōr	sveh′-ti guhr′-goor
Italian *Gregorio*, grĕ-gô′-ryô [greh-go′-ryo].		
Sveti Juraj (Yugosl.)	svĕ′-tĭ yōō′-rī	sveh′-ti yoo′-rai
Italian *San Giorgio*, sän jôr′-jô [sahn jor′-jo].		
Sveti Lovrenc (Yugosl.)	svĕ′-tĭ lô′-vrĕnts	sveh′-ti lo′-vrents
Sveti Marko (Yugosl., isl.)	svĕ′-tĭ mär′-kô	sveh′-ti mahr′-ko
Italian *Stradiotti*, q.v.		
Sveti Naum (Yugosl.)	svĕ′-tĭ nä′-ōōm	sveh′-ti nah′-oom
Sveti Petar (It., isl.)	*S.-C.* svĕ′-tĭ pĕ′-tär	sveh′-ti peh′-tahr
Italian *Asinello*, q.v.		
Sveto Brdo (Yugosl.)	svĕ′-tô bər′-dô	sveh′-to buhr′-do
Svilajnac (Yugosl.)	svē′-lī-näts	svee′-lai-nahts
Svir (Pol.) See *Świr*.		
Svirstroi (Rus.)	svēr′-stroi′	sveer′-stroi′
Svishtov (Bulg.)	svĭsh′-tŏf	svish′-tof
Rumanian *Şiştov*, shĭsh′-tôf [shish′-tof].		
Svisloch (Pol.) See *Świsłocz*.		
Svityaz (Pol.) See *Świtaź*.		

Sviyagino (Rus.)	svĭ-yä′-gĭ-nŏ	svi-yah′-gi-no
Svoboda (Rus.)	svŏ-bô′-dä	svo-bo′-dah
Svobodny (Rus.)	svŏ-bôd′-nĭ	svo-bod′-ni
Svojinovo (Yugosl.)	svô′-yĭ-nô-vô	svo′-yi-no-vo
Svolvær (Nor.)	svôl′-văr	svol′-vehr
Svrljig (Yugosl.)	svər′-lyĭg	svuhr′-lyig
Svrljiški Timok (Yugosl., riv.)	svər′-lyĭsh-kĭ tē′-môk	svuhr′-lyish-ki tee′-mok
Swa (Burma, riv.)	swä′	swah′
Swatow (Ch., Kwang-tung)	*Eng.* swä-tou	swah-tau
Chinese *Shan-t'ow*, q.v.		
Swevezeele (Belg.)	swā′-və-zā′-lə	sway′-vuh-zay′-luh
Świca (Pol., riv.)	shvē′-tsä	shvee′-tsah
Swięciany (Pol.)	shvyăN-chä′-nĭ	shvyaN-chah′-ni
Russian *Sventsyani*, svĕn-tsyä′-nĭ [sven-tsyah′-ni].		
Swinemuende *or* Swinemünde (Ger.)	svē′-nə-mün′-də	svee′-nuh-mün′-duh
Świnica (Pol., Cz., mt.)	*Pol.* shvĭ-nē′-tsä	shvi-nee′-tsah
Świr (Pol.	shvēr′	shveer′
Russian *Svir*, svēr′ [sveer′].		
Świsłocz (Pol.)	shvē′-slôch	shvee′-sloch
Russian *Svisloch*, svē′-slŏch [svee′-sloch].		
Świtaź (Pol.)	shvē′-täzh	shvee′-tahzh
Russian *Svityaz*, svē′-tyäz [svee′-tyahz].		
Sychevka (Rus.)	sĭ-chôf′-kä	si-chof′-kah
Syevernaya (Rus.)	Variant of *Severnaya*, q.v.	
Sylt (Ger., isl.)	sĭlt′	silt′
Syme (Dodec.)	sē′-mē	see′-mee
Syracuse (U.S.A.)	*Eng.* sĭr′-ə-kūs	sihr′-uh-kyoos
	or sĭr′-ə-kūz	sihr′-uh-kyooz
Italian *Siracusa*, q.v.		
Syriam (Burma)	sĭ′-rĭ-ăm	si′-ri-am
Syrmia (Yugosl.)	*Eng.* sûr′-myə	suhr′-myuh
Serb-Croat *Srem*, srĕm′ [srem′]. Hungarian *Szerém*, sĕ′-rām [seh′-raym].		
Syros (Gr., isl.)	sē′-rô(s)	see′-ro(s)
Syzran (Rus.)	sĭz-rän′(y)	siz-rahn′(y)
Szabadka (Yugosl.)	See *Subotica*.	
Szamos (Hung., Rum., riv.)	sŏ′-môsh	so′-mosh
Szamotuły (Pol.)	shä-mô-to͝o′-lĭ	shah-mo-tu′-li
Szarvas (Hung.)	sŏr′-vŏsh	sor′-vosh

Szczakowa (Pol.)	shchä-kô′-vä	shchah-ko′-vah
Szczara (Pol., riv.)	shchä′-rä	shchah′-rah
Russian spelling *Shchara*.		
Szczawnica (Pol.)	shchäv-nē′-tsä	shchahv-nee′-tsah
Szczuczyn (Pol.)	shcho͝o′-chĭn	shchu′-chin
Russian spelling *Shchuchin*.		
Szeben (Rum.) See *Sibiu*.		
Szê-ch'wan (Ch., prov.)	*Eng.* sĕ-chwän	seh-chwahn
	Ch. sŭ-chwän	suh-chwahn
Szeged (Hung.)	sĕ′-gĕd	seh′-ged
Székelyudvarhely (Rum.)	See *Odorhei*.	
Székesfehérvar (Hung.)	sā′-kĕsh-fĕ′-hār-vär	say′-kesh-feh′-hayr-vahr
Szekszárd (Hung.)	sĕk′-särd	sek′-sahrd
Szentes (Hung.)	sĕn′-tĕsh	sen′-tesh
Szentgotthárd (Hung.)	sĕnt-gôt′-härt	sent-got′-hahrt
English *Saint Gotthard*, q.v.		
Szentgyörgyi, Albert (Hung. leader)	sĕn′-dyûr-dyĭ, ŏl′-bĕrt	sen′-dyœr-dyi. ol′-behrt
Szepesh (Cz.) See *Spiš*.		
Szerencs (Hung.)	sĕ′-rĕnch	seh′-rench
Szigeti, Joseph	*Eng.* sĭ-gĕt′-ĭ	si-get′-i
(Hung. violinist)	*Hung.* sĭ′-gĕ-tĭ	si′-geh-ti
Szigetvár (Hung.)	sĭ′-gĕt-vär	si′-get-vahr
Szkwa (Pol., riv.)	shkvä′	shkvah′
Russian spelling *Shkva*.		
Szolnok (Hung.)	sôl′-nôk	sol′-nok
Szombathely (Hung.)	sôm′-bät-hā *or* -hĕ(y)	som′-baht-hay
Szopienice (Pol.)	shô-pyĕ-nē′-tsĕ	sho-pyeh-nee′-tseh
Szydłowiec (Pol.)	shĭ-dlô′-vyĕts	shi-dlo′-vyets
Russian *Shidlovets*, shĭ-dlô′-vĕts [shi-dlo′-vets].		
Tabanovci (Yugosl.)	tä′-bä′-nôv-tsĭ	tah′-bah′-nov-tsi
Tabar (Oc.)	tä-bär′	tah-bahr′
Tabarca (Tun.)	tä-bär′-kä	tah-bahr′-kah
The accent of the ancient *Thabraca* would fall on the first syllable.		
Taber, John (U.S. representative)	tā′-bər	tay′-buhr
Tabiteuea (Oc.)	tä′-bē-tĕ′-o͞o-ĕ′-ä	tah′-bee-teh′-oo-eh′-ah
Tabor (Cz.)	tä′-bôr	tah′-bor
Tabriz (Iran)	tä-brēz′	tah-breez′
Tacloban (P.I.)	tä-klô′-bän	tah-klo′-bahn

Tadjerouine (Tun.)	tä-jĕr-wēn′	tah-jehr-ween′
Tafaraoui (Alg.)	tä-fä-rä′-wē	tah-fah-rah′-wee
Tagalog (P.I.)	tä-gä′-lŏg	tah-gah′-log

Also *Tagal*, tä-gäl′ [tah-gahl′].

Taganrog (Rus.)	tä-gän-rôk′	tah-gahn-rok′
Tagbilaran (P.I.)	täg-bē-lä′-rän	tahg-bee-lah′-rahn
Tagiura (Libya)	tä-jōō′-rä	tah-joo′-rah
Tagus (Port., Sp., riv.)	*Eng.* tā′-gəs	tay′-guhs

Portuguese *Tejo*, tĕ′-zhŏŏ [teh′-zhu]. Spanish *Tajo*, tä′-hô [tah′-ho].

Tah-ch'êng (Ch., Sinkiang)	tä-chŭng	tah-chuhng

Also spelled *T'a-ch'eng*. Also called *Chuguchak*, q.v.

Ta-hei-ho (Manchu.)	dä-hā-hŭ	dah-hay-huh
Tahiti (Oc.)	tä-hē′-tē	tah-hee′-tee
	or tī′-tē	tai′-tee

The former is the older pronunciation, but by 1903, according to Prof. Henry E. Crampton, the accent had shifted to the first syllable in the natives' pronunciation, the intervocalic *h* had weakened, and the word in effect became dissyllabic with a very long first syllable. The name of Chief *Opuhara* changed in the same way from ô-pōō-hä′-rä [o-poo-hah′-rah] to ô-pōō′-hä-rä [o-poo′-hah-rah] *or* ô-pōō′-rä [o-poo′-rah]. The great King *Pomare*, once called pô-mä′-rĕ [po-mah′-reh] was referred to as pô′-mä-rĕ [po′-mah-reh]. Such shifting of accent in native speech may account for the contradictory information we receive, as for instance, in the case of *Rabaul* and *Tarawa*. And it is always well to remember that in most languages of the world, including the Austronesian, the stress accent of English is quite out of place. For one thing it is much too heavy. Usually what we would consider a level stressing of all the vowels approaches a native pronunciation more closely than undue emphasis upon any one of them. Still over the American radio we must speak American English! Of the two pronunciations of *Tahiti*, the older, stressed on the second syllable, is probably what most of our listeners expect to hear. When our soldiers and sailors return from the South Seas, they may change the standard.

Tai Chi-t'ao (Ch. leader)	dī jē-tou	dai jee-tau
Tai-chow (Ch., Chekiang)	*Eng.* tī-chou	tai-chau
	Ch. tī-jō	tai-joh
Tai Hang Shan *or* Tai Hang Mts. (Ch., Shansi, Hopei, Honan)	tī-häng	tai-hahng
T'ai-ho-k'u (Formosa)	*Eng.* tī-hō′-kōō	tai-hoh′-koo
	Ch. tī-hŭ-kōō	tai-huh-koo

Chinese *T'ai-p'eh*, tī-pĕ [tai-peh].

T'ai-hŭ (Ch., Kiangsi)	tī-hŭ	tai-huh
Taikkyi (Burma)	tīk'-chē'	taik'-chee'
Taikyu (Korea)	tī-kū	tai-kyoo
Tainaron (Gr., cape)	tĕ'-nä-rô(n)	teh'-nah-ro(n)
Also called *Kavo Matapas*, kä'-vô mä-tä-päs' [kah'-vo mah-tah-pahs'].		
Taira (Jap.)	tī-rä	tai-rah
T'ai-p'eh (Formosa) See *T'ai-ho-k'u.*		
Taishet (Rus.)	tī-shĕt'	tai-shet'
Taitsy (Rus.)	tī'-tsĭ	tai'-tsi
T'ai-wan (isl.) See *Formosa.*		
T'ai-yüan (Ch., Shansi)	tī-yüän	tai-yü-ahn
Also called *Yang-ch'ü*, q.v.		
Tajo (Port., Sp., riv.) See *Tagus.*		
Tak (Thai)	täk'	tahk'
Taka (Oc.)	tä'-kä	tah'-kah
Takil (Rus.)	tä-kēl'	tah-keel'
Takrouna (Tun.)	täk-rōō'-nä	tahk-roo'-nah
Takuapa (Thai)	tŭ'-kwä-pä'	tuh'-kwah-pah'
Talasea (Oc.)	tä-lä-sĕ'-ä	tah-lah-seh'-ah
Talaud (NEI)	tä'-lout	tah'-laut
Also called *Talaur*, tä-lour' [tah-laur'].		
Talbot (Austral., cape)	tôl'-bət	tol'-buht
Taldom (Rus.)	täl-dôm'	tahl-dom'
Ta-li (Ch., Shansi, Yünnan)	dä-lē	dah-lee
Ta-lien(-wan) (Manchu.)	dä-lyĕn(-wän)	dah-lyen(-wahn)
Also called *Dairen*, q.v.		
Talkeetna (Alaska)	tăl'-kēt'-nə	tal'-keet'-nuh
Talle, Henry O. (U.S. representative)	tä'-lē	tah'-lee
Tallinn (Est.)	täl'-lĭn	tahl'-lin
Russian *Revel*, q.v.		
Talovaya (Rus.)	tä-lŏ-vä'-yä	tah-lo-vah'-yah
Talsi (Latvia)	täl'-sē	tahl'-see
Russian *Talsen*, täl(y)'-sĕn [tahl(y)'-sen].		
Taman (Rus., pen.)	tä-män'(y)	tah-mahn'(y)
Tamatam (Oc.)	tä'-mä-täm	tah'-mah-tahm
Also called *Pulap*, q.v.		
Tamatave (Madag.)	tä-mä-täv'	tah-mah-tahv'
If this name stays in the news, it will become tăm'-ə-tāv' [tam'-uh-tayv'].		
Tambov (Rus.)	täm-bôf'	tahm-bof'
Tambu (Oc., mt.)	täm'-bōō	tahm'-boo

Tamezred (Tun.)	tä-mĕz-rĕd′	tah-mez-red′
Tamil (India)	tăm′-ĭl	tam′-il
Tamiš (Balkan riv.)	*S.-C.* tä′-mĭsh	tah′-mish
Rumanian *Timişul*, q.v.		
Tampere (Fin.)	täm′-pĕ-rĕ	tahm′-peh-reh
Swedish *Tammerfors*, täm′-mər-fôrs′ [tahm′-muhr-fors′].		
Tampico (Mex.)	*Eng.* tăm-pē′-kō	tam-pee′-koh
	Sp. täm-pē′-kô	tahm-pee′-ko
The English pronunciation is so well established that it should be preferred in English reports.		
Tamsalu (Est.)	täm′-sä-lo͞o	tahm′-sah-loo
Tana (Nor.)	tä′-nä	tah′-nah
Tanabuli (Oc.)	tä-nä-bo͞o′-lē	tah-nah-boo′-lee
Tanambogo (Oc.)	tä-näm-bô′-gô	tah-nahm-bo′-go
Tanana (Alaska)	tăn′-ə-nŏ	tan′-uh-no
Tananarive (Madag.)	tä-nä-nä-rēv′	tah-nah-nah-reev′
Ţăndăre (Rum.)	tsən-də-rā′	tsuhn-duh-ray′
Tandjoeng Selor (NEI)	tän′-jo͝ong sĕ′-lôr	tahn′-jung seh′-lor
Tanga (Oc.)	täng′-ä	tahng′-ah
Tangerang (NEI)	täng-ə-räng′	tahng-uh-rahng′
Tangier (Sp. Mor.)	tăn-jĭr′	tan-jihr′
Tangkoebang Prahoe (NEI)	täng′-ko͞o-bäng prä′-o͞o	tahng′-koo-bahng prah′-oo
Tangoucha (Tun.)	tän-go͞o′-shä	tahn-goo′-shah
Also called *Djebel Tangouch*, q.v.		
Tang-shan (Ch., Kiangsu)	däng-shän	dahng-shahn
Tang-yang (Ch., Hupeh)	däng-yäng	dahng-yahng
Tanimbar (NEI)	tä-nĭm′-bär	tah-nim′-bahr
Also spelled *Tenimbar*, q.v.		
Tanjong Pandan (NEI)	tän-jŏng pän′-dän	tahn-jong pahn′-dahn
Tanjong Priok (NEI)	tän′-jŏng prē′-ŏk	tahn′-jong pree′-ok
Tanner, Väinö A. (Fin. leader)	tän′-nĕr, vī′-nû	tahn′-nehr, vai′-nœ
Tannu Tuva (Rus. protec.)	tän′-no͝o to͝o-vä′	tahn′-nu tu-vah′
Tanta (Egypt)	tän′-tä	tahn′-tah
Taongi (Oc.)	tä-ông′-ē	tah-ong′-ee
Also called *Pokaakku*, q.v.		
Taormina (Sicily)	tä′-ôr-mē′-nä	tah′-or-mee′-nah
Tap (Rus., lake)	täp′	tahp′
Tapa (Est.)	tä′-pä	tah′-pah
Russian *Taps*, q.v.		
Tapoly (Cz., Hung., riv.)	See *Topl'a.*	

Taps (Est.)	*Rus.* täps′	tahps′
Estonian *Tapa*, q.v.		
Taptugara (Rus.)	täp-tōō-gä′-rä	tahp-too-gah′-rah
Tapuaemanu (Oc.)	tä-pōō-ä-ĕ-mä′-nōō	tah-poo-ah-eh-mah′-noo
Taqa, el (Egypt)	tä′-kä, ĕt	tah′-kah, et
Tarakan (NEI)	tä-rä-kän′	tah-rah-kahn′
Taranto (It.)	tä′-rän-tô	tah′-rahn-to
Classical *Tarentum*, tä-rĕn′-tŏŏm [tah-ren′-tum].		
Tarawa (Oc.)	*Eng.* tä-rä′-wä	tah-rah′-wah
	native tä-rä-wä′	tah-rah-wah′
	or tä′-rä-wä′	tah′-rah-wah′

For the native pronunciation the Royal Geographical Society places an accent on the last syllable and the U.S. Board on Geographical names follows suit. Former Senator Hiram Bingham in a letter to the New York Times, November 28, says that while his father was missionary to the islands the accent was on the first syllable. Lippincott's New Gazetteer places a secondary accent on the first syllable and a primary accent on the last syllable. It remains to be seen whether the recent Englishing with accent on the second syllable is the form that will persist in the English-speaking world. See the remarks at *Tahiti*. Note also that *Kanaka* may be accented on the first or on the second syllable.

Tarbes (Fr.)	tärb′	tahrb′
Tarcoola (Austral.)	tär-kōō′-lə	tahr-koo′-luh
Tarentum (It.)	tä-rĕn′-tŏŏm	tah-ren′-tum
Italian *Taranto*, tä′-rän-tô [tah′-rahn-to].		
Târgoviște (Rum.)	tûr′-gô-vēsh′-tĕ	tuhr′-go-veesh′-teh
Târgul Jiu (Rum.)	tûr′-gŏŏl zhē′-ŏŏ	tuhr′-gul-zhee′-u
Târgu and *Târgul* are variants, the *-l* being the article.		
Târgul Mureș (Rum.)	tûr′-gŏŏl mŏŏ′-rĕsh	tuhr′-gul mu′-resh
Hungarian *Marosvásárhely*, mŏ′-rôsh-vä′-shär-hā [mo′-rosh-vah′-shahr-hay].		
Târgul Ocna (Rum.)	tûr′-gŏŏl ôk′-nä	tuhr′-gul ok′-nah
Târgul Săcuesc (Rum.)	tûr′-gŏŏl sə-kwĕsk′	tuhr′-gul suh-kwesk′
Tarhuna (Libya)	tär-hōō′-nä	tahr-hoo′-nah
Tarifa (Sp.)	tä-rē′-fä	tah-ree′-fah
Tarn (Fr., riv.)	tärn′	tahrn′
Tarnobrzeg (Pol.)	tär-nôb′-zhĕk	tahr-nob′-zhek
Tarnopol (Pol.)	*Pol.* tär-nô′-pôl	tahr-no′-pol
	Rus. tär′-nŏ-pŏl(y)	tahr′-no-pol(y)
Tarnów (Pol.)	tär′-nŏŏf	tahr′-nuf
Tarnowitz (Pol.) See *Tarnowskie Góry*.		

Tarnowskie Góry (Pol.)	tär-nôf′-skyĕ go͝o′-rĭ	tahr-nof′-skyeh gu′-ri
German *Tarnowitz*, tär′-nô-vĭts [tahr′-no-vits].		
Taroa (Oc.)	tä-rô′-ä	tah-ro′-ah
Tarquinia (It.)	tär-kwē′-nyä	tahr-kwee′-nyah
Tarragona (Sp.)	tä-rä-gô′-nä	tah-rah-go′-nah
Tartu (Est.)	tär′-to͞o	tahr′-too
Russian *Jurjev*, q.v., or *Yurev*. German *Dorpat*, q.v.		
Tashkent (Rus.)	täsh-kĕnt′	tahsh-kent′
Tasman Sea (Austral.)	tăz′-mən	taz′-muhn
Tasmania (Austral.)	tăz-mā′-nĭ-ə	taz-may′-ni-uh
Tătărăşti (Rum.)	tə-tə-rûsht′	tuh-tuh-ruhsht′
Also called *Tărtar Bunar*, tə-tär′ bo͝o-när′ [tuh-tahr′ bu-nahr′].		
Tatar Pazardzhik (Bulg.)	tä-tär′ pä-zär-jēk′	tah-tahr′ pah-zahr-jeek′
Tatarski (Rus., strait)	tä-tär′-skĭ	tah-tahr′-ski
Tatau (Oc.)	tä-tou′	tah-tau′
Tatoï (Gr.)	tä-toi′	tah-toi′
Tatra, High (Cz., Pol., mts.)	*Eng.* tä′-trä, hī′	tah′-trah, hai′
Tatsinskaya (Rus.)	tä-tsĭn′-skä-yä	tah-tsin′-skah-yah
Ta-t'ung (Ch., Chinghai, Shansi)	dä-to͝ong	dah-tung
Ta-tung-kow (Manchu.)	*Eng.* tä-to͝ong-kou	tah-tung-kau
	Ch. dä-do͝ong-gō	dah-dung-goh
Taungbaw (Burma)	toung′-bô′	taung′-baw′
Taungdwingyi (Burma)	toung-dwĭn-jē′	taung-dwin-jee′
Taunggyi (Burma)	toung′-jē′	taung′-jee′
Taungup (Burma)	toung′-o͝op′	taung′-up′
Tauragė (Lith.)	tou-rä-gā′	tau-rah-gay′
German *Tauroggen*, tou-rôg′-ən [tau-rog′-uhn].		
Tauroggen (Lith.) See *Tauragė*, q.v.		
Taus (Cz.) See *Domažlice*.		
Tauu (Oc.)	tou′-o͞o	tau′-oo
Tavanatangir (Oc.)	tä-vä-nä-täng′-ēr	tah-vah-nah-tahng′-eer
Tavolzhanka (Rus.)	tä-vŏl-zhän′-kä	tah-vol-zhahn′-kah
Tavoularis, G. (Gr. collab.)	tä-vo͞o-lä′-rēs	tah-voo-lah′-rees
Tavoy (Burma)	tə-voi′	tuh-voi′
Tawi Tawi (P.I.)	tä′-wē tä′-wē	tah′-wee tah′-wee
Tawngpeng (Burma)	tông′-pĕng′	tawng′-peng′
Tayabas (P.I.)	tä-yä′-bäs	tah-yah′-bahs

Taygetos (Gr., mt.)	tī′-yĕ-tôs	tai′-yeh-tos
Ta-yü (Ch., Kiangsi)	dä-yü	dah-yü
Tazov (Rus.)	tä′-zŏf	tah′-zof
Tbilisi (Rus.) See *Tiflis.*		
Tchad (Afr., lake)	chăd′	chad′
Tczew (Pol.)	tchĕf′	tchef′
German *Dirschau*, dĭr′-shou [dihr′-shau].		
T'ê-an (Ch., Kiangsi)	tŭ-än	tuh-ahn
Tebessa (Alg.)	*Eng.* tĕ-bĕs′-ə	teh-bes′-uh
	Fr. tĕ-bĕ-sä′	teh-beh-sah′
Teboulba (Tun.)	tə-bo͞ol′-bä	tuh-bool′-bah
Tebourba (Tun.)	tə-bo͞or′-bä	tuh-boor′-bah
Teboursouk (Tun.)	tə-bo͞or-so͞ok′	tuh-boor-sook′
Techa (Libya)	tĕ′-kä	teh′-kah
Tê-ch'ing (Ch., Chekiang)	dŭ-chĭng	duh-ching
Tecuci (Rum.)	tĕ-ko͝och′	teh-kuch′
Tegal (NEI)	tĕ-gäl′	teh-gahl′
Tegelen (Neth.)	tā′-k(h)ə-lən	tay′-k(h)uh-luhn
Tehran *or* Teheran (Iran)	*Per.* tĕ-hrän′	teh-hrahn′
	Eng. tĕ-ə-rän′ *or* -răn′	teh-uh-rahn′ *or* -ran′
	or tĭ-ə-răn′ *or* -rän′	ti-uh-ran′ *or* -rahn′
T'ê-hsing (Ch., Kiangsi)	tŭ-shĭng	tuh-shing
Tejo (Port., Sp., riv.) See *Tagus.*		
Tekija (Yugosl.)	tĕ′-kĭ-yä	teh′-ki-yah
Tekirdağ (Turk.)	tĕ-kēr′-dä	teh-keer′-dah
Greek *Rodosto*, q.v.		
Telechany (Pol.)	tĕ-lĕ-hä′-nĭ	teh-leh-hah′-ni
Russian spelling *Telekhani.*		
Telemark (Nor.)	tĕl′-ə-märk	tel′-uh-mahrk
Teleneşti (Rum.)	tĕ-lĕ-nĕsht′	teh-leh-nesht′
Teleorman (Rum.)	tĕ′-lyôr-män′	teh′-lyor-mahn′
Tell el Eisa (Egypt)	tĕl′ ĕl ä-ē′-sä	tel′ el ah-ee′-sah
Tell el Makh Kkad (Egypt)	tĕl′ ĕl mäk′ käd′	tel′ el mahk′ kahd′
Teloek-betceng *or* Telok-betong (NEI)	tə-lo͞ok′-bĕ-to͝ong′ *or* tə-lŏk′-bĕ-tŏng′	tuh-look′-beh-tung′ tuh-lok′-beh-tong′
Telschi (Lith.) See *Telšiai.*		
Telšiai (Lith.)	tĕl-shyī′	tel-shyai′
Russian *Telschi*, tĕl′(y)-shĭ [tel′(y)-shi].		
Temerin (Yugosl.)	tĕ′-mĕ-rĭn	teh′-meh-rin
Temerza (Tun.)	tĕ-mĕr′-zä	teh-mehr′-zah
Temes (Balkan riv.) See *Timişul.*		

Temesvár (Rum.)	*Hung.* tĕ′-mĕsh-vär	teh′-mesh-vahr
Rumanian *Timişoara*, q.v.		
Temišvar (Rum.) See *Timişoara*.		
Temnac (Alaska, Attu)	tĕm′-năk′	tem′-nak′
Temnić (Yugosl.)	tĕm′-nĭch	tem′-nich
Tempelhof (Ger., Berlin)	tĕm′-pəl-hōf	tem′-puhl-hohf
Temryuk (Rus.)	tĕm-rūk′	tem-ryook′
Temryukski Zaliv (Rus.)	tĕm-rūk′-skĭ zä-lēf′	tem-ryook′-ski zah-leef′
Temštica (Yugosl.)	tĕm′-shtĭ-tsä	tem′-shti-tsah
Tenaru (Oc., riv.)	tĕ-nä′-rōō	teh-nah′-roo
Tendanye (New Guinea)	tĕn-dän′-yĕ	ten-dahn′-yeh
T'êng-ch'ung (Ch., Yünnan)	tŭng-chŏŏng	tuhng-chung
Also called *T'eng-yüeh*, q.v., and *Momein*, q.v.		
Tengeder (Libya)	tĕn-jĕ-dĕr′	ten-jeh-dehr′
T'êng-yüeh (Ch., Yünnan)	tŭng-yüĕ	tuhng-yü-eh
Also called *T'eng-ch'ung*, q.v., and *Momein*, q.v.		
Tenimbar (NEI)	tĕ-nĭm′-bär	teh-nim′-bahr
Also spelled *Tanimbar*, q.v.		
Tenos (Gr., isl.)	tē′-nô(s)	tee′-no(s)
Tepelena (Alb.) See *Tepelenë*.		
Tepelenë (Alb.)	tĕ-pĕ-lĕ′-nə	teh-peh-leh′-nuh
Teplice Šanov (Cz.)	tĕ′-plĭ-tsĕ shä′-nôf	teh′-pli-tseh shah′-nof
Teplo Pristanište (Yugosl.)	tĕ′-plô prē′-stä-nĭ-shtĕ	teh′-plo pree′-stah-ni-shteh
Teramo (It.)	tĕ′-rä-mô	teh′-rah-mo
Terbuf (Alb., lake)	*Eng.* tûr′-bōōf	tuhr′-boof
Albanian *Knetë e Tërbufit.*		
Terceira (Azores)	tĕr-sā′-rə	tehr-say′-ruh
Teregova (Rum.)	tĕ-rĕ-gô′-vä	teh-reh-go′-vah
Terek (Rus., riv.)	tĕ′-rĕk	teh′-rek
Teresina (Brazil)	tĕ-rĭ-zē′-nə	teh-ri-zee′-nuh
Terezin (Cz.)	tĕ′-rĕ-zĭn	teh′-reh-zin
Terespol (Pol.)	tĕ-rĕ′-spôl	teh-reh′-spol
Tergnier (Fr.)	tĕr-nyĕ′	tehr-nyeh′
Terijoki (Fin.)	tĕ′-rē-yô-kē	teh′-ree-yo-kee
Terkoz (Turk., lagoon)	tĕr′-kôz′	tehr′-koz′
Termini Imerese (Sicily)	tĕr′-mē-nē ē-mĕ-rĕ′-zĕ	tehr′-mee-nee ee-meh-reh′-zeh
Termoli (It.)	tĕr′-mô-lē	tehr′-mo-lee
Ternate (NEI)	tĕr-nä′-tĕ	tehr-nah′-teh

Terneuzen (Neth.)	tər-nû′-zən	tuhr-nœ′-zuhn
Ter Poorten, Hein (Du. leader)	tər pōr′-tən, hīn′	tuhr pohr′-tuhn, hain′
Terpsithea (Gr.)	tĕr-psē-thĕ′-ä	tehr-psee-theh′-ah
Terracina (It.)	tĕr-rä-chē′-nä	tehr-rah-chee′-nah
Terralba (Sard.)	tĕr-räl′-bä	tehr-rahl′-bah
Terranova (It.)	tĕr-rä-nô′-vä	tehr-rah-no′-vah
Terravecchia (It.)	tĕr-rä-vĕk′-kyä	tehr-rah-vek′-kyah
Terschelling (Neth., isl.)	tər-sk(h)ĕl′-ĭng	tuhr-sk(h)el′-ing
Teruel (Sp.)	tĕr-wĕl′	tehr-wel′
Tešanj (Yugosl.)	tĕ′-shän(y)	teh′-shahn(y)
Teschen (Cz., Pol.)	*Ger.* tĕsh′-ən	tesh′-uhn
Czech *Těšín*, q.v., Polish *Cieszyn*, q.v.		
Tešica (Yugosl.)	tĕ′-shĭ-tsä	teh′-shi-tsah
Těšín (Cz., Pol.)	*Cz.* tyĕ′-shēn	tyeh′-sheen
German *Teschen*, q.v.		
Tessel (Neth., isl.)	tĕs′-əl	tes′-uhl
For another spelling and an English pronunciation, see *Texel.*		
Testour (Tun.)	tĕs-to͞or′	tes-toor′
Teterev (Rus., riv.)	tĕ′-tĕ-rĕf	teh′-teh-ref
Teteven (Bulg.)	tĕ′-tĕ-vĕn(y)	teh′-teh-ven(y)
Tetipari (Oc.)	tĕ-tē-pä′-rē	teh-tee-pah′-ree
Tetschen (Cz.)	*Ger.* tĕt′-shən	tet′-shuhn
Czech *Děčín*, q.v.		
Tetyukhi (Rus.)	tĕ-tū′-hĭ	teh-tyoo′-hi
Tevai (Oc.)	tĕ-vī′	teh-vai′
Tevere (It., riv.)	tĕ′-vĕ-rĕ	teh′-veh-reh
English *Tiber*, tī′-bər [tai′-buhr], should be preferred in an English context.		
Texel (Neth., isl.)	*Eng.* tĕk′-səl	tek′-suhl
	Du. tĕs′-əl	tes′-uhl
Also spelled *Tessel*, q.v.		
Thai *or* Siam	tī′ *or* sī-ăm′	tai′ *or* sai-am′
Thakhek (Indo-Ch.)	tä-kĕk′	tah-kek′
Thala (Tun.)	tä′-lä	tah′-lah
Thalia	*given name* thāl′-yə	thayl′-yuh
	Muse thə-lī′-ə	thuh-lai′-uh
Thanbyuzayat (Burma)	thən-bū-zə-yŭt′	thuhn-byoo-zuh-yuht′
Meaning *corrugated-iron rest-house.* In contrast is *Shwedaung*, q.v., meaning *golden peacock.*		
Thanh-hoa (Indo-Ch.)	tän(y)-whä′	tahn(y)-whah′
Thar (India, desert)	tär′ *or* tŭr′	tahr′ *or* tuhr′
Thargominda (Austral.)	thär′-gō-mĭn′-də	thahr′-goh-min′-duh

Tharnes (Alb., pass)	*Eng.* thär′-nĕs	thahr′-nes
Tharrawaddy (Burma)	thă-rə-wŏd′-ĭ	tha-ruh-wod′-i
Thasos (Gr., isl.)	thä′-sô(s)	thah′-so(s)
Thaton (Burma)	thə-tōn′	thuh-tohn′
Thayetkon (Burma)	thə-yĕt′-kōn′	thuh-yet′-kohn′
Thayetmyo (Burma)	thə-yĕt′-myō′	thuh-yet′-myoh′
Thazi (Burma)	thä′-zē′	thah′-zee′
the before consonants	*th*ə	*th*uh
before ū [yoo]	*th*ə	*th*uh
before vowels	*th*ĭ	*th*i
Avoid the overemphatic "thee." Compare the remarks on the indefinite article, *a.*		
Thebes (Gr.)	thēbs′	theebs′
Greek *Thevai,* thē′-vĕ [thee′-veh].		
Theiss (Europ. riv.) See *Tisza.*		
Thelepte (Tun.)	tĕ-lĕp′-tĕ	teh-lep′-teh
Theodore (Alaska, Attu)	thē′-ō-dōr	thee′-oh-dohr
Russian *Feodor.*		
Theodoroi, Agioi (Crete)	thĕ-ô′-*th*ô-rē, ī′-yē	theh-o′-*th*o-ree, ai′-yee
Also called *Thodoroi,* thô′-*th*ô-rē [tho′-*th*o-ree].		
Theodoros, Agios (Crete, isl.)	thĕ-ô′-*th*ô-rôs, ī′-yôs	theh-o′-*th*o-ros, ai′-yos
Also called *Thodorou,* thô-*th*ô-ro͞o′ [tho-*th*o-roo′].		
Theofanides, Stavros (Gr. leader)	thĕ-ô-fä-nē′-*th*ēs, stä′-vrôs	theh-o-fah-nee′-*th*ees, stah′-vros
Theophilou (Crete, point)	thĕ-ô-fē′-lo͞o	theh-o-fee′-loo
Thera (Gr., isl.)	thē′-rä	thee′-rah
Also called *Santorini,* sän-dô-rē′-nē [sahn-do-ree′-nee].		
Thermaic Gulf (Gr.)	*Eng.* thər-mā′-ĭk	thuhr-may′-ik
Greek *Thermaikos Kolpos,* thĕr-mä-ē-kôs′ kôl′-pôs [thehr-mah-ee-kos′ kol′-pos].		
Thessalonike (Gr.)	thĕ-sä-lô-nē′-kē	theh-sah-lo-nee′-kee
Usually called *Saloniki,* q.v., or *Salonica.*		
Thessaly (Gr.)	*Eng.* thĕs′-ə-lĭ	thes′-uh-li
Greek *Thessalia,* thĕ-sä-lē′-ä [theh-sah-lee′-ah].		
Thevai (Gr.) See *Thebes.*		
Thibar (Tun.)	tē-băr′	tee-behr′
Thibica (Tun.)	tē′-bē-kä	tee′-bee-kah
Thielt (Belg.)	tēlt′	teelt′
Thienen (Belg.)	*Flem.* tē′-nən	tee′-nuhn
French *Tirlemont,* tēr-lə-môN′ [teer-luh-moN′].		
Thiganousa (Gr., isl.)	thē-gä-no͞o′-sä	thee-gah-noo′-sah
Also called *Venetiko,* vĕ-nĕ′-tē-kô [veh-neh′-tee-ko].		

Thisted (Den.)	tē′-stěth	tee′-ste*th*
Thodoroi (Crete) See *Theodoroi.*		
Thodorou (Crete, isl.) See *Theodoros.*		
Tholen (Neth., isl.)	tō′-lən	toh′-luhn
Thonon (Fr.)	tô-nôN′	to-noN′
Thorn (Pol.) See *Toruń.*		
Thorshavn (Den.)	tôrs-houn′	tors-haun′
Thourout (Belg.)	*Fr.* tōō-rōō′	too-roo′
Flemish *Torhout,* q.v.		
Thrace (Gr.)	*Eng.* thrās′	thrays′
Greek *Thrake,* thrä′-kē [thrah′-kee].		
Thueringen *or* Thüringen (Ger.)	tü′-rĭng-ən	tü′-ring-uhn
English *Thuringia,* thū-rĭn′-jə [thyoo-rin′-juh].		
Thyssen, Fritz (Ger. leader)	tĭs′-ən	tis′-uhn
Tiangzup (Burma)	tyäng-zŏŏp′	tyahng-zup′
Tiaret (Alg.)	tyä-rĕ′	tyah-reh′
Tiber (It., riv.)	*Eng.* tī′-bər	tai′-buhr
Italian *Tevere,* q.v.		
Tibet (Ch. dependency)	*Eng.* tĭ-bĕt′	ti-bet′
Chinese *Hsi-ts'ang,* shē-tsäng [shee-tsahng] *or* Si-ts'ang, q.v.		
Ticino (It., riv.)	tē-chē′-nô	tee-chee′-no
Tiel (Neth.)	tēl′	teel′
Tien-pai (Ch., Kwangtung)	dyĕn-bī	dyen-bai
Also called *Tinpak,* q.v.		
T'ien-shui (Ch., Kansu)	tyĕn-shwā	tyen-shway
Tientsin (Ch., Hopeh)	*Eng.* tĭn-tsĭn	tin-tsin
Chinese *T'ien-chin,* tyĕn-jĭn [tyen-jin].		
Tiflis (Rus.)	*Eng.* tĭf′-lĭs	tif′-lis
	Rus. tĭf-lēs′	tif-lees′
Georgian *Tbilisi,* tbĭ-lē-sē′ [tbi-lee-see′].		
Tighina (Rum.)	tē-gē′-nä	tee-gee′-nah
Russian and German *Bender,* bĕn′-dər [ben′-duhr].		
Tiglione (It.)	tē-lyô′-nĕ	tee-lyo′-neh
Ti-hwa (Ch., Sinkiang)	dē-whä	dee-whah
Also called *Urumchi,* q.v.		
Tijesno (Yugosl.)	tē′-yĕ′-snô	tee′-yeh′-sno
Tikhoretsk (Rus.)	tĭ-hŏ-rĕtsk′	ti-ho-retsk′
Tikhvin (Rus.)	tēk(h)′-vĭn	teek(h)′-vin
Tikopia (Oc.)	tē-kô-pē′-ä	tee-ko-pee′-ah
Tikotsin (Pol.) See *Tykocin.*		
Tikveš (Yugosl.)	tēk′-vĕsh	teek′-vesh

Tilburg (Neth.)	tĭl′-bûrk(h)	til′-bœrk(h)
Tilos (Dodec.)	tē′-lô(s)	tee′-lo(s)
Italian *Piscopi*, q.v.		
Tilsit (Ger.)	tĭl′-zĭt	til′-zit
Tim (Rus.)	tēm′	teem′
Timashevskaya (Rus.)	tĭ-mä′-shĕf-skä-yä	ti-mah′-shef-skah-yah
Timbaki (Crete)	tēm-bä′-kē	teem-bah′-kee
Time (Rus.)	tē′-mĕ	tee′-meh
Timika (Oc.)	tē-mē′-kä	tee-mee′-kah
Timişoara (Rum.)	tē-mē-shwä′-rä	tee-mee-shwah′-rah
Hungarian *Temesvár*, q.v. Serb-Croat *Temišvar*, tĕ′-mē-shvär [teh′-mee-shvahr].		
Timişul (Balkan riv.)	*Rum.* tē′-mē-shŏŏl	tee′-mee-shul
Serb-Croat *Tamiš*, q.v. Hungarian *Temes*, tĕ′-mĕsh [teh′-mesh].		
Timor (NEI and Port. col.)	tē′-môr	tee′-mor
A recommendation that the principal accent be placed on the last syllable appears to be not well founded.		
Timoshenko, Semyon (Rus. marshal)	tē-mŏ-shĕn′-kŏ, sĕm-yôn′	tee-mo-shen′-ko, sem-yon′
Tinakula (Oc.)	tē-nä-kōō′-lä	tee-nah-koo′-lah
Tindja (Tun.)	tĭn′-jä	tin′-jah
Tine (Tun., riv.)	tēn′	teen′
Ting-hai (Ch., Chekiang)	dĭng-hī	ding-hai
Ting-nan (Ch., Kiangsi)	dĭng-nän	ding-nahn
Tinian (Oc.)	tē-nē-än′	tee-nee-ahn′
Tinn (Nor.)	tĭn′	tin′
Tinnoset (Nor.)	tĭn′-ō-sə	tin′-oh-suh
Tinpak (Ch., Kwantung)	*Eng.* tĭn-păk	tin-pak
Chinese *Tien-pai*, q.v.		
Tioucha (Tun.)	tē-ū′-shä	tee-yoo′-shah
Tirana (Alb.) See *Tiranë*.		
Tiranë (Alb.)	tē-rä′-nə	tee-rah′-nuh
Tiraspol (Rus.)	tĭ-räs′-pŏl(y)	ti-rahs′-pol(y)
Tiriolo (It.)	tē-ryô′-lô	tee-ryo′-lo
Tirlemont (Belg.) See *Thienen*.		
Tirnovo (Bulg.) See *Trnovo*.		
Tirol (Austria)	*Eng.* tĭr′-ŏl	tihr′-ol
	Ger. tē-rōl′	tee-rohl′
Tisa (Europ. riv.)	*S.-C.* tē′-sä	tee′-sah
Hungarian *Tisza*, q.v. German *Theiss*.		
Tishovtsi (Pol.) See *Tyszowce*.		
Tisza (Europ. riv.)	*Hung.* tē′-sŏ	tee′-so
German *Theiss*, tīs′ [tais′]. Serbian *Tisa*, q.v.		

Titerno (It., riv.)	tē-tĕr′-nô	tee-tehr′-no
Tito, Marshall	tē′-tō	tee′-toh
Nickname of Josip *Brož*, q.v.		
Tityron (Crete, pen., mt.) See *Rodopou.*		
Tiulenev, I. V. (Rus. general)	tū-lĕ′-nĕf	tyoo-leh′-nef
Tivar (Yugosl.)	*Alb.* tē′-vär	tee′-vahr
Serb-Croat *Bar*, q.v.		
Tivoli (It.)	*Eng.* tĭv′-ə-lĭ	tiv′-uh-li
	It. tē′-vô-lē	tee′-vo-lee
Tiznit (Mor.)	tĭz′-nĭt	tiz′-nit
Tjapoe *or* Tjapu (NEI)	chä-pōō′	chah-poo′
Tjiandjoer (NEI)	chyän′-jōōr	chyahn′-joor
Also spelled *Chianjur*, q.v.		
Tjilatjap (NEI)	chē-lä′-chäp	chee-lah′-chahp
Tmimi (Libya)	tmē′-mē	tmee′-mee
Toau (Oc.)	tô-ou′	to-au′
Tobi (Oc.)	tô′-bē	to′-bee
Also called *Tokobi*, tô-kô′-bē [to-ko′-bee].		
Tobolsk (Rus.)	tŏ-bôl(y)sk′	to-bol(y)sk′
Toboroi (Oc.)	tô′-bô-roi	to′-bo-roi
Tobruk (Libya)	tō′-brŏŏk′	toh′-bruk′
Also spelled *Tobruch* and *Tobrukh.*		
Toburba (Tun.) See *Tebourba.*		
Tochigi (Jap.)	tô-chē-gē	to-chee-gee
Todi (It.)	tô′-dē	to′-dee
Todmorden (Austral.)	tŏd′-môr-dən	tod′-mor-duhn
Toender (Den.)	tûn′-ər	tœn′-uhr
Toensberg (Nor.)	tûns′-bĕr	tœns′-behr
Toenset (Nor.) See *Tynset.*		
Toiokh (Ch.)	tô′-yôk(h)	to′-yok(h)
Tokaido (Jap.)	tô-kī-dô	to-kai-do
Tokaj (Hung.) See *Tokay.*		
Tokay (Hung.)	*Eng.* tō-kā′	toh-kay′
	Hung. tô′-koi	to′-koi
Tokelau (Oc.)	tô-kĕ-lou′	to-keh-lau′
Tokmak (Rus.)	tŏk-mäk′	tok-mahk′
Tokobi (Oc.) See *Tobi.*		
Tokowinai (Oc., mt.)	tô-kô-wē′-nī	to-ko-wee′-nai
Tokio (Jap.)	*Eng.* tō′-kĭ-ō	toh′-ki-oh
	Jap. tô-kyô	to-kyo
Tolan, John H. (U.S. representative)	tō′-lən	toh′-luhn

Tolbukhin, Feodor (Rus. general)	tŏl-bo͞o′-hĭn, fyô′-dŏr	tol-boo′-hin, fyo′-dor
Toledo (Sp., U.S.)	*Eng.* tə-lē′-dō	tuh-lee′-doh
	Sp. tô-lĕ′-*thô*	to-leh′-*tho*
Toli-toli (NEI)	tô′-lē-tô′-lē	to′-lee-to′-lee
Tolovana (Alaska)	tō′-lə-văn′-ə	toh′-luh-van′-uh
Tolstoy, Aleksei (Rus. writer)	tŏl-stoi′, ä-lĕk-sā′	tol-stoi′, ah-lek-say′
Tomaszów (Pol.)	tô-mä′-sho͝of	to-mah′-shuf

Russian *Tomashov*, tŏ-mä′-shŏf [to-mah′-shof].

tomato	tə-mā′-tō	tuh-may′-toh
	or tə-mä′-tō	tuh-mah′-toh

American dictionaries agree on this order. The first is without doubt the general American pronunciation. On a particular program, however, there may be a reason for preferring the pronunciation with the "broad ah." There is also an old-fashioned pronunciation, tə-măt′-ə [tuh-mat′-uh].

Tomor (Alb., mt.)	*Eng.* tô′-môr	to′-mor

Albanian *Mal i Tomorrit*; locally *Çukat*, cho͞o′-kät [choo′-kaht].

Tomorrica (Alb.) See *Tomorricë.*		
Tomorricë (Alb.)	tô-môr-rē′-tsə	to-mor-ree′-tsuh
Tomsk (Rus.)	tômsk′	tomsk′
Tönder (Den.)	tûn′-ər	tœn′-uhr
Tonkin (Indo-Ch.)	tŏn′-kĭn′	ton′-kin′

English *Tonking.* Chinese *Tung-ching*, do͝ong-jĭng [dung-jing].

Tonsaasen (Nor.)	to͝ons′-ôs-ən	tuns′-os-uhn
Tönsberg (Nor.)	tûns′-bĕr	tœns′-behr
Tönset (Nor.) See *Tynset.*		
Toowoomba (Austral.)	tə-wo͞om′-bə	tuh-woom′-buh
Topčider (Yugosl.)	tôp′-chĭ-dĕr	top′-chi-dehr
Topl'a (Cz., Hung., riv.)	*Cz.* tô′-plyä	to′-plyah

Hungarian *Tapoly*, tä′-pôl(y) [tah′-pol(y)].

Toplica (Yugosl.)	tô′-plĭ-tsä	to′-pli-tsah
Toplou (Crete)	tô-plo͞o′	to-ploo′
Topola (Yugosl.)	tô′-pô-lä	to′-po-lah
Topoli (Rus.)	tô′-pŏ-lĭ	to′-po-li
Toponica (Yugosl.)	tô′-pô′-nĭ-tsä	to′-po′-ni-tsah
Torcola (Yugosl., isl.)	*It.* tôr′-kô-lä	tor′-ko-lah

Serb-Croat *Šćedro*, q.v.

Torda (Rum.) See *Turda.*		
Torfinnsbu (Nor.)	to͝or′-fĭns-bo͞o	tur′-fins-boo
Torhout (Belg.)	*Flem.* tōr′-hout	tohr′-haut

French *Thourout*, q.v.

Torino (It.)	tô-rē′-nô	to-ree′-no

English *Turin*, q.v.

Torlonia (It.)	tôr-lô′-nyä	tor-lo′-nyah
tornadic	tôr-năd′-ĭk	tor-nad′-ik

Note the short *a* of the second syllable in contrast to the long *a* of *tornado*—tôr-nā′-dō [tor-nay′-doh].

Tornio (Fin.)	tôr′-nē-ô	tor′-nee-o
Tornya (Rum.) See *Turnu.*		
Torokina (Oc.)	tô-rô-kē′-nä	to-ro-kee′-nah
Törökszentmiklós (Hung.)	tû′-rûk-sĕnt′-mĭ-klôsh	tœ′-rœk-sent′-mi-klosh
Torontál (Hung.)	tô′-rôn-täl	to′-ron-tahl
Toropets (Rus.)	tŏ-rô′-pĕts	to-ro′-pets
Torp, Oscar (Nor. leader)	tôrp′	torp′
Torre Annunziata (It.)	tôr′-rĕ än-no͞on′-tsē-ä′-tä	tor′-reh ahn-noon′-tsee-ah′-tah
Torre Archirafi (Sicily)	tôr′-rĕ är-kē-rä′-fē	tor′-reh ahr-kee-rah′-fee
Torrens (Austral., lake, riv.)	tŏr′-ənz	tor′-uhnz
Torres (Austral., strait)	tŏr′-ĭz	tor′-iz
Torto, Fiume (Sicily)	tôr′-tô, fyo͞o′-mĕ	tor′-to, fyoo′-meh
Tortorici (Sicily)	tôr-tô-rē′-chē	tor-to-ree′-chee
Toruń (Pol.)	tô′-ro͝on(y)	to′-run(y)

German *Thorn*, tôrn′ [torn′].

Torzhok (Rus.)	tŏr-zhôk′	tor-zhok′
Tosk (Alb.)	*Eng.* tôsk′	tosk′

Southern Albanian. Albanian *Toskë*, tôs′-kə [tos′-kuh], and *Toska.*

Tosno (Rus.)	tôs′-nŏ	tos′-no
Touggourt (Alg.)	*Fr.* to͞o-go͞or′	too-goor′

Also called *Tug(g)urt*, q.v.

Toujane (Tun.)	to͞o-zhän′	too-zhahn′
Toul (Fr.)	to͞ol′	tool′
Toulon (Fr.)	to͞o-lôN′	too-loN′
Toulouse (Fr.)	to͞o-lo͞oz′	too-looz′
Toum (Tun.)	to͞om′	toom′
Toungoo (Burma)	toung′-go͞o′ *or* toung′-o͞o′	taung′-goo′ taung′-oo′
Tourane (Indo-Ch.)	to͞o-răn′ *or* to͞o-rän′	too-ran′ *or* too-rahn′
Tourcoing (Fr.)	to͞or-kwăN′	toor-kwaN′
Tourloti (Crete)	to͞or-lô-tē′	toor-lo-tee′
Tournai (Belg.)	to͞or-nĕ′	toor-neh′
Tours (Fr.)	*Eng.* to͞orz′ *Fr.* to͞or′	toorz′ toor′

The French pronunciation is common even in English contexts.

Towe, Harry L. (U.S. representative)	tō′-ē	toh′-ee
Tozeur (Tun.)	tô-zûr′	to-zœr′
Trabzon (Turk.)	träb′-zôn′	trahb′-zon′
Also called *Trebizond*, q.v.		
Trafalgar (Sp., cape)	*Eng.* trə-făl′-gər	truh-fal′-guhr
	Sp. trä-fäl-gär′	trah-fahl-gahr′
Trakhoulas (Crete, point)	trä′-hōō-läs	trah′-hoo-lahs
Trakya (Turk.)	trä′-kyä′	trah′-kyah′
Trälleborg (Sw.)	trĕl′-ə-bôr′(y)	trel′-uh-bor′(y)
Trang (Thai)	träng′	trahng′
Tranquebar (India)	trăng-kwĭ-bär′	trang-kwi-bahr′
Transvaal (U. of S. Afr.)	trăns-väl′	trans-vahl′
Transylvania (Rum.)	*Eng.* trăn′-sĭl-vā′-nyə	tran′-sil-vay′-nyuh
Trapani (Sicily)	trä′-pä-nē	trah′-pah-nee
Trasimeno (It., lake)	trä-sē-mĕ′-nô	trah-see-meh′-no
Trašte (Yugosl.)	trä′-shtĕ	trah′-shteh
Trastevere (It., Rome)	trä-stĕ′-vĕ-rĕ	trah-steh′-veh-reh
Trautenau (Cz.) See *Trutnov.*		
Travnička (Yugosl.)	träv′-nĭch-kä	trahv′-nich-kah
Třebíč (Cz.)	trzhĕ′-bēch	trzheh′-beech
Trebinje (Yugosl.)	trĕ′-bĭ-nyĕ	treh′-bi-nyeh
Trebisacce (It.)	trĕ-bē-sät′-chĕ	treh-bee-saht′-cheh
Trebizond (Turk.)	*Eng.* trĕb′-ĭ-zŏnd′	treb′-i-zond′
Now officially *Trabzon*, q.v.		
Trebnje (Yugosl.)	trĕb′-nyĕ	treb′-nyeh
Trecastagni (Sicily)	trĕ-kä-stä′-nyē	treh-kah-stah′-nyee
Tréguier (Fr.)	trĕ-gyĕ′	treh-gyeh′
Trembowla (Pol.)	trĕm-bô′-vlä	trem-bo′-vlah
tremendous See *grievous.*		
Tremiti (It., isls.)	trĕ′-mē-tē	treh′-mee-tee
Trenčín (Cz.)	trĕn′-chēn	tren′-cheen
Trento (It.)	trĕn′-tô	tren′-to
English *Trent*, trĕnt′ [trent′].		
Trentola (It.)	trĕn′-tô-lä	tren′-to-lah
Tre Pietre (It.)	trĕ′ pyĕ′-trĕ	treh′ pyeh′-treh
Tréport, le (Fr.)	trĕ-pôr′, lə	treh-por′, luh
Tretten (Nor.)	trĕt′n	tret′n
Treungen (Nor.)	trā′-ŏŏng-ən	tray′-ung-uhn
Trèves (Ger.)	*Fr.* trĕv′	trev′
German *Trier*, q.v.		
Trgoviški Timok (Yugosl.)	tər′-gô-vĭsh-kĭ tē′-môk	tuhr′-go-vish-ki tee′-mok
Triada, Agia (Crete)	trē-ä′-*th*ä, ī′-yä	tree-ah′-*th*ah, ai′-yah

Triaga (Tun.)	trē-ă′-gä	tree-a′-gah
tribunal	trī-bū′-nəl *or* trĭ-	trai-byoo′-nuhl *or* tri-
tribune	trĭb′-ūn′	trib′-yoon′

As a word in unemphatic speech the first syllable usually has more stress than the second. As the name of a newspaper the second syllable may have the heavier stress. The pronunciation trī′-būn [trai′-byoon] occurs in British speech, but trĭb′-būn [trib′-byoon] is the BBC choice.

Trichinopoly (India)	trĭch-ĭ-nŏp′-ə-lĭ	trich-i-nop′-uh-li
Tricqueville (Fr.)	trēk-vēl′	treek-veel′
Trier (Ger.)	trēr′	treer′

French *Trèves*, q.v.

Trieste (It.)	*Eng.* trĭ-ĕst′	tri-est′
	It. trē-ĕs′-tĕ	tree-es′-teh
Trigno (It., riv.)	trē′-nyô	tree′-nyo
Trikala (Gr.)	trē′-kä-lä	tree′-kah-lah
Trincomalee (Ceylon)	trĭng′-kə-mə-lē′	tring′-kuh-muh-lee′
tri-partite	trī′-pär′-tīt	trai′-pahr′-tait
Tripoli (Libya)	*Eng.* trĭp′-ə-lĭ	trip′-uh-li
	It. trē′-pô-lē	tree′-po-lee
Tripolis (Gr.)	*Eng.* trĭp′-ə-lĭs	trip′-uh-lis
	Gr. trē′-pô-lē(s)	tree′-po-lee(s)

Also called *Tripolitsa*, trē-pô-lē-tsä′ [tree-po-lee-tsah′].

Tripolitania (Afr.)	*Eng.* trĭp′-ŏ-lĭ-tā′-nĭ-ə	trip′-o-li-tay′-ni-uh
	It. trē′-pô-lē-tä′-nyä	tree′-po-lee-tah′-nyah
Triton (Crete, cape)	See *Vouxa.*	
Trivandrum (India)	trĭ-văn′-drəm	tri-van′-druhm
Trn (Bulg.)	tərn′	tuhrn′
Trnava (Cz., riv.)	tər′-nä-vä	tuhr′-nah-vah
Trnjane (Yugosl.)	tər′-nyä-nĕ	tuhr′-nyah-neh
Trnovac (Yugosl.)	tər′-nô-väts	tuhr′-no-vahts
Trnovo (Bulg.)	tər′-nŏ-vŏ	tuhr′-no-vo

Also called *Tirnovo*, tēr′-nŏ-vŏ [teer′-no-vo].

Trobriand (Oc.)	trō′-brĭ-änd′	troh′-bri-ahnd′
Trocchio (It.)	trôk′-kyô	trok′-kyo
Trogir (Yugosl.)	trô′-gĭr	tro′-gihr
Troina (Sicily)	trô-ē′-nä	tro-ee′-nah
Troitsk (Rus.)	trô′-ĭtsk	tro′-itsk
Troitskoe (Rus.)	trô′-ĭts-kŏ-yĕ	tro′-its-ko-yeh
Troitskosavsk (Rus.)	trô′-ĭts-kŏ-säfsk′	tro′-its-ko-sahfsk′
Trojan (Balkan mts.)	*S.-C.* trô′-yän	tro′-yahn

Albanian *Mal i Trojanit*, mäl′ ē trô-yä′-nēt [mahl′ ee tro-yah′-neet].

Trojan (Bulg.)	trô′-yän	tro′-yahn
Trollheimen (Nor., mts.)	trôl′-hā-mən	trol′-hay-muhn
Trolltinnene (Nor., mt.)	trôl′-tĭn′-ə-nə	trol′-tin′-uh-nuh
Tromsoe *or* Tromsö (Nor.)	trŏŏms′-û	trums′-œ
Popular English trŏmz′-ō [tromz′-oh].		
Trondheim (Nor.)	trôn′-hām	tron′-haym
Formerly called *Trondhjem*, trôn′-yĕm [tron′-yem] and at one time *Nidaros*, nē′-dä-rōs [nee′-dah-rohs]. Avoid trôn′-hīm [tron′-haim].		
Tronfjell (Nor., mt.)	trōn′-fyĕl	trohn′-fyel
Tropea (It.)	trô-pĕ′-ä	tro-peh′-ah
Troppau (Cz.) See *Opava*.		
Troutman, Wm. I. (U.S. representative)	trout′-mən	traut′-muhn
Troyan (Balkan mt.)	*Eng.* troi′-ən	troi′-uhn
Albanian *Mal i Trojanit.* Serb-Croat *Trojan*, q.v.		
Troyes (Fr.)	trwä′	trwah′
Trpanj (Yugosl.)	tər′-pän(y)	tuhr′-pahn(y)
Trstenik (Yugosl.)	tər′-stĕ-nĭk	tuhr′-steh-nik
Trsteno (Yugosl.)	tər′-stĕ-nô	tuhr′-steh-no
Italian *Cannosa*, q.v.		
Trubchevsk (Rus.)	trōōp-chĕfsk′	troop-chefsk′
Truk (Oc.)	*Eng.* trŏŏk′ *or* trŭk′	truk′ *or* truhk′
	native trōōk′	trook′
Trutnov (Cz.)	trōōt′-nôf	troot′-nof
German *Trautenau*, trou′-tə-nou [trau′-tuh-nau].		
Trypiti (Crete, cape)	trē-pē-tē′	tree-pee-tee′
Trysil (Nor.)	trü′-sĭl	trü′-sil
Tržič (Yugosl.)	tər′-zhĭch	tuhr′-zhich
Tsangpo (Tibet, riv.)	tsäng-pô	tsahng-po
Tibetan name for the *Brahmaputra*.		
Tscheliadz (Pol.) See *Czeladź*.		
Tschenstochau (Pol.) See *Częstochowa*.		
Tserigo (Gr., isl.) See *Kythera*.		
Tserigoto (Gr., isl.) See *Aigila*.		
Tseziz (Latvia) See *Cēsis*.		
Ts'ien-t'ang (Ch., Chekiang, riv.)	chyĕn-täng	chyen-tahng
Also spelled *Ch'ien-t'ang*.		
Tsimlyanskaya *or*	tsĭm-lyän′-skä-yä	tsim-lyahn′-skah-yah
Tsymlyansk (Rus.)	tsĭm-lyänsk′	tsim-lyahnsk′
Tsi-nan (Ch., Shantung) See *Chi-nan*.		
Ts'in-an (Ch., Kansu)	tsĭn-än	tsin-ahn

Tsin-chow (Ch., Kansu)	jĭn-jō	jin-joh
Also spelled *Chin-chow.*		
Ts'ing-hai (Ch., prov.)	chĭng-hī	ching-hai
Also spelled *Ch'ing-hai*, q.v.		
Tsing-kiang (Ch., Fukien)	*Eng.* tsĭng-kyăng *Ch.* jĭng-jyäng	tsing-kyang jing-jyahng
Also spelled *Tsin-chiang.* Also called *Ch'uan-chow*, q.v.		
Ts'ing-tao (Ch., Shantung)	*Eng.* tsĭng-tou *Ch.* chĭng-dou	tsing-tau ching-dau
Ts'ing-tien (Ch., Chekiang)	chĭng-dyĕn	ching-dyen
Tsi-ning (Ch., Shantung) See *Chi-ning.*		
Tsin-yün (Ch., Chekiang)	dzĭn-yün	dzin-yün
Tsirimokos, Elias (Gr. leader)	tsē-rē-mô′-kôs, ē-lē′-äs	tsee-ree-mo′-kos, ee-lee′-ahs
Tsironikos, N. (Gr. collab.)	tsē-rô′-nē-kôs	tsee-ro′-nee-kos
Tsitsihar (Manchu.)	tsē-tsē-här *or* chē-chē-här	tsee-tsee-hahr chee-chee-hahr
Chinese *Lung-chiang*, lo͝ong-jyäng [lung-jyahng].		
Tsolakoglu (Gr. collab.)	tsô-lä′-kô-glo͞o	tso-lah′-ko-gloo
Hellenizing of a Turkish name.		
Tsouderos, Emmanuel (Gr. leader)	tso͞o-*th*ĕ-rôs′, ĕ-mä-no͞o-ēl′	tsoo-*th*eh-ros′, eh-mah-noo-eel′
Tsushima (Jap., isl.)	tso͞o-shē-mä	tsoo-shee-mah
Tsugaru (Jap., str.)	tso͞o-gä-ro͞o	tsoo-gah-roo
Tsuruga (Jap.)	tso͞o-ro͞o-gä	tsoo-roo-gah
Tsurupinsk (Rus.)	tso͞o-rū′-pĭnsk	tsoo-ryoo′-pinsk
Tsyekhotsinsk (Pol.) See *Ciechocinek.*		
Tsymlyansk (Rus.) See *Tsimlyanskaya.*		
Tuamotu (Oc.)	to͞o-ä-mô′-to͞o	too-ah-mo′-too
Tuapse (Rus.)	to͞o-äp-sĕ′	too-ahp-seh′
Tuban (NEI)	to͞o′-bän	too′-bahn
T'u-ch'ang (Ch., Kiangsi)	to͞o-chäng	too-chahng
Tuchkof (Rum.) See *Ismail.*		
Tuchola (Pol.)	to͝o-hô′-lä	tu-ho′-lah
Tuđemile (Yugosl.)	to͞o′-dyĕ′-mĭ-lĕ	too′-dyeh′-mi-leh
Tufi (New Guinea)	to͞o′-fē	too′-fee
Tug(g)urt (Alg.)	to͝o-go͞ort′	tu-goort′
French *Touggourt*, q.v.		
Tuglie (It.)	to͞o′-lyĕ	too′-lyeh
Tuguegarao (P.I.)	to͞o-gĕ-gä-rou′	too-geh-gah-rau′

Tugurski (Rus., bay)	tŏŏ-gōōr′-skĭ	tu-goor′-ski
Tujna (Yugosl.)	tōō′ĭ-nä *or* tōō′(y)-	too′i-nah *or* too′(y)-
Tukum (Latvia)	*Rus.* tŏŏ-kōōm′	tu-koom′
Latvian *Tukums*, q.v.		
Tukums (Latvia)	tŏŏ′-kŏŏms	tu′-kums
Russian *Tukum*, q.v.		
Tula (Rus.)	tōō′-lä	too′-lah
Tulagi (Oc.)	tōō-lä′-gē	too-lah′-gee

Mr. Johannes Anderson, a New Zealand authority, writes that *Tulagi* is an early missionary spelling of *Tulangai*, tōō-läng-ä-ē [too-lahng-ah-ee]. The letter *i* was used for *ai*, and *g* for *ng*. (Compare *Pago Pago* for *Pango Pango*.) So when we believe we are going native with tōō-lä′-gē, instead of using a possible English tū-lā′-gī [tyoo-lay′-gai] or tū-lăg′-ĭ [tyoo-lag′-i], we are probably still wrong though conscientious.

Tulcea (Rum.)	tŏŏl′-chä	tul′-chah
Tulchin (Rus.)	tōōl′(y)-chĭn′	tool′(y)-chin′
Tulear (Madag.)	tü-lĕ-är′	tü-leh-ahr′
Tuloma (Rus., riv.)	tōō′-lŏ-mä	too′-lo-mah
Tumanni (Rus., cape)	tōō-män′-nĭ	too-mahn′-ni
Tundzha (Balkan riv.)	tŏŏn′-jä	tun′-jah
T'ung-chow (Ch., Hopeh)	*Eng.* tŏŏng-chou *Ch.* tŏŏng-jō	tung-chau tung-joh
Tung-hsiang (Ch., Kiangsi)	dŏŏng-shyäng	dung-shyahng
T'ung-ku (Ch., Kiangsi)	tŏŏng-gōō	tung-goo
T'ung-kwan (Ch., Shensi)	tŏŏng-gwän	tung-gwahn
T'ung-liao (Manchu.)	tōōng-lyou	toong-lyau
T'ung-lu (Ch., Chekiang)	tŏŏng-lōō	tung-loo
T'ung-shan (Ch., Kiangsu)	tŏŏng-shän	tung-shahn
Tung-t'ing (Ch., Hunan, lake)	dŏŏng-tĭng	dung-ting
Tung-yang (Ch., Chekiang)	dŏŏng-yäng	dung-yahng
Tunis (Tun.)	tū′-nĭs	tyoo′-nis
Tunisia (Afr.)	tū-nĭsh′-(y)ə	tyoo-nish′-(y)uh

A quasi-foreign pronunciation, tū-nē′-shə, -zhə [tyoo-nee′-shuh, -zhuh] is also heard.

Tunja (Balkan riv.) See *Tundzha*.

Tunnell, James M. (U.S. senator)	tŭn′-əl	tuhn′-uhl

Turanj (Yugosl.)	tōō′-rän(y)	too′-rahn(y)
turbine	tûr′-bīn *or* tûr′-bĭn	tuhr′-bain *or* tuhr′-bin
American engineers prefer tûr′-bīn [tuhr′-bain]. As the word is a technical one, it may be wise to follow their example, especially on technical programs.		
Turčiansky Svätý Martin (Cz.)	tōōr′-chyän-skĭ svă′-tĭ mär′-tĭn	toor′-chyahn-ski sva′-ti mahr′-tin
Turda (Rum.)	tŏŏr′-dä	tur′-dah
Hungarian *Torda*, tôr′-dŏ [tor′-do].		
Turek (Pol.)	tŏŏ′-rĕk	tu′-rek
T'ur-fan (Ch., Sinkiang)	tŏŏr-fän	tur-fahn
Türi (Est.)	tü′-rĭ	tü′-ri
Russian *Allenkul*, q.v.		
Turija (Yugosl., riv.)	tōō′-rĭ-yä	too′-ri-yah
Turin (It.)	tū′-rĭn *or* tū-rĭn′	tyoo′-rin *or* tyoo-rin′
Avoid tōō-rēn′ [too-reen′]. Italian *Torino*, q.v.		
Turirog (Rus.)	tōō′-rĭ-rôg′	too′-ri-rog′
Turkinsk (Rus.)	tōōr′-kĭnsk	toor′-kinsk
Turkmen (Rus.)	tŏŏrk-mĕn′	turk-men′
Turku (Fin.)	tŏŏr′-kŏŏ	tur′-ku
Swedish *Åbo*, q.v.		
Turnhout (Belg.)	tûrn′-hout	tœrn′-haut
Turnu (Rum.)	tŏŏr′-nŏŏ	tur′-nu
Hungarian *Tornya*, tôr′-nyŏ [tor′-nyo].		
Turnu Măgurele (Rum.)	tŏŏr′-nŏŏ mû′-gŏŏ-rĕ′-lĕ	tur′-nu muh′-gu-reh′-leh
Turnu Severin (Rum.)	tŏŏr′-nŏŏ sĕ-vĕ-rēn′	tur′-nu seh-veh-reen′
Turtagroe *or* Turtagrö (Nor.)	tŏŏr′-tä-grû	tur′-tah-grœ
Turtucaia (Rum.)	tŏŏr-tŏŏ-kä′-yä	tur-tu-kah′-yah
Bulgarian *Tutracan*, tŏŏ′-trä-kän′ [tu′-trah-kahn′].		
tushonka (Rus. stew)	tŏŏ-shôn′-kä	tu-shon′-kah
Tutow (Ger.)	tōō′-tō	too′-toh
Tutuba (Oc.)	tōō-tōō′-bä	too-too′-bah
Tutuila (Oc.)	tōō-tōō-ē′-lä	too-too-ee′-lah
Tuyio (Oc.)	tōō-yē′-ô	too-yee′-o
Tuzla (Yugosl.)	tōōz′-lä	tooz′-lah
Tuzlanska (Yugosl.)	tōō′-zlän-skä	too′-zlahn-skah
Tvedestrand (Nor.)	tvād′-ə-strän	tvayd′-uh-strahn
Tveitsund (Nor.)	tvāt′-sŏŏn	tvayt′-sun
Tvertsa (Rus., riv.)	tvĕr-tsä′	tvehr-tsah′
Tyin (Nor.)	tü′-ĭn	tü′-in
Tyinholmen (Nor.)	tü′-ĭn-hôl-mən	tü′-in-hol-muhn
Tykocin (Pol.)	tĭ-kô′-tsĭn	ti-ko′-tsin
Russian spelling *Tikotsin*.		

Tympaki(on) (Crete)	tēm-bä′-kē(-ôn)	teem-bah′-kee(-on)
Tynset *or* Toenset	tün′-sĕt	tün′-set
or Tönset (Nor.)	*or* tŭn′-sĕt	tuhn′-set
Tyrifjord (Nor.)	tü′-rē-fyōr	tü′-ree-fyohr
Tyrma (Rus., riv.)	twēr′-mä	tweer′-mah
Tyrnavos (Gr.)	tēr′-nä-vôs	teer′-nah-vos
	or to͞or′-nä-vôs	toor′-nah-vos
Tyrol (Austria) See *Tirol.*		
Tyrrhenian Sea	*Eng.* tĭ-rē′-nĭ-ən	ti-ree′-ni-uhn
Italian *Mare Tirreno,* mä′-rĕ tĭr-rĕ′-nô [mah′-reh tihr-reh′-no].		
Tyszowce (Pol.)	tĭ-shôf′-tsĕ	ti-shof′-tseh
Russian *Tishovtsi,* tĭ-shôf′-tsĭ [ti-shof′-tsi].		
Tytärsaari (Fin., isl.)	tü′-tăr-sä-rē	tü′-tehr-sah-ree
Tyumen (Rus.)	tū-mĕn′(y)	tyoo-men′(y)
Tzarevo (Bulg.)	tsä′-rĕ-vŏ	tsah′-reh-vo
Also called *Vasiliko,* vä-sē-lē′-kŏ [vah-see-lee′-ko].		
Tzê-ch'i (Ch., Kiangsi)	dzŭ-chē	dzuh-chee
Also spelled *Tzŭ-ch'i.*		
Tz'ê-k'u (Ch., Sikang)	tsŭ-ko͞o	tsuh-koo
Also spelled *Tz'ŭ-k'u.*		
Tzia (Gr., isl.) See *Keos.*		
Tzoutzouras (Crete, point)	dzo͞o′-dzo͞o-räs	dzoo′-dzoo-rahs
Tz'ŭ-ch'i (Ch., Chekiang)	tsŭ-chē	tsuh-chee

u and *v* are interchangeable in Greek after *e* and *a*. It may be necessary to look up both spellings.

Uaddan (Libya)	wäd-dăn′	wahd-dan′
Ub (Yugosl.)	o͞ob′	oob′
Úbeda (Sp.)	o͞o′-bĕ-*th*ä	oo′-beh-*th*ah
Ubili (Oc.)	o͞o-bē′-lē	oo-bee′-lee
Ubonraj Dhani (Thai)	o͝o-bōn′-räj′-ə tä′-nē′	u-bohn′-rahj′-uh tah′-nee′
Ubort (Rus., riv.)	o͞o-bôrt′	oo-bort′
Ude (Mongolia)	o͞o-dĕ	oo-deh
Udine (It.)	o͞o′-dē-nĕ	oo′-dee-neh
Udomlya (Rus.)	o͝o′-dŏm-lyä	oo′-dom-lyah
Udorndhani (Thai)	o͝o-dôn′-tä′-nē′	u-dawn′-tah′-nee′
Udovice (Yugosl.)	o͞o′-dô′-vĭ-tsĕ	oo′-do′-vi-tseh
Udskaya Guba (Rus.)	o͞od′-skä-yä go͞o-bä′	ood′-skah-yah goo-bah′
Udski Ostrog (Rus.)	o͞od′-skĭ ŏs-trôg′	ood′-ski os-trog′
Udyl (Rus., lake)	o͞o-dĭl′	oo-dil′

Uea (Oc.)	o͞o-ĕ′-ä	oo-eh′-ah
Uerdingen (Ger.)	ür′-dĭng-ən	ür′-ding-uhn
Ufa (Rus.)	o͞o-fä′	oo-fah′
Ugliano (Yugosl., isl.)	See *Uljan.*	
Uglovka (Rus.)	o͞o-glôf′-kä	oo-glof′-kah
Ugra (Rus., riv.)	o͞o′-grä	oo′-grah
Ujae (Oc.)	o͞o-jä′-ĕ	oo-jah′-eh
Ujelang (Oc.)	o͞o′-jĕ-läng	oo′-jeh-lahng
Ujpest (Hung.)	o͝o′ĭ-pĕsht′ *or* o͝o′(y)-	u′i-pesht′ *or* u′(y)-
Újvidék (Yugosl.) See *Novi Sad.*		
Ukmergė (Lith.)	o͞ok′-mĕr-gĕ	ook′-mehr-geh
Russian *Wilkomir*, q.v.		
Ulak (Alaska)	ū′-lăk	yoo′-lak
Ulan Bator (Mongolia)	o͞o-län bä-tôr	oo-lahn bah-tor
Ulbanski (Rus., bay)	o͝ol-bän′-skĭ	ul-bahn′-ski
Ulan Ude (Rus.)	o͞o′-län o͞o′-dĕ	oo′-lahn oo′-deh
Ulbo (Yugosl.)	*It.* o͞ol′-bô	ool′-bo
Serb-Croat *Olib*, q.v.		
Ulcinj (Yugosl.)	o͞ol′-tsĭn(y)	ool′-tsin(y)
Italian *Dulcigno*, q.v.		
Uleåborg (Fin.) See *Oulu.*		
Ulefoss (Nor.)	o͞o′-lə-fôs	oo′-luh-fos
Uliagan (New Guinea)	o͞o-lē-ä′-gän	oo-lee-ah′-gahn
Uliassutai (Mongolia)	o͞o-lyä-so͝o-tī′	oo-lyah-su-tai′
Ulithi (Oc.)	o͞o-lē′-tē	oo-lee′-tee
Uljan (Yugosl.)	o͞o′-lyän	oo′-lyahn
Italian *Ugliano*, o͞o-lyä′-nô [oo-lyah′-no].		
Uljma (Yugosl.)	o͞ol′(y)-mä	ool′(y)-mah
Ullensvang (Nor.)	o͝ol′-əns-väng	ul′-uhns-vahng
Ulm (Ger.)	o͝olm′	ulm′
Ulmin (Rus.)	o͞ol-mĭn′	ool-min′
Ulvik (Nor.)	o͝ol′-vēk	ul′-veek
Ulyanovsk (Rus.)	o͞o-lyä′-nŏfsk	oo-lyah′-nofsk
Umba (Rus., riv.)	o͞om′-bä	oom′-bah
Umboi (Oc.) See *Rook.*		
Umčari (Yugosl.)	o͞om′-chä-rĭ	oom′-chah-ri
Umeaa (Sw.)	ü′-mĕ-ō	ü′-meh-oh
Umnak (Alaska, isl.)	o͞om′-năk	oom′-nak
Unalaska (Alaska, isl.)	ŭn′-ə-lăs′-kə	uhn′-uh-las′-kuh
	or o͞on′-ə-lăs′-kə	oon′-uh-las′-kuh
Unalga (Alaska, isl.)	ə-näl′-gə	uh-nahl′-guh
Unea (Oc.)	o͞o-nĕ′-ä	oo-neh′-ah
Unecha (Rus.)	o͞o-nĕ′-chä	oo-neh′-chah
Ungvár (Cz.) See *Užhorod.*		

Unie (It., isl.)	o͞o′-nyĕ	oo′-nyeh
Serb-Croat *Unije*, o͞o′-nĭ-yĕ [oo′-ni-yeh].		
Unije (It., isl.) See *Unie*.		
Unimak (Alaska, isl.)	o͞o′-nĭ-măk	oo′-ni-mak
Uppsala (Sw.)	*Eng.* ŭp′-sä′-lə	uhp′-sah′-luh
	Sw. o͝op′-sä′-lä	up′-sah′-lah
Uracas (Oc.)	o͞o-rä′-käs	oo-rah′-kahs
Ural (Rus., mts.)	*Eng.* ū′-rəl	yoo′-ruhl
	Rus. o͞o-räl′	oo-rahl′
Urbakh (Rus.)	o͞or′-bäk(h)	oor′-bahk(h)
Ürdingen (Ger.)	ür′-dĭng-ən	ür′-ding-uhn
Uriarte (Sp. general)	o͞o-ryär′-tĕ	oo-ryahr′-teh
Uripiv (Oc.)	o͞o-rē-pēv′	oo-ree-peev′
Uritsky (Rus.)	o͞o-rĭts′-kĭ	oo-rits′-ki
A square in Leningrad named after a murdered commissar.		
Urmi (Rus., riv.)	o͞or′-mĭ	oor′-mi
Uroševac (Yugosl.)	o͞o′-rô′-shĕ-väts	oo′-ro′-sheh-vahts
Uruguay	*Eng.* ū′-ro͝o-gwā	yoo′-ru-gway
	Sp. o͞o-ro͞o-gwī′	oo-roo-gwai′
The pronunciation ū′-ro͞o-gwī [yoo′-roo-gwai] is neither English nor Spanish.		
Uruguayan	ū′-ro͝o-gwā′-ən	yoo′-ru-gway′-uhn
	or o͞o′-ro͞o-gwī′-ən	oo′-roo-gwai′-uhn
Urumchi (Ch., Sinkiang)	o͞o-ro͞om′-chē	oo-room′-chee
Also called *Urumtsi* and *Ti-hwa*, q.v.		
Urupinsk (Rus.)	o͞o-rū′-pĭnsk	oo-ryoo′-pinsk
Urusan (Korea)	o͞o-ro͞o-sän	oo-roo-sahn
Urusha (Rus.)	o͞o-ro͞o′-shä	oo-roo′-shah
Uryumkansk (Rus.)	o͞o-rūm-känsk′	oo-ryoom-kahnsk′
Urziceni (Rum.)	o͝or-zē-chĕn′	ur-zee-chen′
Usedom (Ger., isl.)	o͞o′-zə-dōm	oo′-zuh-dohm
Ushant (Fr.)	*Eng.* ŭsh′-ənt	uhsh′-uhnt
French *Ouessant*, q.v.		
Ushba (Rus., mt.)	o͝osh′-bä	ush′-bah
Ushumun (Rus.)	o͞o-sho͞o-mo͞on′	oo-shoo-moon′
Uskoci (Yugosl.)	o͞o′-skô-tsĭ	oo′-sko-tsi
Üsküdar (Turk.)	üs-kü′-där	üs-kü′-dahr
Also called *Scutari*, q.v.		
Usman (Rus.)	o͞os-män′(y)	oos-mahn′(y)
Ussuri (Rus.)	o͞os-so͞o′-rē	oos-soo′-ree
Ustachi (Croat fascist party) A variant of *Ustaši*, q.v.		
Ustaoset (Nor.)	o͝os′-tä-ō′-sə	us′-tah-oh′-suh
Ustaši (Croat fascist party)	o͞o-stä′-shĭ	oo-stah′-shi

Ust Busulutsk (Rus.)	o͞ost bo͞o-zo͞o-lo͞otsk′	oost boo-zoo-lootsk′
Ust Dvinsk (Latvia)	*Rus.* o͞ost′ dvēnsk′	oost′ dveensk′
Latvian *Daugavgrīva*, q.v.		
Ústí (Cz.)	o͞o′-stē	oo′-stee
Ustica (It., isl.)	o͞o′-stē-kä	oo′-stee-kah
Ustyuzhna (Rus.)	o͞os-tūzh′-nä	oos-tyoozh′-nah
Utėna (Lith.)	o͞o′-tā-nä	oo′-tay-nah
Russian *Utseny*, q.v.		
Utica (Tun., U.S.)	ū′-tĭ-kə	yoo′-ti-kuh
Utique (Tun.)	*Fr.* ü-tēk′	ü-teek′
The English form, preferable in radio usage, is *Utica*, q.v.		
Utirik (Oc.)	o͞o′-tē-rēk	oo′-tee-reek
Utrata (Pol., riv.)	o͝o-trä′-tä	u-trah′-tah
Utrecht (Neth.)	*Eng.* ū′-trĕkt	yoo′-trekt
	Du. ü′-trĕk(h)t	ü′-trek(h)t
Utseny (Lith.)	*Rus.* o͝o-tsĕ′-nĭ	u-tseh′-ni
Lithuanian *Utėna*, q.v.		
Uttaradit (Thai)	o͝ot′-ə-rə-dĭt′	ut′-uh-ruh-dit′
Uudenmaa (Fin.)	o͞o′-dĕn-mä	oo′-den-mah
Uuksa (Fin.)	o͞ok′-sä	ook′-sah
uusi	o͞o′-sē	oo′-see
An element, meaning *new*, in Finnish place names.		
Uusikaupunki (Fin.)	o͞o′-sē-kou′-po͝ong-kē	oo′-see-kau′-pung-kee
Swedish *Nystad*, nü′-städ [nü′-stahd].		
Uusikirkko (Fin.)	o͞o′-sē-kĭrk-kô	oo′-see-kihrk-ko
Uvac (Yugosl., riv.)	o͞o′-väts	oo′-vahts
Uzbek (Rus.)	o͝oz-bĕk′	uz-bek′
Also called *Uzbekistan*, o͝oz-bĕ-kĭ-stän′ [uz-beh-ki-stahn′].		
Uzerthe (Fr.)	ü-zĕrt′	ü-zehrt′
Uzès (Fr.)	ü-zĕs′	ü-zes′
Uzh (Rus., riv.)	o͞ozh′	oozh′
Užhorod (Cz.)	o͞ozh′-hô-rôt	oozh′-ho-rot
Hungarian *Ungvár*, o͝ong′-vär [ung′-vahr].		
Užice (Yugosl.)	o͞o′-zhĭ-tsĕ	oo′-zhi-tseh
Uzlovaya (Rus.)	o͞oz-lŏ-vä′-yä	ooz-lo-vah′-yah
Uzunköprü (Turk.)	o͝o-zo͝on′-kûp-rü	u-zun′-kœp-rü

v, *b*, and *bh* are interchangeable in Greek and *b* and *v* in Spanish and other languages. It may be necessary to look up all these spellings.

v and *u* are interchangeable in Greek after *e* and *a*. It may be necessary to look up both spellings.

vaara	vä′-rä	vah′-rah
An element, meaning *barren mountain*, in Finnish place names.		
Vaasa (Fin.)	vä′-sä	vah′-sah

Vác (Hung.)	väts′	vahts′
Vadheim (Nor.)	väd′-hām	vahd′-haym
Vadino (Rus.)	vä′-dĭ-nŏ	vah′-di-no
Vadsoe *or* Vadsö (Nor.)	väds′-û	vahds′-œ
Vaduz (Liecht.)	vä′-do͝ots	vah′-duts
Værnes *or* Vernes (Nor.)	văr′-nĕs	vehr′-nes
vagary	və-gĕr′-ĭ	vuh-gehr′-i

A pronunciation with accent on the first syllable is not recommended.

vagrant	vā′-grənt	vay′-gruhnt
Váh (Cz., riv.)	väk(h)′	vahk(h)′

German spelling *Waag*. Hungarian *Vág*, väg′ [vahg′].

Vaitolahti (Rus.)	vī′-tō-läk(h)-tē	vai′-toh-lahk(h)-tee
Vaitupu (Oc.)	vī-to͞o′-po͞o	vai-too′-poo
Vajdahunyad (Rum.)	See *Hunedoara.*	
Vajguras (Alb.)	vī-go͞o′-räs	vai-goo′-rahs

Also called *Kuçovë*, q.v. Italian *Petrolia*, q.v.

Vakuf, Donji (Yugosl.)	vä′-ko͞of, dôn′-yĭ	vah′-koof, don′-yi
Valbona (Alb., riv.)	See *Valbonë.*	
Valbonë (Alb., riv.)	väl-bô′-nə	vahl-bo′-nuh
Vâlcov (Rum.)	vûl′-kôv	vuhl′-kov

Russian *Vilkovo*, vēl′-kŏ-vŏ [veel′-ko-vo].

Valdai (Rus.)	väl-dī′	vahl-dai′
Valdepeñas (Sp.)	väl-dĕ-pĕ′-nyäs	vahl-deh-peh′-nyahs
Valdés, Basilio J. (Fil. leader)	väl-dĕs′, bä-sē′-lyô	vahl-des′, bah-see′-lyo
Valdez (Alaska)	văl′-dĕz	val′-dez
Valdres (Nor.)	väl′-drəs	vahl′-druhs
Valea lui Mihai (Rum.)	vä′-lyä lo͝oĭ mē-hī′	vah′-lyah lui mee-hai′
Valencia (Sp.)	*Eng.* və-lĕn′-chə *or* -shĭ-ə	vuh-len′-chuh *or* -shi-uh
	Sp. vä-lĕn′-thyä *or* -syä	vah-len′-thyah *or* -syah
Valga (Est., Latvia)	väl′-gä	vahl′-gah

Latvian *Valka*, väl′-kä [vahl′-kah]. Russian *Valk*, q.v.

Valjevo (Yugosl.)	vä′-lyĕ-vô	vah′-lyeh-vo
Valk (Est., Latvia)	*Rus.* välk′	vahlk′

Estonian *Valga*, q.v. German spelling *Walk*. Latvian *Valka*.

Valka (Est., Latvia)	See *Valga.*	
Valkenburg (Neth.)	väl′-kən-bûrk(h)	vahl′-kuhn-bœrk(h)
Valki (Rus.)	väl′-kĭ	vahl′-ki
Valladolid (Sp.)	*Eng.* văl′-ə-dō′-lĭd	val′-uh-doh′-lid
	Sp. vä-lyä-*th*ô-lē*th*′	vah-lyah-*tho*-lee*th*′
Valle Spizza (Yugosl., bay)	*It.* väl′-lĕ spēt′-sä	vahl′-leh speet′-sah

Serb-Croat Zaliv *Spič*, q.v.

Valmiera (Latvia)	väl′-myĕ-rä	vahl′-myeh-rah
Russian and German *Wolmar*, q.v.		
Valmy (Fr., Alg.)	väl-mē′	vahl-mee′
Valognes (Fr.)	vä-lôn′(y)	vah-lon′(y)
Valona (Alb.)	*It.* vä-lô′-nä	vah-lo′-nah
Albanian *Vlonë*, q.v.		
Valsch (NEI)	väls′	vahls′
Valuiki (Rus.)	vä-lōō′ĭ-kĭ	vah-loo′i-ki
Vamos (Crete)	vä′-môs	vah′-mos
Van Diemen (Austral., gulf)	văn dē′-mən	van dee′-muhn
Vangunu (Oc.)	väng′-ōō-nōō	vahng′-oo-noo
Vanikoro (Oc.)	vä-nē-kô′-rô	vah-nee-ko′-ro
Vanimo (Oc.)	vä′-nē-mô	vah′-nee-mo
Van Loon, Hendrik (Am. author)	văn lōn′, hĕn′-drĭk	van lohn′, hen′-drik
Van Mook, Hubertus (Du. leader)	vän mōk′, hŏŏ-bĕr′-tŏŏs	vahn mohk′, hu-behr′-tus
Vannes (Fr.)	vän′	vahn′
Van Nuys, Frederick (Late U.S. senator)	văn nēs′	van nees′
Van Nuys (Calif.)	văn nīz′	van naiz′
Van Stavaren, J. J. A. (Du. leader)	vän stä′-və-rĕn	vahn stah′-vuh-ren
Vanves (Fr.)	väNv′	vahNv′
Van Zandt, James E. (Former U.S. representative)	văn zănt′	van zant′
vár	vär′	vahr′
An element, meaning *castle* or *fortress*, in Hungarian place names.		
Varangerfjord (Nor.)	vä-räng′-ər-fyōr	vah-rahng′-uhr-fyohr
Varaždin (Yugosl.)	vä′-räzh′-dĭn	vah′-rahzh′-din
Italian *Varasdino*, vä-räs-dē′-nô [vah-rahs-dee′-no].		
Vardar (Balkan riv.)	vär′-där	vahr′-dahr
Greek *Vardaris*, vär-*th*ä′-rēs [vahr-*th*ah′-rees]; *Vardarios*, vär-*th*ä′-rē-ôs [vahr-*th*ah′-ree-os]; and *Axios*, q.v.		
Varde (Den.)	vär′-də	vahr′-duh
Vardoe *or* Vardö (Nor.)	värd′-û	vahrd′-œ
Varela, José Enrique (Sp.)	vä-rĕ′-lä, hô-sĕ′ ĕn-rē′-kĕ	vah-reh′-lah, ho-seh′ en-ree′-keh
Vargas, Getulio (President of Brazil)	vär′-gəs, zhĕ-tōō′-lyŏŏ	vahr′-guhs, zheh-too′-lyu
Vargas, Jorge B. (Fil. leader)	vär′-gäs, hôr′-hĕ	vahr′-gahs, hor′-heh
Variš (Yugosl.)	vä′-rĭsh	vah′-rish

Varna (Bulg.)	vär′-nä	vahr′-nah
Varnsdorf (Cz.)	värns′-dôrf	vahrns′-dorf
Varoš (Yugosl.)	vä′-rôsh	vah′-rosh
Varshava (Pol.) See *Warsaw.*		
Varta (Pol.) See *Warta.*		
Värtsilä (Fin.)	vărt′-sē-lă	vehrt′-see-la
Varvaresos, K. (Gr. leader)	vär-vä-rĕ′-sôs	vahr-vah-reh′-sos
Varvarin (Yugosl.)	vär′-vä′-rĭn	vahr′-vah′-rin
Varvasena (Gr.)	vär-vä′-sĕ-nä	vahr-vah′-seh-nah
Varzuga (Rus., riv.)	vär-zōō′-gä	vahr-zoo′-gah
Vaşcău (Rum.)	väsh-kû′-ŏŏ	vahsh-kœ′-u
Vasilevichi (Rus.)	vä-sĭ-lĕ′-vĭ-chĭ	vah-si-leh′-vi-chi
Vasilevka (Rus.)	vä-sē′-lyĕf-kä	vah-see′-lyef-kah
Vasilevsky, Alexander Mikhailovich (Rus. general)	vä-sĭ-lĕf′-skĭ, ä-lĕk-sän′-dər mĭ-hī′-lŏ-vĭch	vah-si-lef′-ski, ah-lek-sahn′-duhr mi-hai′-lo-vich
Vasiliko (Bulg.) See *Tzarevo.*		
Vasilkov (Rus.)	vä-sĭl(y)-kôf′	vah-sil(y)-kof′
Vaslui (Rum.)	vä-slŏŏ′ĭ	vah-slu′i
Vasojevići (Yugosl.)	vä′-sô′-yĕ-vĭ-chĭ	vah′-so′-yeh-vi-chi
Vassenden (Nor.)	väs′-ĕn-ən	vahs′-en-uhn
Vatheos Lemen (Gr.) Also called *Vathy*, q.v.	vä-thĕ′-ô(s) lē-mēn′	vah-theh′-o(s) lee-meen′
Vathy (Gr.)	vä-thē′	vah-thee′
Vatilau (Oc.)	vä-tē-lou′	vah-tee-lau′
Vatra Dornei (Rum.)	vä′-trä dôr′-nā	vah′-trah dor′-nay
Vatutin, Nikolai (Rus. general)	vä-tōō′-tĭn, nĭ-kŏ-lī′	vah-too′-tin, ni-ko-lai′
Vecchiarelli, Carlo (It. general)	vĕk-kyä-rĕl′-lē, kär′-lô	vek-kyah-rel′-lee, kahr′-lo
Vecht (Neth., riv.)	vĕk(h)t′	vek(h)t′
Vedea (Rum., riv.)	vĕ′-dyä	veh′-dyah
Vegesack (Ger.)	vā′-gə-zäk	vay′-guh-zahk
Veglia (Yugosl.) Serb-Croat *Krk*, q.v.	*It.* vĕ′-lyä	veh′-lyah
Vehčane (Yugosl.)	vĕk(h)′-chä-nĕ	vek(h)′-chah-neh
Vejle (Den.)	vī′-lə	vai′-luh
Velenje (Yugosl.)	vĕ′-lĕ-nyĕ	veh′-leh-nyeh
Veles (Yugosl.)	vĕ′-lĕs	veh′-les
Velešte (Yugosl.)	vĕ′-lĕ-shtĕ	veh′-leh-shteh
velika, -e, -i, -o	vĕ′-lĭ-kä, -ĕ, -ĭ, -ô	veh′-li-kah, -eh, -i, -o

An element, meaning *large* or *great*, in Yugoslav place names. It may be necessary to look up the other part of the name. The similar word in Czech is stressed on the first syllable; in Bulgarian, Polish, and Russian, on the second syllable.

Velikaya (Rus., riv.)	vĕ-lē′-kä-yä	veh-lee′-kah-yah
Veliki Burluk (Rus.)	vĕ-lē′-kĭ bo͞or-lo͞ok′	veh-lee′-ki boor-look′
Velikie Luki (Rus.)	vĕ-lē′-kĭ-yĕ lo͞o′-kĭ	veh-lee′-ki-yeh loo′-ki
Velikii Tokmak (Rus.)	vĕ-lē′-kĭ tŏk-mäk′	veh-lee′-ki tok-mahk′
Velizh (Rus.)	vĕ′-lĭsh	veh′-lish
Vella Lavella (Oc.)	vĕl′-ä lä-vĕl′-ä	vel′-ah lah-vel′-ah
Velletri (It.)	vĕl-lĕ′-trē	vel-leh′-tree
See *Grosseto*, note.		
Velyun (Pol.) See *Wieluń*.		
Velzen (Neth.)	vĕl′-zən	vel′-zuhn
Vena Fiorita (Sard.)	vĕ′-nä fyô-rē′-tä	veh′-nah fyo-ree′-tah
Venafro (It.)	vĕ-nä′-frô	veh-nah′-fro
Venčane (Yugosl.)	vĕn′-chä-nĕ	ven′-chah-neh
Venden (Latvia) See *Wenden*.		
Vendsyssel Thy (Den., isl.)	vĕn′-süs-əl tü′	ven′-süs-uhl tü′
Venetiko (Gr., isl.) See *Thiganousa*.		
Veneto (It.)	vĕ′-nĕ-tô	veh′-neh-to
Venezia (It.)	vĕ-nĕ′-tsyä	veh-neh′-tsyah
English *Venice*, q.v.		
Venezia Euganea (It., dept.)	vĕ-nĕ′-tsyä ĕ-o͞o-gä′-nĕ-ä	veh-neh′-tsyah eh-oo-gah′-neh-ah
Also called *Veneto*, q.v.		
Venezuela (S.A.)	*Eng.* vĕn′-ĭ-zwē′-lä	ven′-i-zwee′-lah
	Sp. vĕ-nĕ-swĕ′-lä *or* -thwĕ′-	veh-neh-sweh′-lah *or* -thweh′-
Vengrov (Pol.) See *Węgrów*.		
Venice (It.)	*Eng.* vĕn′-ĭs	ven′-is
Italian *Venezia*, q.v.		
Venizelos, Sophocles (Gr. leader)	vĕ-nē-zĕ′-lôs, sô-fô-klēs′	veh-nee-zeh′-los, so-fo-klees′
Venta (Latvia, riv.)	vĕn′-tä	ven′-tah
Ventotene (It., isl.)	vĕn-tô-tĕ′-nĕ	ven-to-teh′-neh
Ventspils (Latvia)	vĕnts′-pēls	vents′-peels
Russina *Vindava*, q.v. German *Windau*, q.v.		
Veraval (India)	vē′-rə-vəl	vee′-ruh-vuhl
Vercelli (It.)	vĕr-chĕl′-lē	vehr-chel′-lee
Verde (Afr., cape; Port., isls.)	*Eng.* vûrd′	vuhrd′
See *Cape Verde*.		

Verige (Yugosl., It., str.) Italian *Le Catene*, q.v.	*S.-C.* vĕ′-rē-gĕ	veh′-ree-geh
Verkhne Dneprovsk (Rus.)	vĕr′-k(h)nĕ dnĕ-prôfsk′	vehr′-k(h)neh dneh-profsk′
Verkhne Tambovskoe (Rus.)	vĕr′-k(h)nĕ täm-bôf′-skŏ-yĕ	vehr′-k(h)neh tahm-bof′-sko-yeh
Verkhne Udinsk (Rus.)	vĕr′-k(h)nĕ o͞o-dēnsk′	vehr′-k(h)neh oo-deensk′
Verkhove (Rus.)	vĕr-hô′-vyĕ	vehr-ho′-vyeh
Verma (Nor.)	vĕr′-mä	vehr′-mah
Vernadovka (Rus.)	vĕr-nä′-dŏf-kä	vehr-nah′-dof-kah
Vernes *or* Værnes (Nor.)	văr′-nĕs	vehr′-nes
Veroia (Gr.)	vĕ′-rē-ä	veh′-ree-ah
Verona (It.)	*Eng.* və-rō′-nə	vuh-roh′-nuh
	It. vĕ-rô′-nä	veh-ro′-nah
Versec (Yugosl.) See *Vršac.*		
Verviers (Belg.)	vĕr-vyĕ′	vehr-vyeh′
Vesegonsk (Rus.)	vĕ-syĕ-gônsk′	veh-syeh-gonsk′
Vesoul (Fr.)	və-zo͞ol′	vuh-zool′
Vest-Agder (Nor.)	vĕst′-äg-dər	vest′-ahg-duhr
Vesteraalen (Nor., isls.)	vĕs′-tər-ô-lən	ves′-tuhr-o-luhn
Vestfjorden (Nor.)	vĕst′-fyōr-ən	vest′-fyohr-uhn
Vestfold (Nor.)	vĕst′-fôl	vest′-fol
Vestnes (Nor.)	vĕst′-nĕs	vest′-nes
Vestvaagoe *or* Vestvågö (Nor., isl.)	vĕst′-vôg-û	vest′-vog-œ
Veszprém (Hung.)	vĕs′-prām	ves′-praym
Veternica (Yugosl., riv.)	vĕ′-tĕr-nĭ-tsä	veh′-tehr-ni-tsah
Veurne (Belg.) French *Furnes*, fürn′.	*Flem.* vûr′-nə	vœr′-nuh
Via Appia (It., road) English the *Appian Way*, ăp′-ĭ-ən [ap′-i-uhn].	vē′-ä äp′-pyä	vee′-ah ahp′-pyah
Via Casilina (It., road)	vē′-ä kä-sē-lē′-nä	vee′-ah kah-see-lee′-nah
Via Flaminia (It., road) English the *Flaminian Way*, flə-mĭn′-ĭ-ən [fluh-min′-i-uhn].	vē′-ä flä-mē′-nyä	vee′-ah flah-mee′-nyah
Vianen (Neth.)	vē-ä′-nən	vee-ah′-nuhn
Vianos (Crete)	vyä′-nôs	vyah′-nos
Viareggio (It.)	vyä-rĕd′-jô	vyah-red′-jo
Viborg (Den.)	vē′-bôr	vee′-bor
Viborg (Fin.) See *Viipuri.*		
Vibo Valentia (It.)	vē′-bô vä-lĕn′-tyä	vee′-bo vah-len′-tyah
Vicenza (It.)	vē-chĕn′-tsä	vee-chen′-tsah

Vichuga (Rus.)	vĭ-cho͞o′-gä	vi-choo′-gah
Vichy (Fr.)	*Eng.* vĭsh′-ĭ	vish′-i
	Fr. vē-shē′	vee-shee′
Videseter (Nor.)	vē′-də-sā-tər	vee′-duh-say-tuhr
Vidin (Bulg.)	vē′-dĭn	vee′-din
Vidlič (Yugosl., mts.)	vēd′-lĭch	veed′-lich
Vidlitsa (Rus.)	vēd′-lĭ-tsä	veed′-li-tsah
Vidrnjak (Yugosl., riv.)	vē′-dər′-nyäk	vee′-duhr′-nyahk
Vidzeme (Latvia, prov.)	vēd′-zĕ-mĕ	veed′-zeh-meh
Vienna (Austria)	*Eng.* vĭ-ĕn′-ə	vi-en′-uh
German *Wien*, q.v.		
Vienne (Fr.)	vyĕn′	vyen′
Vientiane (Indo-Ch.)	vē′-ən-tyĕn′	vee′-uhn-tyen′
Viersen (Ger.)	fēr′-zən	feer′-zuhn
Vierzon (Fr.)	vyĕr-zôN′	vyehr-zoN′
Vigan (P.I.)	vē′-gän	vee′-gahn
Vigo (Sp.)	vē′-gô	vee′-go
Vigri (Pol.) See *Wigry*.		
Viipuri (Fin.)	vē′-po͝o-rē	vee′-pu-ree
Swedish *Viborg*, vē′-bôr(y) [vee′-bor(y)]. Russian *Vyborg*, vwē′-bŏrk [vwee′-bork].		
Vijniţa (Rum.)	vēzh′-nē-tsä	veezh′-nee-tsah
Vijosa (Alb., riv.) See *Vijosë*.		
Vijosë (Alb., riv.)	vē-yô′-sə	vee-yo′-suh
Greek *Voïousa*, voi-o͞o′-sä [voi-oo′-sah], and *Aoos*, q.v.		
vik	vēk′	veek′
Norwegian meaning *small bay* or *inlet*; an element in place names. In compounds like *Narvik*, vēk′ [veek′] will be Anglicized to vĭk′ [vik′].		
Vikesund (Nor.)	vē′-kə-so͝on	vee′-kuh-sun
Vila (Balkan mt.)	*S.-C.* vē′-lä	vee′-lah
Albanian *Mal i Vilës*, mäl′ ē vē′-ləs [mahl′ ee vee′-luhs].		
Vila (Oc.)	vē′-lä	vee′-lah
Vileika (Pol.) See *Wilejka*.		
Viliya (Pol., riv.) See *Wilja*.		
Viljandi (Est.)	vĭl′-yän-dĭ	vil′-yahn-di
Russian *Fellin*, q.v.		
Vilkaviškis (Lith.)	vĭl-kä-vēsh′-kĭs	vil-kah-veesh′-kis
Russian *Wilkowischki*, q.v.		
Vilkovo (Rum.) See *Vâlcov*.		
Villach (Austria)	fĭl′-äk(h)	fil′-ahk(h)
Serb-Croat *Beljak*, bĕl′-yäk [bel′-yahk].		
Villacidro (Sard.)	vēl-lä-chē′-drô	veel-lah-chee′-dro
Villacoublay (Fr.)	vēl-lä-ko͞o-blĕ′	veel-lah-koo-bleh′

Villamor, Jesús (Fil. leader)	vē-lyä-môr′, hĕ-so͞os′	vee-lyah-mor′, heh-so͞os′
Villarroel, Gualberto (Bolivian leader)	vē-lyär′-rô-ĕl′ (*or* -yär′-), gwäl-bĕr′-tô	vee-lyahr′-ro-el′ (*or* -yahr′-), gwahl-behr′-to
Villa San Giovanni (It.)	vēl′-lä sän jô-vän′-nē	veel′-lah sahn jo-vahn′-nee
Villetta Barrea (It.)	vēl-lĕt′-tä bär-rĕ′-ä	veel-let′-tah bahr-reh′-ah
Villmanstrand (Fin.) See *Lappeenranta.*		
Vilna (Pol.)	*Eng.* vĭl′-nə *Rus.* vēl′(y)-nä	vil′-nuh veel′(y)-nah
Polish *Wilno,* q.v.		
Vilnius (Pol.) See *Wilno.*		
Vilyanov (Pol.) See *Wilanów.*		
Vinča (Yugosl.)	vēn′-chä	veen′-chah
Vinchiaturo (It.)	vēn-kyä-to͞o′-rô	veen-kyah-too′-ro
Vinci (Yugosl.)	vēn′-tsĭ	veen′-tsi
Vindava (Latvia)	*Rus.* vĭn-dä′-vä	vin-dah′-vah
Latvian *Ventspils,* q.v. German *Windau,* q.v.		
Vinh (Indo-Ch.)	vĭn′ *or* vĭn′(h)	vin′ *or* vin′(h)
Vinica (Yugosl.)	vē′-nĭ-tsä	vee′-ni-tsah
Viničani (Yugosl.)	vē′-nĭ-chä-nĭ	vee′-ni-chah-ni
Vinje (Nor.)	vĭn′-yə	vin′-yuh
Vinjetinnene (Nor., mts.)	vĭn′-yə-tĭn′-ə-nə	vin′-yuh-tin′-uh-nuh
Vinkovci (Yugosl.)	vēn′-kôv-tsĭ	veen′-kov-tsi
Vinnitsa (Rus.)	vēn′-nĭ-tsä	veen′-ni-tsah
Vinstra (Nor.)	vĭn′-strä	vin′-strah
Vir (Yugosl.)	vēr′	veer′
Italian *Puntadura,* q.v.		
Virbalis (Lith.)	vēr-bä′-lĭs	veer-bah′-lis
Russian *Werzhbolovo,* q.v.		
Virovitica (Yugosl.)	vē′-rô-vē′-tĭ-tsä	vee′-ro-vee′-ti-tsah
Virpazar (Yugosl.)	vēr′-pä-zär	veer′-pah-zahr
Virts järv (Est.)	vĭrts′ yărv′	vihrts′ yehrv′
Viru (Oc.)	vē′-ro͞o	vee′-roo
Virzhbnik (Pol.) See *Wierzbnik.*		
Vis (Yugosl.)	vēs′	vees′
Italian *Lissa,* q.v.		
Vişăul de Jos (Rum.)	vē-shû′-o͝ol dĕ zhôs′	vee-shœ′-ul deh zhos′
Vişăul de Sus (Rum.)	vē-shû′-o͝ol dĕ so͞os′	vee-shœ′-ul deh sus′
Visayan Isls. (P.I.)	vē-sä′-yən	vee-sah′-yuhn
Spanish *Bisayas,* bē-sä′-yäs [bee-sah′-yahs].		

Višegrad (Yugosl.)	vē′-shĕ-gräd	vee′-sheh-grahd
Vishkov (Pol.) See *Wyszków.*		
Vishogrod (Pol.) See *Wyszogród.*		
Visla (Pol., riv.) See *Vistula.*		
Višnja Gora (Yugosl.)	vēsh′-nyä gô′-rä	veesh′-nyah go′-rah
Višnjica (Yugosl.)	vēsh′-nyĭ-tsä	veesh′-nyi-tsah
Visočica (Yugosl., riv.)	vĭ′-sô′-chĭ-tsä	ve′-so′-chi-tsah
Visočka Ržana (Yugosl.)	vē′-sôch-kä rzhä′-nä	vee′-soch-kah rzhah′-nah
Vistula (Pol., riv.)	*Eng.* vĭs′-cho͝o-lə	vis′-chu-luh

Polish *Wisła,* vē′-slä [vee′-slah]. Russian spelling *Visla.* German *Weichsel,* vīk′-səl [vaik′-suhl].

Vitačevo (Yugosl.)	vē′-tä′-chĕ-vô	vee′-tah′-cheh-vo
Vitanje (Yugosl.)	vē′-tä-nyĕ	vee′-tah-nyeh
Vitebsk (Rus.)	vē′-tĕpsk	vee′-tepsk
Viterbo (It.)	vē-tĕr′-bô	vee-tehr′-bo
Vitiaz (Oc., str.)	vē′-tyĕs	vee′-tyes

The assumption is that the name is Slavic in origin.

Viti Levu (Oc.)	vē′-tē lĕ′-vo͞o	vee′-tee leh′-voo
Vítkovice (Cz.)	vēt′-kô-vĭ-tsĕ	veet′-ko-vi-tseh
Vitolište (Yugosl.)	vē′-tô′-lĭ-shtĕ	vee′-to′-li-shteh
Vitória (Brazil)	vē-tôr′-yə	vee-tor′-yuh
Vitoševac (Yugosl.)	vē′-tô′-shĕ-väts	vee′-to′-sheh-vahts
Vittoria (Sicily)	vēt-tô′-ryä	veet-to′-ryah
Vittorio Veneto (It.)	vēt-tô′-ryô vĕ′-nĕ-tô	veet-to′-ryo veh′-neh-to
Vi Van Dinh (Indo-Ch. leader)	vē vän dĭn′ *or* dĭn′(y)	vee vahn din′ *or* din′(y)
Vivarit, Liqen i (Alb., lake) See *Butrint.*		
Vizagapatam (India)	vī-zăg′-ə-pə-tăm′	vai-zag′-uh-puh-tam′
Vizcaya (Sp., prov.)	vēth-kä′-yä *or* vēs-	veeth-kah′-yah *or* vees-

Also called *Biscaya,* q.v. English *Biscay,* bĭs′-kā [bis′-kay].

Vize (Turk.)	vē′-zĕ′	vee′-zeh′
Vizeu (Port.)	vē-zĕ′-o͝o	vee-zeh′-u
Vizianagram (India)	vĭz′-ĭ-ə-nŭg′-rəm	viz′-i-uh-nuhg′-ruhm
Vizzini (Sicily)	vēd-zē′-nē	veed-zee′-nee
Vkra (Pol., riv.) See *Wkra.*		
Vlaardingen (Neth.)	vlär′-dĭng-ən	vlahr′-ding-uhn
Vladički Han (Yugosl.)	vlä′-dĭch-kĭ hän′	vlah′-dich-ki hahn′
Vladimir (Rus.)	vlä-dē′-mĭr	vlah-dee′-mihr
Vladimirci (Yugosl.)	vlä′-dĭ-mĭr-tsĭ	vlah′-di-mihr-tsi
Vladimir Volinski (Pol.) See *Włodzimierz.*		
Vladivostok (Rus.)	vlä′-dĭ-vŏs-tôk′	vlah′-di-vos-tok′
Vlahčane (Yugosl.)	vläk(h)′-chä-nĕ	vlahk(h)′-chah-neh

Vlasenica (Yugosl.)	vlä′-sĕ-nĭ-tsä	vlah′-seh-ni-tsah
Vlašić planina (Yugosl., hills)	vlä′-shĭch plä′-nē′-nä	vlah′-shich plah′-nee′-nah
Vlasina (Yugosl., riv.)	vlä′-sĭ-nä	vlah′-si-nah
Vlasinsko Blato (Yugosl., marsh)	vlä′-sĭn-skô blä′-tô	vlah′-sin-sko blah′-to
Vlaška (Yugosl.)	vlä′-shkä	vlah′-shkah
Vlaški Do (Yugosl.)	vlä′-shkĭ dô′	vlah′-shki do′
Vlasotince (Yugosl.)	vlä′-sô-tĭn-tsĕ	vlah′-so-tin-tseh
Vlasulja (Yugosl., mt.)	vlä′-sōō-lyä	vlah′-soo-lyah
Vlieland (Neth., isl.)	vlē′-länt	vlee′-lahnt
Vlissingen (Neth.)	vlĭs′-ĭng-ən	vlis′-ing-uhn
English *Flushing*, q.v.		
Vlodava (Pol.) See *Włodawa*.		
Vlona (Alb.) See *Vlonë*.		
Vlonë (Alb.)	vlô′-nə	vlo′-nuh
Italian *Valona*, q.v. Greek *Avlon*, äv-lôn′ [ahv-lon′].		
Vloshchova (Pol.) See *Włoszczowa*.		
Vlotslavsk (Pol.) See *Włocławek*.		
Vltava (Cz., riv.)	vəl′-tä-vä	vuhl′-tah-vah
German *Moldau*, môl′-dou [mol′-dau].		
Voeringfoss (Nor.)	vû′-rĭng-fôs	vœ′-ring-fos
Vogël, Fand i (Alb., riv.)	vô′-gəl, fänd′ ē	vo′-guhl, fahnd′ ee
The smaller tributary of the *Mat*, q.v.		
Voghera (It.)	vô-gĕ′-rä	vo-geh′-rah
Voiron (Fr.)	vwä-rôN′	vwah-roN′
Voïussa (Alb., riv.) See *Vijosë*.		
Vojnić (Yugosl.)	voi′-nĭch	voi′-nich
Vojnik (Yugosl., mt.)	voi′-nĭk	voi′-nik
Vokeo (Oc.)	vô-kĕ′-ô	vo-keh′-o
Volchansk (Rus.)	vŏl-chänsk′	vol-chahnsk′
Volda (Nor.)	vôl′-dä	vol′-dah
Volendam (Neth.)	vō′-lən-däm′	voh′-luhn-dahm′
Volga (Rus., riv.)	*Eng.* vŏl′-gə	vol′-guh
	Rus. vôl′-gä	vol′-gah
Volhynia (Pol.)	*Eng.* vŏ-lĭn′-yə	vo-lin′-yuh
Polish *Wołyń*, vô′-lĭn(y) [vo′-lin(y)]. Russian *Volyn*, vŏ-lwēn′(y) [vo-lween′(y)].		
Volkhov (Rus., riv.)	vôl′-hŏf	vol′-hof
Volkovisk (Pol.) See *Wołkowysk*.		
Volkhovstroi (Rus.)	vôl′-hŏf-stroi′	vol′-hof-stroi′
Vollenhove (Neth.)	vŏl′-ən-hō′-və	vol′-uhn-hoh′-vuh
Volnovakha (Rus.)	vôl′-nŏ-vä′-hä	vol′-no-vah′-hah
Volochisk (Rus.)	vŏ-lŏ-chĭsk′	vo-lo-chisk′

Vologda (Rus.)	vô′-lŏg-dä	vo′-log-dah
Volokolamsk (Rus.)	vŏ′-lŏ-kŏ-lämsk′	vo′-lo-ko-lahmsk′
Volos (Gr.)	vô′-lô(s)	vo′-lo(s)
Volosovo (Rus.)	vô′-lŏ-sŏ-vŏ	vo′-lo-so-vo
Volozhin (Pol.) See *Wołożyn.*		
Volsk (Rus.)	vôl(y)sk′	vol(y)sk′
Volturno (It., riv.)	vôl-tōōr′-nô	vol-toor′-no
Volujica (Yugosl., point)	vô′-lōō′-yĭ-tsä	vo′-loo′-yi-tsah
Volyn (Pol.) See *Volhynia.*		
Vomero (It., Naples)	vô′-mĕ-rô	vo′-meh-ro
Von Arnim, Jürgin (Ger. general)	fôn är′-nĭm, yür′-gĭn	fon ahr′-nim, yür′-gin
Vonitsa (Gr.)	vô′-nē-tsä	vo′-nee-tsah
Vonkhotsk (Pol.) See *Wąchock.*		
Voorhis, Jerry (U.S. representative)	vōr′-ēz	vohr′-eez
Voorhout (Neth.)	vōr′-hout	vohr′-haut
Voorne (Neth., isl.)	vōr′-nə	vohr′-nuh
Voorst (Neth.)	vōrst′	vohrst′
Vordingborg (Den.)	vôr′-dĭng-bôr	vor′-ding-bor
Voreioi *or* Voreiai Sporades (Gr., isls.)	vô′-rē-ē *or* vô′-rē-ĕ spô-rä′-*th*ĕs	vo′-ree-ee *or* vo′-ree-eh spo-rah′-*th*es
English the Northern *Sporades*, spôr′-ə-dēz [spor′-uh-deez].		
Vöringfoss (Nor.)	vû′-rĭng-fôs	vœ′-ring-fos
Vormsi (Est., isl.)	vôrm′-sĭ	vorm′-si
Russian and German *Worms*, q.v.		
Voronezh (Rus.)	vŏ-rô′-nĕsh	vo-ro′-nesh
Voroninski (Rus.)	vŏ-rô′-nĭn-skĭ	vo-ro′-nin-ski
Voronov, Nikolai (Rus. general)	vô′-rŏ-nŏf, nĭ-kŏ-lī′	vo′-ro-nof, ni-ko-lai′
Voronovo (Rus.)	vô′-rŏ-nŏ-vŏ	vo′-ro-no-vo
Voronya (Rus., riv.)	vŏ-rô′-nyä	vo-ro′-nyah
Voroshilov, Klementi E. (Rus. general)	vŏ-rŏ-shĭ′-lŏf, klĕ-mĕn′-tē	vo-ro-shi′-lof, kleh-men′-tee
Voroshilovgrad (Rus.)	vŏ-rŏ-shĭ′-lŏf-grät	vo-ro-shi′-lof-graht
Voroshilovsk (Rus.)	vŏ-rŏ-shĭ′-lŏfsk	vo-ro-shi′-lofsk
Vorozhba (Rus.)	vŏ-rŏsh-bä′	vo-rosh-bah′
Vorskla (Rus., riv.)	vôrsk′-lä	vorsk′-lah
Võru (Est.)	vû′-rōō	vuh′-roo
Russian *Werro*, q.v.		
Vorys, John M. (U.S. representative)	vōr′-əs	vohr′-uhs
Voskopoja (Alb.)	vô-skô′-pô-yä	vo-sko′-po-yah
Voskresensk (Rus.)	vŏs-krĕ-sĕnsk′	vos-kreh-sensk′

Voskresenskoe (Rus.)	vŏs-krĕ-sĕn′-skŏ-yĕ	vos-kreh-sen′-sko-yeh
Voss (Nor.)	vôs′	vos′
Vossenack (Ger.)	fôs′-ə-näk	fos′-uh-nahk
Vostok (Oc.)	vəs-tôk′	vuhs-tok′
Voukolies (Crete)	vōō-kô-lyĕs′	voo-ko-lyes′
Voulgaris, Petros (Gr. leader)	vōōl′-gä-rēs, pĕ′-trôs	vool′-gah-rees, peh′-tros
Vouxa (Crete, cape)	vōō′-ksä	voo′-ksah

Also called *Bouza*, bōō′-zä [boo′-zah]; *Triton*, trē-tôn′ [tree-ton′]; and *Trypiti*, trē-pē-tē′ [tree-pee-tee′].

Vozarci (Yugosl.)	vô′-zär-tsĭ	vo′-zahr-tsi
Voznesensk (Rus.)	vŏz-nĕ-sĕnsk′	voz-neh-sensk′
Voznesensky, Nikolai (Rus. leader)	vŏz-nĕ-sĕn′-skĭ, nĭ-kŏ-lī′	voz-neh-sen′-ski, ni-ko-lai′
Vračar (Yugosl., mts.)	vrä′-chär	vrah′-chahr
Vraćevšnica (Yugosl.)	vrä′-chĕf′-shnĭ-tsä	vrah′-chef′-shni-tsah
Vrakhori (Gr.) See *Agrinion*.		
Vranište (Yugosl.)	vrä′-nĭ-shtĕ	vrah′-ni-shteh
Vranje (Yugosl.)	vrä′-nyĕ	vrah′-nyeh

Bulgarian *Vranya*, vrä′-nyä [vrah′-nyah].

Vranjevo (Yugosl.)	vrä′-nyĕ-vô	vrah′-nyeh-vo
Vranjska Banja (Yugosl.)	vrän′(y)-skä bä′-nyä	vrahn′(y)-skah bah′-nyah
Vranovci, Gornji (Yugosl.)	vrä′-nôv-tsĭ, gôr′-nyĭ	vrah′-nov-tsi, gor′-nyi
Vrapčište (Yugosl.)	vräp′-chĭ-shtĕ	vrahp′-chi-shteh
Vratarnica (Yugosl.)	vrä′-tär′-nĭ-tsä	vrah′-tahr′-ni-tsah
Vrattsa (Bulg.)	vrät′-sä	vraht′-sah
Vražogrnac (Yugosl.)	vrä′-zhô-gər′-näts	vrah′-zho-guhr′-nahts
Vrbas (Yugosl.)	vər′-bäs	vuhr′-bahs
Vrbaska (Yugosl.)	vər′-bä-skä	vuhr′-bah-skah
Vrbnica (Yugosl.)	vərb′-nĭ-tsä	vuhrb′-ni-tsah
Vrbnik (Yugosl.)	vərb′-nĭk	vuhrb′-nik

Italian *Verbenico*, vĕr-bĕn′-ē-kô [vehr-ben′-ee-ko].

Vrbovsko (Yugosl.)	vər′-bôv-skô	vuhr′-bov-sko
Vrčin (Yugosl.)	vər′-chĭn	vuhr′-chin
Vreeswijk (Neth.)	vrās′-wīk	vrays′-waik
Vrginmost (Yugosl.)	vər′-gĭn-môst	vuhr′-gin-most
Vrgorac (Yugosl.)	vər′-gô-räts	vuhr′-go-rahts
Vrhnika (Yugosl.)	vərk(h)′-nĭ-kä	vuhrk(h)′-ni-kah
Vrmdža (Yugosl.)	vərm′-jä	vuhrm′-jah
Vrnjačka Banja (Yugosl.)	vər′-nyäch-kä bän′-yä	vuhr′-nyahch-kah bahn′-yah
Vršac (Yugosl.)	vər′-shäts	vuhr′-shahts

Hungarian *Versec*, vĕr′-shĕts [vehr′-shets].

Vrška Čuka (Yugosl., mt.)	vərsh′-kä chōō′-kä	vuhrsh′-kah choo′-kah
Vrteška (Yugosl., mt.)	vər′-tĕ′-shkä	vuhr′-teh′-skhah
Vucht (Neth.)	vûk(h)t′	vœk(h)t′
Vučitrn (Yugosl.)	vōō′-chĭ-tərn′	voo′-chi-tuhrn′
Vuori, Eero (Fin. leader)	vŏŏ′-ô′-rē, ā′-rô	vu′-o′-ree, ay′-ro
Vura (Oc.)	vōō′-rä	voo′-rah
Vursell, Charles (U.S. representative)	vûr-sĕl′	vuhr-sel′
Vutrint (Alb.) See *Butrint.*		
Vyazma (Rus.)	vyäz′-mä	vyahz′-mah
Vyborg (Fin.)	*Rus.* vwē′-bŏrk	vwee′-bork
Vyeprj (Pol., riv.) See *Wieprz.*		
Vyg (Rus., riv.)	vwēg′	vweeg′
Vygozero (Rus.)	vwēg-ô′-zĕ-rŏ	vweeg-o′-zeh-ro
Vyshnii Volochek (Rus.)	vĭsh′-nĭ vŏ-lŏ-chôk′	vish′-ni vo-lo-chok′
Vysokoe (Rus.)	vĭ-sô′-kŏ-yĕ	vi-so′-ko-yeh
Vytegra (Rus.)	vwē′-tĕ-grä	vwee′-teh-grah

Waag (Cz., Hung., riv.) See *Váh.*		
Waal (Neth., riv.)	wäl′	wahl′
Waalwijk (Neth.)	wäl′-wīk	wahl′-waik
Waardenburg (Neth.)	wär′-dən-bûrk(h)	wahr′-duhn-bœrk(h)
Wąchock (Pol.)	vôN′-hôtsk	voN′-hotsk

Russian *Vonkhotsk*, vŏn-hôtsk′ [von-hotsk′].

Wadden Zee (Neth.)	wäd′-ən zā′	wahd′-uhn zay′
wadi	wä′-dĭ	wah′-di

An element, meaning *water course* or *valley*, in Arabic place names. It may be necessary to look up the other part of the name.

Wadi el Akarit (Tun.)	wä′-dĭ ĕl ä-kä-rēt′	wah′-di el ah-kah-reet′
Wadi Kebir (Tun.)	wä′-dĭ kə-bēr′	wah′-di kuh-beer′
Wadi Zigzaou (Tun.)	wä′-dĭ zĭg-zou′	wah′-di zig-zau′
Wafd (Egypt. pol. party)	wäft′	wahft′

Wafdist, wäf′-dĭst [wahf′-dist].

Wageningen (Neth.)	wä′-k(h)ə-nĭng′-ən	wah′-k(h)uh-ning′-uhn
Wagga Wagga (Austral.)	wô′-gə	waw′-guh

When pronounced, the name is usually thus shortened from wô′-gə wô′-gə [waw′-guh waw′-guh].

Wagina (Oc.)	wä-gĭn′-ä	wah-gin′-ah
Waigeu (NEI)	wī-gĕ′-ōō	wai-geh′-oo
Wailu (Oc.)	wä-ē′-lōō	wah-ee′-loo

Waingapoe *or* Waingapu (NEI)	wīn-gä′-po͞o	wain-gah′-poo
Wakayama (Jap.)	wä-kä-yä-mä	wah-kah-yah-mah
Wakkanai (Jap.)	wäk-kä-nī	wahk-kah-nai
Walachia (Rum.)	*Eng.* wŏ-lā′-kyə	wo-lay′-kyuh
Rumanian *Muntenia*, mo͝on-tĕ′-nyä [mun-teh′-nyah].		
Walcheren (Neth., isl.)	wäl′-k(h)ə-rən	wahl′-k(h)uh-ruhn
Walk (Est., Latvia) See *Valk*.		
Wallaroo (Austral.)	wŏl-ə-ro͞o′	wol-uh-roo′
Wallgren, Mon C. (U.S. senator)	wôl′-grĕn, mŏn′	wawl′-gren, mon′
Wan-an (Ch., Kiangsi)	wän-än	wahn-ahn
Wanawana (Oc.)	wä-nä-wä′-nä	wah-nah-wah′-nah
Wangaratta (Austral.)	wăng′-gə-răt′-ə	wang′-guh-rat′-uh
Wang Ch'ung-hui (Ch. leader)	wäng cho͝ong-whā	wahng chung-whay
Wang-kiang (Ch., Anhwei)	wäng-jyäng	wahng-jyahng
Wang Shih-chieh (Ch. leader)	wäng shû-jyĕ	wahng shuh-jyeh
Wan-hsien (Ch., Szechwan)	wän-shyĕn	wahn-shyen
Wanne Eickel (Ger.)	vän′-ə īk′-əl	vahn′-uh aik′-uhl
Wan-nien (Ch., Kiangsi)	wän-nyĕn	wahn-nyen
Wan-t'ing (Ch., Yünnan)	wän-tĭng	wahn-ting
Wan-tsai (Ch., Kiangsi)	wän-dzī	wahn-dzai
Wardha (India, riv.)	wär′-də	wahr′-duh
Wareo (New Guinea)	wä-rĕ′-ô	wah-reh′-o
Warnambool (Austral.)	wôr′-nəm-bo͞ol	wor′-nuhm-bool
Warnsdorf (Cz.)	*Ger.* värns′-dôrf	vahrns′-dorf
Czech *Varnsdorf*, q.v.		
Warsaw (Pol.)	*Eng.* wôr′-sô	wor′-so
Polish *Warszawa*, vär-shä′-vä [vahr-shah′-vah].		
Warszawa (Pol.) See *Warsaw*.		
Warwick (Austral.)	wä′-rĭk *or* wôr′-ĭk	wah′-rik *or* wor′-ik
Wasielewski, Thad F. (U.S. representative)	vä-shă-lĕf′-skĭ, thăd′	vah-sha-lef′-ski, thad′
Wassenaar (Neth.)	wäs′-ə-när	wahs′-uh-nahr
Watdek (Oc.)	wät′-dĕk	waht′-dek
Watom (Oc.)	wä-tôm′	wah-tom′
Wattenscheid (Ger.)	vät′-ən-shīt	vaht′-uhn-shait
Wau (New Guinea)	wou′	wau′
Wavell, Sir Archibald	wā′-vəl	way′-vuhl
Waw (Burma)	wô′	waw′

Weerd (Neth.)	wārt′	wayrt′
Weesp (Neth.)	wāsp′	waysp′
Węgrów (Pol.)	văN′-gro͝of	vaN′-gruf
Russian *Vengrov*, vĕn′-grŏf [ven′-grof].		
Weichel, Alvin F. (U.S. representative)	wī′-kĕl	wai′-kel
Weichsel (Pol., riv.) See *Vistula.*		
Wei-hai-wei (Ch., Shantung)	wā-hī-wā	way-hai-way
Wei-ning (Ch., Kweichow)	wā-nĭng	way-ning
Weiss, Samuel A. (U.S. representative)	wīz′	waiz′
Weissenstein (Est.)	*Ger.* vī′-sən-shtīn	vai′-suhn-shtain
	Rus. vā′-sĕn-shtān	vay′-sen-shtayn
Estonian *Paide*, q.v.		
Wei Tao-ming (Ch. leader)	wā dou-mĭng	way dau-ming
Wejherowo (Pol.)	vā-hĕ-rô′-vô	vay-heh-ro′-vo
Wels (Austria)	vĕls′	vels′
Wên-chow (Ch., Chekiang)	*Eng.* wĕn-chou	wen-chau
	Ch. wŭn-jō	wuhn-joh
Also called *Yung-chia*, q.v.		
Wenden (Latvia)	*Ger.* vĕn′-dən	ven′-duhn
Latvian *Cēsis*, q.v.		
Wene, Elmer H. (U.S. representative)	wēn′	ween′
Werro (Est.)	*Rus.* vĕr′-rŏ	vehr′-ro
Estonian *Võru*, q.v.		
Wervicq (Belg.)	*Flem.* vĕr′-vĭk	vehr′-vik
French *Werwik*, vĕr-vēk′ [vehr-veek′].		
Werzhbolovo (Lith.)	*Rus.* vĕrzh′-bŏ-lŏ′-vŏ	vehrzh′-bo-lo′-vo
Lithuanian *Virbalis*, q.v.		
Wesel (Ger.)	vā′-zəl	vay′-zuhl
Wesenberg (Est.)	*Ger.* vā′-zən-bĕrk(h)	vay′-zuhn-behrk(h)
Estonian *Rakvere*, q.v.		
Weser (Ger., riv.)	vā′-zər	vay′-zuhr
Wesermuende *or* Wesermünde (Ger.)	vā′-zər-mün′-də	vay′-zuhr-mün′-duh
Weshka (Egypt)	wŭsh′-kä	wuhsh′-kah
Wessel (Austral., cape, isls.)	wĕs′-əl	wes′-uhl
Westervoort (Neth.)	wĕs′-tər-vōrt	wes′-tuhr-vohrt
Westfalen (Ger.)	vĕst-fä′-lən	vest-fah′-luhn

Westkapelle (Neth.)	wĕst′-kä-pĕl′-ə	west′-kah-pel′-uh
Westphalia (Ger.)	*Eng.* wĕst-fā′-lĭ-ə	west-fay′-li-uh
German *Westfalen*, q.v.		
Wetar (NEI)	wĕ′-tär	weh′-tahr
Wewak (New Guinea)	wĕ′-wäk	weh′-wahk
There is a possible English pronunciation wē′-wăk [wee′-wak].		
Weygand, Maxime (Fr. gen.)	vĕ-gäN′, mäk-sēm′	veh-gahN′, mahk-seem′
Whelchel, B. Frank (U.S. representative)	wĕl-chĕl′	wel-chel′
White Russia See *Belorussia.*		
Wickersham, Victor (U.S. representative)	wĭk′-ər-shăm	wik′-uhr-sham
Wickham (Oc.)	*Eng.* wĭk′-əm	wik′-uhm
Wieliczka (Pol.)	vyĕ-lēch′-kä	vyeh-leech′-kah
Wieluń (Pol.)	vyĕ′-lo͝on(y)	vyeh′-lun(y)
Russian *Velyun*, vĕ′-lūn(y) [veh′-lyoon(y)].		
Wien (Austria)	vēn′	veen′
English *Vienna*, q.v.		
Wiencke (NEI)	wēng′-kə	weeng′-kuh
Wiener Neustadt (Austria)	vē′-nər noi′-shtät	vee′-nuhr noi′-shtaht
Wieprz (Pol., riv.)	vyĕpsh′	vyepsh′
Russian *Vepr*, vĕp′r [vep′r].		
Wieringen (Neth.)	wē′-rĭng-ən	wee′-ring-uhn
Wierzbnik (Pol.)	vyĕzh′-bnĭk	vyezh′-bnik
Russian *Virzhbnik*, vērsh′-bnĭk [veersh′-bnik].		
Wigglesworth, Richard B. (U.S. representative)	wĭg′-əlz-wûrth	wig′-uhlz-wuhrth
Wigry (Pol.)	vē′-grĭ	vee′-gri
Russian spelling *Vigri.*		
wijk	wīk′	waik′
An element, meaning *town*, in Dutch place names.		
Wijk aan Zee (Neth.)	wīk′ än zā′	waik′ ahn zay′
Wilanów (Pol.)	vē-lä′-no͝of	vee-lah′-nuf
Russian *Vilyanov*, vē-lyä′-nŏf [vee-lyah′-nof].		
Wilcannia (Austral.)	wĭl-kăn′-yə	wil-kan′-yuh
Wildervank (Neth.)	wĭl′-dər-vänk	wil′-duhr-vahnk
Wilejka (Pol.)	vĭ-lā′-kä	vi-lay′-kah
Russian spelling *Vileika.*		
Wilhelmshaven (Ger.)	*Eng.* vĭl′-hĕlmz-hä′-vən	vil′-helmz-hah′-vuhn
	Ger. vĭl′-hĕlms-hä′-fən	vil′-helms-hah′-fuhn

Wilja (Pol., riv.)	vē′-lyä	vee′-lyah
Russian *Viliya*, vē′-lĭ-yä [vee′-li-yah].		
Wilkomir (Lith.)	*Rus.* vēl′(y)-kŏ-mĭr	veel′(y)-ko-mihr
Lithuanian *Ukmergė*, q.v.		
Wilkowischki (Lith.)	*Rus.* vēl′(y)-kŏ-vē′-shkĭ	veel′(y)-ko-vee′-shki
Lithuanian *Vilkaviškis*, q.v.		
Willamette (Ore., riv.)	wĭ-lăm′-ĭt	wi-lam′-it
Willapa (Wash.)	wĭl′-ə-pä	wil′-uh-pah
Willemstad (Neth.; W.I.)	wĭl′-əm-stät	wil′-uhm-staht
Willey, Earle D. (U.S. representative)	wĭl′-ĭ	wil′-i
Wilno (Pol.)	*Eng.* vĭl′-nə	vil′-nuh
	Pol. vēl′-nô	veel′-no
Russian *Vilna*, vēl′(y)-nä [veel′(y)-nah]. Lithuanian *Vilnius*, vĭl′-nĭ-o͝os [vil′-ni-us].		
Wimereux (Fr.)	vēm-rû′	veem-rœ′
Winant, John G. (U.S. ambassador)	wīn′-ənt	wain′-uhnt
Windau (Latvia)	*Ger.* vĭn′-dou	vin′-dau
Latvian *Ventspils*, q.v. Russian *Vindava*, q.v.		
Windorah (Austral.)	wĭn-dō′-rə	win-doh′-ruh
Winschoten (Neth.)	wĭn′-sk(h)ō-tən	win′-sk(h)oh-tuhn
Winterswijk (Neth.)	wĭn′-tərs-wīk	win′-tuhrs-waik
Wisła (Pol., riv.) See *Vistula*.		
Wisłok (Pol., riv.)	vēs′-lôk	vees′-lok
Wisłoka (Pol., riv.)	vĭ-slô′-kä	vi-slo′-kah
Wismar (Ger.)	vĭs′-mär	vis′-mahr
Wissant (Fr.)	vē-säN′	vee-sahN′
Wisznia (Pol., riv.)	vēsh′-nyä	veesh′-nyah
Witten (Ger.)	vĭt′-ən	vit′-uhn
Wittenberg (Ger.)	*Eng.* wĭt′-ən-bûrg	wit′-uhn-buhrg
	Ger. vĭt′-ən-bĕrk(h)	vit′-uhn-behrk(h)
Wkra (Pol., riv.)	fkrä′	fkrah′
Russian spelling *Vkra*. Upper reaches called *Działdówka*, q.v.		
Włocławek (Pol.)	vlô-tslä′-vĕk	vlo-tslah′-vek
Russian *Vlotslavsk*, vlŏ-tslävsk′ [vlo-tslahvsk′].		
Włodawa (Pol.)	vlô-dä′-vä	vlo-dah′-vah
Russian spelling *Vlodava*.		
Włodzimierz (Pol.)	vlô-jē′-myĕzh	vlo-jee′-myezh
Russian *Vladimir Volinski*, vlä-dē′-mĭr vŏ-lēn′-skĭ [vlah-dee′-mihr vo-leen′-ski].		
Włoszczowa (Pol.)	vlô-shchô′-vä	vlo-shcho′-vah
Russian spelling *Vloshchova*.		

Wobbegong (Austral.)	wŏb′-ə-gŏng	wob′-uh-gong

This name, which seems native, is said to be derived from *woebegone*.

Woensdrecht (Neth.)	wo͞ons′-drĕk(h)t	woons′-drek(h)t
Woerther See (Austria, lake)	vûr′-tər zā′	vœr′-tuhr zay′
Wolbrom (Pol.)	vôl′-brôm	vol′-brom
Wolcott, Jesse P. (U.S. representative)	wôl′-kət, jĕs′-ĭ	wawl′-kuht, jes′-i
Wold, Terje (Nor. leader)	vôl′, tĕr′-yə	vol′, tehr′-yuh
Woleai (Oc.)	wô-lĕ-ī′	wo-leh-ai′
Wolfenden, James (U.S. representative)	wo͝ol′-fən-dən	wul′-fuhn-duhn
Wołkowysk (Pol.)	vôl-kô′-vĭsk	vol-ko′-visk

Russian *Volkovisk*, vŏl-kŏ-vēsk′ [vol-ko-veesk′].

Wollongong (Austral.)	wo͝ol′-ən-gŏng *or* wŭl′-	wul′-uhn-gong wuhl′-
Wolmar (Latvia)	*Ger.* vôl′-mär *Rus.* vôl′(y)-mär	vol′-mahr vol′(y)-mahr

Latvian *Valmiera*, q.v.

Wołomin (Pol.)	vô-lô′-mĭn	vo-lo′-min
Wołożyn (Pol.)	vô-lô′-zhĭn	vo-lo′-zhin

Russian spelling *Volozhin*.

Wolsztyn (Pol.)	vôl′-shtĭn	vol′-shtin
Wolverton, Charles (U.S. representative)	wo͝ol′-vər-tən	wul′-vuhr-tuhn

Wołyń (Pol.) See *Volhynia*.

Wonthaggi (Austral.)	wŏn-thăg′-ĭ	won-thag′-i
Woodruff, Roy O. (U.S. representative)	wo͝od′-rŭf	wud′-ruhf
Woodrum, Clifton A. (U.S. representative)	wo͝od′-rəm	wud′-ruhm
Workum (Neth.)	wôr′-kəm	wor′-kuhm
Worley, Eugene (U.S. representative)	wûr′-lĭ	wuhr′-li
Wormerveer (Neth.)	wôr′-mər-vār	wor′-muhr-vayr
Worms (Est., isl.)	*Ger.*, *Rus.* vôrms′	vorms′

Estonian *Vormsi*, q.v.

Worms (Ger.)	*Eng.* wûrmz′ *Ger.* vôrms′	wuhrmz′ vorms′
Wörther See (Austria, lake)	vûr′-tər zā′	vœr′-tuhr zay′
Wotho (Oc.)	wôt′-hô	wot′-ho
Wotje (Oc.)	wôt′-jĕ	wot′-jeh
Woudenberg (Neth.)	wou′-dən-bĕrk(h)	wau′-duhn-behrk(h)

Wrangell (Alaska, Attu)	*Eng.* răng′-gəl	rang′-guhl
	Rus. vrän′-gĕl(y)	vrahn′-gel(y)
Wronki (Pol.)	vrôn′-kĭ	vron′-ki
Września (Pol.)	vzhĕsh′-nyä	vzhesh′-nyah
Wu-ch'ang (Ch., Hupeh)	wōō-chäng	woo-chahng
Wu-chin (Ch., Kiangsi)	wōō-jĭn	woo-jin
Also called *Ch'ang-chow,* q.v.		
Wu-chow (Ch., Kwangsi)	*Eng.* wōō-chou	woo-chau
	Ch. wōō-jō	woo-joh
Wuerttemberg	*Eng.* wûr′-təm-bûrg	wuhr′-tuhm-buhrg
	Ger. vür′-təm-bĕrk(h)	vür′-tuhm-behrk(h)
Wuerzburg (Ger.)	*Eng.* wûrts′-bûrg	wuhrts′-buhrg
	Ger. vürts′-bŏŏrk(h)	vürts′-burk(h)
Wu-hu (Ch., Anhwei)	wōō-hōō	woo-hoo
Wu-i (Ch.) See *Wu-yi.*		
Wu-i-shan (Ch., Chekiang, Kiangsi, mts.)	wōō-ē-shän	woo-ee-shahn
Wu-kang (Ch., Hunan)	wōō-gäng	woo-gahng
Wu-ning (Ch., Kiangsi)	wōō-nĭng	woo-ning
Wuntho (Burma)	wŏŏn′-*thō*′	wun′-*th*oh′
Wuppertal (Ger.)	vŏŏp′-ər-täl	vup′-uhr-tahl
Württemberg (Ger.) See *Wuerttemberg.*		
Würzburg (Ger.) See *Wuerzburg.*		
Wu-shan (Ch., Szechwan)	wōō-shän	woo-shahn
Wu-t'ang (Ch., Chekiang)	wōō-täng	woo-tahng
Wu-ti Ho *or* Wu-ti River (Ch., Yünnan)	wōō-dē hŭ	woo-dee huh
Wu-yi (Ch., Chekiang)	wōō-yē	woo-yee
Also spelled *Wu-i.*		
Wygonowskie, Jezioro (Pol., lake)	vĭ-gô-nôf′-skyĕ, yĕ-zhô′-rô	vi-go-nof′-skyeh, yeh-zho′-ro
Russian *Vigonovskoe, Ozero,* vē′-gŏ-nŏf-skŏ-yĕ, ô′-zĕ-rŏ [vee′-go-nof-sko-yeh, o′-zeh-ro].		
Wyndham (Austral.)	wĭn′-dəm	win′-duhm
Wynyard (Austral.)	wĭn′-yərd	win′-yuhrd
Wysokie Mazowieckie (Pol.)	vĭ-sô′-kyĕ mä-zô-vyĕ′-tskyĕ	vi-so′-kyeh mah-zo-vyeh′-tskyeh
Russian *Mazovetsk,* mä-zŏ-vĕtsk′ [mah-zo-vetsk′].		
Wyszków (Pol.)	vĭsh′-kŏŏf	vish′-kuf
Russian *Vishkov,* vĭsh′-kŏf [vish′-kof].		

Wyszogród (Pol.)	vĭ-shô′-grŏŏd	vi-sho′-grud

Russian *Vishogrod*, vĭ-shô′-grŏd [vi-sho′-grod].

Xavier	*Eng.* zăv′-ĭ-ər	zav′-i-uhr
	or zā′-vyər	zay′-vyuhr
Xenia (Ohio)	zē′-nyə	zee′-nyuh
Xeres (Sp.) See *Jerez.*		
Xions (Pol.) See *Książ.*		
Xyda (Crete)	ksē-*th*ä′	ksee-*th*ah′

y

In Dutch *y* is interchangeable with *ij* and *ei,* though *y* is usually preferred when initial. A consultant may have to look for all three forms before he finds his word.

Yablonovy (Rus., mts.)	yä′-blŏ-nŏ-vĭ	yah′-blo-no-vi
Yablunkov (Cz.)	yä′-blōōn-kôf	yah′-bloon-kof
Yaila (Rus., mts.)	yī′-lä′	yai′-lah′
Yakima (Wash.)	yăk′-ə-mə	yak′-uh-muh
Yakutat (Alaska)	yăk′-ə-tăt′	yak′-uh-tat′
	or yŭk′-ə-tăt′	yuhk′-uh-tat′
Yalta (Rus.)	yäl′-tä	yahl′-tah
Yalutorovsk (Rus.)	yä-lōō-tô′-rŏfsk	yah-loo-to′-rofsk
Yamaguchi (Jap.)	yä-mä-gōō-chē	yah-mah-goo-chee
Yambol (Bulg.)	yäm′-bŏl(y)	yahm′-bol(y)
Yame (Oc.)	yä-mĕ′	yah-meh′
Yamethin (Burma)	yə-mĕ′-*th*ĭn	yuh-meh′-*th*in
Yampol (Rus.)	yäm′-pŏl(y)	yahm′-pol(y)
Yanam *or* Yanaon	yä-näm′	yah-nahm′
(Fr. India)	*or* yä-nä-ôN′	yah-nah-oN′
Yandoon (Burma)	yăn-dōōn′	yan-doon′
Yang-ch'ü (Ch., Shansi)	yäng-chü	yahng-chü

Also called *T'ai-yü-an,* q.v.

Yäng-lou-ssŭ (Ch., Hupeh)	yäng-lō-sə	yahng-loh-suh
Yang-pi (Ch., Yünnan)	yäng-bē	yahng-bee
Yang-tz'e Kiang or	*Eng.* yăng-sē	yang-see
Yang-tz'e River (Ch.)	*Ch.* yäng-tsĕ	yahng-tseh

See *Kiang* for the pronunciation if it is desired. The use of *River* is usually preferable.

Yanina (Gr.) See *Ioanina.*		
Yanov (Pol.) See *Janów* and *Janów Podlaski.*		
Yantra (Bulg., riv.)	yän′-trä	yahn′-trah
Yap (Oc.)	yäp′ *or* yăp′	yahp′ *or* yap′

Yarmolintsi (Rus.)	yär-mô′-lĭn-tsĭ	yahr-mo′-lin-tsi
Yaroslav (Pol.) See *Jarosław*.		
Yartsevo (Rus.)	yär′-tsĕ-vŏ	yahr′-tseh-vo
Yarylgach (Rus.)	yä-rĭl-gäch′	yah-ril-gahch′
Yaselda (Pol., riv.) See *Jasiolda*.		
Yashshera (Rus.)	yä′-shchĕ-rä	yah′-shcheh-rah
Yavino (Rus.)	yä′-vĭ-nŏ	yah′-vi-no
Yawnghwe (Burma)	yông′-whā′	yawng′-whay′
Yeadon (Pa.)	yā′-dən	yay′-duhn
Yeats, Wm. B.	yāts′	yayts′
Yebawgyi (Burma)	yā-bô-jē′	yay-baw-jee′
Yefremov (Rus.)	yĕ-frĕ′-mŏf	yeh-freh′-mof
Yegorevsk (Rus.)	yĕ-gôr′-yĕfsk	yeh-gor′-yefsk
Yegorlyk (Rus.)	yĕ-gŏr-lwēk′	yeh-gor-lweek′
Yeisk (Rus.)	āsk′	aysk′
Yelansk (Rus.)	yĕ-länsk′	yeh-lahnsk′
Yelets (Rus.)	yĕ-lĕts′	yeh-lets′
Yelnya (Rus.)	yĕl′(y)-nyä	yel′(y)-nyah
Yelsk (Rus.)	yĕl(y)sk′	yel(y)sk′
Yemen (Arabia)	yĕm′-ən	yem′-uhn
Yen-an (Ch., Shensi)	yĕn-än	yen-ahn
Yenangyaung (Burma)	yā-nän-joung′	yay-nahn-jaung′
Yen-ch'ing (Ch., Sikang)	yĕn-chĭng	yen-ching
Yenikale (Rus.)	yĕ′-nĭ-kä′-lĕ	yeh′-ni-kah′-leh
Yen-ki (Manchu.)	*Eng.* yĕn-kē	yen-kee
	Ch. yĕn-jē	yen-jee
Also spelled *Yen-chi*.		
Yenotaevsk (Rus.)	yĕ-nŏ-tä′-yĕfsk	yeh-no-tah′-yefsk
Yen-t'ai (Ch., Shantung)	yĕn-tī	yen-tai
Also called *Cheefoo*, q.v., and *Chih-fu*, q.v.		
Yepifan (Rus.)	yĕ-pĭ-fän′(y)	yeh-pi-fahn′(y)
Yerevan (Rus.)	yĕ′-rĕ-vän′	yeh′-reh-vahn′
Also called *Erevan*, q.v.		
Yesagyo (Burma)	yā′-zə-jō′	yay′-zuh-joh′
Ye-u (Burma)	yā-ōō′	yay-oo′
Yevpatoriya (Rus.)	yĕf-pä-tô′-rĭ-yä	yef-pah-to′-ri-yah
Yeya (Rus., riv.)	ā′-yä	ay′-yah
Also spelled *Eya*, q.v.		
Yezd (Iran)	yĕzd′	yezd′
Yi- For Chinese names beginning in *Yi-*, see *I-*.		
Yi-hwang (Ch., Kiangsi) See *I-hwang*.		
Yi-wu (Ch., Chekiang) See *I-wu*.		
Yi-yang (Ch., Kiangsi) See *I-yang*.		

Yo-chow (Ch., Hunan)	*Eng.* yō-chou	yoh-chau
	Ch. yō-jō	yoh-joh
Also called *Yo-yang*, q.v.		
Yokkaichi (Jap.)	yôk-kī-chē	yok-kai-chee
Yokohama (Jap.)	yô-kô-hä-mä	yo-ko-hah-mah
Yokosuka (Jap.)	yô-kô-so͞o-kä	yo-ko-soo-kah
	or yô-kôs-kä	yo-kos-kah
Yo-yang (Ch., Hunan)	yō-yäng	yoh-yahng
Also called *Yo-chow*, q.v.		
Ypres (Belg.)	*Fr.* ē'pr	ee'pr
Flemish *Ieperen*, q.v. The name is so un-English that one must sympathize with the popular British wī'-pərz [wai'-puhrz].		
Ypseloreites (Crete, mt.)	See *Ide Oros.*	
Yreka (Calif.)	wī-rē'-kə	wai-ree'-kuh
Ysel (Neth.)	ī'-səl	ai'-suhl
Also spelled *Yssel.*		
Ystad (Sw.)	ü'-städ	ü-stahd
Ystgaard, Hans (Nor. leader)	üst'-gôr, häns'	üst'-gor, hahns'
Yüan-an (Ch., Hupeh)	yüän-än	yü-ahn-ahn
Yüan-ling (Ch., Hunan)	yüän-lĭng	yü-ahn-ling
Also called *Ch'en-chow*, q.v.		
Yü-chiang (Ch., Kiangsi)	yü-jyäng	yü-jyahng
Yü-ch'ien (Ch., Chekiang)	yü-chyĕn	yü-chyen
Yugoslavia	*Eng.* ū'-gô-slä'-vĭ-ə	yoo'-go-slah'-vi-uh
Serb-Croat *Jugoslavija*, ū'-gô-slä'-vĭ-yä [yoo'-go-slah'-vi-yah].		
Yü-hang (Ch., Chekiang)	yü-häng	yü-hahng
Yü-hwan (Ch., Chekiang, isl.)	yü-whän	yü-whahn
Yü-kan (Ch., Kiangsi)	yü-gän	yü-gahn
Yukhnov (Rus.)	ūk(h)'-nŏf	yook(h)'-nof
Yu-ki (Korea)	ū-kē	yoo-kee
Yü-kiang (Ch., Kiangsi)	yü-jyäng	yü-jyahng
Also spelled *Yü-chiang*, q.v.		
Yü-lin (Ch., Kwangsi, Shensi)	yü-lĭn	yü-lin
Yung-ch'ang (Ch., Kansu)	yo͝ong-chäng	yung-chahng
Yung-ch'ang (Ch., Yünnan)	yo͝ong-chäng	yung-chahng
Also called *Pao-shan*, q.v.		
Yung-chia (Ch., Chekiang)	yo͝ong-jyä	yung-jyah
Also called *Wen-chow*, q.v.		

Yung-ch'wan (Ch., Szechwan)	yo͝ong-chwän	yung-chwahn
Yung-fêng (Ch., Kiangsi)	yo͝ong-fŭng	yung-fuhng
Yung-hsin (Ch., Kiangsi)	yo͝ong-shĭn	yung-shin
Yung-hsiu (Ch., Kiangsi)	yo͝ong-shū	yung-shyoo
Also spelled *Yung-siu.*		
Yung-kang (Ch., Chekiang)	yo͝ong-käng	yung-kahng
Yung-p'ing (Ch., Hopeh)	yo͝ong-pĭng	yung-ping
Yung-têng (Ch., Kansu)	yo͝ong-dŭng	yung-duhng
Yün-hsien (Ch., Yünnan)	yün-shyĕn	yün-shyen
Yün-nan (Ch., prov.)	*Eng.* yo͞o-năn	yu-nan
	Ch. yün-nän	yün-nahn
Yün-nan-fu (Ch., Yünnan)	*Eng.* yo͞o-năn-fo͞o	yu-nan-foo
	Ch. yün-nän-fo͞o	yün-nahn-foo
Yurev (Est.) See *Jurjev.*		
Yurev Polski (Rus.)	ūr'-yĕf pŏl'(y)-skĭ	yoor'-yef pol'(y)-ski
Yü-shan (Ch., Kiangsi)	yü-shän	yü-shahn
Yushkozero (Rus.)	ūshk-ô'-zĕ-rŏ	yooshk-o'-zeh-ro
Yü-tu (Ch., Kiangsi)	yü-do͞o	yü-doo
Yvetot (Fr.)	ēv-tō'	eev-toh'
Ywataung (Burma)	yo͝oä'-toung'	yu-ah'-taung'
Yzeure (Fr.)	ē-zûr'	ee-zœr'
Zaandam (Neth.)	zän-däm'	zahn-dahm'
Zaandijk (Neth.)	zän-dīk'	zahn-daik'
Zaafran (Libya)	zä-fə-răn'	zah-fuh-ran'
Also called *Sidra,* q.v., and *Sirte,* q.v.		
Žabalj (Yugosl.)	zhä'-bäl(y)	zhah'-bahl(y)
Žabari (Yugosl.)	zhä'-bä-rĭ	zhah'-bah-ri
Żabinka (Pol.)	zhä-bēn'-kä	zhah-been'-kah
Russian *Zhabinka,* zhä'-bĭn-kä [zhah'-bin-kah].		
Ząbkowice (Pol.)	zôN-pkô-vē'-tsĕ	zoN-pko-vee'-tseh
Russian *Zombkovitse,* zŏmb-kŏ-vē'-tsĕ [zomb-ko-vee'-tseh].		
Žabljak (Yugosl.)	zhäb'-lyäk	zhahb'-lyahk
Zabłudów (Pol.)	zä-blo͝o'-do͝of	zah-blu'-duf
Russian *Zabludovo,* zä-blo͞o'-dŏ-vŏ [zah-bloo'-do-vo].		
Zabrež (Yugosl.)	zä'-brĕzh	zah'-brezh
Zabul (Iran)	zä-bo͝ol'	zah-bul'
Zaccaria (It.)	tsäk-kä-rē'-ä	tsahk-kah-ree'-ah
Zadar (Yugosl., It.)	*S.-C.* zä'-där	zah'-dahr
Italian *Zara,* q.v.		
Zadonsk (Rus.)	zä-dônsk'	zah-donsk'

Zafrana (Dodec.)	*Gr.* zä′-frä-nä	zah′-frah-nah
	It. tsä-frä′-nä	tsah-frah′-nah
Zagazig (Egypt)	zä-gä-zēg′	zah-gah-zeeg′
Zaghouan (Tun.)	*Ar.* zäg-wăn′	zahg-wan′
	Fr. zäg-wäN′	zahg-wahN′
Zagora, Stara (Bulg.)	zä′-gŏ-rä, stä′-rä	zah′-go-rah, stah′-rah
Zagorsk (Rus.)	zä-gôrsk′	zah-gorsk′
Zagreb (Yugosl.)	zä′-grĕb	zah′-greb
German *Agram*, äg′-räm [ahg′-rahm].		
Zagrebačka (Yugosl.)	zä′-grĕ-bäch-kä	zah′-greh-bahch-kah
Žagubica (Yugosl.)	zhä′-gōō-bĭ-tsä	zhah′-goo-bi-tsah
Zagyva (Hung., riv.)	zŏd′(y)-vŏ	zod′(y)-vo
Zahedan (Iran)	zä-hĕ-dän′	zah-heh-dahn′
Zajac (Yugosl.)	zä′-yäts	zah′-yahts
Zaječar (Yugosl.)	zä′-yĕ-chär	zah′-yeh-chahr
Zákány (Hung.)	zä′-kän(y)	zah′-kahn(y)
Zaklików (Pol.)	zä-klē′-kŏŏf	zah-klee′-kuf
Russian *Zaklikov*, zä-klē′-kŏf [zah-klee′-kof]		
Zakopane (Pol.)	zä-kô-pä′-nĕ	zah-ko-pah′-neh
Zakynthos (Gr., isl.)	zä′-kēn-thô(s)	zah′-keen-tho(s)
Also called *Zante*, q.v.		
Zalaegerszeg (Hung.)	zŏ′-lŏ-ĕ′-gĕr-sĕg	zo′-lo-eh′-gehr-seg
Zălău (Rum.)	zə-lû′-ŏŏ	zuh-luh′-u
Hungarian *Zilah*, zĭ′-lŏ [zi′-lo].		
Zaleszczyki (Pol.)	zä-lĕsh-chĭ′-kĭ	zah-lesh-chi′-ki
zaliv	zä′-lĭf	zah′-lif
An element, meaning *bay*, in Yugoslav and Russian place names. It may be necessary to look up the other part of the name.		
Zaliv Petra Velikago (Rus.)	zä-lēf′ pĕ-trä′ vĕ-lē′-kä-vŏ	zah-leef′ peh-trah′ veh-lee′-kah-vo
Zaltbommel (Neth.)	zält-bôm′-əl	zahlt-bom′-uhl
Zama (Tun.)	*Eng.* zā′-mə *or* zä′-mä	zay′-muh *or* zah′-mah
Zamboanga (P.I.)	säm-bô-äng′-gä	sahm-bo-ahng′-gah
Zamora (Sp.)	thä-mô′-rä *or* sä-	thah-mo′-rah *or* sah-
Zamość (Pol.)	zä′-môshch	zah′-moshch
Russian *Zamoste*, zä-môst′-yĕ [zah-most′-yeh].		
Zanana (Oc.)	zä-nä′-nä	zah-nah′-nah
Zandvoort (Neth.)	zänt′-vōrt	zahnt′-vohrt
Žanjica (Yugosl.)	zhä′-nyĭ-tsä	zhah′-nyi-tsah
Zante (Gr., isl.)	zän′-tĕ	zahn′-teh
Greek *Zakynthos*, q.v.		
Zanzur (Libya)	zän-zōōr′	zahn-zoor′

Zapadna Morava (Yugosl., riv.)	zä′-päd-nä mô′-rä′-vä	zah′-pahd-nah mo′-rah′-vah
Zapadnaya Dvina (Rus.)	zä′-päd-nä-yä dvĭ-nä′	zah′-pahd-nah-yah dvi-nah′
Zaplanje (Yugosl.)	zä′-plä′-nyĕ	zah′-plah′-nyeh
Zaporozhe (Rus.)	zä-pŏ-rôzh′-yĕ	zah-po-rozh′-yeh
Žapsko (Yugosl.)	zhäp′-skô	zhahp′-sko
Zara (It., Yugosl.)	*It.* dzä′-rä	dzah′-rah
Serb-Croat *Zadar*, q.v.		
Zaragoza (Sp.)	thä-rä-gô′-thä *or* sä-rä-gô′-sä	thah-rah-go′-thah sah-rah-go′-sah
English *Saragossa*, săr′-ə-gŏs′-ə [sehr′-uh-gos′-uh].		
Zaraisk (Rus.)	zä-rīsk′	zah-raisk′
Zarasai (Lith.)	zä-rä-sī′	zah-rah-sai′
Zarat (Tun.)	zä-răt′	zah-rat′
Zaravecchia (Yugosl.)	*It.* dzä-rä-vĕk′-kyä	dzah-rah-vek′-kyah
Serb-Croat *Biograd*, q.v.		
Žarkovo (Yugosl.)	zhär′-kô-vô	zhahr′-ko-vo
Żarnowiec (Pol.)	zhär-nô′-vyĕts	zhahr-no′-vyets
German *Zarnowitz*, tsär′-nô-vĭts [tsahr′-no-vits].		
Zarzis (Tun.)	zär′-zĭs	zahr′-zis
Žatec (Cz.)	zhä′-tĕts	zhah′-tets
Zaton (Yugosl.)	zä′-tôn	zah′-ton
Zatonje (Yugosl.)	zä′-tô-nyĕ	zah′-to-nyeh
Zator (Pol.)	zä′-tôr	zah′-tor
Zatrijevač (Yugosl.)	zä′-trē′-yĕ-väch	zah′-tree′-yeh-vahch
Zauia (Libya)	zä′-wĭ-ä	zah′-wi-ah
Also called *Ez Zauia*, q.v.		
Zauta en Nofilia (Libya)	zou′-tä ĕn nô-fē′-lyä	zau′-tah en no-fee′-lyah
Also called *En Nofilia*, q.v., and *Nofilia*, q.v.		
Zaverda (Gr.)	zä-vĕr′-*th*ä	zah-vehr′-*th*ah
Zavertse (Pol.) See *Zawiercie.*		
Zavidovo (Rus.)	zä-vē′-dŏ-vŏ	zah-vee′-do-vo
Zavikhost (Pol.) See *Zawichost.*		
Zavishin (Rus.)	zä-vē′-shĭn	zah-vee′-shin
Zavitaya (Rus.)	zä-vĭ-tä′-yä	zah-vi-tah′-yah
Zawchaung (Burma)	zô′-choung′	zaw′-chaung′
Zawichost (Pol.)	zä-vē′-hôst	zah-vee′-host
Russian *Zavikhost*, zä-vē′-hŏst [zah-vee′-host].		
Zawiercie (Pol.)	zä-vyĕr′-chĕ	zah-vyehr′-cheh
Russian *Zavertse*, zä-vĕr′-tsĕ [zah-vehr′-tseh].		
Zawyet Shammas (Egypt)	ză′-wyĕt shăm-măs′	za′-wyet sham-mas′

Zbąszyń (Pol.)	zbôN′-shǐn(y)	zboN′-shin(y)
Zbrucz (Pol., riv.)	zbrŏŏch′	zbruch′
Russian spelling *Zbruch.*		
Zdołbunów (Pol.)	zdôl-bŏŏ′-nŏŏf	zdol-bu′-nuf
Russian *Zdolbunovo,* zdŏl-bŏŏ-nô′-vŏ [zdol-bu-no′-vo].		
Zduńska Wola (Pol.)	zdŏŏn′(y)-skä vô′-lä	zdun′(y)-skah vo′-lah
Zea (Gr., isl.)	zē′-ä	zee′-ah
Also called *Keos,* q.v.		
Zealand (Den., isl.)	*Eng.* zē′-lənd	zee′-luhnd
Danish *Sjælland,* shĕl′-län [shel′-lahn].		
Zebib (Tun., cape)	zə-bēb′	zuh-beeb′
Zebla (Tun.)	zĕb′-lä	zeb′-lah
Zebrzydowice (Pol.)	zĕb-zhĭ-dô-vē′-tsĕ	zeb-zhi-do-vee′-tseh
German *Seibersdorf,* zī′-bərs-dôrf [zai′-buhrs-dorf].		
Žeden (Yugosl., mts.)	zhĕ′-dĕn	zheh′-den
zee	zā′	zay′
An element, meaning *sea,* in Dutch place names.		
Zeebrugge (Belg.)	*Eng.* zē′-brŏŏg-ə	zee′-brug-uh
	Flem. zā′-brûk(h)-ə	zay′-brœk(h)-uh
Zeeland (Neth., prov.)	*Eng.* zē′-lənd	zee′-luhnd
	Du. zā′-länt	zay′-lahnt
Zeeuwsch-Vlaanderen (Neth.)	zā′-ōōs vlän′-də-rən	zay′-oos vlahn′-duh-ruhn
Żegiestów (Pol.)	zhĕ-gyĕ′-stŏŏf	zheh-gyeh′-stuf
Žegligovo (Yugosl.)	zhĕ′-glĭ-gô-vô	zheh′-gli-go-vo
Žegovac planina (Yugosl., mts.)	zhĕ′-gô-väts plä′-nē′-nä	zheh′-go-vahts plah′-nee′-nah
Zegrze (Pol.)	zĕg′-zhĕ	zeg′-zheh
Russian *Zegrzhe,* zĕ′gr-zhĕ [ze′gr-zheh].		
Zehsis (Latvia) See *Cēsis.*		
Żelechów (Pol.)	zhĕ-lĕ′-hŏŏf	zheh-leh′-huf
Russian *Zhelekhov,* zhĕ′-lĕ-hŏf [zheh′-leh-hof].		
Zelenika (Yugosl.)	zĕ′-lĕ-nĭ-kä	zeh′-leh-ni-kah
Zelenikovo (Yugosl.)	zĕ-lĕ′-nĭ-kô-vô	zeh-leh′-ni-ko-vo
Železnik (Yugosl.)	zhĕ′-lĕz-nĭk	zheh′-lez-nik
Željin (Yugosl., mt.)	zhĕ′-lyĭn	zheh′-lyin
Zelvinou (Alb.) See *Delvinë.*		
Zemgale (Latvia, prov.)	zĕm′-gä-lĕ	zem′-gah-leh
Zemun (Yugosl.)	zĕ′-mōōn	zeh′-moon
Zemzem (Libya)	zĕm′-zĕm′	zem′-zem′
Zenica (Yugosl.)	zĕ′-nĭ-tsä	zeh′-ni-tsah
Zenkov (Rus.)	zĕn(y)-kôf′	zen(y)-kof′
Zenta (Yugosl.) See *Senta.*		
Žepče (Yugosl.)	zhĕp′-chĕ	zhep′-cheh

Zephyrion (Crete, point)	zĕ-fē′-rē(-ôn)	zeh-fee′-ree(-on)
Also called *Agios Ioannes*, q.v.		
Žeravino (Yugosl.)	zhĕ′-rä-vĭ-nô	zheh′-rah-vi-no
Zergian (Alb.) See *Zerqan.*		
Žernovnica (Yugosl.)	zhĕr′-nôv′-nĭ-tsä	zhehr′-nov′-ni-tsah
Zernovo (Rus.)	zĕr-nô′-vŏ	zehr-no′-vo
Zerqan (Alb.)	zĕr′-kyän	zehr′-kyahn
Zerqani (Alb.) See *Zerqan.*		
Zerva, Napoleon (Gr. general)	zĕr′-vä, nä-pô-lĕ′-ôn	zehr′-vah, nah-po-leh′-on
Zeta (Yugosl., riv.)	zĕ′-tä	zeh′-tah
Zetska (Yugosl.)	zĕt′-skä	zet′-skah
Zevenaar (Neth.)	zā-və-när′	zay-vuh-nahr′
Zevenbergen (Neth.)	zā′-vən-bĕrk′-k(h)ən	zay′-vuhn-behr′-k(h)uhn
Zeya (Rus.)	zĕ′-yä	zeh′-yah
Zgropoljci (Yugosl.)	zgrô′-pôl(y)-tsĭ	zgro′-pol(y)-tsi
Zhabinka (Pol.) See *Żabinka.*		
Zharkovski (Rus.)	zhär-kôf′-skĭ	zhahr-kof′-ski
Zhdanov, Andrei A. (Rus. leader)	zhdä′-nŏf, än-drā′	zhdah′-nof, ahn-dray′
Zhirardov (Pol.) See *Żyrardów.*		
Zhitomir (Rus.)	zhĭ-tô′-mĭr	zhi-to′-mihr
Zhizdra (Rus.)	zhĭz′-drä	zhiz′-drah
Zhlobin (Rus.)	zhlô′-bĭn	zhlo′-bin
Zhmerinka (Rus.)	zhmĕ′-rĭn-kä	zhmeh′-rin-kah
Zhukov (Rus. general)	zhōō′-kŏf	zhoo′-kof
Zhukovka (Rus.)	zhōō′-kŏf-kä	zhoo′-kof-kah
Zhulat (Alb.)	zhōō′-lät	zhoo′-laht
Zhulati (Alb.) See *Zhulat.*		
Žiča (Yugosl.)	zhē′-chä	zhee′-chah
Zičijevo (Yugosl.)	zē′-chē′-yĕ-vô	zee′-chee′-yeh-vo
Zidanimost (Yugosl.)	zē′-dä-nĭ-môst′	zee′-dah-ni-most′
Zierikzee (Neth.)	zē′-rĭk-zā′	zee′-rik-zay′
Žijeva planina (Yugosl., mt.)	zhē′-yĕ-vä plä′-nē′-nä	zhee′-yeh-vah plah′-nee′-nah
Zijpe (Neth.)	zī′-pə	zai′-puh
Zilah (Rum.) See *Zălău.*		
Žilina (Cz.)	zhē′-lĭ-nä	zhee′-li-nah
Zilovo (Rus.)	zē′-lŏ-vŏ	zee′-lo-vo
Zilupe (Latvia)	zē′-lŏŏ-pĕ	zee′-lu-peh
Russian *Rosenovskaya*, q.v.		
Zimovniki (Rus.)	zĭ-môv′-nĭ-kĭ	zi-mov′-ni-ki
Zinovevsk (Rus.)	zĭ-nô′-vyĕfsk	zi-no′-vyefsk

Žirije (Yugosl.)	zhē′-rĭ-yĕ	zhee′-ri-yeh
Italian *Zuri*, q.v.		
Zirona (Yugosl.)	*It.* tsē-rô′-nä	tsee-ro′-nah
Serb-Croat *Drvenik*, q.v.		
Žirovnica (Yugosl.)	zhē′-rôv′-nĭ-tsä	zhee′-rov′-ni-tsah
Zit (Tun.)	zēt′	zeet′
Officially *Ste. Marie du Zit.*		
Žitkovac (Yugosl.)	zhēt′-kô-väts	zheet′-ko-vahts
Žitni Potok (Yugosl.)	zhēt′-nĭ pô′-tôk	zheet′-ni po′-tok
Žitorađa (Yugosl.)	zhē′-tô-rä′-dyä	zhee′-to-rah′-dyah
Zittau (Ger.)	tsĭt′-ou	tsit′-au
Zlatar (Yugosl., mts.)	zlä′-tär	zlah′-tahr
Zlatibor (Yugosl., mts.)	zlä′-tĭ-bôr	zlah′-ti-bor
Zlatoust (Rus.)	zlä-tŏ-o͞ost′	zlah-to-oost′
Žljeb (Yugosl., mts.)	zhlyĕb′	zhlyeb′
Złoczew (Pol.)	zlô′-chĕf	zlo′-chef
Russian spelling *Zlochev.*		
Złoczów (Pol.)	zlô′-cho͝of	zlo′-chuf
Zmiev (Rus.)	zmĭ-yôf′	zmi-yof′
Znamenka (Rus.)	znä′-mĕn-kä	znah′-men-kah
Znojmo (Cz.)	znoi′-mô	znoi′-mo
Zócalo (Mex.)	sô′-kä-lô	so′-kah-lo
Zoetermeer (Neth.)	zo͞o-tər-mār′	zoo-tuhr-mayr′
Zolachev (Rus.)	zô′-lä-chĕf	zo′-lah-chef
Zolotonosha (Rus.)	zŏ-lŏ-tŏ-nô′-shä	zo-lo-to-no′-shah
Zombkovitse (Pol.) See *Ząbkowice.*		
Žombolj (Rum.)	*S.-C.* zhôm′-bôl(y)	zhom′-bol(y)
Rumanian *Jimbolea*, q.v.		
Zombor (Yugosl.) See *Sombor.*		
Zonari (Dodec., Rh., point) See *Cum Burnu.*		
Zonguldak (Turk.)	zôn-go͝ol′-däk	zon-gul′-dahk
zoological	zō′-ə-lŏj′-ĭ-kəl	zoh′-uh-loj′-i-kuhl
Avoid the temptation to say zo͞o- in this word and in *zoology.*		
Zović (Yugosl.)	zô′-vĭch	zo′-vich
Zriba (Tun.)	zrē′-bä	zree′-bah
Zsombolya (Rum.) See *Jimbolea.*		
Zuara (Libya)	zo͞o-ä′-rä	zoo-ah′-rah
Zubtsov (Rus.)	zo͞op-tsôf′	zoop-tsof′
Zuetina (Libya) See *Ez Zuetina.*		
zuid *and* zuider	zûĭt′ *and* zûĭ′-dər	zœit′ *and* zœi′-duhr
An element, meaning *south*, in Dutch place names. It may be necessary to look up the other part of the name.		
Zuid Beveland (Neth.)	zûĭt′ bā′-və-länt	zœit′ bay′-vuh-lahnt

Zuider Zee (Neth.)	*Eng.* zī′-dər zē′	zai′-duhr zee′
	Du. zûĭ′-dər zā′	zœi′-duhr zay′
Zuid Holland (Neth., prov.)	zûĭt′ hôl′-änt	zœit′ hol′-ahnt
Zuidlaren (Neth.)	zûĭd-lä′-rən	zœid-lah′-ruhn
Žukovac (Yugosl.)	zhōō′-kô-väts	zhoo′-ko-vahts
Zundert (Neth.)	zûn′-dərt	zœn′-duhrt
Zungaria (Ch., Sinkiang)	See *Dzungaria.*	
Županja (Yugosl.)	zhōō′-pä-nyä	zhoo′-pah-nyah
Županjac (Yugosl.)	zhōō′-pä-nyäts	zhoo′-pah-nyahts
Žur (Yugosl.)	zhōōr′	zhoor′
Zuri (Yugosl.)	*It.* tsōō′-rē	tsoo′-ree
Serb-Croat *Žirije,* q.v.		
Žut (Yugosl., isl.)	zhōōt′	zhoot′
Zutfen (Neth.)	*Eng.* zŭt′-fən	zuht′-fuhn
	Du. zût′-fən	zœt′-fuhn
Also spelled *Zutphen.*		
Žuti Kamen (Yugosl., mt.)	zhōō′-tĭ kä′-mĕn	zhoo′-ti kah′-men
Žužemberk (Yugosl.)	zhōō′-zhĕm-bĕrk	zhoo′-zhem-behrk
Zvenigorod (Rus.)	zvĕ-nē′-gŏ-rŏt	zveh-nee′-go-rot
Zverevo (Rus.)	zvĕ′-rĕ-vŏ	zveh′-reh-vo
Zvezdan (Yugosl.)	zvĕz′-dän	zvez′-dahn
Zvižd (Yugosl.)	zvēzhd′	zveezhd′
Zvolen (Cz.)	zvô′-lĕn	zvo′-len
Zvornik (Yugosl.)	zvôr′-nĭk	zvor′-nik
Zwammerdam (Neth.)	zwäm′-ər-däm′	zwahm′-uhr-dahm′
Zwartsluis (Neth.)	zwärt-slûĭs′	zwahrt-slœis′
Zwickau (Ger.)	tsvĭk′-ou	tsvik′-au
Zwijndrecht (Neth.)	zwīn′-drĕk(h)t	zwain′-drek(h)t
Zwoleń (Pol.)	zvô′-lĕn(y)	zvo′-len(y)
Zwolle (Neth.)	zwôl′-ə	zwol′-uh
Żyrardów (Pol.)	zhĭ-rär′-dŏŏf	zhi-rahr′-duf
Russian *Zhirardov,* zhĭ-rär′-dŏf [zhi-rahr′-dof].		
Zyria *or* Zerea (Gr.)	See *Kyllene.*	
Żywiec (Pol.)	zhĭ′-vyĕts	zhi′-vyets

ø is commonly used in Norwegian orthography for *ö* or *œ.* In this book spellings with both *ö* and *œ* are listed, for each may occur in the English spelling of Norwegian names. The use of ø did not seem important enough, from our point of view, to justify the listing of a third spelling.